ELEMENTS OF

PUBLIC ADMINISTRATION

ELEMENTS OF
PUBLIC
ADMINISTRATION

JAMES W. FESLER

GEORGE A. GRAHAM

V. O. KEY, JR.

AVERY LEISERSON

MILTON M. MANDELL

HARVEY C. MANSFIELD

JOHN D. MILLETT

FRITZ MORSTEIN MARX

DON K. PRICE

HENRY REINING, JR.

WALLACE S. SAYRE

DONALD C. STONE

JOHN A. VIEG

DWIGHT WALDO

Edited by

FRITZ MORSTEIN MARX

SECOND EDITION

Englewood Cliffs, N. J.

PRENTICE-HALL, INC.

1959

𝒞

To

OUR STUDENTS

Perpetual Prompters of Thought

Preface
to the Second Edition

When a book enjoys as large a circle of friends as *Elements of Public Administration* has had the good fortune of winning, it is under an obligation to remain itself. The second edition cheerfully meets this obligation. A joint enterprise of men widely known in the profession, the book describes and evaluates the state of the administrative arts, both to instruct the student and to inform the practitioner.

Although unchanged in basic organization and point of view, the second edition reflects more than a decade of growth in the theory and practice of public administration. Moreover, a change in general attitude has occurred in the course of this growth, expressed in a healthy skepticism toward premature orthodoxies about any "one right way." Happily, for the most part the development has followed the trends and tendencies outlined in the first edition.

By and large, the evolution has brought enrichment. Considerable advance has been made in scientific insight, leading to a more sophisticated approach. The stage appears to be set for further significant progress in research and in the application of research findings. Meanwhile a heap of rubble awaits being cleared away—evidence of the high rate of obsolescence in yesterday's theoretical structures and pragmatic devices in the field of administration, public and private.

Perhaps the best thing that may be said about the second edition is that the team of authors stayed the same. Competing workload pressures resulting from other projects induced members of the team in a few instances to accept the editor as partner in the revision of certain chapters. The editor, in turn, was comforted by the care expended upon the manuscript by an old friend, Helen L. Chatfield, long the distinguished record officer of the Bureau of the Budget, Executive Office of the President; and by the ministrations of an invisible hand called Virginia.

Washington, D.C.   FRITZ MORSTEIN MARX

From the Preface
to the First Edition

This is a demonstration of teamwork. The fourteen men who came together to form the team discovered that they thought very much alike about the field of interest they had in common. When they joined forces, all of them were engaged in the practical business of public administration; all of them were under the influence of fresh experience; and all of them were stimulated by new insights that open up to those placed strategically within the administrative structure.

These exceptional circumstances held forth the promise of a unified and systematic treatment of the subject rather than a symposium made up of unconnected essays. In the exchange of views among the members of the team, the preliminary plan grew into an integrated enterprise to which each member contributed his carefully defined share. Throughout the writing of the book, its character as a combined operation was sustained by the team spirit of each participant.

The principal aim of the book is to deepen the reader's understanding of the administrative process as an integral phase of contemporary civilization. In a sense, therefore, this is a broadly political rather than merely technical study. Its focus is on the fundamental problems of public administration—the problems that assert themselves at countless points within the framework of governmental effort. The analysis here presented attempts to explore both the range of controlling institutional factors and the variables of administrative behavior.

The aim of the book compelled an approach appropriate to it. A glance at the table of contents will show that the customary division of the subject matter has been modified in several important respects. There is also a deliberate recurrence of basic themes, each being developed in progressive specificity as the discussion moves forward. One of these basic themes inevitably runs through the entire volume—that of the implications of democratic governance for public management in all of its ramifications.

Washington, D.C.   FRITZ MORSTEIN MARX

Introducing
the Team

James W. Fesler, Alfred Cowles Professor of Government at Yale University, has also taught at the University of North Carolina. He has served the federal government in such agencies as the War Production Board, the Bureau of the Budget, the President's Committee on Administrative Management, and the first (Hoover) Commission on the Organization of the Executive Branch of the Government. He has been an adviser with the United States technical assistance program in Vietnam. In 1958 he became editor-in-chief of *Public Administration Review*. His main publications are *Executive Management and the Federal Field Service* (1937), *The Independence of State Regulatory Agencies* (1942), *Area and Administration* (1949), and, with others, *Industrial Mobilization for War* (1947) and *The Forty-Eight States* (1955).

George A. Graham, formerly professor of politics at Princeton University, is director of governmental studies, Brookings Institution. During World War II, he served in the Bureau of the Budget, where he was in charge of the War Supply Section and the War Records Section, and later of the Government Organization Branch in the Administrative Management Division. He was chairman of the Task Force on Indian Affairs of the first Hoover Commission and staff director of the Task Force on Personnel and Civil Service of the second Hoover Commission. In 1951 he was consultant to the Douglas Subcommittee on Ethical Standards in Government, Senate Committee on Labor and Public Welfare, and later (1956-57) director of the Ford Foundation's public affairs program. His writings include *Personnel Practices in Business and Governmental Organization* (1935), *Education for Public Administration* (1941), *Regulatory Administration* (1943), of which he was co-editor, and *Morality in American Politics* (1952).

V. O. Key, Jr., professor of government at Harvard University, has also taught at Johns Hopkins and Yale Universities. He is a former president of the American Political Science Association. During World War II he was associated with the Administrative Management Division of the Bureau of the Budget. He is the author of *The Administration of Federal Grants to States* (1937), *Politics, Parties, and Pressure Groups* (4th ed., 1958), *Southern Politics* (1949), *A Primer of Statistics for Political Scientists* (1954), and *American State Politics: An Introduction* (1956).

Avery Leiserson heads the Department of Political Science at Vanderbilt University. He has also taught at Princeton University and the Universities

xi

of Chicago, Washington, and Michigan. His government experience includes service with the National Recovery Administration, 1934-35; the National Labor Relations Board, 1938-40; the National Defense Mediation Board, 1941; the Bureau of the Budget, 1942-45; and as public member of the Chicago Regional Wage Stabilization Board, 1951-52. He is the author of *Administrative Regulation: A Study in Representation of Interests* (1942) and *Parties and Politics: An Institutional and Behavioral Approach* (1958).

Milton M. Mandell has been chief of the Management Testing Unit of the United States Civil Service Commission since 1945. He has also been a consultant to the city of Philadelphia, the state of Connecticut, and the Commonwealth of Puerto Rico. He has lectured at Cornell University, the University of Chicago, Dartmouth College, Ohio State and New York Universities, and other institutions of higher learning. He is the author of "The Selection of Executives," in M. Joseph Dooher and Elizabeth Marting, eds., *Selection of Management Personnel* (1957), and *Employment Interviewing* (1956); and co-author of *Selecting Supervisors* (1956).

Harvey C. Mansfield, chairman of the Department of Political Science at Ohio State University, has also taught at Yale and Stanford Universities. He is managing editor of the *American Political Science Review.* He was on the staff of the President's Committee on Administrative Management in 1936, served in the Office of Price Administration during World War II, and has been consultant to the Bureau of the Budget, the National War College, the Commission on Intergovernmental Relations, and other federal and state agencies. He is author of *The Lake Cargo Coal Rate Controversy* (1932) and *The Comptroller General* (1939); and co-author of *Arms and the State* (1958).

John D. Millett, formerly professor of public administration at Columbia University, has been president of Miami University since 1953. He was a staff member of the first Hoover Commission. During World War II he served on the staff of the Commanding General of the Army Service Forces in the War Department, and later in Europe. He is the author of several books in the fields of public administration and higher education, the most recent being *Government and Public Administration* (1959).

Fritz Morstein Marx has taught at the Pennsylvania School of Social Work, Princeton, New York, Harvard, Columbia and Yale Universities, Queens College, and American University, where he is adjunct professor of political science. He serves as a staff assistant in the Office of the Director, Bureau of the Budget. He has been editor-in-chief of *Public Administration Review.* His latest book is *The Administrative State: An Introduction to Bureaucracy* (1957).

Don K. Price, a Rhodes scholar in 1932, is dean of the Graduate School of Public Administration, Harvard University. He was formerly vice president of the Ford Foundation and earlier deputy chairman of the Research and Development Board in the Department of Defense. From 1939 to 1953 he was connected in various capacities with Public Administration Clearing House, last as associate director. He has also been attached to the Administrative Management Division of the Bureau of the Budget. He was the first managing editor of *Public Administration Review.* The latest of his main publications is *Government and Science* (1954).

Henry Reining, Jr., is dean of the School of Public Administration, University of Southern California. He previously taught at Princeton, George Washington, and American Universities. From 1935 to 1945 he was educational director of the National Institute of Public Affairs at Washington, which sponsored governmental internship programs for college graduates showing high promise and which was instrumental in launching the federal management training program. He has been consultant to the United Nations and to federal, state, and local agencies. His overseas assignments have led him to Brazil, Turkey, the Philippines, Iran, and Pakistan. He is a former president of the American Society for Public Administration. He is the co-editor of *Regulatory Administration* (1943) and co-author of *Governmental Reorganization* (1951).

Wallace S. Sayre is professor of public administration at Columbia University. He was previously associated with New York and Cornell Universities and City College of New York. He served as personnel director of the Office of Price Administration in the closing years of World War II. More recently he has been director of research for the New York State Commission on the Government of New York City. He is a member of the Mayor's Advisory Council, New York City, and has been editor-in-chief of *Public Administration Review.* His latest writings have dealt with basic problems of municipal management as well as of the public service.

Donald C. Stone is dean of the Graduate School of Public and International Affairs, University of Pittsburgh. Much of his career has been devoted to the development of the art and science of public administration, nationally and internationally. He has been director of research of the International City Managers Association, subsequently organized Public Administrative Service, and served from 1939 to 1948 as Assistant Director of the Bureau of the Budget, in charge of its Administrative Management Division. Later he become Director of Administration of the Economic Cooperation Administration and the Mutual Security Agency. For four years he was president of Springfield College. A past president of the American Society of Public Administration, he is chairman of its Committee on Research Needs and Resources and chairman of the Committee of Leaders and Specialists of the American Council on Education. He has taught previously at American University, the University of Chicago, and Syracuse University, and is the author of several books and monographs.

John A. Vieg, visiting legislative research professor at the University of California (Berkeley), is chairman of the Department of Government at Pomona College. During World War II, he served in the Administrative Management Division of the Bureau of the Budget. He has been a Fulbright professor of politics and administration. He has written *The Government of Education in Metropolitan Chicago* (1939) and is co-author of *City Manager Government in Seven Cities* (1940), *The Future of Government in America* (1942), *Wartime Government in Operation* (1943), and *Our Needy Aged: A California Study of a National Problem* (1954).

Dwight Waldo is professor of political science and director of the Bureau of Public Administration at the University of California (Berkeley). He taught previously at Yale and Stanford Universities and the University of Bologna, Italy. His administrative experience includes service in the

Office of Price Administration (1942-44) and in the Bureau of the Budget (1944-46). In his professional writings he has specialized in relating administration and administrative study to the historical, cultural, and theoretical context. His published work in the field of administration includes three books: *The Administrative State: A Study of the Political Theory of American Public Administration* (1948), *Ideas and Issues in Public Administration* (1953), and *Perspectives on Administration* (1957).

Contents

Part I: The Role of Public Administration

Part III: Working Methods

THE ROLE OF PUBLIC ADMINISTRATION

THE ROLE OF PUBLIC
ADMINISTRATION

Chapter 1 •

The Growth of
Public Administration

1. Administration: Everybody's Business

A word of guidance. This book presents its subject in four parts. The first part, on the role of public administration, is an introduction. It seeks to lay a common foundation for the other parts, which will take up in logical order the main institutions and processes of today's administrative system, and the issues and problems inherent in them. Thus the reader may gain a sense of general familiarity before he undertakes to examine the machinery by which modern government performs its many functions.

The opening part consists of five chapters. The first attempts to trace the growth of American public administration in broad strokes. The second outlines its development as a field of scientific knowledge. The next chapter boldly pursues the ghost of "bureaucracy." Then comes a chapter that probes the relationships between administrative practice and democratic theory. Finally, the fifth chapter sets out to show the place occupied by public administration in the contemporary order—political, economic, and social.

In the partisan battles of our day, it is a frequent experience to see the growth of public administration portrayed as a very recent development. No doubt industrial society gives strong impetus to the formation of "big government"—government big enough to cope with the social as well as economic risks of "free enterprise." But even the simplest governments since early times had functions to administer, however primitive the forms of administration. Public administration reflects in its growth the character of different civilizations.

Administration and planned effort. Precisely when or where public administration began no one can say, because no one knows when or where men first thought of themselves as comprising a community, as being a public. Yet its origins surely lie far back, for by the time Hammurabi

3

wrote his code 4,000 years ago, the idea of government as a doer of things was already well established.[1]

Administration, as a matter of fact, is involved in all planned effort, private as well as public. Save for those who drift through life and care not where the current takes them, every man senses from his own experience something of the meaning of administration. For to refuse to let circumstances run their own course and to work instead within the limits they impose to attain some more desirable end—this is the essence of administration. It is determined action taken in pursuit of conscious purpose. It is the systematic ordering of affairs and the calculated use of resources, aimed at making those things happen which one wants to happen and forestalling everything to the contrary. It is the marshaling of available labor and materials in order to gain that which is desired at the lowest possible cost in energy, time, and money. No man, therefore, who singly or in company with others has ever laid out a course of action and tried to carry it through can be without some intimation of the nature of administration. Motivated by whatever desires and interests they have, people are continually setting goals for themselves; administration consists of whatever they do thereafter to attain their goals.

Regardless of the field of human endeavor, there is thus an administrative side to all planned effort. In simple situations where the things that need to be done are obvious and it is fairly clear who can best do what, it is possible for those sharing an objective to work as a team without ever realizing that they are engaged in administration. But when a situation becomes complex so that it is no longer easy to know how to proceed or whether the resources available will be adequate for the end in view, administration demands conscious and conscientious attention.

Purpose as organizing force. Conscious concern with administration arises first, and principally, among the comparatively few to whom it falls

---

[1] For a review of administrative systems in early imperial states (Eastern and Western), see Toynbee, Arnold J., *A Study of History,* Vol. VII, p. 344 *ff.,* London: Oxford University Press, 1954. See also Weidlund, Jane and Others, *Comparative Public Administration: A Selective Annotated Bibliography,* especially pp. 9-10, Ann Arbor: Institute of Public Administration, University of Michigan, 1957. The European evolution has been sketched with great skill by Sir Ernest Barker, *The Development of Public Services in Western Europe, 1660-1930,* London: Oxford University Press, 1944. For the federal government, administrative history has found authoritative treatment by Leonard D. White in the following volumes: *The Federalists* (1789-1801), *The Jeffersonians* (1801-1829), *The Jacksonians* (1829-1861), and *The Republican Era* (1867-1901), all New York: Macmillan, 1948, 1951, 1954, and 1958, respectively. Of great value is the same author's tracing of the growth of public administration in the United States during the first three decades of the twentieth century (before the New Deal!): *Trends in Public Administration,* New York: McGraw-Hill, 1933 (published under auspices of President Herbert Hoover's Research Committee on Social Trends). For early American state government, a series of special monographs is particularly enlightening; see, for instance, Louis Hartz, *Economic Policy and Democratic Thought: Pennsylvania, 1776-1860,* Cambridge, Mass.: Harvard University Press, 1948. A recent assessment of the functional balance in the federal system is provided in the *Report* of the Commission on Intergovernmental Relations, Washington, 1955.

to outline programs, devise procedures, and direct or supervise operations. But in a more general way such concern also develops among the many— those through whom the cooperative effort becomes a reality; and how they "see" their role usually makes a considerable difference in the success or failure of the enterprise. When they accept the purpose of their work and look forward to sharing in its fruits, administration becomes the means whereby they are enabled to be proficient at their jobs, and they work accordingly. When they reject the purpose or see no prospect of sharing in the fruits, administration is likely to be regarded as a means of exploiting them against their will. Under such circumstances, not even a genius in management can achieve more than poor results.

Every purposeful individual has administrative problems of his own, regardless of where he lives or works. Ordinarily, however, the terms "administration" and "management" refer to the organization and direction of cooperative or collective activity. The two words are often used interchangeably. In general, administration is the broader term, embracing such responsibilities as devising an appropriate organization, establishing priorities of work, and harnessing all efforts toward attainment of the ends sought. Management, in its distinctive sense, covers those activities which are designed to make the enterprise succeed within the framework of structure, policy, and resources.

Common character of administration. It is therefore in the sphere of cooperative or collective effort that administration has its primary significance. Whether social, religious, economic, or governmental in character, every organization depends on administration for accomplishing its aims. And the larger the organization, other things being equal, the greater is the need for administration to be formally and extensively developed. On the question of whether administration is chiefly art or science it must suffice here to observe that, while it is and must be both, it is steadily coming to be more than an art.[2] From either angle, however, it is equally obvious that the primary precepts and standards of administration comprise a single discipline. Its rules and insights may be utilized in numerous and widely different fields; at the core, they nevertheless form but one body of theory.

Like other sciences, the developing science of administration has several branches. All of them, however, are parts of a larger whole. It is a serious misconception to assume that business administration and governmental administration comprise entirely separate spheres, completely distinct from each other. The fact is that they have rather more in common than otherwise. As disciplines they differ not so much in theory as in the uses to which they are put. Government and business profit alike, if not equally, as the science of administration advances.

---

[2] See Chapter 2, "The Study of Public Administration."

Business affords the most obvious illustration of private administration. But one finds highly developed administration of a nongovernmental character in other institutional realms. One important example is ecclesiastic administration. The Roman Catholic Church and the Greek Orthodox Church come to mind as historic illustrations. Colleges and universities have contributed much to the growth of administrative experience. The universities of Paris, Oxford, Heidelberg, Palermo, Cairo, Salamanca, Kiev, and Harvard are but a few of many outstanding institutions of learning which could not have accomplished their intellectual mission through hundreds of eventful years without devoting thought to matters of administration. Even today few problems are more complex than those of giving common focus to the interests of professors, students, parents, alumni, trustees, and donors or taxpayers—especially when it is recognized that most of these "parties at interest" are free agents, not subject to compulsion.

Scope of public administration. At its fullest range, public administration embraces every area and activity governed by public policy. It may even be taken to include the formal processes and operations through which the legislature exercises its power; for there is much adroit management in the conduct of legislative business. In a literal sense, public administration also includes the functions of the courts in the administration of justice and the work of military agencies as well as those of a civilian character. By established usage, however, public administration has come to signify primarily the organization, personnel, practices, and procedures essential to effective performance of the civilian functions entrusted to the executive branch of government. In its general aspects, public administration centers its concern in those matters common to all or nearly all administrative agencies. It has to do first and foremost with those factors of basic importance found throughout the whole range of administrative activity.

Application of the body of knowledge called public administration to a particular function like that of welfare may shift from the level of the town hall to that of the statehouse, from there to the national stage, and on beyond to international affairs. It may range on a single plane—that of local government, for example—from the bogs and bayous of a Louisiana parish to the desert lands of a county in Nevada or the wooded hillsides of a New England town. It may impress identical features on such different functions as health, education, conservation, transportation, and telecommunication. Or it may weave back and forth from a patently governmental function like the arrest and detention of a thief, to a quasi-governmental, quasi-commercial one like the operation of an electrical utility, and again to what most citizens would regard as a public function par excellence, the delivery of the mail. Despite the shifting scenes, certain problems inevitably recur, and certain insights are found to be applicable in every special field. Generically, the conduct of public administration is everywhere the same; this common body may be called the elements of public administration.

Elements of public administration. The fundamentals of organization, procedure, and method essential to efficient service in all fields alike, irrespective of level, area, function, or purpose, may be grouped in various ways. Broadly speaking, they can be brought under three principal headings. These are: (a) assumption of appropriate roles in policy-making by both the chief executive and the legislature; (b) ability of the chief executive and his principal aides and subordinates to incorporate the policies adopted into workable plans of operation, sustained by appropriate grouping of component activities; and (c) skill on the part of those in charge of operations in so directing, coordinating, instructing, and motivating the working force that the objectives embodied in the policies and plans will be efficiently accomplished. Expressed differently, the elements of public administration encompass the role of the chief executive face to face with the legislature; the relations between him and his immediate associates in the top structure of the administrative hierarchy, on the one hand, and between these and the higher operating officials, on the other; and the relations between supervisors and employees on the level of operations, where administrative action has the greatest impact on the general public.

Every science has its problems of nomenclature. One of the problems of nomenclature in public administration has been to develop agreement on terms that would clearly denote its major spheres. Although usage has not become settled, the highest responsibilities—those involving determination of broad policy and formal relations with the legislative body—are generally referred to as being executive in character. Those primarily oriented internally, toward the general scheme of operations, are usually described as administrative. Those relating to the actual direction and supervision of the body of employees are often labeled managerial. Thus one may say that managers supervise the fulfillment of work programs under the general direction of administrators, who in turn carry responsibility for broad assignments given them by executives.

Administration as servant of policy. Whether the sphere of interest be public or private, administration is always the servant of policy. Management— the largest part of administration—denotes means, and means have no significance except in terms of ends. Though often blurred, the dichotomy of ends and means forms a basis and supplies a justification for studying public administration as a distinct and separable sector of government. Americans usually conceive of government as involving three coordinate functions—legislative, executive, and judicial. But there is equally good, if not better, logic for dividing the roles along two main lines: responsibility for laying down public policy and responsibility for administering the public business in accordance with such policy. It is true the leadership of the executive department is obliged to labor in both vineyards. Presidents, governors, and mayors (save when relieved of administrative duties by a city manager) are required to serve both as political leaders and administrative chiefs. Except for such administrators in chief and their principal subordinates, however, those engaged in administration do not themselves establish the basic policies they execute. Their prime job is to give effect to policy.

Translated into governmental terms, the ends-means schema thus provides the foundation for distinguishing between politics and administration.[3] As long as its relativities are borne in mind, this is a useful distinction. It is of practical value also in helping citizens understand what they can most wisely do in making democracy work. The political tests of policy are mainly two: enlightenment and representation. The citizen can force his government to meet these tests by the proper use of his vote. In contrast there is only one main test of public administration, and it is difficult and often impossible for the citizen to apply: Are the means used effective in terms of their cost in achieving the end sought? The best way for the citizen to ensure that his government meets this test is not by trying to measure administrative efficiency himself but by demanding that his elected representatives insist on the use of suitable measures of performance *within* the administrative system.

As a general proposition, policy and politics (in the sense of the political process of policy determination) are primary to administration, both logically and chronologically. Policy defines the aims and ends of governmental action. On the highest level, public policy is whatever the politically chosen representatives make it. They set the goals and lay out the main lines for attaining these goals through administrative action. Once this is done, those responsible for administrative action must bend every effort to accomplish the program. It is not their business to try to substitute any greater wisdom they may think they have for the wisdom of the people's chosen representatives. The time to record their doubts is at the stage of policy consideration or reconsideration. Here they will usually be heard with full appreciation of their judgment. The more they regard themselves principally as agents of policy, the likelier will the public leave them free to do their work with a minimum of interference or resistance on political grounds.

2. The American Background

Governmental heritage from Britain. In Europe, the pioneering role in developing the administrative institutions of modern government fell to

---

[3] For two classic statements of this distinction, see Wilson, Woodrow, "The Study of Administration," *Political Science Quarterly,* 1887, Vol. 2, pp. 197-222, and Goodnow, Frank J., *Politics and Administration,* New York: Macmillan, 1900.

Brandenburg-Prussia during the seventeenth and eighteenth centuries. The creative impulse came from public-spirited rulers wielding absolute power. These were conditions without counterpart in American history. Five European nations participated in the exploration and early settlement of what is now the continental United States. Only one of them, Britain, left a deep imprint upon our administrative institutions. British antecedents furnished the models for the towns which still are the fundamental units in New England and for the counties which form the basis of local government in the South. The mixed patterns of towns, townships, cities, and counties which have developed in other regions of the country also arose from these beginnings. The combinations and modifications that took place have been due mainly to geographic and economic factors, and also to the fact that those who migrated from one section to another simply carried some of their customs with them.

The *ad hoc* or special-purpose governmental districts so ubiquitous in American local administration—for schools, water, drainage, health, recreation—are likewise to a degree of English origin. Generically, they may be traced back to the concept of the limited or single-purpose local public corporation as developed in Anglo-Saxon jurisprudence. This is not to suggest, however, that British precedent supplies the only reason for the existence of 50,000 school districts (reduced from more than 127,000 within the last generation). More important was the need for a convenient governmental unit through which early Americans, especially in the northern colonies, could realize their ambition of providing free common schooling for all children. In addition, once the pattern of reserving sections of the public domain for the support of education had been established, the necessity arose for a device whereby the people of the Northwest Territory (1787), and also of all other areas subsequently opened for settlement, could organize to take advantage of their educational opportunities. How the district system should be modified and simplified to meet the conditions of the present day are questions for which contemporary students of public administration must find answers.

Until the launching, during World War I, of the movement for state administrative reorganization, perhaps the best way to describe the impact of the British example on state government would have been in terms of "reverse English." American experience with royal colonial administration had been such that the people reversed the model of the powerful chief executive when they themselves came into control after 1776. In organizing their new state governments they vested preponderant power in the legislative assembly. Aside from the hard-won exception of the presidency, it took the nation approximately a century to overcome its fears and suspicions of centralized administrative authority, even under popular and legislative control. Administrative integration under a strengthened executive has been the key to much of the recent progress made in state government.

Constitutionalism and freedom. Insofar as the form and character of American national government is concerned, the Constitution on which it is based comprises a bundle of compromises. One of the reasons why compromise was so essential in the historic summer of 1787 was the insistence of many of the Founding Fathers that the document incorporate numerous features of the British system of government. They aimed at building a structure combining both aristocratic and democratic characteristics, but did so in such a way that over the years the popular features could gradually be expanded. Every mature citizen may judge for himself how well they succeeded.

Finally, there is the matter of English ideals of liberty, equality, and justice. Our British heritage has not consisted merely of mechanics related to administrative areas and structures. In some ways the most significant elements have been those conceptions of individual freedom, due process, and equal justice which, adding up to the "rule of law," are perhaps the richest political treasure of American as well as of Anglo-Saxon civilization. Americans have introduced as many modifications in their administrative as in their linguistic heritage. Yet these have not replaced the foundations.

Influence of the frontier. As part of the "cutting edge of civilization," public administration is always affected at any given time by what civilization is trying to cut. When it is the wilderness of untamed forests, prairies, swamps, and deserts with which American government had to contend for three hundred years as the pioneers made their way westward across the continent, the effects are of one kind. When civilization is cutting economic or social barriers in a highly industrialized and urbanized society, the effects are of a different nature.

The physical frontiers against which American civilization was pushing from the days of the landings at St. Augustine, Jamestown, and Plymouth, until the last of the good "free land" was staked and claimed around 1890, left their imprint upon the emerging administrative system. Sparsity of population and the simple life which the pioneers and first settlers led, together with their fierce spirit of self-reliance, caused the activity of government to be restricted at the outset to little more than the maintenance of the peace, the recording of land titles, and the administration of justice. As a result, the ideal of limited government became deeply ingrained in American political thought. This in turn encouraged the view, asserted on a national scale by Andrew Jackson, that the duties of public employees were, or admitted of being made, so simple that as a general rule they could be performed in a reasonably satisfactory manner by the ordinary citizen. Honesty and normal intelligence were thought to be the only essential qualifications.

These influences have expressed themselves chiefly in two ways. One has been the widespread conviction that government should both stay out of business and keep out of its way—the twentieth century adaptation of Jefferson's preference for that government which governed least. The other influence has been a simple faith in direct relationships between the citizen and his public servants, coupled with a stubborn refusal to combine defectively small governmental units into larger and more resourceful ones. Until near the close of the nineteenth century, virtually every important administrative office—whether in town, city, school district, county, or state—was on an elective basis. Many still are, particularly in the counties. Moreover, terms of elective office are invariably short, seldom running over two years. As for appointive positions, the presumption prevailed from the early days that there should be frequent rotation in office and that every newly elected official had the right to dismiss incumbents inherited from his predecessor and fill their posts with appointees of his own choosing.

Hamiltonian and Jeffersonian traditions. Another historic influence upon modern American administration has been the unceasing contest between the two differing governmental theories espoused by the opposing titans of Washington's first cabinet.

Hamilton, brilliant, logical, and conservative, believed that commercial strength constituted the only sure foundation for national welfare and favored bold use of federal authority to advance that end. His program for building up a business class through tariff protection and other aids to industry inevitably entailed a considerable exercise of centralized power. This caused opposition at a time when previous experience led most people to reject every debatable employment of public authority as a danger to individual liberty. Hamilton, however, had no fear of power in government provided that those who wielded it could be held responsible for their acts. Though often challenged politically, this philosophy has been one of the significant factors in American government and is stronger today than ever before.

Jefferson disagreed with Hamilton's economic ideas, but not with a policy of fostering the development of commerce under state auspices or of using such power as was indispensable to the attainment of an end that would greatly enhance the public welfare. In Jefferson's vision the country was destined under the right leadership to develop into an agrarian democracy in which every man could find security for his family in the cultivation of his own acreage or in independent work as an artisan. As a result, Jefferson saw little need for national administration other than that required for the conduct of foreign relations. Beneath this belief, however, lay a more fundamental conviction. Jefferson held the opinion that power tends to corrupt the man in whom it is vested, making imperative its limitation to the barest minimum. Despite the fading of

Jefferson's agrarian ideal, his philosophy of limited and decentralized administration is one of the most effective rallying cries for many who are earnestly concerned over "centralized control."

Public administration and the national economy. Adam Smith's *The Wealth of Nations,* published in the year of the American declaration of political independence, served in a sense as a declaration of economic independence on behalf of the rising business or middle class. As such its basic ideas came to have an enormous vogue throughout the whole Western world. It is no exaggeration to say that during the nineteenth century they came to supply the dominant theme in popular thought on the relations between government and business. The philosophy of classical economics which took its rise from this epic volume was far more than a reasoned protest against the theory and practice of mercantilism. It had a positive character of its own, the implications of which were of cardinal importance for public administration.

Politics and economics, according to Adam Smith, were largely separate spheres. For the most part, the less they had to do with each other, the better. Every man had his own property or skill and the impulse of self-interest to lead him to put them to the best employment. The wisest thing government could do, therefore, was to leave the world of business strictly alone, aside from doing such necessary things as building and maintaining public works. This had considerable appeal to Americans. With a virgin continent opening up in the eighteenth and nineteenth centuries, they either had property of their own (land being naturally the main type) or could acquire it to be relatively self-sufficient. Consequently, the philosophy of governmental nonintervention did no such violence to the economic facts of life as it would today. Widespread ownership of land, actual and potential, provided at least some justification for *laissez faire* theories.

It required, therefore, a long and slow development, through decades blotted with innumerable instances of helpless poverty and social injustice, to raise political thinking above the standard of freedom from regulation of any kind to the higher standard of freedom under regulation designed to safeguard the general welfare. Until this new development was well under way, public administration had only halting and tentative relationships with the American economy. Today governmental activities sustain and regulate production and consumption in many ways.

Protection of the public interest. During the first half-century following American independence, it was the disposition of state governments in the East to guide economic activities as "planning states." But as industrialization gained full force, government came to permit free enterprise and private competition to take their normal course. Vigorous assertion of the idea of a public interest, whether in the use of natural resources or in fair competition in the market place, did not develop until late in the nineteenth century. Jurisdiction over economic matters lay generally with the states; their inaction often resulted in hardship and injustice for numerous individuals. It was only after the Middle Western states had enacted the Granger laws in the 1870's that government began to intervene extensively in the economic sphere.

Conceivably, the executive arm of the national government might have been employed to prevent the occurrence of abuses as the economy of the country expanded. However, any effort toward effective use of public authority for such purposes would have met strong opposition by the new business leadership. From the history of governmental regulation during the late nineteenth century it is evident that public administration was in a sense the unwanted child of a nation bent on material gain. Gross rapacity and prodigal waste first had to demonstrate the folly of assuming that competition worked like an invisible hand to insure the protection and promotion of the common good. Only then did the representative bodies again begin to emphasize the positive note in the American philosophy of government—the idea that government exists to safeguard the general welfare. Only then did they begin to enact the statutes and create the agencies which became the stepping stones for contemporary public administration.

3. The Expansion of Governmental Functions

American pragmatism. With some measure of justification, it has been said of Americans that as a nation they are not much given to systematic political speculation. Many have argued, without benefit of particulars, that the sphere of state activity should be sharply limited and that government should "stay out of business." No one, however, has succeeded in making a list of proper and improper functions of government that has won public approval over an extended period. William Graham Sumner's *What Do Social Classes Owe Each Other?* (1883) and Herbert Spencer's *Man Versus the State* (1884) both endeavored to demonstrate analytically why it was unwise to enlarge the range of governmental action. Yet the functions of government were increased even during the decades in which these books were enjoying their greatest popularity. Though favoring in theory a restricted scope of government, Americans have shown no less consistency in basing their action on "practical considerations" whenever these have pointed strongly in the opposite direction.

This is the line of argument implied in Cleveland's famous sentence, "It is a condition and not a theory which confronts us." In the last analysis "government has to do what it has to do." The people cannot be expected to adhere blindly to a theory when the price of such adherence would be acute social injustice or failure to reach an objective to which they are strongly attached.

Limits of nonintervention. American administrative history abounds in illustrations of extensions of governmental responsibility to meet current needs. Consider, for instance, the compromise with *laissez faire* involved in the erection of national tariff walls, in the establishment of the three "clientele" departments in Washington—Agriculture, Commerce, and Labor—and in the creation of government corporations. Each of these developments represents something of a variation on the theme of the theory of politico-economic division, yet each has come to be accepted. Curiously enough, those who show the greatest interest in urging government to pursue or persist in a positive course of action are often quite unconscious of what they do in terms of this theory. The reason is simple. If a particular group can manage to persuade government to intervene in the economic sphere on behalf of its own special interest, that naturally seems all to the good; it is "interference" only in the eyes of those who are affected adversely—to them it is all wrong.

Few groups in the body politic have given more lip service to the theory of the separation of government and business than the leaders of industry. Yet they have long favored tariff protection—a clear illustration of artificial interference with the dispensations of the "invisible hand" of free and "natural" competition. As practical men they simply refused to allow intangible principles to stand in the way of tangible results.

Establishment of clientele departments: Agriculture. Governmental intervention in the field of agriculture began nationally in an almost unnoticed activity of the Patent Office—the distribution of seeds and cuttings received from American consuls abroad. After performing this humble service for a number of years, the Patent Office in 1839 was given its first agricultural appropriation: $1,000. This was to be used for continued collection and distribution of seeds, for making several investigations of interest to farmers, and for the collection of agricultural statistics. Succeeding years brought increased appropriations without additional functions. Then, in 1862, under the urging of the United States Agricultural Society whose members wanted additional "service" from the government, Congress took the decisive step of passing the "organic act" which created "at the seat of government of the United States a Department of Agriculture."

It is a far cry from these modest beginnings to the gigantic operations of the department today. But two strong threads have provided connecting ties throughout every stage of the development. One is the continuous desire of organized farmers for governmental aid to agriculture. What the United States Agricultural Society did in persuading Congress to establish a new department in the midst of the Civil War typifies what organized agriculture has tried to do ever since—gain for itself in the solution of its problems the friendly assistance of government. The other thread is the willingness of the public to "go along," especially when it thinks that the general welfare would be served.

Next: Commerce and Labor. The Department of Commerce and Labor, created in 1903, was the second major clientele agency established within the structure of national administration. In terms of its germinal bureaus, it rose from such practical considerations as the necessity for proper patent registration (Superintendent of Patents, 1802), the need for inspection of steamboats to insure their seaworthy condition (Steamboat Inspection Service, 1838), and the demand on government for maintaining a testing laboratory of its own in order to assure itself of getting full and precise value in the purchase of supplies (National Bureau of Standards, 1901). In terms of its creation as a combined entity, the Department of Commerce and Labor owed its origin to the fact that around the turn of the century the President and Congress alike were convinced that administrative needs would better be served by bringing together in a single agency twelve existing bureaus doing broadly related work.

The unit within the Department of Commerce and Labor that has perhaps aided the American business community most directly came into being as the Bureau of Foreign and Domestic Commerce. Established by an act of Congress, it was charged specifically with the "promotion and development of the foreign and domestic commerce of the United States." Organized business worked actively for the passage of the measure setting up the new bureau and has since then looked upon the department, not unreasonably, as its special source of sympathetic governmental assistance.

Like the Department of Commerce (from which in 1913 it was formed by separation), the Department of Labor was composed initially of two bureaus which had been created in preceding years. The older of these was the Bureau of Labor, established by Congress in 1884 for the purpose of collecting and analyzing information on labor conditions and located in the Department of the Interior. Named the Department of Labor a few years later and given independent status though not cabinet rank, it was in 1903 again designated as a bureau and grouped with a number of other agencies to form the Department of Commerce and Labor. The other original unit of the newly formed Department of Labor was the Children's Bureau, which had been in existence for less than a year. As its name implies, the Children's Bureau was created for the purpose of gathering information and preparing reports, nationwide in scope, on problems of child care and child welfare. The considerations leading the President and Congress to combine the two bureaus into a department of cabinet rank were political and administrative. With organized labor's increasing success in making the public aware of the problems of the working class, it appeared to be both good politics and sound administration to accord labor the same kind of recognition that had already been given to agriculture and business.

Rise of government corporations. American pragmatism is plainly evident in the creation of these three great clientele departments. So, too, in the circumstances under which the major governmental proprietary undertakings have been launched. With popular opinion generally adverse to the government's "going into business," most proposals to set up a publicly owned or publicly operated business enterprise have one or two strikes against them even before they start. Yet government corporations are by no means uncommon on the American administrative scene. Many urban communities throughout the country have established their own corporate enterprises in the field of municipal utilities. When the residents of a local community find themselves unable to obtain satisfactory water, electric, gas, or transit service at reasonable rates through private firms, they often take what seems to them the logical second course of using their local government to establish and operate the facilities needed.

As a rule, the states have had less need to undertake business activities of their own. For a variety of reasons, however, the national government has made considerable use of corporate organization. During World War I, for instance, a government corporation was formed for the purpose of expediting an emergency shipbuilding program. Several corporations were formed during the depression years in the thirties to foster economic recovery, especially to make and administer loans to business firms. The Tennessee Valley Authority, created in 1933, was given corporate status so that it might enjoy the greatest possible measure of administrative flexibility in its unique program of regional development. In World War II, to take but one example, the federal government organized the United States Commercial Company because of the need for an agency through which it could act with convenience and dispatch and with a minimum of publicity in waging certain forms of economic warfare.

Growth of administrative activities. In response to what Mr. Justice Holmes called "the felt necessities of the time," the United States, like other modern nations, has experienced during the last century a great transition. A new civilization arose from the steam engine, the locomotive, the automobile, the telephone, the radio, the airplane, and other marvels of science and technology.

The nature of this transformation may be seen very plainly in the tremendous expansion of municipal administration. During the period from the early 1800's down to the 1930's, Cincinnati and Detroit grew from communities whose municipal services could be numbered on the fingers of one's hands to metropolitan regions whose services totaled between three and four hundred. And the number has continued to increase. The log of administrative development for both of these cities makes it clear that activities in the fields of health, utilities, education, recreation, and social welfare are the ones that absorb most energies of urban government in the present age.[4] Comparative studies of state and county governments likewise show upward trends in the number and variety of their administrative activities.[5] Their rate of increase, however, is lower than that of the cities, owing to the fact that the main currents of modern life—the trends toward national economic organization and urban residence—have affected states and counties to a lesser degree.

In the case of the national government the trend line rises steeply. Comprehensive statistical indices are available only for selected periods; but the crude data themselves give eloquent testimony to the steadily increasing use the American people have made of their central government.[6] Annual budget expenditures and civilian personnel figures have both risen at rates in advance of the rate of population growth. Although the table given here does not suggest the nature of the new responsibilities the national government has acquired in recent decades, it does afford some indication of the extent to which the volume of governmental activities has grown.

INCREASE IN NATIONAL POPULATION, ANNUAL EXPENDITURES, AND CIVILIAN PERSONNEL BY DECADES DURING THE CENTURY 1850-1950

Year	Population of Continental United States (in millions)	Annual Expenditures of the National Government, excluding debt retirement	Civilian Employees in the Federal Executive Service
1850	23.2	$ 39,543,492	33,300
1860	31.4	63,130,598	49,200
1870	38.6	309,653,561	53,900
1880	50.2	267,642,958	107,000
1890	63.0	318,040,711	166,000
1900	76.0	520,860,847	256,000
1910	92.0	693,617,065	391,350
1920	105.7	6,403,343,841	562,252
1930	122.8	3,440,268,884	588,206
1940	131.7	8,998,189,706	1,370,110
1950	160.7	40,166,835,915	2,109,642

[4] Cf. Upson, Lent D., The Growth of a City Government, Detroit: Bureau of Municipal Research, 1931; Cincinnati Municipal Reference Bureau, Cincinnati (1802-1936): The March of City Government, Cincinnati, 1937.

[5] For a charting of the administrative growth of state government, see Hurt, Elsey, California State Government: An Outline of its Administrative Organization from 1850 to 1936, 2 vols., Sacramento: California State Printing Office, 1937-39.

[6] See Wooddy, Carroll H., The Growth of the Federal Government, 1915-1932, New York: McGraw-Hill, 1934. This study was published as one of the monographs supporting the report of President Hoover's Research Committee on Social Trends. For developments since 1932, see the reports of the two (Hoover) Commissions on the Organization of the Executive Branch of the Government, Washington, 1949 and 1955, respectively. See also above, note 1. The most comprehensive analysis is: Fabricant, Solomon, The Trend of Government Activity in the United States since 1900, New York: National Bureau of Economic Research, Publication No. 56, 1952.

The salient fact about the character of most of the newer activities of the federal government is that they are designed to cope with the impact of technology on American society.

4. Increasing Competence for Increasing Responsibilities

Even a brief survey of the growth of public administration would not be complete without mention of the perennial struggle that has been waged for competent personnel; of the major gains registered in the fields of administrative structure and procedure; and of the effects produced by national emergencies.

Professional versus amateur. Concerned as it is primarily with means rather than ends, administration is a phase of government in which accomplishment can be measured with a degree of objectivity. It is, moreover, a phase in which it is possible to describe with relative precision the particular qualities or abilities that individuals ought to have for the positions to which they may be assigned. Conceivably, therefore, a system might have been established early whereby appointments to the public service would have been conditioned upon demonstration of the skills or talents required for the proper performance of official duties.

The facts do not bear out such a supposition. Whether because they are democratically inclined or for other reasons, the great majority of the people of the United States have long had a pronounced preference for amateur government. One device, still widely used in state and local government, is that of placing so many offices on an elective basis that the electorate is compelled—or allowed—to choose not only its political representatives but a considerable body of administrative officials as well. A second formula, now for the most part happily abandoned, is that of annual elections, based on the theory that where short terms end, there tyranny begins. Rotation in office comprises a third approach.

Rotation in office. Washington and Adams, the first two presidents of the United States, prided themselves on being good republicans, but neither claimed to be a democrat in the Jeffersonian sense. They believed that politics and administration were matters wisely left to the better classes— "the rich, the well-born, and the able"—and that the best families would inspire their ablest sons to seek careers in the government service. Allowing for Jefferson's deep distrust of social station, his inherent inclinations were also toward "talent and virtue." However, following his election in 1800, he discovered that two practical considerations obliged him to dismiss a number of Federalist appointees and replace them with Republicans. One was the fact that some of the Federalist holdovers showed no zeal for carrying out Republican policies. The other was the pressure for positions put upon the new President by members of his own party.

Agitation in favor of the principle of rotation in office in 1820 caused Congress to adopt the famous Four Years Law. This act provided that federal district attorneys, collectors of customs, naval officers, money agents, registrars of land offices, paymasters in the army, and several other classes of officials should serve four-year terms rather than at the pleasure of the President, as they had formerly. Even without this law, it is more than likely that Andrew Jackson during his administration (1829-1837) would have managed to dismiss a considerable number of the Whigs he found in the executive branch at his inauguration. There can be little doubt, however, that the law helped him to effect those changes in public personnel he thought necessary to place the government under the contol of "the people"—that is, those who had voted him into office. The four-year rule was later modified; but it contributed materially to the establishment of the spoils system in the United States. For half a century, from the 1830's to the 1880's, the overwhelming majority of appointments in American administration—national, state, and local—were made on the basis of party patronage.

Patronage and economy. During the first two-thirds of the nineteenth century, the functions of government continued to be relatively simple in character. After the Civil War, the raw materialism of industrialization, economic instability and insecurity, the loosening of personal ties as a result of increasing urbanization, the opportunities for large-scale graft latent in municipal construction and utilities, and the mounting need for professionally trained personnel to handle the new technical functions and administrative services—all these led to conditions that made reform imperative.

Disclosures of inefficiency and corruption touching every level of government aroused cities and states and the nation itself to a re-examination of democracy long overdue. Gradually a demand emerged for the establishment and enforcement of higher standards of official competence and for the introduction of tighter procedures wherever public money or property was involved.[7]

In national administration, the milestones marking the progress of reform were the Pendleton Act, which inaugurated the rule of merit in the recruitment of federal personnel (1883); the expansion of the new civil service by executive orders, especially under Cleveland and Wilson; and the Classification Act, to bring a rational order into civil service positions (1923). Meanwhile corresponding improvements in personnel administration were accomplished within their own jurisdictions by a growing number of states and cities.

---

[7] *Cf.* Steffens, Lincoln, *The Struggle for Self-Government,* New York: Doubleday, 1906, being an attempt to trace American political corruption to its sources in six states of the United States; Foulke, William D., *Fighting the Spoilsmen,* New York: Putnam, 1919.

Advances in structure and procedure. These efforts toward building a professionally competent and politically nonpartisan civil service have gone hand in hand with equally important improvements in administrative structure and procedure. Congress on several occasions took action in the interest of better administration. It gave support to the Commission on Economy and Efficiency under President Taft by creation of a Bureau of Efficiency (1913-33). It greatly enhanced executive control over the departmental system and strengthened fiscal accountability by passing the Budget and Accounting Act (1921). It enabled President Roosevelt in the Reorganization Act of 1939 to simplify the structure of the executive branch and to organize his own office for planning, management, and control, in line with the astute recommendations of the President's Committee on Administrative Management.[8]

Three main developments symbolize the progress made in raising the level of efficiency in state administration. Beginning with Illinois under the leadership of Governor Frank O. Lowden in 1917, approximately half the states in the Union have taken action to unify their administrative organization under the governor. Many states have also been obliged to give special consideration to the caliber of management in several of their functional departments in order to qualify for the increasing number of grants-in-aid available from the national government, especially under the Social Security Act of 1935. Lastly, the states make it a practice, chiefly through the Council of State Governments,[9] to exchange information and experience on all kinds of administrative problems.

In the field of urban government, the principal improvements in local administration include the formation in 1894 of the National Municipal League; the strengthening in many mayor-council cities of the appointive and directive powers of the mayor; the movement for organized municipal research which started with the establishment of the New York Bureau of Municipal Research in 1906; the drive for the introduction of systematic methods of municipal budgeting and purchasing; the growth of the council-manager plan of local government; and the formation of national professional associations of all major groups of local administrative officials, together with the establishment in 1931 of the Public Administration Clearing House. Widely known by its house number ("1313") in Chicago, this

---

[8] See the report of the President's Committee on Administrative Management and its supporting documents, Washington: Government Printing Office, 1937. Louis Brownlow served as chairman of the President's Committee, and Charles E. Merriam and Luther Gulick were its other two members. For a different approach, one should read, along with the Brownlow Report, the report of the Brookings Institution to the Senate Committee (Senator Byrd, chairman) set up to investigate the executive agencies of the federal government, Senate Report No. 1275, 75th Cong., 1st Sess., Washington, 1937.

[9] The publication program of the Council of State Governments includes the magazine *State Government* and a periodically issued handbook entitled *The Book of the States.*

cluster has become an important influence in local administration throughout the country.[10] In educational administration, the main advances are the well-nigh universal development of the superintendent of schools into the chief administrative officer of the local school system; the formation of the National Education Association and other professional organizations; and, finally, the movement for school districts both large enough in pupil population and strong enough in financial resources to operate programs conforming to acceptable minimum instructional standards. Less progress can be reported for rural administration in general.

Impact of emergencies. As tragedy is the test of character in personal life, so crisis is the test of capacity in administration. Accumulation of abuses in both government and business threatened to build up to serious difficulties in the United States during the decade preceding World War I. These were largely forestalled by a series of reforms embodied in what Theodore Roosevelt liked to call his Square Deal, by Taft's adherence to the "trust-busting" program, and more fully by the measures adopted as a result of Woodrow Wilson's campaign for the New Freedom—all leading to increased administrative strength. With the declaration of war in 1917 the nation's resources in public administration were put to a substantial test. The country was required on short notice to draft and train a large army, produce enormous quantities of food and war materials, and raise vast sums in loans and taxes. The measure of success achieved was accurately reflected in a comment by a leader on the losing side: "They knew how to wage war." Yet World War I had only one significant permanent effect on public administration: The executive branch never returned to its prewar dimensions either in number of agencies and government employees or in total size.

In contrast, the impact upon public administration of the Great Depression was momentous. Many of the measures taken to cope with it were decried as changes in the "American system"—indeed, in the national "way of life." The emergency resulted in both a striking enlargement of the administrative machinery and the assumption by government of far greater responsibility for the nation's economic well-being than ever before. Demanding closer collaboration between Washington and the states, between the states and the localities, and between the localities and Washington, the emergency also forced something of a transformation within the American governmental system. Competitive federalism began to yield by degrees to cooperative federalism.

World War II overtook the United States before the country had pulled

---

[10] Aside from such sources of current information about local administration as the (now) *National Civic Review* (published by the National Municipal League), the monthly *Public Management,* and the *Municipal Yearbook* (both put out by the International City Managers Association), mention should be made of the official organs of the various functional associations within and without the "1313" group.

itself completely out of the depression. Instead of shrinking in size or authority, the national government was vested with still greater powers and obliged to expand its activities and personnel beyond all precedent. The end of the war brought significant retrenchment; but, as after World War I, the level of government activities settled upon a substantially higher plateau. In part, this simply reflected the general growth of the country, and the rising gross national product. In part, it showed the continuing burdens of the war, as in the services for veterans, for instance. In part also, it gave a measure of the country's involvement in the "cold war," with many new responsibilities. Lastly, however, it indicated what Americans today expect of government and its administrative services.

Chapter 2 ●

The Study of

Public Administration

1. The Work of the Pioneers

Beginnings of administrative research. In all countries sufficiently advanced to require a reasonably mature system of public administration in executing public policy, great value is attached to the mastery of the administrative process. This process includes: the designing of appropriate administrative structures and the organizing of their component units; the formulating of work programs, standards of performance, and ways of measuring results; the budgeting of public revenue and expenditures and the accounting for funds; the recruiting, training, and directing of a suitable staff; the assumption of responsibility for the conduct of operations, on the one hand, and for planning proposed policy changes on the other; and the making of proper arrangements for the conduct of relations with other administrative agencies, the legislature, private individuals, organized groups, and the general public.[1]

Consideration of the importance of these elements may suggest the existence of an extensive body of cumulative experience, study, and analysis. European scholarship in the field of "cameralism"—ranging from economic policy to the management of crown lands—began to build up systematic knowledge as early as the seventeenth century. In the United States, however, the study of public administration is only fifty years old, if its birth date is accepted as 1906, the year the New York Bureau of Municipal Research was established. So brief a period did not give Ameri-

---

[1] For a full discussion of the range and the elements of the administrative process, see Waldo, Dwight, *The Study of Public Administration*, New York: Doubleday, 1955. For influential earlier assessments from different vantage points, see Gaus, John M., and Others. *The Frontiers of Public Administration*, ch. 1, Chicago: University of Chicago Press, 1936; Gulick, Luther, and Urwick, Lyndall, eds., *Papers on the Science of Administration*, New York: Institute of Public Administration, 1937. Two valuable bibliographies are: Seckler-Hudson, Catheryn, *Bibliography on Public Administration* (annotated), Washington: American University, 4th ed., 1953; United Nations Technical Assistance Administration, *International Bibliography of Public Administration*, New York, 1957.

can government any architects of administration as influential as Thomas Cromwell in England, Colbert in France, Frederick William I in Germany, or Mikhail Speranski in Russia. On the other hand, during these fifty years the utilization of scientific research for the development of public administration has won American scholarship and experimentation a place of honor throughout the world, though not uncritical acceptance.

Creation of the New York Bureau symbolized the beginning of a profession and a science of administration in three essential respects: accumulation of descriptive materials about the purposes, powers, structure, and functioning of governmental agencies; application of analytical techniques and technical standards; and employment of a full-time expert staff, prepared to accept responsibility for recommending specific measures for the improvement of administrative organization and management. For more than ten years the New York Bureau made studies and reports covering almost all the municipal activities of the city. It relied on well-conceived methods of establishing working relationships with the city government, of developing productive opportunities for investigation, and of getting its recommendations adopted. These methods not only constituted the earliest American experience in continuing administrative research but also set a prototype for use throughout the country.

Waves of governmental reform. The research-bureau movement, of course, did not materialize suddenly out of thin air. It developed after a period of more than twenty years of political agitation and experimentation with political "reform." Most of the reformers were people who, though unwilling or unable to go into politics themselves, thought that the political life of the nation should be purified and that "better" men should enter public service. The reformers included such advocates of the merit system in government employment as Carl Schurz and Dorman B. Eaton; journalists and publicists like E. L. Godkin, Henry Adams, and Henry Demarest Lloyd; and practical businessmen, lawyers, clergymen, teachers, and other citizens who organized city clubs to promote "good government." These individuals and civic-minded groups left a lasting legacy in the formation and the working approach of civil service commissions, and in other devices of reform. Their political activities were less successful. Although they helped to elect "good" candidates to office in many cities, usually these men were voted out soon and the party bosses came back into power. Lacking broad sympathetic support, the independent civil service commissions were in such instances often controlled or isolated by partisan forces.

Around the turn of the century, thoughtful analysis of these experiences resulted in various inquiries into the facts of governmental life. One form of inquiry was represented by the brilliant newspaper and magazine reports of the "muckrakers," whose exposure of the deeper economic roots of political corruption had a wide if short-lived influence.[2] Characteristic realism and a propensity for quick generalization led these writers to take the simple position that the economic system controlled the politicians; that the politicians controlled civil service commissions and operating officials; and that the remainder of public administration, insofar as it was not dishonest or corrupt, was simply the unimportant routine execution of public business. If this approach spent itself in a frontal onslaught upon "the system," it did arouse America's civic conscience. It also underscored the point that the state of public administration could hardly be divorced from the state of society.

Organized dissemination of knowledge. Another type of inquiry expressed itself in the collection and dissemination of information on municipal facts and events by the National Municipal League, founded in 1894, and the formulation by that body after 1900 of its standard "model laws" for the organization and powers of local and state governments. The research activities of the League and the more active promotional tactics of its offshoot, the National Short Ballot Organization, were of great assistance to the developing profession of public administration.

On the whole, however, these and similar private organizations concentrated on reporting developments in better government structure and the framing of charters, ordinances, and constitutions. They borrowed heavily from the lawyer's professional skill in drafting documents, trusting that precision in using words would direct behavior accordingly—which it does in part, but only in part. They tended to leave the study and improvement of administrative management, processes, and standards to "technicians."

Role of Progressivism. A third type of inquiry was associated between 1896 and 1912 with the political movement called Progressivism. Progressivism has often been identified with the personalities of its leaders.[3] One common bond between them was the conviction that if new policies of economic regulation were to stick, those policies must be removed from the hands of legislative bodies and administered by expert boards on the basis of technical investigation and nonpolitical determination of the facts. Early systematic thinking about the independent regulatory commission was linked with Progressivism in the states; and in at least one state, Wis-

---

[2] Steffens, Lincoln, *Autobiography,* New York: Harcourt Brace, 1931; Whitlock, Brand, *Forty Years of It,* New York: Appleton, new ed., 1925; and the autobiographies of Robert M. LaFollette, Sr., and Theodore Roosevelt.

[3] *Cf.* Croly, Herbert, *Progressive Democracy,* New York: Macmillan, 1915, which is perhaps the best statement of its political program. See also Chamberlain, John, *Farewell to Reform,* New York: Viking; 1933; Bowers, C. G., *Beveridge and the Progressive Era,* Boston: Houghton Mifflin, 1932. Progressivism was really faith in a method, rather than a coherent philosophy or economic program, coupled with an abiding belief that the people would support expert administration if properly led and given the facts by responsible political leaders.

consin, it was based on close collaboration between the state capitol and the state university. This collaboration also made possible in 1901 the establishment of one of the first legislative reference libraries in the United States. Moreover, it paved the way for considerable research and participation by university professors in the drafting of state legislation. The ensuing period witnessed the initial adoption in many states of effective legislation regulating public utilities, workmen's compensation, conservation of natural resources, and conditions of employment.

If the trends inherent in the progressive movement prior to 1912 had continued, perhaps the study of public administration would have developed on a subject-matter basis, as separate series of professional or expert techniques, each peculiar to a distinct area of economic policy. What actually happened, however, was something different. Development of the theory of the administrative process exemplified by the independent regulatory commission was largely taken over by the economists and lawyers, while the political scientists divided themselves into two groups. One group busied itself with structural problems in the relations between the federal government and the states, state control over local government, the role of the political chief executive face to face with the legislative body, and the proper organization of the executive branch. The other group joined forces with the municipal research-bureau movement in the conviction that progress toward good government would follow only from full-time detailed study and technical analysis of the methods of conducting the government's business. In its best products, the output of each group reinforced the foundation of the work of the other.

Contribution of the universities. The contribution of the universities to the rise of public administration was rather indirect, with the exception of a few outstanding individuals. Woodrow Wilson contributed his pioneer paper entitled "The Study of Administration" to the infant *Political Science Quarterly* in 1887. James Bryce is said to have drawn heavily upon the series of Johns Hopkins studies in historical and political science (beginning in 1882), as well as upon the services of Professor Frank J. Goodnow, in preparing his influential *American Commonwealth* (1888). Many students of Simon Patten at the University of Pennsylvania, Richard T. Ely and John R. Commons at Johns Hopkins and Wisconsin, A. L. Lowell at Harvard, and of the faculty of History, Government, and Public Law at Columbia University, later distinguished themselves in the practice and the analysis of public administration. However, during the earlier period the study of government and politics was just disentangling itself in the college curriculum from philosophy, political economy, and a jurisprudence dominated by the private law of property.[4]

---

[4] See Beard, Charles A., *Economic Interpretation of the Constitution*, Introduction, New York: Macmillan, rev. ed., 1932; Dorfman, Joseph, *Thorstein Veblen and His America*, esp. chs. 3-6, New York: Viking, 1934; Merriam, Charles E., *American Political Ideas, 1865-1917*, New York: Macmillan, 1920.

The academic progenitors of public administration in the eighties and nineties were economists, political scientists, and sociologists who taught their students how to analyze the economic and political processes through which public authority is exercised, without much speculating about the concepts of political philosophers and supreme court judges. Even so, legal materials constituted so much of the subject matter with which students of government dealt in those days that Goodnow, who is generally considered the father of American public administration, wrote most of his books in the fields of administrative and constitutional law. In this respect, he followed in his intellectual orientation the example of his academic teachers in Paris and Berlin. One may concede that a true profession of public administration could not have arisen until after trained men began to study at first hand the working processes of government. But American administrative research owes its academic forefathers a large debt for their critical and realistic temper, their awareness of the institutional determinants of public policy, and their distrust of the purely legalistic approach.[5]

2. The Advancement of Knowledge

Relativity of efficiency. Full-time research bureaus were established in twelve large cities between 1906 and 1915. Their slogan was efficiency and economy. The experience of their staffs in administrative research soon revealed the fugitive nature of this objective, when conceived as a source of immediate reduction in governmental expenditure. It was discovered that efficiency and economy had to be achieved primarily as a by-product of getting at the basic facts of administrative purpose, structure, and procedure. Leaving out instances of outright venality and political privilege, it was found that there was always a certain degree of efficiency in existing methods and routines. Apart from the question of whether a given function should or should not be performed, the goal of efficiency and economy raised the question of purpose—that is, whether procedures were to be considered from the limited standpoint of particular officials and particular interests or from that of the public purpose the individual agency was supposed to achieve. Thus research-bureau workers were led to a search for principles of management in order to secure acceptance for those practices which advanced the purpose of the organization as a whole, as compared with procedures and habits which

---

[5] Organizations of public officials such as state and local health officers, police chiefs, superintendents of insurance, and tax educational administrators existed before 1906. These early organizations were in many cases more social groups than promoters of research in the standards of their profession, however; and they were separatist and vocational in interest. See White, Leonard D., *Trends in Public Administration*, chs. 20, 22, New York: McGraw-Hill, 1933. Earlier events are discussed in Short, Lloyd M., *The Development of National Administrative Organization in the United States*, Washington: Institute of Government Research, 1923.

had grown up for historic reasons or had been established by officials with narrower objectives in view.

For example, from the angle of a municipal department head, it might be preferable to go directly to the city council for funds, without seeking agreement with the mayor or the city manager. Broader perspective would be necessary for him to envision the advantages of budgetary coordination at a central point. Yet only thus could a balanced consideration of the work plan of the city government as a whole be attained before submitting the estimates of expenditure to the council. In the same way, individual officials did not mind the scattering of similar functions among several agencies and the existence of varying methods of performing similar operations by different organizations. Yet there was obvious merit in the principle that functional consolidation and establishment of uniform standards be secured in the larger interest, even at the expense of particular officials who might have achieved considerable efficiency within their own operations. Economy was not simply a matter of eliminating functions or services, most of which were ardently supported by citizen groups, but one of giving proper consideration to the specific question of whether particular expenditures were or were not justified.

Use of outside experts. Thus administrative research tried to develop principles and techniques of public management. The executive budget, personnel classification and salary standardization, and centralized purchasing all found systematic application and expansion in local governments in the decade following 1906. It was wholly natural that Dr. Frederick A. Cleveland of the New York Bureau of Municipal Research was appointed by President Taft in 1910 to direct the work of the United States Commission on Economy and Efficiency. The Commission and its staff for the first time applied to the entire executive branch of the federal government the full measure of painstaking research into administrative duties, organization, procedure, and housekeeping methods, exhibiting in a long series of factual monographs the results of detailed legislative control over the departments. In his final report, Dr. Cleveland formulated what is perhaps the classic statement of the purpose of the executive budget as a scientific tool of administration,[6] a contribution which laid an early foundation for the Budget and Accounting Act of 1921. Similarly, the Congressional Joint Commission on Reclassification of Salaries drew heavily upon the experience of the local research bureaus in their work of job description and classification; on that foundation was built the scheme embodied in the Classification Act of 1923—a guidepost for federal personnel administration.

The drive for administrative reorganization of state governments began

---

[6] "The Need for a National Budget," 62nd Cong., 2nd Sess., House Doc. No. 854, Washington, 1912. *Cf.* also his *Organized Democracy,* New York: Macmillan, 1913.

in 1909. Staff work and reports in preparation for the New York and Illinois Constitutional Conventions of 1915 and 1917 were notable especially for the quality and method of research. These reports documented three early premises of organizational thinking: (1) concentration of responsibility by consolidating functions into a small number of departments each headed by a single official appointed by and responsible solely to the chief executive; (2) functional integration by grouping similar or related activities into the same department; and (3) centralized controls over finance, government purchasing, and personnel.

Executive responsibility for administration was the dominating theme. Coupled with the short ballot, the executive budget, and application of the merit system to all but politically appointed department heads, these main propositions conceived as principles were applied with variations in about half the states between 1917 and 1932. Many of the changes were based upon recommendations derived from surveys by three private organizations staffed with specialists in administrative analysis: the Institute of Government Research of the Brookings Institution (Washington), the National Institute of Public Administration (successor to the New York Bureau of Municipal Research), and Griffenhagen and Associates (Chicago). Their surveys usually resulted in thorough, factual reports, with recommendations based on intensive analysis and classifications of activities into major functions. Such reports were filed with the governors or legislative bodies for appropriate action.[7]

Critical reactions. Entirely aside from the general rule that the survey staffs were to take no active part in getting their recommendations adopted, the principles recommended in most of the state surveys came in for quite a bit of criticism. It was questioned whether the political executive would have the time or inclination to become a general manager for administration. The notion that the voters would ever choose their mayors, governors, or presidents on the basis of administrative competence was ridiculed. Doubts were raised as to whether the political head should be entrusted with authority over all finance and personnel matters. Finally, instances were pointed out in which there were persuasive reasons for preferring administrative boards over single-headed agencies.[8]

This debate revealed the confusion and ambiguity of concepts and of scientific methods that had crept into the thinking of students of public

---

[7] The capstone of this kind of outside survey work, in method and result, was the monumental study of federal administration by the Brookings Institution for the Senate (Byrd) Committee Investigating Executive Agencies, 75th Cong., 1st Sess., Senate Report No. 1275, Washington, 1937.

[8] See Hyneman, Charles S., "Administrative Reorganization: An Adventure into Science and Theology," *Journal of Politics,* 1939, Vol. 1, p. 62 *ff.*; Walker, Harvey, "Theory and Practice in State Administrative Reorganization," *National Municipal Review,* 1930, Vol. 19, p. 249 *ff.*; Coker, Francis W., "Dogmas of Administrative Reform," *American Political Science Review,* 1922, Vol. 16, p. 399 *ff.*

administration.[9] It is interesting to notice, by comparison, the high degree of unanimity reflected in the adoption by Congress of the Budget and Accounting Act of 1921, by which the President was given his first genuine staff agency, the Bureau of the Budget, acting for him as his budget planner and budget controller, his organization and methods analyst, and his coordinator of legislative proposals. On the one hand, the concentration of authority in the presidency was a constitutional fact, not a wish; and on the other, this reform was the work of Congress itself, with Representative Good of Iowa serving as the unerring pilot.

Challenge to traditional approach. By assuming a separation of policy-making from administrative efficiency, the private survey teams had tried to arrive at valid principles, at least on the technical level of operations. However, validity of principles depends upon agreement: (1) on the diagnosis of the problem; and (2) on the objective sought. The arguments over state reorganization in the 1920's foreshadowed the famous conflict in 1937 and 1938 between the President's Committee on Administrative Management and the Brookings Institution. It illustrated the degree to which broad agreement upon a great many concrete propositions for administrative improvement can be distorted by differences over the priority of problems, and by the intrusion of political issues and value judgments which may or may not be relevant to specific proposals. The President's Committee eschewed the survey method of functional analysis and classification which the Brookings Institution had utilized; it selected its objectives in terms of the problems conceived by the President and his advisers to be of compelling importance. In both its investigations and its recommendations, it sought to develop answers to these problems.

The 1937-38 debates, accompanied by cries of presidential "dictatorship," showed most students of administration that public management is not a science of "principles." The concept of the scientific investigator— standing apart from his material of human beings while collecting and weighing his facts and ultimately arriving at the right conclusions—had to be reexamined for governmental research. It was based in part upon Frederick W. Taylor's ideas of scientific management,[10] which called for the study and formulation of the proper methods of job performance in advance, followed by adjustment of the human factor to those methods.

---

[9] See Beard, Charles A., "Administration: A Test of Ideal and Power," ch. 10, in his *Public Policy and General Welfare,* New York: Farrar and Rinehart, 1941. The best analysis of the American literature of public administration from a methodological standpoint is Waldo, Dwight, *The Administrative State: A Study of the Political Theory of American Public Administration,* New York: Ronald, 1948. *Cf.* also Wallace, Schuyler C., *Federal Departmentalization,* New York: Columbia University Press, 1941; Simon, Herbert A., *Administrative Behavior: A Study of Decision-Making Processes in Administrative Organization,* New York: Macmillan, reprinted with new introduction, 1957.

[10] Taylor's main work is *The Principles of Scientific Management,* New York: Harper, 1919.

This approach or technique was developed and applied to the details of specific job operations at the shop level by a trained engineer or superintendent within the factory hierarchy, with authority over the workers. It lacks immediate applicability to management research into program questions. Conditions are different when the research staff is wholly outside the hierarchy of responsibility and has no powers or sanctions over the human element other than publicity and persuasion. The same is true when the purpose of analysis is not to improve job performance, but to achieve proper structural relationships. A different condition also prevails when the objective of study is not to help the operating official do a better job, but rather is to change his job. Moreover, although being outside the government has certain advantages of freedom and public pressure, it presents difficult problems in developing and maintaining working contacts with operating officials. Publicity is a one-shot weapon which, when improperly used, may result in the destruction of working relationships.

On the other hand, special inquiries under independent auspices can more readily escape the fixed ideas or the stalemate of forces within the organization to be studied. Perhaps the best recent illustrations are the two Commissions on the Organization of the Executive Branch of the Government (1947-49 and 1953-55, both chaired by former President Hoover). But it deserves notice that the second, aiming explicitly at elimination of federal functions, left a less impressive record, perhaps because the aim itself put too heavy a burden on objectivity.

Rise of administrative self-analysis. Two main developments have arisen to modify the methods of citizen research agencies. One was signified by the creation at Chicago in 1933 of the Public Administration Service. PAS emphasized the importance of work planning and scheduling in administrative operations. It also specialized in the development of units of work measurement and systems of administrative reporting, which its staff stood ready not only to recommend but to install.[11] This approach was based on the importance of helping the administrator to run his agency effectively, in contrast with a preoccupation with logical organization and proper allocation of functions.

The other source of competition with traditional administrative research was the development during the twenties and thirties at all levels of government of specialized staff facilities as official instruments of management analysis. The work of continuous study of governmental organization and operations as a basis for the annual scrutiny of departmental budget estimates; the supervision of the methods of approving and recording

[11] Ridley, Clarence E. and Simon, Herbert A., *Measuring Municipal Activities,* 2d ed., Chicago: International City Managers Association, 1943; Public Administration Service, *The Work Unit in Federal Administration,* Chicago, 1937; Stone, Donald C., *The Management of Municipal Public Works,* Chicago: Public Administration Service, 1939.

obligations and expenditures; the application of the personnel classification plan to the recruitment, selection, promotion and transfer of employees—these and similar central staff activities add up to a continuous process of inquiry into the programs and methods of the various agencies. Perhaps the outstanding contribution of the President's Committee on Administrative Management was the way in which it highlighted the value of staff and control agencies as tools of coordination for the chief executive. Its report reviewed the federal experience of twenty years with the Bureau of Efficiency (1913-33) and laid the foundation for the program of the Budget Bureau's Division of Administrative Management after 1939.

Consolidation of central responsibility for general efficiency in the agency of budgetary coordination symbolizes another aspect of strengthened governmental management. Recurrent processes of estimates review and program coordination are invigorated by an energetic pursuit of management improvement. This blending of management-mindedness with budgetary and other governmentwide controls in the Executive Office of the President represents the latest development of federal administrative planning on the highest level.[12] It affords the President the benefit of a general-staff approach in the exercise of his administrative responsibilities.

The decade of the thirties thus witnessed a shift of the center of gravity in governmental research from private citizen-supported agencies outside the government to central staff agencies within the government itself. At the same time, the idea of central agencies as direct controllers of line officials retreated before the concept of central assistance in line operations by clarification of administrative objectives, stimulation of work planning and scheduling, and cooperation with departmental managers in establishing standards of performance. The information about agency activities thus gained makes available to the chief executive an invaluable flow of intelligence divorced as nearly as may be from vested departmental interests.[13] The next step was the gradual if uneven formation of management staffs in the line agencies themselves. Their growth brought into being a desirable counterinfluence, both by limiting the range of responsibilities regarded as normal for central staff agencies and by increasing the opportunities for technical cooperation throughout the executive branch.

Reaffirmation of the political context. After fifty years productive of research findings, refinement in administrative analysis and control, and evolution of a professional spirit among students and practitioners of administration, it is not surprising that eventually a new view developed of the old question about the relation of politics and administration. Little

---

[12] See Hobbs, Edward H., *Behind the President: A Study of Executive Staff Agencies,* Washington: Public Affairs Press, 1954, and the literature cited there.

[13] For a discussion of policy planning as distinct from administrative planning, *cf.* Key, V. O., "Politics and Administration," in White, Leonard D., ed., *The Future of Government in the United States,* Chicago, University of Chicago Press, 1942.

room is left for speculation about the fitness of persons experienced and trained in the administrative arts to contribute to the formulation of policy. The real problem is one of appropriate form, procedure, and accountability for the career man's contribution to policy-making—a contribution in fact continuously called for by his political superiors. General discussions about the "managerial revolution" have drawn attention to it, but have imputed a greater assurance and solidarity among those presumably forming the managerial group than actually exists.

The issue is bound up with other complex problems. These include: (1) the appropriate code of behavior in the area between the setting of administrative policy under law and legislative policy-making; (2) the proper balance between the judgments of subject-matter specialists and line operators on the one hand and those of management planners and staff "generalists" on the other; (3) the perspectives of the lawyers in the entire realm of law-making and rule-making; and (4) the nature of "bureaucratic ideology." On this last point, some feel that administrative agencies are responsible for achieving desirable social purposes and may have to fight for them in the legislative arena. Others think administrative agencies should confine themselves to getting their assignments done within the policies established by the legislative body. Again, the two positions may not be very far apart once the question of the appropriate form, procedure, and accountability has been answered.

Discussion during the past generation of such questions as those of administrative finality, administrative discretion, and administrative responsibility reveals a shift in administrative research. Concern with technical expertness and specialized experience has yielded to study of the factors involved in the management of an organization and the objectives or values toward which governmental organizations should strive. The earlier assumption about the role of public administration in a democratic society is no longer controlling. Once the argument seemed to rest mostly on the thesis that democracy and efficiency in administration were not incompatible. The question was how to make democratic administration efficient and effective in the face of arbitrary political interference in administrative matters. Today the importance of technical competence and professional standards is not underestimated. But it is assumed that the criteria of efficiency in democratic administration are broader than and superior to technically sound procedure and financial economy in the execution of established policies. Efficiency, in its ultimate significance, has been linked with the attainment of the values acknowledged by the society to be served.

At each of these successive stages of the American development, the results attained found expression in widely accepted and quickly conventionalized patterns, both in terms of what to aim for and how to go about it. But the momentum was sustained. Every time, before matters settled sufficiently to give rise to a single dominant school of thought, another intellectual break-through occurred, leading to a fresh appraisal of what was yesterday's self-evident "truth." Granting that all of this reflected in some measure the law of fashion and to a larger extent a characteristic restlessness for immediate practical benefits, on balance the outstanding gain has been the rise of a remarkable degree of sophistication in looking upon the administrative process. This is demonstrated in the current tendencies of administrative research, which we shall examine presently. First, however, it is desirable to turn to a subject closely related to the trends reviewed thus far: What demands should be made of those who want to enter the service of government?

3. Training for Public Administration

Educational aspects. The advancement and maturity of public administration as a profession may be appraised, apart from its assumptions and its techniques, by the types of training provided and the standards of admission required of aspirants for entrance. Of course, there is no single vocational group specializing in "public administration." The public service includes every profession and every skill within the range of functions and activities performed for the community. Yet proper training for government work has been a matter of deep interest to civic reform organizations of public officials, and political science departments in colleges and universities all over the country. In the last generation, there has been an increasing crystallization of ideas and methods of approach.

However diverse the forms of government action may be, the management of public business is recognized as a field of career activity for which it is possible to provide training and incentives to attract the highest ability. In an authoritative survey,[14] Professor George A. Graham has taken the position that training for public administration is not a special professional apprenticeship but part of the broad problem of educational policy. Its ideal is continuous growth and widening experience for the able individual, as he prepares himself to meet successive tests of competence for tasks of greater responsibility. To attract ability and talent into the public service, government recruitment must be coordinated with graduation from the several levels of school and college. Government must encourage efforts on the part of its workers to advance themselves by providing training arrangements both for appropriate specialization and for widening their intellectual horizons, along the lines of the federal employee training legislation passed in 1958.

---

[14] Graham, George A., *Education for Public Administration,* Chicago: Public Administration Service, 1941.

Points of emphasis. A comprehensive policy would not favor the establishment of a separate program in educational institutions emphasizing preparation for the public service exclusively. It would, on the contrary, foster efforts to establish a universitywide program designed to be of use to both prospective aspirants for government employment and those who are interested primarily in relating their higher learning to the realities of public affairs. Such a program would seek to provide appropriate guidance, information, and interdepartmental arrangements for selection of courses, standards of examination, and requirements of evidence of creative ability. Similarly, after entrance into the public service, there would not be a special staff college for prospective government managers or executives only. Rather, there would be a process of competition for opportunities under forward-looking supervision and of promotion across divisional or departmental lines, based upon a servicewide policy.

Public administration is not identified by a distinctive technique of its own, a single type of activity, or a unified subject matter upon which agreement can be reached for purposes of establishing a special curriculum. On the contrary, substantial agreement exists that at the undergraduate level a broad liberal education is the best prescription. It should include a realistic awareness of the operation of economic institutions and the role of government in modern society, supplemented if possible by some work in such empirical-analytical procedures as statistics or accounting. It should stress the ability to speak and write effectively. This would be a better preparation than training for a specific job. In postgraduate work, all types of professional schools are potential sources of recruits for government work. Professional training in the natural sciences, engineering, education, medicine, social work, law, economics, and governmental research, culminating in professional degrees, is increasingly accepted, together with training in political science and public administration, as experience which civil service commissions will consider as qualification for intermediate positions in the classified service. In pre-entry training for public service, therefore, we find little disposition to provide a single specific occupational preparation.

Contrast with Great Britain. Since the University of Minnesota Conference in 1931, much attention has been devoted to the question of whether the elements of public management constitute a subject matter that can be taught apart from application to technical fields of administrative activity such as public health, public works, public welfare; and, if so, whether it would prepare the student for administrative work. Actually, no program of training for public service has attempted to teach the knowledge and art of government management in a vacuum. Syracuse University, pioneering with a special program of graduate training aimed at government service, used the block or "end-on-end" method of instruction to impart both the techniques of management and understanding of special areas of subject matter. Its graduates found ready markets for their services, particularly in budget and personnel agencies.

Recruitment for the civil service in the United States has never followed the lines recommended by the Trevelyan-Northcote and Macaulay reports for Great Britain in 1853-54.[15] These reports advocated the recruitment of the top men in the graduating classes of the British universities, regardless of the subject of their specialization, for the entrance grade of the higher civil service, coupled with a suitable period of post-entry training and qualification. In this country, at least up to 1934, the policy of civil service recruitment was based upon the assumption that government work can be classified into occupational groupings within vertical services. After the amount of training and experience required for the job classification within each such service was determined, qualified applicants were recruited by competitive examination. This policy placed a premium upon professional or vocational experience, and upon evidence of fitness for meeting the practical requirements of particular jobs. The policy came in for a good deal of criticism on the ground that, in the absence of clear career lines, able young men and women of general competence, lacking specific experience, are likely to look elsewhere for their life work.

The decade from 1934 to 1944 was notable for the efforts made to improve the quality of intake in the entrance grades for professional employment in the public service. In 1934, largely upon the initiative of a member drafted from academic life, the late Professor Leonard D. White, the United States Civil Service Commission conducted an examination for junior civil service examiner, for which academic training constituted the principal requirement. In 1936, a broader category of social science analysts was established as a register from which appointments might be made by departments seeking general ability rather than specific experience. From January, 1935, through March, 1939, more than 5,000 such junior professional appointments were made by federal agencies.[16] In 1934, the National Institute of Public Affairs was established in Washington; annually it offered about fifty men and women just out of college the opportunity to study at first hand the operations of federal agencies in the capacity of learners, or interns. Eventually, the federal agencies themselves picked up this work, and the Institute disbanded. Programs of municipal internship

---

[15] See Eaton, Dorman B., *Civil Service in Great Britain,* New York: National Civil Service Reform League, 1881; White, Leonard D. and Others, *Civil Service Abroad,* New York: McGraw-Hill, 1935; Stout, Hiram M., *Public Service in Great Britain,* New York: Harcourt, Brace, 1938; Kingsley, Donald, *Representative Bureaucracy,* Yellow Springs: Antioch Press, 1944; Robson, William A., ed., *The Civil Service in Britain and France,* New York: Macmillan, 1956.

[16] Report of President's Committee on Civil Service Improvement, 77th Cong., 1st Sess., House Doc. No. 118, p. 25, Washington, 1941. Appointments made from other lists built up from the usual kind of competitive examination were less than half (2,421) this number.

also received impetus and encouragement at such institutions as Syracuse University, Wayne University, and the University of Cincinnati. Apprenticeship programs were experimentally developed by several of the national organizations of public officials associated with the Public Administration Clearing House at Chicago, the Michigan Municipal League, and Los Angeles County. For the federal government, the general civil service entrance examination developed in the fifties represents the most promising bid for the college graduate who can offer ability rather than occupational experience. Moreover, the material attraction of the normal entrance grade has been enlarged by higher pay.

Post-entry training. Until the more recent adoption of government programs for the development of potential executive talent, post-entry or in-service training represented mainly an opportunity of advancement for the middle and lower ranks of public employment, particularly in the clerical and manual occupations. Universities, where located in proximity to large groups of government workers, such as the University of Southern California, have established courses for public employees, particularly in the fields of budgeting and accounting, police and fire administration, tax assessment and sanitary inspection. A source of financial aid is available to states and municipalities under the George-Deen Act of 1936 for vocational training in public-service occupations.

In the national capital, one program of in-service training is that of the Department of Agriculture's Graduate School. Others are those of American University and George Washington University, both also at the seat of the federal government, which offer evening courses in practically all the social sciences, including public administration. With others throughout the land, these institutions have trained men and women who started as clerks and messengers for administrative and professional positions. In the federal service, post-entry training is not highly formalized, except for such special programs as those of the State Department's Foreign Service Institute, the Federal Bureau of Investigation, and the Internal Revenue Service.[17] It consists in part in authorizing selected individuals to seek additional education outside their jobs at government expense, and in part in providing in-service programs directly related to the need for raising the performance level in the discharge of particular functions.

Group structure of the public service. Perhaps the main reason why post-entry training has not been more closely coordinated with official channels of advancement lies in the American distaste for a formal division of the public service into integrated grade groups around which career incentives might develop. The Commission of Inquiry on Public Service Personnel (1935) proposed separate careers for administrative, professional,

---

[17] For another development, see Reining, Henry, Jr., "The First Federal In-Service Internship Program," *Personnel Administration*, 1944, Vol. 7, p. 8 *ff*.

clerical, skilled-trade, and unskilled employees. These proposals have hardly received the serious public attention they deserve.[18] In spite of careful explanations that an administrative class would serve as a vertical ladder leading from junior staff positions or below to administrative assistants and on to the top, the impression continues to prevail that such an arrangement would serve the interests of privilege. It would, it is said, reserve the top positions under the political secretaries and assistant secretaries for a special group who would be favored at the expense of able persons in the clerical, technical, or professional services.

Until the emergence of an integrated administrative career group in American personnel practice, however, top administrative positions will be filled in various ways—by appointment from outside the service and by promotion from the ranks of professional and technical as well as administrative employees. Under these conditions, pre-entry programs of training for public administration will have to rely more upon general motives of public service and competitively inviting job opportunities in government than upon the specific attractions of a career in management.

Higher career opportunities. Even without legislative sanction of an administrative career group, much could be done to maintain such an ideal as a long-range objective. Constructive suggestions looking forward to the establishment of an "administrative corps" were made by the Reed Committee on Civil Service Improvement in 1941.[19] These included: identification of positions in specified grades as a group; maintenance of an inventory of personnel in these positions for use in making appointments to higher administrative posts; reporting of vacancies in higher positions; recommending candidates with tested qualifications to appointing officers; and follow-up on action. It was asserted that tapping and training personnel for positions in the lowest grade of the administrative group should be a continuing objective of agency personnel officers at all times, while a liberal policy permitting transfer of such personnel between agencies would widen their experience and develop general administrative skill.

A fresh start along broadly similar lines was proposed by the second Commission on the Organization of the Executive Branch of the Government, presided over by former President Herbert Hoover (1953-55). It embodied in its recommendations dealing with federal personnel an interesting formula for strengthening both the political element and the administrative cadre in the top structure of the administrative system. These ideas, in turn, had been suggested in a memorable report prepared by a task force chaired by Harold W. Dodds, a political scientist distinguished both as civic leader and as president of Princeton University, with Professor Graham, previously mentioned, directing the staff work. The report took

---

[18] *Better Government Personnel*, p. 5-6, 37-47, New York: McGraw-Hill, 1935.
[19] *Op. cit.* above in note 16, p. 3, 56-62, 86-97. See also White, Leonard D., *Government Career Service*, Chicago: University of Chicago Press, 1935.

the position that the role of political executives in the direction of the departments should be more fully recognized, and their sphere be enlarged. This point was ingeniously balanced against the demand that the highest career grades be pulled together into a senior service group, available to meet the needs of the government as a whole. Some preliminary steps were taken in 1958, but it is still too early to forecast the outcome of this proposal. By and large, the rank and file was unsympathetic; and top civil servants were mostly dubious, as they had been about the creation, some eight years earlier, of the departmental post of assistant secretary for administration as a career position.

4. The Frontiers of Research

Currents and countercurrents. The decade from 1940 to 1950 stands out in retrospect as one extraordinarily rich in evolutionary currents in the intellectual advance of the study of public administration in the United States. These currents partly supported and partly battled against one another. It was like a re-enactment of the fanciful scene of the rider jumping into the saddle and racing off in all directions at once.

The explanation, in the main, must be found in two facts. On the one hand, the academic treatment of public administration had settled on a plateau which to venturesome minds left the subject at considerable distance. The stored-up restlessness was straining to gain a better vantage point. On the other hand, wartime service in civilian as well as military agencies gave hundreds of teachers of public administration their first chance of direct participation in the conduct of large-scale government. They soon discovered that "the books had not told all." Filled with a revolutionary experience, they looked forward to "telling the story differently." The combination of those two facts created an explosive urge to try out fresh approaches. One may therefore say without exaggeration that nearly all of today's probing in the study of public administration had a beginning in the forties.

Two markers may be selected to indicate the nature of the fermentation. The opening marker was the foundation of the American Society of Public Administration (1940), breaking its own path in self-conscious independence from the American Political Science Association (since 1903). From the start, a strong contingent in the new organization was formed by the body of status-minded practitioners. Most of these were men and women who represented the professional element in the sphere of public management—specialists in budgeting, planning, programming, organization and methods work, personnel administration, and the like. In the society's quarterly, *Public Administration Review*, theory as well as practice found recognition. But the emphasis, by and large, was less upon cautious empirical testing of scientific propositions than upon an exchange of experience gained at the working benches of administration. Indeed, had the new society not been shepherded in its formative period by the ubiquitous monitor of solid knowledge, Louis Brownlow's foundation-financed Public Administration Clearing House, the management specialist might have come to squat in a very shallow trench. Now that Public Administration Clearing House has gone out of business, the basic orientation of the American Society for Public Administration cannot readily be predicted. If it is not in peril of turning into a high-class trade union, the reason lies in good part in the stature which administrative research has acquired in the meantime.

Evidence of that stature is supplied by the second marker placed to show the productive vigor of the forties. This was the appearance in 1950 of "the most different" textbook in public administration by Herbert A. Simon, D. W. Smithburg, and V. A. Thompson. Here the primary concern was with data rather than with theories, with detached observations rather than with practical prescriptions addressed to doers. Drawing upon the contributions of the different branches of social science research rather than treating public management as a bundle of self-sufficient techniques and processes, focused upon human behavior and group action rather than the role of public administration in a democratic political system, this book deserves a place of distinction, despite the criticism to which it has been exposed on grounds good and bad.

New perspectives. Between these two markers, various other tendencies asserted themselves. Different as they were, however, all were linked to one central factor. Students of public administration had come to look about themselves; and as they did, they were bound to gain new or sharper perspectives.

The vanguard of scholarship pushed ahead to escape self-isolation in a narrow functional context. In search of strengthened foundations, it reached out into such adjacent fields as sociology, psychology, anthropology, and even political theory. Research in behavior attracted much interest. At the same time, students of public administration developed their field in depth, by moving into policy analysis and a fuller exploration of decision-making in its political as well as administrative aspects. The shift was one from "know-how" to the unraveling of program issues and the reconnoitering of the whole range of institutional motivation.

This change brought into view such value questions as those implicit in public ethics. It also drew attention to the characteristics of career bureaucracies. It gave significance to neglected topics, such as the role of "middle management," in contrast with the structure and performance of specialized staff work. As a means of illuminating the anatomy of institutional action, administrative case study won increasing favor, eventually attaining a high level of incisiveness, in keeping with the general drive for "reality." Scrutiny of the historic record of administrative organization and operations added another dimension, and comparative exposition of different administrative systems came into its own once more.

The new was bound to collide with the old. Prematurely hardened orthodoxies, including the very concept of "principles" of administration, were sharply challenged. But the old showed remarkable resilience and adaptability, as becomes clear when one examines the several editions of Leonard D. White's influential *Introduction to the Study of Public Administration* (since 1929). The yield of the decade from 1940 to 1950 included the first publication of our own book, *Elements of Public Administration*. Greeted here and abroad as a principal guide not only to emerging tendencies but also to a coherent view, this systematic treatise described public administration as an integral part of its political environment. The administrative system, in the American context, was shown to be the machinery of service of the democratic state, instead of representing a self-contained technology.

Second thoughts. Much of what is taken up in later chapters provides an exploration of the present-day frontiers of public administration. Here it is enough to present a quick sketch of the background. Before that is done, two things may be stressed in general.

First, today's study of public administration is anchored in the proposition that scientific knowledge is a welcome guide for action even when its main advice, at this stage, is one of caution against getting entrapped by half-truths, instead of being sure of "the one right way." For some time to come, research will be absorbed in probing its hypotheses and testing its conclusions. The ground is being cleared, and new contours are being plowed; but the harvest is still far away. And secondly, in looking forward to the harvest, students of public administration may find it desirable to keep their fingers crossed. They are less likely to be carried away again as much as they have been in the past by the fast-flowing stream of public advocacy and popular reform. In measuring their opportunities and respecting their limitations, they may share in part the more somber attitude of the natural scientist. Arnold J. Toynbee has conveyed this attitude in *A Study of History* by quoting the president of the British Association for the Advancement of Science as follows:

> In the present-day thinker's attitude towards what is called mechanical progress, we are conscious of a changed spirit. Admiration is tempered by criticism; complacency has given way to doubt; doubt is passing into alarm. There is a sense of perplexity and frustration, as in one who has gone a long way and finds he has taken the wrong turning. To go back is impossible; how shall he proceed? Where will he find himself if he follows this path or that? ... It is impossible not to ask: Whither does this tremendous procession tend? What, after all, is its goal? What is its probable influence upon the future of the human race?

Function versus structure. Even during the thirties, the accumulation of research materials had produced both a systematization of knowledge and considerable philosophic inquiry into the nature, purpose, and scope of public administration. The textbooks stressed such matters as sound administrative structure and procedures of good administrative housekeeping. They also raised the question of the proper content of public administration.

But the experience of management research in private industry revealed the error of stating principles of organization as ends, or even as major purposes. Industrial management thereafter had come to start from the basic purpose of the organization itself. It encouraged research to develop the best ways and means of achieving that purpose. Paralleling this approach, government research turned to the public purpose sought to be achieved. In it was seen the rationale for all other things—organization, the planning of operations, the creating of staff units to assist in their conduct, and the establishment of goals and standards as well as methods of measuring results in relation to the standards selected.

This analysis of management shifts the emphasis from structure to function. It also defines the key problem as the establishment of effective working relations between the component parts of the organization. The emphasis upon planning and coordination as essential elements of management helped to reorient the thinking of public administration toward the functions of top direction. Process gave room to program, and program had to allow for personality. The interplay of these three factors is a central theme of administrative research today.

Man in organization. Discussion of the elements of organization, however realistic, aims at general concepts, and hence tends to depersonalize the problems of management. Arthur W. Macmahon and John D. Millett developed a more productive approach through an analysis of the role of personalities in the major departments in the federal government.[20] Their idea was that a description of background, training, and career experience of administrators at the levels of bureau chief and assistant secretary should adduce useful evidence of managerial traits. The result was a valuable interpretation of varying types of administrative supervision and departmental coordination arising from the diversity of personal development and the adjustments made by key officers.

Biographical research was also utilized by Gaus and Wolcott in their exemplary study of the United States Department of Agriculture.[21] Instead of drawing wider inferences from personal data, however, Gaus and Wolcott used such material as one of several colors with which they painted the panorama of administrative evolution through seventy years of political response to powerful economic and technological pressures. Their study opened broad vistas of research opportunities in administrative history, focused on the positive role of a public agency in bringing professional and

---

[20]Mamahon, A. W., and Millett, J. D., *Federal Administrators*, New York: Columbia University Press, 1939.

[21] Gaus, John M., and Wolcott, Leon O., *Public Administration and the United States Department of Agriculture*, Chicago: Public Administration Service, 1940.

scientific tools to bear upon the economic problems of a large segment of the population. It offered chapter-and-verse illustrations of the way a public agency formulates programs and policy, leading onward toward constructive public service through the educational character of its own experience, despite the barriers interposed by strong political influences.

The stimulating effects of these works can be found in a whole shelf of more recent studies dealing with administrative policy-making, organizational leadership, and the occupational traits of the career man in government. Such writings furnish a necessary antidote to the sweeping indictments of the "age of organization" hurled forth by James Burnham (*The Managerial Revolution*, 1941) and William H. Whyte (*The Organization Man*, 1956).

Theory of relationships. The lifting of the sights of administrative research to focus upon the social and economic environment has been largely due to the penetrating writings of Mary Parker Follett and the more systematic work at the Harvard Business School under the leadership of Elton D. Mayo. Miss Follett's earlier work in political and social theory had led her to a keen appreciation of the influence of organization in modern society. At the same time she had reacted strongly against the ideologies of group and class conflict, which constituted both factual explanation and political hope for many intellectuals who were aware of antisocial policies and controls over modern large-scale production. During the last fifteen years before her death in 1933 she became interested in business management and organization as a field for application of the principles of unity and organized cooperation that she had developed in her political studies.

In this new field of interest she was impressed much more with the conditions tending toward cooperation in the behavior of men working in groups than with assumptions about inevitable conflicts of interest. It was Mary Follett's abiding faith that the factors tending toward disunity and internal conflict could be faced frankly; that to this end enlightened management would open up channels for collective consideration of the conditions in which frictions arise; and that such frictions stemmed for the most part from the frustrations and disappointments of individuals working under conditions out of which they derived no sense of personal creativeness or contribution.[22]

The research of the Harvard Business School into the springs of human motivation in business organizations has given us the benefit of considerable scientific documentation of Miss Follett's insights.[23] These studies applied to industrial research both anthropological findings and sociological concepts.

---

[22] Her collected papers are reprinted in Metcalf, H. C., and Urwick, L., eds. *Dynamic Administration,* New York: Harper, 1941.
[23] *Cf.* Mayo, Elton D., *The Human Problems of an Industrial Civilization,* New York: Macmillan, 1933; Whitehead, T. N., *Leadership in a Free Society,* Cambridge: Harvard University Press, 1936; Roethlisberger, Fritz J., and Dickson, W. J., *Management and the Worker,* Cambridge: Harvard University Press, 1943; and Roethlisberger, *Management and Morale,* Cambridge: Harvard University Press, 1941.

The record of the Harvard team's association with the Western Electric Company to conduct experiments in personnel relations constitutes an early high-water mark of intensive research into group behavior under controlled conditions. A few outstanding findings may be mentioned:

> First, there is in each organization a system of informal personal relationships which condition work habits and attitudes more effectively than the official hierarchy of authority.
>
> Second, large organizations consist of many working groups, each small enough to effect cohesion. Morale centers around such groups, where direct personal relationships function in relation to a set of nonlogical or emotional incentives and standards. These group standards must be integrated with the purpose of the organization as a whole and not permitted to develop intergroup conflicts.
>
> Third, the function of attaining a sense of interrelation between the working groups composing the organization as a whole is a full-time job which top management cannot leave to chance or to the part-time attention of supervisory personnel.

From these findings and their further refinement has sprung the host of writings dealing with "human relations" in the life of organizations. A heady term, it has turned sour in the hands of quacks eager to sell standardized techniques. But the key to the "spirit" or the "mind" of an agency arises in the interaction of human beings.

Progressive management. The importance of the personnel function in organization can hardly be overstressed, but its relation to the central task of top management remains to be stated. In response to the Harvard group, an outstanding business executive, Chester I. Barnard, developed perhaps the most systematic analysis of the executive function since Henri Fayol. Barnard defined organization as an "impersonal system of coordinated human efforts." He identified the executive's job as: (1) providing the system of communication; (2) securing essential services from individuals; and (3) establishing the purposes and objectives of organization.[24] In his formulation, technical efficiency and morale are not the primary ends of organized effort. They are factors bearing upon the permanence or duration of an organization, whose existence through time depends upon its effectiveness in attaining both the concrete ends of concerted activity and essential human satisfactions.

Perhaps the most noteworthy American experiment in modern managerial freedom to accomplish broad objectives of public policy—the Tennessee Valley Authority—has been analyzed most revealingly in an able piece of administrative reporting by its then chairman, David E. Lilienthal.[25] The

---

[24] Barnard, Chester I., *The Functions of the Executive*, esp. chs. 7 and 15, Cambridge: Harvard University Press, 1938.
[25] *TVA: Democracy on the March*, esp. p. 159-161, 199-202, New York: Harper, 1944. To indicate the "given" limitations to all such experiments, this book should be supplemented by Selznick, Philip, *TVA and the Grass Roots: A Study in the Sociology of Formal Organization*, Berkeley: University of California Press, 1949.

author argued that TVA exemplifies sound democratic administration—decentralized operations, voluntary citizen cooperation and local community participation, placing responsibility for both planning and execution of administrative policy upon a single agency, a personnel policy based strictly upon merit but allowing for constructive flexibility, and an enforcement policy of education and persuasion that relies for coercive sanction only upon the power of eminent domain in the public interest.

The essence of democratic administration, Lilienthal says, is doing things *with* people, not *to* them, and placing the responsible administrators close to the people where they must share the people's problems. Method, he asserts, is all-important; "it is as inseparable from purpose and ends as our flesh is from our blood." Give to management powers of affirming and initiating what shall be done; fix upon it responsibility for results; see that the experts take action with people instead of simply applying legal coercion—if we do so, we may be sure that management will work as well for the public interest as for any incentive of private profit. But management's freedom to pursue the public interest arises ultimately from the alignment of forces in the larger environment, regional as well as national. Management can influence the character of this alignment to some extent by its own planning choices, but cannot simply make or unmake it. In the end, "democratic management" gets its cue from the nature of the political system of which it is a part.

Agenda of administrative research. Research in public administration thus has pushed steadily back the barriers between the various specialists in the administrative arts. Study of the modes of policy formation and the relationships in organization has brought about an understanding of the psychological processes of personal identification with the individuality and achievements of the organization as a whole.

Because of the requirement to keep the public needs linked to the essence of popular rule, increasing interest has developed in the borderline problems lying between political theory and public administration. What canons should govern the creative and formative roles of administrators in advising on the best means of defining particular objectives and establishing the administrative machinery for achieving them? How should administrative agencies react to private group demands and drives for power? How can political leadership be brought to utilize properly the concepts and techniques of administrative planning in the formulation of public policies and programs? Can new forms of administrative accountability to legislatures and to the public be devised which will increase mutual respect and lessen suspicion and distrust? Can the educational system be used with greater

See also Simon, Herbert A., "Recent Advances in Organization Theory," in *Research Frontiers in Politics and Government*, pp. 23-44, Washington: Brookings Institution, 1955; Wasserman, Paul, and Silander, Fred S., eds., *Decision-Making: An Annotated Bibliography*, Ithaca, N. Y.: Graduate School of Business and Public Administration, Cornell University, 1958.

effectiveness to bring about adequate understanding of the problems of public management and to generate a willingness to enter the public service in the minds of promising individuals representing all sections of the population?

These are problems of the highest order. In their solution, we need the benefit of familiarity with concrete administrative settings, on the one hand, and with foreign administrative experience, on the other. The first need is met by case study.[26] As for the second, comparative study, long largely ignored, is currently moving forward with new vitality.[27] But we need not only look around; we must also look back. Administrative history has greatly gained in stature, not the least by the pioneering work of Leonard D. White.[28]

5. Administration—Art or Science?

Aims of scientific approach. In modern Western civilization, the term "science" is an honorific word. Considerable effort has been made to justify its use in identifying the knowledge and skills that are applied in administrative practice. A science of administration would be a body of formal statements describing invariant relationships between measurable objects, units, or elements. Unquestionably, administrative research has produced definite precepts and hypotheses that are applicable to concrete situations. But what administrators visualize as particularly valuable goes beyond that. They are interested in the techniques of systematizing the process of securing and sifting relevant information so that the factors involved in arriving at a policy decision can be stated and the consequences of alternatives can be analyzed and balanced.

The objective of public or private management is to arrive at a determination of appropriate action in terms of both a plan and particular decisions in conformance with the plan. From this angle, administrative research looks toward the systematic ordering of functions and human relationships, so that organizational decisions can and will be based upon the certainty that each step will actually serve the purpose of the organization as a whole.

---

[26] Systematic development of case materials was promoted by the Committee on Public Administration of the Social Science Research Council (its case series began in 1940, Washington, D.C.). Since 1951, the Inter-University Case Program (also Washington, D.C.) has carried this work forward. The outstanding collection is Harold Stein, ed., *Public Administration and Policy Development: A Case Book,* New York: Harcourt, Brace, 1952.

[27] *Cf.* Morstein Marx, Fritz, *The Administrative State: An Introduction to Bureaucracy,* Chicago: University Press, 1957 (with bibliography). See also Weidlund, Jane and Others, *Comparative Administration: A Selective Annotated Bibliography,* Ann Arbor: Institute of Public Administration, University of Michigan, 1957.

[28] See his monumental studies entitled *The Federalists* (1789-1801), *The Jeffersonians* (1801-1829), *The Jacksonians* (1829-1861), and *The Republican Era* (1867-1901), New York: Macmillan, 1948, 1951, 1954, and 1958, respectively.

Concerns of the technicians. Naturally, there are levels of routine and technical proficiency on which uniform mechanical operation is possible and desirable. Research should continually seek to simplify and standardize work methods, ranging from the relatively simple operation of sorting incoming mail for distribution to the complex process of formulating a work plan for an entire organization in the annual budget. However, the establishment of standardized processes and mechanical efficiency does not penetrate to the central function of management. Absorption into this more limited aspect of the science of administration differentiates the operational expert and technician from the manager-administrator.

Techniques of budgeting, accounting, personnel management, purchasing, storage and handling of materials, and reporting are indispensable, not the least because the facts involved in recurring problem-situations are thus brought into sharper focus for the administrator. Yet they are significant to him in an immediate sense only as they raise issues requiring his executive determination, or call for changes in the general policy of the organization. Administrative progress, in this sense, consists in the reduction of problems to routines which can be disposed of satisfactorily at the lower levels.

Science and social dynamics. Focusing upon the problem areas of social organization, the question becomes a different one. How far is it a matter of science to exercise judgment in selecting among alternatives of policy, in determining specific action in pursuit of the purpose of the organization, or in interpreting the requirements of the public interest in particular cases?

If this question were to be answered in scientific terms, the answer would have to be stated, as in all matters of social relations, in categories upon which general agreement could be obtained. There is no such agreement in sufficiently specific terms on the purposes and powers of public officials, or on a formula for human behavior whereby conflicts of interest and will can be predicted and determined in advance. In the philosophy and practice of democracy, however, it has been learned that men can agree upon constitutional procedures through which personal and intergroup conflicts can be resolved by reference to general policy, basic objectives, and social priorities.

Through the joint action of citizens as well as public officials, public policy can be tested, tried out, and changed as the result of administrative experience and alert leadership. The science of administration in a democracy will always be in part a matter of trial and error. It will grow through the insight and ability of administrators as they devise ways of adjusting their programs to the conflicting demands and ideals of their consumer publics and their political overseers.

Alliance of theory and practice. This view of a democratic science of administration assumes a unity of theory and practice, and at the same time envisages a general—but not closed—functional differentiation between its students and its practitioners. That is to say, administrative research must be oriented toward actual behavior and the working problems of administrators; continuous efforts must be made to encourage such research and to bring its results to the attention of busy administrators. But administrative research must not be turned into the handmaiden of officials to justify their preferences at any given moment.

The profession of administration should include both the research worker and the executive. They should be willing to collaborate in selecting problems for study and in making data and experience available. In the formulation and interpretation of findings, however, there will always be room for initiative and responsibility outside the official sphere.

Chapter 3 •

Bureaucracy—Fact and Fiction

1. Semantics and Realities

Language of contempt. One collective designation for those who man the services of government is the "bureaucracy." The tyranny of words is nowhere better exhibited than in the use of that word.[1] Governments do their work as much through administration as through politics. It might therefore be supposed that in a democracy where administrators are subject to direction by politicians and where politicians derive their power from the people, popular allusions to those who manage the public business would have pleasing connotations. Perhaps that is the way it will be some day. For the present, however, this is clearly not the case. The name "bureaucracy" is often one of derision and contempt, harsher, to be sure, in some contexts than in others, but even at its mildest a word inviting one to sneer or scorn.

As is evident in a thousand ways, the human animal is fearfully and wonderfully made. Man knows he needs the discipline of authority. But even as he maintains it, he still resents it and chafes under it. Rationally he realizes that freedom is unworkable without responsibility. Emotionally his desire is for liberty without restraint. In this sense "cussin' the bureaucrats" is but the expression of human nature. Is there a citizen anywhere who does not occasionally need the convenience of an impersonal scapegoat to bear the blame for his own blunders?

Habit and memory furnish another explanation. Popular government, as now conceived, was born in the age of Jackson. Both in America and in those lands across the sea whence so many of our forebears came, government of the people, by the people, and for the people triumphed only after centuries of autocratic or aristocratic rule during which administration was frequently overbearing. Consequently, it was in some measure out of their own mean experience that the common people came to damn their public "servants." It became a habit—and the habit has persisted.

[1] See Merton, Robert K., and Others, eds., *Reader in Bureaucracy*, Glencoe, Ill.: Free Press, 1952; Morstein Marx, Fritz, *The Administrative State: An Introduction to Bureaucracy*, Chicago: University of Chicago Press, 1957 (both with bibliography).

Officiousness and frailty. Officiousness is another factor accounting for the unflattering character of many of the popular references to governmental employees. Civil servants are ordinary mortals; they have the defects and weaknesses typical of human nature. Each man loves, as Shakespeare said, "his own brief moment of authority." However, some seem unable to avoid showing their glee, and of these the public service probably has a normal ratio. It is so in all countries. Every government has a portion of otherwise satisfactory employees who do their work in a fashion that rubs the public the wrong way. This "insolence of office" naturally comes in for greater criticism in democratic lands. Yet even the Germans found ways of scoffing at Brownshirt "bureaucrats" while Hitler was in power. Nor have the people of the Soviet Union hesitated to lampoon their own overreaching "functionaries." The combat troops of all armies illustrate in their scorn for martinets and for paper-soldiers berthed at headquarters the military equivalent of these civilian attitudes.

Further probing leads to a more serious fact: Occasionally bureaucrats do abuse their position and authority. By and large, the governmental processes of modern democracy constitute adequate protection against official misconduct. But these procedures are not always fully used, nor are they always faithfully observed. Here and there a public servant attempts to make his public office yield a private gain or buckles under pressure and uses his power to confer an unfair advantage on some special group. It should be added, however, that this happens more often among bureaucrats in political posts. Although the guilty are not always caught and forced to make amends, and serious cases time and again arouse public indignation, the gross volume of such abuse has long been on the decline.

Administrative self-promotion. More common and harder to cope with is a wholly different kind of fault, arising from excess of zeal in the promotion of what is honestly believed to be the public interest. That is the inclination of some public administrators to take too expansive a view of their functions. In order to accomplish a public good that might otherwise be deferred or lost, they may push the range of their discretion beyond the limits intended by the legislature. It was a mistake, Woodrow Wilson argued, to relegate administration to the category of things "which clerks could arrange after doctors had agreed upon principles." But it is equally a mistake—and in a democracy a dangerous one—to conceive of administration as the heroic center of government. Such a conception might encourage the view that the executive is free independently to correct through administrative orders any legislative "errors" of omission or commission.

Administration has been called the core of modern government. This is true in the sense that it is today essential in all states, popular and despotic alike. It is the only branch of government that is continuously in operation; and it is the one in which the overwhelming majority of public employees work and the vast bulk of public funds is spent. Yet policy-making through representative assemblies remains primary in a democracy. To organize government so that administrative officials are responsible to those whom the people desire to exercise political power—this is the formula for freedom. Except as the chief executive may direct, the participation of civil servants in the making of public policy is confined to advising him and the legislature in their own field of expert knowledge and offering recommendations or technical assistance. The administrative official may argue with foresight, with ingenuity, and with a sense of urgency. Having presented his views, however, he has done everything he may properly do.

The "great game of politics" has its basic rules like any other. It is up to the administrator to abide by them no less than the politician and the citizen. The democratic way to secure the adoption of a particular public policy is by fighting for it in full assumption of political responsibility. That is the reason why the public takes offense at men who, as administrators, try to "decree" policies they need not stand up for as politicians.

Procedural rigmarole. Red tape—or what the average citizen has in mind when he uses the phrase—also supplies part of the explanation for the stereotyped conception of bureaucracy. The point should be granted without argument. To the 90 per cent of the public who want to do "the right thing" and generally know how to do it, many a government procedure must seem unnecessarily complicated. This is true especially of those to whom it fails to occur that most of the detailed requirements relating to such matters as permits, licenses, and contracts are to save the majority from the ignorance, selfishness, or carelessness of the other 10 per cent. By and large, it is hard and costly social experience that accounts for most of the irritating specifications in bureaucratic procedure—that and nothing more.

When at the threshold of World War II motormaker William Knudsen assumed a post of great importance in the defense effort of the nation, he said of Washington red tape, "In Detroit we call it system." So saying he not only gave it a fair and simple characterization, but also furnished a clue to the reason why it can be so irritating. As long as the individual fits the regular pattern for which the system is devised, it clicks like a clock. But it cannot simultaneously be capable of perfect adaptation to a unique situation —let alone a person's whim and fancies. Resenting authority to begin with, man resents it even more when, no matter what the reason, it seems to be blind to his own special circumstances. Yet in countless instances this appearance can hardly be avoided. There are numerous types of situations in which the power to fix general rules must necessarily be centered, while information relevant to their just and proper utilization lies largely at the point of application. Delegation of discretion may not always be a feasible answer. When public administration has to rely on absentee authority, it must accept the consequences in popular resentment and dissatisfaction as a "risk of operation"—just as they are accepted in private business in similar circumstances.

The assembly lines in the great automobile plants are designed to move at the speed and in the order that will enable the workers to produce the maximum number of cars per day. This does not mean that a customer will always be able to get the car he wants when he wants it and at the price he thinks right—or that individual workers will not find the pace inconveniently fast or slow. So with the red tape of a government agency. Though designed to enable employees, working at a set rate, to provide the public with service conforming to acceptable standards, it will inevitably fail to meet precisely the needs of every single citizen. Methods and procedures calculated to yield the greatest good for the number simply will not fit the details of each and every case.

Subjectivity and objectivity. The final explanation of why the word "bureaucracy" has a bad ring is that, for their own purposes, various groups are constantly trying to discredit public administration. The economic stakes involved in "keeping government out of business" are great, and the financial resources available to promote suitable propaganda are frequently on the same scale. Much of the inspiration for the battle against "bureaucratic regimentation" is generated by nothing nobler than the desire to make it difficult or impossible for democracy to enact or enforce regulations needed to protect the public interest. Bureaucracy is besmirched because this seems to offer a way of winning the battle over public policy.

Through distortion and caricature, the term "bureaucracy" has come to imply bungling, arbitrariness, wastefulness, officiousness, and regimentation. This is far from what the word means in free translation—"desk government," or management by bureaus. It thus denotes the sum total of the personnel, apparatus, and procedures by which an organization manages its work and accomplishes its purposes. The organization may be public or private, governmental, commercial, educational, ecclesiastical; but if it is of any size, it must be a bureaucracy, in this sense.

So seen, then, bureaucracy is a feature of all large-scale undertakings, whether the General Motors Corporation or the United States Government —and General Motors employees are quite as well aware of the fact as are federal workers. In relation to government, however, the term is also used in the nomenclature of the scholar to denote the entire executive establishment, but especially the permanent or career personnel and their operating processes. On its administrative side, therefore, the whole problem of government consists—as Carl J. Friedrich has properly emphasized—in the development and maintenance of a bureaucracy that is competent, responsive, and responsible.

2. The Sources of Red Tape

Red tape and green tape. Efficiency in administration depends at bottom upon devising and directing a routine, a regimen, a system. Admittedly, it is never possible to reduce all the components of a process to the point where they can be handled by a formula. It is nevertheless the aim in all management to discover and introduce such a division of labor as will enable the total job to be performed satisfactorily and at the lowest possible cost.

From the standpoint of efficiency in general, public and private administration are basically alike. They operate under similar types of managerial motivation and compulsion. Many of the sources of red tape in the governmental bureaucracy are no different from those which account for the "green" tape in the business bureaucracy.[2] But the parallel holds true only part of the way. Administrators in government are obliged to consider a number of factors beyond those to which business ordinarily extends its concern. These are the things that make the government tape red instead of green. Typically they are social considerations—Aristotle would have called them political.

In some fields, the ultimate objectives of public management tend to coincide with those of commercial undertakings; but this is the exception rather than the rule. Government generally aims at ends more complex and more intangible than business. Men look to government for justice, law, peace, and order; for the maintenance of liberty, equality, and opportunity; for impartiality in the enforcement of economic regulations and for even-handedness in the administration of economic assistance—not so much for service that is swift and cheap as for service that is safe and sure. True, they want such service to be economically efficient. But they also want it to satisfy these other more basic expectations. They do not run their government to make money. They run it in order to establish and preserve an environment in which they themselves can make a decent living. The standard of success in business is the greatest economic gain to the individual entrepreneur or firm at the lowest economic cost. The standard for government is the greatest social-and-economic gain for the public at the lowest social-and-economic cost to all.

Requirements of efficiency. To avail itself of the economies latent in specialization and large-scale organization, government no less than business must submit to the compulsion of working out a detailed sequence of steps in which the various jobs on each unit of production can best be done. Assembly-line techniques offer marked advantages over those of custom

---

[2] For an amusing and withal an instructive account of what can happen when a customer gets entangled in the "green tape" of private business, see Appleby, Paul H., *Big Democracy*, pp. 58–59, New York: Knopf, 1945.

craftsmanship. They also have their price. They entail the imposition of an order of progression, the fixing of a rate or rhythm of operation, and the discipline of a regular routine. Set order, fixed pace, and adherence to routine—these are the things of which red tape is made, for they are of the essence of "system."

Likewise common to both government and business is the desire for predictability of performance. Both for his own peace of mind and in the interest of maximum productivity, a manager wants and needs to know how many units of goods or services his staff or plant can produce per week or per month and at what cost. Whether in government or business, his only hope for such predictability lies in the possibility of maintaining sufficient regularity of operations, both qualitatively and quantitatively, to permit calculation of results in advance of their occurrence. Yet the very regularity for which he strives and on which he depends for his success may prove monotonous to his workers.

These, however, are not the only common sources of bureaucratic tape or system. It is also nourished by institutional inertia and indifference, wherever either is allowed to gain a foothold. It flourishes whenever the lure of order, once established, has a chance to invest every precedent with the sanctity of final authority. And it positively luxuriates wherever management becomes so attached to the comfort of accustomed routine that it attempts at all costs to avoid even the momentarily disruptive effects of a change in procedure.

Government of laws. What of the red tape peculiar to public administration? To begin with, there is an administrative counterpart to that key principle in democratic politics which insists in the name of freedom on a government of laws rather than of men. Public administration uses red tape because it is expected to proceed according to objective rules rather than the subjective intuition of government officials. Who would have it otherwise? Red tape is perhaps the best insurance the public has that all citizens receive equal treatment at the hands of government.

Another closely related source of red tape is the insistence of the public on full accountability in governmental management, not alone for the final result but also for each and every step by which it is reached. This means that bureaucrats are required to do their work in such a way that, actually or contingently, their every move may be opened to public scrutiny. A civil servant must perform his duties in such a manner that they can be defended and justified even if brought under the most minute and critical review. The result is what might be expected—almost as much concern at times over not doing anything wrong as over trying to do something right. To make matters worse, the tangible rewards for creative imagination are likely to be meager. Business management prides itself on paying handsomely for initiative and invention. In governmental administration, the premium on constructive innovation is hardly ever of comparable magnitude. Nor is this for the reason that public management does not appreciate the value of such incentives. The trouble lies in its being hedged about by restrictions that practically preclude it from fully using them. In the United States, legislative impositions of detailed procedural requirements has caused controls to be piled upon controls beyond all need.

3. The Charge of Despotism

Effects of the industrial age. Having essayed an explanation and evaluation of the red tape and inefficiency ascribed to bureaucracy, it is now in order to examine the merits of two graver indictments—those of despotism and regimentation. Both relate to supposed abuses of trust or power by the executive branch of government. Let us first consider the charge that bureaucracy seeks to usurp the judicial function, and thereafter the claim that it is contriving to usurp the legislative function as well.[3]

The separation of powers has never meant the same thing in Britain as in America, particularly in the relations between the executive and legislative branches. But with respect to the relations between the executive and judicial branches, it has had approximately the same significance. One of the common assumptions in both countries has been that the rights and liberties of the citizen would not be secure unless all men, public officials and private citizens alike, were under a "rule of law" guaranteed by a hierarchy of independent courts. So long as public administration was largely limited to police activity, the ordinary courts of law were able to dispose of nearly all types of questions calling for adjudication—whether they arose out of criminal offenses in the usual sense, civil-law transactions, or noncompliance with administrative regulations. But as the impact of technology upon society became more pervasive, every government has been obliged steadily to extend the range of its concerns. Thus arose the question of the proper handling of an increasing body of technical controversies. The answer was often the creation outside the judicial branch of novel administrative agencies or tribunals, staffed with specialized personnel and authorized to employ procedures adapted to the subject matter involved.

Because they were in the vanguard of industrialization, America and Britain have had to make changes in administrative structure and procedure comparable to those undertaken by other nations which were outside the common-law version of the "rule of law." As in the case of most departures from old ways, the new administrative tribunals did not always function perfectly, particularly in their early years. Occasionally they made errors

---

[3] For a fuller treatment, see Chapter 23, "The Judicial Test," and Chapter 15, "Legislative Control."

of procedure which but for subsequent review by the law courts might have led to a miscarriage of justice. From the beginning, however, certain groups within the body politic have been unwilling even to acknowledge the necessity for new instrumentalities of this kind. Insisting that the rule of law was being vitiated rather than aided by these new departures, they have condemned the new instrumentalities as agencies of a new despotism.[4]

Charge of usurpation. In his *New Despotism,* the late Lord Hewart, Britain's doughty defender of the "rule of law," gave sweeping expression to this criticism. "A little inquiry," he wrote, "will serve to show that there is now, and for some years past has been, a persistent influence at work which, whatever the motives or the intentions that support it may be, undoubtedly has the effect of placing a large and increasing field of departmental authority and activity beyond the reach of the ordinary law."[5] Taking for granted the adequacy of "the ordinary law"—perhaps more accurately, "the ordinary courts"— and thus in a way begging the whole question, the author averred that the people of Britain were in danger of losing their liberties through the growth of administrative absolutism.

Hewart ignored the inconvenient question of the competence of the ordinary judges to ascertain the facts over a wide range of highly technical matters, let alone the practical significance of such facts. He simply argued that individual rights and liberties were now in jeopardy because the "ardent bureaucrat" had lately come to operate under "some such faith" as this:

1. The business of the Executive is to govern.
2. The only persons fit to govern are experts.
3. The experts in the art of government are the permanent officials, who, exhibiting an ancient and too much neglected virtue, "think themselves worthy of great things, being worthy."
4. But the expert must deal with things as they are. The "four-square man" makes the best of the circumstances in which he finds himself.
5. Two main obstacles hamper the beneficent work of the expert. One is the sovereignty of Parliament, and the other is the rule of law.
6. A kind of fetish-worship, prevalent among an ignorant public, prevents the destruction of these obstacles. The experts, therefore, must make use of the first in order to frustrate the second.
7. To this end let him, under Parliamentary forms, clothe himself with despotic power, and then, because the forms are Parliamentary, defy the Law Courts.
8. This course will prove tolerably simple if he can (a) get legislation passed in skeleton form, (b) fill up the gaps with his own rules, orders, and regulations, (c) make it difficult or impossible for Parliament to check the said rules, orders, and regulations, (d) secure for them the force of statute, (e) make his own decision final, (f) arrange that the fact of his

---

[4] Perhaps the best illustration of the literature in which this view is presented is Hewart of Bury, *The New Despotism*, New York: Cosmopolitan Book Corp., 1929 (reissued London: Benn, 1945).

[5] *Ibid.,* p. 5.

decision shall be conclusive proof of its legality, (g) take power to modify the provisions of statutes, (h) prevent and avoid any sort of appeal to a Court of Law.

9. If the expert can get rid of the Lord Chancellor, reduce the Judges to a branch of the Civil Service, compel them to give opinions beforehand on hypothetical cases, and appoint them himself through a businessman to be called "Minister of Justice," the copingstone will be laid and the music will be the fuller.[6]

If all this or even the main part of it were generally true,[7] it would be a devastating indictment—but not so much of the bureaucrats as of the legislature, and thus of the electorate. Had Lord Hewart and American critics of like mind been content to specify some of the cautions which should be observed in adapting the "rule of law" to the conditions of a technological civilization, they could have performed a valuable service. Instead, all they have done is to "prove" too much.

Legislative delegation. As Pennock observed in opening his study of administration and the "rule of law,"[8] "Before the days of the automobile there was no need for policemen to direct traffic. Before our population had multiplied and become concentrated in congested urban areas, sanitary inspectors were not so necessary as they are now. Before the development of large-scale business enterprise, the sale of securities required no supervision by the government." These changes illustrate some of the technical problems with which public administration has been confronted through the progress of applied science. It is almost axiomatic that no invention is ever quite an unmixed blessing. New mechanisms or processes often bring new dangers as well as new advantages. They pose for government the question of how best to secure their potential benefits for the people without at the same time disturbing or endangering the social order.

Ordinarily the legislative body is the first to take positive action in dealing with new situations of this kind. Generally it waits, and sometimes it procrastinates, until sufficient evidence has accumulated to demonstrate clearly that existing prescriptions and procedures are inadequate to protect the public interest or to safeguard individual welfare. Then it sets forth as best it can the criteria of the common good, and vests the power to apply them in an agency either within the executive branch or independent of it—and normally outside the judicial branch as well. Far from forsaking the ideal of justice, however, what the legislature has in mind in assigning such tasks is to develop a more resilient rule of law, one insuring more relevant knowledge simpler in procedure and less given to delay, and less expensive

---

[6] *Ibid.*, pp. 13–14, by permission of the publisher, Farrar & Rinehart, New York.

[7] For a point-by-point rebuttal of Hewart's charges in terms of the British bureaucracy, see Finer, Herman, *The British Civil Service,* ch. 7, London: Fabian Society and Allen & Unwin, 1937.

[8] Pennock, J. Roland, *Administration and the Rule of Law,* New York: Farrar & Rinehart, 1941.

to the litigant,[9] yet withal equally just. In brief, the legislature has tried to cope with the practical problem of devising ways and means for the equitable and expeditious settlement of a mounting mass of technical controversies.

It is always difficult to devise concrete criteria and standards for new fields that will square perfectly with those to which men have grown accustomed under familiar conditions. Instead of pretending to a knowledge they lacked, legislative bodies have had the wisdom to vest in specialized tribunals or other comparable agencies, under statutory guidelines of a general character, secondary responsibility for deciding what specific requirements would be appropriate in new situations. Recognizing that some degree of discretion would have to be vested somewhere, legislatures have conferred it, at least for the purpose of establishing the relevant facts, upon officials possessed of technical knowledge. Of course, such officials are required to observe in their work fundamental rules of both evidence and responsibility. Thus, statutes defining standards have used such phrases as "reasonable rates," "public convenience and necessity," "unreasonable discrimination," "action necessary or desirable in the public interest," "adequate facilities and services," "maintenance of a fair and orderly market" and the like.[10] The interpretation of these phrases has been left largely to the regulatory agencies and, as a last resort, to the courts.

Quasi-judicial agencies. In the federal government, quasi-judicial agencies operating under legislative delegation in this sense include the following: Interstate Commerce Commission, 1887; Federal Trade Commission, 1914; Federal Communications Commission, 1934; Securities and Exchange Commission, 1934; National Labor Relations Board, 1935; and Civil Aeronautics Board, 1940. These agencies are also known as independent regulatory commissions and boards. Congress has also enacted scores of regulatory measures calling for the exercise of considerable discretion under appropriate rules by the departments represented in the President's cabinet. State legislatures have found it advisable to follow a similar course within their jurisdiction; likewise city councils, particularly in the larger cities. And the end is not yet. Although the question of whether to vest regulatory authority in agencies within or outside the executive branch is still a moot one, American experience with administrative tribunals is by now sufficiently broad and varied for some general conclusions. Those who have studied it carefully are generally agreed that both the resulting limitations to court control over public administration and the partial replacement of judicial by administrative guarantees of "liberty

---

[9] In their concern for the preservation of the "rule of law," bench and bar have tended to ignore the matter of the costs of justice to the litigant in terms of both time and money, especially the latter. Its importance as a factor in the creation of administrative tribunals has been considerable, in America and abroad.

[10] See Pennock, *op. cit.*, p. 31.

under law" have not brought the citizen under a new despotism. On the contrary, without the aid of regulatory agencies he might well be unable to maintain his liberties against the powerful organized interests which have risen about him.[11]

Administrative tribunals are here to stay; the problem is how to perfect them.[12] This is as much a question of how to improve their personnel as it is one of procedure. Ideally, most of the professional staff of a regulatory agency should have a mastery of both the technical subject matter with which it deals and the legal principles and procedures that govern such matters as the conduct of hearings and the taking of evidence. However, these are two distinct specializations, and few men can acquire expertness in both. The legal profession, which is now becoming reconciled to the need for administrative adjudication, naturally believes that the best way to secure a proper balance between private rights and public interests in the regulatory process is through stress on legal training. Yet lawyers must not be allowed to substitute their judgment on technical matters for that of the subject-matter experts. Obviously, the practical course for every quasi-judicial agency to take is to staff itself with personnel of both types and make sure that consideration is given to both sets of factors.

4. The Battle Against Regimentation

British experience with "delegated legislation." Parallel to the accusation that the bureaucracy has been usurping the function of the courts

---

[11] For a more specific discussion, see Chapter 10, "Independent Regulatory Agencies."

[12] Much pertinent information is to be found in the reports of the United States Attorney General's Committee on Administrative Procedure, Washington, 1940–41; the report on *Administrative Adjudication in the State of New York*, submitted to Governor Herbert H. Lehman by Robert M. Benjamin and staff, Albany, 1942; and the *Tenth Biennial Report of the Judicial Council of California to the Governor and the Legislature*, Sacramento, 1944. Some indication of the number and variety of state administrative agencies engaged at least partially in adjudicatory work may be gained from the following list of agencies described by the California Judicial Council as conducting "formal, adjudicatory licensing and disciplinary proceedings": Board of Dental Examiners, Board of Medical Examiners, Board of Osteopathic Examiners, Board of Nurse Examiners, Board of Optometry, Board of Pharmacy, Board of Public Health, Department of Public Health, Board of Examiners in Veterinary Medicine, Board of Accountancy, Board of Architectural Examiners, Board of Barber Examiners, Board of Registration for Civil Engineers, Registrar of Contractors, Board of Cosmetology, Board of Funeral Directors and Embalmers, Structural Pest Control Board, Yacht and Ship Brokers Commissioner, Secretary of State, State Fire Marshal, State Mineralogist, Director of Agriculture, Labor Commissioner, Real Estate Commissioner, Commissioner of Corporations, Department of Social Welfare, Department of Institutions, Board of Pilot Commissioners for the Bays of San Francisco, San Pablo and Suisun, Board of Pilot Commissioners for Humboldt Bay, Board of Pilot Commissioners for the Harbor of San Diego, Fish and Game Commission, Board of Education, Board of Equalization, Insurance Commissioner, Building and Loan Commission. As an illustration of the continuous nature of this development, mention may be made of the proposal of the governor of California (1959) that the legislature create an adjudicatory commission for automobile accident claims to relieve the courts of an excessive burden of suits and to increase the prospects for reasonable settlement of such claims.

is the charge that it has also encroached upon the legislature. Administrative adjudication does indeed have a counterpart in administrative rule-making. Most of those who damn the new despotism are therefore also prone to denounce bureaucratic "regimentation."

It may conduce to a sounder analysis of American developments to look first at Britain. Although there is in England greater readiness to accept the necessity of administrative regulations than in the United States, the House of Commons has concerned itself with the matter of "delegated legislation" several times in the past generation. The Donoughmore Committee on Ministers' Powers recommended in its report[13] a closer scrutiny by Parliament of the promulgation of subordinate legislation by the executive branch; but this led to no significant action. In 1944, however, it was acknowledged by the government that additional safeguards should be adopted, especially because in the future ministers might have to issue rules and orders in greater volume than ever before. The Commons then proceeded to create

> a Select Committee, ... whose duty it should be to carry on a continuous examination of all statutory rules and orders and other instruments of delegated legislation presented to Parliament; and to report from week to week whether in the opinion of the committee any such instrument is obscure or contains matter of a controversial nature or should for any other reason be brought to the special attention of the House.

By its term of reference, the Select Committee is charged with guarding the powers of Parliament and the liberties of the citizen alike by inquiring into the character and effect of the most important types of delegated legislation. Though lacking authority to send for ministers, it can obtain departmental answers to technical questions and other requests for relevant information. The Committee especially examines measures that would impose charges on the public revenues or be immune from challenge in the courts. Two classes of orders come in for particular scrutiny. The first includes those which by law do not become effective unless approved by affirmative resolution of Parliament. The second and larger group consists of rules and orders which automatically go into force unless opposed. On this basis the British have gone ahead with their use of "delegated legislation."

Color of partisanship. In the United States, Congress, state legislatures, and city councils have placed upon administrative agencies responsibility for putting the flesh of life and action on the bare bones of skeleton legislation. The bureaucrats proceed as best they can with these difficult tasks only to find themselves accused of all manner of evil-doing. Why? Because, as often as not, having been unable to prevent the passage of the statute itself, those opposed to its objectives retreat to their last line of defense. The

---

[13] London: H. M. Stationery Office, 1932, Cd. 4060.

real parties to the argument over public regulation of economic activity are the representatives of the people in the legislature and the spokesmen for the interest groups which desire to avoid being placed under such regulation. But those who raise the cry of regimentation try to befuddle the public into thinking that the issue lies instead between tyrannical bureaucrats on the one side and well-meaning citizens on the other.

Tactics of this kind have always been used by those trying to evade their obligations. Of all the fictions about bureaucracy, one of the most flagrant is the contention that it is the bureaucrats who are responsible for the imposition of governmental controls on economic activity. Such controls are established by the duly chosen representatives of the whole people. The bureaucrat is their agent, by whom such controls are made effective.

Matrix of a mixed economy. The abuses and insecurities that occur when men insist on using liberty as though it were license have forced an almost continuous retreat from the philosophy of governmental nonintervention in the economic sphere. The American economy is a mixed economy. Private and public undertakings intermingle. "Either-or" studies of the role of government in economic life have value only in pointing out the perils of going to extremes. Many aspects of production and distribution can be competently handled by private enterprise under law and regulation. Others are so basic to the maintenance of public health and decency that their management cannot safely be entrusted to those who would have to operate under the limitations inherent in the profit motive. In between lie various fields which lend themselves about equally well to private, public, cooperative, or combined efforts.

How far public ownership and operation need to be carried and how far governmental regulation of private enterprise will have to go are certainly not questions to which bureaucrats will—or should be—allowed to give the final answer. Fundamentally, these are matters of high public policy. No one can predict with certainty what functions of regulation or control governmental management will be performing a generation hence. This does not mean, however, that no clues are available to suggest what the future will bring. For a people as pragmatic as the Americans, the lamp of experience provides a very good light. The likelihood of socialism is at a minimum. Government will go on in the future as in the past—gradually adapting forms and processes to changing conditions and circumstances.

In America's long record of evolutionary rather than revolutionary adjustment, there is much reassurance for those inclined to be anxious about the morrow. It should be sufficient to keep them from rejecting the universe and the century in which they live. The volume of governmental regulation of economic activities is doubtless destined to expand further, but this would spell regimentation only if the citizens allowed their sense of responsibility to die.

5. The Need for Understanding

Psychology of public employment. Democracy rests on understanding between the citizen and his government. If this is to have any real meaning there must be understanding between the citizen and his civil servants parallel to that between the citizen and his political leaders. And the maxim works both ways: The bureaucrat's need to understand the citizen matches the citizen's need to understand the bureaucrat. As a practical matter, however, the more urgent necessity in the present age is for greater citizen understanding of the administrative process.

Consider the ordinary man or woman "working for the government." He is recruited from no special rank or class or circle within American society; his background is the same as that of the average citizen. He is increasingly obliged to give objective proof of competence—first, to get his job, and thereafter to gain promotion or advancement. His compensation may be sufficient to enable him to support his family on an acceptable scale of living, but it is never of large proportions.

He does his work hedged about by a mass of rules and regulations which have accumulated over the years as the embodiment of popular attitudes toward conditions of public employment. Much of what he does may be floodlighted at any time by pitiless publicity; all of it is subject to the most intensive and pervasive scrutiny. His chances of taking advantage of his economic and social environment in furtherance of his own ends, should he be so minded, are fewer and more circumscribed than are those of thousands upon thousands of his fellow citizens who are privately employed.

Ethics of government service. Yet why presume that he will be so minded? In the first place, no person desiring to lay his hands on material riches would be attracted to the public service. The bulk of government employees are public servants because that is what they want to be—because the idea of serving the community through its government appeals to them as the best of all ways to make their living and to spend their lives.

For most public servants the taking of an oath of loyalty merely formalizes a resolution already made. It amounts to an outer expression of an inner dedication—the legal aspect of a code of ethics by which the public employee is guided in all his official acts and by which he expects all his fellow workers to proceed. An administrative official no more seeks his position in order to be able to sit in arbitrary judgment over the public than does a judge.

Let the government business be what it may, when it comes before the administrator for action, his whole disposition is to ask himself a series of questions on this order: What do the Constitution and the statutes say on the matter? What was the intent of the makers of policy in passing the law? What discretion am I obliged or expected or allowed to exercise?

How can I best exercise that discretion to promote and preserve the public interest? There need be little mystery about the workings of bureaucracy for anyone honestly interested in finding out the facts. Administrative officials make mistakes in judgment just as do other human beings. However, any intimation that the typical official counts that week lost in which he has not perpetrated some evil on the public is as base as it is ludicrous.

Veil of official anonymity. One thing that would doubtless make it easier for the public to overcome its misconceptions about the civil service would be a better understanding of the reasons for official anonymity. There are two main aspects of the matter. One is the maintenance of anonymity by bureaucrats in their capacity as advisers to their political chiefs. The other is their avoidance of public identification with the work of governmental administration.

Any administrative system operating under a government of laws requires some degree of official anonymity. This is simply the reverse side of the basic principle that administrative agencies are fundamentally impartial and impersonal instruments through which government performs its functions. The officials of such agencies are not supposed to place upon their actions the stamp of their own individual personalities. On the contrary, their job is merely to be the efficient device through which the will of the people finds tangible expression.

Yet various difficulties arise when in his official life the bureaucrat endeavors not to be John A. Smith, William B. Jones, or Edward C. Brown and tries instead to be something like a disembodied executor of public policy. For one thing, he runs up against the fact that though theoretically the people want him to submerge his personal views or preferences and function only as "the Administrator," "the Bureau Chief," or "the Licensing Officer," many of those with whom he has to deal want him to handle their cases on the basis of "What's the law between friends?" Friends? Yes and no. Certainly it is not uncommon experience for administrative officials to have citizens presume upon personal acquaintance with them by asking for favored treatment. And there are always plenty of others looking for an opportunity to establish such acquaintance so that they may presume upon it. The official's reaction is usually what might be expected. Knowing that even acquiescence in such presumptions could be ruinous, he relies as much as possible upon official anonymity to discourage them. He can easily go too far: his desire to underscore the impersonal character of his work sometimes leads to excessive formality in address and conduct.

Officialese and fear of error. Basically, this reserve is the explanation for the development and use by governmental officials of that wooden diction known as officialese or gobbledygook. Percival Q. Adams of 1456 Jefferson Street, Missouriville, Missouri, probably considers his application for a license or his tax return a matter quite as intimate as it is momentous to him. He does not want the licensing officer or the tax collector to treat him as if he were merely a number. He does not like to see himself referred to in the third person. Nor does he appreciate the deliberate way in which administrative officials usually avoid speaking of themselves in the first person when writing him about things for which they are supposed to be personally responsible. At its worst, officialese becomes so inverted and involved as to be little short of maddening. The bureaucrat may think his formalities nicely calculated to make the citizen "keep a proper distance." The citizen is more likely to feel that the bureaucrat has built a wall between them.

Official anonymity also stems from the bureaucrat's understandable desire to escape being made the victim of unreasonable and indiscriminate criticism. The body politic accepts years of competent and faithful service without comment or commendation. But let a bureaucrat make some little slip—or merely be charged with making one—and the chances are that he and his agency will have to pay a price in loss of popular support and esteem out of all proportion to the error. Is it any wonder, therefore, that to the bureaucrat the public sometimes looks like a wild beast to be avoided if at all possible? There are always people anxious for their own purposes to exploit the alleged faults and shortcomings of government employees. What reaction could be more natural for bureaucrats than to contrive to reduce their exposure to such people to the absolute minimum?

Teams and cogs. Having considered the needs and the uses of official anonymity in relations between the official and the citizen, let us look at the matter now from the internal angle, that is, within the government itself. No administrative agency can succeed in the discharge of its functions unless its staff works as a team or as a related group of teams. Each employee should, of course, have an individual assignment, and, with regard to his particular job, should to some degree be on his own. Yet this consideration must always be subordinated to cooperative needs, so that the net result becomes an "organized" product embracing the whole work of the agency.[14] Every member of the staff must learn that what he does commits the agency itself to some extent. How to instill this essential discipline among all the employees under him and yet not kill their spirit of initiative is one of the toughest problems the head of any agency has to face—and it has to be faced continuously.

Not every man confronted with this problem manages to solve it satisfactorily. Some administrators generate in their staffs so great a fear of committing the agency to something wrong as to keep their employees from being positive or effective about anything. Others may require their personnel to conform in their mode of work to so narrow and rigid a

---

[14] For an elaboration of this concept, see Appleby, *op. cit.* above in note 2, p. 78 *ff.*

routine that all become in practice little more than robots, cogs on the wheels of government. Fortunately, there are always some top officials who exercise a special initiative in highlighting for their subordinates the public purposes for which the agency was created and the specific services which it must render in carrying out its responsibilities. Through the practice of office democracy and active concern for the welfare and self-development of all employees, such officials prove to each member of the staff that he is a fellow worker whose work is vital to the success of the agency.[15]

Responsibility for political counsel. Official anonymity has perhaps its greatest value in the continued role of bureaucrats as advisers to their political chiefs. It is a basic obligation of administrative officials in the high echelons to give their political chiefs the soundest advice of which they are capable and, under the laws, to carry out their policies with loyalty and efficiency, irrespective of how much or little of counsel they accept. Lacking the authority to make public policy, however, permanent officials should not be identified with the responsibility for making it.

Only yesterday the professional bureaucrat advised the predecessor of his present political chief. On some tomorrow he will be advising his chief's successor. If today he is to try as hard to help his present chief succeed as he tried to help others in the past and as he expects to help still others in the future, it can only be on the basis that his counsel will not be publicized. Under the protection of anonymity, his code of ethics calls for excluding from his mind all considerations except those related to the policy of his political chief and the general welfare.

Fact over fiction. Granted that every governmental bureaucracy contains its share of drones and dullards, of self-servers and time-servers, of minor tyrants and soulless automatons, these comprise all told but a fraction of all public employees. Man for man and woman for woman, there is no reason for believing them to be different from their fellow Americans who are self-employed or work in private industry. The American bureaucracy is now so fully in the public view that no citizen can indict it without indicting the nation itself.

The fictions about bureaucracy will go on circulating, but there is reason to expect that they will do so at a gradually decreasing rate. Year by year the circle of popular understanding will grow wider. As it does, the public will more generally come to appreciate the limitations under which it has made its civil servants work. American democracy has thousands of exceptionally gifted and devoted employees who not only make no fuss about being bureaucrats but, on the contrary, are proud of their status and grateful for their tasks. It is unthinkable that the day will not dawn when their work will receive the recognition it deserves.

---

[15] See Chapter 4, "Democratic Administration."

Chapter 4 •

Democratic Administration

1. Legislative-Executive Relationships

New tyrants? The men who drafted the Constitution of the United States had had experience with both hereditary monarchy and a confederation in which a legislative assembly possessed exclusive power. As they considered the kind of executive head they wished to create, it seemed that they must choose between tyranny and anarchy. Being sensible men, they refused both. Instead, they invented, after much groping, a national chief executive with broad powers who was to be chosen periodically, not by the legislature, but by majority vote—and, as it turned out, by popular election.

The adoption of the Constitution did not end controversy over the powers and functions of the President. The presidency has been popular enough to last longer without fundamental change than the office of any other chief executive in any major nation. But many have disliked it, feared its influence, and believed that to protect our liberty we should restrict its initiative and independence.

In recent years, the contest over the powers of the presidency has broadened into a debate over the functions of the executive branch, of the agencies of government and their personnel. In these terms, of course, the issue is more realistic in the light of recent world history. It is no single "man on horseback," but a dominant machine or party or class, that can threaten a nation's liberty. The administrative personnel employed by government, therefore, may well consider what their role should be in a democratic society.

Critics of the part that present-day public administration must play have given administrators something to think about. Mr. James Burnham, for example, has cheerfully assured us that public administrators, along with corporation managers, are going to exploit the rest of us, who will constitute the new proletariat.[1] Others have warned that the modern service state will reduce us all to servility just because we have asked its administrators to organize our welfare and security.

---

[1] Burnham, James, *The Managerial Revolution,* New York: John Day, 1941.

Such charges are not new. They have a familiar ring to those who have heard the same arguments used in municipal politics. When cities, in order to get their streets paved or their milk inspected, hire city managers or strengthen the powers of their mayors, outraged critics often protest that the democratic system is being undermined. These attacks appear to carry weight in proportion to the lack of fundamental agreement over the objectives of government. In cities where there has been little factional dispute over fundamental policy, arguments of this sort are largely ignored.

Democracy versus efficiency? Whenever such attacks are taken seriously in municipal, state, or federal affairs, they lead the public to turn to the stock prescriptions for weakening the executive power—that the legislature be put in control of the details of administration by statute, that questions of policy be left to the lawmakers, that the national government stay out of state and local affairs, and that government in general stay out of business. Yet no administrative official can work by these maxims. If he thinks that democracy is defined by such maxims and still tries to do his job, he is likely to decide that the management of public affairs cannot be democratic and efficient at the same time.

Some administrators, no doubt, have come to this defeatist way of thinking. Just as Lord Melbourne thought that religion was a fine thing so long as it did not interfere with a man's private life, so some governmental managers may think that democracy is a fine thing so long as it does not meddle with the management of public affairs. Nor is this merely an error of governmental managers. In advancing the old argument that government should be run like a private corporation, certain political reformers have meant that government should be efficient, while others have meant that the way it is run should be none of the public's business.

However, many of the men and women who have distinguished themselves as public servants have shown little disposition to look on politics as a millstone round the neck of governmental management. On the contrary, they understand that, in a broader sense, efficient administration and democratic administration are one and the same. American society has operated with a comparatively high degree of consent and a low degree of compulsion. These characteristics may well offer the public administrator more opportunity for enterprising service than any political Utopia devised by critics. But such service must flow from accountable conduct.

Dangers of oversimplification. The importance of keeping administration accountable to a representative body will never grow less, no matter how strong a sense of professional responsibility public officials may develop, no matter how exact may become their standards of service. The fundamental powers and prerogatives of the legislature are as essential today as they were when men first risked life itself to assert them. It is hard to imagine how a government can be democratic unless its legislature is elected periodically by a free vote; unless the members of the legislature and the legislative proceedings are free of executive coercion and corruption; and unless public officials administer their offices according to the statutes and spend money according to the legislative appropriations—all in an environment of free thought and free speech.

If we start with such a political assumption, how seriously should the administrator take the argument that the legislature should frame policy in complete independence of the executive branch and also assert its control over the details of public affairs?

It does not make sense to expect the legislative and the executive branches to work in general harmony, and then to condemn the legislature for too sympathetic consideration of executive proposals. To some extent the public is led into such inconsistency by the etiquette of a system of separation of powers, in which leaders of the legislature are likely to be jealous of the influence of the chief executive and his agencies. However, some of the most violent feuds over legislative-executive relations in the United States have developed in cities with council-manager government, in which the city manager is the appointee of the council and has no formal independence of it whatever. Perhaps the basic reason is that the American people, considering themselves responsible for creating their governmental arrangements by rational acts of will, expect the machinery automatically to conform to the logic of charters and constitutions. Obviously, the public does not police compliance with these documents on its own initiative. However, the legislator or the executive official who chooses to raise an issue of procedural relationships between the branches of government can usually count on popular attention.

There are always reasons for raising such issues. Legislators frequently find it expedient to argue that the executive is usurping legislative prerogatives, thus calling on the corporate pride of lawmakers to reinforce an argument of policy. Lobbyists like to bolster their case with the phraseology of the classic attacks on tyranny; a press agent for a vested interest can do no better than sound like Tom Paine. And newspaper reporters, who seem to specialize in public disagreement, often find procedural issues the best material available, in the absence of consistent disagreement on policy.

The administrative official himself is hardly likely to be impressed by these issues. He knows that all the major aspects of his program depend on general agreement. In local government, when he thinks in practical terms, he has to regard the mayor, for example, as being his boss for some purposes, the council for others. He is realistic enough to understand also that in a great many matters of administration or even policy he must make decisions himself without being under the immediate control or guidance of either the mayor or the council, and that in lesser matters his subordinates also must be similarly independent of him. Without delegation of this kind, no governmental organization can operate.

Control by delegation. In this perspective, many questions simply solve themselves. What, for instance, of the century-old complaint that administrative agencies are issuing too many orders, and that the legislature is giving up its right to settle questions by statute? A federal administrative official knows that his bureau now settles by its own orders many matters that only a few decades ago were the subject of departmental action, or even an order by the President. As the volume of work increased, the numerical quantity of decisions naturally increased in greater proportion at lower levels. The practice of leaving minor matters to be handled at lower levels strengthened the control of the higher executive at each level. Indeed, only a systematic practice of directing the lower official to take responsibility for details can enable a higher official to control him. The same principle must be applied to legislative control. Just as the President can direct the executive branch only if he concentrates his personal attention on the most important matters and delegates the minor ones to others, so Congress can determine national policy by legislation only if it focuses on the great issues and leaves the lesser ones to be handled by the President.

Similarly, an alert executive is eager to have his subordinates develop and propose new policy. Administration is quite unlike the writing of poetry or other forms of personal inspiration; as the old wisecrack has it, an administrator is one who never writes what he signs or signs what he writes. This is inevitable because the creation of policy is a collective process—one of gathering ideas and facts and combining them into a program. When a city manager finds the proposal of a department head acceptable, it is a sign of good teamwork; when the council finds the proposal of a city manager acceptable, some faction will surely accuse it of being a "rubber stamp." If a legislature, uncoerced and unintimidated, agrees after open discussion with the proposals of the chief executive, is it not a sign of effective democracy rather than of shameful submission? It is pure romance to consider disapproval of a subordinate's recommendation a sign of independence. The supervisor—whether legislative or executive—gets his policies carried out by inducing his subordinates to develop and execute his general program. To do so, he must reach an understanding with them about his goals, so that he rarely needs to reject a specific proposal and start all over again.

A large legislative body will always find it difficult or impossible, even through committees, to keep in touch with all the advance planning of administrative agencies and to control the detailed application of policy. The legislator is tempted by short-run interest and pressure from his constituents to make up for this limitation by political interference with matters that for best performance ought to be delegated—the selection of individual officials, the location of field offices, the letting or cancellation of contracts, the modification of administrative orders. This temptation is apt to defeat the whole purpose of legislative supervision, which is to define the major lines of policy for the executive branch to follow.

Democracy and legislative supremacy. Let us consider the classic example of parliamentary government. It is easy to see how a legislature may keep administration generally responsive to its control by only the broadest kind of supervision. The British Parliament delegates far more rule-making power to the executive branch than would be constitutionally possible in the United States. Such delegation covers the whole subject of governmental organization. The outlines of departments and their divisions, and also the membership and structure of the Cabinet itself, are not fixed by legislation but by Orders in Council, Treasury memoranda, or even less formal documents. Moreover, while the House of Commons discusses the main policies proposed by the Prime Minister, it rarely alters them. In effect, individual members acting for themselves cannot get amendments to any important legislation considered by the House, and the House has not altered the executive budget during this century. Members of the House have never been able to interfere with administrative details; by the time that the Cabinet and the civil service came under the control of the House, the doctrine of collective responsibility of the ministers as the Cabinet induced them to keep other members of the House from interfering with the direction of their departments.

For our purpose, the primary fact is that British administration became democratic as the legislature restricted itself to a very general kind of supervision. Nor can we consider it paradoxical that general legislative control should be improved by the prevention of legislative actions aimed at details. It was one of the main purposes of our Constitution to take certain types of executive actions out of the hands of the legislature, breaking boldly with a habit that had developed in nearly every early state legislature and in the Congress of the Confederation. As Thomas Jefferson wrote a friend shortly before the Constitutional Convention met, "I have ever viewed the executive details as the greatest cause of evil to us, because they in fact place us as if we had no federal head, by diverting the attention of that head from great to small subjects."[2]

However, it was and is still possible for Congress, in sharp contrast to the House of Commons, to keep its fingers on all kinds of executive details through its standing committees. Any one who believes this difference an inherently national one should consider the contrast in local government. General management of British cities rests with committees of the city councils, council members being elected by wards. Most large American

---

[2] To Edward Carrington from Paris, August 4, 1787. *The Life and Selected Writings of Thomas Jefferson*, p. 428, New York: Modern Library, 1944.

cities, and nearly all the better governed ones, are administered either by strong mayors or city managers, while the individual members of the comparatively small councils do not participate in the direction of administrative affairs. The most delightful aspect of the matter is that Americans are apt to call the parliamentary system undemocratic whenever they learn how much power it places in the Prime Minister, while British municipal officials consider the city-manager plan and the strong-mayor plan quite dictatorial and un-British, whatever administrative merits these plans may possess.

Legislators versus legislatures. In general, a legislature does not make administrators responsive to representative control either by settling details in statutes or by refusing on principle to support policies proposed by the executive branch. This point is often obscured, however, because a legislature does not speak to the public with a single voice. Being composed of a majority and a minority, it may in general stand behind the chief executive, and at the same time—through a vocal minority in control of certain committees—appear to oppose him vigorously. It is then only natural for the newspapers to give the public the impression that the executive branch is carrying out a policy over the opposition of the legislature. What is called "executive usurpation" often resolves itself into a case in which the majority of the legislature fails to defend against minority attack the policy that it is generally supporting.

If it is entirely democratic for an administrator to carry out the intent of the legislature in the face of attacks from individual legislators or legislative committees, another point becomes apparent. Representative control can be fully accomplished only if the chief executive and the legislature work in basic harmony—the former to maintain effective control over his departments and bureaus, the latter to keep its individual members and committees from using tricks of procedure to block its general program. The real issue of representation and responsibility is not simply between the chief executive and the legislature, but between the two, on the one hand, and each and all of the departments, bureaus, and legislative committees that seek to go their own ways, on the other. The great advances in attaining administrative responsibility to the legislative branch which have been achieved in the United States have been made possible by strengthening the chief executive, who alone can present to the legislature a coherent program, over and through which broad and democratic control can be exercised.

In exercising such control, the legislature needs staff assistance in the review and interpretation of facts, the appraising of programs, the drafting of bills, and other technical work. It must have committee secretariats, legislative reference aids, and parliamentary counsel to fit itself for its tasks of general surveillance, just as a chief executive needs the tools of management that are appropriate to executive control. However, the committees must keep decisions in their own collective hands and direct their staff toward matters of proper legislative concern. Any legislative staff that is allowed to reach into the particulars of agency operations becomes in effect a rival administrative department, with all of the power of the executive officials and none of their responsibility for results.

2.   The Public as Star Customer

Methods of opinion analysis. A legislature, even if bicameral, is essentially a single body. As a body, it can act only on a limited number of important problems. Its influence, however, extends beyond its formal acts. An alert administrative agency does not merely comply with statutes; it seeks to anticipate the drift of public opinion, to develop policy proposals today that will meet the legislative demands of tomorrow. For this reason it wishes to keep in touch as closely as possible with public opinion. It may do so partly by new and specialized methods of analysis, but it is likely to depend mainly on compiling and appraising in a systematic way the information that flows in as a result of its ordinary operations.

One of the new and specialized methods is the opinion survey. What the marketing survey does for a business organization, the opinion survey does for administrators eager for the views of the star customers of the government, the general public. As Dr. Gallup and his competitors keep in touch with broad national issues, so public agencies use similar polling techniques to keep informed of what the general public or specific groups think of their programs. The Department of Agriculture, for example, has conducted scientific surveys of public opinion with its own specialists, not only for its own use but also for other departments. Many cities have made similar surveys with the help of research institutes or universities, to say nothing of less professional studies. In addition to these sampling surveys, nearly all government departments study the current trends in public opinion as reflected in newspaper and trade-journal comment.

Advisory committees. Most administrative policies, however, do not touch the public as a whole. Administrative agencies are, therefore, usually more interested in the opinion of one or another special group that is principally affected by their programs. The formal advisory committee is one means of keeping in touch with such opinion. Many agencies have developed an extensive system of such committees and general rules to guide their operations. Such rules often establish a procedure by which affected private interests may be consulted by the agency, but will not be permitted to block action that is indicated by the public interest. Still more important are the degree of public support for the purposes of the agency, the effectiveness of its organization and operations, and the cohesiveness of the private interests and their willingness to cooperate with the government. If these conditions are favorable, a governmental agency may be more intimately in touch with the private interests than any advisory group itself could be.

Day-by-day administrative relationships. Best of all as a means of keeping in touch with the special opinion of affected interests are the day-by-day administrative relationships. Through consideration of large quantities of individual cases, officials may judge not only the nature of the opinions of those affected but also their general temper.

Of course, the stream of information between public officials and citizens should flow both ways. One of the most curious aspects of the attacks on "bureaucracy" in recent years [3] has been the opposition to publicity programs or to the spending of money for reports to the public, as if it were improper or undesirable for a governmental agency to ask for the cooperation of the public, rather than to rely on sanctions. While some agencies have tried to develop programs of persuasion, especially in seeking compliance with requirements newly established by statute, most have stressed straight information.

Reporting to the public. In general, the quality of purely factual reporting has unquestionably improved in recent decades. Cities have competed with each other to issue the most informative and interesting annual reports. A few states have followed their example, and several federal agencies prepare periodic reports that are encyclopedias of information for whole areas of our social activities. The Yearbook of the Department of Agriculture has long been an indispensable reference work in its field.[4] Nor is it simply a matter of providing information on government programs for the voter to weigh and analyze. Most useful—and most significant of the present role of administration—are the periodic and special reports which become the basis for all sorts of private activity. The weather reports, the census compilations, the specialized periodicals such as the *Federal Reserve Bulletin* and the *Survey of Current Business*—publications like these furnish essential data for many and varied private operations.

The daily work of the governmental press agent, disguised by various more dignified terms, has its place in the total democratic process. He is often the closest and most frequent adviser of administrative officials on the general aspects of their programs. His bias is all in favor of what the public will like, for his success is measured by the degree of public approval he wins for his agency. Too often he thinks of advancing the

---

[3] See Chapter 3, "Bureaucracy—Fact and Fiction."

[4] A reader interested in the general philosophy of an editor of government reports who combines an understanding of general public affairs with an appreciation of scientific techniques and—rarest of all—a literary style should read the volume of essays by the editor of the Agriculture Yearbook: Hambidge, Gove, *The Prime of Life*, New York: Doubleday Doran, 1942.

personal fortunes of his boss, and too rarely does he take a long and impartial view of the administrative program. But his shortcomings are to some degree corrected by the independence of newspaper reporters and editors. His general influence on administration is surely on the side of adjusting it to the taste of the public.

Commissions of inquiry. Advisory committees and public reporting have their influence on departmental policies. Even more important is the effect on national policy of programs developed by special advisory groups, including both public officials and private citizens. Such programs have no mandatory effect, but the influence of painstaking research and thoughtful recommendations may be tremendous in the long run. Anyone who reads the reports of President Hoover's Committee on Recent Social Trends and of his Commission on Home Building and Home Ownership will discover in them the outlines of the subsequent decade's national policy on social welfare and housing. More recent examples are the two Commissions on the Organization of the Executive Branch of the Government (1947-49 and 1953-55, both chaired by Herbert Hoover) and the Commission on Intergovernmental Relations (1953-55), each leaving a large package of reports and special studies.

The basic changes in national policy are rarely the invention of either legislators or administrators working alone. They require the consensus of interested men and women of special knowledge and the support of private organizations, as well as the agreement of officials, the promotion of popular understanding through press and radio, and the sanction of elected representatives.

3. Public Participation

Cooperative government. It is hard to talk realistically about government as long as we think of it as something apart from ourselves. A governmental program does not exist for its own sake, but as a part of a larger purpose tied into the social order. This must be remembered when we hear government described as something equivalent to coercion intruding into our private affairs.

Authority wielded by government employees, intruding into the everyday life of the citizen to deliver his mail, to relieve him of his garbage, to teach his children, to keep him from driving on the wrong side of the road —are these "intrusions"? And it may also be asked whether private corporations themselves, and their property, do not need to be protected and supported by the authority wielded by government employees. It is at variance with fact to see public administration as the employment of authority against citizens. Nor does it make sense to think of it as being controlled solely or even primarily by government employees.

When we judge the political character of public administration, and before we decide that it is either oppressive or paternalistic, we should remind ourselves that nearly every main function of government is now administered by cooperation among levels of government or between public and quasi-public or private agencies. Not only has the public become the star customer of government, but business, labor, and a host of organized group activities have all been rolled into one broadly unified cooperative system. In this system the traditional values of liberty have not been lost. Yet a higher degree of harmony has been attained than would ever be achieved through a coercive approach.

In general, the system that for want of a better name has sometimes been called "cooperative government" is one in which a broad program is carried out, not by a single national agency such as the Post Office Department, but by federal, state, and local agencies working in cooperation with each other, with quasi-governmental or private institutions, with business and labor. For its greatest efficiency, cooperative government requires a high degree of mutual trust and common understanding, correlated action by several or perhaps even thousands of legislative bodies, and considerable voluntary support from private individuals or institutions.

Combined operations among levels of government. One of its aspects is the cooperation of federal, state, and local agencies in almost all the important programs of government, whether in education, social security, agriculture, public health, the regulation of commerce, housing, highways, public works, or any other fields. Rather than list the programs in which intergovernmental cooperation is essential, it would be better to challenge the reader to name an important one in which it is not. He may start with the business of the post office, but he will be hard put to it to find another. He had better not mention national defense, usually considered a predominantly federal function, until he has studied the influence of the state militia and the National Guard on our military history, and the way in which the National Guard is formally linked to the structure of the Defense Department. And as national defense has become more and more a matter of technological and industrial power, it is significant that much basic scientific research for national defense is conducted by private institutions—academic and industrial research laboratories. These benefit from an independent status and thus greater leeway in approach, even though they are working within the framework of governmental policy.

The system of cooperative government was greatly expanded during World War II. Never before had governmental operations and planning been so decentralized in the United States as at the time when their purpose became utterly concentrated and their potential authority great beyond any peacetime precedent. The Selective Service System turned over to local boards of volunteers, set up by state agencies, the task of manning the armed forces. Much the same policy was followed by our price and rationing administration. Anyone who thinks of the war program as something dictated from Washington may study the war activities of the Council of State Governments, the American Municipal Association, and the United States Conference of Mayors. State and local governments not only had to carry out national programs in many obvious and some unexpected ways,[5] but they were often ahead of federal agencies in realizing and pointing to the need for new policies.

Although state and local governments still use the jargon of states' rights and local autonomy, in practice they know that they cannot live in independence. They must work with federal agencies and influence federal activities in order to justify their existence.

One particularly good example, though in some ways it is unique, is the scheme of agricultural administration. It has been influenced by concentrated economic forces to a lesser degree than have comparable activities in the fields of commerce and industry. As a result, the traditional American individualist, the farmer, has retained wider opportunities for direct participation in cooperative government. He has taken part in the development of an intricate cooperative system of public subsidy, joint marketing, production control, soil conservation, public credit, freely available scientific research, and technical education in state universities, extension courses, and on the farm. From the administrative point of view, this is especially interesting because it illustrates so well how some functions can best be handled by national agencies, especially if they deal with broad economic problems like farm credit or aid to weaker groups like the program of the Farmers Home Administration; how other functions are best entrusted to state agriculture departments; others to land-grant colleges; and still others to the joint efforts of experiment stations and extension services, in which the county agent works at one and the same time for all levels of government and for private associations of farmers—and on the side helps carry on incidental programs of welfare and education.

Benefits of intergovernmental collaboration. To see the benefits of a cooperative system, it is not necessary to believe that local government is closer to the people, or more important to the people, or more democratic, than national government. None of the traditional local functions deals with as many people every day as does the postal service; none of them affects the lives of citizens in ways as important as do international diplomacy and war. And all functions exercised by state and local governments are more likely to fall under the control of irresponsible groups, whether tightly controlled machines or powerful economic interests, than is the

---

[5] For example, the provision of emergency war housing required the amendment of city building codes, and the national fiscal policy depended partly on cooperative state and local taxing and spending programs.

case in the federal government. Moreover, the business of the nation commands the citizen's first attention. The newspaper editor knows what people are interested in when he puts Washington affairs on the front page, and local council news, if any, inside with the hair-tonic ads.

Yet there is a great deal to be said for arrangements under which public officials with a national point of view have to deal on a basis of mutual respect with public officials representing a local point of view. Quite a few broad governmental programs may well be divided into specific functions, some under exclusive federal or local control and others under mixed control, but with representatives of all levels of government in a position to criticize independently the arrangements, and to speak up if they are disregarded. Even if the federal government is the exclusive source of funds or has the final word in any dispute, the participation of local agencies may be a source of initiative, of independent criticism, and of administrative personnel who have been trained in the exercise of political responsibility rather than as anonymous components of a larger organization.

Inclusion of business and labor. It is interesting to note, moreover, how the cooperative system has been extending itself, not only to local governments and public institutions, but to business corporations that are sometimes thought to be motivated only by their balance sheets. Perhaps the general drift toward the view that private property, too, is a public trust is partly responsible. And perhaps the way in which the management of business has become largely separated from ownership has opened the road to cooperation with the government.

This is not to suggest that business interests are sacrificing themselves out of public spirit. It is only to say that they now see their place in a larger system more clearly than was the case half a century ago. They have been drawn into the administration of national programs by the legislation that they have sponsored, by regulations imposed on them, by contractual arrangements with public authorities, and through the activities of their trade associations.

Property, as the lawyers say, is only a bundle of rights. Legislators and administrators have followed the advice of Aesop by dealing with each right separately, so that the national interest in the use of property may find expression while private interest is not destroyed. There is indeed no general principle about government-business relations that is uniformly binding. Like state and local governments, business enterprise has to justify its existence by its usefulness in the public interest. One cannot expect too much of such a general responsibility by itself, but it is probable that government-business relations will be worked out according to specific and empirical standards, field by field. And as business corporations come into the picture, so do labor unions.

Group initiative under national standards. The modern tendency is for the federal government to see to it that private organizations or state and local governments do certain things according to certain standards, instead of doing them itself. The Civil Aeronautics Administration, for instance, licenses private flying schools and private repair shops to examine the pilots and inspect the maintenance of aircraft—functions comparable to those which the early Steamboat Inspection Service assigned to its inspectors. Thus an agency empowered to establish its own regulations, instead of being bound by detailed legislation, is apt to discover that administrative effectiveness dictates the same policy as does the desire to leave private enterprise independent of detailed government control, subject to standards established in the public interest.

In all these cooperative arrangements, private associations play an essential part. De Tocqueville remarked a century ago that the leadership in public affairs which would be assumed by a public functionary in France or a grand gentleman in England was taken in America by a private association.[6] Some of these are organizations of people bound together only by public spirit and civic interest in a single subject; some, like trade and professional associations or organizations of public officials, are bound together by a common occupational interest.

It must not be imagined that such a system always works toward the public welfare. It has the disadvantage of diffusing responsibility and encouraging various groups to blame their own shortcomings on each other. To keep the main lines of policy in the hands of responsible public officials is essential if a governmental program is to be democratically administered. To let local agencies use national funds for purposes other than those determined by responsible national authorities, or to leave to a private interest the responsibility of regulating itself, cannot be justified on any grounds of democratic decentralization. However, the existence of many organizations which command the loyalties of citizens is the best guarantee that no single agency can demand and abuse that loyalty. The people may safely call on their governmental executives for vigorous leadership as long as they have many channels through which to contribute to the development of policies and to protest those that seem to be determined by self-interest or professional prejudice.

4. Representing the Public Interest

Interdependence of public and private interests. The system of mixed governmental and private efforts has not solved all political and administrative problems; sometimes it may seem that it has only complicated them. In politics, it has made the old issues of left wing versus right wing, government ownership versus private enterprise, appear unrealistic. In ad-

---

[6] *Democracy in America,* Vol. 2, p. 106, New York: Knopf, 1945.

ministration, it has added so many dimensions to the functions and responsibilities of public management that the negative formulas of the nineteenth century have been rendered inadequate. The problem is no longer simply how to prevent special privilege; it is one of organizing the larger public interest.

The most conspicuous kind of nineteenth-century privilege in the United States—party spoils—is fast becoming obsolete. Today's problem is more subtle than the prevention of patronage in jobs or contracts. It is to keep the system of cooperative government from freezing into a structure of guilds or competing pressure groups. The distinction is not mainly one of form or pattern, but of purpose and attitude. We cannot solve the problem by saying that government must not aid private interests, for the interests of private organizations and governmental agencies are so thoroughly intertwined that many of the distinctions between them have become only incidental.

The interdependence of private and public interests is nothing fundamentally new in America. It is as old as the land grants to railroads and homesteaders, as Henry Clay's "American system" of tariffs and internal improvements, and as the subsidized and chartered private companies that established most of the thirteen colonies in the New World while the other Americas were being developed by alliances of military and ecclesiastic hierarchies.

Threefold collaboration in policy-making. Today we see most national policies—which govern the larger private interests as well as purely governmental business—worked out in three-fold collaboration, with participation by congressional committees, by administrative officials, and by representatives of private interest groups.

It is clearly essential to democratic government that the legislature be free to consider and reject the proposals of administrative officials and of pressure groups, and that it give no particular official or private interest an exclusive right to be heard. Yet the "bureaucrats" and the "lobbyists" have a vital role in the formulation of policy, for they shape up the smaller questions into large issues capable of legislative consideration. Congress would be faced with chaotic conditions if, for instance, it insisted on reading petitions from individual businessmen instead of hearing the testimony of trade-association executives.

To develop a program in democratic fashion, it is indispensable to examine present administrative experience, study the probable effect of new proposals on all interests concerned and on related programs, and then subject the proposals to legislative hearing and debate. While the representative of the special-interest group plays a necessary part in this process, the public administrator has much the same special knowledge and a broader kind of responsibility. His role in the formulation of policy—for final legislative consideration, amendment, and approval or rejection—is and should be an influential one. It is accepted as such whenever any group, in or out of the legislature, tries to work out a practical program. Heated denunciation of the influence of bureaucrats on legislation is usually only a tactical maneuver in the battle over policy.

The administrative official has several assets that make it accord with the public interest for him to exert great influence in the evolution of policy. He may develop impartial scientific and professional standards for the measurement of the effect of policies. He may judge the working of those policies by close observation in actual practice. His regard for theories is likely to be tempered by a shrewd appreciation of what is possible and practical and what is not. And yet he can be the spokesman of interests that are not cohesive or powerful enough to hire press agents or influence legislators by well-tailored arguments. This function is especially important since consumers—being equivalent to the general citizenry—rely mainly on their government to protect their interests against the powerful lobbies of producers and salesmen.

All the advantages that the administrative official possesses in the formulation of policy are reflections of the responsibility of his position. It is his task to further the purposes defined by law and executive order, which are a part of a general program supported by the electorate. He is directly accountable to his superiors, and indirectly to the legislature, whose control over appropriations is a powerful weapon for the enforcement of responsibility. His professional bias and his governmental responsibility alike impel him to work for the public interest. In practice, his influence is considerable. Careful studies of the origins of legislation—of the sources of the drafts of bills acted on by the legislature—show that in federal and state governments alike the administrative official is accepted as the ghost writer of the lawmaker.

Informality of policy-making process. On the other hand, no matter how much of scientific methods or objective standards is applied in the development of a policy, a public official is subject to the error of overemphasizing his own specialty. The more zeal he shows for the public welfare, the greater is the probability of error. This kind of distortion is increased by the tendency of the official to ally himself with legislators who have similar preferences and with interest representatives holding a similar point of view.

Such informal alliances to further the public interest by advancing special programs make it impossible to determine exactly who was responsible for what. The effective responsibility for the content of public policy cannot be measured simply in the number of bills that are prepared by lobbyists, by administrative officials, or by individual legislators. For the more important decisions in the formulation of policy are usually made in informal discussions in which those concerned try to work out an agreement before the proposal is formally prepared for legislative consideration.

Even if no informal discussions are held, a proposal drafted by an administrative official will be influenced greatly by his judgment of what the legislative committee will probably accept and of what will arouse strong opposition by private interests. It should, therefore, be stressed that the very informality of this process is a democratic characteristic. The legislature and the chief executive are enabled, if they consider it in the general public interest, to refuse to accept the organized point of view of the interest group or the administrative department, and to try through other combinations of private interests and public administrators to line up a workable new program.

For while government departments and organized private interests are basic machinery in our social system, they can be positive forces in a democracy only if they are kept in line with the general public interest. It is not enough for them to refrain from encroaching on the rights of others; they must actively contribute to the general welfare. To enforce this fundamental responsibility it is necessary to prevent any single collection of interests—whether a government department, a trade association, a labor union, or what not—from monopolizing an activity so completely that it can deal with the people on its own terms.

Experimental approach. For this reason it may sometimes be politically wise not to consolidate major bureaus or departments even though they have related functions, especially if they are pursuing different experimental approaches to a problem and if their consolidation would result in dropping such productive experimentation. Thus a two-party system is better than a one-party system, not because the two parties necessarily have different philosophies, but because each helps prevent the other from subordinating the general welfare to its prejudices and interests. Similarly, at the top level of administration where broad considerations are properly involved, it may sometimes be desirable to avoid a neat pattern which puts all related functions under the same agency, in order to leave the chief executive more freedom of choice.

For example, in the middle 1930's the field of housing was divided into sharply defined groups, each with its own solution to the housing problem. The real-estate boards, the building and loan associations, the commercial banks, the lumber dealers, the welfare workers, the advocates of decentralized subsistence homesteads, the advocates of slum clearance—each of these private groups was sure that its solution alone was right, each identified it with its own philosophy, each lined up in support of an administrative agency dedicated to something like its approach, each cultivated the Congressmen whose committees were likely sources of support. To amalgamate the various administrative agencies in the field of housing at that stage would have been to commit the country to a partial approach. After ten years of enlightening experimentation, however, all groups were much better prepared to admit the possibility of making the several programs operate in harmony rather than in opposition to each other. It was then feasible to bring the several administrative establishments into a single agency, each retaining a measure of its independence and each fitting itself into a comprehensive program.

General interest over special interest. The program of a government is never merely the sum of its departmental programs; it may be much more or much less. It is much less if the basic purposes of the departments are inconsistent. It is much more if their operations are linked together, each furthering the activities of the others and all submerging their jurisdictional disputes in a general current of agreement.

But the legislature alone cannot accomplish such administrative coordination. The democratic process of subordinating the special interest to the general interest depends to a high degree on the leadership of the chief executive in the sponsorship and application of policy. No one is in a better position to observe how present developments will require changes in policy. No one else can as effectively use the agencies of centralized management— budgeting, planning, personnel. No one else can equally well back up his formal orders to the executive establishment with administrative sanctions.

The broader the responsibility of an administrator, the more concerned he must be with the general aspects of the government's program, and the less with narrow questions of technical efficiency. The specialist in management efficiency or scientific research who resents "political" interference from above may be properly objecting to partisan exploitation of his job. It is just as likely, however, that he resents having the technical aspects of his work adjusted to fit a general program. Similarly, the bureau chief naturally dislikes having his aims subordinated to those of the department, and in turn the department head may seek to be as independent as possible of the chief executive.

It is plain that the adjustment of each level's work to make it fit into a larger pattern is the essential process in administration. As long as this process is carried on in an atmosphere of free criticism, and with the chief executive responsible to the people, it is a truly democratic process. The formal machinery is not as important as the fact that the chief executive is held responsible by the public for the whole program of the government. His direct responsibility to the people is strong in the American democratic tradition. Let us remember that the Electoral College was reduced to a fiction soon after it had been established, and that in many a city the voters have chosen council members for their support of the city manager rather than for their own views or personalities.

The chief executive is most effective in contributing to the democratic workings of administration if he combines with his machinery of coordination a policy or a philosophy that will stir the interest and inspire the support of his departments, the legislative body, and the general public alike.

5. Departmental Democracy

Individual freedom versus institutional restraint. If the purpose of democracy is to make government serve the highest ends of man, instead of making man serve the lowest ends of government, we cannot be sure that public administration will remain democratic in the long run simply by achieving satisfactory working relations between governmental agencies, the legislature, and the general public. We must consider the way the governmental agencies are organized and operated, for it is always possible for an organization to defeat its own ends by becoming an end in itself.

Within an organization, democracy is by no means the same thing as lack of discipline or authority. An army, for example, can be quite democratic even though an officer has authority to order his men to certain death. The question is whether the administrative organization permits its members to retain their independence as citizens in matters that do not concern their official duties, and whether it gives them a chance, in performing those duties, to make full use of their talents to further the general welfare.[7]

Public officials and employees do not need to surrender their personal rights or liberties as citizens. Perhaps the low point of public confidence in government, at least in the English-language tradition, was reached for a few years in the late eighteenth century when the British Parliament denied civil servants the right to vote. That limitation was soon removed, but Great Britain continued to restrict the political activities of civil servants more severely than did the United States at that time. America made the opposite error of letting political parties use government employees for their own purposes, until civil service rules established the proposition that a public servant must not campaign in party contests.

Political participation of civil servants. It would probably be an error for this nation to adopt the general principle that civil servants, though necessarily under certain restraints, may not take part in organizing the promotion of public policy. The permanent tenure of the civil servant, and the possibility of change at any time in the political direction of public administration, make it inconvenient to permit him to take a public stand on an issue between his present political superiors and their rivals who could become his superiors tomorrow. Even so, it is a little hard to see why it is proper for civil servants to organize to get their salaries raised and improper

---

[7] See also Chapter 21, "Morale and Discipline." *Cf.* in general Waldo, Dwight, "Development of a Theory of Democratic Administration," *American Political Science Review,* 1952, Vol. 46, p. 81 *ff.* (for comments see *ibid.,* p. 496 *ff.*).

for them to take part in more inclusive organizations in support of other policies. After World War II, Britain adopted, especially for her "industrial" government employees, more liberal rules for political participation than are applied in the United States.

At one extreme there must obviously be some limitation; at the other extreme there need be none. An officer in a high position should not publicly oppose his political superior's policy without resigning; and if he does oppose it in public he should be discharged. At the other extreme, an employee with duties totally unrelated to policy ought to be permitted to take any stand he likes on issues of policy.

The most difficult problems arise between these two extremes. An official with a long-range interest in the public service will often find compromise necessary. As long as he is conscious of working toward his general objective as a servant of the public, compromise is simply a function of his position. Government, of course, needs men whose primary interest and competence are focused in the administrative process itself, and who can help conduct administrative affairs regardless of changes in policy. However, in a dynamic democracy there is also room for men who, while not active in the business of running electoral campaigns or party organizations, are primarily interested in policies and programs, and are quite willing to work for these either inside or outside the government.

Now that the number of civil servants is so great, it is especially important to safeguard their political rights. As long as we keep our system of co-operative government, we will never be threatened by a gigantic bureaucracy all of whose members vote for its boss—if there ever was such a bureaucracy under popular rule. The cooperation of state and local governments and private institutions in national administration helps guarantee the freedom and diversity of political views.

Sense of general purpose. At the same time, administrators themselves ought to be concerned with the political implications of their own departments and the departmental working processes. The purpose of every organization is partially defeated whenever it tends to become absorbed in itself and in the interests of its personnel, rather than in the accomplishment of its general objectives. The administrator ought not to be blind to the dangers of such introversion, for it is a fault from which none of his management formulas can save him.

There is, first of all, one obvious danger. Any person may easily slide into the error of believing that his organization exists primarily for him and for his particular category of associates. This is a matter of degree. In general, the more the civic status of public employees is preserved, the less incentive they have for considering their pay and working conditions their prime objectives. It is quite proper to demand the protection of employee rights and to organize to that end. It is also quite proper to take an interest in the development of a career service, based on adequate personal incentives. At the same time, neither the citizen nor the civil servant ought to confuse the security or conditions of government employment with the essential purposes of public administration.

The distinction is not always simple, but there are several approaches that will help an agency head to make it clearer. One is to see that employees have full opportunity to use their abilities in the most effective ways. No single organization can do so completely, for the purpose of the organization itself is a limitation. A welfare agency, for example, could hardly make the best use of a promising physicist. Within reasonable limits, however, intelligent methods of recruiting and classifying employees and of assigning them work that will suit and develop their talents are apt to further at once the efficiency and the democracy of administration.

Employee development. Large organizations can do even more by adopting programs of in-service training and executive development to encourage the fullest growth and use of all potential abilities. Nothing weakens an administrative organization or a government as a whole more seriously than artificial barriers to the advancement of men and women with capacity and leadership. The traditional practice of American civil service commissions of considering only the immediate usefulness of a recruit, and making little or no effort to discover and develop general administrative ability at an early stage, cannot be justified on grounds of democracy; it is merely shortsighted. It is possible to develop administrators without producing an undemocratic administrative elite.[8]

In encouraging employees to put forth their best efforts, a great deal depends on indefinable matters of personality and atmosphere. It may not be too fanciful to suggest, however, that the qualities which enable a citizen to assert his political independence while respecting the opinions and personalities of others are similar to those which aid the administrator to bring out the best efforts of his subordinates. The dictatorial administrator who makes personal issues out of differences of judgment is likely to stifle the advice on which he must rely for guidance. On the other hand, one always yielding to the personalities of his subordinates—one who fails to bring to their attention the points on which they fall below standards, and who juggles his organization to suit their peculiarities—may merely find the more scrupulous to be confused and uncertain, and the less scrupulous to be either scheming for their own purposes or challenging his leadership. A good measure of intelligent extroversion, combined with a sensitivity for the rights and feelings of others, will help the administrator to keep his agency's attention on the job to be done rather than on its internal problems. If he has these qualities, and a supply of intellectual discrimination as well,

---

[8] *Cf.* Chapter 2, "The Study of Public Administration," sec. 3, "Training for Public Administration."

he may profit from the research that is being done on human relations in administration. Equally important, he may be able to avoid the excessively specialized techniques that have threatened to make human relations into a cult, rather than a normal phase of the administrative process.

Vice of departmentalism. Another danger is the assumption that the organization exists for its own sake. The logical transition here is easy: *esprit de corps* makes for effective work, and *esprit de corps* is furthered by expansion of the functions or jurisdiction of the organization. In mild doses this is good medicine, but as a steady diet it is politically fatal. Undue concentration of loyalty in the agency is somewhat akin to the specialist's devotion to his own specialty. The formula of having the expert "on tap but not on top" is easier to quote than to apply in practice.

Several cures have been tried for this ailment. One is to introduce counterinfluences in the form of governmentwide concerns—agencies to aid the chief executive in his widely embracing managerial duties, such as a planning office or a budget bureau, or special coordinating machinery. Another is to give multiple functions to a single agency or a single unit of government. On this principle the Tennessee Valley Authority was created; much earlier the entire system of British local government was reorganized on the same principle, to substitute a single unit of government in each area for a number of specialized authorities. Still another cure is the systematic promotion or transfer of administrative personnel from one department to another. The British civil service adopted this idea for the higher levels more than three decades ago, and in Germany it is much older, if not consistently practiced. Such transfers have probably done much to make civil servants think more of the general welfare and less of jurisdictional disputes. Perhaps the same effects will be fostered under the scheme, proposed for the federal government, for a "senior career service." Up to now, advance to the top has usually been most predictable when one stuck unwaveringly to one agency, or even one bureau within it.

If transfers of this kind are good between departments, why not apply them between the various levels of government and between government and private institutions? Government is only one part in the whole organization of society, and the changes in its functions during the past century have made the line between it and private activities far less sharp. Today, the governmental administrator cannot adequately judge his agency's operations merely by the conventional standards of management; he must consider its effects on society as a whole. To give him the necessary breadth of view, we may need a wider interchange of top personnel among levels of government and between public and private life. The specialists in techniques and in various subject-matter fields are necessary, and will want to make life careers of their work. However, they are not likely to develop the breadth of sympathy and imagination that an administrator of the highest level must have if he is to do his job in the development as well as in the execution of policy.

The spoils system was little better than looting the public treasury. But the theory of rotation in office is not the same as that of partisan spoils. In a general sense it has always applied in American life, private as well as public. Visitors from more static or more stable societies invariably wonder at the American's tendency to change from job to job, or to occupy several jobs at once. Perhaps we should bring up to date, with proper adaptation, the theory that Jefferson and Jackson held about public office. It is not that public administration is so simple a matter that anyone can master it in a short time. On the contrary, it is so complex that few can comprehend the problems that arise at its higher levels without having had wider experience, and not in government alone.[9]

Inroads of perfectionism. A further trap awaits the administrator who seeks to do the job assigned to him by law and executive direction. It is the danger that the administrative process will become an object in itself, that the very art of generalization will be converted into a specialty. Some managers allow their personal analytical and critical processes to absorb their attention. As a result, they fail to let subordinates do their jobs in their own ways, thus obstructing the development of diverse abilities and the release of individual energies throughout the organization. Others become hypnotized by the procedures of management. A manual of procedures has its uses, but like other written rules it is apt to turn sterile unless it is the elaboration of a common will, a real agreement of minds within the organization on objectives and on the type of teamwork by which they are to be effected.

Delegation depends on the assumption that some other man can do the job as well as the delegating superior, once general direction is established. The popular axiom, "If you want a job well done, do it yourself," is the opposite of administration. Yet a kind of perfectionism sometimes creeps into management. It is shown by a preference for making all decisions at headquarters rather than leaving enough of them to the field, on the theory that headquarters will make no mistakes, even if a bottleneck develops. It is shown by a preference for flooding the field with detailed instructions; it is thought best to make sure that all is settled in terms of the letter of the directives. It is shown by a preference for centralized national administration in all circumstances, so that there be a uniform policy and no local variations, even if the program fails to win general understanding and acceptance.

Yet these perfectionist assumptions usually break down because the very

---

[9] Of course, this proposition is quite different from the historic use of rotation in office for patronage purposes; *cf.* Chapter 1, "The Growth of Public Administration," sec. 4, "Increasing Competence for Increasing Responsibility."

nature of public affairs requires administration with flexibility and initiative on lower levels. It is, therefore, just as desirable to get the views of the men in the field as it is to get the views of the department head. In a quite literal sense, headquarters must serve the field officers and the field officers must serve the public if the organization is to be democratically efficient in its administration.

Democratic self-education. The purposes of democratic society deserve the best administration that can be had. No less will do the job. And the administrator who today is doing his best hardly need worry about the stale charges of despotism and dictatorship. On the contrary, he should be heartened by the way in which the administrative process has broadened and become more democratic during the past generation.

This broadening of participation in our national administration must not be credited to any single group or party. It is the result of a gradual strengthening of public responsibilities throughout the nation, and of a freer exchange of ideas and personnel among all levels of government and private organizations, including business corporations. In its more successful programs, contemporary government makes it plain to the citizen that while the best administration is certainly democratic, the most democratic administration is also the most efficient.

In order to provide a cohesive force for this cooperative system, we should encourage among our administrative officials responsible participation in the development of policy.[10] The old proposition that policy and administration are mutually exclusive spheres of activity never fully applied anywhere. Particularly, it never fitted the United States. And today, when the political fate of the world depends on our ability to coordinate technologies while encouraging initiative, it is necessary for administrative officials to help in the charting of our social policies, even though they must remain fully responsible to legislative control and to direction by democratically chosen executives.

Our social frontiers will move forward not according to abstract theories but as fast as we can educate one another to the possibility of effective cooperation. This process of democratic self-education is one of the main aspects of public administration. To it the administrative official must contribute his full share.

---

[10] To be sure, no one would want to minimize the basic distinction between responsible and irresponsible participation in policy development. Some of the standards of responsibility in this sphere have been outlined in the present chapter. Others are suggested in Chapter 1, "The Growth of Public Administration," sec. 1, "Administration: Everybody's Business," and Chapter 3, "Bureaucracy—Fact and Fiction," sec. 1, "Semantics and Realities." See also Chapter 22, "Essentials of Responsibility."

Chapter 5 •

The Social Function of

Public Administration

1. The "American System" and the Service State

Wartime record. Toward the end of World War II, in their official report on war and postwar adjustment policy released early in 1944, Bernard Baruch and John Hancock passed judgment on the performance of the American economy. With the trained eye of experienced business leaders, they cast an appraising glance at "all of the economic systems of the world" and concluded that "the American system has outproduced the world." But they added a very significant qualification on the manner in which this "miracle"—as they put it—had been achieved. "With the coming of war," they observed, "a sort of totalitarianism is asserted . . . planning and execution rest upon one over-all purpose and a single control."[1] This tribute to both the power of the American people's common determination and the role of government in directing the mobilization of the nation's resources could be read as a lesson for peace as well as war.

War is not the only teacher of patriotism and civic solidarity. True dedication of men's individual efforts to the organic development of democratic society might bring forth on a national scale the "moral equivalent of war," to use the title William James gave one of his most memorable essays. If we can attain greater service from our economy by effective cooperation under the auspices of "one over-all purpose and a single control," should we not hasten to seek the better life by adopting for peacetime use the wartime features of the "American system" which proved the key to victory?

Peacetime relevance of wartime achievement. An affirmative answer could find support in the character of American wartime experience. The United States reached not only unprecedented levels of productivity and national income but also a high mark of direct citizen participation in governmental activities such as selective service administration, civilian defense, and price and rationing administration. The democratic structure

---

[1] Senate Doc. No. 154, 78th Cong., 2d Sess., pp. 3, 7, Washington: Government Printing Office, 1944.

of government remained intact, and the individual's fundamental liberties were not undermined. In the sphere of business, the "American system" retained its identity as an enterprise economy, in the main individually owned and managed for private gain. By harnessing its full productive strength, the United States succeeded in building a vast war economy atop a peace economy. At no time in its history had the American people accomplished anything like it.

Yet Americans were far from assuming that the scheme that served them well in war would provide them with a sound working formula for peacetime living. Winning a war is a goal for which nations close ranks almost automatically. Safeguarding prosperity in the context of the democratic way of life is an equally worthy end, but one for which it has been hard to evolve a generally acceptable organizational pattern. As a matter of fact, to many groups in the United States, the essence of the "American system" lies precisely in the absence of any semblance of a "single control," any "regimentation," any "sort of totalitarianism." Spokesmen of some of these groups have often insisted that the "American system" itself demands that government "stay out of business" and leave the economy to its "natural laws."

Long-range trend toward the service state. However vigorously this doctrine has been expounded, it is clear that the United States has never attempted to practice it consistently. Suffice it to mention the Articles of Confederation, formulated in 1777, which authorized government to "go into business" by establishing its "sole and exclusive right and power" to run the postal service. Indeed, next to its unparalleled technological advance, perhaps the most striking thing about the "American system" in the historic perspective is the steady growth of direct and indirect public controls. These are effected by regulation, by taxation, by central management of money and credit, by enforcement of standards of safety, by governmental insurance of risks, by preserving industrial peace, by grants and subsidies, and by the conditions attached to a host of specialized services to meet particular group needs. For better or for worse, all of this is part of the "American system."

Nor can it be argued that the gradual emergence of such public controls arose from anybody's conspiratorial scheming or lust for power, or from zest for interference on the part of government. Traditionally suspicious of authority, Americans resorted to new controls only in the face of strong popular pressures or conditions that cried out for remedy. On this score, there is no basic difference in the records of the Republican and Democratic parties. In each instance, governmental action, preventive or curative, presented itself as the lesser evil, when compared with an unimproved *status quo*. Sometimes the action taken was futile; sometimes it was foolish. Sometimes it was clumsily devised and incompetently executed. Even if it met public expectations, satisfaction usually was not unmixed. After all, is not the lesser evil still an evil?

One important fact, however, stood out. As the framework of public concern and superintendence widened, the industrial society managed to narrow the dangerous chasm between wealth and poverty, increase its economic health, and raise the national standard of living. Government, by expanding its functions in the social and economic realms, simultaneously built a floor under man's feet below which he could no longer drop, thus broadening the meaning of democracy. This was the "trend toward the service state" which Leonard D. White had found in evidence in the administrative evolution of American government during the first three decades of the twentieth century.[2] It is still continuing.

Assurance versus fear. Even today, however, the implications of this trend are by no means universally appreciated. Like parents who do not see their children grow, most of us would not know a trend if we met one. Those who became aware of the "trend toward the service state" were more inclined to decry it than to weigh its deeper consequences. Time and again we were chilled by prophecies of impending doom. How could free enterprise or, for that matter, *any* freedom survive if government continued to reach out farther and farther? How could the nation's economic efficiency —the very basis of its existence—hold up if government meddling drained all initiative from private management? Questions such as these inspired gloom rather than assurance. Yet, although political power changed hands, no party clothed with governmental responsibility found it practical to call a halt and defy the "trend toward the service state." Is it reasonable to assume that governments simply did not know what they were doing?

It is a more reasonable alternative to accept the propositions that the service state is democracy brought up to date; that the extension of governmental responsibilities aims at the assertion of democracy in the nerve centers of modern industrial society; and that modern industrial society can endure in relative freedom only through such assertion. This is not a new or abrupt turn. It is the chief means of preserving the Western political heritage. As one of the ablest defenders of the "middle way" has expressed it, "The liberty which our Anglo-Saxon ancestors have fought to maintain for fifty generations has been liberty under law, and law means regulation."[3] Liberty under law is at the same time liberty bolstered by law, for both the economically strong and the economically weak. In this sense, the service state is the charter for the common man. Here Jefferson's concern for the rank and file and Hamilton's vision of active government promoting the public interest link up with each other in one unified formula.

Test of the service state. World War II was an undoubted test of the

---

[2] *Trends in Public Administration,* p. 341, New York: McGraw-Hill, 1933.

[3] John Dickinson, in presenting the government side of the constitutionality of the Bituminous Coal Conservation Act of 1935, Senate Doc. No. 197, 74th Cong., 2d Sess., p. 15, Washington: Government Printing Office, 1936. Dickinson's general position is concisely outlined in his *Hold Fast the Middle Way,* Boston: Little, Brown & Co., 1935. This book has hardly found the attention it deserves.

"American system." It was also a test of the service state. In terms of existing governmental machinery, the United States was far better equipped at the outset than it had been on the threshold of World War I. On this basis, the country proceeded to put itself, for the duration of the national emergency, under "a sort of totalitarianism." Thus forearmed, with all the great resources of the nation at its command, the United States set a world record of production. The triumph of the "American system" was a triumph of creative enterprise backed by the service state.

But a real issue remains. Obviously, no one would contend that what democracy needs is "a sort of totalitarianism." Wartime demands are extraordinary. Nations cannot afford to be slow in getting into their stride. We confront an entirely different situation in peacetime. Short of emergencies, real or imagined, citizens are more circumspect and hesitant about means even when they agree on ultimate ends. They bicker and quarrel among themselves for selfish reasons. They sneer at authority, if only for the fun of it. And authority, in turn, cannot be supported by those standards of exceptional latitude which are the essence of war powers under the Constitution. Thus peacetime government is beset by many problems in pursuit of the well-being of the nation.

Basic issues. For one thing, the absence of a sense of urgency such as is generated in time of war greatly reduces the potentialities of national unity. Thus the task of political leadership is made vastly more difficult. More important still, can one readily assume that the step-by-step evolution of the service state as a whole will be guided by tested standards of both ideological consistency and utilitarian feasibility—or at least by responsible experimentation? In other words, will democratic government manage to prevent the service state from slipping over into the grooves of a new police state or a centrally controlled economy indifferent to the people's need and preferences?

This question, in turn, is linked with two others. First, is popular rule able, in the era of mass democracy, to cope effectively with longer-range policy choices, especially those in which immediate gains must yield to ultimate ones? Are sound choices of this order of magnitude conceivable only by shifting much of the burden of deciding to the statesman, bolstered by the expert in and out of government? And second, will popular rule succeed in developing a productive division of labor between the political representatives of society, the elective agents of final policy choice, and the arm of policy, the merit bureaucracy? Will the political cadre learn to make good use of the administrative cadre, and will the administrative cadre learn to function well under changing political leadership? There is no reason to take either a hopelessly pessimistic or a blindly optimistic view in these matters. But it can hardly be denied that the eventual outcome will be of crucial significance to both the record of twentieth century democracy and the future course of the service state.[4] In this outcome the performance of public administration—in integrity as well as in competence —is bound to play a large part.

2. The Needs of the Service State

Making democracy succeed. In the light of peacetime's much-increased opportunities for disruptive disagreement, the postwar assignment faced by the United States as a nation, at home and abroad, looked formidable, to say the least. Nor has it grown easier with time. Internationally, enduring peace itself may be lost unless the American role as a senior partner of potentially decisive influence in world politics is played with both strength and wisdom. In the domestic sphere, government is virtually committed to perpetuation of the wartime "miracle" of productive capacity and maximum employment. Historically, this obligation of the service state goes back to the British White Paper on Employment Policy—issued before the end of World War II—which bluntly declared in its first sentence, "The Government accept as one of their primary aims and responsibilities the maintenance of a high and stable level of employment after the war." The discharge of such broad governmental responsibility, together with the corollary of "taking action at the earliest possible stage to arrest a threatened slump," entailed a "new approach" [5] and specific machinery for its application. In the United States the machinery was created by the Employment Act of 1946: the Council of Economic Advisers in the Executive Office of the President and a joint economic committee in Congress.

This machinery is expected to work without expansion of regulatory power in the usual sense. Proper reliance on devices other than regulatory ones is a traditional aspect of the service state. Fiscal policy is a good illustration. As World War II taught democratic governments how to direct the enterprise economy for national purposes, so they learned in the stress and strain to use fiscal policy in its several dimensions—expenditures, taxes, borrowing, and management of the public debt.

Through fiscal policy, government can influence the volume and direction of spending, the rate and character of investment, the course of inflationary or deflationary developments—a wide range of factors that enter into the business cycle. However, determinations in the field of fiscal policy must rest on a large body of factual knowledge as well as sound theory. Each determination, moreover, requires some implementing action through ap-

---

[4] On the proposition that those governing should be given considerable leeway for this purpose, see Lippmann, Walter, *Essays in the Political Philosophy*, Boston: Little, Brown & Co., 1955. On the need for a better understanding of the division of labor between final policy choice and the continuing aspects of public management, see Morstein Marx, Fritz, *The Administrative State: An Introduction to Bureaucracy*, Chicago: University of Chicago Press, 1957.

[5] Cd. 6527, pp. 3, 16, London: His Majesty's Stationery Office, 1944.

propriate administrative mechanisms. Even indirect controls such as those of fiscal policy depend for their success on adequately staffed statistical and research services, and a variety of regulatory mechanisms which can be brought to bear on policy execution. Of course, when government in effect assumes responsibility for underwriting prosperity, it must be fully equipped for the task. We would not choose a dentist who prides himself on doing everything with a single instrument.

Continuity of progress. In the face of a continuing need for improvisation and experimentation, the "trend toward the service state" is in itself a valuable legacy. Fortunately, it is a legacy that bears the imprint of times of peace, and for this reason lends itself better to peacetime application than would any innovations springing from wartime necessities.

True enough, in capturing for democracy and for accountability to the public some vital areas of social and economic life, the service state has met stubborn resistance by those who had previously staked claims to immunity and exemption for their own ends. *Laissez faire* had its enchantment for the few when the many did not stir. But even in its heyday the doctrine of government nonintervention was elastic enough to allow for tariff protection as well as various other aids to agriculture and business. The idea of protection was bound to carry over into other fields such as free competition and social security. Industrial society cannot endure without a considerable degree of stability, grounded in law and regulation.

As the developing industrial society plunged repeatedly from heights of prosperity into valleys of depression, it learned to fashion safeguards against recurrent calamities. Eventually, these safeguards extended all the way from regulation to promotion, from policing to insurance—all done by government in support of the private enterprise system. Nor must we forget the remarkable growth of governmental lending activities, which reached an unprecedented scope with the establishment, at the close of the Hoover Administration, of the Reconstruction Finance Corporation. In its lifetime, this agency alone probably did as much for business as was accomplished for the unemployed by the public works programs during the depression in the thirties.

Surviving contradictions. Have there been planners of the service state? Not in the sense in which we think today of planning. The service state was not conceived on any general plan. As governments sought remedies against economic and social ills over more than half a century, they inserted public controls in piecemeal fashion and at a variety of points. If in the end the cumulative effects of these efforts came to resemble something like a coherent scheme, it was by accident rather than by prior intent or design. However, at the time World War II broke out the outlines of a general pattern had become apparent even in the United States.[6]

---

[6]Perhaps the best comprehensive description of the service state in the United States before World War II is contained in Lyon, Leverett S., and Associates, *Govern-*

It is true that contradictions in structure remained visible, but they were negligible in comparison with the unresolved and more fundamental contradictions in public attitudes toward the service state. On the one hand, no open-minded observer could fail to notice that the "American system" had long ceased to be one of private enterprise exclusively, that it had become in fact a mixed economy in which both the private and the public sectors fulfilled essential tasks, in many ways complementary in nature. It was apparent that a decisive weakening of the public sector would merely restore earlier conditions of social and economic vulnerability. On the other hand, all too many Americans are still captives of obsolete slogans and stereotypes which depict the service state as a parasite feasting on the body of the "American system." These fundamental contradictions, more than anything else, account for the fickle climate of opinion in which the service state operates. How can the nation acquire the highest degree of skill in operating the governmental machine when it permits itself to be obsessed with the idea that the machine will destroy it?

It is precisely the perennial denunciation of the service state that interferes most seriously with the gradual refinement and perfection of responsive and responsible government. Beyond this question of public confidence—identical in the main with confidence in democracy and democratic procedure—one must not ignore other elementary needs of the service state. First, there is the need for resourceful public management. Second, there are the related needs for program planning and continuity of policy. Third, there is the need for conscious synthesis of fundamental motivations—political, economic, and social. Each of these needs involves the interplay of all three branches of government: legislative, executive, and judicial. No one branch—and no one level of government—can singly satisfy these needs. To that extent, cooperation among the three branches and among all levels is imperative. So is civic participation, as prime mover for common needs.

As long as its elementary needs are only partly met, the service state remains little more than an idea. As long as its needs are answered only in a haphazard way and without sufficient attention to their interrelations,

ment and Economic Life, 2 vols., Washington: Brookings Institution, 1939-1940. For more recent analysis, see Steiner, George A., *Government's Role in Economic Life,* New York: McGraw-Hill, 1953; McIver, Robert M., *Democracy and the Economic Challenge,* New York: Knopf, 1952; Edwards, Corwin D., *Big Business and the Policy of Competition,* Cleveland: Press of Western Reserve University, 1956; Hamilton, Walton H., *The Politics of Industry,* New York: Knopf, 1957; Mason, Edward S., *Economic Concentration and the Monopoly Problem,* Cambridge, Mass.: Harvard University Press, Harvard Economic Studies, Vol. 100, 1957; Colm, Gerhard, and Geiger, Theodore, *The Economy of the American People: Progress, Problems, Prospects,* Washington; National Planning Association, Planning Pamphlet No. 102, March 1958. A historical treatment of the relationship of science and government is to be found in Dupree, A. Hunter. *Science in the Federal Government: A History of Policies and Activities to 1940,* Cambridge, Mass.: Belnap Press of Harvard University Press, 1957. See also Redford, Emmette S., *Administration of National Economic Control,* New York: Macmillan, 1952.

it will fail to mature. There is a vast difference between maintaining large-scale governmental organization, operating at limited capacity, and actually securing the greatest benefits from that organization.

Requirements of public management. This is not the place to set forth in detail the basic requirements of public management under conditions of the service state. That will be done in subsequent chapters. Here passing reference to the most obvious implications must be sufficient. Resourceful management in government presupposes several things. One is rationality in working methods as well as in professional outlook. Another is acceptance of the implications of the system of public responsibility characteristic of popular rule. In addition, there must be standards of competence and guaranties of stability applicable to the public service. Above all, the public sector of the "American system" must be nourished with administrative and professional talent at least in the same degree to which such talent has been drawn into the private sector since the advent of industrialization. This raises the problem of making public employment attractive in terms of both general prestige and career opportunities.[7]

Nor can the United States delay for long a practical reconciliation of the desirable scope of administrative self-reliance, initiative, and inventiveness with effective forms of general control and administrative responsibility. Thus far, legislative control has succeeded neither in securing true accountability for administrative conduct nor in promoting vigorous management in governmental agencies. On this score, in the balance of policy guidance and resourceful management, the record of private business generally is more satisfactory than that of government. As one knows also from the experience with judicial control over administration, responsibility is weakened rather than strengthened if it is exacted primarily in negative forms of invalidation. For an effective solution, again, the professional spirit of the career element in the administrative system may prove of greatest importance.

Requirements of program planning. Equally important is adequate organization for program planning and continuity of policy. A people united in the pursuit of its main national objectives is likely to give unified direction to its public undertakings. When unity of purpose is not fostered by program-minded parties, distortion of general policy through organized pressures and vested interests is bound to become serious. However, the impact of these forces of distortion may be lessened by governmental arrangements designed to bring forth something like a rationally conceived national agenda. Planning is an inseparable aspect of industrial civilization. It is

---

[7] An outstanding earlier American report on this problem is: Commission of Inquiry on Public Service Personnel, *Better Government Personnel*, New York: McGraw-Hill, 1935. The task force report on *Personnel and Civil Service* (1955) of the second (Hoover) Commission on Organization of the Executive Branch of the Government (George A. Graham served as task force staff director) has been praised as the best official report on the subject in the United States.

recognized by industry as a source of profit and an insurance against loss. Government cannot do without it in carrying on the business of the nation.[8] While today this assertion is perhaps uncontroversial, it cannot be said that Americans are unanimous on such questions as the proper location of the planning function and the scope of its mandate. Congress in 1943 deprived President Franklin D. Roosevelt of the National Resources Planning Board, but in 1946 supplied his successor with the Council of Economic Advisers.

Acknowledgment of the importance of planning does not carry with it any commitment on the questionable alternative between economic freedom and a planned society. The degree of planning, realistically speaking, will always depend on practical needs, not on abstract preferences expressed in oversimplifications. In view of its large responsibilities, government cannot be indifferent to the waste and peril of contradictions in policy. Consistency of policy, on the other hand, calls for combined action, legislative and administrative.

One can best hope to attain a reasonable degree of synthesis of fundamental motivations on the basis of concrete proposals of the executive branch placed before the legislature. This is one way of defining the national agenda. Such an agenda could clarify the tasks of government in relation to our economic and social life. As one result, the respective functions of the private and the public sectors of our mixed economy would be circumscribed more explicitly. This would reduce substantially the dangers of friction and disruption and proportionately increase the general efficiency of the "American system."

3. Public Administration—Instrument of Government

Prominence of public administration. The most distinctive characteristic of the service state is the prominence of public administration. As government shifts from a relatively passive to an increasingly active role, it inevitably expands its machinery of action. This machinery assumes the character of a permanent establishment because government is compelled to take on continuing responsibilities which can be fulfilled only through continuity of operations.

Typically, continuing administrative operations fall within the province of the executive branch. Typically also, their conduct requires the delegation of administrative power to each individual agency. Although even the weakest administrative system must have at its disposal some degree of administrative power, in our day such power has acquired an importance in the life of the citizen equal to that of legislative power and in certain ways

---

[8]For an authoritative account of a significant "chapter in American planning experience," see Merriam, Charles E., "The National Resources Planning Board," *American Political Science Review,* 1944, Vol. 38, p. 1075 *ff.* See also Chapter 6, "Planning."

much greater than that of judicial power. This development, being a manifestation of the "trend toward the service state," has been in evidence as long as the trend itself. Well before the birth of the New Deal, Ernst Freund, a leading authority on administrative law, observed that "administrative power appears as one of the established political facts in present-day government." [9] His judgment was not ahead of the times, even though it was not yet reflected in the editorial pages of the newspapers.

Demands on legislative leadership. The prominence of administration in contemporary social life does not imply a corresponding decline of legislative power. On the contrary, as modern government has become bigger than big business, the scope and magnitude of its operations render farsighted direction ever more significant. If we may speak of any change in the essential nature of legislation, that change would lie in mounting demands on legislative leadership. When administrative agencies touch upon the activities of millions of citizens, it is a matter of highest concern whether or not the legislative marching orders for administrative officials are framed effectively and in full recognition of the public interest. The increased significance of administrative power in our day leaves American government as much a government of laws as it ever was under the Constitution.

Administrative power is not self-generative. No government agency can take action without a statutory foundation for action. No government agency is legally free to push action beyond either the bounds of lawful means or the limitations drawn in the annual budget adopted by the legislative branch. However, statutory definition of administrative marching orders can draw only major outlines. It would be unable to penetrate into the mountain of detail that is necessary for effective deployment of governmental agencies in pursuit of objectives laid down in law. Thus the legislature is called upon to meet the difficult task of establishing priorities of goals and giving general direction through statutory policy pronouncements, though at the same time allowing administrators sufficient leeway to utilize the resources at their disposal to the best possible public advantage. Few would maintain, in the face of this task of broad superintendence, that the service state is apt to reduce the legislative branch to the function of dignified ornament. Active government sorely needs wise legislative guidance.

Role of the judicial power. Nor can it be said that the prominence of administration detracts from the institutional role of the judicial power. To be sure, the judicial power may isolate itself. Courts have often gravitated toward becoming exponents of conservative attitudes. If any documentation is needed in this respect, it may be found in the history of judicial review of the constitutionality of legislation. In fact, in the United States the

---

[9]*Administrative Powers over Persons and Property,* p. 584, Chicago: University of Chicago Press, 1928. For today's emerging issues, see Gellhorn, Walter, *Individual Freedom and Governmental Restraints,* Baton Rouge: Louisiana State University Press, 1956.

service state has suffered its most grievous initial defeats from the recalcitrance of the judiciary. The memory of the sharp conflict between the New Deal and the Supreme Court is still fresh. That conflict could have been predicted, for during the New Deal the United States tried to make up for lost time in meeting the instabilities of the industrial economy and thus advanced at a more rapid pace. What was new was not the direction of the advance but its relative speed. As the speed increased, the courts strained to intensify their traditional braking effort.

Granting that no court is safe when stepping between a determined people and its needs and aims, there remains the question of applying judicial power in defense of essential canons of justice. Administrative agencies must be kept within the scope of their statutory mandate and the range of lawful means, without crippling resourceful public management. The judicial power denies itself opportunities for constructive influence in administration if it operates primarily as a negative force. Even in protecting the citizens against unlawful encroachments, the judiciary can help to build a positive code of administrative conduct. In the service state, the presence or absence of a code of this kind is a matter of great consequence. But courts disqualify themselves from making a decisive contribution to the development of such an administrative code when they permit their best energies to become absorbed in efforts to block the growth of the service state on principle.

Characteristics of administration. As an instrument of government, public administration occupies a central place because of its capacity for achieving results by its own operations. It is eminently suited to function as an agent of policy, to give policy immediate meaning by affecting economic and social behavior. Not being tied down to the formalized procedures appropriate for judicial decisions, it is elastic in its approach. It is the government's business establishment par excellence. Whereas policy can only attempt to establish a general rule, administration carries the application of the general rule into the boundless diversity of concrete situations. In giving specific application to the general rule, administration can take into account the numerous variables of different conditions. Because of this flexibility, it can obtain compliance in varying situations without either jeopardizing the consistency of the general rule or making the general rule a crushing force incapable of appropriate differentiation.

Administration thus presents itself as a process of fitting—as a means of giving policy concise expression in a highly diversified society. For this purpose, administration needs direction. A mechanical tool can eat its way through a sheet of steel, repeating its operation with never-changing precision. Administration, by way of contrast, deals with the dynamics of an organic society made up of human beings. Even in routine transactions, therefore, administrative procedure must be alert to the expressions of need and change that run through economic and social life. It must ascertain facts without bias, appraise them astutely, bring policy to bear upon the emerging picture, and shape its decisions in wakeful appreciation of the intent of policy and the results to be produced.

In each of these phases, administration must aim at coherence without becoming a helpless victim of precedent and operating convenience. In each phase it must keep itself open to the need for innovation and constant improvement of methods and procedures. In each phase it must set its course in such a way as to prove itself the servant of the people, of the *general* public in contrast to a particular public. A consideration of these postulates is all we need in order to understand the necessity for securing the highest caliber of administrative stewardship.

4. The Enlistment of Administrative Judgment

Legislative marching orders. As an instrument of government, public administration moves on marching orders written into laws and regulations. Being the agent of policy, it must on principle accept legislative superintendence as well as executive command. It is not free to exercise a veto power in the name of greater *expertise*. This principle is easily stated, but it raises many subtle points of administrative ethics. Government agencies, responsible for defined fields of public activity, are prone to develop a stake in their programs. That is not bad in itself, because administrators will on the whole render better service when they have faith in their missions. But it is also true that their wholehearted identification with the task assigned them may collide with their obligation to bow to direction even when such direction reflects changes of policy that rip into established programs. In situations of this kind, the deeper loyalty of service must triumph over secondary loyalties to cherished ends and means. Administration as an agent has no moral right to plot against its legislative principal, however much the principal may seem to be in error.

This does not mean that administration is free to use its mind only in performing its duty as an agent of policy. Throughout the executive branch, we find today a considerable assortment of staff services of high quality. No less impressive is the store of sound administrative judgment derived from cumulative experience. Many of the management services that have been built up at various points of the governmental structure are wholly on a par with those developed in private enterprise. In managerial skill, too, government has ceased to be generally inferior to business. How obsolete in this respect the catchwords of bygone days are is attested by the degree of unpublicized informal cooperation among different groups of specialists in private and public employment in a great many professional associations. Give-and-take in the exchange of helpful information has become a mutual process from which government and business profit alike in equal proportions.

Political feasibility of policy. With so much pertinent judgment and experience on tap, it would be folly to insist, in the interest of abstract purity of functions, that legislative direction should never seek expert counsel from the administrative sphere. As a matter of fact, such counsel is constantly sought and utilized by the legislature as well as by the chief executive and the political leadership in the departments. It must be admitted, however, that the chief executive, being in a better position than the legislature, can more expeditiously equip himself with machinery designed to make available for his use the whole body of administrative information. The creation in 1939 of the Executive Office of the President illustrates the way in which machinery of this character may be linked with the head of the government's business establishment. Central staffs attached to the chief executive are in a position to develop and maintain continuing reporting relationships with the departmental system through which appropriate information flows up, to provide a reasonably complete picture. Much of this information is immediately translated into intelligence to serve internal control purposes. A considerable volume, however, feeds into the policy-making process, either by pointing up issues that require solution or by supplying supporting data for tentative policy suggestions.

Successful government involves the accomplishment of feasible objectives. Determination of feasibility depends on a number of factors. Politically, a feasible objective is one that is wanted by sufficiently strong groups of the population or for which popular endorsement may be obtained through effectively stimulated public debate. Determination of such feasibility is a question that elected representatives of the people are generally better qualified to decide than administrators. It includes, for example, a choice among goals that cannot all be achieved at the same time. Here, again, political sense is generally more important than administrative experience. However, once political feasibility has been ascertained, there is still the problem of the appropriate governmental approach. Big business though it is, government, like any other business, has to think in terms of available resources, organizational as well as financial.

Administrative feasibility of policy. A politically feasible objective may not be attained at all if the administrative system is too feeble for the task. Even stronger administrative machinery may be dangerously overworked if a politically feasible objective of considerable magnitude is tackled in one reckless effort. It may be necessary to progress step by step, and to time the steps at wider intervals.

On each of these points, administrative judgment is able to contribute substantially to the determination of sound policy. The same is true of defining the administrative design that will offer assurance of the most effective and least expensive advance toward the established goal. Practical alternatives can be analyzed before action is taken. Such planning cuts the chance of breakdown to a minimum. It also provides protection against costly organizational and operating errors. In short, it is a valuable aid in achieving economy of effort.

Blending of judgments. Although it is thus clear that administrative advice is an important ingredient in the making of policy, we must not assume that there is a precise borderline between consideration of political feasibility and examination of administrative feasibility. The more both merge, the better will be the result. Because administrative advice has no obvious representation in the political councils, it must be drawn in systematically. Moreover, in their policy planning, legislative bodies must allow for administrative alternatives in order to evolve a statutory formula that will best lend itself to prompt execution. Conversely, administrative officials, in advising on policy, reduce the range of their assistance if they fail to give careful thought to the legislative balance of power, the enunciated or anticipated preferences of the chief executive, and the probabilities of public reactions. Ideally, political and administrative thinking should blend into a joint process.

A radical separation of powers, like that in the governmental system of the United States, is on the whole unfavorable to such blending, especially when legislative and executive prerogatives are jealously guarded. But there are avenues through which one can come near the ideal. The chief executive has many opportunities for transmitting to the legislative branch recommendations based on careful staff work. The legislature, in its committees, may avail itself of testimony from those administrative officials who are most familiar with the subject matter under discussion. In addition, informal cooperation between the staff employed by legislative committees and staffs of various agencies often makes for fruitful connections. Such comparing of notes and interchange of findings are sometimes more productive than public presentation of testimony before legislative committees, which shape their basic inferences in closed executive session. In general, however, modern government is still far from a rational scheme through which political reasoning and administrative judgment can be merged in the formulation of policy. Despite this partial failure, the role of administrative judgment as a source of informed policy decisions has steadily expanded in the conduct of government business.

Administrative freedom of expression. In furnishing counsel on policy matters, administrative officials may foster perilous illusions if their environment encourages servility and spinelessness. They are of no help whatsoever, and can easily turn into a positive menace, when conditions induce them to echo the voices of the mighty. Administrative judgment must rest on integrity. It cannot be both trustworthy and pleasing to everyone. It must enjoy freedom of expression. Advice amounts to nothing when it is fearful of disagreement.

The climate of administrative judgment is not made by administrators alone. It is the product of many things: public attitudes toward the government's business establishment; the stereotypes employed in cartoons and editorials; aggressive and defensive propaganda coming from particular special interests; legislative resentments; administrative self-complacency. Sometimes Americans have experienced deep-rooted doubts whether their national ways and habits, especially in the legislative sphere, leave room for public administrators who pour their hearts into their work, think for themselves, and make no bones about the state of affairs and what ought to be done about it. These doubts may merely demonstrate that the service state is still in its youth. But one cannot escape the conclusion that when there is competence for counsel on policy in the administrative system, it is only common sense to use and strengthen it.

5.   The Contribution of Service

Popular basis of administrative services. A fairly detailed listing of all of the services that in the United States are performed by government—federal, state, and local—would fill many pages. None of these services was forced upon the community by a wild-eyed officialdom. Each came into being in response to public demands to which legislative bodies paid deference—a perfectly natural development in a democracy.

The power of votes and the threat of reprisals in subsequent electoral campaigns hang like dark clouds over the legislative scene. If every public demand could be subjected to popular referendum, many loudly advocated propositions would show themselves without wide support and therefore would die a natural death without gaining the upper hand in pressure politics. A legislature guided by the program of the majority party or the joint action program of a coalition of parties may know itself in broad accord with most of the voters. Without parties that take their programs seriously, as in the United States with its weak party system, representative assemblies are highly exposed to group agitation, because the public at large is normally amorphous and unorganized. It is divided by conflicting loyalties that pull simultaneously not only toward party, but even more strongly toward class, general inclination of outlook, real or imagined self-advancement, religious denomination, occupational organization, and an abundance of other interests, large and small. In this bewildering and ever-changing pattern, the public falls apart into many publics. And the better organized for political pressure each public is, the greater is its chance of overriding the public at large. This explains in the main the failure of effective consumer representation in the political arena. Everybody is a consumer, but he is many other things besides—farmer, veteran, trucker, or union member. Here, in part, is the reason why the service state is neither of one cast nor free from inconsistencies.

Habit of self-restraint. Of course, it would be a strange misconception to contend that the test of democracy is unfailing wisdom. As individuals, we commit sad errors of judgment in matters of great importance, do foolish things for unaccountable reasons, cling tenaciously to absurd prejudices, cast prudence to the winds when we feel like it. Can we hope to do much better collectively? Actually, we do better in the realm of public affairs because here each participant is entitled to invoke the test of reason. Here, then, reason follows us like a faithful dog, even though we may choose to ignore it. Here there is considerably more argument and counterargument than we would be willing to put up with in our private affairs. And here we also have more free advice from various sources—in the United States, for instance, from the League of Women Voters, the National Association of Manufacturers, the Secretary of State, our Congressman, the head of the Bureau of Labor Statistics, to mention but a few. Sometimes we entirely change our minds on the basis of such advice, though even when we do we usually line up with the side that generally talks our language or promises us the largest slice of cake. Yet on the whole we are rather particular about the price of the cake and more anxious to restrain our appetites than we are in our private spending.

This relative eagerness for self-restraint is a wholesome tendency. It should be no more than that. It was more than that for a considerable time, especially in the closing decades of the past century when the great economic interests reaped the harvest of the American continent. In those days the masters of new fortunes found it easy to convince themselves that the United States must make this tendency toward political self-abnegation into an axiom of governance. They happily retrieved the idea that the best government is one that governs least, one that entrusts control to the natural drift of the economy and the profit motive. Only when it became apparent that the country fared none too well under this prescription did alert minds cast about for a better one.

Governmental reinforcement of the enterprise economy. Thus the structure of our public services came forth without a supporting ideology, even running counter to the general line of editorial comment. Americans bought the service state in relatively small pieces, each piece when it was needed to fill cracks and breaches in the industrial order. The mixed economy took form, not because it was thought good, but because necessity dictated successive reenforcements of the private sector of the national economy through governmental action which added to the public sector. The contribution of the administrative system, viewed as a whole, lies primarily in its function as a broad support of the enterprise economy.

It may be presumed that private business would be able to run our unemployment and old-age insurance schemes as well as does government—if sufficient profit could be found in it. It is conceivable for business to service itself on some cooperative basis in about the same way it is being serviced at public expense by such agencies as the Department of Commerce. It is perhaps possible for the several large farmer organizations to maintain specialized staffs that could jointly undertake the research job now done by the Department of Agriculture in such fields as plant industry, soils, and agricultural engineering. However, if one thinks of the balance sheet of national efficiency, it is not difficult to spot the comparative weakness of such solutions. Each of these governmental services—and they are examples chosen at random—benefits not only from widest access to data, but also operates in direct accountability to the public at large. Fiscal accounting under budgetary control, and expenditure justification to the satisfaction of the legislature, are not in themselves the most important factors. More significant is the general public sharing of both the data accumulated and the record of operations in accumulating these data. Government must come very close to scientific accuracy in its analytical activities and to impartial service to all.

Benefits of regulation. This is true also of the regulatory process. Regulation has sometimes been slapped down on interests that have outraged the public sense of equity. But punitive regulation has always tended to throw new burdens of ill-feeling on the community and to overstep its legitimate aims in the heat of battle. Ordinarily, the punitive impetus does not survive for any length of time, and methods are later adjusted to meet the practical business at hand. We need only look at the gradual transformation since 1887 of the relationships between carriers and shippers on the one hand and the Interstate Commerce Commission on the other.[10] First viewed almost as the Evil One, the Commission became with time a sort of guardian angel to the interests subject to its regulation.

Evidence shows that regulatory bodies, when they have established themselves, develop a peculiar affection for those subject to their powers. This is hardly surprising. The function of regulation is to police—in the interest of a better state of affairs. The goal is constructive, and the procedure must correspond to it. Thus regulatory bodies come to see the public welfare from the angle of the welfare of those to be regulated. Even so they are forced, by their public status, to justify their actions as expressions of the general interest, beneficial to the economy and those regulated alike. To give full weight to the common good when the performance of regulatory bodies needs corrective action is the task of the legislature or, more precisely, of free public criticism.

Popular accountability of administration. The service motive is not an exclusive property of government. No big company today overlooks opportunities for selling itself on claims of superior service. We hear these claims every day in the commercial plugs over the radio; we read them on trolley and bus posters and in the advertisements of popular magazines. Business wants to serve—as well as government. However, as voters we have much

---

[10]See the tribute to a strong-minded administrator in this field, who died in harness: Swisher, Carl B., "Joseph E. Eastman: Public Servant," *Public Administration Review,* 1945, Vol. 5, p. 34 *ff.*

closer control over public business and public services than private enterprise would be willing to allow its customers.

We have a sharp eye on our public servants, and they know it. We can chastise them by public complaint and legislative grilling. We can take business away from them by cutting down appropriations. We may often censure too rashly, but the irascible temper which we habitually reserve for governmental errors and failings keeps administrative officials on their toes. Administration cannot withhold itself from the public. It is politically committed to responsive service.

6. Public Administration—Social Buffer

Growth of substantive knowledge. The broad scope of governmental activities in the service state has had consequences extending beyond the mere expansion of public services. When government is interposed at many points in modern society, it gains extraordinary opportunities for developing a flow of information or intelligence whose output is converted into public knowledge.

Take something as vital as dependable statistics on unemployment. Before the hundreds of thousands of Smiths, together with the Joneses, the Thompsons, and all the others, had been duly entered in the records of the social security system, it was necessary in the United States to guess at the volume of unemployment. Now, as an incidental by-product of providing social security services, the government can always know with a high degree of exactness. Fortified with up-to-date information, the government is in a position to plan policy with considerable assurance. It is also able to obtain early warning of impending slumps and take remedial action before being overtaken by events. It can even put its finger on specific areas where economic maladjustments have become acute, and probe into underlying causes.

Government's intelligence function. The intelligence function of modern government is in many ways crucial to the fate of the economic and social order. Jeremy Bentham, no friend of "big government," for this reason pressed the case for centrally assembled vital statistics more than a century ago. Accumulation and interpretation of adequate data lie at the heart of maintaining a high level of employment. The role of the federal government in attaining maximum employment is predicated on the availability of a large array of detailed statistical information. It must cover such activities as consumer spending; business expenditures and outlays, including construction, additions to inventories, and exports; and state and local expenditures, including projected public works. Moreover, retrospective data alone would not be adequate. They must be supplemented by data that seek to predict future facts.

Industrial society would be stopped in its tracks and left to face complete uncertainty if the body of government intelligence failed to measure up to its needs. This is unlikely when government, in its interlocking with the enterprise economy, has multiplied its eyes and added finer lenses. The sharper picture forms a sounder basis of action, for both government and private business.

Public research and analysis. The more it knows, the better government can judge. Seeing more, it is no longer so easily eluded by those interests whose doings shy from light, nor is it quickly misled and confused by the assertions of optimists and pessimists alike. Drawing on its far-flung intelligence, government can substantiate its hunches and projections, and is less helpless in rebuttal. In our civilization, research and analysis of information, together with scientific fact-gathering and wider dissemination of knowledge, are national resources of greatest practical value, because they give industrial society a surer touch in shaping its institutional and technological environment. Truth is an objectifying influence in the identification of the public interest and in the pursuit of public ends. It takes the wind out of the sails of partisan clamor and intentional or unintentional misrepresentation.

The acquisition of knowledge is a field of primary concern to democratic government. Its ascendancy was properly stressed in the epoch-making report of Great Britain's Machinery of Government Committee under Haldane's chairmanship at the end of World War I.[11] In the United States, annual federal expenditures for peacetime research and development have grown into the billions of dollars after World War II. But research is not confined to laboratories alone. The whole administrative establishment of government, although its main task is to perform specific public functions, is at the same time a gigantic test tube with which nations gradually expand their social knowledge. In this way they not only enlarge the body of information to guide the policy-making authorities; they also make clearer the issues in need of public discussion. It is harder to fool the people when the facts and figures are in the open, thus making wild statements uncomfortable for their authors.

Getting at the facts. Through its administrative system, government has been able to organize its intelligence function. Without something like the administrative machinery that has been built up over the years, government intelligence would necessarily be secondhand and thus of dubious merit. The risk of accepting at its face value the brief of an interest group or the complaint of a constituent is well known to every seasoned lawmaker. With literally hundreds of thousands of government employees in daily touch with countless economic and social activities and different parts of the population, administrative agencies meet few obstacles in providing for continuing public reconnaissance, in gauging pressures and tensions in the

---

[11]Cd. 9230, London: His Majesty's Stationery Office, 1918.

industrial order, and in getting at the relevant facts. On the other hand, general awareness by the public of the intelligence function of government has a restraining effect on the voraciousness of special interests and the tactics of pressure groups. To this extent, administration places itself deliberately between contending forces, each of which could have its way only at the expense of all of us.

More explicit and more direct is the buffer function of the administrative system in the immediate exercise of authority, either of a regulatory nature or as the organizer of public services. Here government, by being on the scene, seeks to enforce the ground rules of democratic society. This task includes not only the job of safeguarding defined standards of economic conduct and decent living but also that of preserving the essential framework of individual initiative and accomplishment. Administrative power is brought to bear upon the economic power wielded by large-size organizations which, if left unchecked, would play havoc with the basic interests of the individual as well as with those of the community at large. It is true, of course, that administrative agencies are not always strong enough to muster sufficient resistance under the impact of determined pressures.[12] But one should not lose sight of the fact that in the struggle of organized forces for superiority, government has gone far toward running interference for the underdog.

Concern for the underdog. Concern for the underdog is deeply ingrained in the American way of life. Yet, in the day-by-day operation of the economy Americans are inclined to a startling degree to condone sharp prosecution of selfish ends. A broad strand of social philosophy in the United States supports the fears which Mr. Justice Brandeis aptly expressed in speaking of the curse of bigness. It is equally American, however, to write bigness in big letters—to take pride in the colossal and still greater pride in the supercolossal. The native soil has favored the growth of economic empires, and the captains of these empires have ranked above the politicians. When bigness is allowed to write its own constitution in the name of *laissez faire,* little is left of the buffer function of the administrative system. Public officials, however firmly established their service ideology may be, cannot withdraw into the ivory tower. They cannot defy public opinion or what successfully poses for it. How well administration performs its buffer functions is, therefore, mainly up to all citizens.

These conflicting reactions toward bigness have beclouded the fact that the ultimate criterion of effective organization in democratic societies is its contribution to the life of the common man. There have been times when shrewd play on their emotions made Americans more fearful of big govern-

---

[12] A pioneer study of this problem is Herring, Pendleton, *Public Administration and the Public Interest,* New York: McGraw-Hill, 1936. For another informative study, see Blaisdell, Donald C., *American Democracy under Pressure,* New York: Ronald, 1957.

ment than of big business. One thing is clear, however. In a common man's democracy, government must be big enough to measure up to the order of magnitude prevailing in the economic sphere.

But big government becomes a load, even a danger, when it grows top-heavy, autocratic, or sluggish. Public administration can fulfill its social function only when civil servants keep their eyes on the common good, instead of becoming busy operators enslaved to the apparatus of authority and their own ambition. It is equally necessary that the custodians of political power—in the legislature as well as on the highest executive levels —accomplish their task under representative government. They must combine devotion to the interest of the electorate with sensitivity to the rules that govern the exercise of both political and administrative responsibility.

PART II

ORGANIZATION AND
MANAGEMENT

Chapter 6 ●

Planning

1. Types of Planning

Pointless controversies. In approaching the broad field of organization and management, we can do no better than begin with a discussion of planning. Planning is preparation for action. It is the vital first step in any major administrative action. Planning is a means to an end. It is the process of formulating the objectives to be realized by administrative enterprise. Decisions about financial requirements, organization, personnel needs, physical facilities, supplies and equipment, work processes, and many other phases of administration flow from the determination of purpose. There can be no efficient management of work performance without planning.

For some time in our country, especially during the thirties, the word "planning" came to have something of a sinister connotation. This was especially true in discussions about government and public administration. To many, planning suggested communism. Indeed, the word was often held to be synonymous with economic enterprise conducted under government direction rather than under the rules of the market place. Much of this controversy occurred at the same time when private enterprise in the United States was giving more attention to business planning than ever before. Today the former alarm about the word planning has largely disappeared. It is generally realized that planning is an administrative process essential to governmental endeavor, as it is to all group effort. It seems to be understood today that planning as a process is completely neutral insofar as value judgments and purposes are concerned.

No doubt planning is a major technique of government used by the Communist regime of the Soviet Union. But this fact does not mean that therefore all non-Communist states must abandon planning. Indeed, one of the arguments frequently advanced by Communist apologists is that only a Communist regime takes careful forethought for tomorrow. Even many believers in democracy have come to assume that a major difference between the Soviet Union and the United States is that the former engages in planning while the latter does not. Any argument of this kind falls into the same trap that hampered public discussion in the thirties. Here again

113

planning becomes equated with some particular governmental system and with a particular set of economic goals. This is a corruption of the word "planning." Those who manage the affairs of government and of business enterprise in our country believe in planning and practice planning. They reject the particular goals and especially the means of governmental planning in the U. S. S. R. They do not believe in the all-competent state which owns the productive resources of the nation and turns over to a small elite the matter of determining the productive goals and the governmental services to be achieved year by year.

Planning in a pluralistic society. In the United States there are over 100,000 different governments. Their jurisdiction varies. The one central government cannot order the forty-nine state governments what to do. Federal law may set certain standards of acceptable governmental and administrative conduct, but this is at best a negative rather than a positive control. In turn, our state governments by process of law set certain standards for the operation of some 3,000 counties, some 17,000 cities, about the same number of villages and townships, over 50,000 school districts, and another 14,000 special districts. But, here again, the controls are only partial and minimal. The citizenry still enjoys substantial authority to fix its own goals for local action. As for the economy, there are some five million farms in the United States, and at least one million major farm units the value of whose output is over $6,000 a year. The number of industrial, transportation, communication, construction, commercial, financial, retail trade, and service enterprises in the United States is estimated to be well above four million. As many as 700,000 business corporations file income tax returns with the Internal Revenue Service.

The truth is that there is no central source of planning in the United States—no "master plan" for the economy or for government formulated in one place by one small group of men. But this does not mean that there is no planning. The reverse is the case. Planning goes on in most if not every one of the various governments and business enterprises. The larger the government or the business, and the greater the administrative load it carries, the more detailed and formal will be its planning processes.

Planning in the United States is thus characterized by its diffuse character. This is consistent with the values of a free society, which awards importance to the worth of the individual and which tolerates, indeed encourages, a pluralism of competing social groups. Such planning has many participants. With great diversity in governmental and economic achievement, great variation exists in the competence with which particular plans are prepared and carried out. Yet all of this is a part of planning in a free society.

Planning under control. In public administration, the planning process is an important part of the way in which administrative agencies participate in political decision-making. Such agencies exercise power, but only within set limits. For one thing, an administrative agency may exercise authority only as indicated by law. This means that an agency must seek a change in law to broaden the scope of its work, or even to carry out its work in a different way. Moreover, the exercise of the agency's authority remains under the control of the chief executive and the legislature. In these ways an administrative agency is kept answerable to higher political authority. In addition, each year—or in certain states every two years—an administrative agency must seek an appropriation of funds with which to operate. The recommendation of the necessary appropriation rests with the chief executive, and the legislature decides the issue. The result is that an administrative agency must periodically justify its activities in presenting its budget estimates, and any widespread public criticism of how it performs its work is likely to result in a reduction of funds. Here, again, is a substantial control by higher political authority, and there are still others. In short, when we say that an administrative agency exercises power, it is necessary to observe the institutional framework within which this power is actually exercised. In a free society, it is not unlimited or irresponsible power that administrative agencies enjoy.

The essential point to notice is that planning is the usual way in which administrative agencies play some part in determining public policy. An administrative agency undertakes to review the policies under which it operates. In the process, it decides that other policies are desirable. The agency must then seek to obtain such statutory authorization or higher executive sanction as it deems necessary in order to gain approval for carrying out the new policies. This is administrative planning. It is also administrative participation in the political process, because in the end it is the legislature and the chief executive who must agree that a change is desirable. Or an agency decides that its program goals should be altered. It believes that such a change is within the realm of its discretion, without a decision by the chief executive. Yet it may need additional appropriations, or some change in appropriations. There is thus executive and legislative opportunity to review the contemplated change in program goals. Once again, this is administrative planning and simultaneously administrative participation in the political process.[1]

This interplay of political and administrative planning is most clearly evident in the preparation and enactment of the annual budget, usually

---

[1] For planning in general, and particularly in relation to the economy, see Dahl, Robert A., and Lindblom, Charles E., *Politics, Economics, and Welfare,* New York: Harper, 1953; Williams, John H., *Economic Stability in a Changing World,* New York: Oxford University Press, 1953; Redford, Emmette S., *Administration of National Economic Control,* New York: Macmillan, 1952; Galbraith, John K., *American Capitalism,* Boston: Houghton-Mifflin, 1952, and *The Affluent Society,* Boston: Houghton-Mifflin, 1958; and Boulding, Kenneth E., *The Skills of the Economist,* Cleveland: Howard Allen, 1958.

initiated by the executive branch and decided ultimately by the legislative branch. Both in the federal government and in most of the states and municipalities, the budget is a prime planning document.[2]

Policy planning. One part of the planning process by government is concerned with policies. Policies are broad decisions usually involving value judgments, setting forth the basic social purposes of governmental action. Policy decisions are so important that they are often set forth in statutes. Indeed, it is current practice in the federal government and in some state governments to begin any major piece of legislation with a declaration of policy. Policy planning is the very essence of an administrative agency's concern with its present and future operations.

For example, it is federal policy to generate hydroelectric power produced at large multipurpose dams, but not to market this power on a retail basis. Rather, agencies that operate hydroelectric stations seek to sell the power to municipal power systems, to cooperatives, and to private power companies. Within the limits of this policy, written into law, a subsidiary policy issue arises. Shall federal agencies sell their power only at the site of its generation? Or shall they build distribution systems that will enable them to reach various possible markets? The answer to this policy decision has depended in large part upon executive and legislative attitudes. If a federal agency builds its own distribution system, it can reach out to give preference to particular wholesale consumers, such as municipally owned power systems or cooperatively owned power systems. If a federal agency sells the electric energy it generates only at the site, it must give preference to those consumers who can afford to build the necessary distribution facilities. Those inclined to believe that electric power sold by private companies is too costly to the consumer will favor municipal and cooperative distribution. Those who believe that the charges to consumers for electric power are fairly regulated by state utility commissions, and that private enterprise in any event is preferable to municipal and cooperative enterprises, will favor sale at the site. These policy decisions are influenced by value judgments about the right and wrong of particular economic behavior.

Another example may be taken from the field of foreign affairs. After World War II, the United States decided by legislation to extend assistance for rehabilitation to those countries devastated by war. For the most part, this assistance was intended to prevent starvation and disease while production was being restored and cities were being repaired. Then, in 1947, the Secretary of State proposed a different policy—a policy of economic assistance extended to those nations, especially in Europe, which would undertake long-term plans for expansion of productive facilities and output. Under the first policy, the U.S.S.R. had been glad to receive nearly half a billion dollars of relief assistance. Under the second policy, the Soviet

---

[2] For fuller discussion, see Chapter 25, "Fiscal Accountability." See also Chapter 16, "The Formulation of Administrative Policy."

government decided not to cooperate, and the countries of Western Europe alone adopted long-range plans. In 1950, after the start of war in Korea, the United States again shifted its policy in favor of extending economic assistance to friendly nations in order to help build up their military strength against possible Communist aggression. In the twelve-year period between 1945 and 1957, the United States extended economic aid to foreign countries in the amount of 60 billion dollars. Of this total, nearly 11 billion dollars were in the form of loans and 49 billion dollars were outright grants. Of the total grants, 29 billions were for expansion of economic output and 20 billions for military security.

What were the supporting considerations? First, it was believed to be in the best interests of the United States for humanitarian reasons to help prevent starvation and disease in various countries that had suffered substantial war damage to their cities and their productive resources. It was all the more appropriate to make this decision in the light of our own immense productive resources and our virtual immunity from any war damage to property. Subsequently, the United States made the decision to help other nations to rebuild their productive economies. Such help was predicated in the first instance upon a system of European economic cooperation that would result in specialization by a nation in those fields of output where it enjoyed some particular advantage in natural resources, technological skill, or productive facilities. It was thought that economic development would help Western Europe to resist Communism through rising standards of living, and might also eliminate future demands upon the United States for help in meeting consumer needs. With the renewal of armed conflict in 1950, and with the evidence that the Soviet Union was determined to exploit any situation where the Western nations might be politically or economically embarrassed, the United States determined by law that it was in its best interests to help friendly nations to build up their military strength. This meant sharing America's defense output with other countries. If this output were to be used by American forces only, a substantial increase in military personnel would have been necessary, and the United States would have had to take on the manning of a worldwide defense system along with its military supply.

Or let us look at still another example. Most of the states have determined by law that all boys and girls between the age of six and sixteen years shall have the opportunity to attend a free elementary and secondary school. This policy decision is based upon a number of considerations, such as the importance of education in giving all youth the chance to make the most of their abilities, and the importance of an educated electorate in a democracy. In the administration of this policy, school administrators confront subsidiary policy issues. As a matter of policy, should all be taught the same subjects? Should they be taught at the same rate of speed? Should all advance on a chronological basis through ten or twelve years of schooling, or advance only on the basis of achievement? These are policy questions because they involve judgments about competing values, such as the importance of encouraging able youth to work at their full capacity as against encouraging youth of average ability to complete an "academic" program.

In all of its fields, public administration constantly raises policy questions which must be decided by administrators, by the chief executive, or by the legislature, and which may need to be interpreted by the judiciary. These policy decisions lie at the very heart of administrative activity. In turn, policy decisions involve planning. They require a determination or reassessment of human values at stake in the objectives of an agency. These objectives must be clearly formulated. They must be periodically re-examined. They must be divided into their essential elements, with full consideration of the policy implications. They must be communicated widely and be understood throughout the administrative agency. Policy planning is a vital part of public administration.

Program planning. Policy planning sets a large or general framework for administrative activity. This is followed by program planning, which consists of detailed preparation of projects or activities to give effect to the policy adopted. Again, one or two illustrations may make clearer what is meant by program planning.

After due consideration of its advantages and disadvantages (policy planning), the policy decision to provide military assistance to our allies would have remained a pious expression of hope or intent if it had not been translated into action. Program planning is the first step in translating intentions into accomplishment. A number of questions must be answered in formulating a program. How large a military force, nation by nation, is the United States going to help maintain? What will be the composition of this force—ground, air, and sea? What kinds of weapons will be employed? How much of the needed military supply will the United States provide? What is American productive capacity for meeting these needs? What will be the impact of our foreign aid program upon our own strategic plans? These and similar questions must be examined in the preparation of work programs for carrying out the policy decision to extend military aid to friendly nations.

One other example may be mentioned. We have noted that a major policy objective in our elementary and secondary school system is equality of educational opportunity. This requires a series of programs. There must be a program of courses of instruction, a curriculum. What emphasis shall be put on reading, writing, and arithmetic? What part shall be given to art and music? What part to physical education? Where shall some differentiation in course study be introduced, recognizing that some students possess a greater aptitude for academic study than others? How much technical education shall be provided for students who excel in manual dexterity, on the one hand, and for those who have a natural aptitude for working with mechanical and electrical devices, on the other? What qualifications shall be expected of the staff? Where can the staff be recruited? How much will it be paid? What buildings will be required and where will they be located? And the most important question of all: How many children will there be to educate? Such are the questions that must be answered in the process of program planning by an administrative agency entrusted with elementary and secondary education.

Planning factors. In these illustrations one discovers a certain procedure common to the substantive questions to be answered through program planning. The first step is to determine the objectives of a work program in terms of magnitude. This may involve, for example, population forecasts. Certainly, one of the most important single factors in any program planning by most administrative agencies is this element of future population growth. Those who specialize in population studies can forecast future population upon the basis of varied assumptions. It is even possible to make some forecasts of population distribution based upon past trends.[3] Especially with the expectation of continued growth in the United States over the next fifteen to twenty years, the size and location of the population have become a prime consideration in program planning.

Some governmental activities, however, are not affected directly by population size. This is true of the national defense. The objectives for defense programs are formulated in terms of strategic goals and expected technological achievements. A program for the conservation of natural resources must rest on estimated demands for raw materials and an orderly rate of utilization, with full regard for replacement or other conservation measures. A program for development of power-generating stations utilizing nuclear energy depends upon the state of research and upon economic objectives. A program for improvement of air traffic control depends upon traffic volume, safety goals, and technical capacity.

In all cases, program planning begins with the formulation of objectives for some governmental service, expressed in quantitative terms insofar as possible. By doing so, an agency has some sense of what it hopes or expects to achieve in the years immediately ahead. Furthermore, such program goals are usually expressed in both long-range and short-range expectations. The long-range goals may be fixed in time periods of five or ten or fifty years, to be undertaken in yearly installments, either evenly or differentially spaced over the longer period.

Once objectives are decided for both long and short periods, the next

---

[3] See Bogue, Donald J., ed., *Applications of Demography: The Population Situation in the United States in 1975*, Oxford, Ohio: Scripps Foundation for Research in Population Problems of Miami University, 1957.

step is to determine the resources that will be needed in personnel, facilities, and operating services and supplies. These resources must be provided through appropriations or other financing. When money is available, there is still the time factor. Time is required to purchase and obtain delivery of supplies, recruit and train personnel, and build and operate the necessary facilities. In some instances, as in many military procurement programs, the productive resources may not be available to meet the time table. It may be desirable to have 1,000 heavy jet bombers delivered in a particular year, or to have a certain number of intercontinental ballistic missiles available by a certain date; but it may be impossible to achieve these goals. The alternatives are to change the delivery schedules or to increase the productive resources.

The difference between what an agency is doing at the present time and what it expects to do in four or five years constitutes a gap, which must be filled by future work programs. For this reason, program planning necessarily involves careful attention to the ways and means by which a gap may be filled. If objectives are to be achieved, the work program must make it possible to build up a service or activity to the desired program goals.

In some instances, a great deal of statistical data and even extensive research may be necessary in order to achieve program objectives. Let us assume, for example, that the United States decides to power bomber aircraft with nuclear energy. Many advantages could be derived from nuclear-propelled aircraft, such as the long periods of operation without refueling. But it is one thing to want nuclear-powered aircraft, and another thing to build it. It may take years of research and development before such a goal is reached. Thus, some program goals may depend upon the acquisition of new knowledge through research, or the development of new technological capacity. There is inevitably a close relationship between program planning and research.

Organization for planning. The job of planning—both of policy and of program—is an essential task of management. This means that the chief planner in any administrative organization is the chief administrator. Concern with planning cannot be separated from the general concern with management in all its ramifications. In turn, no administrator can ever delegate his authority to plan. He may need assistance in order to perform his planning duties, but he cannot expect to shift his planning responsibility to someone else.

Sometimes it is said that a fundamental conflict exists between planning and operations. Some observers of administrative activity have concluded that there are operating officials who concentrate their attention upon the work of the moment and show little interest in the future. More and more, however, administrators have come to realize that to concentrate undue attention upon current work is to be unprepared to handle the work of tomorrow. More and more, top officials have come to understand that planning is a vital part of the administrative process which they cannot afford to ignore.

The relationship of planning to operations was illustrated in a striking manner in the Pacific theater during World War II. The United States Navy established two fleet commands under two admirals, complete with their own staffs. First one command spent some time in planning a particular naval operation, such as the invasion of the Mariana Islands. When the time came to undertake this campaign, the fleet command that had prepared the plan was placed in charge of the actual operation. The other command headquarters then prepared plans for the next operation, such as the invasion of Okinawa. This command headquarters took over the responsibility for the actual operation. In short, the same ships— carriers, cruisers, battleships, destroyers, and escort and supply vessels— were used under two different fleet designations and under two different commanders. This arrangement indicates the close relationship between planning and operations.

When an organization gets so involved in day-to-day work that there seems no time to plan future activities, undoubtedly the administrator is at fault. The kinds of decisions that are made on current problems will determine future developments, whether intended or not. An administrator has the choice of permitting the current workload to absorb the organization's time and energy or of insisting that time be found to plan longer-range goals. The choice is his. But he may need staff assistance in performing his planning responsibilities. He may set up a special unit for this purpose, or he may expect his various assistants to give a substantial part of their time to planning for future needs. Several advantages flow from having a management group generally to pay attention to planning, along with other duties. In this way the connection between current operations and long-term objectives and programs can be constantly reinforced. Special problems in the organization for planning have arisen at the municipal level and in the federal government; these will be discussed in the next section. We may note here that on occasion a chief executive may establish some *ad hoc* committee or commission to study an emerging problem and recommend desirable action. Other examples of this organizational device are the royal commission of inquiry and the so-called departmental committee in England.

Planning is closely linked with political debate, because decisions involving new provisions of law and decisions about various types of expenditures are always subject to possible public criticism and political argument. This is not to say that such decisions necessarily arouse partisan controversy. Much depends upon what political leaders pick as issues having popular appeal in their efforts to retain or win elective office. It seems illusory, however, to believe that governmental planning will not give rise to political argument.

2. Problems of Planning

Sustaining the economy. It is impossible to discuss specific problems of governmental planning without reference to administrative activity. We shall now try to sketch in broad terms several planning issues that have occupied public attention in recent years, and that are likely to receive more attention in the years ahead.

The Employment Act of 1946 declared that it is "the continuing policy and responsibility of the Federal Government to use all practicable means" to develop "its plans" and resources, consistent with a free competitive enterprise system, to promote "maximum employment, production and purchasing power." This legislation committed the federal government to the proposition that the way in which it planned its policies and programs should have a positive influence upon the functioning of the American economy. The legislation fixed as a goal of government the promotion of maximum employment, production, and purchasing power, to be achieved within the framework of existing governmental activities. The Employment Act certainly contemplated no doctrinaire or radical change in the relationship of the federal government to the American economy. But it did provide new planning machinery in giving the President a Council of Economic Advisers and Congress a joint committee to review the President's proposals.[4]

In the years since 1946, the state of health of the American economy has been a major preoccupation of national policy. For the most part these years have witnessed a continuing increase in production and employment, accompanied by a more or less steady inflation. There was some economic recession in 1949, again in 1953-54, and once again in 1957-58. Yet there were more years of productive expansion than of contraction. This development was influenced by several factors. One was the federal government's concern with foreign relations and national defense, and particularly after 1950 with the intensification of conflict with the Soviet Union. This required substantial outlays for economic and military assistance to other countires, as well as large-scale development and procurement of weapons needed for national defense. The federal government was therefore compelled to spend large sums of money and to levy heavy taxes regardless of economic philosophy. Furthermore, internal problems could not be ignored, such as the farm economy, road construction, education, and water resource development. Large-scale

---

[4] On the Council of Economic Advisers, see Nourse, Edwin G., *Economics in the Public Service*, New York: Harcourt, Brace, 1953.

governmental activity, with large-scale expenditure and income programs, continued almost unabated during the years after World War II.

Economic analysis and recommendations. Under the Employment Act, the President each year submits to Congress an economic report. In this document, he sets forth the essential facts about the functioning of the American economy, together with a review of governmental policies and programs affecting the level of employment, production, and purchasing power. If the President believes that adjustments in policies and programs may be desirable in order to influence economic development in some desirable way, he submits recommendations to Congress in his economic report and in subsequent special messages. Each economic report has reviewed current trends and presented proposals for governmental action. For example, the last economic report of President Truman, in January 1953, declared that "in no previous period have the economic programs of government shown so high a degree of internal consistency, or so clear a relationship to the needs of the over-all economy." President Truman spoke also of the collaboration between the executive and legislative branches in the enactment and administration of economic policies. He expressed the opinion that in the years after 1946 both government and private enterprise had achieved a better understanding of the other's problems. At the same time he summed up the philosophy of the legislation of 1946 by saying that "private enterprise, under our free system, bears the major responsibility for full employment," and that it is "the duty of government to help improve the environment in which private enterprise works."

The economic report of President Eisenhower transmitted to Congress in January 1956 dealt at some length with current economic problems. It made the point that prompt government action in easing credit conditions, in providing tax reductions, and in reinforcing income security for individuals had been successful in meeting the recession of 1953-54. The report then explained a series of government policies which were necessary at a time of economic expansion, such as had occurred on so sizable a scale during the calendar year 1955. These included holding the tax line, containing the rise in stock market credit, reducing the ease of consumer borrowing, and releasing some government stockpiles of raw materials. The report went on to sketch desirable long-term goals, such as agricultural adjustments, reduction of unemployment in certain distressed areas, raising productivity, improvement in the economic status of older people, extending home ownership and urban redevelopment, and greater stability in the expanding economy.

Eisenhower's economic report of January 1958 was different in tone. It began with the acknowledgment that 1957 had demonstrated "how rapidly changes can occur in the problem of maintaining growth with reasonable stability of prices in a dynamic, free enterprise economy." The report mentioned again the responsibility of government to pursue policies that would help prevent inflation. Yet the conditions existing at the end of 1957 required action also to encourage business activity. This included an easing of credit restrictions, and some increase in expenditures for national security and certain other governmental needs, both federal and state.

It is impossible here to examine in detail the many different aspects of governmental economic and fiscal policy, the ways in which these policies influence the economy, or the factors in free economic enterprise that may promote continued economic growth in production, employment, and consumption. The important thing is that economic developments have become a major concern of the federal government, and that economic reporting and forecasting, along with the needed adjustment of government policies and programs, have become a continuing part of federal administration. To a lesser but nonetheless notable extent, similar developments have been occurring in state government.

Planning for national security. The greatest single administrative activity of the federal government for nearly twenty years has been national defense.[5] Of total federal expenditures, the lion's share has gone to national security. Nor is there much likelihood that this proportion will change substantially for many years to come. As national defense is the largest administrative endeavor of the federal government, so also is it the largest planning effort. Indeed, planning is at the heart of military activity. Constant attention is given to meet the anticipated situations that might threaten the security and the national interest of the United States.

In recent years a good deal of controversy has revolved about national defense policies and programs. That is understandable. In spite of the immense sums that have been committed for national defense, a large part of the task of the Department of Defense has been to allocate funds and personnel to those instruments of warfare believed to provide maximum security for the United States. Such decisions are not easy to make; they inevitably arouse those who for their own reasons believe that the wrong decisions are being made. For example, in 1949 there was controversy about whether the national defense was not too largely concentrated upon the B-36 bomber, now obsolete. The Navy appears to have been one party in raising this criticism. The then heavy bomber of the Air Force was said to be too slow for effective striking power, was tied to overseas bases, and would have great difficulty in reaching a Soviet target. In addition,

---

[5] Of many volumes on foreign affairs and national defense, perhaps the most stimulating is Kissinger, Henry A., *Nuclear Weapons and Foreign Policy*, New York: Harper, 1957. See also Finletter, Thomas K., *Foreign Policy: The Next Phase*, New York: Harper, 1958; Agar, Herbert, *The Price of Power*, Chicago: University of Chicago Press, 1957; Millis, Walter, *Arms and Men*, New York: Putnam, 1956; and Osgood, Robert E., *Limited War: The Challenge to American Strategy*, Chicago: University of Chicago Press, 1957.

it was entirely an offensive rather than a defensive weapon. More recently, much the same sort of argument has arisen about the B-47 and B-52 bombers in comparison with other military needs, such as the intercontinental ballistic missile.

Military planning concepts. For the most part, national defense planning has involved three principal elements in the years since World War II. They are the concept of the kind of war in which the United States might be engaged, the concept of the weapons system with which such a war might be waged, and the concept of direct military strength required for such a war.

At the conclusion of World War II, American military thinking was largely committed to the view that the United States itself would be the target for any future world conflagration. The reasoning was simple. During World War II, the productive strength of the United States, along with Soviet manpower and massing of large land forces, had played the decisive role. The United States had been given a good deal of time to convert its productive resources to turning out war material. After the Japanese attack in 1941, there was still time to mobilize the economy. Not until 1944 came the launching of the large-scale offensives in Europe and the Far East. The point was obvious. Any future aggressor, reading the lesson of the past, would see that his first objective must be to eliminate the potential military power of the United States. The answer of military planners was to keep in existence a sizable military force and a sizable military procurement program, ready to strike back immediately and effectively at any aggressor. With this concept of future war, the government proceeded to develop the atomic bomb as the major weapon and the Air Force as the principal source of military strength. The doctrine of "massive retaliation" proclaimed by Secretary of State Dulles in 1954 was an expression of this concept of war, and it continues to dominate a great deal of American defense planning. Yet in 1950 the United States became involved in a limited war in Korea in which it was not directly attacked and during which our own shores were not immediately threatened. It was only with great difficulty that American armed forces, constituting the preponderant United Nations strength in Korea, were able to achieve a military stalemate and an uneasy truce after 1953. In 1958, American troops carried out a military occupation of Lebanon in the Middle East. Many observers came to believe that the United States was more threatened by "limited war" than by any direct, large-scale attack.

The concept of war that prevails in military planning both affects and is affected by the concept of a weapons system. After 1945, the United States seemed to be dominated in its security thinking by its apparent advantage in the development of nuclear bombs. These were to be delivered to the target area by manned aircraft. Then in 1957 it suddenly appeared that the Soviet Union might be ahead of the United States in the development of ballistic missiles, and that these weapons with atomic and nonatomic warheads might be more powerful than manned aircraft. A further question was whether a nuclear-propelled bomber might be technically possible, as the nuclear-propelled submarine had become a reality. Would nuclear propulsion return the manned aircraft to an effective role in national security? Would missile launching give the Navy and Army new roles to fulfill in the conduct of war?

These questions introduce the third concept—that of military strength in terms of weapons, composition of the armed forces, and current production of military output. How large a stockpile of atomic bombs is desirable? How large a number of heavy bombers is needed in order to make massive retaliation possible? How rapidly can the technological development of new weapons be speeded up? How rapidly can and should new weapons be produced on a large scale? How large an armed force is needed to handle modern weapons and to wage successfully either a limited or an all-out war? How well trained must such an armed force be? These are only some of the questions that must be answered in military planning. Obviously, defense planning is an immense, complicated, far-reaching endeavor. Our very existence as a nation, together with the survival of the Free World, depends upon how well this task is performed.

Urban planning. At the state and local levels of government, no problem looms as more vexatious or compelling than that of urban congestion and organization.[6] In 1950 about 55 per cent of the total population of the United States resided in some 200 metropolitan areas. By 1975 it has been estimated that about two-thirds of the population will live in the 200 largest metropolitan areas. Moreover, about 60 per cent of the population within these areas live in the central city. It is very likely that by 1975 at least one-half of the metropolitan population will reside in suburban communities. Indeed, in the near future as much as half of the total population of the United States will reside in some fifteen "superurban" regions.

One of these regions extends down the Atlantic seaboard from Maine through Virginia, and out the Mohawk Valley to Buffalo. Another region extends from Pittsburgh in one direction through Cleveland and Detroit and in another direction through Columbus, Cincinnati, Indianapolis, and Louisville. A third such urban region is around Chicago, including northwestern Indiana and southeastern Wisconsin. Other regions surround

---

[6] On the metropolitan and urban problem, see Walker, Robert A., *The Planning Function in Urban Government,* Chicago: University of Chicago Press, 2d ed., 1950; Coleen, Miles L., *Renewing Our Cities,* New York: Twentieth Century Fund, 1953; Meyerson, Martin, Terrett, Barbara, and Ylvisaker, Paul V., eds., "Metropolis in Ferment," *Annals of the American Academy of Political and Social Science,* 1957, Vol. 314; Gulick, Luther, *Metro: Growth and Problems of Government in the Metropolitan Areas of the U. S. A.,* Washington: Governmental Affairs Institute, 1957; and Woodbury, Coleman, ed., *Urban Redevelopment* and *The Future of Cities and Urban Redevelopment,* Chicago: University of Chicago Press, 1953. See also the report on St. Louis published in 1957 by the Metropolitan St. Louis Survey.

Minneapolis, St. Louis, Kansas City, Dallas-Forth Worth, Denver, Salt Lake City, San Francisco, and Los Angeles. Four remaining regions extend along the Appalachian highlands from North Carolina to Atlanta, along the eastern coast of Florida, the Gulf coast from Mobile to Houston, and the western valley of Washington-Oregon.[7]

Principal problems. The urban complex has to contend with three broad sets of problems. Let us begin with traffic. In the urban regions, the main highways have encouraged a fringe development which means for all practical purposes that one never leaves an urban or congested living area. New superhighways will not halt this growth; if anything, they will do the opposite, because traffic flow is speeded up. The problem of traffic is to provide rapid means of automobile and truck movement between and within urban areas. To a large extent, the highways of the past have provided a fairly free flow of traffic between urban communities, with almost a complete paralysis of movement within the urban community. More recently, to the extent made possible by public works, some urban communities have built great freeways within the city limits. But, here again, traffic congestion persists when the inflow and outflow for such freeways are through narrow local streets with inadequate parking facilities. The highways of the future may help to solve the current problems of urban fringe congestion, but unless the central cities are enabled to move traffic more rapidly and to provide adequate parking, any improvement will be only partial.

A second set of problems involves the future fate of the core city as a business and residential center. This problem is only partly one of traffic flow. Much also depends upon rebuilding the trade and office facilities of the core city, and upon eliminating the slums as residential areas. Urban renewal is an immense endeavor. It will require imagination in planning and substantial expenditures of funds in execution.

A third of problems stems from the question whether the units of government are satisfactory for the urban complex. Each metropolitan area today is beset with difficulties in organizing itself effectively for performing various governmental activities. The difficulties are many: pride and vested interest in separate local governments, inadequate tax revenues, inefficient performance of services, and intercommunity rivalry for industrial location and other advantages. It no longer makes sense to provide water and sewage disposal services on a community-by-community basis. The result has been the growth of metropolitan water districts. The same kind of problem arises in connection with education, public health, public welfare, traffic, and many other services. Sometimes certain duties are transferred from the city to the county, as in health and welfare. Sometimes a

---

[7] *Cf.* Tunnard, Christopher, "America's Super-Cities," *Harper's,* August 1958, Vol. 217, p. 59.

new area of government is created, such as a metropolitan park board or a metropolitan transportation authority. Yet progress in finding the best service areas is slow.

It would not be an exaggeration to say that the urban area today is a contest between improvement and collapse. In more and more large metropolitan communities, such as in Kansas City, St. Louis, Cleveland, Dayton, New York, and Pittsburgh, groups of business and civic leaders have banded together to make extensive studies of the metropolitan problem. State legislatures each session are faced with more and more proposals for consolidation of local governments, core-city annexation of surrounding areas, or establishment of new units of government. The future will witness an ever-increasing concern with the urban complex, and mounting insistence that governmental agencies and nongovernmental bodies launch long-range plans to make metropolitan living more satisfactory.

To sum up, planning is not alone a tool of efficient management in the public service. It is the very hope of our civilization's continued existence.

Chapter 7 •

Concepts of Organization

1. Organization—Forms and Factors

Variety of Administrative Agencies. When we speak here of organization, we have in mind the large-scale, organized, or formal structure of agencies established to perform the *administrative* tasks of government. This definition allows us to confine ourselves to giving only fleeting recognition to certain agencies set up for the primary purpose of assisting the legislative, executive, and judicial branches of government in the performance of their particular duties. Using the federal government as an example, we find among the so-called legislative agencies the Government Printing Office, the Architect of the Capitol, the General Accounting Office, and the Library of Congress. The Administrative Office of the United States Courts assists the Supreme Court in directing the business affairs of the federal judiciary. In turn, the President has a number of specialized bodies to help him in the exercise of his executive power; these include the Cabinet and the Executive Office of the President, in which are placed such agencies as the White House Office, the National Security Council, the Bureau of the Budget, and the Council of Economic Advisers.

For our discussion, we shall pass by agencies such as these and focus our attention more narrowly upon agencies set up to perform the operating tasks of government, to administer public policy, and to carry out the substantive duties determined to be necessary for the public welfare. When we begin to examine the agencies so defined, we discover at the outset that they are quite varied in their structure and type. There is no such thing as a common species of administrative agency in American government. Again, we may refer to the federal government to illustrate the point.

First of all, we need to mention the ten executive departments.[1] These vary greatly in numbers of employees, in expenditures, and in the relation of the department head to the constituent operating units. One of the executive departments, the Department of Defense, has three military departments and various overseas commands. No other executive department

---

[1] See also Chapter 9, "The Departmental System."

has such a structure. Yet executive departments are one kind of federal administrative agency. Of another kind are, secondly, the regulatory commissions and boards, such as the Interstate Commerce Commission, the Federal Trade Commission, the National Labor Relations Board,[2] and others. But there are also, thirdly, still other important agencies, each headed by a plural body, such as the Atomic Energy Commission, the National Mediation Board, and the Railroad Retirement Board. Next come, fourthly, equally important additional agencies like the latter, but headed by a single administrator, such at the Veterans Administration, the Federal Mediation and Conciliation Service, and the Housing and Home Finance Agency. In the fifth place, there are nonregulatory agencies set up as government corporations, with a board of directors as head, such as the Tennessee Valley Authority and the Federal Deposit Insurance Corporation.[3] Finally, we encounter peculiar plural agencies which are difficult to categorize, such as the Board of Governors of the Federal Reserve System, the Farm Credit Administration, and the Federal Home Loan Bank Board. They, were created by act of Congress, and their boards are appointed by the President with the consent of the Senate, but they obtain their operating funds by assessment upon constituent semi-public corporations.

This kind of variety is equally evident in the states and in local government. Here we even discover administrative boards and individual officers who are elected directly by the voters. In brief, one finds no such thing as a standard type of administrative agency in American government. Rather, there are many different kinds of agencies which perform the administrative work of government.

Factors in organization structure. Public administration differs from private enterprise in the complexity of the organizational factors with which it must contend. First of all, in public administration the basic organizational outlines are determined in accordance with prevailing political expectations. The organizational pattern of public agencies provides a basis of work specialization and a structural status acceptable to the legislature, the executive, interest groups, and the citizenry at large. Organizational design in public agencies involves the public interest.

In the second place, there is the technical factor that organizational structure is expected to promote efficiency and effective service by those who are entrusted with the authority and responsibility for administrative activity. It is important to bear in mind that the technical judgment of organizational effectiveness may originate outside an agency itself. To those who are actually in charge of an organization, the existing structure may appear quite satisfactory. The outside critic, however, may argue that it violates standards of effective administrative conduct.

----

[2] See also Chapter 10, "Independent Regulatory Agencies."
[3] See also Chapter 11, "Government Corporations."

In the third place, organizational structure is influenced by the reactions of those who comprise its components. Organization is people working together. Organization is a social environment. It is, accordingly, a structure of anticipated individual behavior. But the individual is not an automaton, to be manipulated at will by some higher authority. He has his own aspirations, ideas, and emotions. As such, he is much concerned in his working group about organizational arrangements, since these may vitally influence his own life and interpersonal relationships.

In public administration these political, technical, and personal factors must all be analyzed in order to understand organizational patterns. To be sure, the three factors are interrelated and on occasion may not be easy to separate even for study or analysis. Yet, one should not examine organizational structure from a single point of view. All three must be given proper consideration.

2. Political Factors

Organizing the atomic energy program. Organizational structure establishes the range of activities as well as the status of an administrative agency. Both of these are matters of great political interest.[4] When we speak of political interest, we mean that the organs of political decision-making in the American scheme of government find issues of public concern involved in organizational arrangements. In other words, organization in public administration is a problem involving legislative and executive points of view and, beyond these organs of decision-making, the points of view of interest groups as well as of the public at large. In the American scheme of government it is the legislature that is the main architect of organizational structure.[5] Whenever a new governmental program is about to be launched, or some existing program is being expanded, a number of organizational questions arise as part of the decisions to be made. Indeed, such questions are usually an integral part of the consideration given to any governmental activity.

Numerous illustrations will readily occur to anyone who follows debate on legislative matters. Two or three examples will here suffice. In 1946 the federal government set out to establish a continuing program of research, development, production, and military use of fissionable materials. During World War II, the War Department had launched a large-scale effort to produce an atomic bomb. This endeavor met success when a first bomb was dropped upon Hiroshima in Japan and a second bomb on Nagasaki early in August 1945. The whole atomic bomb program was

---

[4] The political factors in the organizational structure of public administration have not received nearly so much attention as the subject deserves. Usually, they are treated incidentally to the consideration of some other issue, such as administrative discretion or regulatory administration.

[5] *Cf.* Chapter 15, "Legislative Control."

then handled as a military enterprise within the framework of War Department authority, organization, and appropriations. When the war came to an end, one possibility was to leave the existing arrangements alone. But too much public interest in the whole subject had developed for this possibility to be very real. Instead, a special committee was created in the Senate to study the matter. Military officials, the Bureau of the Budget on behalf of the President, and the scientific advisers in various federal agencies prepared recommendations. Individual scientists of outstanding reputation were asked to give testimony, and representatives of business also took an interest in the subject. The result was the passage of the Atomic Energy Act of 1946, which set up a continuing federal program.

Comprising a very important part of this legislation were its organizational provisions. The law began with a statement of findings and a declaration of purpose, which included encouragement of private research, the control of scientific and technical information, and government control of production and use of fissionable materials. The very next part of the act proceeded to establish organizational machinery, beginning with an Atomic Energy Commission of five members. In addition, the statute provided for a general manager, a division of research, a division of production, a division of engineering, and a division of military application. Furthermore, the director of this last division was to be a member of the armed forces. The law also specified that there should be a general advisory committee of nine members and a military liaison committee. What is noteworthy is the extent to which Congress by statute set forth organizational details for the government's program in atomic energy. The law did not simply create a commission and then leave the organizational detail to its discretion. Rather, the various interests involved, including that of the armed forces and that of the public, found expression in the statutory prescription of the organizational design for the federal government's activities in the development of atomic energy.

Organizing for higher learning. As a second illustration, we may mention another but quite different matter of current concern. In Ohio there has never been any sizable number of junior or community colleges created under private or public auspices to handle part of the load of education beyond the high school. Early in the 1950's it became apparent that during the sixties the college-age population would substantially increase. Reports by the Ohio College Association and then by the Governor's Commission on Education Beyond the High School called attention to the need for additional facilities. It was generally agreed that much of this expansion should be provided in the main urban areas and should consist of instruction through two years.

The organizational question was whether these two-year junior colleges should be set up, insofar as public action was concerned, by local school districts, as in Texas and California, or be created as branches of existing state universities, as in Indiana. There were many arguments on both sides. In favor of local school districts were such factors as the existence of high school facilities which might be utilized, the current programs of technical and vocational education being offered by many school districts, and the fear that state universities might not take much interest in junior-college branches. In favor of university sponsorship were such factors as greater assurance of keeping programs to two years, existing accreditation which could be extended to the branches, and the possibility of higher standards of instruction. In addition, fiscal issues had to be resolved. First of all, if a local school district took over sponsorship of junior colleges, how would young people from neighboring school districts be treated? Secondly, what proportion of educational cost would fall on the local school district, and with what consequences for the tax burden upon real property? In the third place, what part of the cost would fall on students, and would local school districts be able to collect fees?

These were important policy questions to be determined in the light of the educational objectives of the state of Ohio. Yet the questions appeared in the context of an organizational problem. Indeed, they seemed to present a struggle for educational power between large urban school districts eager to operate junior colleges and the state universities eager to expand their branch activities. Obviously, here again are organizational p.oblems of great public interest and problems that would eventually have to be resolved by legislative action.

Organizing the armed forces. Let us examine still a third example. The long story of organization for national defense is too intricate to recount in detail, but it is possible to spot the principal issues that have arisen and that in varying degree were settled by laws enacted in 1947, 1949, and 1958. The first issue organizationally was to recognize the claim of the Air Force to a status equal to that of the Army and the Navy. This was finally achieved in 1947. The second issue was to achieve some degree of integration of the Army, Navy, and Air Force. American experience in World War II all around the globe had demonstrated the importance of joint action. No one force could claim an exclusive military role. Rather, coordinated efforts of all three forces were required. This was obtained with some degree of success by means of the Joint Chiefs of Staff functioning in Washington under the immediate supervision of the President as commander in chief and by means of unified commands in various theaters of operation. The question then was what kind of joint organization to continue after 1945.

The National Security Act of 1947 answered this question by creating originally a new kind of organization known as the National Military Establishment headed by a Secretary of Defense. The law provided that the Secretary was to exercise *"general* direction, authority, and control" over the three executive departments of the Army, Navy, and Air Force.

Furthermore, he was given authority to "supervise and coordinate" the preparation of military budgets by the three departments. He was to be assisted by a Joint Chief of Staff, a Munitions Board, and a Research and Development Board. But the difficulty with this arrangement was that it conferred only general power upon the Secretary of Defense. By 1949 the Congress was ready to move in the direction of overcoming this defect in organization, especially when the tragic suicide of the first Secretary of Defense, James V. Forrestal, was ascribed to collapse brought on by the difficulties of handling his arduous task. Accordingly, the Department of Defense was created as one executive department, and the three constituent departments became mere "military departments." The language conferring authority upon the Secretary of Defense was changed to eliminate the word "general" and to provide "direction and control" over the budgets of the military departments. In 1953 the functions of the Munitions Board were abolished and vested directly in the Secretary of Defense by a reorganization plan of the President. The same was done with the Research and Development Board.

In 1958, still further changes were made. Again the organization of the Department of Defense had come under widespread criticism, this time because of the belief that the United States was lagging behind the Soviet Union in the development of intercontinental ballistic missiles. The new law retained the separate identity of the three military departments. But it specified that each department was to function under the "direction, authority, and control" of the Secretary of Defense, to whom the civilian secretary of each military department was made responsible for efficient operation of his department. In addition, the President was authorized to establish through the Secretary of Defense "unified combatant commands." These were to report directly to the President through the Secretary, but not to be subject to control by one of the military departments. Furthermore, the Secretary of Defense was empowered to transfer, reassign, consolidate, or abolish functions of the military departments, even though such action could not become effective without a report to the Armed Services Committee of both the House of Representatives and the Senate. If these committees approved, the action would become effective within 30 days of its being reported to them. If one of the committees adopted a resolution of disapproval, then another 40 days were to elapse, in which time either house could affirm the resolution of disapproval, thus vetoing the Secretary's proposed action.

The point simply is that over a period of eleven years Congress considered three major pieces of legislation dealing with national defense organization and only gradually was willing to vest more authority in the hands of a Secretary of Defense. The question of the degree of power to be given to the Secretary of Defense and thus to be taken away from the three armed forces was a grave organizational matter of public interest. It had to be resolved slowly as circumstances appeared to dictate.

Range of political issues. In expressing its public interest in organizational matters, a legislature tends to be concerned with several common problems. These arise in the context of many different policies and programs of government, at the federal, state, or local level. One question is that of the number of administrative agencies. Most interest groups advocating the establishment or expansion of some government program favor the creation of a single administrative agency to handle the activity. The reason is obvious. The interest group believes that it will better be able to make its own point of view prevail—or at least ensure that its point of view is given careful attention—if a separate agency is organized. Furthermore, many an interest group fears that if the program close to its heart is to be merged with those of some existing agency, the character of the work to be performed may be hampered or substantially changed. For example, the maritime shipping interests do not wish the governmental activities concerned with them to be merged with the Interstate Commerce Commission, primarily occupied with railroad regulation.[6]

Another organizational question of major public interest is the degree of supervisory authority over an administrative activity to be exercised by the chief executive. Because basic matters of administrative structure are fixed by law, it is inevitable that some of the latent antagonisms that exist between the legislative and the executive branches should find expression in such legislation. The legislature often believes that it can better deal with the departments when they are not too ready to respond to direction by the chief executive. The legislature may favor fixed terms of office for department heads, rather than indefinite terms. It may require reasons why an agency head should be removed. It may endeavor to limit administrative discretion insofar as possible, because the greater is the degree of discretion enjoyed by an agency, the stronger may be the case for higher executive supervision. The legislature is reluctant to build up an administrative apparatus for the chief executive by which he can exercise continuing control over administrative agencies. Moreover, the legislature does not worry too much about the large number of administrative agencies which the chief executive has to supervise.

Another question is that of agency leadership. Should the head of an agency be a single individual or a board? Legislatures often tend to prefer a board, because a board can more readily be isolated, or protected, from executive domination. In the field of public education, for example, the prevailing pattern of primary and secondary school administration is the separate school district, with an independently elected school board

---

[6] *Cf.* Chapter 14, "Interest Groups in Administration."

which appoints a full-time professional administrator. At the level of higher education it is customary to have a board of regents or trustees, sometimes elected and sometimes appointed by the governor. This board is usually free from detailed administrative supervision by the chief executive. The same situation prevails in regulatory administration. Regulatory authority of the federal and the state governments is frequently vested in commissions or boards, especially where price-fixing and licensing powers are involved. The feeling is that the interests affected will have greater assurance of fairness from a board than from one official. In turn, the board is isolated to some degree from executive oversight.[7]

A fourth question is whether it may be desirable to establish a government corporation to carry out certain activities. In general, where a particular activity produces a substantial amount of revenue through service charges, much can be said for creating a government corporation. Then the income from charges may be devoted to the service, and it is easier to keep expenditures to the total of earnings when a corporation is established. A corporation, moreover, may plan and carry out long-range plans without the need for annual or biennial appropriations. On the other hand, legislatures are not enthusiastic about such fiscal independence in governmental agencies. A fifth question is that of the relationship between a federal agency and its counterpart among state agencies, or between state agencies and similar agencies of local government. Legislatures tend to be protective of local interests and seek reassurance in organizational terms that the work of local administrative bodies will not be absorbed by a central agency.

One final matter may be mentioned. Although seldom expressed in law, legislatures take a great deal of interest in the local or field offices created by federal or state agencies. Administrators have to be very careful about where such offices are located, what work they handle, and when to discontinue or merge any of them. The local citizenry and its legislative representatives are usually but mildly concerned with administrative efficiency. They are much interested in the dollars-and-cents advantage to a particular community in having such an office located there, in addition to the point of prestige and convenience. In many different ways, then, organization in public administration is a matter of public interest. This is another way of saying that there are political issues to be resolved in the organization and reorganization of administrative agencies.

3. Technical Factors

Criteria of organizational grouping. Division of labor is the basis of organization. The fundamental work units of any organized group are determined according to the prevailing knowledge and skills of a particular

---

[7] See Chapter 10, "Independent Regulatory Agencies."

society. The technical problems of organizational structure arise usually in terms of building needed abilities and skills into some kind of coordinated major purpose.[8] Over a period of time, especially in government, a number of major purposes have come to be recognized. These include the conduct of foreign relations, provision of national defense, protection of persons and property, collection of taxes, promotion of public health, assistance to agriculture, provision of education, regulation of commerce, construction of roads and streets, encouragement of economic enterprise, delivery of mail, and still other such purposes.

The technical analysis of organizational structure employs several criteria. The one most commonly utilized is *efficiency*. This term may be employed in different ways, but the usually accepted meaning is that of increased output in terms of manpower, plant, and other resources employed. In other words, the goal of efficiency is to render more or better service or to produce more or better goods with the same or fewer resources. There are other criteria besides efficiency. One of these is *convenience of service.* The work done by government must be placed in reasonable reach of those who are entitled to its benefits. Another criterion is *quality of service.* The work of government must meet desirable standards of performance; these include sufficiency and timeliness. A fourth criterion is *equality of service,* or fairness. Government work must be performed on an equal basis for all. The alternative is to accept the undemocratic proposition that there is an elite group of citizens who are entitled to special privileges and various other grades of citizens who are of inferior status. The criterion of equality is based on the principle that individuals are equal before the law, and that those in similar circumstances or conditions shall be treated on a like basis.

The four elements of efficiency, convenience, quality, and equality are the fundamental criteria usually employed in evaluating the technical performance of organization. Yet these criteria are by no means self-evident, or simple to apply. Certain factors of personal judgment are always involved in using such standards. And there is no automatic weighting among the four criteria. Considerations of efficiency may at times be at variance with considerations of convenience of service. Considerations of equality may at times be at variance with considerations of quality of service. It is because of this personal element of judgment about organizational effectiveness that public administration remains an art while it develops into a science. The student of organization must understand the elements involved

---

[8] On the technical aspects of public administration, one of the best studies is Gulick, Luther, and Urwick, L., eds., *Papers on the Science of Administration,* New York: Institute of Public Administration, 1937. This should be supplemented by Fesler, James W.. *Area and Administration,* University, Alabama: University of Alabama Press, 1949. For critical comment see Wallace, Schuyler C., *Federal Departmentalization,* New York: Columbia University Press, 1941, and Waldo, Dwight, *The Administrative State: A Study of the Political Theory of Public Administration,* New York: Ronald, 1948.

in proposing lines of improvement. But organizational analysis involves judgment and cannot be reduced to scientifically accurate prediction of future behavior.

Basis of organization. The first problem that arises when one tries to promote effective performance within an organizational structure is that of subdividing larger purposes as the basis for constructing administrative units. Ordinarily, the first degree of specialization is the establishment of an administrative entity that is separate from the other administrative entities and subject only to the supervision of the chief executive and the legislature. This may be termed the primary basis of organization. As we have explained, this primary basis of organization is ordinarily determined by law and may be the product of public or political interest rather than of technical standards. The two considerations, however, may be closely connected. Moreover, organizational patterns are dynamic rather than static, and changing political and technical circumstances may result in organizational changes.

From a technical point of view, the major consideration is to group together related activities on the basis of a common purpose. Yet it is not easy to decide what shall be regarded as a common purpose. Let us look at some examples to illustrate the various factors at play in determining organizational structure. At the local level of government—in town, village, county, or city—we look upon protection of persons and property as an important purpose. In a city of 50,000 there might be a Department of Public Safety, with a Division of Police and a Division of Fire Protection. Or in another city of the same size we may find a separate Police Department and a separate Fire Department. Indeed, this latter organizational arrangement tends to prevail in most cities throughout the United States. In the federal government, the Tennessee Valley Authority performs functions in the field of river control on the basis of the common purpose of providing flood control, navigation, power generation, and auxiliary activities in a particular geographical area. For the remainder of the United States, such functions are exercised by several different federal agencies— the Army Corps of Engineers, the Department of the Interior, the Department of Agriculture, the Department of Health, Education, and Welfare, and the Federal Power Commission. The Corps of Engineers is concerned primarily with flood control and river navigation; the Department of the Interior with irrigation of arid lands in the seventeen western states; the Department of Agriculture with planning agricultural production and marketing; the Department of Health, Education, and Welfare with pure water supply and sanitation; and the Federal Power Commission with the licensing of hydroelectric power development.

Still another kind of problem is suggested by the Department of Agriculture. This agency is organized on the basis of a clientele, the farm population of the country engaged in agriculture as a productive enterprise, which receives a wide range of services in support of both a way of life and a sector of production. Such services include agricultural education and research, soil conservation, marketing and price support, regulation of produce and live stock exchanges, farm-home loans, rural electrification, and finally the Forest Service. Interestingly enough, however, the most extensive system of farm credit is set up as a separate agency, the Farm Credit Administration. Although from 1939 to 1953 a part of the Department of Agriculture, this agency was separated by the Farm Credit Act of 1953, in the expectation that the system of land banks, intermediate credit banks, and banks for cooperatives would function in a fashion similar to the Federal Reserve System and that the government investment in the capital of these banks might eventually be reduced or eliminated. Another agency organized on the basis of clientele served is the Veterans Administration, which operates a medical service, a pension system, an insurance business, and incidental services such as educational benefits and loan guarantees for housing.

Alternatives of common purpose. At the level here discussed, the problem of finding a pattern of organization for related activities has a dual nature; the considerations are both political and technical, with the political factor tending to be dominant, as it should. But the technical factor is not missing, as the long evolution of American defense organization after 1945 well illustrates. Technically the basis for grouping activities as having a common purpose may be found in several things. These are purpose (or function), technique (such as construction or legal service), geographical area, or clientele group served.

The technical factors in organizational planning operate primarily at the level below that of the basic administrative unit, which is the department or agency itself. The agency head may enjoy substantial discretion in building or rearranging the internal organizational structure. But this is not always so. Indeed, one distinction that may be made between administrative agencies is the extent of organizational authority granted the agency head. In the federal government, the legal authority in some instances is substantial, as in the State Department, the Department of Agriculture, the Veterans Administration, and the Post Office Department. Sometimes the legal authority is limited, as in the case of the Interior Department, the Atomic Energy Commission, the Labor Department, and others. Even when the legal authority exists, however, it is another question whether it is feasible to exercise it.

In brief, within the broad framework of a department one finds various kinds of organizational structure, bringing together activities which may be related by purpose, technique, geography, or clientele. It is not easy to say that one pattern of grouping is superior to another. Sometimes experimentation is possible, so that results provide an answer. Sometimes comparative experience is available to guide organizational decision-making.

Sometimes changing circumstances must be considered, such as the burden of work.

Organization for supervision. Another main consideration in determining a desirable organizational pattern is that of supervisory requirements. Ordinarily, related activities are grouped together because they have some substantial impact upon the product or service to be attained, whether in interrelationships, timeliness, convenience to the clientele, or on other grounds. But supervision is a two-way proposition. The goal of supervision is to bring and keep together the various working units. To be effective, however, the burden of supervision imposed upon a level of organization must be reasonable.

For many years organizational specialists have talked about "span of control." The idea was that there was only a limited number of work units or of persons which any supervisor could effectively direct and control. Indeed, the magic number was often asserted to be seven. Experience, and psychological research, have both confirmed that there is a limit to the supervisory capacity of an administrative officer. But this limit is subject to different considerations, such as the newness or growth of a function, the degree of supervision required, and the variety of work performed.

In an agency that has long done its work, where the volume of work is not changing greatly, where the variety of work done is limited, and which employs few highly specialized techniques, an administrator can assume a larger supervisory burden than where one finds the exact reverse of these conditions. As a rule of thumb, it may be said that levels of supervision tend to increase, and the number of work units assigned to a supervisor tends to decrease, as the workload of an agency and the interrelationships of work units increase, and as work techniques become more and more complicated.

Organization for management. A further element in the technical construction of organizational patterns has to do with providing an administrator with personal assistance, with adequate organization for management. Usually we think of administrative organization in terms of a pyramid, or of a ladder. The many small work units make up the broad base of the pyramid, or the first rung of the ladder. Next, a number of these first-rung work units are grouped together under a supervisor or foreman. Then a number of first-line supervisors and their work units are grouped together under another supervisor, who may be known as a director or chief. At a third, a fourth, and a fifth level there will be further supervisors, and the groups they supervise will have some common basis for being related to one another.

Management organization refers to the structure of assistance that is provided the supervisor. As one ascends the pyramid or ladder of organizational structure, the task of the supervisor or administrator becomes more complicated. No longer is it possible to think of supervision in a personal or individual sense. The administrator needs help. Management becomes a collegial job. And top management in particular tends to become a large-scale task in itself, participated in by many specializations. As a result, management organization is a special technical problem for administrative agencies.

Aspects of management. It is difficult to discuss management organization without discussing management. Three broad types of management responsibility have been recognized in most administrative agencies. The first has to do with directing the substantive affairs of the agency. If the agency is concerned with education, certain substantive aspects of education may become the subject of central supervision. If the agency is concerned with public health, the same may happen with respect to certain substantive aspects of preventive medicine. Management organization for supervision of the substance of an agency's work will depend upon two principal factors. One is the nature of the operating divisions of the agency. Such operating divisions may require a great deal of interdivisional collaboration. If so, management—or staff—supervision of the important elements of these interdivisional relationships will become necessary. The actual determination of what relationships thus to supervise on a continuing basis depends upon the peculiarities of each agency. The other factor is the extent to which top management decides to get into long-range planning and into research and development. Assistance to management is required if a top administrator sees no need for giving all of his attention to day-to-day operations, but wants to influence the work of his agency by planning for what will be done in the next five or ten years. Such management assistance would concentrate on planning the agency's goals in the future, or on carrying forward the research and development which may determine technological improvements, new products, or new types of service.

A second task of management is operation of the enterprise. Operating problems include budgeting and finance, personnel, legal services, administrative improvement, and public relations. The management of any enterprise requires attention to these common operating problems. Hence organization for management is needed to help the administrator perform these duties. Thirdly, management extends to the performance of certain internal maintenance or housekeeping tasks. These include the construction and maintenance of the physical plant, the purchase of supplies, and the provision of mail and transportation, printing and reproduction, and other specialized internal services. No agency can function without these housekeeping services. Each requires usually a specialized organizational unit.

Two problems are ordinarily encountered in the construction of organization for management. One is the extent to which the operating and the housekeeping activities shall be centralized at the top level. Shall there be a centralized accounting office, for example? Shall there be a centralized purchasing office? Factors of geography and of size usually provide the answer to such questions. A second common problem is that of achieving a clear understanding of what phases of a management activity shall be performed at various levels of organization. For example, if accounting is decentralized to lower levels of supervision, top managment will require a unit on its own level to exercise general oversight of all accounting activities. It is not always easy to draw a clear-cut distinction between accounting policy and reporting, on the one hand, and the actual keeping of primary accounting records, on the other. The same kind of difficulty arises in other fields of management.

Field offices. Another important technical subject in the construction of the organizational pattern of public administration is the creation of field offices.[9] The work of government cannot all be performed in some headquarters city. In a large school district, elementary schools will be scattered in several parts of the area. This may even be the case with the secondary schools. Maintenance of state highways requires district offices in various parts of the state. The Forest Service must have offices in its forest areas. The Department of State has diplomatic and consular offices in other countries. Most government work requires some kind of decentralization.

Two major issues tend to arise in the organization of field offices. The first is that of the number of field offices to create. The main considerations are (1) convenience for the clientele of a service and (2) an area large enough to ensure full utilization of the service. Thus a road maintenance district should be large enough to keep trucks and specialized repair equipment fully employed. Many school districts in the United States are too small to support a high school of adequate size to permit, for instance, some teachers to specialize in instruction of college-bound students. The location of field offices also depends upon such factors as the availability of land and of the desired labor force, the existence of adequate transportation and communication facilities, and the desirable relationships to other governmental agencies. All of these considerations play their part in determining the number and particular location of field offices.

The second major organizational issue is that of the jurisdiction of the field office. In general, an agency has two choices in creating a field organization. One may be described as decentralization by specialty, the other as decentralization by hierarchy. In decentralization by specialty, all the main operating units of the headquarters office set up their separate field offices as they see fit. Thus, for example, the medical department of the Veterans Administration determines the number and location of veterans hospitals, without concern for the field office needs of the other operating elements of the agency. On the other hand, in decentralization by hierarchy,

---

[9] *Cf.* Chapter 12, "Field Organization."

the field office reproduces the total program of the parent agency within a particular geographical area. For example, under the Department of Defense Reorganization Act of 1958, the President through the Secretary of Defense may establish "unified combatant commands." These commands in a particular strategic area would have Army, Navy, and Air Force units, together with the necessary supporting forces. In effect, the combatant command would reproduce the range of duties and specialized parts of the Department of Defense.

There are advantages and disadvantages to both kinds of field office organization, as there are with most patterns of organization structure. In decentralization by specialty, there is a close and usually harmonious working relationship between the field office and the headquarters office. In decentralization by hierarchy, it may be the lot of the field office chief to supervise a variety of work. Some of the specialists in the headquarters office will worry that their particular activity may not be fully appreciated or properly utilized by him. Decentralization by hierarchy proves an acceptable arrangement only when much local collaboration between the various specialized activities is necessary, and when the headquarters specialists are able to retain a substantial degree of technical supervision over their specialized work at the local level.

Summary. We can thus see that there are problems to solve in setting up units of work specialization, in grouping such units for purposes of supervision, in creating necessary management units, and in establishing field offices. These are common organizational concerns, found in many different kinds of activities. The solution to organizational problems depends in part upon certain rational criteria or standards such as efficiency and convenience, quality, and quantity of service. In part it depends upon changing circumstances, the state of technology, external pressures, and changes in workload.

The determination of organizational structure on the basis of rational criteria requires careful analysis, and adjustment from time to time. Organization needs to be dynamic and sufficiently flexible to meet changing requirements.

4. Personal Factors

Group identification and leadership. As was said earlier, organization is a pattern of interpersonal relationships. Organization thus takes on certain characteristics which arise from the social psychology of human beings working together.[10] The work group is not an artificial social creation but

---

[10] See particularly Presthus, Robert V., "Toward a Theory of Organizational Behavior," *Administrative Science Quarterly*, 1958, Vol. 3, p. 48 *ff*. See also Chapter 13, "Informal Organization."

Much research effort and writing have gone into the subject of group administrative behavior. See Simon, Herbert A., *Administrative Behavior*, New York: Maca functional and acceptable necessity for most individuals. Furthermore, once they become members of a work group, most indivduals soon identify their own welfare with that of the group. They come to believe that the group is important and resent external attack. When a newcomer joins the group, he is on trial for a while until the group is ready to accept him as one of its own.

Such group identification has its advantages and disadvantages. On the one hand, social cohesion makes it possible for a group to work together and to achieve a common purpose which might not otherwise be possible. On the other hand, social cohesion can also become a static factor. The group tends to fix standards of work performance that suit the talents and abilities of the majority of the group. There may be a reluctance to try new methods of operation. There may be hostility to any external encouragement to greater effort. Social cohesion can thus become an obstacle to social progress.

Each group will recognize leadership. The actual leadership in the group is not always found in those formally vested with the leadership function. Sometimes formal and informal authority coincide; sometimes the two are different. Many factors account for leadership, but almost all have in common that the leaders excel in some particular way. They may have more knowledge, more strength, more skill, or more sensitivity to the moods and drives of the individuals who comprise the group.

Status and prestige. An organizational pattern is a structure of authority. The administrator has the authority to carry out the objectives which an organization exists to achieve. In turn, various unit heads of operating departments and management divisions are delegated a part of this authority. And so down the chain of command this authority is subdivided and extended to the smallest component of an organization.

Now this authority is never absolute. In social groups one test of authority is legitimacy. But another test, equally important, is acceptability. Individuals must accept the exercise of authority on their own grounds. If authority becomes capricious, uncertain, or harmful, there will be obstruction, and ultimately revolt. In this reaction to authority, individuals and groups are often motivated by considerations of status and prestige, for themselves individually and for their group. They want to be appreciated and rewarded. They want their contribution to the enterprise as a whole properly acknowledged. Status and prestige are not simply matters of compensation. Indeed compensation may often be a lesser consideration for an individual, unless he is living on the very margin of

millan, 2nd ed., 1957; Hoslett, Schuyler D., ed., *Human Factors in Management,* Parkville, Missouri: Park College Press, 1946; and Dubin, Robert, *Human Relations in Administration,* New York: Prentice-Hall, 1951. A helpful recent volume of readings is Stacey, Chalmers L., and DeMartino, Manfred F., eds., *Understanding Human Motivation,* Cleveland: Howard Allen, 1958.

subsistence. Otherwise, compensation is only one evidence of status, and a lesser one. Other factors in status are titles, access to the top administrator, location and furnishings of an office, the kind of building assigned, relationships to others, the recognition given to associates, and similar considerations. Prestige is a highly personal motivation, but the leader of a group knows that the recognition accorded him expresses recognition to the group of which he is a part. Failure to provide recognition is an insult to the group as well.

As a general proposition, a key individual in a group seeks to advance the group's status and prestige. Evidence of recognition of such status will be eagerly awaited and highly valued when received. Any organizational action that appears to cast some adverse reflection upon the status and prestige of a group member or the group will be resented, and may in time disrupt organizational relationships. Accordingly, adjustment in organizational structure must be planned in terms of what the consequences will be for the status and prestige of particular individuals and their group. Seldom is it possible to achieve acceptance of change if the change is widely interpreted as a reduction in prestige for a particular group. In these circumstances organizational change will be resisted. If the change is made nonetheless, it must be carried through over such resistance.

Anxiety. Another important motivating factor in the social life of a work group is anxiety. Many individuals worry about themselves, whether they will be accepted by others, whether their health is good or not, whether they will be able to support themselves, whether their work performance will be adequate, and so forth. Thus anxiety becomes a force in group behavior in any organization.

Individual anxiety may be quickly transferred to the group. Rumor, hearsay, or gossip may fan individual anxiety into group alarm. Usually the object of such anxiety will be such matters as fear of change, loss of employment, diminution in work responsibility, transfer of some persons away from the group, addition of a large number of newcomers, change of leaders, and adoption of new work methods which some members of the group may not be able to master. These and many other personal and group anxieties affect behavior in an organization. The result is opposition to change and to authority.

Here, again, accomplishment of organizational adjustment depends on success in allaying individual and group anxieties, in building confidence, and in providing reassurance about the work and the career chances of all who are affected.

General conclusion. In concluding this chapter, we may repeat that in constructing and reconstructing the organizational patterns of public administration, many considerations must be met. These need to be reconciled in some fashion. The reconciliation achieved is the currently prevailing pattern of organization. This pattern should not be static, however, because changing circumstances often necessitate changing patterns of organizational structure.

Organizational structure can contribute to administrative accomplishment because it provides a pattern of individual and group effort, encourages necessary output of government goods and services, and stimulates the drive for public progress. The relationship between organization and accomplishment is not expressed in some precise quantative measure. Although the relationship exists, we cannot eliminate the element of personal judgment about the exact nature of the relationship. Thus we are dependent upon political and administrative leadership constantly to press for needed organizational improvement.

Chapter 8 •

The Chief Executive

1. Dual Function: Policy and Administration

Means and ends. At its highest reach, administrative management is so completely fused with leadership in policy development that in most governments and in nearly all private organizations both functions are intentionally lodged in the same man. This is the central fact setting off the position of the chief executive from those of all lesser officers, whether they be called executives, administrators, or managers. An understanding of this most important of all offices in public administration calls for analysis of five basic factors: the duality of the chief executive's role; his leadership and authority; the external relationships he must cultivate and sustain; the tools he needs for effective control; and the staff facilities comprising the arms of modern management.

Study of administration, as distinguished from other phases of government, rests on the feasibility of differentiating broadly between political ends and administrative means. This is not to deny that there are higher and lower levels both of administration and of policy, and that differing degrees of initiative and discretion have to be exercised throughout the entire range of political power and administrative authority. In other words, lesser ends are themselves means toward greater ends, and higher means are intermediate ends reached by lower means. Life is tangled and connected, and schemes of analysis have value only if their limitations are steadily borne in mind. Yet it is profitable to look at things separately, when the general context is not ignored. When the accent is placed on public policy—or ends—to visualize decisions made by individuals holding political responsibility, it is well to remember that nonetheless secondary policy decisions are normally left to administrative officers. Below the plane of high policy lie planes of administrative policy, on which questions of alternative courses of action also have to be decided. Conversely, if the accent be on means—as alternatives of administration—it should not be forgotten that above these questions of means lie political issues. Administrative preferences are frequently obliged to yield to necessities of politics.

147

In the whole realm of government, perhaps no one appreciates the truth and the importance of this proposition so much as the chief executive. The President of the United States, the governors of New York, California, and Pennsylvania, and the mayors of New York City, Chicago, Los Angeles, Philadelphia, Detroit, St. Louis, and Boston—all illustrate, by their fumbles as well as their achievements, the range and complexity of the responsibilities inherent in this office. Abilities of the same kind if not of the same order are needed at the helm of every sizable executive establishment, and likewise in the direction of every large administrative department.

Political leadership and administration. Before proceeding to an analysis of the chief executive in his major roles, it may be useful to recall that the responsibilities of policy development and administrative direction are often assigned to different officials rather than concentrated in a single individual. Outside the field of government it is common practice, especially among business corporations, to vest responsibility for basic policy in a board of directors headed by a chairman and to delegate responsibility for management to a president or general manager. Election as "chairman of the board" means recognition of demonstrated initiative and intelligence in policy leadership. While the president or general manager may also be a director, his first duty is the effective execution of whatever policies the board may adopt. Nor are business corporations the only organizations employing such a division of basic responsibilities. The presidents of many private colleges and universities and of other nongovernmental institutions stand in the same relation to the chairmen of their boards.

Fewer examples of such separation occur within government. Perhaps the most striking illustration is furnished in the municipal sphere by what ought to be called, for the sake of completeness, the mayor-council-manager plan. The theory behind this soundest of all forms of local government is plain. Policy leadership is the responsibility of the council, and particularly of its chairman, the mayor—whether he be chosen by the council or elected by the voters. The city manager's job is confined to advising with the mayor and council on matters requiring their decision and to administering the work program which they adopt. Other examples may be found in the field of public education. Insofar as underlying theory is concerned, the relations between local boards of education and superintendents of schools are like those prevailing under the council-manager plan. The same applies to the relations between state boards of education and the presidents, chancellors, and provosts of state colleges and universities.

One other aspect remains to be mentioned. In the more recent past, not a few governmental agencies—national, state, and local—have found it productive of good administration within their own organizations to distinguish consciously between policy concerns and management responsibilities. They have sought, in the words of Donald C. Stone, to create "a common focus for management facilities either in an administratively minded department head or in a general administrator working in close association with the policy leadership of the agency." Separation of responsibilities for policy initiative and general management offers many practical advantages. Yet the distinction between political head and administrative manager is usually sharper in name than it is in fact. The separation of these roles is successful only where the relationships between such officials are characterized by mutual confidence—confidence sustained through frequent conference and counsel. The practical working arrangements between the two elements will vary from jurisdiction to jurisdiction. The net result should be such a modification of the functional separation as to produce, in Bagehot's phrase, an "intimate detachment" between the two spheres—like that between the British minister and his permanent undersecretary.

Combination of responsibilities. Though bifurcation does occur, the general rule in government is combination of policy initiative and top management in a single official, the chief executive. But he must know how to cooperate with the legislature and respect its prerogatives if he is to head an effective government. This is the principal clue to the nature of the office of President, and of the offices of governor and mayor as well. Each serves simultaneously as political leader and administrative chief. The powers and prerogatives of their offices may be inadequate to the double task; yet they are supposed to be effective in both capacities. They are expected either to surmount the handicaps under which they have to labor or to contrive to reduce their ill effects.

Every president since John Adams has realized that no one could hope to be a successful leader of national policy if he did not first succeed in being the effective leader of his own political party. On the administrative side, every president—at least since Theodore Roosevelt—has likewise recognized the need for better managerial arrangements. In the states and cities, developments have been roughly parallel. Governors and mayors have long recognized the indispensability of organized support among the voters in order to be influential in making or changing public policy. Generally speaking, however, it has only been since the first practical tests of state administrative reorganization that governors have begun to be comparably effective as administrative chiefs. Though that reform movement came into its own with Governor Frank O. Lowden in Illinois in 1917, approximately a third of the states remain relatively untouched by it.[1] As for municipal chief executives, they have usually been ineffective as administrators until the city revised its charter and adopted the so-called strong-mayor form of government. Many American municipalities, par-

---

[1] See Lipson, Leslie M., *The American State Governor: From Figurehead to Leader*, Chicago: University of Chicago Press, 1939, and Ransone, Coleman B., Jr., *The Office of Governor in the United States*, University, Alabama: University of Alabama Press, 1956.

ticularly those with larger populations, have effected such charter revision. However, there remain hundreds upon hundreds of communities where the administrative lot of the municipal executive is not a happy one.[2]

2. Leadership and Authority

Cloak of legal power. Formally, the position of chief executive embodies tremendous responsibility and authority. But no one in such a position is likely to achieve more than indifferent success unless he conceives his job first of all in terms of opportunity for enduring service to the public. This is the mark of the great chief executive in democratic government: He looks upon the office as giving him for his term the noblest assignment within the power of the people—the privilege of leadership in action designed to promote the general welfare. The greatest of American presidents, governors, and mayors have not been content to do only what they had to do. Nor have they relied upon legal authority alone to achieve their goals. Although willing to use legal authority when obliged to do so, they have had deep convictions about the uses to which the power of government should be put. They have preferred to gain their ends through leadership rather than through the assertion of power.

Every public office requires a legal definition of its competence. Such definitions have their merits. They are valuable for establishing fields of jurisdiction among various officers. They are also indispensable for enabling the courts to decide cases involving the duty or discretion of an administrative official, on the one hand, and the right of a private citizen, on the other. But it is clear that at the top of the administrative hierarchy such legal delineations are insufficient to raise an official to the stature of a chief executive. Clothes do not make the man; neither do the vestments of power make a president. Legal authority a chief executive must have. However, unless it is in effect a confirmation of leadership already accepted or emerging, the chances are that it will profit him little.

Constitutions and charters invest a chief executive with the legal competence to recommend and veto legislation, appoint and dismiss subordinate officials, prepare and—upon legislative approval—execute budgets, represent the government at all manner of official functions, and direct the entire executive establishment. The placement of these several powers in his hands is obviously essential to the performance of his main duties, but it is far from being all that is essential. Legal powers are, so to speak, the executive's bones. Flesh and blood, mind and spirit, he must supply himself.

Personal qualifications. One of the things of mind and spirit the executive must bring to his job is strength and balance of personality. Without

---

[2] For a sound treatment of the executive function in city government, see Adrian, Charles R., *Governing Urban America: Structure, Politics, and Administration*, New York: McGraw-Hill, 1955.

this deeper authority latent within himself, the prospect of his developing vital relationships will be almost nil, in administration as well as in politics. For an administrative head, it is one thing to have the legal right to command; it is something quite different to have effective direction over an executive organization. The former is a matter of formal power. The latter is largely a matter of appeal and influence. It requires, first of all, evidence of interest, intelligence, and energy. Unless there be about the executive a single-mindedness that will enable him to generate and sustain a general concern for the fulfillment of the goals of his program, he cannot hope to assert the authority that signifies the true leader. If he does not care, no one will care; there will be no program. Let him beware at all times of being content merely to sit in the executive's chair; his job consists not of being but of doing. Only if he demonstrates by continuous interest that he has made the aims of the total enterprise his very own concern will he stand out as head of the organization.

Basic intelligence—as contrasted with great learning—is so indispensable that nothing more is needed here than the merest mention of it. No man willingly takes orders from someone who is plainly "hard of thinking," regardless of how eminent or exalted his position. The hardness may stem from deficiency of brain power, from set bias, or from infirmity of age; it makes no difference. There is no substitute for the ability to think.

Energy is another prime necessity. He could never be more than a nominal executive who, though showing steady interest and intelligence, was devoid of physical and nervous vigor. It is not surprising that presidents, premiers, and other top executives find their tasks a heavy drain upon their energies. That is an inescapable aspect of their work. There is point to the argument that a man's age and vigor have a direct bearing on his fitness for high executive office. Exceptions may be justified by exceptional facts; but, as a general rule, no one should be asked or expected to undertake arduous executive responsibilities beyond the age of 70. The risks to the public welfare are too great.

These qualities—interest, intelligence, and energy— are fundamental to strength of personality. But they must also be in balance. Unless the individual's traits are so combined that they enable him to win and hold the devotion of other men, he will have little chance of meeting the demands made on him. Others must be able to feel that they know him and can trust him, because he is the captain of their team. President Franklin D. Roosevelt epitomized the right point of view at his first inaugural: "For the trust reposed in me I will return the courage and the devotion that befit the time. I can do no less. . . . The people of the United States . . . have made me the present instrument of their wishes. In the spirit of the gift I take it."

Mark of leadership. More specifically, an executive must have that quality about his personality which enables him, without sacrificing integrity of purpose, to lubricate human relationships. It is this kind of influence that induces men to *act* on their big agreements rather than to *argue* over their little differences. It is this kind of influence that induces them to sustain enthusiasm for a general program even after it has become clear that they are not going to be able to "have things exactly their own way." The chief executive can indulge in high self-confidence only if his identification with the program of his government is so complete that those around him will accept that confidence as proof that "Together we can and will do it!" General Eisenhower rose to a nearly perfect identity of individuality and program during his "crusade in Europe." The seal of that perfection lay in his being quite as ready to take the blame when something went wrong as to accept the glory when victory crowned the efforts of his soldiers and his staff. His inability to achieve a like identity in leading his peacetime "crusade" as President may well serve for all students of administration as a reminder of how difficult a feat this is. To be truly effective, in Lyndall Urwick's words, "command must represent a common objective." Whether this is achieved depends primarily upon the spirit that emanates from the commander's personality.

Someone has defined leadership as the ability to make other men "feel two inches higher." The observation applies to administrative leadership as much as to any other kind. The greatest executives are always marked by generosity of attitude toward those under them, by a willingness to overstate rather than understate their subordinates' accomplishments.

One other basic element in administrative leadership remains to be mentioned. In some ways it is the most important of all. That is a talent for ideas, the ability to conceive solutions to current political, economic, and social problems which the public will approve or, at the least, can be persuaded to accept. In the final analysis, a chief executive succeeds or fails in the substantive policies he espouses—and if he espouses none, he is not a chief executive. No matter what other qualifications a man may possess, if he lacks the capacity for initiating concrete proposals to meet the urgent issues of his day, he has no warrant for seeking or accepting executive office. Nor is he likely to gain such office if he has to win in an election against someone who does have positive ideas to offer.

Political and administrative talent. Anybody can rant about the need for efficiency and economy in government. Every normally articulate citizen inveighs against unnecessary overlapping and duplication of governmental activities. No ordinarily alert official has yet been found who has denied the need for coordination and cooperation among agencies. But these are not policy issues. They are standards, and they are universally accepted. Up to now no Democrat has been caught alive who would admit that a Republican could be more firmly attached to such standards than he—or *vice versa*. And none ever will.

With respect to public policies, however, the situation is markedly different. Whether a chief executive is concerned about social issues and willing to take a stand on proposals for their solution is something the electorate can easily find out. It is impossible for him to get by with pretense or evasion, except temporarily. A man aspiring to elective executive office must be prepared to disparage the claims of the opposition candidate —and there may be times when this alone will "put him in." However, the fundamental thing the people want to know is not what the incumbent has done wrong but how the contender would do things differently.

In a purely administrative or managerial position, commitment to such goals as "economy and efficiency" is all that can be expected. But these mechanical or mathematical virtues, even embellished by platform technique, do not suffice to make a president or a governor. Nor can a chief executive worthy of the name be produced by synthetic composition—so much political leadership and so much executive ability. The assumption may have done him an injustice, but Thomas Dewey was handicapped as presidential candidate by the suspicion, widely entertained, that he was not a "natural." Few of his critics could deny that he appeared to have made a good record "as an administrator." But they were able to persuade the voters that that was all there was to him: he was simply an "efficiency machine." Be this as it may, the fact remains that over and above administrative capacity a chief executive must have some natural talent for political leadership. If he has the latter in abundance, it may compensate for deficiencies in the former, because soundness of policy generally eases administrative tasks. The rule does not apply with equal force in reverse, however, because there is no substitute for enlightened vision.

American presidents: Washington and Jefferson. From Washington to Eisenhower, the American presidency illustrates considerably varying types of executive leadership. Among the thirty-three men who have occupied the position, several stand out as administrators of extraordinary talent. Washington's signal success in launching the new government is traceable to his ability to take ideas from both Hamilton and Jefferson, weld them into a single program, and then enlist the aid of both men in its execution. The inferior of both Hamilton and Jefferson in originating plans and proposals, he was their superior in devising combinations of policy on which it was possible to reach agreement for action. What made Washington's leadership acceptable and effective, however, was not simply his intelligence at finding high common denominators. There were also his known competence in management and his proven personal disinterestedness. The secret of his achievement as President did not lie, of course, in the legal authority with which he was endowed by the Constitution. It lay in the confidence the public had learned to put in him because of the character of his leadership.

In analyzing the reasons for Jefferson's high stature as President, one is tempted to wonder what kind of record his rival Hamilton would have made. The answer lies in the fact that Hamilton was probably not electable. With all his brilliance, he had too little gift for compromise. An executive he could have been—and indeed a very great executive he was—but not a chief executive, sensitive to working relationships. Jefferson did not begin to equal Hamilton in administrative skill, but in the realm of political thinking he had a clear advantage over the scintillating New Yorker. Indeed among all the Presidents probably none accomplished so much with such slight administrative wherewithal as Jefferson. His record proves as does no other that in the highest office in American government, political ingenuity is far more important that administrative talent.

Jackson and Lincoln. President Jackson exhibited an executive personality profoundly different from that of any of his predecessors, and quite at variance, too, from that of any occupant of the White House since. Considering himself the spokesman of the hitherto more or less unenfranchised common man, and particularly of the rising West, he took office with the conviction that he had a mandate from the electorate to restore the government to the people. To him, this entailed beating back the growing concentration of financial power in private hands and preserving and strengthening the Union against all hazards. In his view, a president would be guilty of dereliction of duty if he held himself under no higher obligation than to furnish Congress with information on the state of the Union and to administer such laws as the legislature might adopt. He saw with exceptional clarity that under the American Constitution effective government depends mainly upon the chief executive. If the President failed to offer positive leadership, no one else could substitute for him.

Lincoln's genius, like Jefferson's, lay far more in the political than in the administrative realm. Where other men, abler and more experienced in governmental management, lost their heads and embraced proposals that could not possibly have united the nation, he devised a policy at once moderate, positive, and capable of evoking enthusiastic popular support: the limitation of slavery to those areas where it already existed and the preservation of the Union. It was his championship of these policies, attended as it was by unfailing steadiness, humility, and magnanimity, that earned for him his pre-eminent rank in the American hall of fame.

Creative policy versus economical administration. Time lends a perspective to appraisals of the administrative capacity of Washington, Jefferson, Jackson, and Lincoln which will be lacking for years to come in the case of those who have lived in the White House more recently. It is impossible to assess with equal accuracy the capacities and accomplishments of Cleveland, Theodore Roosevelt, Wilson, and Franklin D. Roosevelt, not to mention Truman and Eisenhower. Yet there is one thing that can be said of these later presidents quite as safely as of the earlier ones. They were distinguished far more for creative policy than for economical and efficient administration.

Nor does the rule work only one way. The national chief executives who are least well remembered are precisely those who lacked the impulse or the capacity to be imaginative about their office. They tended to look upon their powers in narrowly legal terms or seemed unable to conceive of any higher public service than that of reducing the tax rate. Buchanan, Grant, McKinley, Harding, and Coolidge rank among the lesser lights of the White House for one and the same reason. As they pursued no distinctive public policies, the nation has not been much interested in such economy or efficiency as they may be said to have achieved.

Business leaders. What has been said about the test of success for the chief executives of the nation is also borne out in the records of American business leadership. Captains of private enterprise, too, must rely on influence rather than on formal authority if they are to rise to the heights. In the nature of things, the object of business executives is to make money through the efficient production and sale of goods and services. Consequently, policy problems do not assume for them the breadth and proportions they necessarily do in the case of governmental chief executives. With this significant qualification, however, the conditions for executive success in government and business are much the same.

John D. Rockefeller, Andrew Carnegie, James J. Hill, Owen D. Young, Walter S. Gifford, and Alfred P. Sloan became great business executives because they were, first of all, leaders of men. The secret of their authority among their associates and subordinates lay in the continuous demonstration of their superiority in intelligence, in imagination, in shrewdness, in daring, and in personal magnetism—the very qualities recognized by their collaborators as most essential at the highest rung of the executive ladder. Admittedly, differences in volume of stock ownership, in family relationships, and in personal friendship all have a bearing on the selection of top officials in business corporations. At least among the larger firms, however, the basic criterion is usually capacity for leadership. Responsibility is likely to come to those who are most ready and anxious to accept it.

Governors and mayors. It is to be expected that the relationship between authority and leadership in the case of state and municipal chief executives should correspond very closely to that characteristic of the presidency. The great governors have invariably been the champions of the general welfare in response to the vital issues of their day; they have seldom been acclaimed as efficient administrators of established programs. It does not alter the fact that in some cases their most singular achievement has been to raise the whole tone and level of public administration. This has often been the necessary prerequisite to an attack upon emerging problems of basic policy.

La Follette of Wisconsin, Smith, Roosevelt, and Lehman of New York, Olson and Stassen of Minnesota, Arnall of Georgia, Warren of California, Stevenson of Illinois, Williams of Michigan, Ribicoff of Connecticut—

these may or may not be the greatest governors to have held office in the twentieth century. But they are among the elect. And in every instance, their reputation has turned on political leadership rather than on adminis-trative accomplishment.

Generally speaking, policy issues on the municipal level are relatively less important than those on the state level, and considerably less than on the national plane. Even so the prestige of a municipal chief executive also depends mainly on the kind of program he sponsors and the dynamic qualities of his personality. LaGuardia in New York City, Hoan in Mil-waukee, Seasongood in Cincinnati, Maverick in San Antonio, Wyatt in Louisville, and Dilworth in Philadelphia—none of these distinguished mayors has contented himself with being merely a faithful steward of "things as he found them." On the contrary, all have carried forward new programs supplementing or supplanting the old, programs that held the promise of making for better community life rather than merely more efficient administration.

3. External Relationships

Relations with the judiciary. The chief executive's relations with in-dividuals and groups outside the executive branch are bound to absorb much of his time and energy, regardless of whether the form of govern-ment be presidential or parliamentary. But in the United States, given the separation of powers and the traditions attendant upon it, such external relations can hardly fail to be of the keenest and most continuous concern to the head of the federal government's administrative machinery. Within the governmental framework itself his responsibilities are three. He must establish and maintain good relations with the legislature, with the judiciary, and—depending upon the circumstances—with other chief executives. It will be useful to look at each of these separately.

Let us begin with executive-judicial relationships, exactly because ordi-narily they pose no problems of consequence. Assuming that the measures a chief executive takes himself or proposes for legislative action raise no issues of constitutionality, he should have little difficulty in living in peace with the judiciary. Moreover, the president rarely encounters restrictive court review in the exercise of his own constitutional powers.[3] Prudent choice in his appointment of judges will naturally pay dividends, but opportunities to make such appointments may come infrequently, especially in the federal government.

However, as the epic battle of 1937 between Franklin D. Roosevelt and the Supreme Court demonstrated, a "strong man" in the presidency is apt not only to bring forward new policies but also for this very

---

[3] *Cf.* Schubert, Glendon A., Jr., *The Presidency in the Courts,* Minneapolis: Uni-versity of Minnesota Press, 1957. See also Rossiter, Clinton, *The American Presi-dency,* New York: Harcourt, Brace, 1956.

reason to run up against the latent conservatism of the judiciary. In such a situation, matters cannot easily be resolved through the President's appointive power, because vacancies on the bench may be slow to occur. There is, in fact, no constitutional mechanism readily available for attaining constructive adjustment under these conditions. The only remedy lies in the President's hold on popular support. Not even the Supreme Court can afford to stand between a resourceful national leader and the majority of the people.

Relations with the legislature. In his relations with the legislature, the chief executive faces a different situation. Both the legislative and executive branches have political functions to perform. Unless they can agree on the need for public action, government may simply have to mark time. And not merely that. Through its sanctions over policy proposals requiring statutory enactment, its control over the public purse, and its power of confirmation with respect to major appointments, the legislature can do much to aid or obstruct day-by-day administration. What this adds up to is that presidents, governors, and mayors must try to get along with their legislative assemblies as a continuous task. This is true despite the fact that the categorical separation of powers effected by the Constitution, together with the general tradition born of it, has encouraged each branch of government to be constantly sensitive about its prerogatives and its coordinate position.

The prospect of effective government under these circumstances depends upon several considerations, each of which the chief executive must exploit to full advantage. In the first place, he can capitalize on the fact that in the United States, notwithstanding the forces of pressure politics, there is a wide consensus on the principle of the priority of the public welfare over private interests. He must seek to formulate his recommendations for new legislation in terms of that consensus. Secondly, by virtue of his role as the leader of his party, he can appeal in the name of the party and its platform for support of his program from the members of the party in the legislative branch. Indeed, he may also win support from the other party, to compensate for the degree to which his own party fails him. In the third place, he can demonstrate the depth and sincerity of his desire for cooperation with the legislature by showing at all times a generous respect for its high place in the grand scheme of democracy, and by consulting freely with its leaders on all matters of mutual concern. Lastly, he can try, in a manner that avoids the appearance of organized pressure, to use the widespread popular interest attaching to his office. Thus he is able to generate among the people a climate of opinion that will dispose both branches of government toward a common approach in solving the problems of the day. "Fireside chats" and televised press conferences or addresses can exert an enormous influence, especially in combination with good hard bargaining behind the scenes.

Agency contacts with legislators. It has been noted previously that every major administrative agency has its own contacts with the legislature, either with a legislative committee or with individual members. Inevitably these cross connections have an important bearing on the way in which the chief executive gets along with the legislature as a whole. In the national government the contribution of agency-congressional relationships to the President's success in redeeming his campaign pledges and giving effect to his program can be considerable. Courtesies extended by administrative agencies to Senators and Representatives, including prompt supply of technical information and special attention to the needs of important constituents, can do much to create an active good will on the part of Congress toward the Administration as a whole.

On the other hand, these relations have another aspect, and one often grimly detrimental from the President's standpoint. Agency officials sometimes form understandings with members of Congress that almost amount to defensive alliances against the fulfillment of certain portions of the chief executive's program. Obviously no president can be indifferent to the evils of such a situation. Yet he may not be in a position to correct it with ease. For if the uncooperative agency official has strong backing "on the Hill" or from organized groups having the ear of influential elements in the legislature, he becomes virtually untouchable. The chief executive's only recourse is to try to outmaneuver or isolate the insubordinate subordinate. To this extent, administrative hierarchy may break down. Nor is the legislative majority better able to check its own entrenched intransigents in such cases.

Relations with other chief executives. When it comes to his relations with other heads of governments, the chief executive will find them light or burdensome depending largely on the level of action involved. The President has few responsibilities more engrossing than those arising in the conduct of foreign affairs. Increasingly, he finds that he must work with the heads of other national governments, particularly those with similar ideals and interests. Even when his foreign policy glides through clear waters, these relations are apt to absorb as much of his time and thought as those with all the state governors and municipal executives put together. There is probably no standard by which presidents and contenders for the presidency will be measured more sharply than their standing and influence, actual or potential, in the international sphere.

Governors and mayors are rarely confronted with issues as important as those faced by the President. Moreover, in the American tradition there are even fewer working contacts between governors and mayors than would be good for the public business. On the whole, a mayor's relations with other chief executives are likely to be confined to two kinds. First, he will attend conferences on mutual problems with the mayors of neighboring cities. Secondly, he will participate with other mayors in the activities of his state's league of municipalities and either the American Municipal Association or—in the case of the larger cities—the United States Conference of Mayors. As for the governors, their main dealings are with the governors of adjoining states and with the mayors of their state's largest cities. On matters other than party politics, the governer's contacts with the mayors of smaller cities or with the governors of more distant states are normally quite infrequent, except as the latter type of relationship develops under auspices of the Governors' Conference or the Council of State Governments.

Relations with political parties. Outside the structure of government proper, the problems of the chief executive fall again into several classes. In point of importance, party relationships probably rank first: his strength within his party and the party's strength lie at the very core of his effectiveness as chief executive. Both must be steadily cultivated. It therefore behooves him to counsel frequently with party leaders, to keep the party united and aggressive, and so to guide its fortunes that it may win and hold the favor of the voters.

He may count himself fortunate if without inordinate anguish of soul he can handle the distribution of public honors and political appointments in a way that serves these ends. The management of matters of this kind makes up a large segment of what may be called party business. Despite the help traditionally furnished by the party's national chairman, "the Chief" often finds a lot of his own time and energy absorbed in this way. He must also be available as principal speaker as well as for advice on questions of party finance or even on the times and places of party rallies, to say nothing of party conventions and their agenda. Meantime he must secure as much cooperation as possible from the other party—and from disaffected elements within his own.

Public opinion. Because of the basic importance of free communication in democratic government, the President's relations with the press are of peculiar significance, as are those of a governor or a mayor. Nothing is more essential to a chief executive's success than that he keep in touch with the people. Newspapers, magazines, the radio, television, and moving pictures make two-way contact possible every day in the week. An efficient and tactful press secretary will therefore rank among the most indispensable personal aides.

Even with the ablest assistance on this score, however, the President will be obliged to give personal attention to what publicity he wants and what political intelligence services he needs. In his direct use of the various media he will be wise to make the most of his particular gifts of expression and to hide his shortcomings. If the press and radio and Hollywood take a friendly line and he learns how to cooperate with them, they can do a great deal to build him up and keep him favorably in the public eye. Regardless of what history may record of him, here and now he will be what they say he is.

Interest groups. Interest groups pose a tough problem for every politician who dedicates himself to the common good, whether he be in the executive or the legislative branch. For ordinarily a special interest tends to assume something no chief executive mindful of his trust would grant—that what it wants for its own good will also be good for all the people. It is clear, however, that he cannot ignore organized interests. In the first place, it is of the essence of democracy that men should be free to work together in pursuing the interests they share. But it is equally essential that government subject the struggle for power among all interest groups to such regulation and control as is needed to safeguard the public welfare. A potent factor is the powerful influence interest groups often exert over how their members vote. Consequently, each party is anxious to win as much of their support as possible or at least to avoid their antagonism.

Business, labor, agriculture, veterans, civic organizations, and professional patriots probably constitute the principal interest groups that presidents and governors confront. Municipal chief executives see less of organized agriculture and more of neighborhood councils, social welfare organizations, and taxpayers' associations. Each of these groups makes up a part of the body politic, which the chief executive is to serve. The great public for which he likes to think he works all too often turns out to be nothing more than a loose composite of little or lesser publics. To generate a sense of community is a critical part of his job. Only thus can the various groups be induced to keep their selfish impulses under reasonable restraint and so to make a positive contribution to the proper functioning of government. But if he fails in this regard, whether as a result of personal weakness or of circumstances beyond his power, he will learn at first hand what havoc pressure politics may cause.

4. Internal Direction and Control

Administrative planning and direction. The preceding section, treating of external relationships, dealt principally with the political phases of the chief executive's life. In this and the succeeding section, we shall focus on the functions he performs and the means he employs within the executive branch itself, the presidency being taken as a prototype.

As administrator in chief, the President's first task is to decide what consensus he may assume or evolve between himself and the legislature, what are to be the main policies of his Administration, and by what basic programs he will work for their attainment. Such anticipations are subject to change; yet he needs some point of departure. Next, he must arrange for plans to be developed. This begins with the analysis of specific policy issues and moves forward to an outline of alternative methods of solution. He must also give thought to an organizational structure fitting the logic of his policies and programs. All of this requires a reliable supporting cast.

One of the President's principal responsibilities is to select the men and women who as agency heads will fill the major executive positions within his organization. They in turn will have to be depended upon to nominate their deputies and subordinates. The selection and appointment of key officers are, however, still in the category of preliminaries. All of these officials have to be directed to their tasks. It falls to the chief executive to convey to them a clear conception of their missions.

He must require annually of each agency a systematic work program, supported by estimates of expenditures. In order to develop a balanced program for the executive branch as a whole, he needs to integrate the various agency programs into a single comprehensive plan of operations as well as finance. This is known as the annual budget. No document he submits to the legislature is of greater importance. Upon its presentation to Congress in justification of requests for funds, it is scrutinized by the Appropriations Committee of each chamber. Its subsequent adoption by the legislature, usually with various modifications, transforms it into a means of control, whereby the President can assure himself that the work program of the government will be accomplished as specified.

Executive coordination and administrative reporting. Even with reasonably clear policies and plans, a satisfactory scheme of organization, able top personnel, alert direction in the individual agencies, and careful programming and scheduling of administrative activities, there is no foolproof guarantee that everything and everybody will mesh nicely so that each agency can be left to run by itself. One of the President's most complicated functions is that of coordinating the efforts and operations of the entire executive branch. The budget itself is a chief instrument of coordination. Through it the President may even attain a modicum of concerted action on the part of the regulatory commissions and boards which, except for the power of appointment, are not under his command. But the budget cannot be expected to overcome singlehandedly the tradition of institutional individualism throughout the executive branch. Hence it should be easy to understand that effective coordination of administrative operations is a heavy responsibility and a never-ending one.

Finally, the President must constantly keep his eyes on the total administrative picture. He must make himself a central point for the flow of reporting. The budget provides some basis for the systematic gathering and analysis of information. Yet the President needs other channels of intelligence as well. He must be able to find out whatever he needs to know in order to report effectively to Congress, the press, or the public. This calls for special arrangements to provide him with the kind and quantity of information he wants whenever he wants it.

Constitutional supports. These being the President's main administrative functions, what specific powers and devices does he rely upon to perform them? His prerogative in the field of policy initiative derives from that clause in article II of the Constitution which provides that he "shall from time to time give to the Congress information of the state of the Union, and recommend to their consideration such measures as he shall judge necessary and expedient." In proposing a line of public policy, no chief executive would want to act on the spur of the moment. He naturally welcomes ideas and suggestions, formal and informal, from a wide variety of sources both inside and outside the government. These, however, have to be sifted and evaluated, and a final selection has to be made. Most of the sifting and appraising can be entrusted to the President's staff organization in his Executive Office. Often, however, he will need further help in "making up his mind." He may put the matter to the Cabinet or consult with individual members. He may call in the leaders of Congress. Or he may seek the confidential counsel of a Colonel House, a Harry Hopkins, or a George Humphrey. There is perhaps undue fluidity in this pattern, but without a more highly developed Cabinet this is to be expected. By and large, it works quite effectively.

No provision in the Constitution specifically requires or authorizes the President in so many words to "plan" his general program. Yet his need and right to do so would appear to be implied in the constitutional provision that "he shall take care that the laws be faithfully executed," and in another clause appearing earlier in article II that "he may require the opinion, in writing, of the principal officer in each of the executive departments, upon any subject relating to the duties of their respective offices." Even without these clauses, however, the necessity for him to anticipate the future would remain. He would have to prepare for it even though his authority might derive from "the law of the situation" [4] rather than the law of the Constitution.

With respect to administrative organization, the President's powers are limited. The administrative agencies which form the executive branch no less than the so-called independent regulatory commissions and boards are the creations of Congress. None of them can be broken up or recombined in different ways or merged with other agencies except by statutory authorization. There is a strong case to be made for investing the President with permanent authority to adapt administrative structure to governmental needs, but so far no such continuing authority has ever been granted. Specifically circumscribed grants of power were made in the Reorganization Acts of 1939, 1945, and 1949. But they were all temporary, though representing by prolongation something like an uninterrupted chain in practical effect. Only in time of war is the President likely to obtain extensive authority of this kind, such as in the two War Powers Acts of World War II and the Overman Act of World War I.

---

[4] For the insight embodied in this phrase, students of administration are indebted to a brilliant—and practical—woman, Mary Parker Follett. See her "Individualism in a Planned Society," in Metcalf, Henry C., and Urwick, L., eds., *Dynamic Administration,* New York: Harper, 1942.

Power of direction. The power of appointment and—by implication—of removal is one of the most telling the chief executive possesses. Article II of the Constitution provides that he

> ...shall nominate, and by and with the advice and consent of the Senate, shall appoint ambassadors, other public ministers and consuls, judges of the Supreme Court, and all other officers of the United States, whose appointments are not herein otherwise provided for, and which shall be established by law: but the Congress may by law vest the appointment of such inferior officers, as they think proper, in the President alone, in the courts of law, or in the heads of departments.

The removal power, held by the Supreme Court to be corollary to the appointing power,[5] continues to be extensive, but was definitely qualified in the Humphrey case [6] with respect to members of regulatory commissions and boards. In the words of Edward S. Corwin: "As to agents of his own powers, the President's removal power is illimitable; as to agents of Congress' constitutional powers, Congress may confine it to removal for cause...."

In the exercise of his directive function over the administrative agencies —but not the independent regulatory boards and commissions—the chief executive is supported by several provisions of the Constitution. The very first sentence of article II says: "The executive power shall be vested in a President of the United States of America." That broad grant would perhaps suffice of itself to empower the President to issue such orders as he finds necessary or expedient in directing the administrative operations of the executive branch. In addition, however, certain other provisions are relevant. One is the express stipulation in section 2 of the same article that he "shall be commander in chief of the Army and Navy of the United States, and of the militia of the several states, when called into the actual service of the United States." Of greater importance is the more general clause, already cited, that he "shall take care that the laws be faithfully executed."

But uncontested authority to direct the executive branch does not insure informed and competent administration. The problem is how to make it effective. One of the first needs is a system of administrative communication that will flash up to the chief executive the institutional intelligence he requires from all sectors of the organization and simultaneously guarantee that his own orders and his general line of approach will get through without distortion or delay to those in the lower echelons.

Statutory implementation. Work programming and budgeting are basic to sound administration, but the President has had the machinery to perform these functions effectively only since 1921. The Budget and Accounting Act of that year furnished him specialized staff assistance in a Bureau of the Budget operating primarily by reliance on his own directive power.[7] The

---

[5] Myers v. United States, 272 U.S. 52, 118 (1926).

[6] 295 U.S. 602 (1935). See also Chapter 10, "Independent Regulatory Agencies."

[7] For the background and aims of this legislation, see Morstein Marx, Fritz, "The

administrative histories of the states suggest the same lesson: that until a government adopts the principle of the executive budget—and preferably with the item veto that is lacking in the federal government—it is futile to expect control of administration. Adoption of such a system will not automatically bring an administrative millennium. Without it, however, the gates to progress are only halfway open.

Like the directive power, of which it may be said to be a derivative, the power to coordinate is general in character. It rests fundamentally upon the same clauses in the Constitution as the directive power. Beyond that it is made explicit in the Budget and Accounting Act and other statutes, in which Congress has reaffirmed the President's obligation to unify the operations of the various administrative agencies it has created. One notable example is the Employment Act of 1946, under which the President is to avail himself of a Council of Economic Advisers to convey to the legislature ways and means of safeguarding the health of the national economy through concerted governmental action.

As the central source of information about the national administrative system, the chief executive is the logical official to report on it to Congress and the public. The legislature may require such reports in the same statutes by which it authorizes or directs him to launch new undertakings, such as the mutual security program after World War II. The annual message on the State of the Union and the yearly budget message serve a similar reporting purpose.

By far the larger body of data and proposals emerges, however, through administrative reporting within the executive branch. This is the method —and the only one—by which the President can hope to keep himself abreast of what is going on. He must have a means of finding out what is being done in his name at the administrative front-lines by the hundreds of thousands of federal employees deployed all over the country, not to mention American outposts abroad. Without staff work to harness this vast flow of information, it could easily turn into an unmanageable torrent. Facts, figures, and suggestions must be transformed continuously and systematically into information that will be serviceable to the chief executive for control purposes.

5. Arms of Management

Need for assistance to the President. "The President needs help." So wrote the President's Committee on Administrative Management headed by Louis Brownlow in its report of 1937. In assigning functions and responsibilities to the executive branch, the Constitution and the statutes simply ordain that "the President" shall do thus and so. Obviously no man,

Bureau of the Budget: Its Evolution and Present Role," *American Political Science Review*, 1945, Vol. 39, p. 653 *ff.*, 869 *ff.*

whatever his genius, could personally perform the many and heavy tasks which the chief executive is thus obliged to take on. It is to him in his institutional capacity—to his office—that the assignments are made; and, except where Congress has itself fixed the means, he is expected, within the bounds of statutory authority and funds appropriated, to recruit, organize, and direct whatever personnel may be required for the work to be accomplished.

Here we have, if not the biggest, clearly one of the biggest management jobs in the world. How does the President handle it? What aides and arrangements does he need to help him get his work done? The great line departments carry the main burden of translating federal policies into operating programs; but what are the means by which the President makes sure that they know of *his* intentions and can satisfy himself that they are succeeding in their tasks?

It was the general conclusion of the President's Committee on Administrative Management that: (1) the President needed administrative assistants, in addition to his personal secretaries; (2) in the tasks of executive management, he should be bolstered by three main "arms," one for planning, one for budgeting, and one for personnel; (3) with such internal arrangements as would meet the special problems presented by regulatory commissions or boards and government corporations, all line agencies should be consolidated into twelve departments, each headed by a secretary of Cabinet rank; and (4) there should be a reordering of the functions of the General Accounting Office to insure two things—that, on the one hand, an end be made to auditing prior to spending, with its tendency to keep the wheels of administration from turning, and that, on the other, the executive branch be made more truly accountable to Congress by a more searching and more constructive post-audit.

Executive Office of the President. How fully House and Senate would have accepted these recommendations if President Roosevelt had not followed their submission with his provocative message on Supreme Court reform, no one can say. The Reorganization Act of 1939 incorporated only part of the proposed measures. The President was granted six administrative assistants in an enlarged White House Office. Far more important, a foundation was laid for the establishment of the Executive Office of the President, perhaps the most significant step forward in federal administration since the Budget and Accounting Act of 1921. The Executive Office was made up of a National Resources Planning Board, the Bureau of the Budget, a Liaison Office for Personnel Management, an Office of Government Reports, and an Office for Emergency Management.[8]

---

[8] As its name suggests but does not fully explain, this office is normally dormant. It serves its purpose in the main by providing an ever-ready legal and administrative framework within which temporary emergency agencies can be created when required, provided that funds are made available for such agencies by Congress.

The last subsequently afforded the President a convenient legal base for inaugurating many of the great wartime control agencies.

Notwithstanding the abolition in 1943 of the National Resources Planning Board by a surprise move of Congress and the subsequent administrative evaporation of the Office of Government Reports, the Executive Office of the President has continued to serve its essential purposes as originally contemplated. Its principal component, the Bureau of the Budget, has gone far to give the President highly diversified staff assistance. Under the Employment Act of 1946, the vacant spot in the field of planning was filled by a Council of Economic Advisers. No less significant is the addition in 1947 of the National Security Council and other machinery for the planning of resources mobilization.

Realigning the executive branch. As to changes in departmental structure, those adopted under the several Reorganization Acts in the form of presidential reorganization plans are by no means insignificant. Leaving aside the point that authority to reorganize administrative structure is by nature a continuing necessity and should therefore not be granted for a limited time only, how can the chief executive best use such power? If he wants to make it serve general needs, he will try to accomplish four main goals.

First, he will weigh opportunities for regrouping and consolidation among and within line or operating agencies to effect better service, avoid duplication, and reduce the span of control for himself and for his "team," the agency heads. It has even been argued that the number of major departments can and should be smaller than it is. Experience suggests, however, that no change quite so drastic would win acceptance.[9] Moreover, too much concentration might in turn overtax the departmental leadership.

Centralized services. Second, the President may want to re-examine alternative arrangements for the conduct of central staff and auxiliary services such as budgeting, personnel, purchasing, accounting, printing, and the like. Here the aim would be to gain for the federal government whatever advantages can be derived from centralized staff and housekeeping activities, while leaving in each department adequate means as well as full authority and responsibility for performing its functions.

Establishment of the General Services Administration in 1949 is a case in point. But it is perhaps too much to expect an agency of this kind to reach its fullest usefulness without considerable experimentation and a flexible approach. Similarly, much has happened to eliminate impediments to sound management which once were latent in the authority of the General Accounting Office to intervene unproductively in administrative operations. There is every reason for insisting on a careful audit of all records, after administrative transactions have been completed. But there is no reason for the kind of supervision the Comptroller General contrived to

---

[9] See Chapter 6, "Planning."

exert over federal administration in the thirties. Congress needs an auditor general for the final examination and certification of accounts. His usefulness is greatly increased when he not only submits a comprehensive annual report but also provides a current appraisal of the fiscal operations and general performance of the executive branch as a whole.

Staff arms for the President. Third, the President must consider time and again the adequacy of his own staff assistance. The theoretical premises of the Executive Office of the President have proved sound. Increasingly since 1939, the Bureau of the Budget has grown into that great arm of overhead management and program analysis which was the intent of the Budget and Accounting Act. In Arthur Macmahon's descriptive phrase, the bureau has become the "embodiment of the presidency" in federal administration.[10] Through its staff offices—Budget Review, Management and Organization, Legislative Reference, Accounting, and Statistical Standards—and its control divisions—Military, International, Commerce and Finance, Labor and Welfare, and Resources and Civil Works—the chief executive obtains continuing assistance in the preparation and execution of the annual budget; in the achievement of better organization and management throughout the executive branch; in the clearance and coordination of agency proposals for legislation or report to Congress on pending bills; in the improvement of accounting systems and financial management in all agencies; in the coordination of federal statistical services; and in the analysis of governmentwide or departmental programs, of issues or implications of fiscal policy, and of the progress of administrative operation.

The situation is different with regard to forward-looking policy planning. Harried as the President tends to be by immediate concerns, he requires first-rate advice if he is to think wisely—or think at all—about the state of the Union a decade or a generation hence, instead of a year or two. There was provision for that kind of help as long as the National Resources Planning Board was still in existence. Since 1943, when Congress cut off its appropriations, it has been necessary for the President to rely on catch-as-catch-can planning wherever he could get it, even if only in bits, as by temporary commissions of inquiry. The Council of Economic Advisers and the National Security Council furnish help in their respective realms, but neither in the way nor to the degree represented formerly by the National Resources Planning Board.

The case for a director of personnel to give the President expert counsel and, as civil service administrator, to direct the operations of the present Civil Service Commission, has continued to be persuasive. The arrangement of having a Presidential Assistant for Personnel Management within the Executive Office has been quite serviceable. Yet it remains a makeshift arrangement, and has not always stayed put. The President is as much

---

10 Macmahon, Arthur W., "The Future Organizational Pattern of the Executive Branch," *American Political Science Review,* 1944, Vol. 38, p. 1182.

in need of having his own director of personnel as any other chief executive. Few problems lie closer to the heart of administration than that of staffing—of attracting, recruiting, placing, and developing competent employees so that they can produce at top capacity. The solution of this problem should grow out of simplest design. It should not have to depend upon the circumstances of the President's relations with the Civil Service Commission.

Policy coordination. The fourth goal of administrative reorganization involves the development of machinery for policy coordination, particularly in domestic affairs—though the possibility of distinguishing foreign from domestic becomes steadily more difficult. The Director of War Mobilization and Reconversion toward the end of World War II was often referred to as "Assistant President" or "Coordinator of Domestic Affairs." The President needs a regular arrangement to coordinate domestic policy, much as the Secretary of State oversees foreign affairs. By way of improvisation and circumstance, this was the service Sherman Adams sought to perform for President Eisenhower until circumstances destroyed his usefulness—policy coordination rather than the managerial coordination provided by the head of the Bureau of the Budget.

An alternative might be for the President to make greater use of his Cabinet. Ample delegation of authority and responsibility by the President to the heads of the line establishments and integration of his own staff contribute greatly to his success in administration. However, the affairs and concerns of the departmental system ramify so widely and intertwine so perplexingly that the chief executive must try to arrange for the main agencies to share their problems with him through discussion and decision in the Cabinet. As a collegial body, the Cabinet can serve as a forum for debating policy recommendations and can aid the President in formulating his program. Cabinet committees may be assigned the task of finding a common approach to major issues and of devising a pattern of combined operations for resolving them effectively. Cabinet meetings may include key men from the Executive Office.

In the past, it has been one of the distinctive facts about the federal government that the Cabinet lives in a kind of dormant state as a device for making policy. In recent years, President Eisenhower has overcome such dormancy by personal effort. But it will be a main task for every President to define by his own choice what role the Cabinet might play as an instrument of policy coordination.

Chapter 9 •

The Departmental System

1. General Features

Purpose of departmentalization. We speak of departments when dealing with parts of a whole. The whole may be a unified territory; thus, the French *départements* are areas into which the country is divided for governmental purposes. Or the whole may be the total structure of political organization; thus, Americans often refer to the three main powers of government, set apart from one another under the Constitution, as the legislative, executive, and judicial departments. Or the whole may be the machinery of administration combined in the executive branch; thus, practical minds have long recognized the need for some division of labor in the administrative system by grouping more or less related functions under integrated agencies, which in many instances are formally designated as departments. It is with departmentalization in this last sense that we shall here be concerned.

Departmentalization, being in essence a division of labor, is intended to make more effective rather than split up the whole within which it is applied. When organizations grow to the point where direction and control can no longer be exercised in face-to-face contact between the leader and the rank and file, intermediate stages of leadership must be supplied. Such arrangements, it is true, mark out the component parts within the whole and draw dividing lines internally. But in this way it is made possible to keep the organization in formation and to attain efficient use of specialized skills. In determining the scope of responsibility on each intermediate stage or at each point of subdivision, consideration must be given to two elementary propositions. First, it is essential to achieve the greatest measure of operating unity within every subdivision. Second, it is necessary to establish sound working relationships among all subdivisions.

This is in the main a matter of economy of control. Like top leadership itself, subleadership is hopelessly overburdened when compelled to pull together scattered fragments of different activities. The span within which effective control can be accomplished is inevitably limited. In addition, however, it is easy to see that the demands on subleadership are not always of the same character. In large-scale organizations, public and private, the higher intermediate stages usually require special capacity for ranging over broader fields and for marshaling far-flung activities in close relationship to the aims of the organization as a whole. On the other hand, subleadership on the lower intermediate stages down to the first-line supervisor increasingly calls for technical competence with respect to specific operations. Even the first-line supervisor, however, is in a very practical sense an agent of the leader of the entire organization, assisting him in attaining the ends of the organization at large.

The way in which the whole is reinforced through identification of its parts and through their interrelations provides the general framework of administrative organization. The characteristic forms of hierarchy—lines of command, levels of responsibility, and channels of administrative communication—find their proper place within this framework. Departmentalization represents the highest intermediate stage of leadership in relation to the chief executive, but it is only one stage. Level upon level, division of labor and delegation of authority progress downward throughout the departmental system. Nevertheless, the first order of division, the departmental pattern, is of decisive importance in giving shape to the bulk of the lower structure. That is why departmentalization, however academic much of the discussion about it may sound, is far from being an academic matter.

Structure of the departmental system. In one form or another, and under varying labels, departmentalization occurs in all organized enterprise except the smallest kind. Some large American companies, for instance, maintain more than twenty departments, such as production, traffic, and sales on the one hand; and engineering, research, economics, and public relations on the other. But the term is often left without a distinct meaning, being sometimes even applied to subdivisions of other departments.[1] In the field of state government, assuming the benefits of an executive reorganization, the governor may have below him a consolidated administrative system consisting of most of the following departments: administration, finance and taxation, highways and public works, conservation, agriculture, insurance and banking, labor, education, public health, and institutions and public welfare.[2] By contrast, the mayor of a big city may exercise authority, wholly or in part, over a larger number of departments, including perhaps fire, health, hospital, public welfare, institutions, building, city planning, street laying-out, public buildings, public works, transit, park, market,

---

[1] See National Industrial Conference Board, *Company Organization Charts,* Studies In Personnel Policy, No. 139, New York, September 1953; Dale, Ernest, *Planning and Developing the Company Organization Structure,* American Management Association, Research Report No. 20, New York, 1952.

[2] See Council of State Governments, *Reorganizing State Government: A Report on Administrative Management in the States and a Review of Recent Trends in Reorganization,* Chicago, 1950; Buck, A. E., *The Reorganization of State Governments in the United States,* New York: Columbia University Press, 1938.

weights and measures, and library and art.[3] Again, a village manager may do well with only a few departments—say, police, fire, health, public works, and water and electricity.

The number of federal agencies officially designated as executive departments in the United States is no more than ten. Listed on the basis of seniority, they are: State and, next, Treasury (both since 1789); Defense (1949), with its three service departments, Army (formerly War: 1789), Navy (1798), and Air Force (1947); Justice (1870) and Post Office (1872), both with early forerunners; Interior (1849); Agriculture (1862), Commerce (1903), and Labor (1913); and finally, Health, Education, and Welfare (1953).[4]

Considering the actual scope of federal activities, it may look at first glance like a marvelous accomplishment that the chief executive of the nation can direct these activities through so few departments—less than a third of the number of departments that cluster about the Prime Minister in England. But the first glance is sadly deceptive. Historically, the United States started out well enough. The Founding Fathers, with a remarkably acute sense of administration, took great care in drawing the outlines of a unified executive branch of simple structure. A total of only nine executive establishments required the attention of George Washington (1790), and there were but two more under Lincoln (1864). However, significant departures from this simple design occurred during the period after the Civil War, especially with the creation of establishments independent of the President save mainly for his appointing power.

A landmark in this new development was the creation of the Interstate Commerce Commission (1887), a regulatory body politically well-nigh uncontrolled in the exercise of its control functions, initially over the railroads and eventually over the whole national transportation system, except aviation. Through the years, a battery of similar agencies came forth on this general model. If one adds the emergence of other kinds of administrative agencies, including government corporations and separate authorities, the picture confronting the chief executive becomes one of diversity and diffusion. How can he perform his constitutional duties as head of the administrative organization, asked the President's Committee on Administrative Management in 1937, when he must deal directly with one hundred federal agencies of one kind or another?[5]

---

[3] As one illustration, mention may be made of City of Boston Finance Commission, *Final Report of the Administrative Survey,* February 1, 1950.

[4] General reference may be made in this context to the *United States Government Organization Manual,* an official handbook which appears in up-to-date editions at short intervals and which may be obtained from the Superintendent of Documents, Government Printing Office, Washington 25, D.C.

[5] The findings and recommendations of the President's Committee on Administrative Management and its staff, published as *Report with Special Studies,* Washington: Government Printing Office, 1937, represent an important source for the study of federal administration, as does the voluminous output of the first and second (Hoover)

The Reorganization Act of 1939 and its successors of 1945 and 1949 authorized the President, subject to statutory limitations and a congressional veto of disapproval in each instance, to bring about improvements in the structure of the executive branch. The total effect of legislative as well as executive measures over twenty years has been a reduction in the number of federal agencies to about sixty. This may be regarded as a striking achievement, especially considering the intervention of World War II and the war in Korea. From another angle, however, an executive branch consisting of some sixty agencies may yet seem to pose stupendous problems of direction, coordination, and general management.

Much the same situation prevails in American state and local governments. Independent boards and commissions, together with other unattached authorities of comparable status, in many jurisdictions compete with that part of the departmental machinery which is controlled by the governor or mayor. The chairman of a municipal police commission, for example, may exercise greater power than the nominal executive head of the city. Moreover, most state and local governments are still enmeshed in the consequences of the long ballot of old, which was based on the philosophy that public offices should be filled by election. Elective officials such as treasurer and comptroller, holding office by statutory or even constitutional sanction, can be thorns in the flesh of the state or local chief executive. Since the beginning of this century, measurable progress has been made toward raising governors and mayors to true responsibility for the executive branch, and the continuous spread of the council-manager plan of municipal government has worked in the same direction. However, an integrated system of administration is even now the exception rather than the rule, despite many instances of state and local reorganization.

Factors in departmentalization. Failure to evolve a fully satisfactory executive structure should not be seized upon as evidence of government floundering. There is no doubt that departmentalization is fraught with complexities.[6] These are in part technical, in part political. From a tech-

---

Commissions on Organization of the Executive Branch of the Government (Washington: Government Printing Office, 1949 and 1953).

[6] A cross section of recent writings on organization is represented by the following works: Brech, Edward F. L., *Organization: The Framework of Management,* London: Longmans, Green, 1957; Weiss, Robert S., *Process of Organization,* Ann Arbor: Survey Research Center, Institute of Social Research, University of Michigan, Publication No. 17, 1956; Argyris, Chris, *Personality and Organization: The Conflict between System and the Individual,* New York: Harper, 1957; Mooney, James D., *The Principles of Organization,* rev. ed., New York: Harper, 1947; Meyer, Poul, *Administrative Organization: A Comparative Study of the Organisation of Public Administration,* London: Stevens, 1957; Selznick, Philip, *Leadership in Administration: A Sociological Interpretation,* Evanston, Ill.: Row, Peterson, 1957; Jones, Manley H., *Executive Decision-Making,* Homewood, Ill.: R. D. Irwin, 1957; Davis, John A., *Regional Organization in the Social Security Administration: A Case Study,* New York: Columbia University Press, 1950; Martin, Roscoe, *Grass Roots,* University, Ala.: University of Alabama Press, 1957. The difficulties inherent in departmentalization found early recognition in American organization theory. See Gulick, Luther, "Notes on the Theory of Organization," in Gulick, Luther, and Urwick, L., eds.,

nical point of view, it is difficult to determine with assurance the proper basis of departmental organization in the individual instance. Should it be the major purpose to be served or the main function to be exercised, such as national defense, social welfare, and urban development? Or should it be the nature of the process or the primary skill involved in it, such as engineering, licensing, and data-processing? Or should it be the group of people to be given special service, such as farmers, veterans, and small businessmen? Or, finally, should it be the territory or area on which activities would center, such as New England, the Missouri valley, and downstate Illinois? Speculating on the feasibility of each such basis, one is bound to discover soon that its strict and exclusive application leads simultaneously to two undesirable consequences. First, activities that belong together as components of a concrete administrative product—however it may be defined—are torn apart at various points and in varying ways. Second, if reasonable concessions are made to a combination of activities in what might be termed an organic manner and with an eye to the administrative product, activities of the same kind appear in conjunction with others at many different places in the executive branch.

Classification of conceivable bases of departmental organization, being essentially governed by convenience, is therefore merely a useful starting point for trying to piece together the jigsaw puzzle. How to utilize the classification for practical ends is quite another matter. Admitting its inability to lay down a few simple rules of the game, the Brookings Institution, advising a congressional committee more than twenty years ago, suggested a cautiously eclectic approach:

> No single factor can be decisive throughout the entire organization. One factor may help us to decide at one point; elsewhere, another factor may be more helpful. At every point one determinant must be balanced against another. For some functions and some agencies there may be no one best course of action. A choice may be presented between alternatives, one as desirable as the other.[7]

This does not sound very encouraging, but it contains more than a grain of truth. A study of departmentalization, like all administrative analysis, requires careful penetration into the total situation in which the

<hr>

Papers on the Science of Administration, p. 3 *ff.,* New York: Institute of Public Administration, 1937; Brookings Institution, Report to the Byrd Committee on *Organization of the Executive Branch of the National Government,* Senate Report No. 1275, 75th Cong., 1st Sess., Washington: Government Printing Office, 1937; Wallace, Schuyler C., *Federal Departmentalization: A Critique of Theories of Organization,* New York: Columbia University Press, 1941. By comparison, the first (Hoover) Commission on Organization of the Executive Branch of the Government went rather far in stressing the concept of major purpose as the basis of departmental organization. See also Chapter 7, "Concepts of Organization." On the problems surrounding departmental leadership on the federal level, see Bernstein, Marver H., *The Job of the Federal Executive,* Washington: Brookings Institution, 1958; David, Paul T., and Pollock, Ross, *Executives for Government,* Washington: Brookings Institution, 1957.

7 *Op. cit.* in note 6 above, p. 43.

problem to be solved is lodged. Technical knowledge, even when tested in the hard school of practical experience, is of little avail unless its application is preceded by painstaking and skilful diagnosis, not only of the ill to be remedied, but also of all the factors that bear upon both the ill and the possible remedies.

Aside from its technical difficulties, departmentalization is also beset by institutional pathology as well as by political issues. No sooner has a department been established than it will become engrossed in itself. However extraordinary the conglomeration of activities packed into it, it will presently associate itself with each of them in unfaltering fondness. Talk about shifting any of these activities to some other department—as subsequent events may indicate to be the better logic—and heated argument breaks loose. Then too, the departmental mentality naturally inclines toward taking an expansive view of the department's mandate. As the department grows bigger, it inevitably begins to impinge upon related activities carried on by other departments. Again, there will be a lot of fussing and fuming when lines of demarcation must be redrawn. Each time the department will muster persuasive reasons for keeping what it has "always" had, or what "belongs to it"—at least by implication; and these contentions are likely to evoke a vigorous echo among the loyal clientele of pressure groups that have lined up on the department's ramparts. Usually the noise alone is enough to intimidate the advocates of disinterested change.

Moreover, executive reorganization is a somewhat obscure art and more than a little suspect among the entrenched interests inside and outside the departmental system. Suspicion begets hostility and resistance. Within the departments, institutional resistance may be deliberate, but it may arise also from the inertia of settled form. The cumulative effect has been one of inordinate immobility of departmental structure. Looking at this structure, we may be reminded of "monsters with great defensive power developed at the expense of movement and intellect," as Pendleton Herring once aptly put it.[8]

---

[8] "Executive-Legislative Responsibilities," *American Political Science Review*, 1944, Vol. 38, p. 1161. On the general subject of executive reorganization, see (in addition to the references above in note 6) Hobbs, Edward H., *Executive Reorganization in the National Government*, University, Miss.: University of Mississippi, 1953; Emmerich, Herbert, *Essays on Federal Reorganization*, University, Ala.: University of Alabama Press, 1950; Morstein Marx, Fritz, "Federal Executive Reorganization Reexamined; A Symposium," *American Political Science Review*, 1946. Vol. 40, p. 1124 *ff.*, and 1947, Vol. 41, p. 48 *ff.* (contributors: Wayne Coy, Joseph P. Harris, Don K. Price, Lloyd M. Short, Robert M. LaFollette, Jr., and Avery Leiserson); President's Advisory Committee on Management, *Report to the President*, Washington, December 1952 (reprinted in *Public Administration Review*, 1953, Vol. 13, p. 38 *ff.*); Temple University, *Survey of Federal Reorganization*, Philadelphia, 1953, 2 vols.; Meriam, Lewis, and Schmeckebier, Laurence F., *Reorganization of the National Government*, Washington: Brookings Institution, 1939; Graves, W. Brooke, comp., *Reorganization of the Executive Branch of the Government of the United States: A Compilation of Basic Information and Significant Documents, 1912-1947*, Washington: Library of Congress, Legislative Reference Service, Public Affairs Bulletin, 1949. See also above note 5.

In the face of such "monsters," the feeble voice of organizational common sense is none too effective. Exceptional circumstances must come to the fore in order to provide the psychological moment for thoroughgoing functional realignment. Circumstances of this kind are relatively rare. But they are frequent enough in the sweep of decades to warrant continuous organizational planning by a central staff agency, such as the Bureau of the Budget in the Executive Office of the President. Continuous planning is necessary because changing national needs and emerging reorientation of policy usually affect the departmental system to a greater or lesser extent. Here, as elsewhere, preparedness pays. When the day for constructive action arrives, the whole opportunity may hinge on the immediate availability of previously developed proposals for reorganization.

In the absence of such exceptional occasions for overhauling the executive branch as a whole, the reorganization plans of the President after World War II have brought about less spectacular improvements in two directions. First, agency heads have gained greater freedom to reorganize the internal structure of the machinery under their direction. Second, the administrative role of most of the chairmen of independent regulatory commissions and boards has been strengthened, without changing the collegial form of reaching political decisions.

Undirected growth. The many difficulties that surround departmentalization account in large measure for the fact that the structure of the executive branch in the federal government has been traditionally the product of "undirected growth," in Leonard D. White's descriptive phrase. To put it differently, rarely if ever have proponents of reform tried to project existing and emerging governmental activities in terms of a comprehensive organizational plan. On the other hand, judging by past experience with state and local reorganization, one must admit that a neatly conceived general formula yields only limited results, unless its application is accompanied by a change of institutional atmosphere. This would have to include a corresponding strengthening of departmental management, a better personnel system, and greater legislative self-restraint in tampering with the departmental scheme on partisan impulse. Reorganization has often been abused as a political football.

The alliance between institutional inertia, vested interests, and political partisanship throws an enormous weight of support behind the departmental *status quo*. To be sure, stability of organization is an asset, because for greatest efficiency everyone must know his way within the organization as a matter of habit. Indeed, such habit born of repetition or indoctrination may minimize the effects even of grossly deformed organization. However, stability becomes a vice when it is maintained at the price of structural simplicity and functional balance. It shows itself as a particularly serious vice when one considers the usual time lag between established governmental form and the dynamic quality of social and economic life. On

practical grounds, therefore, the best solution would be a permanent legislative-executive arrangement under which appropriate organizational adjustments and modifications in the executive branch could be made in harmony
with changing needs. The legislature would provide the general frame of
reference, and the chief executive would take action within the scope of
his authorization. This is what Herbert Hoover, then Secretary of Commerce, proposed in 1924 before the Joint Congressional Committee on
Reorganization of the Administrative Branch.

Reorganization procedure. The Reorganization Act of 1939 and those
of 1945 and 1949—though granting the President only temporary authority
—followed the line of Hoover's reasoning. Under those acts, reorganization plans formulated by the President became effective by lying for a
specified period before Congress, which reserved to itself the right of disapproval.[9] Until the prolongation act of September 4, 1957, such disapproval had to have reasonably firm legislative support. The new version,
for the first time, requires no more than a mere plurality of either chamber,
which could be a handful of members on the floor.

Generally speaking, the reorganization plan procedure has proved very
successful. A large number of reorganization plans presented by the President have become effective; few were disapproved by Congress. It must
be added, however, that the prospect of congressional disapproval naturally
limits the range of issues the President would consider it practical to try
to tackle.

Because departmentalization aims to increase the effectiveness of the
whole rather than to produce segments, the number of main divisions is
important especially from the angle of the chief executive. His physical
span of control is naturally limited, though differing with different personalities. For each personality the limit is easily reached, especially if
we keep in mind that a smaller number of agencies reporting to the President in turn may mean too wide a span of control for the agency heads,
with the effect of shifting the problem to their own level. Moreover, fewer
departments may mean a larger number of other agencies. Inflexible restriction of the number of departments is therefore no adequate answer,
whether such restriction be imposed constitutionally, as it has been in
several states, or by statute, as it was in the Reorganization Act of 1939,
primarily as a check on the President's range of structural choice.

Quasi-departments. Although no new "departments" were to be created
under the Reorganization Act of 1939, three quasi-departments came into
being: the Federal Security Agency, the Federal Works Agency, and the
Federal Loan Agency. Each absorbed into itself a multitude of administrative establishments, many of which had formerly not known a common

---

[9] For an early appraisal of this novel procedure see Millett, John D., and Rogers,
Lindsay, "The Legislative Veto and the Reorganization Act of 1939," *Public Administration Review*, 1941, Vol. 1, p. 176 *ff.* See also the literature cited above in note 8.

denominator. One may doubt very much whether the grouping of quite diversified lending activities under a quasi-department—and hence without close relationship to broader substantive programs—was a sound move. The fact remains, however, that the creation of these three new agencies brought welcome relief to the overburdened chief executive. Internal integration within each new agency proceeded slowly. It is hardly surprising that initially there was more similarity to a sort of holding company than to a department.

Obviously, the assumed common denominator does not spring from mere pronouncement. It must be fostered systematically over a longer period before it translates itself into a point of view commonly shared throughout the agency. In general, formation of quasi-departments is an ingenious device for providing the executive branch with an experimental fringe. Activity groupings may thus be tried out in practice, and full departmental status may be bought by demonstration of performance. The Federal Loan Agency did not last long, and the functions of the Federal Works Agency after ten years fell to the General Services Administration (1949); but the Federal Security Agency eventually became the Department of Health, Education, and Welfare, by way of a reorganization plan (1953). Another quasi-department is the Housing and Home Finance Agency, an essentially permanent establishment originally created as the National Housing Agency, which resulted from a merger of several federal programs under the First War Powers Act of 1941 and thus required further action for its continued effectiveness; that action, again, took the form of a reorganization plan (1947).

2. Interdepartmental Coordination

Staff establishments. Interdepartmental coordination is a task at once too big and too important to be left to any one official, the chief executive not excluded. But part of the task may be entrusted to officers or offices that serve the chief executive in a staff capacity and exercise authority essentially in his name and by his direction. This is not a novel idea. Provision for such assistance arose as an essential factor from the demand for strengthened executive responsibility which had dominated the governmental reform movement in the United States since the first decade of the twentieth century, especially in state and local government. It was expressed most frequently in the centralization of expenditure control under a budget agency attached to the office of the governor, mayor, or city manager.

A milestone was set in 1917 when Illinois adopted such a budget system. Municipalities followed the same path. The Budget and Accounting Act of 1921 carried the new formula into the federal government. By giving the President a special agency, the Bureau of the Budget, to help him prepare the budget as the annual work plan of the government for consideration and adoption by Congress, this act reversed the former trend toward departmental self-determination and independence. In shaping the agency estimates of appropriations into a general program, the Bureau of the Budget could correlate the activities undertaken throughout the executive branch, thus bringing about interdepartmental coordination as well as improvement of administrative management.

With the establishment in 1939 of the President's Executive Office, the Bureau of the Budget, as part of it, developed into one of the "principal management arms of the Government."[10] Through alert use of its diversified professional staff, it was able to furnish practical help at numerous points in the conversion of the administrative system from peacetime conditions to wartime necessities, and back again to a half-peace after World War II. In addition to direct assistance to individual agencies, the Budget Bureau was successful in spreading knowledge of tested methods and practices. The broad range of its reviewing and consulting functions supplied the bureau with unusual opportunities for spotting undetected weaknesses of organization and management.

Simultaneously, the Budget Bureau kept its eyes on the attainment of concerted action by federal agencies in both administrative planning and synchronized execution. This entailed continuing working contacts with planning staffs and operating officials in various parts of the executive branch. In addition to the leverage obtained through such working contacts, the bureau exercised its budgetary authority for coordinating purposes. The same end was furthered in the bureau's review, for conformity with the President's program, of agency proposals for legislation or executive orders, and of agency reports to congressional committees on pending bills. Another means of coordination presented itself in the bureau's responsibility, under the Federal Reports Act of 1942, for approving agency plans for statistical inquiries addressed to the public. In all of its functions, moreover, the bureau benefits from its relationships with the other parts of the Executive Office of the President, especially the White House Office, containing the President's personal staff; the Council of Economic Advisers, created by the Employment Act of 1946; and the National Security Council, a statutory Cabinet committee established by the National Security Act of 1947.

Professional staff organization, grouped about the head of the executive branch, has also become fairly common in state and local governments.

---

[10] This is the language of Executive Order No. 8248 of September 8, 1939, which may be called the original charter of the President's Executive Office. See on this staff organization Hobbs, Edward H., *Behind the President: A Study of Executive Office Agencies,* Washington: Public Affairs Press, 1954; Morstein Marx, Fritz, *The President and His Staff Services,* Public Administration Service, No. 98, Chicago, 1947. A highly informative symposium on the Executive Office of the President in its original form by Louis Brownlow and others was published in *Public Administration Review,* 1941, Vol. 1, p. 101 *ff.* Comparable developments in state government are described by Ransone, Coleman B., *The Office of Governor in the United States,* University, Ala.: University of Alabama Press, 1956.

This is true especially of the larger municipalities and the more populous states. Abroad, too, similar developments have become noticeable, although under parliamentary government such staff elements have usually been attached to the office of the Prime Minister.

Special coordinating agencies. Compared with the implicit and broadly inclusive coordinating mandate of the Bureau of the Budget, the innovations of World War II for pulling together governmental activities in order to organize the productive resources of the country took the form of explicit and specific grants of authority. The evolving pattern, defined by executive orders issued by the President under his wartime powers, found its sharpest expression in the tasks assigned to the Office of War Mobilization (1943). The head of this office, often called Assistant President, was charged with the duty "to unify the activities of the federal agencies . . . engaged in or concerned with production, procurement, distribution, or transportation of military or civilian supplies, materials, or products." He was also to "resolve or determine controversies between such agencies," unless these were to be settled on a lower level. In exercising his functions, he was entitled to "issue such directives on policy or operations to the federal agencies . . . as may be necessary to carry out the programs developed, the policies established, and the decisions made," and to call for progress reports from any of the agencies subject to his directives. In basic conception, this pattern was reaffirmed in the War Mobilization and Reconversion Act of 1944, in which the renamed Office of War Mobilization and Reconversion emerged as a statutory establishment.[11]

Although it stood at the apex of the special coordinating machinery for wartime use, the Office of War Mobilization still had to share its lofty heights with others, primarily the representatives of the military services, including the Joint Chiefs of Staff, and spokesmen of foreign policy, especially the Secretary of State. Despite being a makeshift arrangement, the special coordinating machinery was able to take care of countless questions that normally would have plagued the chief executive without really requiring his consideration. Delegation of some of his authority to the "right man" proved to be the answer to the riddle of how to keep the President in the role of "the boss" without demanding a week's time of each of his hours.

This sounds quite simple. But the specific character of such delegations had to be worked out experimentally. Men had to be found to try their hand at tentative assignments, never knowing at the start how they would

---

[11] The progress of demobilization planning has been traced by Key, V. O., "The Reconversion Phase of Demobilization," *American Political Science Review*, 1944, Vol. 38, p. 1137 *ff.* On the principal agency, see Somers, Herman M., *Presidential Agency: The Office of War Mobilization and Reconversion*, Cambridge, Mass.: Harvard University Press, 1950. See also Macmahon, Arthur W., "The Future Organizational Pattern of the Executive Branch," *American Political Science Review*, 1944, Vol. 38, p. 1179 *ff.*, and the writings cited above in note 10.

get along, with so many unknown factors. And prestige had to be built up for these men so that operating officials would actually take orders without thoughts of appeal or evasion. All of this called for more than mouth-filling clauses written into executive orders. Certainly the institutional gap between the Office of War Mobilization and the Bureau of the Budget would have caused difficulties save for generally satisfactory working relationships, insisted upon by President Roosevelt himself. Yet, despite these problems, the United States fell back upon essentially the same pattern in the emergency of the Korean conflict. It should be added, however, that the Office of Defense Mobilization, surviving afterward as part of the Executive Office of the President, has been reduced to the tasks typical of a peacetime agency for resources mobilization and civil defense.

Role of the Cabinet. Nothing has been said thus far about the Cabinet as a coordinating mechanism, and for good reasons. It is customary to point out that in the United States, in contrast with Great Britain, the assembly of department heads as a consultative body is devoid of consitutional standing, in the states as well as in the federal government. Nor is the matter different in our municipalities. Where governor's or mayor's councils exist, they are generally special advisory establishments for particular purposes. They are not essential bodies bearing anything like collective responsibility for the conduct of the executive branch.

Whereas in both World War I and World War II the British War Cabinet served as the foremost device for maintaining the unity of the departmental system, in the United States the accelerated pace of critical times seems to bring about almost the opposite result. Although Woodrow Wilson found it convenient to meet regularly with the key figures of his war administration, working relations among various agencies rarely dominated the agenda. Franklin D. Roosevelt took no inspiration from Wilson's example and managed to keep the circle of his close wartime advisers for the most part in fairly constant motion. The parallel with the fluidity of the "brain trust" of the thirties suggests itself, including the rate of turnover. The Cabinet's contribution was reduced to the fact that it continued to meet, mainly as the President's captive audience, without ever becoming a central organ of either administration or policy.

One reason for the difference between British and American practice in this respect deserves special mention. In England, the Cabinet draws much benefit for the effective conduct of its business from a small but high-powered secretariat. In its developed form, this secretariat is the institutional offspring of World War I. It examines all matters for the docket, except last-minute items of great urgency, to see that they are cleared to the point where the issue can be disposed of by a decision.

In the United States, notwithstanding the existence of the Executive Office of the President, comparable arrangements have been slow to take form. During the presidency of Franklin D. Roosevelt, Cabinet meetings tended to revolve around summaries of developments presented by the President himself, with a sprinkling of departmental items brought up by the individual secretaries, but rarely of true interest to the Cabinet as a whole. Under President Truman, preparation of Cabinet meetings was given increased attention. President Eisenhower, long familiar with military staff work, lent his personal support not only to a more genuinely consultative role of the Cabinet but also to the establishment of an orderly flow of Cabinet papers, including the maintenance of a record of action. Although not meant to be a point of substantive scrutiny, the new office of Cabinet Secretary could be regarded as a link to the secretariat-like staff functions available from the several parts of the President's Executive Office. No doubt, durable vitalization of the Cabinet is hardly in the offing as long as the secretariat remains underdeveloped.

Use of interdepartmental committees. Before we leave the subject of interdepartmental coordination, a word on the use of special committees is in order. Such committees combining representatives of several agencies for joint deliberation of matters of common interest or wider ramification are nothing new. We find illustrations on all three levels of government— federal, state, and local. Shortly after its establishment, the Bureau of the Budget, for example, began to surround itself with a growing array of interdepartmental committees which, under varying names, set out to achieve better management. Collectively, they came to be known as the Federal Coordinating Service, under a chief coordinator who in turn reported to the director of the bureau. The Coordinating Service was supported by a regional organization of its own, which maintained close connections with the more than 300 federal business associations composed of federal field officials in as many cities throughout the land. In the early twenties, these interdepartmental arrangements showed considerable drive in the improvement of governmental business practices. But in the course of time the effort spent itself, and the Coordinating Service died of stagnation. It was formally abolished in 1933. Atrophy also weakened the remaining federal business associations, although a number have remained active.

Many interdepartmental committees, however, continued to function in the executive branch. One notable example was the Central Statistical Board, later transferred to the President's Executive Office and now performing its coordinating tasks as the Office of Statistical Standards in the Bureau of the Budget. Although an accurate count is made difficult because of the varying degrees of formality in the creation of interagency committees and comparable working groups, the total number in the federal government runs to several hundred. Of these, only a few are Cabinet committees or deal with matters of equal governmentwide significance.

With all that, it cannot be said that there is a comprehensively interlocking committee system, built upon objective standards of need. Nor should one expect too much from it if there were such a committee system. In the nature of things, interdepartmental committees seldom feel a directing push from above. They function on condition of agreement, and may deteriorate into trading posts where stubborn parties bicker for their own advantages. Apparently, such committees work best on the basis of specific terms of reference, with a membership picked for sufficient authority or technical knowledge to ease mutual commitment, and under alert and vigorous leadership. When these conditions prevail, interdepartmental committees may repay many times the administrative effort invested in them.[12]

Avenues of progress. In the perspective of interdepartmental coordination, the departmental system shows itself as a massive conglomeration that does not readily respond to the reins held by the chief executive. Administrative agencies are apt to become personifications of a purpose anchored in legislative enactments and guarded by interests that regard themselves as the lawful beneficiaries of that purpose. The result is reluctance toward wholehearted acceptance of executive control. Centrifugal tendencies are therefore innate in the departmental structure. A concert of action is attainable only through a common service attitude displayed by the career element or through resourceful assertion of direction from the top.

Realistically speaking, when common service attitudes are not solidified, coordinative effort must play the role of a counterpressure. It is never supreme, but it may go far toward accomplishing a relatively high degree of general orientation. Organization charts of the executive branch tend to display reassuringly straight lines of command and responsibility. In certain ways, however, it might be more appropriate to think of a feudal pattern of higher and lower fiefs in which the vassals are sometimes torn between conflicting loyalties, and where designation of rank is often a very misleading index of actual power and influence.

On the national level, the general organization of the executive branch in the United States must be responsive to three needs. First, to strengthen top coordination in planning as well as in execution, it is necessary to decrease the exorbitant strain on the chief executive by providing for preliminary stages of synthesis through consolidation of agencies or of planning machinery or through stronger machinery for interdepartmental cooperation. This need is particularly acute in such fields as national defense, foreign affairs, economic stability, and industrial peace. Second, as soon as one thinks of the implications of organizational regrouping, the question of the independent regulatory commissions and boards presents itself. Independence from the chief executive, together with the scattering of regulatory assignments among such agencies, does not accord with the need for dealing

---

[12] For the earlier chapters of federal experience in this field, see Reynolds, Mary T., *Interdepartmental Committees in the National Administration,* New York: Columbia University Press, 1939.

with the economy on the basis of unified policies. And third, an imaginative and flexible approach is needed to bring about integrated staff work within the Executive Office of the President, with full utilization of the contributions made by agency staffs all down the line.

3. The Secretary's Business

External affairs. In the government of the United States, the title of secretary is confined to the heads of eight of the ten executive departments; the remaining two department heads are designated as Attorney General and as Postmaster General. The heads of other agencies bear such designations as administrator, director, and chairman (who in important matters must defer to the commission or board over which he presides). However, in this discussion of the secretary's business we shall apply the term generically, as encompassing the tasks of the governmental executive on the level of agency head. It should be mentioned at the same time that agencies differ enormously among themselves in size of organization, importance of responsibility, and volume of public resonance—from the supercolossal Department of Defense to the relatively tiny Smithsonian Institution, devoted to the "increase and diffusion of knowledge among men." Moreover, certain agencies regard themselves as "legislative agencies," such as the General Accounting Office. Again, although most agencies are permanent establishments, some are of temporary character. Such temporary agencies come forth in greater number during national emergencies— economic depressions as well as wars. However they may differ in durability, most of them are very much like regular agencies. Their heads face about the same working conditions and tribulations.

Like the chief executive himself, the governmental executive on the level of agency head must cope with two main categories of business: external matters and internal matters. Both categories compete for his attention. He cannot safely neglect the one for the other. In this respect, however, the governmental executive finds himself in a position not entirely different from that occupied by the executive in private enterprise. To be sure, the governmental executive, being always visible to the public, moving about in a "goldfish bowl," is more heavily burdened with external matters. His business seems to be that of everybody else; and if his department happens to be in the limelight, he may spend mountains of time as witness before congressional committees, in White House conferences, and with the press. But private management has recently become very much aware of the necessity of being alert to general public reactions as well as to those of its customers, stockholders, and employees. Ever since the late Ivy Lee made himself the father of a new profession by "humanizing" the Pennsylvania Railroad and the senior Rockefeller, the art of public relations has enjoyed high rating among the external concerns of business executives.

With all that, when there is talk of the executive function in the technical sense, the weight of this function is usually assumed to rest in the internal realm, in the direction of an administrative organization toward accomplishment of its purposes. By comparison, external business is treated as if it were auxiliary to the executive function, providing for the surrounding conditions under which this function—indeed, the total task of the organization —can best be carried out. Such a distinction, however, is artificial. As a matter of fact, one can hardly draw a precise borderline between external and internal aspects. Quite apart from questions of administrative policy where public repercussions are often a crucial factor, even seemingly innocent details of day-by-day management have an alarming capacity for catching unexpected attention outside the agency's four walls. Most problems that come before the governmental executive are potentially the sort of thing likely to stir up public debate, and require at least a second thought from this angle.

Living in a goldfish bowl. Fortunately, the large majority of items passing across the desk of the governmental executive fail to attract outside notice. But he can never be sure in advance. Newsmen have their peculiar pipelines. Congressmen fish up a great many interesting things about regulations, instructions, and orders which agency field officials bring to bear upon constituents "back home." Grilling may be merciless when the time comes around for committee hearings on the agency's budgetary estimates, or on legislative proposals advanced by it, to say nothing about the curiosity of investigating committees. Of course, public wakefulness is not only necessary in a democracy but also a most desirable stimulant of agency action in the general interest. Yet the governmental executive frequently has a tough time trying to do anything without offending some organized group or running up against the highly personal views of a powerful figure in the legislature.

Because of the burden of external matters, the governmental executive must be something of a politician, at least to the point of appreciating politicians and gaining their confidence. He needs to cultivate contacts with those active in the arena of politics, especially if he was borrowed from the world of business. His political friends are valuable sources of counsel on matters of agency strategy and tactics. They can be instrumental in promoting the public reputation of the governmental executive as a "crack administrator," even if his professional management staffs will never cease to shake their heads in privacy. Friends good and true, in the legislature and in interest organizations, are also able to carry the ball for him when the game becomes fast.

The management requirements of the service state are such as to discourage the use of executive offices in the administrative system as political plums. Competence—at least of a sort—has become increasingly a minimum qualification. On the other hand, a temporary tour of duty with Uncle

Sam does not produce an experienced administrator. Whatever the background of the governmental executive, he cannot for any length of time relax his vigilance over his agency's public relations. This requires administrative arrangements as well as much hard work on his part in mingling socially with the right crowd and in building good will. Nor should we forget his equally exacting chore of maintaining himself close to the chief executive and those who have his ear—members of the "kitchen cabinet," White House staff, and perhaps also their ladies.

Finally, there are the agency head's colleagues at the helm of other agencies. Some of them may have sharply competitive instincts. Others may demonstrate personal antagonism. But rare is the agency that can live by itself, without cooperation from other agencies. It would be very bold to presuppose the existence of wholehearted cooperation among all members of the executive family, however vigorous the references to "team work." In the development of cooperation, the way in which the governmental executive personally gets along with his brethren is a matter of great importance.

Character of executive function. Turning to the executive function itself, we may describe its core in brevity as direction and control—the former in the sense of providing for the right kind of action, and the latter looking toward the attainment of accountability for the execution of policy. These two terms embrace a variety of implied and interrelated functions. Direction entails planning, coordination, and programming—even research. Control involves organization, supervision, documentation, and reporting. Other functions extend into both spheres. Budgeting, for instance, is simultaneously a tool of planning and a basis of accountability. Personnel administration also serves both direction and control.

However one might group the ingredients of the executive function, no grouping can dispose of the plain fact that the governmental executive himself operates in a relatively small circle. In other words, in exercising the executive function he is at the pole from which his actions radiate into his agency. In planning his actions and in securing compliance throughout the agency, he must necessarily rely on many aides, who thus act as extensions of the executive function. Because human beings are anything but robots, these aides perform their tasks, not as inanimate cogs, but as individuals who exert measurable influences upon one another, and also upon the governmental executive himself. This makes the latter a more resourceful and better-informed chief. But it is at the same time a control and a limitation placed upon him.

Classes of executive aides. The aides who share in the exercise of the executive function fall into fairly distinct classes. They may be divided broadly into political and professional officers. Typically, undersecretaries, assistant secretaries, and special assistants are political appointees, though today they rarely owe their positions simply to obligations of patronage.

Indeed, sometimes these political officers have risen from the career ranks of the departments; and the still experimental position of Administrative Assistant Secretary, provided in certain federal departments, is intended to be a career position. The professional element is mostly supplied through the classified civil service. In the federal government, the majority of bureau chiefs or heads of staff and auxiliary functions like budgeting have reached their posts from below; this would not be true of many state and local governments.

Most of the federal bureaus carry on activities of a line character—that is, they administer functions that directly touch the public. But one should never trust official nomenclature. An outstanding example of a bureau serving in a staff capacity is the Bureau of Labor Statistics in the Labor Department. Many other staff units are known as offices or divisions. Such staff units—for planning, management, budget, statistics, personnel—contribute to the infusion of professional thinking into the institutional environment in which the agency head spends his days.

Attaining an institutional product. The governmental executive thus enjoys the advantage of having at his call not only various types of aides but also a profitable blend of judgments—political and professional, staff and line, general and special. If he is alert in securing the proper mixture for each occasion, he will rarely make a fool of himself. However, the proper mixture cannot be found in any book of recipes. The crux of the executive function lies therefore in the disciplined collaboration of all the aides who enter into the exercise of direction and control.

In an agency that has settled down to its business and has become a going concern, such collaboration is likely to arise without requiring constant prodding from the executive head. Notwithstanding personal animosities and incompatibilities of one kind or another, the individuals concerned may come to adjust themselves to a pattern familiar to all. Each learns the modes of thought of the others, including their idiosyncrasies and their blow-up points. As this process continues, the governmental executive is able increasingly to restrict himself to feeding his aides fresh ideas and to getting conclusions hammered out for practical application. It is in this sense that some students of management have spoken of the executive as the catalyst or as the ratifier of staff judgment. This is quite different from the naive conception of the titan who roars orders.

Departmental leadership, then, calls for much more than a chief who thinks of himself as a ruler and "gets things going." He cannot whip subordinates into doing well. He cannot overrule them blindly. He has no way of preventing his orders from being bent and twisted in the process of execution by operating officials who say they "didn't understand them." In widening the horizon of his organization, in holding it to its main goals, in welding its resources together, in straightening out internal and external difficulties, the governmental executive shows himself a true leader by being mindful of the human factor. The more he succeeds in persuading, the less will he be driven to theatrical gestures of authority. In the long run, his accomplishments will not stand up if they fail to live in the minds and attitudes of his subordinates. This means that he may have to accept, at least temporarily, the veto of his key officials. Nor can he push ahead in too many directions at once. He must have considerable patience in making his influence felt. Only thus can he educate his organization to think and act on his terms. Only thus can he give real force to his leadership.

4. The Bureau Pattern

Special concerns versus general purposes. Exercise of the executive function employs many individuals besides the agency head himself. Despite such relief as may be achieved through distribution of responsibilities among officials sharing in the application of directive power or bolstering the directive power by staff work, the agency head is still heavily burdened. Generally speaking, he alone is able to attend to the necessary contacts with the chief executive, the legislative leaders, and his colleagues in the departmental system. He alone is in a position ultimately to reconcile political answerability for the actions of his agency with vigorous pursuit of agency programs. He alone can undertake to keep fresh in all minds a unified conception of purpose and approach.

Faced with these prime duties, he would invite failure and defeat if he allowed his energies to be dissipated in details and trivialities. Of course, small things are often more important than they seem to be at first glance, especially if they have a political twist. In trying to shun small things, the governmental executive therefore cannot afford to dispose of sage discrimination. He must develop an eye for the significant detail. Yet he should normally stick to his proper level, without reaching down into the operating machinery time and again, perhaps even personally rewriting a proposed instruction he finds unsatisfactory. If he does not stay on his level, he is likely not only to give inadequate time to his main role but also to befuddle his supporting cast and throw working relationships on lower levels out of gear.

In confining himself generally to his own level, the governmental executive would have little ease of mind if he could not be reasonably sure of the caliber, loyalty, and thought processes of his key subordinates. This again underscores one of his principal obligations—that of establishing close *rapport* with the subleadership of his organization so that his attitude on the larger issues can become active on a broad scale. Subordinates can directly handle many issues when they know of his general attitude. They can acquire a pretty dependable sense of differentiation in determining what matters should go up to him and what matters they can settle in their spheres.

It is difficult specifically to spell out such differentiation in writing, but in the working style of a well-directed agency the differentiation is usually quite precise to all concerned. Equally important is the willingness of the governmental executive to make the most of his associates by handing them things he cannot accomplish without assistance. He is the chief conductor of a concert of specialists; as such he needs only his score, a baton, and the eyes of his orchestra. When problems come up, he should promptly turn them over to his trained hands for a first analysis.

Such smooth interplay of individuals is most likely when the top command of an agency, down to the assistant secretaries and their personal aides, does not suffer from too frequent turnover and appreciates the contribution of the career service. In important ways these two matters are linked together. When it is hard to draw the departmental leadership from other walks of life; when tours of duty are consequently rather short; when there is no reserve of experienced political executives to fall back upon— under these conditions departmental direction will inevitably suffer. So will the institutional relations between the political leadership in the agencies and the career element.

Centrifugal pull. Most of the staff and auxiliary services aiding the agency head are appendages to his own office, perhaps combined under a career Administrative Assistant Secretary. But the operating branches, traditionally organized as bureaus or their equivalent, are one further step removed. Each—in its divisions, sections, units, and field establishments— may control many hundreds and even thousands of employees. And the number of such bureaus within one agency may run to a dozen. The sheer bulk of these operating branches, absorbed in their particular business, means for the agency's center—the secretary's level—an enormous centrifugal pull, or a constant "downward drag." As one thoughtful former undersecretary has remarked, "throughout my stay in Washington I have been impressed with the fact of too great separation on the part of the bureaus from the departments." [13]

This separation is not simply overcome by placing groups of bureaus in charge of assistant secretaries or coordinating directors. Organizational arrangements, review procedures, and personal exertion are needed to provide the strong counterpressure that is required in moving the bureaus into closer association and harmony and in "converting matters that come from the special bureau pyramids into the general." [14] Nor can such efforts be expected to yield results automatically. They supply stepping stones that lead to varying degrees of functional integration insofar as the responsible officials can be induced to make use of them.

Bureau intransigence. As departments are prone to struggle for their jurisdictional prerogatives and find inconspicuous ways of defying or evad-

---

[13] Appleby, Paul H., in an interesting exchange of letters with Professor Arnold Brecht on departmental organization, published in *Public Administration Review,* 1942, Vol. 2, p. 63.
[14] *Ibid.,* p. 66.

ing central control, so bureaus within departments prefer to be "left alone" by the departmental high command. To a degree, this tendency is inherent and ever present. It is frequently reinforced by bureau self-sufficiency, both in squatting on a special function and in holding hands with a specific clientele. The result may be institutional intransigence paired with subservience to interest demands coming from the outside. The one is as troublesome to the agency head as the other.

Here, as in the sphere of the chief executive, we can notice distinctly the unintended consequences of the historic growth of administrative organization in the government of the United States. The administrative body first grew to full size in its extremities, then began to develop its head. In their relative proportions, hands and feet—the operating extremities—are oversized, and the control center of the nervous system is still too weak. To change the metaphor, in too many instances the relationship between the bureaus and the secretary's office resemble the figurative tail wagging the dog.

Weight of professionalization on bureau level. The genesis of the federal administrative system is also reflected in a related fact. The staff resources for policy advice and management that are directly available to the agency head are not only younger and weaker than most of the operating bureaus; they are also more heavily weighted with politically congenial "outsiders"— compared with the civil service element.[15] Thus general management and control, as applied to the entire department, have to contend with a greater measure of professionalization on the subordinate operating levels. The answer here would be a fuller recognition of the career idea in the top ranges of the administrative hierarchy, without denying the agency head an appropriate number of political advisers and assistants in his entourage.

In Germany, for instance, where the career principle for the higher service emerged more than two and a half centuries ago, the central departments have traditionally operated as very small establishments, with the operating machinery organized as separate entities under departmental policy guidance. The department head exercised his authority essentially through the permanent undersecretary, who had under him some three to five divisions, most of which were composed of less than a dozen higher civil servants, not counting supporting personnel. These civil servants— principals, as their counterpart is called in British administrative parlance —looked after their special fields, in which each was "expected to be the foremost expert of the country, at least so far as it relates to government." [16]

---

[15] A valuable source of information is Macmahon, Arthur W., and Millett, John D., *Federal Administrators,* New York: Columbia University Press, 1939. See also Hensel, H. Struve, and Millett, John D., *Departmental Management in Federal Administration,* Washington, (first) Commission on the Organization of the Executive Branch of the Government (Hoover Commission), Task Force Report, 1949.

[16] Brecht, Arnold, and Glaser, Comstock, *The Art and Technique of Administration in German Ministries,* Cambridge: Harvard University Press, 1940, p. 25. It is pertinent to observe that in the United States, as a rule, federal departments have

The principals thus were the links between the department and the separate subordinate bureaus under it. Dealing with career men like himself on the bureau level, the individual principal kept the bureaus under his jurisdiction in touch with departmental policy and conversely received all necessary information from them. At first glance, this may appear to be a still more marked separation of the bureaus from the departments. Actually, conversion of business from the special bureau context to the general departmental context was more easily attained through a small but highly skilled top organization composed of experienced civil servants.

Reaffirming unity of purpose. Although his bureaus may have assertive individualities of their own, it should not be inferred that the agency head in the United States is helpless in the face of subtle obstinacy. His staff services are capable of acting for him at many points of the departmental organization in the combined roles of prompters, mediators, missionaries, and watchdogs. The departmental budget officer, for example, can be extremely useful in keeping operating bureaus in line with the general program of the agency head. Nor need the pressure for synthesis come exclusively from the top. Interbureau committees may be utilized to provide gentle compulsion for the operating services to take account of a broader conception than that of their own cherished microcosm. Consultative methods, systematically applied, can contribute substantially to the formation of what may well be called the departmental mind. Regular staff conferences, bringing together responsible officials on various levels of the departmental pyramid and from different bureaus, offer another device of coordination; the staff conference has yielded tangible benefits where it has found thoughtful sponsorship and intelligent support.

To be sure, forms of administrative structure and management, though experience may favor one over another, are never better than the living substance they are to serve. This living substance is the departmental "manpower"—men and women who together represent humanity in all of its embodiments. That they have passed entrance examinations is perhaps the least significant thing about them. Much more important, in the competition of personal motives, is their conviction of service and their adjustment to the discipline of working together for an end above personal gain. In these respects they are subject to various influences, good and bad—including those which spring from the dynamics of the political order. The character of departmental leadership is only one of these influences, but the more such leadership is bolstered by effective administrative arrangements and traditions, the less is there reason for citizens to fear the bungling or bullying of uninspired mediocrity.

---

met with suspicion on the part of the Appropriations Committees of Congress when proposing reinforcement of the staff organization at the immediate disposal of the department head.

Chapter 10 •

Independent Regulatory Agencies

1. Types of Independent Agencies

Meaning of independence. The ideal administrative structure of government is often pictured as a neatly symmetrical pyramid in which each stone is a unit of the executive branch and the capstone is the chief executive. Tidy instincts make us expect that no stray stones will be scattered about on the ground surrounding the pyramid. In practice, government is not organized that way, and there is a considerable body of opinion that it should not be so organized. We need only glance at any government in this country or abroad to see that while many public agencies are subject to immediate control by the chief executive, there are a number of agencies having some degree of independence. It is these so-called independent agencies that will receive particular attention in the present chapter.

"Independence," as a word, has acquired a confusing variety of meanings in the governmental setting. Usually the word means freedom of an agency from immediate control by the chief executive and, in some cases, by the legislature. In certain uses, however, "independence" in government refers to integrity and devotion to the public interest—a natural derivative from the first meaning if legislatures and chief executives are thought of as "political" in the opprobrious sense of that term. By natural progression, this emphasis on integrity and the public interest may lead to giving "independence" the meaning of freedom from control by private interest groups. Sometimes independence even means an agency's freedom to act without fear of highly restrictive legal barriers erected by courts of law. Finally, those who use independence in the sense of freedom from executive and legislative control may arrive, through a different chain of reasoning, at an "independence" that means direct responsibility to the electorate; this is common at the state government level.

The confusion of meanings does not create insuperable obstacles to consideration of the status of independent agencies. Confusion arises simply from applying the same term to two things. The first is the end sought—the formulation and administration of public policies without undue pressure from political and economic interests. The second is the supposed means to that end—the organizational status of "independence" or isolation from political and economic centers of power.

191

There are five main types of agencies for which independent status is often urged and obtained. First are the regulatory agencies, charged with exercising broad governmental powers in connection with electric power, transportation, insurance, banking, liquor control, securities issuance, fair trade practices, labor relations, radio and television, and other important economic areas. The second type is the government-in-business enterprise, usually organized as the government corporation, to which the next chapter is specifically addressed. Third are certain service agencies, such as educational institutions, welfare departments, and highway commissions. They may have independence either because their work is professionalized and nonpolitical, or because their staffs and budgets are so large as to tempt the governor into urging appointments and contract awards that will reward his friends. The fourth group consists at the state level of such officials as the state treasurer, the secretary of state, and the attorney general, who largely for traditional and political reasons may be directly responsible to the electorate. Finally, there are the auditors who, because they are expected to report independently on the legality of expenditures by executive officials, are wisely made independent of control by the chief executive.

Surprisingly, it is difficult to determine when an agency is independent. In fact, both complete independence from, and complete subordination to, the chief executive and the legislature are myths. All governmental institutions draw too much from the same wellspring of ideas and are too exposed to the same "climate of opinion" to be thought of as truly independent for long. Independent agencies follow the election returns, though sometimes with considerable reluctance and delay. On the other hand, it is a familiar feature of bureaucracy that even in the more highly integrated executive branch, individual departments, bureaus, and sections can muster a considerable resistance to direction by superior authority. We are, therefore, dealing with a matter of degree—more or less independence—not with complete independence or complete dependence.

Institutional safeguards of independence. Ingenious designers have by now developed most of the institutional arrangements that promise to increase an agency's degree of independence. The most common device is that of the commission or board form of organization. It is supposed that a group of three, five, or seven men will be less subservient to the chief executive than a single department head. If decisions must be made by such a multiple-member commission, there is likely to be emphasis upon discussion, deliberation, consideration of all relevant opinions, and compromise. The very delay involved in calling a formal meeting of the commission before a decision is made is an influence against precipitate compliance with the chief executive's orders.

Conceivably, of course, even a commission could be made subservient if its members were party loyalists all allied with the chief executive, or if they were beholden to him for their tenure and could be removed at any time he thought appropriate. In fact, some commissions and boards are created as agents of the chief executive, with no thought that they will be or should be independent. Advocates of independence must therefore go beyond mere creation of commissions.

Many commissions are required to be bipartisan; that is, no more than a bare majority of the members may belong to the same political party. However, political scientists are agreed that the requirement of bipartisanship puts a premium on extensive political activity as a qualification for membership, and therefore fails to lift commissions out of politics into an atmosphere of true independence. Furthermore, with each major party at present such a congeries of discordant factions, a bipartisanship requirement alone cannot prevent a shrewd chief executive from picking a majority of members who share his views on public policy in the area of the commission's responsibility. While party labels still mean different orientations toward public policy when applied to each party as a whole, such labels may be quite meaningless when attached to individuals.

Another supposed assurance of independence is the staggered-term arrangement. Terms of members of each commission are scheduled on an overlapping basis so that no individual chief executive during his term of office has an opportunity to appoint a majority of members of any commission. Thus it is assured that no commission will be subservient to him. This safeguard breaks down if the same chief executive is elected for more than one term or if the same political party or faction captures the post of chief executive for several terms in succession. Furthermore, not only newly appointed commissioners but also hold-overs whose terms will expire during the chief executive's term are likely to be hospitable to his views on policy.

Appointment and removal of members. Statutory or constitutional restriction on the exercise of the executive's appointive power is another device resorted to in the name of independence. Many such restrictions are scarcely worth notice, for they are almost meaningless—statutory insistence that an appointee be of good moral character, or have professional or business experience, or be free of a criminal record. The requirement of senatorial confirmation of appointments has failed to be a safeguard against bad or unsuitable choices by the President, has increased political influences in the selection of commissioners, and has blocked the reappointment of able commissioners who have offended regulated industries by their zeal.[1]

Sometimes the chief executive's freedom of choice is considerably restricted by the requirement that he select appointees from a limited panel of names prepared by some presumably nonpolitical group. Thus, neutral

---

[1] See Harris, Joseph P., *The Advice and Consent of the Senate*, p. 267 *ff.*, and his valuable case study of the natural gas industry's success in accomplishing senatorial rejection of the reappointment of Leland Olds as a member of the Federal Power Commission, p. 178 *ff.*, Berkeley and Los Angeles: University of California Press, 1953.

citizens—for example, presidents of the principal universities in the state—may be authorized by law to nominate to the governor candidates from whom he shall select members of an important regulatory commission. In other instances, the legislature may actually force the governor to select all commission members from a panel of names submitted by a single special-interest group. This, of course, reflects considerable distrust of the governor and a surprising confidence in the interest group's sympathetic regard for the public interest. Often such a provision betokens abdication by the legislature in favor of self-regulation by an industry, profession, or other economic group. Sometimes several competing interest groups are brought into the nomination process, and the chief executive is required to select a certain number of his appointees from nominees of each of the interest groups. Through such a balancing of special interests in its membership it is supposed that the commission's decisions will come close to representing the public interest—a supposition, it may be added, that students should regard with skepticism.

The removal power is more important than any other formal criterion of independence. A commissioner who can be removed at any time is in a poor position to challenge the policy of the chief executive. Actually, few statutes place commissioners entirely beyond the executive removal power. The alternative of legislative impeachment is too cumbersome a process to serve as the sole recourse against dishonest or inefficient public officials. But the chief executive is generally restricted to certain specific reasons for removal. "Inefficiency, neglect of duty, or malfeasance in office" are customary grounds for removal in statutes creating independent commissions. Even when the statute is silent on removal, the President is not free to remove commissioners of quasi-judicial agencies on policy grounds. Removal, of course, is an extreme step that is rarely taken. Yet its existence or nonexistence as an ultimate sanction of the President's authority conditions the atmosphere in which commissioners consider his views on regulatory policy.

Financial support and basic authority. Freedom from reliance upon the chief executive and the legislature for financial support is an important criterion of independence. We should not underestimate the importance of executive budgets and legislative appropriations as power-bestowing and power-withdrawing instruments—and, by natural deduction, instruments giving the chief executive and even individual legislators an influence upon the commission that they might not have otherwise. Commissions that finance themselves are generally free of this executive-legislative type of control. The Board of Governors of the Federal Reserve System is supported directly by assessment upon the reserve banks. And many state commissions on banking, insurance, public utilities, agricultural marketing, and professional licensing support themselves in whole or in part through assessment of fees on the companies and individuals subject to their regulatory authority. As a means to independence, financial self-support is an excellent instrument; but it runs counter to the whole emphasis in democratic history upon legislative possession of the power of the purse.

The architects of independent establishments have rarely succeeded in freeing such agencies from dependence on the legislative body for grants of regulatory authority. Congress and the state legislatures create and abolish the powers of independent agencies. Every so often, therefore, an agency, however independent by all the criteria here reviewed, must ask the legislative body for extensions of its jurisdiction and for more effective sanctions with which to enforce its decisions. It must also enter the legislative arena whenever a bill is proposed to abolish or weaken the agency.[2]

Political factors. Two final factors are important in freeing agencies from dependence on the chief executive, even though they are not recognized by the statute books. One is the alliance of agencies with pressure groups whose economic and political power is sufficient to protect their wards against even such controls as are authorized by law. A chief executive and a legislature may readily be balked in their attempts to control the regulatory agencies if a utilities commission wins the favor of the utility companies, the banking commission comes to be regarded as the banks' creature, the fish and game commission is strongly backed by the well-organized sportsmen's associations, the labor department can run for support to the great labor organizations, and the medical licensing board can turn to the influential medical association.

The second factor is the ability of the agency to develop political power sufficient to resist the chief executive's encroachments upon its independence. The courting of pressure groups is, of course, a major step in this direction. In addition, the chief executive will be less likely to "cross" the agency if the agency head controls a major faction in his and the chief executive's political party; or if the agency head has established a public prestige that rings him 'round with the protective support of newspaper editors, educational leaders, civic organizations, professional associations, and women's clubs; or if he has assiduously cultivated the good will of legislators and party leaders.

In theory, the responsiveness of regulatory agencies to public opinion stems from their dependence on the popularly controlled legislative and executive branches. In practice, however, many regulatory agencies are assured a substantial degree of independence. Thus theory and practice are in conflict.

---

[2] A few state agencies are established and granted their powers by constitutional provision; dependence on the legislature is therefore lessened, but on occasion such agencies may have to participate actively in a campaign to influence an election on proposed constitutional amendments.

2. Nature and Conduct of Regulatory Business

Essence of regulation. The basic questions in organizing for regulation are (a) whether regulatory agencies should act independently of the chief executive, and perhaps also of the legislative body; (b) whether independent status actually leads to independent conduct; (c) whether the means chosen to assure independent status really contribute to that status; and (d) whether independent conduct, independent status, and the means for assuring independent status carry other costs that must be weighed in any judicious appraisal of independent regulatory commissions or boards. These questions can only be approached through an understanding of what the regulatory process is.

Regulation is governmental circumscribing of the range of permissible conduct of individuals and groups. The simplest regulations require that stop lights be observed, that houses not be robbed, that children attend school. In this type of regulation, characteristically the legislative body adopts a clear-cut rule defining public policy. It is a simple task then for policemen and truant officers to arrest apparent violators; and the courts have no serious problem, assuming sufficient evidence is presented, in deciding finally whether or not the law has actually been violated.

The black-and-white simplicity of this kind of regulation can be overemphasized. There is, in fact, much administrative discretion in enforcement of clear-cut ordinances and statutes; but it is informal and, for that reason, overlooked in much legal writing. Policemen may substitute reprimand for arrest in traffic violations. Police chiefs and mayors may silence Sunday "blue law," antigambling, and antiprostitution ordinances by a deliberate nonenforcement policy. Public prosecutors may choose which cases to take to court and which to let slide.

Rule-making and case-by-case decision. In the more complex types of regulation, the most dramatic feature is the extent to which legislative bodies formally delegate broad discretionary power to administrative agencies. The legislatures despair of defining in crystal-clear terms the norms of conduct to govern economic or social life. Instead, they pass laws requiring that railroad and power rates be "just and reasonable," that restaurants and dairies be "sanitary," that employers provide "reasonable protection to the lives, health, and safety" of their employees, that commercial practices not be "unfair or deceptive" or include "unfair methods of competition." The volume of legislative business, the lack of expertness on the part of the average legislator, and, perhaps, a disposition of the lawmaking body in some instances to "pass the buck," have all contributed to the trend toward vague statutes whose precision is acquired by administrative and judicial action long after the legislature has completed its work. Whatever the cause, the administrative and judicial areas of discretion have been vastly increased by legislative inability to define precisely what acts are to be regarded as unlawful.

Once the legislature has decided to delegate broad discretionary authority, the question of whether such authority should be exercised through techniques of a legislative, judicial, executive, or other character is posed. Most regulatory agencies use a combination of these approaches, but it is important to note the practical significance of the several approaches because the emphasis given each differs. If emphasis is placed on a legislative technique, the agency will set about doing what the legislature failed to do—define with some exactness the types of acts that will be treated as unlawful. This it will do through the issuance of rules and regulations. For example, in most states there are industrial safety codes, issued by the state labor department, which describe specifically the types of safety precautions employers must take if they are to conform to the legislature's demand that employers provide safe conditions of employment. In formulating such general rules, the regulatory agency can engage in thorough research to inform itself of all relevant economic facts, and can seek the advice of all affected interests.

On the other hand, if the discretionary authority is to be exercised along judicial lines, the agency will decide each case as it comes along, without paying much attention to the need of industry and citizens for more reliable and comprehensive guidance than either the vague statute or the spotty pattern of case decisions affords. Many an agency passively depends upon private individuals, companies, or labor unions to bring cases formally to its attention. Some agencies take the initiative themselves in seeking out probable violators and bringing them into formal hearings for the taking of evidence. Still others operate under statutes that require that each individual or company proposing to take a particular line of action—such as open a liquor store, extend a railroad's tracks, practice medicine, or raise rates—apply to the agency for permission before going ahead with the proposed action; the permission may take the form of a license, a certificate of convenience and necessity, or a rate order.

The case-by-case approach reaches its greatest usefulness when the function is genuinely one of settlement of disputes between two parties; as, for example, when an injured workman seeks compensation from an employer, or when a freight shipper seeks reparation for damages suffered as a result of a railroad's violation of the Interstate Commerce Act. This clearly is different from a situation where public policy needs to be defined, where the public interest needs to be vigorously advanced in an industrial area in which that interest has previously been subordinated to private interests, and where an important segment of the economy needs to know the "rules of the game."

Administrative approach. A third approach to regulation is usually thought of as administrative in character. Most clearly connected with this approach is the regulatory function of inspection. It is the inspector who checks fire precautions in theaters and office buildings; visits factories to determine observance of industrial safety codes and wage and hour laws; looks over barber shops, dairies, and restaurants to ensure sanitary conditions; stops cars on the highway to prevent spread of the Japanese beetle; and examines bank records to protect depositors against loss of their savings.

The inspector is no mere automaton answering "yes" or "no" to a form question as to whether his inspection reveals a violation. The modern inspector is often a missionary, charged with telling people subject to his jurisdiction not only what the regulations are and the penalties for their violation, but also why the regulation is necessary and deserves voluntary compliance. Inspection and enforcement, in other words, thrive best when those subject to them are so educated and persuaded that actual violations are few.

This very emphasis on the inspector's educational function lends breadth to his discretionary powers. For discovery of a first and second violation is often used as an opportunity for an educational interview with the violator, rather than for punishing him.

It is noteworthy that for laxity in enforcement by the inspector there is generally no judicial remedy.[3] Nor is there a recourse against a city inspection bureau that suddenly reverses a policy of laxity and enforces the letter of the law by ordering a motion picture theater closed as unsafe without expensive alterations or by assigning "unsanitary" ratings to particular restaurants. Inspection, being a specialized kind of policing, offers wide opportunities for reciprocation of favors between regulator and regulatee.

Mixture of approaches. Regulatory officials and scholars alike have often questioned the attempts to define regulatory approaches as either legislative, judicial, or executive. One basis of their questioning is the frequency with which two or three of these approaches are combined in the same agency. In practice the rules-and-regulations approach, which is of a legislative character, and the case-by-case approach, which is more judicial in orientation, are often found together. For instance, in some states the workmen's compensation board both formulates industrial safety codes and hears individual cases of workmen claiming compensation for injuries sustained in industrial accidents. In addition, regulatory agencies have executive or administrative responsibilities. A notable case among the independent agencies is the Interstate Commerce Commission. Its most publicized work is rate-fixing for railroads and trucking companies, a legislative kind of task in which courtlike procedures are followed. But

---

[3] For an excellent case study of inspectional earnestness coupled with laxity in applying sanctions, see Martin, John Bartlow, "The Blast in Centralia No. 5: A Mine Disaster No One Stopped," *Harper's Magazine*, 1948, Vol. 196, p. 193 *ff.*, an abridgement of which appears in Waldo, Dwight, ed., *Ideas and Issues in Public Administration*, pp. 2-22, New York: Macmillan, 1953.

the Commission also enforces safety standards by having its staff inspect annually a million freight cars, 100,000 locomotives, and 40,000 motor vehicles.

In fact, the mixture of legislative, executive, and judicial approaches has been one ot the principal arguments for establishment of the independent commissions. The reasoning runs that, under the doctrine of the separation of powers, none of the three great branches of government may exercise powers constitutionally belonging to either of the other two branches. Consequently, a regulatory agency exercising a combination of legislative, executive, and judicial powers cannot constitutionally belong to any one of the three branches. Hence, the regulatory commissions must be independent. This reasoning overlooks the fact that a number of the executive departments and agencies perform all three types of function. It also betrays its own weak logic, for the tripartite separation-of-powers doctrine provides no fourth branch into which the left-over "things that don't fit" can be cast.

Possibility of fresh categories. The second defect in the attempt to apply the classic categories to regulatory action is that this classification loses sight of the variety of means that are available for achievement of the objectives of public policy.[4] Fact-finding, analysis, negotiation, and persuasion are among the most important of these means; yet they slip from view if one's thinking is held to traditional channels. A commission regulating a whole industry or activity can scarcely conform to standards of rational decision-making unless, with the help of its professional staff, it has acquired a thorough knowledge of the economics, technology, history, and problems of the industry or industries of concern to it. As the commission approaches individual cases of importance or novelty, it will need to refine, focus, and add to that knowledge. It may do so by detailed investigation of the records of the company involved. It may also do so by sharpening its awareness, so far as facts are available, of how a decision directed to the particular company will affect other companies in similar circumstances, and suppliers, customers, workers, stockholders, and creditors of the company.

Analysis, as well as fact-finding through research, plays a part in regulation. While facts narrow the range of alternative courses, analysis starting from the facts may involve assigning of priorities to basic social values, giving weight to the interests of the consuming public and other unrepresented interests, projecting trends of industrial development into the future, anticipating reactions to possible decisions, even guessing at matters for which facts are not available. Analysis, as a phase of regulation, is at

---

[4] A thoughtful and detailed analysis of regulatory approaches will be found in Redford, Emmette S., *Administration of National Economic Control*, New York: Macmillan, 1952.

its best an intellectual process blending facts, values, logic, and strategy in an effort to arrive at a result that is equitable both to the immediately affected parties and to the larger interest of the general public.

Negotiation and persuasion are vital elements of regulation where results are measured in prevention of evils, rather than simply in punishment of those guilty of the evils. The Federal Trade Commission encourages whole industries to hold trade-practice conferences under its sponsorship and to adopt rules that interpret the law in words specifically meaningful to the particular industries. The conferences may also adopt recommendations, not legally enforceable, that encourage members to go even further than the law may require in avoiding unfair and deceptive practices. Furthermore, in individual cases the Commission negotiates stipulations whereby, after informal conference or correspondence, companies agree to stop such practices as false advertising and mislabeling of products. The Securities and Exchange Commission informally advises marketers of securities to withdraw and improve registration statements they have filed if these fail to meet the Commission's standards of accurate and full disclosure, so as to avoid the embarrassment to the marketers of having a stop order issued.

Much cost and time are required for a regulatory agency to hold lengthy hearings and then, perhaps, to have to defend a decision through a succession of courts. This explains a tendency to settle informally for half a loaf rather than to get the full loaf that absolute standards might suggest. Thus, a state utility commission may negotiate with a company for a cut in rates that is more modest than what it could perhaps achieve by formal proceedings.

Whose categories? The regulatory process looks different to different observers. This is partly because each starts from what is familiar and usually from his own set of basic values. The lawyer may think of a court, of protection of the individual charged with crime, and of the long struggle against executive prerogative. He values the independence of the judiciary, the procedure of the courtroom, the decision of a single dispute, and the opportunity for appeal to a higher court. The legislator thinks of the breadth of policy-making power, of the investigative and consultative procedure of legislative committee hearings, and of the long struggle of legislative bodies to wrest power from the chief executive. Many legislators are also lawyers. Their interpretations of regulatory structure and process thus often make use of judicial analogies.

The administrator, not inclined to distrust his own integrity and fairness, thinks of regulation as execution of the laws, which declare public policy. Regulatory decision-making to him is simply what any good administrator tries to do, whether he is a regulator or not—state the problem accurately, learn the facts, get expert advice, relate short-term decisions to long-term policy, expand decisions affecting a few individuals to a general rule covering all who are in the same situation, and maximize consent without sacrificing objectives. But the administrator may like to run his own show, free of interference by the chief executive, free of the red tape of elaborate procedural requirements, free of any court's claim of a right to make "the final error" in reviewing a regulatory agency's decision, free of the importunities of legislators on behalf of those constituents who have cut corners sharply marked by regulatory laws and regulations.

The lawyer, the legislator, and the administrator all take positions that are quite understandable, given their differing backgrounds and ways of life. Each also expresses truth, though it is but partial truth. And all have some reasons for objecting to domination of the regulatory process by the chief executive.

3. The Record of Independence

Independent regulatory commissions. In the federal government, the independent regulatory agencies have never been large either in number or in expenditures and staffs. Their significance results rather from the economic areas over which they have jurisdiction. There are only nine so-called independent regulatory commissions and boards: the Interstate Commerce Commission, the Board of Governors of the Federal Reserve System, the Federal Trade Commission, the Federal Power Commission, the Federal Communications Commission, the Securities and Exchange Commission, the National Labor Relations Board, the Federal Maritime Board, and the Civil Aeronautics Board.[5] Together they account for only about 11,000 employees out of the 2.3 million in the whole federal government. Their combined expenditures are less than $75,000,000 out of a total of about $70 billion.

But these bodies in the aggregate have vast powers over transportation by rail, bus, truck, pipeline, ship, and airplane; communication by telephone, telegraph, radio, and television; the "rules of the game" by which industry and trade are kept fair and competitive; the supply of electric power from hydroelectric projects on government-owned lands and on navigable waters and the interstate transmission of electric power and

---

[5] The listing corresponds to that of Cushman, Robert E, *The Independent Regulatory Commissions,* p. 4 ff., New York: Oxford University Press, 1941, and of the (first Hoover) Commission on Organization of the Executive Branch of the Government, *Regulatory Commissions,* p. 1, Washington: Government Printing Office, 1949. Herbert Hoover, chairman of this Commission, believed that the United States Tariff Commission and the Tax Court were also independent regulatory commissions. The Commission's task force on this subject acknowledged that the Atomic Energy Commission had certain regulatory powers and was an independent commission, but excluded it on grounds of its substantial operational work and the uniqueness of many of its problems. Marver Bernstein's *Regulating Business by Independent Commission,* Princeton: Princeton University Press, 1955, covers seven commissions, excluding the Board of Governors of the Federal Reserve System and the Federal Maritime Board, as each has certain distinctive characteristics.

transportation of natural gas at reasonable rates; the supply of money and credit, the issuance of stocks and bonds, and the operations of stock exchanges; and the maintenance of collective bargaining and fair labor practices on the part of employers and unions.

Most of these commissions and boards have five or seven members, though the important Interstate Commerce Commission has eleven. The members are appointed by the President with the advice and consent of the Senate, and the chairmen (except for the Interstate Commerce Commission) are designated by the President. Staggered terms of four to seven years (except for the 14-year terms of the Board of Governors of the Federal Reserve System) and a requirement of bipartisan membership (not required for the Federal Reserve Board or the National Labor Relations Board) are intended to contribute to independence from the current chief executive. Statutory restrictions on the President's removal power are not so common as is widely believed. In the case of five commissions and boards, he can remove members only "for cause" or "for inefficiency, neglect of duty, or malfeasance in office." This applies to the Interstate Commerce Commission, the Board of Governors of the Federal Reserve System, the Federal Trade Commission, the National Labor Relations Board, and the Civil Aeronautics Board. But the statutes omit such restrictions in the case of the Federal Power Commission, the Securities and Exchange Commission, the Federal Communications Commission, and the Federal Maritime Board.[6] However, the courts currently would not interpret the silence of Congress as authority for the President to remove members at will.

Other regulatory agencies. Regular executive departments and other single-headed agencies exercise regulatory powers not unlike those entrusted to the independent commissions. An outstanding example is the Department of Agriculture, with its regulation of packers and stockyards and commodity exchanges (roughly paralleling the regulation of railroads and securities exchanges by independent commissions) and its responsibility for administration of some forty regulatory statutes. Other departments —Commerce, Interior, Labor, Treasury, and Health, Education, and Welfare—also control important economic activities. In wartime, vast regulatory authority is entrusted to single-headed agencies for such functions as price control and rationing, production control and allocation of materials, transportation, and manpower utilization.

Among the single-headed departments, two problems have been paramount. One is the special-interest taint of the three "clientele departments"

---

[6] The omission of restrictions on the removal power with respect to the Federal Power Commission, the Securities and Exchange Commission, and the Federal Communications Commission is an accident of history. The statutes creating these three commissions were passed during a period in which restrictions on removal would have seemed unconstitutional. See (first) Commission on Organization of the Executive Branch of the Government, *Task Force Report on Regulatory Commissions,* p. 14, Washington: Government Printing Office, 1949.

that would be the most likely single-headed agencies for peacetime exercise of regulatory powers: Agriculture, Commerce, and Labor, traditionally spokesmen respectively for the interests of farmers, businessmen, and labor unions.[7]

The second problem about single-headed departments has been the extent to which particular kinds of regulatory work may be slighted because of the influence of the department head or the President. The Justice Department, for instance, having limited funds and staff like any other agency, must choose where it wishes to concentrate these resources. Under one administration, prosecutions for violation of antitrust laws may be relatively infrequent. Under a different kind of administration, and without any change in the law, the Justice Department may launch a full-scale crusade against monopolies. One of the principal justifications for the independent commissions is the argument that, because of their staggered-term arrangement and relative freedom from executive domination, they have greater continuity of policy than executive departments. But such continuity may simply turn into lack of animation.

Constitutional problems. The Constitution provides for separate legislative, executive, and judicial departments. Where do the independent regulatory commissions and boards fit? If they are intended to be independent of the President's control, must not some legal formula be found by which they can be placed outside the executive branch? The Supreme Court has thrice given attention to the problem. The Myers case in 1926, the Humphrey case in 1935, and the Wiener case in 1958, all dealing with the President's power of removal, provide the guideposts.

In the Myers case [8] the Supreme Court held that Congress could not constitutionally restrict the power to remove any executive official—in that case, a postmaster—whom the President had appointed either alone or with the advice and consent of the Senate. A dictum in the opinion, written by Chief Justice Taft, clearly indicated that the President had an unfettered right under the Constitution to remove members of quasi-legislative and quasi-judicial bodies.

Nine years later the Supreme Court rejected the Myers case dictum. The background facts are revealing. The Federal Trade Commission, created in 1914 under the Wilson Administration, had been given important powers to attack unfair methods of competition and unlawful trade practices and to investigate business misconduct. Its vigorous attitude, particularly evidenced by the commission's blistering attack on the monopolistic practices of the meat-packing industry, aroused the bitter resentment of much of the business world. It is not surprising that under the more conservative administrations of Presidents Harding, Coolidge,

---

[7] See, for one example of the problem, Rourke, Francis E., "The Department of Labor and the Trade Unions," *Western Political Quarterly,* 1954, Vol. 7, p. 656 *ff.*
[8] 272 U. S. 52 (1926).

and Hoover, a conscious effort was made to put men on the Federal Trade Commission who would have less crusading zeal and who, to a considerable extent, would exercise the commission's powers at something less than their maximum extent. William E. Humphrey, appointed to the commission by President Coolidge in 1925, dominated it between 1925 and 1933 because on most important issues he could count on the votes of the other two Republican commissioners. Now collusion with, rather than control of, trusts and monopolies by the Federal Trade Commission was talked about on the floor of the House of Representatives.

Shortly after Franklin D. Roosevelt was inaugurated, he asked Commissioner Humphrey to resign, pointing out that Humphrey's policy was not in harmony with the President's policy on the work of the Federal Trade Commission. On the Commissioner's refusal, the President removed him. Eventually, the Humphrey case reached the Supreme Court. Humphrey's position had rested on the Federal Trade Commission Act, which provided for presidential removal of commissioners "for inefficiency, neglect of duty, or malfeasance in office." The chief executive, the argument went, had violated this act in removing Humphrey not for any of these reasons, but for incompatibility with the President's views on policy matters. The President's position, on the other hand, was that Congress had no constitutional power to limit his reasons for removal.

The Supreme Court ruled against the President.[9] It held that Congress may by statute specify the causes for which members of commissions or boards can be removed by the President, wherever the body exercises primarily quasi-legislative and quasi-judicial duties and only incidentally administrative or executive functions—and the Court classified the Federal Trade Commission as such a body. In such circumstances, the statute is binding on the President, and he cannot remove for causes not specified in the statute. Some commentators have concluded that the Supreme Court thus recognized a headless fourth branch of the government, consisting of the independent regulatory commissions and boards. A commission such as the Federal Trade Commission, said the Court, is "wholly disconnected from the executive department" and is instead "an agency of the legislative and judicial departments."

But what if Congress says nothing about removal in a statute creating a commission? Does such silence leave the President unfettered in his exercise of the removal power? Or does it make the commissioners irremovable—at least in the absence of gross misbehavior? President Eisenhower thought the former; the Supreme Court decided the latter. In 1948 Congress confronted the problem of arranging for paying the claims of internees, prisoners of war, and religious organizations that suffered personal injury or property damage by the enemy during World War II.

---

[9] Humphrey's Executor v. United States, 295 U.S. 602 (1935).

As the Court pointed out, Congress could have done the job itself, passing laws that named persons and amounts to be paid. Or, as the bill originally provided, the job could have been turned over to an executive official. Or the District Courts or the Court of Claims could have handled the claims judicially. But Congress instead established a War Claims Commission of three members, with jurisdiction to "receive" the claims and "adjudicate" them "according to law." The Commission's life was limited, its expiration being fixed eventually for 1955. This served to fix the terms of the commissioners automatically, and no provision for removal was included.

Wiener was a Truman appointee to the Commission. In 1953 President Eisenhower asked for his resignation, but Wiener refused. So, in December of 1953, Eisenhower removed him, writing, "I regard it as in the national interest to complete the administration of the War Claims Act . . . with personnel of my own choosing." The Supreme Court unanimously ruled the removal illegal.

Justice Frankfurter, in his opinion for the Court,[10] found no difference between what Roosevelt had tried to do in the Humphrey case and what Eisenhower had tried to do in the Wiener case. He thought the President's power of removal here turned on the nature of the function that Congress vested in the War Claims Commission. He emphasized "the intrinsic judicial character of the task" and concluded that the Commission "was established as an adjudicatory body." The inference followed that "Congress did not wish to have hang over the Commission the Damocles' sword of removal by the President for no reason other than that he preferred Commission men of his own choosing." The only qualification to Frankfurter's sharp line of cleavage between "those who are part of the executive establishment and those whose tasks require absolute freedom from executive interference" is his observation that Wiener's case did not raise a question of his "rectitude." While not crossing that bridge yet, the Court seemed to imply that even independent commissioners cannot wholly escape a reckoning with some agent of the public conscience, perhaps even the President.

Modifications of independence. Emphasis on the constitutionality of restricting the President's power to remove commissioners can lead to exaggerated notions of the independence of commissions. Emphasis on the way in which political realities blunt the effectiveness of such mechanical devices as staggered terms, bipartisanship, and limited removability can lead to exaggerated notions of the commissions' dependence on the President. Recent official proposals clearly indicate that the commissions have not yet come to rest in a wholly independent or wholly dependent status; they further indicate that "mechanical" arrangements do matter, for such arrangements help to mark out the channels of influence.

---

10 Wiener v. United States, 357 U.S. 349 (1958).

The principal formal change resulting from the first Hoover Commission's study of the regulatory commissions concerned the selection and role of the commission chairmen. As late as 1948 the President designated the chairmen of but five regulatory commissions. In four other commissions the members selected their own chairmen; in two of these instances, the "selection" involved simply rotating the chairmanship annually; in the other two, the choice frequently fell on a member informally suggested by the President. This variety was brought into substantial uniformity in 1950, in accordance with a recommendation of the Hoover Commission's task force on regulatory commissions. The chairman of every regulatory commission, except the Interstate Commerce Commission which continues its rotation practice, is now chosen by the President from among the members of the commission. The intent was partly to "enable the President to obtain a sympathetic hearing for broader considerations of national policy which he feels the commission should take into account," while leaving to the commission itself the decision of what weight should be given to his views.

The change was not universally applauded. Six years after it went into effect a committee of Congress sounded an alarm at the "most recent invasion of the independence of these regulatory bodies by the Chief Executive." The committee assembled data intended to demonstrate "how Presidentially appointed chairmen of the Federal regulatory commissions and agencies . . . , subject to control by the Chief Executive, have exercised the great powers residing in them to whittle away at the remaining vestige of independence of their respective agencies."[11] As is often the case, a vigorous minority report challenged the facts and conclusions of the majority.

All of the commissions, except the Board of Governors of the Federal Reserve System, are subject to legislative and executive procedures that modify independence. They submit their annual budget proposals to the Bureau of the Budget for review, possible scaling down, and incorporation in the President's annual budget for transmission to Congress. The commissions must clear proposed data-gathering survey questionnaires with the Bureau of the Budget, as do all executive agencies. When a commission has a legislative proposal to submit to Congress or has formal views to present on legislation being considered by Congress, it is expected to clear with the same bureau so that Congress can be advised whether the proposal or views are in accord with the President's program. When a

---

[11] *The Organization and Procedures of the Federal Regulatory Commissions and Agencies and Their Effect on Small Business*, p. 76, Report of Subcommittee No. 1, House Select Committee on Small Business, 84th Cong., 2d Sess., House Report No. 2967, 1956. In 1959 another House committee formally proposed: "The chairman of each commission should be selected by the members thereof and his term as chairman should be for not longer than a 3-year period." *Independent Regulatory Commissions*, p. 11, Report of Special Subcommittee on Legislative Oversight, House Committee on Interstate and Foreign Commerce, 85th Cong., 2d Sess., House Report No. 2711, 1959.

lower court decides a case against a commission, the commission must secure the approval of the Solicitor General in the Department of Justice and act through him in asking the Supreme Court to review the court's decision. All of these are normal aspects in the life of executive agencies. But the legislative committee report we quoted insists that the regulatory commissions, as "arms of Congress," be exempt from such requirements. It recommends, for instance, that each commission submit its appropriation requests directly to Congress.

Experience in the states. In the states, certain factors have given the problem of independent commissions a setting different from that of the federal government.[12] Many legislatures meet less frequently—that is, only once every two years. Thus it is more difficult for independent commissions to argue that, though independent of the executive, they are given effective supervision and coordination by the legislative branch. In the second place, the general atmosphere of many state governments is more definitely political, with emphasis on patronage, favoritism, and subservience to pressure groups. In states where this atmosphere exists—and it does not exist in all—the departments responsible to the governor, those responsible directly to the people, and the independent commissions are all affected. The agencies that come nearest to escaping this atmosphere are those with professionalized staffs, such as the state health department, the state welfare department, and the state university.

Such service agencies with professional staffs are likely to have a tradition of both integrity and skill. If they receive federal grants, federal regulations may govern in part their expenditures, personnel selection, political activity, organization, and basic standards of operation. Their professional caliber may enlist for them the outside support of like interests, while their purposes—health, education, welfare—assure some support from enlightened public opinion. Finally, they have largely administrative rather than policy decisions to make. In contrast, the heart of economic regulation is policy, and the electorate is ill-served if it has no effective way to bring sanctions against the state regulatory commissions, which seem to float in mid-air, unanswerable directly to either of the two political branches of government, executive and legislative. These factors suggest that, if a choice had to be made, the people would be better advised to let service agencies, rather than regulatory bodies, have a high degree of independence. Both the degree of political favoritism running through the conduct of public affairs in some states and the fear of strengthening the office of governor when experience reveals the possibility that a charlatan may be elected to the post, result often in a general desire for the independence of all agencies—service and regulatory—that have important work

---

[12] Fesler, James W., *The Independence of State Regulatory Agencies*, Chicago: Public Administration Service, 1942. See also American Assembly, *The Forty-Eight States*, New York: Graduate School of Business, Columbia University, 1955.

to do. While this has an appealing appearance of "facing the realities," it leaves the governor with little responsibility, removes administration of a large number of governmental policies from effective public control, and in some cases causes a relative increase in the control of agencies by special-interest groups. No one is left to call regulatory officials on the carpet promptly if they are neglecting the public interest. The spur to action is gone, for the public itself is not overly vigilant about the day-to-day acts of regulatory agencies. On the other hand, the special-interest groups are likely to be well organized in their efforts to soften the rigors of regulation.

4. The Price of Independence

Need for policy coordination. Independent status has certain characteristics that carry price tags. One is the central fact that an independent body can make decisions without regard to what is done or needed in other parts of the government. So there is a loss in coordination of public policies and governmental operations. Another is that an independent body sets its own standards of performance. How well it does its task may be affected by the absence of the stimulus and accountability that external control can provide.

Regulatory commissions make policies that are often more important than those made by executive departments. They may do so by action or by inaction. Two problems arise. The first is whether substantial powers over economic policy should be vested in governmental agencies that are not clearly subject to officials who in turn are responsible to the people. It can be argued that policy is the very thing to be kept under effective popular control, if democracy is to be a meaningful principle of government. The second problem is that, simply as a practical matter, the policies that are being adopted and executed by the scores of agencies, executive and independent, need to be coordinated to the degree that they impinge on one another. Clearly, the citizenry has a right to demand that someone prevent its government's right hand from undoing what its left hand has been trying to do. The very size of federal and state administration makes perfect coordination impossible. However, the existence of commissions with great regulatory powers claiming virtual independence of the chief executive seriously handicaps attempts to approximate even a rough-hewn sort of coordination.

Transportation affords a ready example of the need for coordination. Different modes of transportation are in competition for much business, and are complementary to one another in some circumstances, as when trucks deliver freight to railroad centers and airports. Yet the Civil Aeronautics Board, the Federal Maritime Board, and the Interstate Commerce Commission are each fixing rates for the particular transportation industries assigned to them for regulation, with no necessity for assuring that their separate decisions add up to a rational transportation policy. Furthermore, what these commissions and boards do has a bearing on the interests of the executive departments, and the reverse is true as well. Movement of troops, of military and war-plant supplies, and of the mails depends on the adequacy and rates of the transportation industry. Subsidies from the federal budget aid the building and operation of transportation facilities. The vast highway construction program, supervised by the Federal Highway Administrator, speeds truck, bus, and private-automobile transportation—to the disadvantage of the railroads. In addition, the President's economic agencies cannot help but be concerned over the impact on the economy of a threatened collapse of the railroad companies.

Other examples of the need for coordination come readily to mind. Both the Federal Trade Commission and the Department of Justice have responsibilities for enforcing the antitrust laws. Both the Treasury Department and the Board of Governors of the Federal Reserve System are vitally concerned with inflation, deflation, and the price of government securities. Interagency liaison has not sufficed to prevent contradictory policies and actions. The clashing of governmental agencies without ready means of settling their disputes cannot charitably be tolerated in an era when the government's function is conceived as positive in character. Conscious guidance of economic forces to achieve maximum production and employment calls for correlation of governmental activities. The needed consistency seems difficult to obtain so long as some of the most important instruments for guidance of the economy are independent commissions without close ties linking them to one another and to either the legislature or the chief executive. Because the legislature has serious handicaps as a focus for coordination, the question of the role of the chief executive cannot be ignored.

Standards of performance. Quite apart from the weakness of coordination among independent commissions and between them and executive agencies with related functions, there is the further question of how well a regulatory commission performs its own task when it has an independent status. Other factors than independence affect performance, and disentanglement of the web is difficult. The quality of men appointed to the commissions has not been impressive,[13] and for this the President, the Senate, and the political system through which men rise to consideration for

---

[13] *Cf.* Mansfield, Harvey C., *The Lake Cargo Coal Rate Controversy,* p. 141 *ff.*: "The Personnel of the Interstate Commerce Commission," New York: Columbia University Press, 1932; Herring, Pendleton, *Federal Commissioners: A Study of Their Careers and Qualifications,* Cambridge: Harvard University Press, 1936; Harris, Joseph P., *op cit.* above in note 1, p. 267 *ff.*; (first) Commission on Organization of the Executive Branch of the Government, *Task Force Report on Regulatory Commissions,* cited above in note 5, *passim.* Although the quality of commissioners results primarily from decisions of the President and the Senate, the formal independence of commissions sometimes encourages the President to choose weaker men, either because he hopes through them to have some influence on the commissions or because he can thus "take care" of politicians without weakening the part of the government for which he has direct responsibility; he may also think a multimembered commission with some strong members can readily "carry" one or two "weak sisters."

appointment are all partly responsible. But independence itself seems largely responsible for other failures of the commissions to achieve high performance standards.

Passivity, lack of vigor, and inertia tend to displace the energy requisite to advancing toward the goals set out in the basic regulatory statutes. As an investigation of transportation regulation put it, "A regulatory statute may be both wise and practicable, and yet be totally ineffective for the simple reason that the agency takes no decisive action under it. . . . An agency, in fact, possesses through this means a not inconsiderable power to thwart the legislative purpose. . . . An inactive agency will not lack apologists in any event; the difficulty is to find persons or groups able and in a position to apply a spur." [14]

In the states as well, one finds many utility commissions, workmen's compensation and industrial safety boards, banking and insurance boards, and professional licensing boards which show little evidence of a determined effort to define and achieve the public interest. Public utilities commissions, for example, most of them created because the people wanted forceful regulation of the entrenched railroad and electric power companies, have all too generally taken a negative attitude toward exercise of their power.

The causes of such reluctance to act vigorously on behalf of the public are several. The most important are four: (a) the ease of indulging in inertia when there are no incentives to action and when action is bound to make enemies; (b) overemphasis on the judicial approach, springing in part from the belief that commissions and boards were made independent so that they could have much the same character and procedure as courts, and in part from the insistence of courts that due process of law requires court-like procedures in regulation; (c) excessive exposure to the views and influence of the regulated interests, without compensating exposure to governmental and private views expressive of the public interest; and (d) the diffusion among the commissioners of responsibility for both initiative and results.

The Task Force on Regulatory Commissions of the first Hoover Commission, as rather friendly critics, pointed out that "the basic task of most of the commissions is to establish standards of conduct as the legal framework for the regulated industry or activity." This means constant involvement "in seeking to define . . . standards; in reviewing the regulatory program as a whole; and in anticipating emerging problems and planning for their solution." But exactly "these are areas where many commissions are notably weak." [15] Again inertia, lack of initiative, and reliance on judicial types of procedure are to be blamed, along with excessive turnover of commissioners and their being busy with other things. In internal administration, says

---

[14] Board of Investigation and Research, *Report on Practices and Procedures of Governmental Control,* p. 15-16, 78th Cong., 2nd Sess., House Doc. No. 678, 1944.

[15] *Op. cit.* above in note 5, p. 39-40.

the same group, "Many of the commissions suffer badly from inefficiency and delay in handling their work." These weaknesses "point to the fact that many commissions have failed to appreciate the need for orderly administration or to adopt methods adequate to achieve it." [16] For all these deficiencies, the independent status is largely responsible. The diffusion of responsibility and the stalemating which are characteristic of boards or commissions in their operations bear much of the remaining responsibility.

5. Proposed Solutions

Argument over diagnoses. The search for solutions of the regulatory problem is an odd kind of treasure hunt. Each seeker seems to define for himself what he is looking for and where it will be found. Those who favor effective economic regulation in general, place considerable trust in the presidency. They sense a mounting need for better coordination of the government's many responsibilities. Hence they advocate that the activities of the regulatory commissions, or a large part of them, be brought under presidential control. Those who are opposed to effective regulation in general, take issue with the policy orientation of recent presidents. They place considerable trust in judicial impartiality and advocate the maintenance or even strengthening of the commissions' independence—or the transfer of some of their activities to the courts.

These two main categories of seekers of a solution are supplemented by smaller groups concerned with individual fields of regulation. Those long aggrieved by certain practices of private concerns are likely to want not only a statute condemning the practice, but a special agency wholly dedicated to making the teeth of the statute bite. As the political branches of the government are presumed to be the channels of pressure for "the interests," the independent commission seems an ideal regulatory instrument. Oddly, this conclusion coincides with the conclusion of the opposite group—the "special interests" that are subjected to regulation. Often even a regulatory commission whose genesis lay in public criticism of the industry regulated becomes convinced that it must "learn to live with" its ward; this rapidly converts the commission into a sympathetic and indulgent regulator. The regulated industry, in turn, comes to find the relationship quite comfortable, and so defends the commission's independence against wider public control and frequent spurs to action.[17]

---

[16] *Ibid.*, p. 43, 46. The Hoover Commission recommended for the federal regulatory commissions and boards that the chairmen carry much of the responsibility for internal administration; this has been provided for in most instances.

[17] The evolution of commissioners from zealous regulators to tired accommodators of the desires of the industry is skilfully sketched in Bernstein, *op. cit.* above in note 5, p. 74 *ff.* See also Redford, *op. cit.* above in note 4, p. 385 *ff.* In some important areas the interests to be regulated have themselves sponsored the regulatory statute, and advocated establishment of an independent board or commission as the agent of their "self-regulation." Professional licensing, a good example, has been given frequent critical attention; see, for example, Gellhorn, Walter, *Individual Freedom and*

Proposed solutions for the problem of the independent regulatory commissions or boards look toward increased executive control, increased legislative control, increased judicial control, or judicialization of regulatory procedure.

Increased executive control. A finding that the independent regulatory commissions "have not been satisfactory instruments of government regulation," [18] or that if the governmental process were fully understood "the argument for the regulatory board would lose force in most situations," [19] leads to proposals for increasing executive control over the commissions. The degree of disenchantment may even support a case for transfer of their functions to ordinary executive departments, though the case is rarely stated so bluntly. All proposals for increased executive control rest on the belief that the principal responsibility of the commissions is policy-making for important segments of the economy. Only incidental support is sought in the argument that the administrative efficiency of the commissions is of natural concern to the chief executive, though this argument has utility in debates over the constitutional issues.

Recommendations for strengthening the President's hand in policy matters range from minor tinkering with his appointing power to drastic reorganization of the entire commission structure. Thus the first Hoover Commission recommended that the President be given the right to designate the chairman of each commission, who would be put in charge of the commission's internal administration—a recommendation now substantially in effect. Some students of the regulatory process would go further, even to the point of allowing the President to review certain kinds of commission decisions or to send policy directives to the commissions.[20] The most drastic solution—offered by the President's Committee on Administrative Management in 1937—would separate policy-making, prosecuting, and strictly administrative functions, on the one hand, from adjudication, on the other. The former would be placed within the regular departments, while the latter would remain with courtlike commissions. Bifurcation has indeed been attempted occasionally, as with the independent Civil Aeronautics Board and the Department of Commerce's Civil Aeronautics Administration, but the experiments have not been striking successes.

Increased legislative control. The issues involved in legislative control are quite simple. Congressional power to abolish any commission, to write policies and procedures into statutes governing the commissions, to deter-

---

Governmental Restraints, p. 105 *ff.,* Baton Rouge: Louisiana State University Press, 1956; and Fesler, *op. cit.* above in note 12, p. 46 *ff.*

[18] Bernstein, *op. cit.* above in note 5, p. 294.
[19] Redford, *op. cit.* above in note 4, p. 323.
[20] Hyneman, Charles S., *Bureaucracy in a Democracy,* p. 316 *ff.,* New York: Harper, 1950; and Redford, *op. cit.* above in note 4, p. 317 *ff.* For a case study of presidential review of commission decisions, see Committee on Public Administration, *The Latin American Proceeding,* Washington, 1949.

mine appropriations for them, and to investigate them through its committees are not in question. The means to substantial legislative control are fully available, and no one proposes to take them away. The problem, rather, is whether in actual practice the legislative controls make other controls unnecessary. The tendency of Congress is to criticize an extension of presidential control even though this is seriously advocated only because there are needs that have never been adequately met by Congress.

After the most careful appraisal of past experience and future prospects for congressional control, Robert E. Cushman concluded in 1941 that "Congress is likely to content itself with doing nothing for the most part in its dealings with the commissions, and with resorting to some form of drastic action when something approaching a scandal crops up in connection with a commission." [21] It is true that since then congressional committees have been reorganized, expert staffs have been provided for them, and the seniority principle governing membership on important committees has been somewhat modified. In 1957 the House of Representatives authorized a Subcommittee on Legislative Oversight, which proceeded to examine the execution of the laws by six regulatory commissions.[22] Its early results included the resignation of a Federal Communications Commissioner, promulgation of codes of ethics by the commissions, and discovery of what was thought to be responsiveness by two commissions to the interest of the principal assistant to the President in cases involving a personal friend.

Increased judicial control. Increased judicial control of regulatory commissions would contribute little or nothing to the coordination of policy and administration. But historically judicial control has been a major factor in the shaping of other aspects of regulation by commission. The Interstate Commerce Commission and the Federal Trade Commission were often before the courts; their adaptation to an often hostile attitude by the judiciary set models that later commissions have kept in mind in developing their own regulatory approaches.

Those eager to have the courts clip the wings of regulatory commissions have had two courses open to them. One was to expand judicial review of regulatory decisions. But the critical defect of this course was the tremendous volume of those decisions. To assure everyone his day—or year—in court was simply impractical. And this would be especially the case if the courts not only were to consider questions of law but were to go over all the evidence presented to the commission, substituting the court's judgment for that of the commission on what a correct decision on the evidence would be. While some expansion in the reviewing role of the courts has occurred,

21 Cushman, *op cit.* above in note 5, p. 678.
22 *Interim Report* of the House Committee on Interstate and Foreign Commerce, Subcommittee on Legislative Oversight, 85th Cong., 2d Sess., House Report No. 1602, 1958. See also *The Organization and Procedures of the Federal Regulatory Commissions and Agencies and Their Effect on Small Business*, p. 79, cited above in note 11.

the practical necessity of leaving most regulatory decisions undisturbed has halted tendencies to seek a major strengthening of that role.

The second course, given the unavailability of the first, was to insist that the procedures followed by regulatory agencies provide full protection for the companies and individuals under their jurisdiction. The courts themselves increasingly chose this course, while according finality to agency decisions reached through approved procedures. And such groups as the American Bar Association also concentrated more on reform of agency procedures than on increasing the opportunities and the scope of judicial review. This effort brought forth the Administrative Procedure Act of 1946, on whose effects informed opinions differ widely.

Judicialization of regulatory procedure. As the volume of regulatory work requires delegation of much of the workload, "examiners" on the regulatory commission's staff conduct most of the hearings, though the commission itself or individual commissioners may also do so. The Administrative Procedure Act went to considerable lengths to convert the hearing examiners into independent judges. It is the Civil Service Commission, not the regulatory commission, that sets their compensation "independently of agency recommendations or ratings," selects examiners to be promoted, and determines whether there is good cause for removal of any of them. The regulatory commission must assign the examiners "to cases in rotation so far as practicable," instead of doing so according to their special knowledge, their personal competence, and the difficulty of particular cases. The examiners are sharply segregated from the investigative and prosecuting parts of the commissions. And an examiner cannot give confidential advice to the commission where it, rather than he, chooses to make the formal decision, for his recommended decision must be communicated to the parties in the case so that they can submit their criticisms.[23]

For some critics of the regulatory process, however, these steps were not large enough. One of the more drastic proposals sent to Congress by the second Hoover Commission[24] recommended that an Administrative Court of the United States be established. This court would take over immediately such things as jurisdiction over unfair methods of competition and unfair or deceptive practices (now regulated by the Federal Trade Commission and other agencies) and jurisdiction over unfair labor practices (now vested in the National Labor Relations Board). Another recommendation proposed that, for functions remaining with the regulatory

---

[23] The leading study of the hearing-examiner provisions in operation is Musolf, Lloyd D., *Federal Examiners and the Conflict of Law and Administration*, Baltimore: Johns Hopkins Press, 1953. See also on the role of the courts and of courtlike procedures in public administration Chapter 23, "The Judicial Test."

[24] (Second) Commission on Organization of the Executive Branch of the Government, *Legal Services and Procedures*, p. 50 ff., Washington: Government Printing Office, 1955. The Commission itself did not vote in favor of these recommendations, merely passing them along to Congress as the views of the Commission's task force on this subject.

bodies, hearing examiners (to be renamed "hearing commissioners") be assigned to these bodies, to be administratively controlled and directed by a Chief Hearing Commissioner appointed for a term of 12 years and attached to the Administrative Court. The power to remove hearing commissioners would rest with the judges of the Administrative Court. And still more. The requirement of the Administrative Procedure Act that hearing examiners be isolated from the investigative and prosecuting work in quasi-judicial cases would be extended to other types of decisions and not only to hearing examiners but to the commission itself and the individual commissioners.

Elements for a solution. Three additional points remain to be made. These are (a) that analysis of the whole problem within the confines of the separation-of-powers doctrine does not produce a solution; (b) that regulatory commissions need to be thought of as "governmental agencies"; and (c) that "fairness" in regulation is a goal whose operative meaning needs to be realized through various institutional arrangements and in balance with other highly valued goals.

The separation-of-powers way of analyzing the problem is often grossly misleading. *All* federal agencies with regulatory functions are answerable to all three "branches" of government. Most of the statements one can make about legislative control and judicial control of the regulatory commissions are equally accurate for the executive agencies. This is not to say that the control is identical in all circumstances. It varies according to political interest, lobbying strength and litigious tendencies of those regulated, volume of agency decisions, intelligibility to technical laymen (including legislators and judges) of the particular field of regulation, and traditional legal categories (for example, whether the regulation concerns the *right* to use one's own private property or the *privilege* to apply for a permit to use government-owned land). But these factors do not neatly match the organizational categories of independent commissions and regular executive agencies.

The separation-of-powers approach is of no help, either, in determining how independent the commissions should be, or to whom they are principally responsible. Each commission has a mixture of policy-making, adjudicatory, and administrative functions (and, as has been suggested earlier, other functions that do not fit these classic molds). To select one function as dominant requires blinding one's eyes to the others. The Supreme Court, to be sure, has chosen to stress the judicial nature of the commissions' work, which is a useful premise for arguing that the commissions should be independent (by analogy with the independence of the judiciary) and that the President's removal power may therefore be restricted by Congress. But the utility of the premise does not establish its validity.

In the second place, the commissions need to be treated as "governmental agencies" with responsibility for achieving their statutory objectives through optimal use of the resources placed at their disposal—powers, appropriated funds, personnel, services available from other agencies, and the like. Two specific conclusions flow from this proposition. The commission proper (that is, the commissioners) is responsible for the full range of the agency's work. This includes making of policy; development of an expert staff; determination of which companies or which evils to investigate and issue formal complaints about; negotiation of informal agreements and stipulations; decision of innocence, guilt, and penalty to be imposed or remedial action to be required in cases brought to a formal hearing as a result of a complaint formally issued; and enforcement of the decisions arrived at by such means as inspection, requirement of compliance reports, and resort to the courts. Further, while the commission proper carries the responsibility described, the discharge of the responsibility must be institutional in character, the commission sharing responsibilities with its staff according to the volume of work and the different kinds of expertness that are relevant. As much as an executive department head, the commission needs to be able to draw on its staff for studies and advice; it needs to delegate to staff members much of the actual making of decisions that apply the commission's policies in specific cases.

One conclusion stands out from these two ideas that flow from the *agency* concept—the commission's own comprehensive responsibility for the discharge of its statutory obligations and the institutional nature of actual performance of the work. That conclusion is to apply close scrutiny to proposals to isolate the commission from its staff, make some of its staff members individual islands without means of communication with the mainland, and shape the bulk of work to judicial models, in spite of the affirmative responsibilities of the commission for identifying and pursuing with vigor the public interest.

Contest of values. Third, to translate the standard of fairness into an operative principle of governmental regulation is a more complex problem than is generally recognized. This is so because we have insisted on fairness in some circumstances but not in others, because there are many ways rather than one of maximizing fairness, and because fairness competes with other important values that seek expression in governmental arrangements.

A choice between at least two alternatives is posed in any decision in government—whether on foreign policy, on appropriation or allocation of funds, on appointment or dismissal of a civil servant, or on regulation of an industry or a company. Typically, a decision either way will disappoint someone with an interest in having it decided the other way. To assure fairness, should each such situation be structured so that the decider is wholly indifferent to the outcome, so that the advocates of each alternative present their evidence in a formal public hearing with witnesses and a stenographic record, so that the decider is forbidden to take account of information not presented in the hearing, so that he must not consult with anyone else in the government? The government's business, of course, cannot be carried on if all decisions must occur under these circumstances. Then which kinds of decisions should be so formalized? Curiously, it is the most important decisions—those on policy—that are the least confined by prescribed procedures. Yet their impact on private property and personal freedom is greatest. What we do is to emphasize formalities to assure fairness when a decision directly affects only one or two individuals or companies, in analogy to the situation in a court case. The pattern can be extended to cover decisions addressed to groups of companies, such as the eastern railroads or the manufacturers of a particular drug. Yet the same groups of companies are not afforded comparable formal procedures when an agency decides to stockpile a particular drug ingredient, rather than allot it for current use by drug companies.

Fairness is something that is achieved by many methods—the staffing of the civil service, the selection of commissioners and department heads, and the ethical code of public officials; the exposure of decisions to public criticism, legislative investigations, and attack in political campaigns; the passage of proposed decisions through many hands, as a normal part of the administrative process; and such ultimate sanctions as removal and judicial review. As one of these methods, the formal, courtlike hearing has an important place; but it is clearly not a full answer to the problem of fairness in the making of governmental decisions that affect private individuals and companies. Furthermore, fairness is a desired general pattern; its achievement cannot be guaranteed in every case, no matter what method is followed. Judges, as well as other officials, make incorrect decisions; some innocent men are punished and some guilty men escape punishment.

Finally, fairness is one of several "goods" that governmental regulation must seek; therefore it cannot be an exclusive end. Even in the judicial system, one cannot appeal to higher courts indefinitely. Indeed, in only a limited category of cases does one have a right to carry one's case to the Supreme Court for the correction of a lower court's errors. Practical considerations intrude. The government, like the courts, must get on with its business. It can set up regulatory processes, staffing arrangements, and organizational patterns that emphasize fairness as a major goal. But it can seldom accommodate to the limit the conviction of a regulated individual that, because his views did not persuade the agency, there must have been bias, or indifference to his evidence, or the intervention of politics. Nor can it accommodate those regulated interests which advocate elaborate procedures in order to reduce the agency's effectiveness by making its operations overly expensive, by squeezing out consideration of the public interest, and by inducing the agency into passive acquiescence in things as they are. Part of the explanation of the establishment of regulatory commissions is the proven inadequacy of the courts as avenues of remedy for the evils legislated against. The agency must keep its eye on its major task of eliminating those evils. If it converts itself into little more than an administrative court, it goes a long way toward destroying its reason for existence.

The political and economic forces that sustain the independence of the regulatory commissions are not likely to lose their belief in the advantages of independent status and its presumed result, independent action. These forces appear powerful enough to resist any drastic change. Increases in executive control, therefore, are likely to occur through increased use of means already available. These are, particularly, appointment of commissioners sharing the President's policy ideas, budgetary review, presidential influence on congressional policy-making for the commissions, and expanded provision for presidential review over particular kinds of commission decisions.

Chapter 11 •

Government Corporations

1. Central Controls and Managerial Freedom

Special relationship. One recurrent theme in each of the preceding chapters dealing with organization and management has been that of the best design for the relationship of the agencies of administration to the organs of popular control—the elected chief executives and legislatures. The general tendency in the United States during most of this century has been to strengthen the powers of direction of the chief executive over administrative agencies. A parallel trend has been the development of more efficacious congressional controls over many aspects of administration, mainly through improved procedures for the review of appropriation requests and through the establishment of means for the supervision of the managerial aspects of administration.

These tendencies toward the integration of the administrative apparatus have their justification in application to the ordinary administrative departments. But they create special problems for agencies engaged in commercial and quasi-commercial activities involving extensive business dealings with the public. To meet such problems, the government corporation developed as an administrative entity having a specially defined relationship to Congress and, to a lesser extent, to the chief executive and other agencies of administrative direction. That relationship frees the government corporation from certain types of controls and gives it a degree of autonomy in the choice of means for the achievement of its purposes.

Types of departmental control. To understand the place of the government corporation in the general administrative structure, it is well to keep in mind the types of congressional and executive control over ordinary departments. In the process of making administrative agencies accountable to the chief executive, ordinary departments have come to be hedged about by many limitations on their freedom of action. Some of these limitations on departmental autonomy concern the substance of what is being done. The chief executive wants to move in one direction rather than another. He desires to wait for a more propitious time before a department inaugurates a program. He prefers this program emphasis or that. By such controls of departmental policy, the chief executive fulfills his broad political responsi-

219

bility. It may be doubted whether in these substantive matters government corporations enjoy any more, or less, freedom of action than do ordinary departments.

It is chiefly with respect to another type of control that a special regime has come to prevail for governmental operations. The process of administrative integration has brought a variety of types of overhead control, which are directed primarily toward the means or methods of achieving substantive objectives. The department is not only told by higher authority what to do, but it is also bound by more or less detailed instructions on how to do the job. Budget, personnel, accounting, and legal officials on the governmentwide level make it their business to see that such instructions are generally followed.

A department must apply elaborate procedures in estimating its future financial needs and in obtaining appropriations from Congress. It enjoys no assurance of continuity in its programs, for once a year it must seek funds from a Congress that is sometimes friendly and sometimes inexplicably capricious. It must hire its employees subject to intricate procedures and regulations fixed by the Civil Service Commission. In spending money, it must take care lest it violate the voluminous jurisprudence on the subject created in the decisions and interpretations of the Comptroller General.

Such modes of integration within the executive branch are based on statute; they are to make possible a more detailed and more effective control of administrative operations by Congress. A well-prepared executive budget which presents data for informed congressional action is a foundation for legislative control. An effective central personnel agency strengthens Congress. For example, Congress can fix salary scales for classes of work and the Civil Service Commission will see that they are applied. The Comptroller General, legally an agent of Congress, will see that legislation prescribing the manner of expenditure of funds is carried out to the letter.

A fanciful illustration. The thoroughness with which legislative enactments can be enforced throughout the vast administrative structure of the federal government is marvelous and awesome. In a more primitive administrative era, the rule books might be filled with regulations, but they would hamper no one as long as they could be ignored or not as the official saw fit. Modern administrative techniques alter the situation. If Congress should abruptly decide that, beginning with the next fiscal year, no red-haired person was to be employed in the federal service, a complex and far-flung administrative process would be set in motion.

The Civil Service Commission would assemble the experts to advise it in the promulgation of regulations defining "red" hair. It would exclude all people within the definition from its future examinations. It would lay down rules for the departments. To make certain that the act of Congress was carried out, it might prescribe that no color-blind person could be a personnel officer. The Bureau of the Budget would inquire of the departments what steps were being taken to avoid the expenditure of funds for the prohibited purpose.

Each department head would issue stern orders to his personnel offices. Instructions including detailed procedures for the application of the law would flow to the bureau chiefs, the division chiefs, and the section chiefs. From Washington, these orders would go to the federal field establishments —the regional and local offices. The regulation would find its way to outposts of the government in Lebanon, India, and Afghanistan. It would filter down the administrative hierarchy to the lowliest and most remote office. The Comptroller General would require an affidavit from each employee that he or she did not have red hair—probably accompanied by a photograph in color, attested to be a true likeness of the affiant by two disinterested persons! The Attorney General would be asked to rule on the applicability of the law to a completely bald person who once had red hair; and the holding of the Attorney General might be contrary to that of the Comptroller General.

The Federal Bureau of Investigation would put samples of hair through the laboratory to detect evidences of dye. The courts would be called upon to decide whether the law applied to employees of state governments paid in part from federal grants. The Department of State, for the good of the service, would seek from Congress an exception from the law for its locally hired employees in Eire. Congressional committees would be petitioned by discharged persons insisting that their hair was titian and not red as the Comptroller General had held, and demanding special legislation authorizing their employment.

The example is fanciful, but its essence could be duplicated a hundred times. Derived from such controls over methods are the cherished maxims of our political folklore to the effect that government departments are stifled by red tape, paralyzed by intricate procedures, hindered by adherence to precedent, and bound by absurd rules and regulations. Corollary beliefs are that departments are ill fitted to undertake functions requiring speedy action, rapid adaptation to new conditions, inventiveness, and the exercise of judgment unfettered by petty rules. These notions abound most luxuriantly in newspaper editorials, campaign speeches, and kindred sources, and in some degree they possess an undeniable validity.

Corporate escape from controls. In part because of the controls applicable to the operation of ordinary departments and in part because of other reasons, the government corporation is commonly regarded as a means by which the body politic can conduct commercial activities under administrative arrangements approximating those of private enterprise. In a frequently quoted passage, Britain's Herbert Morrison has argued for the use of the corporation in the management of publicly-owned commercial enterprise because such an undertaking "should be able with speed and decision to adapt itself to the changing needs of the modern world." Such characteristics are not without merit in the ordinary department, but they are indispensable in a commercial enterprise, if it is to survive.

Perhaps in its "pure" form, a government corporation would be one in which government owned all or the majority of the stock of an ordinary commercial corporation. Government, like a private stockholder, would look to the managers for the efficient conduct of the enterprise and would measure performance by the volume of dividends and the state of the balance sheet. It would leave to the officers of the corporation proper discretion in the tasks of management: the methods of personnel selection; the rules for purchasing supplies; the terms on which sales would be made; the decision about dividend rates; the question whether to plow earnings back into plant expansion or to borrow for it; and the like. For example, if the federal government should buy 51 per cent of the stock of the American Telephone & Telegraph Company, it could receive the company's dividends, observe the results of operations, and, if dissatisfied, use its majority stock control to replace the management.

Adaptation of the corporate device. The simple analogy between government and private corporations has turned out to be not entirely apt. As a consequence, the corporate pattern within government has undergone a marked evolution to adapt it to the circumstances under which it operates. In the process, the government corporation has come to be subjected to new types of congressional and executive supervision, compatible with the exercise of a degree of freedom from the controls applicable to ordinary departments. In this adaptation the government corporation has both lost and retained characteristics of resemblance to the private corporation; it has both acquired characteristics like those of the ordinary department and retained differentiations.

Perhaps the major adaptation of the corporation in government has been the development of functional equivalents of certain controls exercised over private corporate management. Early enthusiasts for governmental use of the corporate device by and large did not know much about private corporations. They failed to recognize the fact that, though stockholders do not turn out in hordes at stockholders' meetings, private corporate management does work under the discipline of the balance sheet and of the market. Its operations are subject to fairly searching review by the security analysts and by investors. So long as earnings are satisfactory, it may run the business. Incompetence sooner or later gets its come-uppance in the capital markets or in the markets for the products of the corporation.

A major consequence in the evolution of the government corporation has been the creation of procedures that simulate such controls over the private corporation. These procedures took form in the Government Corporation Control Act of 1945. They grew out of a situation in which many government corporations were really not held to account by anybody. The act of 1945 provided for annual reviews by the President and by Congress to assure authoritative consideration of the status of each corporation. The information required for this review permits the raising of questions not unlike those which would be raised with respect to the management of a private corporation and which would be inapplicable in the review of the work of most ordinary governmental agencies.

The Government Corporation Control Act has been called by Harold Seidman "one of the most significant developments in the art of public administration." [1] It was not the work of a day, but marked the culmination in the evolution of several lines of policy regarding the government corporation. In a broad sense, what the law accomplished was to permit government corporations to act on their own judgment in the performance of many transactions for which a department would have to obtain specific authority from Congress or would have to abide by rules imposed externally. In substitution for such controls, the act provides for periodic appraisals of the total operations of each corporation, first by the President, with the assistance of the Bureau of the Budget, and again by Congress.

2. The Development of the Corporate System

Gap between theory and practice. In the growth of the corporate system, an inconsistency appears to have existed between the justifications offered in the extensive literature on government corporations for the use of this form of organization and the actual practice of Congress and the chief executive in the establishment of corporations. Rationalizations of the corporate form were erected on the assumption that it should be resorted to primarily for the administration of self-sustaining commercial undertakings. Operations yielding sufficient revenues to cover costs and perhaps to finance some expansion would permit the existence of an administrative entity with an autonomy comparable to that of the private corporation. Only with such revenues would it be feasible for long for autonomy to prevail, as nearly all the controls applicable to the ordinary department stem from the fact of expenditure from the public treasury.

However desirable perhaps as a goal, in practice these conditions conducive to the granting and maintenance of autonomy rarely prevailed. Only most infrequently was a government corporation created to conduct commercial undertakings of a type that would normally yield sufficient profit to provide the financial foundation for genuine autonomy. Often a corporation undertook a function certain to be unprofitable; then

---

[1] Seidman, Harold, "The Theory of the Autonomous Government Corporation: A Critical Appraisal," *Public Administration Review,* 1952, Vol. 12, p. 94. See also his "The Government Corporation: Organization and Controls," *Public Administration Review,* 1954, Vol. 14, p. 183 *ff.* and "The Government Corporation: Its Place in the Federal Structure," in Hanson, A. H., ed., *Public Enterprise: A Study of Its Organization and Management in Various Countries,* Brussels: International Institute of Administrative Sciences, 1955, p. 41 *ff.* Dr. Seidman read and criticized a draft of this chapter. Grateful acknowledgment of his advice is not meant to saddle him with responsibility for the views and interpretations expressed.

sooner or later the corporation would have to go to Congress for restoration of its impaired capital. Even more frequently the government corporation was charged with functions whose performance of necessity had to be coordinated with other activities of the federal government. Such a corporation might enjoy freedom from procedural controls applicable to the ordinary department, but its policy had to be integrated with that of the regular departments. An Export-Import Bank, for example, could scarcely conduct its foreign lending operations quite independently of the foreign policy of the government. In other instances, corporations performed a mixture of functions, some "corporate," others "noncorporate." The Tennessee Valley Authority generates and sells power, but it also operates flood control works, seeks to prevent soil erosion, and performs other functions of a noncommercial nature.

For these and other reasons, government corporations in the United States have been of "somewhat limited value" [2] in illustrating the use of the corporate form as a means of managing publicly owned commercial enterprises. In the process of adaptation of the corporation to the necessities of operation under political accountability a new sort of institution developed. As early as 1941, a leading student of the subject could conclude that the "government corporation as a concept—as a definite and specialized form of administrative organization—is rapidly ceasing to exist." [3] The benefit of hindsight enables us now to say that the corporation was not so much ceasing to exist as taking on new forms compatible with both the functions performed and the necessities of political accountability.

Government corporations as products of emergencies. The major objective in the creation of most government corporations has been to carry out, under emergency conditions, functions of a commercial nature clothed with a public concern. The choice of the corporate form has been in the main dictated by the desire to avoid the normal administrative restraints by overhead controls, rather than to vest in the corporation autonomy in the determination of its substantive commercial policy.

This general point holds, it is true, only if one considers the entire roster of government corporations, present and past. The system of government corporations has tended to expand markedly in times of military and economic emergency. In the contraction following such crises, a smaller

---

[2] Thurston, John, *Government Proprietary Corporations in the English-Speaking Countries*, p. 6, Cambridge: Harvard University Press, 1937. The corporations that remained after the depression of the thirties and World War II and those that have since been created may turn out to be more relevant to the concept of the corporation as an instrument for the performance of publicly owned, commercial enterprise. Yet it will be a minor miracle if the Saint Lawrence Seaway Development Corporation becomes self-sustaining.

[3] Pritchett, C. H., "The Paradox of the Government Corporation," *Public Administration Review*, 1941, Vol. 1, p. 381.

number of government corporations remains to conduct continuing operations for whose performance the corporate device has been judged more appropriate than an ordinary department. It should be added further that the government's earliest corporate undertaking was more a matter of chance than of choice. The oldest government corporation—the Panama Railroad Company, now succeeded by the Panama Canal Company—came into government ownership under special circumstances.[4] In 1903, the United States acquired the French interest in the canal and in the railroad company which had been incorporated under the laws of New York in 1849. The federal government continued to operate the company under its original charter until 1950.[5] In addition to the railroad, the company operated hotels, commissaries, steamships, dairies, laundries, and other enterprises. In 1950, the Panama Canal Company was created to succeed the Railroad Company; to it was also assigned the operation of the Panama Canal.

Wartime corporations, after serving their purpose, have usually been liquidated in due course. Corporations brought forth by economic emergency, however, have not so uniformly moved through such a life cycle. In some instances the economic emergency caused the formation of corporations that survived to perform functions of lasting importance. Thus, the Federal Deposit Insurance Corporation emerged from the banking crisis of the thirties as a permanent institution.

The first large-scale use of corporations occurred in World War I, when such bodies included the United States Housing Corporation, the United States Grain Corporation, the War Finance Corporation, the Emergency Fleet Corporation, and the United States Spruce Production Corporation. Experience gained at that time brought a recognition of the potentialities of the corporation and furnished precedents for subsequent action.[6]

Great Depression and World War II. The Great Depression was a second occasion for the creation of a considerable number of corporations. The Reconstruction Finance Corporation was formed in 1932 in an at-

---

[4] See Dimock, Marshall E., *Government-Operated Enterprises in the Panama Canal Zone,* Chicago: University of Chicago Press, 1934.

[5] Before 1948, practice in the chartering of government corporations varied widely. In some instances, they were formed under state corporation laws by federal officials who proceeded in the same manner as private incorporators. In others, they were created specifically by acts of Congress. In a few instances, private corporations became "government" corporations by public acquisition of their capital stock. The Government Corporation Control Act of 1945 prohibited the organization or acquisition of any government corporation "for the purpose of acting as an agency or instrumentality of the United States, except by Act of Congress or pursuant to an Act of Congress specifically authorizing such action." The act also required the liquidation by June 30, 1948, of all wholly owned government corporations formed under laws of the states or the District of Columbia, unless reincorporated by act of Congress prior to that date.

[6] See Van Dorn, Harold, *Government-Owned Corporations,* New York: Knopf, 1926.

tempt to stave off economic disaster by loans to business—banks, insurance companies, railroads, and other types of enterprise. The functions of the corporation were broadened after its establishment, and through the spawning of subsidiaries it eventually became a huge holding company. The Home Owners Loan Corporation was another type of emergency credit agency. Created in 1933, it had the function of refinancing home mortgages threatened with foreclosure. By the end of its lending operations in 1936, it had refinanced over $3 billions in home mortgages. Another variety of emergency corporation was the Federal Surplus Commodities Corporation, which was chartered in 1933 for the purpose of buying agricultural surpluses and of distributing them to relief agencies—hardly a profit-making enterprise, but one involving large purchasing operations which could be carried on more handily under corporate arrangements.

The Tennessee Valley Authority, though a permanent institution, was also of depression origin. Created in 1933 with functions of a mixed governmental and commercial nature, it is notable both for its corporate form and as an experiment in multi-purpose regional administration. The Federal Deposit Insurance Corporation, another permanent agency of emergency origin, was charged with the insurance of bank deposits, a risk too great to be carried by private enterprise and difficult of assumption save through compulsory coverage on a large scale. The Federal Savings and Loan Insurance Corporation (1934) had a similar objective in the protection of investments in savings and loan institutions. Federal Prison Industries, Inc. (1934) involved the incorporation of an existing activity, a move perhaps influenced by the frequent resort to use of the corporate device in other activities at the time. The corporation sells to government departments, which are obliged to buy from it, and employs workers who have no alternative market for their labor. It makes money. Other corporations created in the early 1930's included the Commodity Credit Corporation (1933), the Federal Farm Mortgage Corporation (1934), and the Federal Home Loan Banks (1932).

World War II brought another spurt in corporate activity with the creation of a number of corporations, principally as subsidiaries of the Reconstruction Finance Corporation, to carry on war activities which are notoriously of a risky character. The Defense Homes Corporation (1940) was organized to construct homes in areas congested by defense activity. The Defense Plant Corporation (1940) was created to finance and construct plants for war production; it became the owner of billions in plants and machinery. The Defense Supplies Corporation (1940) and the Metals Reserve Company (1940) were established to buy and sell strategic and critical materials. The Rubber Development Corporation (1940) was given the job of developing and procuring natural rubber abroad, principally in Latin America, while the Rubber Reserve Company (1940) was formed to construct synthetic rubber plants. The United States Commercial Company (1942), another Reconstruction Finance Corporation subsidiary, was chartered to engage chiefly in preclusive buying abroad— that is, buying critical materials regardless of price to prevent their falling into the hands of the enemy. In 1945, several of the defense subsidiaries of the Reconstruction Finance Corporation were merged with the parent company and lost their separate identity. In 1953 the Reconstruction Finance Corporation was placed in liquidation, although some of its lending functions were continued by the Small Business Administration.

Government corporations in the field of credit. A major use of the corporate form is in the operation of lending and credit guarantee programs. The earliest venture in this field was the system of Federal Land Banks, authorized in 1916 after long inquiry into the problem of agricultural credit. These banks were for a time mixed in ownership, with part of the stock being owned by the federal government and part by national farm loan associations—that is, borrowers' cooperatives. The Federal Land Banks revolutionized long-term farm mortgage lending practices. Gradually the government's investment in these banks was retired, and in 1947 the federal capital was replaced entirely by stock held by the borrowers' associations.

The farm credit system was broadened in 1923 with the creation of twelve Federal Intermediate Credit Banks, which make loans and discounts for lending institutions engaged in short-term financing of farm production. In 1933 twelve Production Credit Corporations were set up to organize and finance local production credit associations, which in turn would make short-term loans to farmers. These local associations were credit cooperatives, with some of their capital subscribed by the Production Credit Corporations. Under an act of 1956 the Production Credit Corporations were merged with the Federal Intermediate Credit Banks, and provision was made for the eventual retirement of the government's capital in the banks and for their ultimate ownership by the production credit associations.

The system of Federal Home Loan Banks, created in 1932, was modeled on the Federal Land Banks. The Home Loan Banks make advances to their members—savings and loan associations and savings banks—on the security of home mortgages. The capital of the banks was initially subscribed by the federal government, but it has now been repaid. The banks are controlled by their members, subject to the supervision of the Federal Home Loan Bank Board. The Home Loan Banks may borrow up to $1 billion from the Treasury.

In 1948 the Federal Housing Administration was made subject to the Government Corporation Control Act. The Administration operates a a variety of programs to insure banks and other credit institutions against losses on loans. Its revenues come from premiums and fees charged for coverage. The view is expressed from time to time that the Administration's contingent liabilities are probably excessive in the light of its resources and of its charges for loan guarantees.[7]

Scope of corporate system. Given the fact that corporations have been used extensively to cope with emergency problems, the size and composition of the corporate sector of the federal administrative structure differ from time to time. In 1944, there existed about 100 government corporations, the precise number varying with idiosyncrasies in definition. After World War II, many of these corporations were liquidated. The Eisenhower Administration put an end to others. Nevertheless, the residue of more or less permanent government corporations includes many large enterprises of great public importance. The Federal Land Banks, the Federal Home Loan Banks, the Federal Deposit Insurance Corporation, the Federal Savings and Loan Insurance Corporation, the Federal Housing Administration, and the Export-Import Bank play significant roles in the credit and banking field. The Commodity Credit Corporation is an important instrumentality in the maintenance of farm prices through its purchasing and credit operations. The Tennessee Valley Authority is one of the world's largest generators of electric power. The Saint Lawrence Seaway Development Corporation is vested with the responsibility for the construction and operation of great public works. And a number of other smaller corporations perform a variety of governmental functions. Moreover, "revolving fund" operations have developed throughout the government; these closely resemble corporations because their administrators have considerable discretion in the management of a capital sum appropriated by Congress.

3. Overhead Control of Corporate Operations

Changing character. The ordinary government department is subject to overhead controls applied by the Bureau of the Budget, the Department of Justice, the Comptroller General, and the Civil Service Commission. Through decades of evolution these controls and procedures have become, as David E. Lilienthal has said, "stupefying" [8] in their complexity. Although such limitations on departmental action are by no means without utility, they often delay operations. They limit departments in the choice of means to achieve ends; they sometimes smother initiative; and too often they become pointless ritual. Long experience has demonstrated the need for limits on officials who spend other people's money. However, in some types of governmental undertakings, reliance on the traditional prescriptions rather than on alternative methods of measuring performance makes it difficult to accomplish the job assigned to an agency.

---

[7] See (second) Commission on the Organization of the Executive Branch of the Government, *Lending, Guaranteeing, and Insurance Activities,* Washington, 1955; Saulnier, R. J., and Others, *Federal Lending and Loan Insurance,* Princeton: Princeton University Press, 1958.

[8] *TVA—Democracy on the March,* p. 168, New York: Harper, 1944.

The government-owned corporation, immune from most of the controls applicable to ordinary departments, was thought to provide also the alternative means of measuring performance. Yet the present-day government corporation is far removed from the early conceptions of that institution. By a rather tortuous process of evolution, the corporate form was modified to meet the practical necessities of operation within the federal government.

Elements of financial control and the corporate system. Perhaps the most significant deviation from ordinary governmental practices in the operation of government corporations occurs with respect to financial control. The customary rules about finance stem from the constitutional principle that no money be paid from the Treasury except under law. The principle lays the basis for control by the executive and legislative branches over the administrative agencies. The power of the purse is used to determine the amounts to be spent for each of the purposes of government. It is also used to prescribe in greater or lesser detail precisely how the money shall be spent.

Another principle—a necessary corollary of the first—is that public revenues shall be deposited in the Treasury. Without adherence to this maxim, public moneys might be spent directly from revenue without specific appropriation by the legislature. A third fundamental principle is that of annual appropriations. Invariable adherence to it has not been achieved. A few permanent appropriations—that is, standing authorizations for the expenditure of specified amounts each year—remain on the books. Yet annual appropriation is the general practice in the federal government. This is of profound importance. It means that the power of the purse is exerted at annual intervals. The burden of proof and pressure is annually placed upon those who desire money.

The government corporation furnishes a method of modifying these principles. A subscription by government to the capital stock of a corporation or an allocation of funds to the corporation removes the money from the Treasury and from annual appropriation control. The funds may be utilized until exhausted, whether it takes one year or ten. Earnings of the corporation, because they may be corporate funds rather than public revenues, need not be covered into the Treasury but may be retained in the custody of the corporation. They may then be spent at the discretion of the officers of the corporation, though only within the limits of corporate purposes fixed by the charter. If the corporation is engaged in a self-sustaining function, its revenues would enable it to operate on its own resources more or less indefinitely, without annual subjection to the presidential and congressional power of the purse.

It is usually pointed out that in the avoidance of customary regulations about expenditure a superior type of control becomes possible. If a revenue-producing function is involved, analysis of the financial operations by ordinary methods applied by private corporations will furnish a means of evaluating performance. Is the enterprise coming out even or is it yielding a return on the government's investment? Thus the Tennessee Valley Authority attempts to indicate in its financial reports the degree to which its power operations are paying their way. This can be contrasted with the Post Office accounting in which a profit may be claimed while no charges are made for capital, depreciation, or other factors which are weighed in business accounting.

Forecasting financial needs. Fiscal freedom makes the measurement of performance feasible. However, probably of greater importance in the case made for corporate autonomy are certain characteristics of the appropriation procedure for ordinary departments. It is very difficult to forecast the financial requirements of a commercial enterprise. If business is unexpectedly good, the increased revenues must be available to meet the increased operating charges. Moreover, application of the usual appropriation procedures to commercial enterprises is made less practicable by the length of the appropriation cycle. An ordinary department must anticipate its financial needs long in advance of actual expenditure. Thus each summer a department must begin the preparation of its expenditure estimates to cover the fiscal year that will end on June 30 two years later. It must ordinarily present its estimates for review by the Bureau of the Budget about September of the year preceding the beginning of the fiscal year covered by the estimates. It will subsequently justify the estimates as approved by the President to congressional committees, and final action will be taken by Congress shortly before the beginning of the fiscal year.

The difficulties of forecasting revenues and expenditures of commercial enterprise are illustrated by an experience of the Tennessee Valley Authority. Estimates of power revenues and expenses of power production prepared in the summer of 1939 for the fiscal year ending June 30, 1941, were: revenues, $14.7 millions; direct power expenses, $5.6 millions. In fact, however, revenues turned out to be $21 millions and expenses about $9 millions.[9] Under ordinary budget procedure, TVA would have had to go back to Congress for additional appropriations to meet the unforeseen conditions. Under corporate practice, the increased revenues were available without congressional action to meet the increased expenses.

Another example is furnished by the Federal Deposit Insurance Corporation. Its revenues consist of assessments on the deposits of insured banks, together with the earnings from the investment of the capital and surplus of the corporation. The annual disbursements for the protection of depositors have ranged from $265,000 to $74,000,000. The corporation attempts to pay depositors as soon as possible after a bank is closed—the

---

[9] Finer, Herman, *The TVA: Lessons for International Application,* p. 189, Montreal: International Labour Office, 1944

next day if practicable. Any attempt to estimate losses and provide for them by appropriations would be doomed to failure.

Development of review and control of corporation finance. The considerations urged in support of corporate freedom from appropriation controls are persuasive. Yet experience also indicated a need for authoritative review of corporate fiscal operations. The Government Corporation Control Act marked the culmination of the development of procedures for the periodic and systematic appraisal of corporate operations as well as the introduction of a degree of budgetary control over all wholly owned government corporations. That act, however, left a range of fiscal discretion to corporations appropriate to the performance of their business functions.

Even before the adoption of the Corporation Control Act, successive actions by the President and Congress had narrowed corporate autonomy in the determination of expenditure programs. These actions left only the Inland Waterways Corporation, the Panama Railroad Company, and certain agricultural credit corporations in full enjoyment of the power to adopt operating programs for the expenditure of their revenues.

In the development of appropriation control, the first step was the introduction of the requirement that corporations with funds available for expenditure without annual appropriation, obtain approval by the Bureau of the Budget of expenditures for "administrative expenses," a category of expenditure somewhat difficult to define. In 1935, the President directed that the Federal Savings and Loan Insurance Corporation, the Home Owners Loan Corporation, and the Federal Farm Mortgage Corporation submit annually to the Bureau of the Budget estimates of funds needed for administrative expenses, and that they incur obligations only within the limits approved by the budget director.[10] Shortly afterwards, the same rule was applied to the Federal Deposit Insurance Corporation, the Export-Import Bank, the Reconstruction Finance Corporation, and the Electric Home and Farm Authority.[11] Next, the Tennessee Valley Authority was added to the list. In 1942, the requirements were extended to all major corporations until then outside the rule.[12]

The next step in the evolution of overhead control of government corporations was the introduction of congressional review of administrative expenses. The First Deficiency Appropriation Act of 1936 listed nine larger corporations which, beginning with the next fiscal year, were prohibited from incurring any administrative expenses "except pursuant to an annual appropriation specifically therefor . . . ."[13] This provision would have resulted in expenditures being made from the Treasury rather than from corporate funds. That in turn would have brought such administrative

---

[10] Executive Order No. 7126 of August 5, 1935.
[11] Executive Order No. 7150 of August 19, 1935.
[12] Executive Order No. 9159 of May 11, 1942.
[13] 49 Stat. 1648.

expenditures within the purview of the Comptroller General and would have made them subject to all the general rules and regulations applicable to departments. However, the law of 1936 was modified in subsequent appropriation acts. Congressional action took the form of a limitation on the amount of corporate funds which might be spent for administrative purposes, rather than of an appropriation from the Treasury. Thus the language of one pertinent appropriation act for 1945 reads: "Not to exceed $11,500,000 of the funds of the Reconstruction Finance Corporation, established by the Act of January 22, 1932 (47 Stat. 5), shall be available during the fiscal year 1945 for its administrative expenses . . . ." By this means, Congress limited the amount which might be spent for administrative purposes but did not bring the expenditure under the control of legislation and regulations governing ordinary departments.

The question whether to change the original laws governing a corporation to bring administrative expenses under annual congressional review seems to have been determined largely by chance rather than by principle. In some instances, the action taken resulted clearly from the lack of legislative confidence in a particular individual. In other instances, the initiative came from the corporation, motivated by the consideration that it might be better off under a limitation suggested by itself than it would be under more drastic action initiated by Congress.

Congressional limitation of administrative expenses. Subjection of "administrative expenses" to congressional limitation was not necessarily onerous. It left the corporation autonomous in the greater part of its fiscal operations. A lending corporation, for example, might loan, collect, and reloan its funds without congressional limitation on the total scale of lending operations—save such limitation as was imposed by the amount of capital available to the corporation. Congress limited only the "administrative" expenses. Moreover, the ingenious concept of "nonadministrative expenses" and their exclusion from congressional control permitted corporate flexibility in the determination of the amounts spent for certain purposes which in lay language might be called administrative. The differentiation between administrative and nonadministrative expense was not sharp. Generally, continuing overhead costs were included in the administrative category, while expenses arising directly in the management, protection, and care of property by the corporation were nonadministrative.

The distinction was laid down in the appropriation act relating to each corporation. Thus, for fiscal year 1945 the appropriation limitation for the Reconstruction Finance Corporation stated: "Provided, That all necessary expenses in connection with the acquisition, operation, maintenance, improvement, or disposition of any real or personal property belonging to the Corporation or the RFC Mortgage Company, or in which they have an interest, including expenses of collections of pledged collateral, shall be considered as nonadministrative expenses for the purposes hereof."

This formula is typical, but variations in language have prevailed for each corporation or cluster of corporations to which the nonadministrative expense proviso applies. The significance of the exception of nonadministrative expense may be deduced from the fact that in 1944 these expenditures for corporations and credit agencies reporting them were in the aggregate more than five times as great as administrative expenses.

The annual congressional limitation on a corporation's administrative expenses was ordinarily accompanied by no restriction on what might be called "program expenditures." In the case of the Reconstruction Finance Corporation, for instance, the magnitude of its operations were limited by the size of its capital and the rate of turnover of loans rather than by a statutory specification that during the year it might lend so many millions of dollars. However, if a corporation sought additional capital from Congress or authority to borrow, it had to ask for legislative action. When the Tennessee Valley Authority, for example, sought new capital to construct additional works, its estimate would be scrutinized by Congress just as thoroughly as would a similar request by the Bureau of Reclamation.

Budget review and congressional control. By the steps that have been recounted the essential elements of the financial position of government corporations under the Government Corporation Control Act developed. That act differentiated between wholly owned and mixed-ownership government corporations. Insofar as the mixed-ownership corporations were concerned—the Central Bank for Cooperatives and the Regional Banks for Cooperatives, Federal Land Banks, Federal Home Loan Banks, and the Federal Deposit Insurance Corporation—the *status quo* was maintained. No annual budget presentation was required of these corporations by the act.[14]

Wholly owned government corporations—that is, corporations other than those of mixed ownership listed above—were required to submit annually a "budget program" through the usual budgetary channels. The act specified: "The budget program shall be a business-type budget, or plan of operations, with due allowance given to the need for flexibility including provision for emergencies and contingencies, in order that the

---

[14] The President in 1957 proposed that certain of the mixed-ownership corporations be brought under the act and be subjected to annual scrutiny by the President and Congress. Under the proposal, budgetary and financial review would be maintained over all government corporations "which possess authority (1) to issue or have outstanding obligations guaranteed in whole or in part by the United States; or (2) to obtain Government funds by appropriations, borrowings, subscriptions to capital stock or otherwise; or (3) to utilize Government funds obtained by any of the above methods." Thus, the Federal Deposit Insurance Corporation, although the Treasury's investment in it has been retired, may call upon the Treasury for $3 billion, a circumstance that justifies periodic review of the status of the corporation. Incidentally, since the passage of the act of 1945 some of the mixed-ownership corporations have become in fact entirely privately owned through the retirement of the federal investment from corporate earnings. Yet these corporations continue to enjoy a special position as government instrumentalities; and presumably the government, whose capital permitted the development of the enterprises, has a residual interest in them.

corporation may properly carry out its activities as authorized by law." The statute also specified that the budget program contain a statement of the financial condition of the corporation and such other information as would enable Congress to evaluate its past performance and its future program.

The legislation thus provided a special budgetary system for government corporations. Their budget presentations constitute more nearly reports and analyses of the results of business operations (and forecasts of the results of future operations) than they do conventional budget requests by governmental agencies. Moreover, the action of Congress upon the budget proposals of corporations differs from the usual appropriation method. Ordinarily Congress does not make an annual appropriation from the Treasury for the corporation; it merely authorizes expenditures from corporate funds.[15] In making these authorizations, a limitation is commonly placed on the total amount to be available for administrative expenses, a usage that developed before the adoption of the act of 1945.[16] The older distinction between administrative and nonadministrative expenses is maintained, a distinction that permits flexibility in nonadministrative outlays as the level of activity dictates. Although the budget presentations include estimates of the levels of future program expenditures, usually no limitation on their size is written into the appropriation bill. They may be governed by the gross level of business or the rate of turnover of the capital of the corporation.

The periodic presentation of corporate budget programs to the Appropriations Committees creates the opportunity for Congress to give authoritative expression to whatever disposition it has on the details of corporate management. Although the precise authorization language varies from corporation to corporation, by and large Congress has limited itself to an over-all limitation on corporate administrative expenses. The congressional committees, however, keep a sharp eye on outlays for automobiles and frequently limit the use of a corporation's funds for this purpose.[17] Congress also tends to reserve for itself the determination of the use of corporate

---

[15] Thus, the passage in the Independent Offices Appropriation Act for 1957 with respect to the Export-Import Bank began: "The following corporation is hereby authorized to make such expenditures within the limits of funds and borrowing authority available to such corporation, and in accord with law, and to make such contracts and commitments without regard to fiscal year limitations as provided by section 104 of the Government Corporation Control Act, as amended, as may be necessary in carrying out the programs set forth in the budget for the fiscal year 1957 for such corporation . . . ."

[16] For example, the Independent Offices Appropriation for 1957 recited: "Federal intermediate credit banks: Not to exceed $1,932,000 (to be computed on an accrual basis) of the funds of the banks shall be available for administrative expenses . . . ."

[17] The 1957 authorization for the Saint Lawrence Seaway Development Corporation, for example, included this language: "Provided further, That the Corporation's funds shall be available for the purchase of not to exceed four passenger motor vehicles (two for replacement only)."

funds for general office buildings. The Appropriations Committees from time to time "advise" corporations in committee reports, as they do ordinary departments, although this advice is not reflected in the language of the appropriation act.

Overhead control and audit. Justifications for the use of the corporation have often emphasized the freedom from both audit and settlement of accounts by the Comptroller General. That official, in his review of expenditures by ordinary departments, checks conformity with all the legal prescriptions of governmentwide applicability as well as with the legislation and appropriation language applicable to the individual agency. These rules frequently hamper commercial operations. Moreover, the Comptroller General exercises, in effect, the final power to interpret the statutes under which an agency operates through his authority to determine the legality of expenditure in the settlement of accounts.

The corporate effort to escape from the authority of the Comptroller General was, in effect, an attempt to escape from the governmentwide administrative rules applied by the Comptroller General. Thus, to spend legally, an agency must comply with an act requiring competitive bidding in the making of public purchases. If all bids are alike, the accepted etiquette is to advertise again or to draw lots to determine the successful bidder. It has been pointed out that if this procedure had been required of the Tennessee Valley Authority when it received identical bids for cement, it would have had to pay excessive prices. Instead it negotiated lower prices. It was able to bargain, with the intimation that it could construct its own cement plant.[18] Such a tactic would have been illegal under ordinary procedures, and the Comptroller General would have blocked payment on a purchase so made. Naturally, in commercial enterprise, freedom in purchases from hampering routines bulks much larger in importance than in the ordinary department, which usually has to make only small purchases for its office needs.

The statute on purchasing procedures is only one of hundreds of statutes and many more decisions of the Comptroller General which the General Accounting Office applies in reviewing the expenditures of government departments. A few additional illustrations may be cited of such general prohibitions; these can be waived in particular instances only by congressional dispensation, which, needless to say, has been often granted. Land to be used for public buildings may not be bought until the Attorney General clears the title. All printing must be done by the Government Printing Office. All agency contracts must be placed on the custody of the General Accounting Office. Plans for public buildings must be approved by the Public Buildings Administration. In addition to general laws of

---

18 Lilienthal, David E., and Marquis, R. H., "The Conduct of Business Enterprises by the Federal Government," *Harvard Law Review,* 1941, Vol. 54, p. 567.

unequivocal meaning, government departments are subject to a large body of rulings produced by the General Accounting Office in the interpretation of statutory language.[19]

Review by Comptroller General. The relationship of corporations to the Comptroller General underwent a process of evolution similar to that of their relation to the budget process and appropriation procedure. At least some corporations were completely free from review by the Comptroller General and his enforcement of the rules commonly applicable to departments. That state of affairs was gradually modified by changes affecting particular corporations. Finally, in 1945 all corporations became subject to inspection of their accounts by the Comptroller General in a manner somewhat different from that applicable to ordinary departments. Whether a corporation came within the jurisdiction of the Comptroller General, thus being subject to the regulations applied by his office, was determined before 1945 by the basic legislation and appropriation language relating to each corporation. By an executive order of 1934, the President directed that corporations created after March 3, 1933, "the accounting procedure for which is not otherwise provided by law," should render accounts to the General Accounting Office for settlement as prescribed by the Comptroller General.[20] In actual fact, the procedure was generally "otherwise provided by law" for each corporation.

Nor was the practice by any means uniform. At one extreme, corporations such as the Panama Railroad Company and the Inland Waterways Corporation, both created before the date fixed by the executive order of 1934, retained complete freedom from the Comptroller General. Even when Congress limited total administrative expenses for particular corporations, it sometimes made it clear that this action did not bring the manner of making such expenditures within the regulations applied by the Comptroller General. Thus for 1945 the limitation for the Reconstruction Finance Corporation indicated that "except for the limitations in amounts hereinbefore, and the restrictions in respect to travel expenses, the administrative expenses and other obligations of the corporation shall be incurred, allowed, and paid" in accordance with the Reconstruction Finance Corporation Act. In other instances, administrative expenses alone were made subject to review by the Comptroller General. The 1945 limitation on administrative expenses of the Smaller War Plants Corporation provided that no part of the administrative expense allowance might "be obligated or expended unless and until an appropriate appropriation account shall have been established therefor pursuant to an appropriation warrant or a

---

[19] The above examples are from McDiarmid, John, *Government Corporations and Federal Funds*, Chicago: University of Chicago Press, 1938. Mention of rules applicable to ordinary departments should not be taken to mean that government corporations are invariably exempt from their application. The situation differs from corporation to corporation.

[20] Executive Order No. 6549 of January 3, 1934.

covering warrant, and all such expenses shall be accounted for and audited in accordance with the Budget and Accounting Act."

All types of expenditures by Federal Prison Industries, Inc. were placed under review by the Comptroller General and had to be made "in accordance with the laws generally applicable to the expenditures of the several departments and establishments of the government." The Tennessee Valley Authority occupied a position at the time peculiar in relation to the Comptroller General. It was liable to audit by the Comptroller General, but it enjoyed the right to overrule a disallowance by him.[21]

Commercial-type audit. Perhaps good and sufficient reasons existed for excepting the expenditures of many government corporations from general laws and regulations. However, one of the consequences was an unsatisfactory system for the inspection of corporate accounts. Not a few corporations employed private accounting firms to examine their accounts. This practice is of dubious efficacy for public enterprise. To fill the void, Congress in 1945 directed the Comptroller General to audit the financial transactions of all government corporations, but the intent was to require a type of audit different from that applicable to ordinary departments. When the Comptroller General "audits" and "settles" accounts of departments, he determines whether particular expenditures have been made in accordance with law and regulation as interpreted by himself. The Government Corporation Control Act calls for an annual audit in accordance "with the principles and procedures applicable to commercial corporate transactions."

Thus the act does not operate to bring corporate expenditures under the laws and regulations applicable to government agencies generally. The *status quo* that existed before the passage of the act is preserved. If a corporation was authorized by previous legislation to determine the manner of making expenditures, that right would live on. Or if a corporation was bound by the ordinary rules and regulations, as in the example cited above of Federal Prison Industries, that arrangement would also continue. The Comptroller General was directed to report to Congress on the findings of the audit, including "a statement of assets and liabilities, capital and surplus, or deficit; a statement of surplus or deficit analysis; a statement of income and expense; a statement of sources and application of funds; and such comments and information as may be deemed necessary to keep Congress informed of the operations and financial condition of the several corporations." The statute laid the basis for a more satisfactory financial inspection of corporations than had generally prevailed. In effect,

---

[21] An act of 1941 provides that the General Accounting Office "shall not disallow credit for nor withhold funds because of any expeditures which the Board shall determine to have been necessary" to carry out the provisions of TVA's basic statute; 55 Stat. 775. Such language made the TVA board rather than the Comptroller General the authoritative interpreter of the statutes fixing the powers of TVA to make expenditures. A similar end has been achieved in several recent corporate charters by authorizing the corporation "to determine the character and necessity of expenditures and the manner in which incurred, allowed, and paid."

the act superimposed over the pre-existing practice, with respect to each corporation, a commercial-type audit which is designed to raise entirely different questions than those of the traditional government audit. The General Accounting Office then recruited staff and established procedures for the conduct of these audits along lines not dissimilar from those followed by private accounting firms in their audits of private corporations.

Central control of personnel. A federal department is bound by general legislation, administered by the Civil Service Commission, which fixes the manner of recruitment of employees, classification and pay scales, and other aspects of personnel administration. As a consequence, departmental discretion is limited in the selection of staff and in the determination of compensation by both legislation and the tradition and customs of civil service. Government corporations have placed a high value on freedom from civil service rules and procedures, but their special privileges in personnel matters have been narrowed.

The President, by Executive Order No. 7915 of June 24, 1938, provided for bringing into the competitive civil service all positions, "including positions in corporations wholly owned or controlled by the United States," except those exempted by statute. The general terms of the order applied to the Commodity Credit Corporation, the Electric Home and Farm Authority, the Export-Import Bank, and the Federal Deposit Insurance Corporation. The Ramspeck Act of 1940 authorized the President to "cover into the classified service" the employees of all government-owned corporations, except the Tennessee Valley Authority.[22] The President exercised this power by Executive Order No. 8743 of April 23, 1941, which put under the provisions of the Civil Service Act the great majority of positions to which the act of 1940 authorized civil service extension.

In the legislation creating the Tennessee Valley Authority, special attention was given to the personnel question. Congress concluded that the undertaking might have a smaller chance of success if it had to operate under civil service rules. Yet it laid down the following merit-system injunction: "In the appointment of officials and the selection of employees for said Corporation, and in the promotion of any such employees or officials, no political test or qualification should be permitted or given consideration, but all such appointments and promotions shall be given and made on the basis of merit and efficiency . . . ." TVA has won an impressive reputation for its personnel policies and practices. A thorough student of TVA concludes that its record in personnel "has been in considerable measure attributable to its freedom from time-worn Civil Service

---

[22] 54 Stat. 211. The Classification Act of 1949 applied the classification system to government corporations with the exception of the Tennessee Valley Authority, the Virgin Islands Corporation, the Panama Railroad, and certain others. Also exempted from the act were "employees none or only part of whose compensation is paid from appropriated funds."

procedures and regulations." [23] He points out, however, that the Civil Service Commission of today is not the routine-ridden organization that it was in the early 1930's.

Freedom from the "time-worn" procedures of the Civil Service Commission does not ensure by itself better-than-average personnel practices. It merely leaves the way open for innovation and managerial responsibility in personnel administration. In some instances—notably the Home Owners Loan Corporation in its earlier days—the freedom from civil service legislation has provided merely an opening for spoils practices. No corporation other than TVA has gained an outstanding reputation for its personnel policies, although some may have done a good job without much advertising.

4. Corporate Autonomy and Political Accountability

Early misconceptions about corporate autonomy. It is fundamental that means exist by which administrative officers and governmental agencies may be held accountable for their acts to those who bear political responsibility—the chief executive and the legislature. It is also essential for the conduct of commercial operations that a government agency be free from many of the regulations and overhead controls customary for ordinary departmental operations. The present policies toward government corporations represent the result of the gradual development of practices calculated to meet both of these needs.

The broad issue of the place of the corporation in the total governmental structure seems not to have been squarely faced by early advocates of the government corporation. The view at times seemed to be that Congress should subscribe the capital for a corporation and then forget about it. The corporation, because it was a corporation, could be left to operate within the sphere of autonomy fixed by its charter.

The extreme view on corporate autonomy failed to take into account at least two major problems of accountability and direction. First was the problem of accountability for prudence in business management. Second, the corporate program often needed to be geared into the operations of ordinary agencies and always was potentially a matter of concern to the President and Congress in the fulfillment of their broad political responsibilities. Ways and means had to exist for appropriate oversight of corporate programs to meet these responsibilities.

Accountability for operating results. One lesson of experience with government corporations may be that the administrative side of the government cannot be relied upon to enforce an accountability for operating, or business, results of government corporations. Provision needs to be made

---

[23] Pritchett, C. H., *The Tennessee Valley Authority*, p. 306, Chapel Hill: University of North Carolina Press, 1943.

for the communication periodically of adequate operating information and for its routine review by Congress. Earlier thought about government corporations placed excessive reliance on the supposition that they would behave like private corporations. It turned out that the creation of a government corporation did not establish an entity subject to the influences that affect private corporate management. Although a degree of autonomy is enjoyed by a private corporation, various forces operate to enforce managerial responsibility. The financial journals, bankers, investment advisers, and such government agencies as the Securities and Exchange Commission seek and obtain considerable information about the operation of a business concern. Larger stockholders are certainly not without influence. The need to retain the confidence of the financial community is a spur to management. The mores and habits of a business civilization likewise have their effects.

None of these forces operated upon government corporations. It required long trial and error to develop substitutes within the government. Congress, habituated to its annual review of the expenditures of ordinary departments, was somewhat baffled by government corporations. Their novel mode of operation required that they be appraised differently. The sense of frustration that arose in Congress when it dealt with government corporations is illustrated by the following interchange in 1943 between Senator Harry F. Byrd, a committee chairman, and Jesse Jones, then chief of the Reconstruction Finance Corporation:

> *The Chairman.* Will you point out to me now exactly what congressional authority Congress has over these corporations after the first authorization to operate is given to you? . . . We authorize you to borrow $5,000,000,000. After that is done, what authority has Congress over the RFC and how can they exercise it if it has got it?
>
> *Secretary Jones.* I suppose if we misuse the funds, you would have a good deal of authority?
>
> *The Chairman.* How?
>
> *Secretary Jones.* I do not know about that. . . .
>
> . . . .
>
> *The Chairman.* . . . I am asking you what authority Congress has over the RFC after they make their initial authorization.
>
> *Secretary Jones.* I have always thought they had all of the authority.
>
> *The Chairman.* Tell me how they can exercise the authority. You know vastly more about it than I do. They haven't even a report from the RFC in detail.
>
> *Secretary Jones.* We make monthly reports to Congress.
>
> *The Chairman.* You do not make them in detail?
>
> *Secretary Jones.* Pretty well in detail.
>
> *The Chairman.* You do not give the names of the borrowers?
>
> *Secretary Jones.* I think we do. . . .
>
> . . . .
>
> *The Chairman.* Where does that report go?
>
> *Mr. Mulligan.* To the Vice President and the Speaker.
>
> *The Chairman.* Is it a public report?

Mr. Mulligan. Yes, except since the war I do not know whether they have been issued to the general public or not.

The Chairman. Do you make an annual report to Congress?

Mr. Mulligan. In addition to the monthly report a quarterly report to Congress is also required by law.

Secretary Jones. A monthly report and a quarterly report. . . .

. . . .

The Chairman. . . . I have never seen a report on the itemized loans of the RFC.

Secretary Jones. If you will refer to the act, Senator, you will find it requires these things, and these reports are sent in here, and you can go to the Vice President's office and get them.

The Chairman. I am glad to hear you say that.

Secretary Jones. We will be delighted to send them to the individual members who want them. . . .

. . . .

The Chairman. I am talking about the itemized statements.

Secretary Jones. I am talking about the itemized statement. I am talking about the loan to John Smith for X dollars, and the rate of interest. . . .

. . . .

The Chairman. You haven't told me yet what control Congress can exercise over the RFC.

Secretary Jones. I will leave that to Congress.[24]

Congress was not, of course, as helpless as the Senator would have had us believe. Yet, in some instances, corporations did not have to appear routinely and periodically before congressional committees to report upon and explain their operations. In others, corporations partook in a special degree of the administrative attitude that "what Congress does not know will not get one into trouble." Quite frequently corporate reports concealed far more than they revealed about the results of operations. Thus, by enough research to produce a book, a private scholar might conclude that without the subsidy from the Production Credit Corporations, the production credit associations would have had to charge farmers about 1 per cent more on loans in 1943 in order to maintain the same services and accumulate the same reserves as in 1942.[25] That simple fact could not be readily deduced from the data available to Congress. Or, in other instances, government corporations reported profitable operations actually made possible by over-capitalization. That is, their deficits were, in effect, endowed by the government. In reality, neither Congress nor anybody else had, for many corporations, information that showed clearly the business results of their operations.

Review under Government Corporation Control Act. Even before the adoption of the act of 1945, Congress took steps to improve the flow of

---

[24] Joint Committee on Reduction of Non-Essential Federal Expenditures, *Hearings,* pp. 2295-2297, 78th Cong., 1st Sess., pt. 7, 1943.

[25] Butz, E. L., *The Production Credit System for Farmers,* Washington: Brookings Institution, 1944.

information about corporate operations. The more foresighted corporate managers encouraged such action, for they were aware that some of their troubles with Congress came from the inadequacy of information on their operations and the lack of regularized channels of communication with Congress.

The submission of budgetary programs under the Government Corporation Control Act provides a recurring opportunity for systematic reporting of the results of operations to the President and Congress. The corporate statements, included in the federal budget,[26] differ somewhat in form from corporation to corporation with the nature of the function performed. They do not resemble private corporate reports to the extent that it is possible to compare earnings per share from year to year. But they are adaptations of the essentials of commercial accounting to government enterprise and convey far more information about corporate operations than was usually available before the system was inaugurated.

The program covers the preceding fiscal year, includes estimates for the current year, and makes projections for the next year. Ordinarily, the report includes a summary statement of sources and applications of funds for the periods covered. A lending corporation indicates receipts from loan collections, earnings from interest payments, perhaps the yield from guarantee fees, and income from other sources. On the application side, it would show loan disbursements and obligations, administrative expenses, payments of interest to the Treasury, dividend payments to the Treasury, and other categories of outlay. Or a power-generating corporation would show gross revenues from power sales, along with gross operating expenses for the generation of power.

Also included is a statement of the financial condition of the corporation, its assets and liabilities. This statement permits year-to-year comparisons of investment in property, of inventory, of working capital. In addition to liabilities, the statement shows the status of the government investment in the corporation, in the form of capital, loans, or retained earnings. The statement of the financial condition of the corporation reveals aspects of operating results that are generally not shown by ordinary government accounting.[27]

Congress thus receives far better information upon the operations of corporations than it once did. If a corporation is running a deficit, that fact is placed before Congress. If a profit is forecast, its planned disposition is indicated. It may be retained by the corporation, a dividend to the Treasury may be in prospect, or the corporation may plan to invest earnings in plant

---

[26] The most readily available compendium of information about government corporations is the federal budget. The corporate programs and statements are included under the heading, "Public Enterprise Funds," at the end of each major section of the budget.

[27] When a corporation is compelled to make such reports, it must maintain accounts in a manner to yield the necessary data. The maintenance of records that yield cost figures may in itself have its repercussions upon management.

additions. Not all these reports are of a quality to bring cheers from the accountants, but the Comptroller General will, in due course, in his audit report call the attention of Congress to matters not adequately revealed. All of this probably influences corporate management as well as permits Congress to know better what results are being produced from public capital. That is not to assert that government corporations should uniformly earn a profit; but it is sound public policy that Congress know whether an enterprise is profitable or subsidized.

Autonomy and substantive corporate policy. The procedures that have been described tend to enable the President and Congress to evaluate the managerial performance of government corporations in business terms. Their effect is to permit the enforcement of a degree of accountability for corporate operations and so to integrate corporations within the general governmental structure. Perhaps a more significant limitation on autonomy consists of those measures by which substantive corporate programs are brought into line with over-all governmental policy or by which corporate operations are coordinated even in detail with the related activities of ordinary agencies. Given the nature of their functions, few are the government corporations that can be permitted to drift about the administrative cosmos, accountable to no one in particular.

The basic policies for government corporations are made by congressional chartering. Supplementary policy instructions may be made in subsequent legislation modifying the corporate authority or in appropriations for capital purposes. These actions, in some instances, may constitute elements in a general government program. When the President recommends and Congress provides additional capital for the Federal National Mortgage Association, for example, the action may be a part of an integrated national economic policy.

In other instances, corporations—though having a board of directors and the appearance of corporate autonomy—operate in reality as units of other agencies. This integration often finds justification in the necessity for coordination between the activities of the corporation and the work of the controlling department. In its lending, price support, and loan guarantee operations, the Commodity Credit Corporation constitutes, in effect, a bureau of the Department of Agriculture. Federal Prison Industries, Inc. is within the Department of Justice and is managed by those responsible for the federal prisons.[28]

Coordination of the substantive work of corporations has been achieved in some instances by means other than virtual amalgamation with a department. During World War II, for example, the Defense Plant Corporation, the Defense Supplies Corporation, the Metals Reserve Company, and other defense subsidiaries of the Reconstruction Finance Corporation acted as

---

[28] On the problem of integration with departments, see Dimock, Marshall E., "Government Corporations: A Focus of Policy and Administration," *American Political Science Review*, 1949, Vol. 43, p. 899 *ff.*, 1145 *ff.*

bankers and managers to carry out procurement and construction directives of the War Production Board and similar agencies. Presumably, a degree of integration among bank examining authorities is achieved by the fact that the Comptroller of the Currency is a member of the board of directors of the Federal Deposit Insurance Corporation. Most government corporations enjoy certain special privileges that a departmental bureau does not have; but, with such notable exceptions as the Tennessee Valley Authority, they tend to be guided by departmental direction in the exercise of these privileges. That departmental direction, however, may be by the departmental head and not involve the departmental apparatus of supervision to which ordinary departmental bureaus are subject.

Contribution of the corporate device. The corporate arrangement constitutes a modification of ordinary governmental organization of special utility for the conduct of commercial activities. In its present form in the United States, it represents the result of considerable evolutionary trial and error. The product was an institution differing from both private corporations and ordinary departments, yet peculiarly adapted to the practical necessities of its operating environment. Although extensive and important continuing functions are carried on through the corporate device, its most widespread utilization has occurred in times of national emergency. At such times, a single action—establishment and capitalization of a corporation—has put men to work unhampered by the possibility of a running fight with the Bureau of the Budget, the Appropriations Committees, the Comptroller General, and the Civil Service Commission. Once the emergency is over, the operation can be brought into more orthodox governmental patterns or the corporation can be liquidated if its task is completed.

Yet the wide use of the corporation and the considerable literature on the subject throw into bold relief the general problem of administrative deconcentration. The pressure toward uniformity of operating method and toward coordination of policy throughout the huge federal machinery brings with it formidable issues in the maintenance of initiative and in the preservation of conditions favorable to self-reliant management and innovation. Unification and uniformity carry with them an inevitable degree of congestion at the center, and also delay and hamper action. In devising mechanisms for central control, we must guard against the tendency to exert great effort in the achievement of integration and uniformity on matters that really are not of sufficient significance to justify the trouble.[29]

---

[29] In the devolution of administrative responsibility, interesting developments, somewhat akin to the government corporation, have occurred in the fields of defense production and atomic energy. In some instances private corporations, laboratories, or divisions of private corporations operate with the government as their sole customer. Often they perform services radically different from those rendered by the ordinary government supplier. Although the profits, if any, accrue to the private corporation, these units at times tend to be but extensions of governmental organization itself. See also Price, Don K., *Government and Science,* chap. 3, New York: New York University Press, 1954; Newman, James R., "The Atomic Energy Industry: An Experiment in Hybridization," *Yale Law Journal,* 1951, Vol. 60, p. 1263 *ff.*

Perhaps in part from the pattern of the government corporation, many programs conducted by ordinary departments have come to be managed under conditions similar in some, if not all, respects to those governing corporate management. As was pointed out earlier, it is possible simply to establish a revolving fund,[30] into which receipts are paid and from which expenditures are made, with procedures for appraisal of the operation similar to those used in reviewing the work of a corporation. Such an arrangement assures continuity and stability and removes most of the detailed concern associated with annual appropriation procedure.

---

[30] The federal budget carries the financial statements and reports of the numerous revolving funds along with those of government corporations. The variety of activities dealt with by revolving funds may be judged by an examination of the current budget document.

Chapter 12 •

Field Organization

1. The Growth of Field Organization

Center and area. Capitals of nations and states are popularly regarded as the places where the business of government is carried on. Actually this business brings national and state government into hundreds and thousands of communities distant from the capital—that is, into "the field." For it is in the field that taxes are collected, regulatory laws enforced, and governmental services rendered. This being true, effective administration at the capital is not enough. Field administration presents its distinctive problems for which solutions must be sought.

The central government projects itself into the field in other than strictly administrative ways. It draws its legislators from local communities. It depends on local communities to provide strong units of political parties. There are, therefore, at least three lines of communication strung up between the capital and the locality: the administrative, the representative, and the still more specifically political. They provide the citizen with alternative means of access to the distant governmental center and its administrative agencies; they also cross each other from time to time, and on some occasions sparks fly. The structure of the field organization of administrative agencies and the behavior of key field officials are not wholly explicable apart from the total pattern of legislative-political-administrative interrelations and, one might add, the play of state, regional, and national pressure groups, together with the complex web of "personal connections" between local citizens and old friends and neighbors holding administrative positions at the capital.

Field administration, however, has a long history and reveals common elements in a variety of countries. One can, therefore, treat it as something more than a unique product of a particular time, place, and disposition of forces.

Continental prototypes. Historically, field organization has been a tool used for both the centralization and decentralization of government. The centralist emphasis dominated field organization during the centuries when Western civilization was emerging from the Middle Ages. The evolution

246

of the nation-state was a reaction against the feudal organization of society —under which state taxes had long ceased to be collected, justice was meted out by local authorities, the right to travel highways depended on payment of tolls to local lords, the coinage of money was far from a state monopoly, and national armies were mere assemblages of groups of vassals of allied lords. Naturally, the extent of reversal of these centrifugal tendencies depended upon the king's capacity for reducing his dependence upon the feudal lords. This required, among other things, the development of a truly national bureaucracy that would carry the king's law and collect the king's taxes throughout the realm.

Accordingly, in France for instance, the king appointed so-called intendants to represent him in the field, with authority over both local governments and subordinate field officials of the different departments of the national government. The precedent thus set commended itself to the nationalizing leaders of revolutionary regimes after 1789—and to Napoleon. The revolutionary Constituent Assembly, deliberately ignoring the traditional provinces, superimposed on the country's map a largely artificial set of boundaries outlining areal "departments." Napoleon, in his turn, placed at the head of each "department" a prefect representing the central government and subject to summary removal. This scheme of territorial administration has continued since Napoleon's time as a major instrument of centralization. Its distinctive principle is that the prefect represents virtually all of the national government's functional departments. Consequently, most of the functional threads of national government are supposed to be pulled together at his level before they are stretched on to individual communities and citizens. Although the principle has somewhat eroded in practice as governmental work has increased and functional departments have multiplied, the basic doctrine is still accorded substantial respect and has been widely adopted in Europe and Asia.[1]

In Prussia, too—and its precursor, the Electorate of Brandenburg—field officers were used to weld local feudatories into a centralized nation. In the seventeenth century Frederick William, the Great Elector of Brandenburg, shrewdly appointed the district heads of the nobility as his own commissioners to collect taxes and assist his army in finding billets, food, and other necessities; he appointed a general commissioner for each province, and established a General War Commission in Berlin to coordinate the activities of all these officials. Thus was established a field service, which both reduced feudal parochialism and established a financial base for the new royal absolutism. Meanwhile, on the side of civil administration, a different set of field officials was gradually appointed to collect revenues from the king's

---

[1] The leading work is Chapman, Brian, *The Prefects and Provincial France,* London: Allen & Unwin, 1955. See also Diamant, Alfred, "The Department, the Prefect, and Dual Supervision in French Administration: A Comparative Study," *Journal of Politics,* 1954, Vol. 16, p. 472 *ff.*

domain lands and from his "regalian" rights, such as tolls from roads and bridges.

The capstone of Prussian absolutism and its victory over feudalism was laid in the eighteenth century by Frederick William I, the Corporal King of Prussia. An energetic ruler, he completely reorganized both central and field administration. In 1723 he established a General Directory, which for the first time unified the previously separate military and civil administrations. Likewise in the field one provincial board of war and domains replaced the many competing agencies in each province and so centralized the administration of all field activities for the Prussian state. With these provincial boards in the field and the General Directory in Berlin, Frederick William I completed the struggle against feudalism's centrifugal pressures and set the stage for Prussia's spectacular emergence as a great European power under his successor, Frederick the Great.[2]

British development. Considerably before the European continent emerged from feudalism, England had established the ultimate dependence of all lords and lords' vassals upon the king. Accordingly, she never was driven to provide the continental type of counterpoise to the decentralized structure of feudalism—an army of intendants or regents administering local areas on behalf of the king. Instead, centralist tendencies took the form of local sheriffs designed both to represent the king and to protect the rights of local self-government against encroachment by feudal lords; or of justices of the peace appointed by the king from among local landowners. However, popular prejudice against the sheriffs as local representatives of the king resulted in decay of the sheriff's office. Subsequently, the attempt to use local justices of the peace as royal administrative agents came to an end with the civil wars of the seventeenth century. Thenceforth the justices were virtually uncontrolled by London.

The vitality of British local government, the compactness of the country, and perhaps the historical predominance of struggles over policy formation and the role of Parliament may account for the British failure to follow the continental pattern of field integration and, as well, for the small number of local offices of national departments until the present century. Now about four-fifths of Britain's permanent nonindustrial civil servants are located outside the national headquarters offices; all are attached to individual departments, as Britain has no agents, comparable to French prefects, representing the whole national administration in particular areas. In World War II, use of civil defense regions headed by regional commissioners was a gesture toward the prefectoral pattern, but after the war the system was

---

[2] Fay, Sidney B., *The Rise of Brandenburg-Prussia to 1786,* pp. 63, 80, 101-109, New York: Henry Holt, 1937; Barker, Ernest, *The Development of Public Services in Western Europe, 1660-1930,* p. 19 *ff.,* London: Oxford University Press, 1944; Dorwart, Reinhold A., *The Administrative Reforms of Frederick William I of Prussia,* p. 161 *ff.,* Cambridge: Harvard University Press, 1953.

abandoned, to the ill-disguised delight of both national departments and local governments.[3]

Expansion of federal functions. In modern times particularly, it is difficult to disentangle the motives, or for that matter the results, of the growth of field services. To some degree the centralizing factor—so conspicuous in the modern origins of field organization—persists, often with emphasis upon supervision of local governments. At the other extreme is a conscious effort by national governments to permit adaptation of administration to the needs and aspirations of particular regions—in other words, to decentralize the execution of policies that must be formulated nationally. A third, and perhaps most important, factor in the growth of field organization is simply the need to get particular functions performed, with all conscious theorizing about centralization and decentralization pushed aside.

This third factor has dominated the development of the field service of the federal government in the United States. The centralization-decentralization dispute has centered on the respective powers of the Union and the states. The federal field service has been generally accepted as a necessary and unobjectionable complement to those powers that are in fact exercised by the national government. That explains, from the historical standpoint, why the bulk of these field services evolved for such functions as carrying the mail, collecting federal taxes, prosecuting and trying legal cases under federal law, protecting the frontiers, and building and repairing the ships of the Navy. In fact, the story of the growth of the federal field services parallels almost directly that of the expansion of functions of the national government. In many ways the most interesting phases of field adminstration developed only after the federal government undertook important and varied regulatory responsibilities and adopted spending programs designed to equalize and support with national resources the social and economic opportunities of the citizens of the several states.

A case in point is the United States Department of Agriculture. Although established in 1862, the early concentration of this department upon research and reporting meant that for many years there was no need for a large staff, either in Washington or in the field. Even in 1905, all functions could be performed by about 5,000 employees, 70 per cent of whom were stationed in the field. Only two of the department's bureaus had extensive field services.[4] Yet, in 1958, the demands of regulatory, promotional, and re-

---

[3] The most valuable sources on British field administration are Mackenzie, W. J. M., and Grove, J. W., *Central Administration in Britain*, p. 260 *ff.*, London: Longmans, Green, 1957; Dhonau, May L., *Decentralization in Government Departments*, London: Institute of Public Administration, 1938.

[4] Truman, David B., *Administrative Decentralization*, p. 36 *ff.*, Chicago: University of Chicago Press, 1940. For an account of the growth of the functions of the Department of Agriculture, see Gaus, John M., and Wolcott, Leon C., *Public Administration and the United States Department of Agriculture*, p. 3 *ff.*, Chicago: Public Administration Service, 1940. Listing of the Department's field offices re-

search functions had so multiplied that the employees of the department numbered 90,000—almost twenty times the figure for 1905; over 85 per cent of this number were in the field service.

Thus expansion of the service and regulatory functions of government underlies much of the expansion of field services. Indeed, the very fact that national policy could be administered in the field—away from Washington —undoubtedly made more palatable the idea of federal assumption of many responsibilities that earlier had been thought to belong to state and local governments. Similarly, state assumption of local functions has often been followed by arrangements for having these functions administered either through field agents of the state government or through local governments themselves, serving in effect as arms of state administration.

Technological progress. Particularly in the fields of transportation and communication, technological progress has played an important role in the expansion of field services. Technology converts local commerce into national commerce, and so both furthers the shifting of regulatory and promotional functions to the national government and necessitates expansion of the government's field services. It also affects directly the ease of contact between citizens and the national capital and between field agents and the central government.

This ease of contact has contradictory implications. If citizens can readily communicate directly with Washington, the need for establishment and expansion of field services is reduced. Furthermore, citizens can more easily bypass local field officials by dealing directly with headquarters officials at the capital, or through legislative, political, and lobbying intermediaries. On the other hand, advances in communication and transportation enable central officials to be in such constant contact with their field representatives that the setting up of field offices and the formal decentralization of authority need not be a threat to central control. The point is dramatically illustrated by the changed role of American ambassadors to distant countries. As "field agents" of the President, they are daily subject to cabled instructions and often to displacement in negotiations by an airborne Secretary of State or other central representative.

Scope of field organization. The most perplexing and important problems of field organization in this country arise naturally in the federal government, because its functions extend over greater territory than do those of the states. Nonetheless, the states are also faced by the necessity for field organization. In general, the states have lagged considerably behind the federal government in the development of extensive field services. This has been attributable to several factors: (1) the shorter distances between the state capital and the other communities in the state, with the result that ad-

---

quired 70 pages of small type in U. S. Department of Agriculture, *Directory of Organization and Field Activities of the Department of Agriculture, 1957,* Agriculture Handbook No. 76, Washington: Government Printing Office, 1957.

ministration directly from the capital was in most cases reasonably satisfactory; (2) the extent to which governmental functions were performed by counties, towns, and special districts; and (3) the less satisfactory state personnel situation, so that in many departments employees could not be spared for the staffing of field offices.[5]

For all the obviousness of the need for extending administration through field services, it is generally startling to look at the statistics that demonstrate governmental response to this need. In the federal government, for instance, nine employees are stationed in the field for every employee stationed in Washington. Of the total of 2.3 million federal employees in late 1958, about 205,000 were stationed in the Washington metropolitan area and 2,140,000 in the field. The agencies with the largest number of field employees were, in the order of size of field staffs, the Department of Defense, with over a million,[6] the Post Office Department, with half a million, and the Veterans Administration, with 167,000; others, with less than 80,000 but more than 40,000 were, in order, the following departments: Agriculture; Treasury; Commerce; Interior; and Health, Education, and Welfare. In two thirds of the states there are more federal employees than employees of state government, and California has even more federal employees than there are in the Washington metropolitan area.

2. Centralization and Decentralization

Approach to decentralization. Because field organization has developed in the United States not through any master plan but in response to the needs of individual departments and bureaus, naturally there is diversity among the methods of field administration. Yet, within virtually every agency will be found such basic problems as these: the proper degree of decentralization of authority; the conflict of interests between functional experts at headquarters and general administrators in the field; the basic need for intelligent and sympathetic handling of headquarters-field relations; and the complexities of managing a field structure having two or even three successive levels. Each of these intra-agency problems will be considered in turn.

The question of the degree to which authority should be delegated to field agents requires appreciation of the character of field organization as susceptible of different uses. It is an efficient tool for either centralization or decentralization of authority, and, perhaps even more important, for any of the many degrees that are marked on the scale between these two

---

[5] In Michigan, 24 state agencies (of a total of 117) operate 47 separate field organizations. Pealy, Robert H., and Robertson, John C., *Field Organizations of Michigan State Government Departments*, p. 1, Ann Arbor: Bureau of Government, Institute of Public Administration, University of Michigan, 1956.

[6] The figure for the Defense Department gives a misleading impression, as about half of its field employees are wage earners, working in arsenals and shipyards, for instance.

extremes. Whether a given field service leans toward centralization or toward decentralization may be discerned from observation of the importance of matters on which field officials have decision-making authority, compared to matters wholly retained for headquarters decision; the extent of central consultation with field officials on matters that arise and are formally decided at headquarters, and the weight such field opinion carries; the frequency with which field officials must refer matters to headquarters for decision even though they arise at and are partially "processed" in the field; the number and specificity of central regulations and orders governing decision-making in the field; the provision for citizen appeal to headquarters for overruling of field decisions; the degree to which all of the agency's field activities within each geographic area are directed by a single field official; and the caliber of field officials. Neither the mere existence of a field service, nor its carrying of a heavy workload, nor its employment of nine-tenths of the agency's personnel constitutes evidence of decentralization.

Because authority stems initially from the center, decentralization requires positive action. Absence of such action results in centralization. Two points deserve statement. On the one hand, this necessity of positive action, coupled with a variety of centripetal pulls to which agency heads must be sensitive, weights the scales against substantial decentralization. On the other hand, decentralization, like delegation itself, is not so absolute a good that the agency head should fail to discriminate between what should be decentralized and what centralized, or fail to adjust the balance from time to time.

The factors that usually control the degree to which an agency centralizes or decentralizes its authority fall under four broad headings: (1) the factor of responsibility; (2) administrative factors; (3) functional factors; and (4) external factors.

Factor of responsibility. The principle of administrative responsibility acts as a general deterrent to the decentralization of administrative authority. Every agency head in the federal government is answerable for his general administrative program to the President, Congress, and the people. He is responsible to central budgetary, accounting, auditing, and personnel agencies and to the courts for the integrity and legality of his agency's operations. He can also be pilloried at any time by the press, committees of Congress, and political enemies for right or wrong decisions made by him or his subordinates, however picayune the matter.

As a result, agencies hesitate to delegate broad discretionary authority to field officials, who are thought to be less readily controlled than officials regularly stationed at the capital. The effects of this system of responsibility, though well-nigh universal, are more acute in some agencies than in others. Agencies in fields open to corruption, such as award and supervision of public works and supply contracts, agencies carefully watched by alert pressure groups such as veterans' organizations, and agencies in whose field services scandals have recently attracted attention are likely either to centralize decision-making or to issue elaborate regulations that reduce decision-making in the field to a mere matching of cases against specific paragraphs in the regulations.

Administrative factors. The second main cluster of factors influencing decentralization is administrative in character, specifically: age of the agency, stability of its policies and methods, competence of its field personnel, pressure for speed and economy, and administrative sophistication. The age of the agency is basic to several of the other administrative factors mentioned. Time is required for a new agency to get well staffed and organized at headquarters, for key officials to get used to working together, and for an *esprit de corps* to develop that will support high morale in the field. But the time factor poses dilemmas. Logically, a field service is an extension of headquarters, so that field organization and staffing must generally await the clarification of organization and authority at the center. But in an emergency period, such as the Korean War, field services may have to be rapidly organized, without awaiting completion of details in the central economic mobilization agencies.[7] And there may be advantages in this, because the inchoate character of Washington organization permits the field to get rationally organized and to establish beachheads of decentralization without encountering the special demands and resistances of well-dug-in specialized divisions at headquarters.

Stability of policies and methods is fundamental to decentralization. So long as headquarters itself is in ferment over these, the confusion would be worse confounded if field agents were turned loose with unguided decision-making authority.[8] Here, too, a dilemma is posed. For if a new agency's field service is initially staffed with men content to exercise no discretionary authority, their inferior quality later constitutes an argument against decentralizing authority even though policy objectives have been clarified. Nonetheless, it remains true that when an agency has stabilized policies and methods, it can afford to decentralize; at that point, it may also find opportunities to attract abler men to key positions in the field. The competence of field personnel is therefore another administrative factor governing readiness to decentralize. At the heart of the disinclination to delegate substantial authority lies the conviction of many officials that only they themselves have the ability to do the job as well as it should be done. To dissuade them from this point of view requires, among other things, a demonstration that others, both at headquarters and in the field, can do important parts of the job competently. The field officials must

---

[7] For the experience of the Korean War, see Redford, Emmette S., "Problems of Mobilization Agencies in Establishing Field Organizations," *Public Administration Review,* 1952, Vol. 12, p. 166 *ff.*

[8] This problem is admirably traced in Richards, Allan R., *War Labor Boards in the Field,* Chapel Hill: University of North Carolina Press, 1953.

have the confidence, not only of the top executives of the agency, but also of the functional specialists down the line. The fact that a field office can rarely demonstrate as much *technical* competence as the specialized divisions at the agency's headquarters is a chief deterrent to decentralization.

Decentralization is affected also by a further administrative factor—the need for speed and economy in operations, both to satisfy citizens as clients of the agency and to meet budgetary and efficiency goals of the agency itself. Many agencies recognize that officials stationed permanently in particular districts, with authority to take action, will generally have lower travel and communication costs than headquarters officials in a centralized organization. Space costs may be lower than those in the crowded capital. Citizens will generally prefer to deal face-to-face with a near-by official, compared with a central bureau that can only be corresponded with or else be visited at considerable expense.

Administrative sophistication, particularly with regard to management of a field service and its interrelations with the central organization, is a final factor influencing decentralization. Age is a contributing element, for—as has been pointed out—an agency must often develop its field arrangements in an experimental fashion and then wait for their crystallization as an accepted part of the "understandings" about subject matter and administration that central and field personnel are expected to share. This requires time, but time without a growth in maturity of insight by key officials would be of no avail. With such growth might be expected greater appreciation of the relative values of centralization and decentralization, the respective roles of functional experts and general administrators, the techniques for breaking down barriers to mutual collaboration between central headquarters and the field service, and the appropriate distribution of authority and functions in a two-tier or three-tier field organization.

Functional factors. While factors of responsibility and administration set limits to the feasibility of centralization and decentralization for individual departments, the most marked variations among governmental agencies result from the third major group of factors—those concerned with functions. Here the questions are these: How great a variety of distinct functions does the agency have? How essential is technical specialization in the agency's work? Does the function require national uniformity or diversity among regions and localities?

The variety of functions an agency performs may affect its readiness to decentralize operations. An agency with a single function has a relatively simple problem of analysis and decision in order to determine the appropriate degree of decentralization. But if an agency performs a variety of functions, each of its central divisions may insist on a separate set of field offices and districts, may have quite contradictory views on the urgency or the extent of decentralization, and may violently oppose control of its field agents by a field official representing the department head or his chief of field operations. Reconciliation of these different viewpoints may be impossible, with the result that either no decentralization occurs or each division decentralizes as it chooses. In the latter event, the very failure to get agreement on an integrated field service for the whole department may retard the process of decentralization. The department head, with full coordinative authority over officials in Washington but no coordinative machinery in the field, may very well fear the possibility of inefficiency, duplication, or direct conflict if division heads delegate a large degree of authority to their field representatives. It is also true that in cases where two or three divisions need to reach joint decisions, the level in the hierarchy of all three where the decisions will be made will be dictated by the structure of the least decentralized division. Consequently, one or more divisions will always act as "drags" on the decentralization of other divisions in a department performing a variety of functions.

In some agencies there is a pressing need for a variety of technical specialties. This, particularly in a small agency, usually handicaps attempts to decentralize the work. A simple comparison makes this clear. If for a certain purpose an agency is allowed to have a payroll of fifty employees, it is able to concentrate the fifty positions in a central staff within which there can be both general administrators and groups of specialists, such as engineers, chemists, and budget and personnel experts. Or it may want to open perhaps forty district offices in the field and assign to each office one employee representing the whole agency in all of its specialized aspects, leaving only ten at headquarters. This means that, both at headquarters and in the field, practically all positions will have to be filled by employees who are not trained for any of the specialties that could contribute materially to an intelligent job of administration. Ready examples are afforded by the wartime experience of the Office of Price Administration and the War Production Board.[9] At Washington, each agency had an expert on almost every industry and commodity in the United States. But to duplicate this range of expertness in field offices was out of the question. It is a general rule that no agency has in each of its field offices as great a range of specialization as is represented in its headquarters staff. This necessarily acts as a bar to decentralization by agencies requiring the services of technical personnel in reaching most of their decisions.

Variety of functions and need for technical specialization are complemented by a third functional factor—the degree of need for national uniformity as contrasted with the need for regional and local variation. The fact that a function is within the legal jurisdiction of a central government

---

[9] Mansfield, Harvey C., and Associates, *A Short History of OPA*, p. 221 *ff.*, Washington: Office of Price Administration, Office of Temporary Controls, 1947; Redford, Emmette S., *Field Administration of Wartime Rationing*, Washington: Office of Price Administration, Office of Temporary Controls, 1947; Shaw, Carroll K., *Field Organization and Administration of the War Production Board and Predecessor Agencies*, Washington: Civilian Production Administration, 1947.

does not mean that its administration cannot be decentralized. Often functions are shifted to the central government because financial or personnel resources are greater there than at lower governmental levels; because policy formulation needs to be centralized; or because the central government must be looked to for assumption of ultimate administrative responsibility on the highest level. However, unless there are affirmative reasons for absolute uniformity in detailed operations as well as in general decisions of the agency, authority can generally be decentralized to field agents.

The most obvious need for diversity in administration of a function arises in agencies affected by differences in the physical characteristics of the various parts of the country. Agricultural, forest, and water-resource activities are examples. On the other hand, the principal drive toward centralization comes when privileges and penalties are being dispensed or rights determined. Then equity may require an identical administrative decision in every identical set of circumstances, whether the case arises in Oregon, Louisiana, or Maine. Because administrative decisions often involve general elements of judgment, this degree of uniformity cannot be assured under a decentralized system permitting each field agent to reach independent conclusions on the cases arising in his district. Examples of functions demanding uniformity on a national basis are the administrative adjudication of veterans' claims for compensation, the review of tax returns, and the determination of benefit claims under the old age and survivors insurance program. The workload, it is true, can be assigned to field offices, but centrally prescribed regulations and standards must then be so detailed that the field staff performs a largely clerical operation, instead of exercising discretion.

External factors. A final group of factors bearing on centralization or decentralization still calls for discussion. It concerns the need for an agency to look beyond its own internal operations to external problems. The most important are the necessities for bringing the citizen into the administrative process, collaborating with other federal, state, and local agencies, and adapting field activities to political pressures.

The first of these factors may be referred to as the degree of need for support, participation, and representation at the "grass roots" of democracy.[10] If support of a large number of citizens is requisite to successful administration—as is true of farm production control programs, wartime

---

[10] Local citizens' committees and boards present their own difficulties in a field administration program. See, for price control and rationing boards, Putnam, Imogene H., *Volunteers in OPA*, Washington, Office of Temporary Controls, 1947; Redford, *op cit.* above in note 9, p. 85 *ff;* and Aikin, Charles, "Volunteers in Retail Price Control—A Postscript," *Public Administration Review*, 1948, Vol. 8, p. 300 *ff.* For farmers' committees, see Hardin, Charles M., *The Politics of Agriculture*, esp. p. 115 *ff.*, Glencoe, Ill.: Free Press, 1952; Frischknecht, Reed L., "The Democratization of Administration: The Farmer Committee System," *American Political Science Review*, 1953, Vol. 47, p. 704 *ff.*

rationing, and the military draft; or if their participation is needed to impart wisdom to the local decisions made—again a factor in these three programs; or if national policy-makers at Washington need vigorous representation of regional points of view so as to avoid development of unrealistic and extravagantly uniform national plans—under such conditions a decentralized organization is likely to develop.

The degree of need for collaboration with other federal, state, and local agencies is a second external factor in decentralization decisions. Other things being equal, an agency's decisions should be made at the level of authority that is most convenient for other agencies participating in the decision-making process. This means that if federal agencies *A* and *B* have a number of joint activities, their regional officials should have reasonably similar grants of discretionary authority. It means further that if the program is one of federal collaboration with state or local governments, the federal agency administering the program will probably need to establish regional, state, or local offices that can work with these governments. Similarly, pressure for a degree of decentralization develops when an agency's field officials are invited to participate in a regional or river-basin planning commission or development authority. Nevertheless, the need for collaboration with other agencies probably exerts only a secondary influence on a department's determination of the desirable degree of decentralization.

Finally, among external factors, political aspects need to be considered. As the strength of the political parties in the United States lies in their state and local organizations, and as an agency's command of legislative support is not unrelated to the impact of its decisions on legislators' districts, field administration cannot in practice be wholly divorced from politics. Part of this is reflected in the acuteness of political interest in the location of field offices,[11] construction of office buildings in the field, selection of field office directors, and size of local staffs. If partisan and factional patronage govern the selection of key field officials, such as state administrators of federal agencies, the agency headquarters may hesitate to decentralize authority to them. The appointment of employees, awarding of contracts, and making of grants or loans to individuals and business concerns are peculiarly subject to political bias; prudence may require their close control by headquarters. Indeed, because field work is more susceptible to political inroads than departmental work at Washington, an able agency head may avoid even establishing a large field staff lest he be forced to appoint a considerable number of politically sponsored employees. Of course, the inclusion of field positions under the merit

---

[11] Political concern by members of Congress when discontinuance of field offices in their constituencies is proposed is well illustrated in Arnow, Kathryn S., *The Department of Commerce Field Service,* Inter-University Case Series No. 21, University, Ala.: University of Alabama Press, 1954; and Shaw, *op. cit.,* p. 43 *ff.*

system lessens the problem. But an agency may nonetheless find it "politic" to transfer or dismiss a field office head who has become *persona non grata* to a Congressman or Senator in whose constituency the office is located. Often an important and sometimes delicate direct relation exists between a field office head and the lawmakers representing the area legislatively. This need not be a hostile relation. In a "correct" relation, each recognizes the legitimate activity of the other, as well as the bounds of legitimacy. In some cases, the relation can be so friendly that the legislator protects the field office head against discipline by agency headquarters and so serves as his "patron" in the old sense of that term.

3. Field-Headquarters Relations

Roles of functional experts and general administrators. The preceding discussion has suggested certain fundamental requisites for the maturing of field-headquarters relations in an agency: the adjustment of the conflicting interests of functional experts and general administrators; the development of methods for improving mutual field-headquarters understanding and respect; and discovery of a firm formula to govern relations within a complex, multilevel field organization. These are all problems that arise in every field service, whether authority be centralized or decentralized.

The most fundamental of these problems is the relation between functional experts and general administrators. Each agency's headquarters office is subdivided into specialized units dealing with different programs, techniques, controls, and services. Some of them are so-called line or operating divisions, responsible for important segments of the agency's program. For instance, the Department of the Interior includes such line or operating units as the Fish and Wildlife Service, the Bureau of Reclamation, the National Park Service, the Bureau of Indian Affairs, and the Bonneville Power Administration. Headquarters of agencies also include units that contribute special skills, such as engineering, statistics, and legal advice. Still other units exercise management control or perform managerial services, such as budgeting, personnel, and space allocation. But each of the main divisions is responsible to the agency head or to one of his chief deputies. Each has an institutional pride and enthusiasm for its own part of the total program. Each—as can be understood— would dislike to see important phases of its work performed or directed by other divisions and officials.

When an agency's program is projected into the field there arise two basic alternatives. Each division may be allowed to set up its own field service and directly control the performance of the division's functions in the field. At the other extreme, the whole agency may organize an integrated field service, with each regional, state, and district director held responsible for all agency functions performed in his assigned territory.

The first alternative has the defect that execution of the agency program is not integrated in each field area. The second alternative has the defect that functional divisions at headquarters have no direct control over execution of their subject-matter programs in the field. A major problem of administration is to avoid the impasse between the apparently irreconcilable positions of function and area, of functional experts and general administrators.[12] The solutions found in this dilemma stem in considerable measure from the character of headquarters organization. If the agency head is weak, or if the agency is a mere confederation of unrelated functional divisions with no really joint objective or program, the functional point of view is likely to prevail over the agencywide point of view in field organization. Many a federal department embraces so wide a range of functions and includes such powerful and tradition-encrusted bureaus that any single departmentwide field structure seems out of the question. An example is the Treasury Department, with such varied operating bureaus as the Internal Revenue Service, the Bureau of Narcotics, the Bureau of the Mint, the Coast Guard, the Secret Service, and the Bureau of Customs. The Department of Health, Education, and Welfare would also seem to qualify here, but Congress specifically required the Department to organize a departmental field service.

Sheer size of the administrative task, often but not always a companion of multiplicity of autonomous bureaus and distantly related functions, may also be a deterrent to real agencywide field coordination. The volume of orders and informational paper that would have to flow to field coordinators if functional lines of authority were suppressed in such an agency as the United States Department of Agriculture is fearful to contemplate. In general, though the ability of a department's field coordinators to integrate its functions for given areas of the country will depend heavily on the strength of the department head *vis-à-vis* his bureau heads, and on the inherent need for integration of departmental functions because of their contribution to a single purpose.

Lines of command. Formal establishment of an integrated field service by no means ends the problems of function versus area. For there remains a never-ending tussle over (a) the extent to which the agency's regional director must take orders from functional divisions at headquarters, and (b) the amount of direct contact permitted between regional functional divisions and their central prototypes. There are really only two choices, because complete autonomy for the regional director is unattainable. One choice is to require that all programs and major *orders* clear through the administrative hierarchy, while technical *advice* is handled directly between central functional divisions and their regional counterparts. On main instructions to the field, the central functional divisions would make recommendations

---

[12] This problem is the principal focus of Fesler, James W., *Area and Administration*, University, Ala.: University of Alabama Press, 1949.

to the agency head or his deputy. The latter, on the basis of these recommendations, would transmit to his regional directors such orders as he, a general administrator like the regional directors, deemed desirable. The regional director in turn would see that the orders were executed by his regional functional divisions. In this pattern, the functional officials are subordinated at each step to the general administrators. The alternative method, called "dual command," appears at first glance to be almost indistinguishable from the relationship just described. However, the difference is that between subordinating functional specialties to general administration and recognizing a double line of control. Under such dual command, regional functional experts must look for orders both to the regional director and to the functional divisions at headquarters. The arrangement calls for a distinction between "administrative" orders, which would be the regional director's province, and "functional" or "technical" orders, which would be the province of the specialized divisions at headquarters.[13]

Again, as in the question of the feasibility of decentralization, no single formula will fit all agencies. Too much depends on the unity of purpose of the particular agency and the consequent need for integrating all of its functions. A great deal depends also on the effectiveness with which the needed integration is actually achieved by a strong agency head. If headquarters is simply a tent under which autonomous bureaus are gathered for mere appearance's sake, there is no possibility of a strong regional director being able to challenge the flow of "technical" or program—as distinguished from "administrative"—commands. If the agency really has a single purpose, requiring that its functions be geared together, the need for a strong hierarchy of general administrators built into both the headquarters and field organizations is great. A single-purpose agency has, in addition, the incidental advantage that its regional directors can be men and women with some specialized training, able to command respect from the functional divisions. On the other hand, a wide-ranging agency like the Department of Health, Education, and Welfare must choose "generalists" whose contributions to administration the functional experts tend to underrate.

In practice, the dynamism of functional divisions and the professional bond between the staff of each such central division and its regional counterpart weight the scales against the general administrators. This combina-

---

[13] Although the concept of multiple supervision dates back to Frederick W. Taylor's work on scientific management in industry, its applicability to field administration was first emphasized in Macmahon, Arthur W., Millett, John D., and Ogden, Gladys, *The Administration of Federal Work Relief*, p. 265 ff., Chicago: Public Administration Service, 1941. Among recent important examinations of the desirability of multiple supervision in particular national agencies are Davis, John A., *Regional Organization of the Social Security Administration: A Case Study,* New York: Columbia University Press, 1950, and Richards, *op. cit.* above in note 8. See also Cleaveland, Frederick N., "Administrative Decentralization in the U. S. Bureau of Reclamation," *Public Administration Review,* 1953, Vol. 13, p. 17 ff.

tion of influences tends to reduce regional directors to mere providers of common facilities such as space, stenographic pools, and mail routing; freely available speech-makers; and recorders of what goes on—the field "eyes and ears" of headquarters. The centrifugal force of the functional divisions has been so strong that the administrative problem has nearly always been how to strengthen the regional director, and seldom how to increase the role of the functional divisions.

Differences of opinion on how relations between headquarters and the field should be structured stem in part from ambiguities of language and from different estimates of the significance of prescribed formal organization. Decision-makers, in the field as much as in Washington, are influenced in various ways. The preferences of one's direct superiors may weigh less in the making of an actual decision than the views of coordinate colleagues, subordinates, specialists in the same subject-matter, interest groups, individual citizens, and even the decision-maker's wife. If "authority" be defined as whatever "really" influences a decision, then there are many sources of authority.[14] A subordinate may resist a superior's instruction by insisting on conforming to laws, regulations, orders, and professional standards whose authority the superior must acknowledge.

Personnel policies. Whatever the basic formula hammered out between generalists and functionalists may be, an agency has day-to-day problems of headquarters-field relations, most of which revolve about these issues: personnel policies; the headquarters office of field operations; and communications and control. In the case of personnel policies, field relations are often muddied by jealousy over relative salaries, when the average annual salary is significantly higher in the capital. A regrettable lack of mutual understanding also develops when there is no exchange of personnel between headquarters and field stations. The Bridgeman Committee on reform of the British postal service put both of these problems bluntly when it recommended, "As a rule no officer should be appointed to an administrative position of importance at Headquarters until he has had a thorough training in, and experience of, the actual work of the Post Office provinces . . . there should be no difference in status between the administrative staff at Headquarters and in the provinces." [15] In the United States, as a Hoover Commission study reported, over half of the top-level federal officials have had no field experience, and three out of four

---

[14] For a study resting on the presupposition that administrative decisions in the field are not formulated through established administrative procedures, see Gore, William J., "Administrative Decision-Making in Federal Field Offices," *Public Administration Review,* 1956, Vol. 16, p. 281 *ff.* See also a forthcoming study that illustrates how field agents of a specialized career service may be trusted with decision-making precisely because they are so strongly indoctrinated with their agency's policies and methods that they conform even when they seem to themselves wholly free: Kaufman, Herbert, *The Administrative Behavior of U. S. Forest Rangers.*

[15] Great Britain, Committee of Enquiry on the Post Office, *Report,* London: His Majesty's Stationery Office, 1932, Cmd. 4149.

have had from none to not over five years of such experience.[16] The free movement of personnel, both vertically and horizontally, is necessary not only to increase awareness of field problems at headquarters and to open opportunities of promotion for field staff members, but also to counteract provincialism within field districts.

Transfer of field personnel among districts can both widen opportunities for promotion and overcome a localized outlook. However, a regional office having a vacancy may resent the passing over of its own staff members in favor of someone from another region. The national movement of personnel is also handicapped by the need for placating sectional prejudices by the appointment of natives to regional offices, and by the value to an agency of regional representatives who are thoroughly acquainted with the agency's clients in the region and sensitive to the more subtle regional trends. For some functions, however, an "outsider" may be a superior choice, precisely because he can bring to his task an ability to act "without fear or favor" in individual cases and a concern for the effectiveness of national programs rather than for regional and local interests. The usefulness of the outsider for functions calling for a degree of toughness and unquestioned loyalty to the national interest was discovered centuries ago in France and Germany, where foreigners were sometimes brought in to perform such jobs as tax collection.

Headquarters office of field operations. A second major issue of headquarters-field relations is the role and status of the headquarters office of field operations. In an agency having an integrated function and a generalist line of authority, regional directors would theoretically receive all important orders from the agency head, not from the functional divisions. Yet the agency head rarely can give personal attention to each of these orders. Hence he usually establishes an office of field operations through which all functional and other orders proposed for issuance to the field must be cleared. The office can also be expected to reflect the field viewpoint in top-level discussions at headquarters. And it constitutes the instrument through which the agency head can maintain administrative supervision of field operations.

The dangers inherent in this solution are several. The office of field operations may become procedure-minded and fail to develop a broad appreciation of the total agency program. It may lack the prestige and broad-gauged personnel needed for effective participation in policy councils at headquarters. It may overstep its authority by captiously revising programs that have been developed by functional divisions. By barring direct contact between regional directors and headquarters officials, it may depress field morale and undermine central-field understanding. Indeed, the im-

---

[16] (Second) Commission on Organization of the Executive Branch of the Government, *Task Force Report on Personnel and Civil Service,* p. 241, Washington: Government Printing Office, 1955.

pression that it is the principal unit with concern for field operations may reduce the earnestness with which the functional units at headquarters interest themselves in field problems and may even serve to polarize the hostilities between headquarters and field.

Communication and control. The third problem of central-field relations, communication and control, has two aspects—ordinary administrative operation of a far-flung organization, and the formulation of policies. The formal pattern for communication from headquarters to the field is established by such rules as "orders must flow through the office of field operations," and "advice may flow directly from functional divisions at headquarters to their counterparts in the field." But this formalization of channels by no means meets fully all problems. How are regional administrators to keep informed of the flow of technical advice to their subordinates? How can field officials be given adequate understanding of the total program of the agency? How can functional divisions be prevented from dropping "paratroops" into regions to perform special brief assignments—or how can this practice at least be kept from undermining the regional director's responsibility for all agency activities in the region? How can field officials be apprised of central decisions in advance of their appearance under headquarters datelines in the region's newspapers? How can headquarters' answers, given directly to officials of state and local governments, business corporations, and private citizens, be kept consistent with the answers of regional offices to the same people? And how can headquarters be kept informed of communications between regional offices? In addition, there is the important and puzzling question of the volume and type of reports that field officials must file centrally to keep headquarters informed of developments all over the country and to facilitate effective supervision over the field services.

Despite the variety and difficulty of these communication problems, the most fundamental question is probably that of how field officials can be brought to play a constructive part in the formulation of agency policies and procedures. Few able officials are content to be mere executors of central instructions, or mere pedestrian writers of weekly reports "to keep headquarters informed." Their operating and administrative experience with agency programs is a resource that headquarters should not lightly ignore. But more, principal field officials may provide a useful sounding board against which to test newly conceived policy ideas; in the process they may suggest modifications of substance, redesigning of methods, and alterations of timing that will make the difference between success and failure in achievement of the policy goals.

Control and communication interlock. Successful communication and growth of understanding between headquarters and the field reduce the burden that must be borne by the control system. Ideally, controls will assure that headquarters is informed of what's going on in the field, will bring headquarters thinking and the experiences of other field offices to the service of each field office, and will stimulate better performance by the weakest offices. Save for the fact that controls may result in reprimands, personnel transfers, and other disciplinary actions, the methods of control are hard to distinguish from the methods of communication. Reporting, inspection, and after-the-fact review of individual decisions are among the most common control devices. Field offices may be asked to submit weekly statistical and narrative "progress reports" to headquarters. Comparison of accomplishments, methods, and costs of performing the same function in a number of field offices may provide the factual basis for any remedial action that is needed. But field officials, as other human beings, are likely to be restrained in revealing their failures. Further, reporting arrangements often fall into a dull routine, with neither headquarters nor field men attentive to the opportunity offered by such arrangements. Inspection, another essential to control, is often a sharp irritant to field officials. Unless they are skillful, inspectors must either be superficial and ineffective or be "snoopers" trying to get under surface appearances and consequently undermining the field staff's feeling that their office chief has the full confidence of headquarters. A field administrator tolerates with some distaste the brief visits of central agents who subsequently write reports and recommendations on matters he feels would require them months or years to master. One device for preserving the field official's dignity is to let him see the central inspector's report and submit his own comments to accompany it. Another, and perhaps the most important, is for the inspector to be more a counselor, and less an examiner of formal obedience to procedural instructions.

After-the-fact review of individual decisions, like a post-audit in the financial area, may lead to a reprimand for past mistakes, a caution against repeating an error in the future, or a change in law or regulation. The important point is that such a review does not *correct* the error made in the individual case. When coupled with a sampling method of selecting cases, a checking of these against established standards, and an avoidance of nit-picking, the after-the-fact review can be a valuable control in field administration. Finally, for both communication and control purposes no formal, arm's-length arrangements between headquarters and the field can be quite as meaningful as the opportunities for key officials of headquarters and field to confer together. A common feature of field administration, both in the United States and abroad, is the regular meeting of regional directors with the agency head, his deputy, and the heads of functional divisions. However, travel costs limit the frequency of such conferences, often to one each year or each quarter.[17]

---

[17] Communication and control arrangements always seem lifeless when discussed in general terms. Appreciation of their importance and difficulties is best gained by scrutiny of a particular agency's travail. For example, see Flory, Anne P., "Field Administration in OPS [Office of Price Stabilization]," in symposium on *Price Control*

Problems of multilevel field organization. Some agencies have three or four tiers or levels of offices—headquarters, regional offices, state or district offices, and, perhaps, county or community offices. Such an elaborate pattern tends to develop especially in an agency that has a large clientele, a large volume of field work, and a necessity for personal contact with its clients. This may mean hundreds or thousands of local offices: there are over 35,000 post offices; the Bureau of Old-Age and Survivors Insurance has over 500 district offices.

The problems of a multilevel field organization are not easily solved. Each level is likely to have certain functions that are peculiarly its own responsibility, involving decision-making powers and negotiations with business concerns, other agencies, state and local governments, and certain classes of citizens. Each level above the lowest one also has responsibility for supervising and assisting the subordinate offices within its geographic area. Within each regional office, there will be need for interrelating and doing justice to these two responsibilities; in addition, the regional office will confront many of the standard problems already described—the conflict of interest between functional experts and general administrators, the question of the desirability of having a regional division of field relations, the arrangements for communications and controls.

The existence of intermediate offices creates special problems for headquarters. Theoretically, headquarters is relieved of a heavy supervisory workload, and lines of communication and control are neatly laid out, with headquarters dealing with regional offices, regional offices with district or state offices, and these with local offices. Two problems arise, however. Headquarters may decentralize to regional offices, but the regional offices may fail to push decentralization down to lower levels. Even if decentralization occurs within the region, a further problem remains. Intermediate levels tend to insulate headquarters from adequate contact with the "firing line" of local offices. The costs to the agency of thus separating the "noncombatants" at headquarters from the "combatants" in the local offices may turn out to be too great, with the result that arrangements for bypassing the intermediate offices are developed—for example, by direct communication of new policies and orders and by visitation of local offices by inspectors from headquarters. Such by-passing has its own costs, mainly in reduction of the authority and morale of the regional office.

---

in a Cold War, Autumn issue of *Law and Contemporary Problems,* 1954, Vol. 19, p. 604 *ff.* Field-headquarters conferences can be held in the field; see Office of the Administrative Assistant Secretary, United States Department of the Interior, *Strengthening Management in Interior,* Washington: Government Printing Office, July 1958, which reports on field management conferences at Tulsa, Oklahoma, and Yosemite National Park, and incidentally provides an admirable opportunity for the student to discover the views of field officials on the problems discussed in this chapter. For communication and control problems in tax collection, see *The Internal Revenue Service: Its Reorganization and Administration,* a study prepared for Congress' Joint Committee on Internal Revenue Taxation, Washington: Government Printing Office, 1955.

4. Interagency Coordination in the Field

Divergencies in field organization. In the United States, each bureau and agency having field functions has developed its own field service. As a result, the federal government has no integrated field organization such as those established by governments of continental Europe. Instead, it has well over a hundred separate field services. For each of these, the sponsoring agency locates field offices, delineates regional boundaries, and determines the desirable degree of decentralization with primary reference to the administrative and functional requirements of its own operations, but with slight reference to the broader interests of the whole government. To some extent, the diversity in field organization is due to minor considerations of administrative or personal convenience; to political pressures affecting the selection of field centers; and to lack of imagination in appreciating the need for decentralization and the desirability of interagency collaboration.

The importance of these influences can be exaggerated, however. There are sound grounds for handling field operations in connection with agricultural production differently from field operations in taking the census, inspecting steamboats, operating national parks, settling labor disputes, or supervising Indian reservations. Because the clustering and the nature of the phenomena with which government is concerned vary, diversity among the field organizations for dealing with these phenomena is natural. The factors to be considered in laying out regional boundaries, locating field offices, and decentralizing authority can be enumerated without too much difficulty. Yet the relative weight of each factor will vary agency by agency and function by function, with the result that even a consciously logical approach to field organization will lead to differing arrangements.

Yet diversity among field organizations can be pressed too far, and in the United States it has been carried too far. In its extreme version, it would call for a distinctive field service for every function and subfunction of every agency, thus destroying the idea of an integrated field service, even for an agency with a single major purpose. And in cases where the need for diversity is genuine, we must still accommodate in some fashion the necessity for interagency coordination in the field. Attempts to meet this necessity have revolved about five possibilities: increased uniformity in the location of regional boundaries and field offices; incidental coordinating responsibilities of service and control agencies; reliance on informal coordination; appointment of regional coordinators to represent the President; and the use of committees and commissions.

Identity of regional office locations is an ideal that can be more closely approximated than identity of regional boundaries. There is a natural tendency for federal agencies to be represented in the same large cities that enjoy strategic locations as transportation and business centers, with office space, residential housing, schools, and cultural and recreational amenities. New York, Chicago, and San Francisco stand out as frequent choices—although a number of cities, including Los Angeles, surpass San Francisco in population. Boston, Atlanta, and Denver are among the cities that serve as natural regional centers and so attract federal regional offices. Individual departments lacking integrated departmental field services often encourage their bureaus to locate their field offices in common cities and, if possible, in common buildings. In some cities there is a federal office building or a large post-office building that can accommodate a number of agencies as tenants; in other cities federal field personnel, even those in the same bureau, may be scattered among a variety of federally owned and rented quarters. A glance under "United States Government" in the local telephone directory will give a quick appreciation of the number, kind, and office arrangements of federal field offices located in the particular city.

Coordinative influence of service and control agencies. Whatever the ultimate compromise between uniformity and diversity in regional boundaries and headquarters may be, the need for interagency coordination in the field will remain. Historically, coordination was earliest developed in attempts at economies in such common services as office and storage space, trucking facilities, equipment, personnel, and purchasing. This was the working focus of the area coordinators of the Federal Coordinating Service and the federal business associations from 1921 to 1933, both having as patron the Bureau of the Budget. Emphasis continues on the pace-setting role of such agencies as the General Services Administration, the Civil Service Commission, the General Accounting Office, and the Disbursement Division of the Treasury Department.

Because all operating agencies must work with such service and control agencies, these can exert leverage on field administration in three ways. Unless service and control agencies establish field offices of their own and give them authority, the operating agencies cannot link up with them in the field. Instead, much routine paper must flow to Washington headquarters; as long as the General Accounting Office in Washington required that federal agencies submit to it all expenditure vouchers and supporting documents for every individual transaction, the result was "freight carloads of vouchers from all over the United States hauled to Washington." [18] In the second place, service and control agencies can directly affect the selection and development of federal regional centers by their choice of cities for their own regional offices. Virtually all operating agencies will find it convenient, other things being equal, to put their

---

[18] (First) Commission on Organization of the Executive Branch of the Government, *Budgeting and Accounting*, p. 41 ff., Washington: Government Printing Office, 1949. The second Hoover Commission's *Task Force Report on Budgeting and Accounting* (1955) reported "substantial progress in changing over to modern commercial-type audits performed at the site of agency operations" (p. 64).

principal regional management staffs within ready reach of the service and control offices. Third, the influence of the General Services Administration on selection of cities to be blessed with construction of large office buildings can be consciously shaped to the objective of attracting agencies to choose the same cities for their regional headquarters. Still, it remains true that coordination of managerial services alone falls far short of what is needed.[19]

Informal coordination. The temptation to impose an authoritative coordinating system on what is largely an unregulated free-for-all must be qualified by recognition that field coordination does occur, even if informally and imperfectly. Much of this is two-way cooperation. It operates informally on the basis of personal acquaintance between officials of different agencies, depends a good deal on ease of access of each to the other, and deals with specific problems of mutual concern. The last factor, in turn, depends on relatedness of functions of the agencies, the degree of congruity of the geographic areas assigned to their officials, and the similarity in scope of decentralized authority to act for the respective agencies.

Because the conditions stated will not exist frequently enough to assure that informal coordination occurs to the degree needed, conscious effort would need to be invested to bring them to pass. Sporadic efforts have been made to facilitate informal coordination. In the 1920's luncheon clubs of ranking federal field officials—called "federal business associations"—were supported in many cities by the Bureau of the Budget's Federal Coordinating Service. In the Korean War, the principal economic mobilization agencies were required to adhere for the most part to a prescribed scheme of regional boundaries and headquarters cities.

Regional coordinators. The most frequent solution proposed and intermittently acted upon is that of a coordinator appointed for federal activities in each region of the country. The title is misleading. Coordination may mean authoritative orders to federal officials in the region; at the other extreme, it may mean only such things as reporting to Washington on overlappings and conflicts among agencies in the region, using persuasion to get agency officials to meet common problems and to work out their difficulties, and generally encouraging harmony among them and between them and the state governments of the region. It is the minimal concept that has dominated American thinking and practice.

Consistent with this formula, there have been "area coordinators" of the Budget Bureau's Federal Coordinating Service during the 1920's, state directors of the National Emergency Council in the mid-1930's, and the

---

[19] A valuable case study of an effort to establish regional managerial-service offices to serve the otherwise separate field staffs within a single department is Eley, Lynn W., *The Decentralization of Business Services in the Agricultural Research Service,* Inter-University Case Series No. 40, University, Ala.: University of Alabama Press, 1958.

heads of four midwest and western field offices of the Bureau of the Budget from 1943 to 1953.[20] In all cases, the assigned functions were to facilitate cooperation among agencies by persuasion and "good offices" and to submit reports to Washington. The intermittent character of these arrangements is notable; each was terminated, leaving a vacuum rather than a successor.

Nonetheless, the literature of the subject is studded with proposals that there be a representative of the President, or of his office, in each of the various regions of the country.[21] But Congress is reluctant to strengthen the presidency. Congressmen particularly object to any strengthening of the President in the field. Their own lines to local opinion and local interest groups would then be paralleled and rivaled by an executive line. Besides, presidential agents might develop fully packaged plans and negotiate regional support for them; this could curtail the legislators' freedom of maneuver and diminish their role as policy-makers. A presidential representative might focus particularly on the water-resource area where agency rivalry is acute. Congressmen could perhaps not continue to promote politically valuable "rivers and harbors" projects in their districts by the method of "pork-barrel" legislation. Congress is not overly fond of the idea of regional offices because regions exceed any one Senator's or Representative's electoral area and therefore weaken his claims to patronage consideration in appointments. The reluctance of Congress to endorse such innovation is matched in administrative agencies. Federal departments and bureaus prefer autonomy to any outsider's on-the-spot coordination. As we have seen, bureaus resist efforts of department heads to merge bureau field services and may seek to keep the regional director's powers innocuous even if a merger is achieved. Resistance to a presidential coordinator might be even more intense.

Committees and commissions. Between informal coordination, on the one hand, and a designated regional coordinator with governmentwide responsibilities, on the other, lie such devices as committees and commissions composed of representatives of federal agencies concerned with a common subject in a particular area. Recent history is strewn with examples.

There is no such thing as "coordination in general." It is always co-

---

[20] The field work of the Federal Coordinating Service and the National Emergency Council is critically reviewed in Fesler, James W., "Executive Management and the Federal Field Service," in President's Committee on Administrative Management, *Report with Special Studies*, p. 279 *ff.*, Washington: Government Printing Office, 1937. That of the Bureau of the Budget field offices is well covered in Latham, Earl, "Executive Management and the Federal Field Service," *Public Administration Review*, 1945, Vol. 5, p. 16 *ff.*

[21] See Fesler, *op. cit.* in note 20 above, p. 291 *ff.*; Special Committee on Comparative Administration, Committee on Public Administration, Social Science Research Council, *Memorandum on Regional Coordination*, p. 12, 21-23, Washington, March 1943; McKinley, Charles, *Uncle Sam in the Pacific Northwest*, p. 607 *ff.*, Berkeley and Los Angeles: University of California Press, 1952.

ordination about something—a definable subject-matter or problem. Committees, commissions, and conferences designed to bring representatives of *all* federal agencies together are, therefore, of little value as instruments of coordination. Committees focused on an interest common to several agencies do have value. They may inform each representative of the others' activities and plans; help to achieve agreement on removal of superficial frictions; promote action on matters whose solution is of relative indifference to the agencies principally involved; even nudge consent a little further by establishing an atmosphere of rational discussion in which a single committee member would be reluctant to take a stubborn position that he could not support by reasonable explanations.

But committees in the field are usually incapable of reaching solutions to problems on which feelings run deep, agency prestige is at stake, and views of public policy diverge. Committees of agency representatives rarely operate by majority vote; each agency has its own statutory responsibility and is free to withhold its consent. If change in its policies or operations is necessary to success of the proposal favored by the majority in a committee, each agency has what amounts to an absolute veto. The evidence is clear that "just getting men around a table" does not suffice to impose a decision on one of the participants who chooses to resist.

5. Natural Resources and Field Administration

Valley authorities? Development of the nation's natural resources has provided the sharpest of the challenges to traditional modes of field administration.[22] Establishment of the Tennessee Valley Authority in 1933, and the high praise the Authority's subsequent performance commanded, gave concrete evidence that federal functions need not be performed in a river basin by the poorly coordinated field agents of a number of Washington bureaus. Instead, a single federal agency, with its headquarters located in the river basin it serves, can displace a number of the national bureaus for its area and set the terms on which others may operate in it. Despite a number of proposals for establishment of valley authorities in other parts of the country, no counterpart of TVA has come to life.

Prevailing opinion is that the valley authority is not the answer to the problem of field administration. Valleys differ: the Tennessee is one-

---

[22] The literature is substantial. Among the most useful treatments are those in *River Basin Development* and *Water Resources,* which are the spring and summer issues of *Law and Contemporary Problems,* 1957, Vol. 22, p. 155 *ff.* Also see McKinley, *op. cit.* in note 21 above; Hart, Henry C., *The Dark Missouri,* Madison: University of Wisconsin Press, 1957; Martin, Roscoe C., ed., *TVA: The First Twenty Years,* University, Ala., and Knoxville, Tenn.: Universities of Alabama and Tennessee Presses, 1956; first and second Commission on Organization of the Executive Branch of the Government, *Reorganization of the Department of the Interior* (1949) and *Water Resources and Power* (1955), respectively, and corresponding task force reports, all published at Washington: Government Printing Office.

thirteenth the size of the Missouri; indeed, the Missouri basin is a sixth of the United States. The differences lie not only in size. The problems vary: in a western river basin, irrigation for farming and supply of water to cities and industries make high-priority claims, while in the Tennessee basin higher priority is likely to be accorded flood control and navigation. The political and administrative problems differ, too. In a large basin such as that of the Missouri river, the reconciliation of the clashing interests of different parts of the basin can be achieved only by talented exercise of the political art. In western basins, a number of important bureaus of the Interior and Agriculture Departments are far more active than was the case in the Tennessee Valley in 1933; indeed, the bulk of the Interior Department's activities take place west of the Mississippi. The experience of TVA, besides, is not automatically transferable because that agency's uniqueness, experimental character, and command of active interest by the President afforded a favorable climate that could not be assumed to prevail were a number of valley authorities to be established today.

The multiplication of valley authorities would itself create problems not heretofore faced. What is done by one valley authority—say, to the volume of water flowing into a major channel like the Mississippi or to the market for electric power—would require coordination with the interests of nearby valley authorities. If many valley authorities were to take over the natural resource functions, the challenge to the very existence of several important national bureaus would assume large proportions indeed. In addition to arousing vigorous opposition by bureaus, establishment of such authorities would require thinking through of how Washington should adjust its organization for analyzing, determining, communicating, and enforcing national policies on natural resources—responsibilities that presumably would still exist if valley authorities came into being.

Larger planning needs. Yet one more point may be made. To say that valley authorities should displace existing field services concerned with natural resources gives an illusory impression of neat solution of coordination problems. The illusion stems from the fact that "natural resources" is both too comprehensive and not comprehensive enough. The initial focus tends to be on water, and its control and exploitation as it flows in river channels. But "natural resources" is a much more comprehensive and, indeed, vague concept. It includes land (and hence agriculture), minerals (and hence mining), forests (and hence lumbering), and the less dramatic uses of water (and hence recreation, commercial fishing, sewage disposal, and mosquito abatement, among others). Can so large a part of national responsibilities be appropriately turned over to authorities oriented to the interests of their particular regions?

"Natural resources" is also not comprehensive enough. Many federal agencies are not directly charged with natural resource functions. This is true of agencies concerned with tax collection, social security, banking, government lending, collective bargaining and fair labor standards, small business, and law enforcement, to choose examples at random. In other words, valley authorities could not really provide the answer to the need for coordination of more than a few field activities of the federal government. Further, "natural resources" is not comprehensive enough if valley authorities are intended to devote themselves to regional development in its full sense. Partly because of the Tennessee valley example, but also because of a desire to find an instrument superior to what has been tried before and because of an awareness that whoever controls water and electric power has strategic leverage on a region's development, it is common to cast valley authorities in the role of comprehensive planners and developers for a whole region, such as the Pacific Northwest. But there the valley authority would find that at critical points in its planning any of a number of federal agencies could resist persuasion.

A Washington solution? It is not necessary to accept as valid all points in this case against multiplication of valley authorities. But among them there seem to be enough to dampen the earlier enthusiasm. It remains true that the field work of the government in natural resources needs a solution more than does any other field activity. The difficulty appears to require a Washington solution. Most striking is the rivalry of the Army Corps of Engineers and the Interior Department's Bureau of Reclamation.[23] Both are active builders of dams in the western part of the country; each has different priorities—for example, irrigation versus flood control; each has the backing of different local interests; each responds to and commands the support of a different branch of the federal government—the President in the case of Reclamation, and Congress in the case of the Engineers.

Conflict in the field is inevitable, and the only solution lies in organizational changes at Washington. Interagency committees and commissions at the national and basin levels have been unsuccessful. Although this particular conflict between two agencies is the most dramatic, it reflects a recurrent difficulty in focusing attention on interagency coordination in the field. Most of the really important instances of inadequate field coordination turn out to be reflections of lack of policy consistency in legislation, inability of the President to give adequate and effective attention to resolution of interdepartmental conflicts, and deficiency in departmental structure at Washington which fails to bring important related activities under the guidance of a single cabinet member.

Even in the resources field, however, evidence abounds that within a single department there will be such a variety of functions, so strong a bureaucratic insistence on autonomy, and so fragmenting a play of political

---

[23] The classic treatment is Maass, Arthur, *Muddy Waters: The Army Engineers and the Nation's Rivers,* Cambridge: Harvard University Press, 1951. See also McKinley, *op. cit.* in note 21 above, and Hart, *op. cit.* in note 22 above.

and interest-group influences that the department head will be unable to establish effective machinery for coordination in the field. Neither the Department of Agriculture nor the Department of the Interior has an integrated departmental field service. Such efforts as both Secretaries have made to provide minimal field coordination have had to take the form of interbureau regional committees or, in one or two regions, designation of a regional representative of the Secretary with vague authority to promote coordination by his gifts for persuasion.

Chapter 13 ●

Informal Organization

1. Formal and Informal Organization

Organic growth of informal organization. Broadly speaking, formal organization is organization planned; it corresponds to design. By contrast, informal organization is a natural growth; it often collides with formal organization and may even supersede it in part. Central to the distinction between formal and informal organization is the difference between authority and influence. Authority, in this sense, is the legal power of command to direct the behavior of others. Influence is the human capacity for getting others to see things your way so that they will act and even want to act accordingly. How it affects the role of the chief executive we have noticed earlier.[1] But the matter has wider significance. It can hardly escape the sharp-eyed observer that administrative bodies—and indeed all organizations, whether legislatures, political parties, labor unions, business enterprises, universities, churches, armies, or professional associations—respond in fact to a variety of informal patterns of influence among their membership.[2] These are more or less at variance with the acknowledged structure of formal authority on which the organization rests. Three distinct, though often related, sorts of reasons enter into the variance: one, the inherent differences in capacity and personality among the people who at any given time make up an organization, whatever their formal assignments; two, the variety of purposes that animate them; and three, the elements in the situation that make it relatively easy or hard for them to turn purpose into accomplished fact.

Of the first, more in a moment. Of the second, what is relevant here is that everyone lives in a private world as well as in the organization of which he is a part. He has not only his private dreams, ambitions, and antipathies, but also sees the purposes of the organization in his own light. Unless he is altogether cynical, he tends to identify those purposes with what he thinks they should be. So, while every organization has some

---

[1] See Chapter 8, "The Chief Executive," sec. 2, "Leadership and Authority."
[2] For the increasing interest of students of management in this subject, see also Chapter 2, "The Study of Public Administration," sec. 4, "The Frontiers of Research."

publicly avowed mission, usually stated in a charter or statutes, no formula of words is self-executing. A continual competition of purposes goes on, within and around the organization, more or less informally and often unconsciously, to shape its policies and activities. In that sense, control of the organization is control of the purposes of those who make it up. When this is consciously recognized, new appointments at high levels of administrative responsibility may be deliberately made to reverse or modify, to invigorate or de-emphasize, previous policies, by setting new informal organizational forces to work.

On the third score, a military example will serve. In actual battle, the necessities of self-preservation drive together the private and public purposes of soldiers, and discipline and morale become secondary problems. But an army in peacetime, or a well-supplied unit in the backwash of a quiet sector in war, furnishes a host of opportunities and temptations to officers and men to use their leisure to convert the facilities at hand from the remote public mandate of an armed force to their own immediate ends. In the organization of such "privatized" activities, the normal hierarchy of ranks may get badly mixed up.

It is therefore easy to understand that it is an essential task of successful administrative leadership to link the informal patterns of influence to the structure of formal authority. Leadership must provide the integrating forces that will draw all eyes toward common goals. In small groups where the boss is mainly the product of conceded superiority rather than of legal designation, the distinctive effect of influence may blend completely with the group's understanding of who has the last word. As soon as the group grows larger, formal authority needs to be designated. Even at best, however, such authority has no monopoly of leadership. In general, although the boss naturally will want to run the show, everyone else in the group, no less naturally, will want to be as independent as possible, and will have his own ideas of how the show ought to be run. Such individualistic impulses never fully subside in any organization. They give rise to the cell formation typical of informal organization.

Charts and realities. The organization chart shows the formal structure, labels the jurisdiction assigned to each component unit, and indicates the lines of hierarchical authority established to regulate the conduct of business. If the chart is carefully and candidly drawn, the very act of preparing it is almost sure to disclose internal ambiguities calling for resolution. If clarification is achieved in the course of completing the chart, the labor of the chartmaker is already repaid in the smoother operations that can be expected to result from a better understanding of working relationships among the various groups of employees. At best, however, the organization chart presents an idealized picture of the intents of top management, a reflection of hopes and aims rather than a photograph of the operating facts within the organization. To the sophisticated reader, the chart is a useful guide to further questions.

To begin with, the chart, while locating present personnel, speaks rather in terms of positions than of live employees. In such an inevitably composite abstraction of, say, all possible top-grade economists, we have no clue to the kind of man who might be heading the Analysis Section in the Import Division, to the standing he has in his section or in the division, or to the load of work he carries or has failed to carry. Is he the faithful technician who as anonymous assistant to the previous section head used to get up the figures to support the division's policy and who as the "logical" successor now fondles the same set of figures even though changing conditions call for a fresh and imaginative analysis of foreign trade? Or is he the man who was borrowed from the Research Division on a temporary detail to work out a particular problem before the Import Division had an Analysis Section of its own, and who impressed the division chief so much that the section was created to keep him around?

Again, was he perhaps the only promising reinforcement the division chief could think of in order to bolster an ailing operation, and the position of section head the handiest vacancy to bring him into the picture? Or, to suggest only one more line of possibilities, is the position again vacant today as we look at the organization chart? If so, is a replacement in sight and the section's work still definitely part of the whole program? Or is the place not to be filled and the section to be disbanded, so that its box in the chart has already become an anachronism? Plainly, we would need answers not only to these and many more questions about our section head, but also to similar questions about the division chief one step above and others in adjoining positions, before attempting to draw from the chart an appraisal of the role of the Analysis Section.

Attitudes and motivations. However he appears on the chart, the section head stands in a different light to his own subordinates. Here he is the boss, clothed with authority to summon and direct, and all his qualities of leadership are at stake in the assessment of what that authority is worth. To the oldtimer in the section—say, with a standing assignment to tabulate the weekly figures of customs receipts—he may be only another boss, more or less like those who have come and gone. Thus the boss may be viewed with indifference unless it should occur to him that the customs figures ought to be compiled differently, or possibly are no longer needed at all. If he lets people alone who know their tasks and do them without prodding, he is a safe boss; and a safe boss is a good boss in the oldtimer's way of thinking.

To one of the junior economists, however, the boss may be the author of that series of articles which broke new ground in the analysis of the balance of international payments. This junior may have studied the same field, and is cherishing a hope that the boss will develop it within the section—a prospect rich in possibilities of new assignments and recognition for the alert youngster. Another junior of the same rank, though, who because of his addiction to doctrinal heresies was passed over whenever the previous section head had an especially interesting project to assign, is disgusted to find that the present head also has a blind spot regarding these doctrines. Convinced that he is facing a hopeless situation, he has already begun to make discreet inquiries about possible openings in other parts of the agency. In a sense, his mind is no longer on the job.

Variables of this sort must be accounted for in the staff pattern before we can have much of an idea of the concrete work situation. And so with the girls in the section. One or two of them can be counted on to stay overtime if needed, to get out the materials the boss has to have for his conference the first thing in the morning. Others may feel that if he cannot arrange to get his work done during office hours, they are under no duty to bail him out.

Basis of personal organization. Given the crew our section head has to work with—and allowing for such additions and eliminations as he can manage from time to time—he develops a team for *his* purposes. He leans on the strengths he finds, and by-passes the weaknesses. He looks to a smaller nucleus of people for the crucial work, and he meets with them more often. Together they look ahead and lay plans, assemble the strategic information and put it into persuasive form, carry the argument when the occasion for it arises, and consolidate the advance when their program has won endorsement. This is the section head's personal organization—perhaps no more than a thought-man, an action-man, and a personal secretary. Organization charts are silent on the relationships that constitute such personal organizations.

The factors here considered center around the measure of influence that our hypothetical subordinate—the section head—may exert on his immediate superior and on his own section. The example is taken from the middle ranks in the scale of positions, and from a staff or auxiliary function in the organization's work—for the Analysis Section presumably does not actually issue the licenses that are, let us say, the end product of the division's operation. If we shift our example upward or downward in the hierarchy, or from a staff or auxiliary section to an operating section, some of the situations indicated are no longer so plausible, while other new possibilities open up. In particular, the higher we go up the line, the more complex the relationships become.

Growing and shrinking organizations. Again, we have assumed an example from a stable organization. But organization charts are drawn also for rapidly expanding agencies. After Pearl Harbor, for instance, the war agencies were recruiting personnel at an almost overwhelming rate as they struggled to cope with the new tasks that had brought them into being. As their functions grew, their internal structure and external relationships altered. Successive newcomers in these agencies caught hold and came to exert decisive influence, or failed to catch hold and dropped out of sight. From month to month, under the impact of these changes, organization charts became obsolete more rapidly than maps of Europe. In the same way, during the months that followed the close of hostilities, contraction or liquidation and atrophy of functions were the order of the day for most of these agencies. Once more, the patterns of influence within the organization in many cases changed abruptly. This process was duplicated during the Korean emergency—and is likely to be repeated with any new national emergency on a similar scale.

In short, the chart portrays the norms of anatomy. We must look to the informal organization to understand the physiology—perhaps the pathology —of the organism, and the dynamics of its behavior.

2. Elements of Informal Organization

Characteristic factors. The network of influence does not extend from any single center—even under the Soviet system. Relationships based on influence result from the interplay of a combination of factors. Some are unique to the particular scene. Others are recurringly characteristic of many agencies and situations.

In this second group we may discern: (1) the relation of the actual leadership sensed within the organization to the formal location of authority; (2) the personal organizations installed or recognized by the leaders within the framework of the formal structure, to transmit direction and keep the leaders posted on internal conditions; and (3) the ties of allegiance, external and internal, that cut across the lines of command and bind together groups of officials and employees on some basis other than that of loyalty to their formal superiors. It is useful also to distinguish the role of these informal groupings as supplementary channels of communication and intelligence from their potentialities for furthering or hindering the acknowledged aims of the organization. These points call for some elaboration.

Distribution of influence. The magnetism of personal leadership is an irrepressible and often an unpredictable force. Responsibility will frequently evoke it unexpectedly in the head of an organization that is suddenly subjected to new conditions and pressing problems. However, leadership may fail to appear at the point where there was every reason to count on it, and instead turn up elsewhere in the organization. It may indeed be ordinarily denied to the titular head of the organization by the very process of his selection.

Nomination for the presidency, to take a conspicuous case, usually does not go to a man showing exceptional personal qualities of independent leadership, if the party chieftains who control the convention can feel confident of winning with a more manageable and dependable candidate. The chairmanship of a congressional committee, where seniority commonly governs, will only by accident fall to the most gifted personality of the committee. Cabinet officers must often be chosen in recognition of claims other than the leadership they can promise in running their departments. And so with administrative appointments. The conditions of selection too seldom permit native qualities of personal leadership to be the decisive criterion. A new agency may have an active head who is also its actual leader. A crisis in the life of an older agency may give a new head an unusually free hand for reorganization. The typical situation, however, shows a distribution of leadership through the organization that does not coincide with formal authority. All such leadership begets loyalty, and loyalty commands influence.

Why men count. Nominal authority must either seize upon leadership or live in its shadow. A capable department head may be given jurisdiction over an unrelated operation, merely because the operators must report to someone, and no better place for allocation of the function has appeared. If the jurisdiction is already in satisfactory hands, it may be left alone. Authority to this extent tends to follow the pull of leadership. Much the same is true within the departmental organization itself and within each of its component parts.

Because one of the chief staff officers serving as immediate advisers to the department head may have demonstrated special capacity for achieving internal agreements or for exercising sound political judgment or simply for getting work done more promptly than others, he is used more and more as a privileged source of counsel and assistance. Difficult problems—including those outside his formal jurisdiction—drift to him magnetically from the desk of the top executive. Other staff officers, and line officials as well, discover that it is wise for them to check with this colleague in advance on all troublesome matters handed up to the department head. In the end, the staff officer may be doing the job of a permanent undersecretary, while the nominal undersecretary shifts his attention to matters of special interest to him. Or, in a given bureau, division, or section, the employee who establishes himself as a key man will grow in stature as his responsibilities expand *de facto* by spontaneous accrual.

No doubt, such developments introduce into the hierarchy of command much-needed flexibility. They allow an organization to make the most of its strength wherever such strength resides. On the other hand, it is also evident that as a consequence the organization may develop all kinds of strange bulges. From time to time these bulges will be legalized, so to speak, as factual influence is given formal status through the redefinition of authority and through adjustments in the channels of command. However, such formalization may merely aggravate defects in internal balance, structural deformities, and lopsided arrangements. For these reasons the surveyor of organizational structure should always bear in mind the need for reserving judgment until all compensating advantages of a seemingly bizarre pattern have been ascertained. A department is not likely to be impressed with the criticism that its organization chart looks unorthodox when the existing working mechanisms accord with the operating preferences of its strongest personalities and are adequately understood by its personnel.

Variables affecting authority. Another complicating factor arises from the dynamics of leadership. Authority as expressed in legal terms is essentially static. Influence is susceptible of continuous change. Leadership may wane as an official commanding deference shows himself unable to stand the tough grind of responsibility, or as his health and his nerves begin to falter, or as he fails to withstand the jolts and shocks of temporary defeats. Influence is competitive. When leaders stumble and fall by the wayside, rivals will see an opportunity. As these individuals begin to inject their personalities into the stream of operations, new bulges may evolve while earlier ones wither away.

The actual substance of authority is therefore elusive. To support itself, authority cannot merely point to its insignia. It must seek to effect constancy of deference. Thus it requires a basis in persuasion. It must nurture itself in consent. It must bargain for endorsement and negotiate workable covenants with internal forces of opposition. Administrative orders, while traveling downward from level of authority to level of authority, may completely change their meaning when they encounter passive resistance or open antagonism. Authority cannot assert itself when its claims fail to rest on plausible reason or commonly shared attitudes. To a large extent, therefore, authority must be buttressed by rational considerations and appeals. That is why some students regard the top executive primarily as a ratifying agent—one who sanctions the common thinking of his organization. In aiming at such sanction, he must prepare the ground by shaping common thought.

Moreover, the exercise of authority is affected by the nature of its mandate, which in a real sense is always in flux. The statutory formulation of the mission of an administrative organization may remain the same, and yet the scope of actual authority reposing in the top executive is bound to change with changing circumstances, most of them beyond his own control. Shifting legislative alignments, the rise and fall of popular causes, reorientations in general policy, and deteriorating public relations may arrest the individual agency in many ways. These variables account for the fact that there are always matters of great administrative significance within the reach of the legislative mandate of an agency which its top executive would never dare to touch at certain times. Particular issues grow too hot to handle, while others cool off in the battles of public opinion and the contests of political forces. The time-bound cycles of popular elections also play their role in determining the actual scope of legal authority.

Even in the most limited sense—solely in reference to the specific incumbent—the place of formal authority is one of relative importance only. The official vested with authority may be personally weak or strong, timid or aggressive, unimaginative or intellectually alert, phlegmatic or choleric. The same span of legal authority will furnish different individualities with different opportunities for initiative and leadership. Even in reasonably stable organizations, changes in personnel at the points of control are frequent enough to cause conspicuous modifications in the interplay of different personalities. All this does not suggest that formally allocated authority amounts to little. It does suggest that it is never quite the same when circumstances alter.

Forms of personal organization. We have earlier alluded to the phenomenon of personal organization—special structures of relationships built freely for the convenience of individual leaders within the formal framework of the organization. The members of a personal organization may not always be identified as such except to the inner circle they represent. Their individual roles will vary, too. On the level of the top executive, for instance, some members will be primarily sources of confidential information. Others may be placed strategically for the stimulation of prompt response to administrative directives from above; these members of the top executive's personal organization are to "carry the ball" for him in the sphere of operations. While functioning for the most part independently and at different points of the hierarchical structure, all members will maintain contact with one another as well as with "the chief." They will act in concert, though for best effect their synchronized action usually retains the appearance of coincidence and spontaneity.

The existence of such personal organizations formed around individuals at key control points—the department head, chiefs of larger staff or auxiliary services, line officers on various levels of command, and even unit supervisors at the base of operations—in itself attests to the limitations of formal authority. Power of direction may be commensurate with personal responsibility at each control point of the administrative hierarchy, yet direction does not automatically elicit positive response. All large-scale organization, because of both its size and its specialization, is highly vulnerable to internal indifference, intransigence, and obstruction. Left to himself, even the agency head, in the imposing plenitude of his directive power, may have the ugly feeling of perching atop an elephant firmly set to have things his own way. True enough, the executive has his "arms of management"—administrative planning, budgeting, personnel—and his line officials to rely upon. But how much of this supporting cast can be trusted actually to support him?

The new department head. How real this question is perhaps can be seen most readily when we think of a new appointee taking over a government department. This may be an entirely novel experience for him, as it usually is even to a competent corporation executive. There is no one to brief him fully on his first day of office. He is lucky if he knows one or two key people in the department sufficiently well to be sure of their sympathetic help right at the start, and some others against whom he should be on guard. He may be free to bring along a small number of personal assistants—each probably as green at the start on departmental business as he himself. Replacements in the top range of command will have to wait until the new head has had time to reach at least tentative judgments on the internal situation he is facing.

His first thought in testing personalities he has to depend upon will be to have assurance of their loyalty toward him so that he in turn can have full confidence in them and talk to them without mental reservations. Because too many new appointments would mean a heavy mortgage of inexperience, he is never free to fire and hire at will, quite aside from the limitations placed upon him by the civil service system in the name of objective standards and official impartiality. In the main, he must learn to work with the department as he finds it, and teach his immediate subordinates to take to him and work with him. In some instances, he will be able to shift individual officers he spots as congenial into positions in his proximity. As a general rule, however, he has only a restricted opportunity for rearranging the human pattern around him.

In the experience of his first few months, he will therefore attempt to create his own unofficial peerage from within the department. He will turn repeatedly to those who win his confidence first. These will become conscious of their task as intermediaries, and in due course will be treated and used as such by their colleagues. Unofficial peers can be made and unmade by the department head; readjustments in the structure of his peerage may happen rather frequently at the beginning, and will continue to occur at later periods. Slowly, however, a degree of constancy will evolve in his personal organization. At best, its constancy will allow for a recognition of those special talents which are at a premium in this kind of grouping.

Departmental "peerage." One of those rare individuals who have a good grasp of the department as a whole—perhaps the budget officer, perhaps a bureau chief with many years of service and a sufficient variety of successive responsibilities behind him—is likely to be drawn into the personal organization of the top executive. The personal assistants he brought into the department become "charter members," too, though not necessarily for all time to come. It would be erroneous to assume that every one of the political officeholders of the department is simultaneously a member of the peerage in our sense. One of them may be too intimately tied into a powerful interest group that eyes the department head with misapprehension. Another may remain too much adrift in the affairs of the department to win standing within it. On the other hand, some of the permanent officials will be included in the top executive's personal organization because of their strength as leaders, because of the multiplicity of their working contacts with others, or because of their range of practical experience. In addition, his personal organization is apt to reach into such highly sensitive functions as public relations, legislative liaison, and field direction.

Objective qualifications alone are never enough for membership; the decisive factor is a substantial degree of personal compatibility with the intellectual approach and the outlook of the department head. His personal organization is basically made up of "king's men," whether as a tight group or as a loose affiliation. Within it, stars may rise and fall. There may also be occasional cases of desertion. Moreover, his personal organization is never the only one. For greatest utility it must link itself to the personal organizations developed by ranking subordinate leaders. Where a subordinate leader differentiates himself from the fortunes of the department head, the latter's personal organization must attempt to outmaneuver or to checkmate in one way or another the "king's men" of the uncooperative subordinate. Prolonged battles may rage between different personal organizations. Formal agreements in open conference may be in many cases merely the product of informal bargains for support. The price exacted for such support may be an important promotion, an enlargement of functions, or a greater degree of independence in specified areas. Such concessions may interfere with general expectancies based on official rules and customs, causing losses in morale throughout the department. There is hence always a point of diminishing returns.

Yet it is clear that without this type of personal organization, individual leaders in the department cannot hope to know what is really going on, what the attitudes of the working force are, and how to generate momentum for cooperative action in line with their own priorities. Teamwork is not achieved by mere pronouncement of superiors. It requires recognition of the most accomplished players on the team. Indeed, one or two of these may monopolize the actual leadership in the team, leaving the nominal leader in the role of a figurehead. At the same time, it is obvious that effective personal organization calls for adroit handling and appreciation of relationships, coupled with a sense of reality. As with organization in the formal sense, personal organization may easily militate against itself. It may become a burden on the individual leader, setting him off from his wider institutional environment. It may inject elements of arbitrariness or favoritism into general working processes. It may substitute subjective considerations for objective evaluations, disrupting the regularity of operations and destroying the chance of planned advancement toward acknowledged aims.

The balance sheet of personal organization has its debit as well as its credit side. On the debit side is the possibility of doubts seeping through the department about the integrity of management, the soundness of decisions, and the justice of rewards. Personal organization can be a great convenience in attaining impersonal objectives—policy goals. It can also acquire the characteristics of personal government and thus corrupt impersonal objectives. An able department head will periodically examine the balance sheet—and draw his own practical conclusions.

Ties of allegiance. Formal organization suggests a monolithic structure in which all wills are bent toward institutional goals. Acceptance of these goals is at least implicit throughout the entire structure. An outstanding leader at the helm of the organization may not only become a symbolic expression of the validity and continuity of such objectives, but he may also draw forth the allegiance of his subleadership and with it that of the large body of personnel. Even then, however, there remain in each individual certain residual allegiances of varying strength that exert their pulls in different directions. Man is only in part organizable. He lives only in part in his occupation. The fanatic alone is able to pour all of his capacity for allegiance into a single cause.

Normally, every individual responds to a wide range of loyalties—some embedded in his background, some foisted upon him in the school of living, some freely accepted as a matter of deliberate choice. In this agglomeration no single loyalty will dominate all others. For satisfying human experience, however, all loyalties should admit of harmonious blending without contradiction or conflict. The same applies to man as part of an organization in which he spends his occupational life. No more can be expected of him than that the web of his loyalties as a whole keeps him receptive to the goals of the organization he is serving. Yet, even when there is a general accord of loyalties, each loyalty separately continues to have some influence upon him. Depending on the circumstances, each may place him in part or for a time in opposition to the organization for which he works.

This is the basic reason why institutional leadership must constantly attempt to magnify individual loyalty toward the institution. Such effort cannot be confined to a single approach—a single "morale program." It must come to the fore in everything the organization undertakes to accomplish. To foster what military language calls "pride of outfit," institutional leadership must be articulate and persuasive on its objectives and policies, adept in developing a general system of internal inducements, resourceful in broadening the base for participation in policy-making, and inventive in distributing credit for collective accomplishment.

Formal authority becomes effective in the deference it elicits; but no assurance exists that deference will conform to institutional assumptions. Even in reasonably unified organizations characterized by a common feeling of institutional individuality and identity, each member may stand in a different relationship to the organization as a whole. Some members may completely give themselves to the organization, regarding it as their better part. Others may accept institutional authority as a pragmatic compromise essential to their cooperative role in the organization. Still others may be satisfied with a more passive attitude—"live and let live"—while reserving their deeper attachments for personal pursuits outside the organization. Finally, there will be those who, though not necessarily antagonistic to the organization itself, will strive to superimpose on the "powers that be" values derived from loyalties other than those the organization demands.

Outside connections. Loyalties in conflict with deference to formal authority may have external or internal focus; often both types are intermingled imperceptibly. Under the rubric of external factors, for example, we may think of a bureau chief who consciously or unconsciously reflects in his own thinking the preferences of the interest group that looks upon his bureau's function with proprietary eyes. If challenged by his official superiors, he does not hesitate to set up his defense in closed session with the leaders of the interest group. These may treat him as a central figure in their councils, run personal publicity for him, and build him up as a great public servant or a national expert. Blind to more general objectives, he comes to regard his superiors in the department as opposing, perhaps even dangerous forces, against which he must battle tenaciously in order to guard the function of his bureau—and the outside interest that supports him.

Or we may think of an assistant secretary in a department whose credentials for public service stem from political affiliation with a legislative bloc that seeks to dominate the department. His official chief may treat him as a hostile observer posted for sniping, missing no chance of advancing the purposes of the legislative bloc. Everyone suspects him of carrying ammunition to his legislative principals and of tipping them off confidentially on any steps planned by the department that may affect their stake.

We may also think of a regional director out in the field who regards it as his chief mission to go to bat for the interests dominant in his region, without consideration of the need for defining public policy in terms of the nationwide public interest. In much the same way, still other members of the organization, whether in important or unimportant positions, may think of themselves primarily as internal guardians of clientele formations —business or labor, farmers or veterans, oil or silver. The institutional hierarchy—theoretically one structure—is thus fragmented in many ways by allegiances that obstruct the "channels of command."

Internal factors. Within the four walls of the department, too, multiplicity of loyalties has its disruptive effects. Strong loyalty, we may remember, plays a principal part in the formation of personal organizations. Membership in one personal organization therefore usually carries with it a marked degree of exclusiveness, especially toward other personal organizations. This exclusiveness may also turn against the formal organization as a whole; only on the level of the top executive are both personal organization and formal organization oriented toward essentially the same objectives. Quite aside from personal organizations, however, loose protective associations may develop on the principle of reciprocal support in the promotion of policy suggestions or in the mutual insurance of institutional status. In the higher councils of a department, for instance, three or four bureau chiefs may band together in a durable alliance for such purposes as pressing jointly for acceptance of their ideas or bringing their combined strength to bear upon the budget officer. Too often for a constructive frame of mind, they may assume themselves to be right and the departmental leadership to be wrong.

We can observe the same kind of alignment in even the smallest working unit where a few employees sticking together may compel the first-line supervisor to respect them as the controlling power in his shop. They may determine unofficial standards of output and discipline which the supervisor by mere authority is unable to modify. They may in fact set the entire tone of operations and employee behavior.[3] A similar kinship can develop within professional or technically specialized cadres. To illustrate, an economist dealing with administrative officials may find it natural to uphold the judgment of other economists; a lawyer dealing with economists may similarly side with other lawyers; an engineer dealing with lawyers may support the views of other engineers. Or, especially in questions of functional grouping and allocation of responsibilities, individual categories of specialists may be guided primarily by their conception of the stake of their specialty in the proposed arrangements.

In addition, personal association of a comparable character—with corresponding investment of loyalty—may spring from common backgrounds. Graduation from the same college or professional school is one illustration; earlier staff experience in the same research institution or consulting firm is another. Like any other type of large-scale organization, moreover, government departments have their ideological factions—here the "liberals," there the "conservatives." Eager stalwarts of such factions are likely to look upon the department as a potential area of conquest, or at least an object of proportionate influence. Factional struggles may not always be conspicuous, but the sense of loyalty produced in their heat may leave little loyalty for the department itself. Finally we should mention the ties of allegiance among the organized rank and file of employees. The locals of government-employee unions may attract to themselves a substantial share of loyalty, especially in the face of an unsympathetic or laggard departmental leadership.

Thus the actual pattern of human relationships and allegiances within the formal organization is distinguished by complexity. Reference to "channels of command" may becloud the real picture. Uncrowned lead-

---

[3] Informal organization in this sense has been analyzed extensively in the area of industrial production by Roethlisberger, Fritz J., and Dickson, William J., *Management and the Worker,* Cambridge: Harvard University Press, 1943.

ers compete with crowned ones. Informal and often unaccountable groupings brought to life for various purposes press against one another. Nor are the underlying motivations always either clear or durable. Human beings freely exercise their privilege to change their minds on what seems worth their effort. So does man in organization. This explains in part why any given organization may demonstrate great vigor at certain times and may virtually fall apart or drop into a coma at certain other times, even though its general mandate or its formal structure remains unchanged. It also casts a sharp light on the folly of considering a department a mighty steamroller pursuing its aims with mechanical precision. Last but not least, it shows how much is borrowed from imagination when we hear talk about the sinister designs of a single-minded bureaucracy.

3. Formation of Influence

Balance sheet of free growth. Democratic theory stresses the unregimented evolution of free associations of citizens who speak for themselves. The very diversity of these associations is considered an asset. Public preferences can be tested in open argument. Fresh ideas can find direct expression. Workable compromises can be forged in the adjustment of group aims to one another. This is regarded as the soundest way of tapping and mobilizing the political resources of the whole nation. Even those who doubt the productivity of too much diffusion and too much milling around would be very reluctant to sacrifice the values of unimpaired self-expression to a superimposed "order" that would choke group autonomy under a gigantic blanket of directed uniformity. But free political competition is not without pitfalls. It may operate to the detriment of the public interest. There is a great difference between the National League of Women Voters and an economic pressure group eager to advance its material advantage.[4] Pressure politics may degenerate into brash hijacking.

Informal organization offers close parallels. Unless kept in bounds, it may turn into a disorganizing force, undoing at least in part what formal organization is intended to achieve. It may dangerously widen the cracks and crannies which division of labor and segregation of functions inevitably tear into the structure of all formal organization. In certain spots it may actually nullify official responsibility. With all that, informal organization does meet practical needs. Like the free interplay of democratic groups in the civic realm, it is in many respects a source of administrative vitality. It provides additional outlets for group opinion, thus extending and broadening the avenues of institutional planning and thought. Informal leadership, moreover, is in a sense as much a school of responsibility as the

---

4 See Chapter 14, "Interest Groups in Administration," sec. 1, "The Meaning of Interest Representation."

exercise of official authority. In short, informal organization, as a perfectly natural growth, not only eases the rigidities of hierarchy but also can work as a desirable stimulant to a timid or uninspired top command. How far it so works depends mainly on the public spirit of its leaders. This may become clearer through a review of some examples of the formation of influence in informal organization.

Men behind the throne. No ruler—be he an omnipotent dictator or a constitutional president—thinks and acts in splendid isolation. There are always men and women in his entourage who intentionally or unintentionally help him to make up his mind.[5] In quite the same way, the head of a government department, however retiring and introverted by nature, is surrounded by his "inner circle." He may have a regular "cabinet" of his own, made up perhaps of his principal staff and line officers, with whom he discusses matters of general importance at a set hour each week or oftener. On special issues he may confer with smaller or larger groups of officials, excluding those members of his cabinet not directly concerned, and drawing in other officers who do not ordinarily attend the cabinet meetings. Consultative organs of some kind are an administrative necessity; whether they are always intelligently utilized is another question. However, the existence of advisory machinery seldom gives a hint about the way in which the top executive frames his judgments. He may be merely a polite listener. He may simply believe such formally organized consultation to be a proper democratic gesture. Or he may use his cabinet meetings primarily as a method of communicating his decisions to the next-lower level of leadership. How, then, does he reach his decisions?

It is at this point only that we turn from formal to informal organization. The insider may tell us that the cabinet is just a ritual; that there is in fact something like an "inner cabinet" of only three members; and that one of these is not even included in the cabinet itself. Those in the inner cabinet are the "men behind the throne." The one who does not belong to the cabinet itself is the senior personal assistant to the department head. For many years he has been the political shadow of the man who now directs the affairs of the department. The relationship developed long ago in local politics and has been reinforced in the test of changing fortunes as both made their way within the currently dominant major party. This personal assistant has no clearly defined functions. He is a Colonel House or a Harry Hopkins or a Sherman Adams to the department head. Moreover, he is the department's most important liaison to the party leadership and the legislative body as well. He and "the chief" have come to think as one mind. The other two members of the inner cabinet are one of the assistant secretaries and a bureau chief. The assistant secretary

---

[5] For a penetrating discussion, long overlooked, see Bentley, Arthur F., *The Process of Government*, Chicago: University of Chicago Press, 1908; republished Bloomington: Principia Press, 1935.

is the youngest man on the top level, but he has proved himself an invaluable fountain of fertile ideas. That is the reason why he overshadows the undersecretary, who is weighted down by a heavy burden of operating responsibilities. The bureau chief is known neither for imaginative thinking nor for good political judgment. However, he has been with the department for nearly three decades and knows its practical business inside out.

It is with these three men that the department head arrives at his decisions, sometimes at a tray luncheon in his office, sometimes during a brief session preceding a meeting of his cabinet. Because all four know each other very closely, they are able to express themselves in some kind of shorthand language, coming to the point in a few words. There is not only extraordinary economy in their method of oral communication, but each is also fully aware of everyone's general bias, including his own. This introduces desirable checks.

The type of consultative grouping here portrayed resembles a regency, with the king withdrawing, for all practical purposes, into the role of one member. In other institutional settings, the "men behind the throne" may be an equally small body of departmental civil servants, with or without actual veto power; or a more fluid group of little collective strength, throwing the greatest influence in the direction of the subordinate with whom the department head happened to talk last. There is obviously no single "best way" of organizing and using the "men behind the throne." The decisive factor will often be the working habits of the top executive. In such small groups, of course, it is highly advantageous that each individual member consciously complement the abilities and inclinations of the other members. The greatest peril lies in the possibility that the convenience of harmony reduces the group's capacity for stimulating differences; after all, life is much more agreeable when one can roll along with the momentum supplied by the strongest personality.

The personal secretary. Throughout the administrative hierarchy, men of authority would often cut sorry figures were it not for the untiring help they receive from their personal secretaries. As the housekeeper of the administrative estate of her boss, the personal secretary may feel herself to be part of the structure of authority. Outside the province controlled by her boss, her importance is frequently underrated; inside she may be treated like a queen. Her responsibilities reflect those of the boss; and within certain limitations she may even act as his *alter ego*. As the stenographic manual of one federal agency explains:

> To be a real help to the executive, she must know how he would like to have a task performed and do it that way. She must be alert to grasp situations and draw sound conclusions, to take into consideration more than meets the eye or ear. She must be able to follow the wishes of her chief, even to anticipate them.

... The "thinking secretary" proves her ability to take responsibility; to express initiative, originality, and resourcefulness. This thoughtful attitude is the basis for judgment, which is essential in tempering all other traits.

An extremely important point for the secretary to remember is that she represents both her chief and the agency to callers, in person and over the telephone. She must put herself in her chief's place and convey the impression and the information as he would have her do it.

The secretary must become skilful in taking interruptions herself and in interrupting others. She must determine when something is sufficiently important or urgent to justify interrupting her chief at a conference and the method by which she will convey the message to him, remembering that she interrupts not only her chief but others as well.

Because the boss himself generally occupies a dual position as an exponent of the official hierarchy and as a member of one or more informal organizations, his personal secretary must extend her activities in these same different directions. Her main stock in trade is knowledge of things that only her boss knows. Only she can tell where he is at the moment, whether he may be accessible "for a few minutes" during the next few hours, where the memorandum now is that was sent up to him day before yesterday, what matters are still on his desk, what disposition he is likely to make of each matter. In giving information of this kind, in arranging the list of callers and conferences, in adjusting priority among appointments as urgencies change, in drawing the attention of her boss to items that have passed from his mind—in all of her activities she must be thoroughly cognizant of the specific character of the relationship between him and others.

She must have a sure sense of differentiation; some demands on the time of her boss need to be rebuffed, while on others she will yield with ease. Members of his own personal organization may share with her confidential information that she would never think of disclosing to anyone else. Indeed, she may become the manager of the agenda for this personal organization. She must make it her business to hear and to see—drawing even from the gossip of the office and the cafeteria hints and suggestions of profit to her boss. Through her contacts with other secretaries, she may become a special channel of intelligence to other kinds of informal organization.

Small wonder that the personal secretary will often know her boss better than does his wife. He may find it of benefit to pose to her administrative problems to which he has no ready answer. He may leave her a great deal of discretion in handling particular matters with his subordinates. He will feel hopelessly stranded when a cold keeps her from the office. Others working for him will soon learn the importance of approaching him through her. They will try to gain her favor, but she would not be able to conduct her business with full efficiency if she proved an easy victim of flattery.

The invincible constellation. In our discussion of informal groupings we have noticed time and again the extent to which the hierarchical order of authority is modified by the factor of personal standing within the organization.[6] This is true also within the hierarchy itself. There are everywhere individuals on a relatively lower level of authority who overshadow others on a higher level of authority. For example, a ranking staff officer may belong to the department head's personal cabinet, and yet he may not "count." Or a line executive may be entitled to all the vestments of seniority, and yet he knows that his opinions and proposals find no takers unless they are endorsed by someone who does "count." Conversely, those within a department who are familiar with the structure of informal organization will be able to point to four or five unadvertised officials whose agreement on any matter almost always foreshadows the departmental decision. Those are the few one has to see in order to get action—the "invincible constellation."

The informal status of the members of this cardinal group may have quite different foundations. One may be a central figure in the top executive's personal organization. Another may be the action-man among those "behind the throne." No less often will membership in the "invincible constellation" rest on a firmly established reputation for soundness in judging the feasibility and efficacy of proposed action. This is sometimes

---

[6] Study of informal organization is still in its infancy. A useful bibliography is available in de Grazia, Alfred, *Human Relations in Public Administration,* Chicago: Public Administration Service, 1949. Valuable insights were furnished indirectly by Bentley, *op. cit.* above in note 5. More specific materials can be found in Argyris, Chris, *Personality and Organization,* New York: Harper, 1957; Marrow, Alfred J., *Making Management Human,* New York: McGraw-Hill, 1957; Mayo, Elton, *Human Problems of an Industrial Civilization,* New York: Macmillan, 1933; Tead, Ordway, *Human Nature and Management,* New York: McGraw-Hill, 1933, and *Democratic Administration,* New York: Association Press, 1945; Urwick, Lyndall F., *Leadership in the Twentieth Century,* London: Pitman, 1957; Selznick, Philip, *Leadership in Administration: A Sociological Interpretation,* Evanston, Ill.: Row, Peterson, 1957; Barnard, Chester I., *The Functions of the Executive,* Cambridge: Harvard University Press, 1938, republished, 1945; Roethlisberger and Dickson, *op. cit.* above in note 3; Ginzberg, Eli, and Others, *Effecting Change in Large Organizations,* New York: Columbia University Press, 1957; Weiss, Robert S., *Process of Organization,* Ann Arbor: Survey Research Center, Institute of Social Research, University of Michigan, Publication No. 17, 1956; Roethlisberger, Fritz J., *Management and Morale,* Cambridge: Harvard University Press, 1941; Houser, Theodore V., *Big Business and Human Values,* New York: McGraw-Hill, 1957; Gardner, Burleigh B., *Human Relations in Industry,* Chicago: Irvin, rev. ed., 1955; Livingston, Robert T., and Milberg, Stanley H., eds., *Human Relations in Industrial Research Management,* New York: Columbia University Press, 1957; Murphy, Dennis, *Better Business Communication,* New York: McGraw-Hill, 1957; Redfield, Charles E., *Communication in Management: The Theory and Practice of Administrative Communication,* Chicago: University of Chicago Press, rev. ed., 1958; Leavitt, Harold J., *Managerial Psychology: An Introduction to Individuals, Pairs, and Groups in Organization,* Chicago: University of Chicago Press, 1958. On public relations, see further Hill, John W., *Corporate Public Relations: Arm of Modern Management,* New York: Harper, 1958; Harlow, Rex F., *Social Science in Public Relations: A Survey and an Analysis of Social Science Literature Bearing upon the Practice of Public Relations,* New York: Harper, 1957.

a matter of breadth of appreciation of all the factors that may affect specific measures—an attribute of precise thinking and rich experience. Equally often such reputation may simply stem from the fact that luckily previous judgments have usually proved right rather than wrong. Whatever the explanation, the fact remains that the initials of these four or five officials at the bottom of action papers seem to have a magic effect.

Clubs and clusters. As in ward politics, so in the office it often pays to be known as a good fellow, and to be active in good fellowship. Assume that an important man in the organization loves a weekly night of poker and virile conversation, would it not be both a distinction and a privilege to be asked to share in the fun? An inexhaustible supply of jokes may buy the important man's jovial interest in one's career. "An entertaining chap," the important man may think; "I ought to see more of him in the office." And during poker there are always precious opportunities for posting the important man on this or that. Or consider the Indiana Club and all its jolly Hoosiers; they have a hard-working program committee, but no one minds a discreet business conversation in the corner. Or think of the car pool, and how gratifying it is to come to know the section chief so intimately.

Innocuous—and desirable—as these groupings are, they are also sources of influence. Illustrations of a somewhat different character may be taken from the annals of quickly recruited emergency agencies, especially those of World War II and of the Korean emergency. Intensive solidarities developed among occupational groups—businessmen, professors, lawyers, civil servants. Each group tended to see a challenge in the other. Informal leadership, if only for purposes of vigilance, found ready support within the individual group. In fact, spokesmen discovered it to be to their advantage not to be caught in the neutralizing sphere of the official hierarchy, where extremist views could not be expressed in freedom. Similar formations, based on general outlook rather than on occupation, are by no means exceptional in old-line establishments. At times the reformist "Young Turks" may have the upper hand, reducing the "solid element" to the role of the "loyal opposition"—loyal or not so loyal. No matter how frequently the factional position will be reversed, the existence of a "loyal opposition" heightens the sense of public purpose and helps to defeat institutional self-complacency. Again the protégés of a powerful Senator—chairman of one of the key committees—may similarly make up a network of communications and influence working within and across several agencies, informing one another and the Senator's staff of policy trends, placement opportunities, and other bits of useful information.

Nor should we forget the "old school tie" in its American version, which is considerably less prominent than the British prototype. Still, in the administrative staff and auxiliary services we may run into a significant scattering of Minnesota men, Chicago men, Syracuse men, and the like.[7] Quite naturally, they maintain their own system of communication, develop their own sign language, and generally look upon one another with fraternal eyes. This may even be a necessity when they confront the most honorable federation of departmental oldtimers.

Voice of the union. The picture would hardly be complete without some indication of the place occupied in a department by the local or locals of government-employee unions.[8] Unionization has received new impetus in recent years, especially among the rank and file. It should be admitted at the outset that collective bargaining in the public service must take different forms as compared with industry, particularly because compensation and other phases of the work relationship are ordinarily the subject of governmentwide and even statutory regulation. Nonetheless, a considerable field remains for constructive participation of chosen employee representatives in various aspects of management. This is true not only of grievance procedure and the promotion of employee health, welfare, and safety but also of departmental employee relations in general.

By and large, the working contacts of employee locals have been confined to the personnel office, instead of fanning out over the organization. By and large, too, the nature of these contacts has held the local too much to a negative role—raising remonstrances in the face of departmental intentions or actions. That this need not be the case has been demonstrated by the more positive approach pursued from the outset by such agencies as the Tennessee Valley Authority. The ultimate administrative producers are the ordinary employees. Work-simplification programs, for instance, cannot be carried along by first-line supervisors single-handedly. Programs of this kind must enlist every employee. It will not always be easy to win the rank and file, but without first settling all acrimonious questions with their legitimate representatives no appeal for wholehearted cooperation is likely to be successful.

The leadership of an agency local is an example of informal power *par excellence*. It may be a nightmare to the exponents of the official hierarchy. When met with good will and understanding, however, the union can be a source of real support to the department. To fight a running battle with the local entails grave risks to morale. It also may set off sparks on the legislative side, and embarrass the chief executive himself. These considerations invite an attitude of give-and-take, even though negotiating the basic terms of such give-and-take may not be easy.

---

[7] *Cf.* Chapter 2, "The Study of Public Administration," sec. 3, "Training for Public Administration."

[8] *Cf.* Chapter 21, "Morale and Discipline," and Chapter 24, "Personnel Standards."

Chapter 14 •

Interest Groups in Administration

1. The Meaning of Interest Representation

Types of interest groups. Public administration operates in an environment of interest-group activity. Most of the agencies of government are the product of intergroup pressure or conflict, the outcome of which was establishment of a governmental body to perform a service or function that had been carried out unsatisfactorily or not at all under conditions of private initiative. Some of the duties of the oldest federal departments—Foreign Affairs, Treasury, War—included the protection, promotion, or regulation, in Madison's phrase, of "various and interfering interests" which "involves the spirit of party and faction in the necessary and ordinary operations of the government." Even when a public agency secures a legislative mandate to perform a given task without formal relationship to the group or class structure of society, citizens affected by that task watch it constantly, and make their views known through some collective organization or agent.

The variety and scope of interest-group activity defy efforts toward simplification. Students of interest-group activity have concentrated on describing the organization and activities of specific organizations, and on making case studies of agencies and situations in which group pressures have molded or modified legislative and administrative policy. The latter method succeeds in capturing the richness and vitality of governmental experience.[1] Yet we also need to develop concepts and methods of understanding the fundamental motivation and distinctive behavior patterns of interest groups. Above all, we need to appreciate that the "age of organization" is an age of group action, and that power in fully developed societies is the product of group competition as well as its regulator.[2]

A slightly revised version of a classification suggested by Charles A.

---

[1] An outstanding illustration is Herring, Pendleton, *Public Administration and the Public Interest,* New York: McGraw-Hill, 1936.

[2] Next to the famous tenth number of *The Federalist* (1788) and John C. Calhoun, *Disquisition on Government* (1851), the authoritative references are: Bentley, Arthur F., *The Process of Government,* Chicago: University of Chicago Press, 1908, republished Bloomington: Principia Press, 1935, and Truman, David B., *The Governmental Process,* New York: Knopf, 1951.

Beard is presented below to give some idea of the variety of interest groups. It also emphasizes the rise of professional and skill groups outside the category of economic interests that until recently had been presumed to be predominant.

Major Category of Interest and Basis of Organization	Group Organization
I. ECONOMIC ADVANTAGE	
A. Industry, commodity, or service	A. Trade associations and industrial institutes, trade unions, producer cooperatives
B. Federation of particular interests	B. Chamber of Commerce of the United States, National Association of Manufacturers, American Farm Bureau Federation, National Farmers Union, American Federation of Labor and Congress of Industrial Organizations
C. Federation of general interests	C. Consumers' associations, taxpayers' leagues, civic federations
II. SKILL	
A. Profession	A. Bar and medical associations, public relations counselors, social workers, educators
B. Research and communication of experience	B. Scientific societies, organizations of public officials
III. RELIGION	National Catholic Welfare Conference, Federal Council of Churches of Christ in America
IV. REFORM	
A. Moral causes	A. Anti-Saloon League, Women's Christian Temperance Union
B. Improvement of group status	B. Relief recipients, veterans' organizations
C. Equalization of opportunity	C. Negro, nationality, and women's organizations

Interest orientation of public administration. Pressure groups have in common a self-regarding singleness of aim which places priority upon the immediate purpose or welfare of the organized group as such. But administrative agencies are also characterized by a focus of aim and effort, coupled with a highly developed sense of self-importance. A bureaucracy transcends the particularism of pressure groups only by its commitment to the execution of a comprehensive program formulated by the political policy-makers. The operating code of civil servants attempts to avoid group pressures by referring them to general policy or to the necessity for rules and regulations applying to all groups and situations. The weakness of this formal position is that the bureaucracy is itself part of the structure of the community, and the achievement of its purpose is in large measure dependent upon its capacity for winning the cooperation of various other groups in the pursuit of public programs.

If it fails to do so, it loses a valuable opportunity to find takers for its advice on policy. And unless it does so, its own powers and organization may be modified or abolished by legislation induced by pressure from dissatisfied groups or by the legislature's own dissatisfaction with the inability of the bureaucracy to transform the relationships between conflicting groups from controversy to routine. Administrative agencies must give their foremost loyalty to the public purpose entrusted to them. Still, they cannot forget that other social groups share in that purpose and have their own notions as to how it may best be achieved. The public official may be primarily responsible for the formulation of administrative policy, but under democratic conditions his responsibility does not make him the sole judge of the ends of policy. The wise administrator, therefore, keeps open the channels of information and advice between his agency and the private organizations concerned with its operation. Indeed, next to maintaining an independent mind, the only question is whether these channels should be established on a formal basis or maintained as a matter of informal personal contact.

In countries like the Soviet Union, where the scope of governmental responsibility for economic enterprise is much wider than in the United States, this interdependence of governmental and economic organizations becomes an integral part of the political structure. Trusts, trade unions, and cooperatives are in effect decentralized operating divisions of the central policy-making agency controlling the national economy. In that role, industrial bodies and groups participate in the formulation of policy in an administrative rather than a political capacity, losing their independence and their opportunity to criticize openly and to press for changes in the direction of policy.

Interest groups and class theory. Where a distinction is maintained between private initiative and governmental control in economic affairs, interest groups in general accept the prevailing structure and process of policy formation. Reformist rather than revolutionary in orientation, they attempt to make public policy the instrument of their aims. Their techniques include the methods and channels of publicity; withholding or offering financial or voting support; sanctions of cooperation or noncooperation; and personal contacts with public officials through innumerable channels of social, professional, and official association.

Interest-group activity is in a category of thought different from the Marxist concept of class interest, which presumes an irrepressible conflict between the capitalists and the workers. This ideology looks forward to the unification of political and economic activity in the name of an authoritative program identified with the interest of the whole people—or the "classless society." Less inclusive group interests are labeled as collaborationist, diversionist, or reactionary. Believers in the class-interest doctrine may engage in pressure-group tactics pending the realization of the classless society. However, they do so without a sense of responsibility for the immediate effects of policy, for their goal is the achievement of a different social structure and a new political order of ideas, rulers, and institutions.

Demands for interest representation. Historically, the class interests of property were reflected for hundreds of years in the governmental structure and theory of representation underlying policy formation. Since the nineteenth century, however, property representation as such has almost completely been abolished as a qualification for public office. A partial recrudescence of class representation has appeared in recent years. Certain group interests, particularly labor organizations, have raised the demand for specific representation or participation in the formulation of public policy.

As we know, there are always either formal or informal relationships between group organizations and governmental agencies. Furthermore, it is perfectly clear that in the sense of the right to be heard, to be consulted, and to be informed in advance of emerging policy determination, group participation is a fundamental feature of democratic legislation and administration. When, therefore, group organizations press for representation in the official structure of administration, their desire reflects some deeper motivation, whether it be redress of grievances, desire for power, resentment over too limited participation, or fears of insecurity.

What are the forms and types of interest representation, and the ways in which it works? In the following sections three forms will be analyzed, and in the final section some suggestions will be presented for the appropriate conditions and basic assumptions of such interest representation.

2. Clientele Organization

Growth of clientele agencies. Interest representation finds expression indirectly in the structure of government when an agency is created to benefit a special category of citizens, or to promote the welfare of a group having some specified interest or attribute in common. The best known examples are perhaps the services and financial aids provided by the Veterans Administration; the research, promotional, and advisory functions of the Women's Bureau in furthering equal opportunities and nondiscrimination between wage earners of both sexes; the comparable activities and grant-in-aid responsibilities of the Children's Bureau for improving the health, education, and welfare of mothers and children; the regulation and constructive development of Indian life by the Bureau of Indian Affairs. Clientele organization may be contrasted with the more common organization by function, in which the agency is established to perform a function or service for all categories of citizens, such as a public library or a fire department.

A function may be so defined that, in effect, it is restricted to a major industrial or economic group. The Federal Reserve System operates through reserve banks whose operations in turn are restricted to banks. The Securities and Exchange Commission's jurisdiction is restricted to security issuers, traders, and organized exchanges engaged in security transactions. The Interstate Commerce Commission dealt for many years solely with the railroads and their customers. However, when the administrative function is of a regulatory rather than a service or promotional character, the implication is that two or more adversary interests are involved, one of which —having by law been accorded priority—is represented by the public agency. In such cases, the clientele principle is obscured by clothing the group objectives wholly or in part with the public interest. This projection of group interests into public policy characterizes a great deal of modern labor and agricultural legislation.

Disadvantages of clientele organization. From the standpoint of economy and efficiency, the clientele principle is defective because it allows many agencies to perform essentially the same basic function for different classes of people. In practice, of course, the principle is not carried to its logical extreme. Under modern conditions, the justification for clientele agencies is usually based on special circumstances, coupled with a welfare motive that assumes the desirability of governmental ministration to the needs of an unprotected or underprivileged or unrepresented group. The most familiar arguments are that clientele organization is required either to redress existing inequalities or inequities in economic and social life, or to handle technical problems peculiar to an economic process or to a specific class of citizens, in which case the distinction between function and clientele loses its meaning.

The crux of the problem of administrative organization turns upon the extent to which the agency becomes exclusive, competitive, or self-centered in spirit. An agency whose activities are focused and directed toward a particular group is likely to be more narrowly centered than one established to perform its function impartially for all citizens. Analysis of governmental structures will usually reveal, however, some functional agencies which have a focus of purpose so narrow that they become more exclusive and self-centered than a clientele agency whose interests range over a broader segment of the population or national economy. No governmental agency should be so constituted as to enable a single group to prevent the agency from taking the most inclusive view of the public interest in any given situation.

Attempts at internal balance of interest. One way of implementing such a standard would be to create agencies with so broad a jurisdiction, covering so many organized groups, that the interest of no one group could be controlling. At first glance this idea would seem to have been followed in the creation of such federal departments as Agriculture, Commerce, and Labor. The functions of the Department of Agriculture include research, information, service, and regulation of processors, distributors, and financiers as well as a great variety of commodity producers. The Department of Commerce deals with interests represented by hundreds of industrial product and service classifications and associational groupings. The Department of Labor's statistical and regulatory functions affect manufacturers as well as scores of industrial and craft unions. All this splintering of "interests" fails, however, to take account of the pressure influences behind the historical development of the three departments and of the psychological factor that the great federations of agricultural, business, and labor groups look upon each department as their spokesman in the highest councils of the executive branch.

As long as the large interest groups retain any degree of virility and unity, they will expect great weight to be given their views in the appointment of top personnel and general policy matters. No government can neglect this factor. Indeed, provided the operating and technical levels of administration are protected from political interference in appointment or removal of personnel and in the handling of business, it seems at least arguable that the political heads of these departments might be appointed as representatives of farmers, businessmen, or wage earners. Aside from a broader public interest, however, the problem at this level raises another issue, namely, the need of the chief executive for a department head in whom he has complete confidence, while a group representative by definition has another primary loyalty. The dilemma is not insurmountable, but it requires a rare combination of ability, integrity, and flexibility to serve in something like a dual capacity.

Functions of clientele agencies. The functions most often delegated to a clientele agency are of a service character: research and exchange of information. The systematic reports and studies of the agency are used by the clientele group or by other groups to press for desired legislation or changes in administrative policy. Another function is the formulation of standards, whether of equity and health, as in the industrial employment of women and children, or of competence and training to be applied by state professional and trade examining boards. In the latter case, the standards are authoritative rather than advisory. They raise the question of formal delegation of rule-making power to private groups, because such boards are usually composed of representatives of the professional or trade groups that are seeking state regulation of admission to the profession or trade. Inevitably, the standards established have an economic effect in limiting the number of those admitted to the profession or trade. However, delegation of this power to private associations has been justified by courts and legislatures because technical and specialized training cannot be maintained without rigorous tests of proficiency.

Generally speaking, the endowment of clientele agencies with regulatory responsibilities runs counter to deeply felt ideas of equity and fairness. The assumption prevails that an agency responsible for promoting the welfare of a particular group or class of citizens cannot be expected to maintain judicial attitudes of impartiality in a dispute involving an interest adversary to that which the agency is supposed to protect or promote. This has been one of the reasons for the creation of independent regulatory commissions outside the structure of the executive departments, although it is possible to protect the regulatory tribunal, wherever it be located, from political or other interference in the handling of its cases. The Department of Agriculture, for instance, has many regulatory duties which are administered by single-headed bureaus fairly and equitably enough to pass the test of judicial scrutiny by the Supreme Court. But "organizational independence" has retained its strength as a symbol of fairness in most areas of federal regulatory administration.

Experiences of the Great Depression and World War II. Emergency legislation to meet conditions of economic depression, such as the National Industrial Recovery Act of 1933, and the mobilization of industry and agriculture in World War II resulted in a mushroom growth of clientele agencies. The hundreds of NIRA code authorities, hailed at the beginning of the New Deal as experiments in industrial self-government, were later vilified as promoting monopolies and enabling minority groups to legislate for their private ends. But the mood was passing. Faced with the exigencies of defense and war production programs, the Office of Production Management—and subsequently the War Production Board, the Office of Price Administration, the War Food Administration, the Office of Defense Transportation, and the Petroleum Administration for War—all developed an organization based upon industrial processes or commodity groupings, and in many cases staffed by men drawn from the ranks of the industries concerned.

It was recognized that the normal governmental machinery and personnel had to be supplemented to meet the demands of war; that basic policies and controls should not be delegated *in toto* to industrial groups; and that a form of organization had to be evolved that would conduce to maintaining contacts with the regulated groups, securing their advice and active cooperation, giving them prominence in announcing and promulgating administrative policies and regulations, and enlisting them for much of the routine work of administration. The conflicts of policy between the agencies built on industry or clientele and the functional agencies of control above them, like the Office of War Mobilization, yield some classic case studies in administration. It is probable, however, that these conflicts reflected bottlenecks or divergencies in production programs that would have plagued the war effort in any event, regardless of organizational forms.

Two general observations stand out. First, any agency that seeks special treatment, privilege, or protection for particular groups deprives itself of a justifiable claim to the administrative responsibility for executing more inclusive general policies of government. Second, while in special cases a group purpose may be identified with the general welfare and with statutory policy, the primary concern of any organized group is with the naming of administrative top personnel and the content of policy.

3. Staffing for Point of View

Grounds for interest representation. The question may be asked whether it is possible to distinguish between the content or substance of administrative policies and the officers who are responsible for policy-making. In the process of policy formulation, the substance of decisions reached is extremely difficult to dissociate from the personalities and social attitudes of those participating. The "organization product" is rarely an individual idea. It is usually the fruit of a great deal of discussion and exchange. Ultimately it comes forth in the form of a letter, statement, message, or order which has been reviewed and initialed by representatives of many different parts of the organization.[3] Realizing the relatively indeterminate character of administrative policy-making and the importance of participation in the developmental stages, some interest groups—particularly labor organizations—have frequently requested representation in administration on three grounds: first, that such group representation is desirable to equalize opportunities for protecting and safeguarding respective interests; second, that organized groups can make contributions of special knowledge and experience which would not otherwise be available to public agencies; and third, that group participation in policy formulation makes possible the avoidance of mistakes and the integration of diverse viewpoints in advance of formal action on policy proposals.

Before discussing the different forms that group representation may take, we should say that there is a practical difference between demands for representation that arise from distrust of the administrative top personnel and demands for representation to effect changes in agency rules or policies. Administrators may isolate themselves from leaders and currents of group opinion. But by doing so, they lose a valuable opportunity for developing mutual respect and confidence that may be gained through continued formal or informal contacts with outside interests. Self-isolation interferes with the all-important impression of fairness—the public conviction that decisions are made only after full investigation and consideration of the facts, which includes taking into account the positions and views of group

---

[3] *Cf.* Appleby, Paul H., *Big Democracy,* ch. 8: "Wanted: An Organization Product," New York: Knopf, 1945.

spokesmen. Such institutionalized contacts and the application of elementary principles of judicious procedure can go far to protect administrators from charges of bias, unfamiliarity with their job, inside manipulation, and "politics" in making decisions.

Demands for group representation that are motivated by a desire to influence policy can be met in a variety of ways. Members of regulatory boards and commissions are usually prohibited—though not always fully effectively—from having any financial interest in concerns to be regulated and from engaging in any other vocation, trade, or employment. In such agencies, the demands and views of affected groups are expected to be considered through legal procedures of investigation and notice and through opportunity for hearing prior to a formal decision, regulation, or order. A more direct device—which will be considered in the next section—is the appointment of a representative administrative board, whose members are nominated by interest groups. A third technique is the appointment of administrative personnel on grounds of special vocational experience or affiliation. One form of this device is the creation of a special staff unit to maintain contacts with outside groups and to present their grievances, claims, or suggestions to the appropriate officials.

Administrative appointment of interest representatives. The appointment of individuals to public office because of group affiliation squarely conflicts with the civil service concept of appointment by virtue of merit established by competitive examination. Fortunately, the two principles are not incompatible. Group affiliation or vocational experience may go hand in hand with merit and qualification. The question of propriety in appointing group representatives who retain connections of personal loyalty or financial interest in private organizations has to be answered upon other grounds.

During World War II, one type of such representation was the practice of agencies like the War Production Board to appoint $1-a-year men. The Office of Defense Transportation in certain cases employed its top personnel on a "without compensation" basis, the private employer—a railroad—paying the executives their regular salaries. The Petroleum Administration for War adopted the practice of paying regular government salaries, but many of its executives received the difference between their public pay and their private salaries from their previous employer. Representatives of labor organizations appointed to top administrative posts usually followed the principle of accepting government positions but served only part-time. They and their labor alternates received compensation on a when-actually-employed basis. At lower levels, public employees appointed as labor representatives accepted government salaries and devoted full time to their responsibilities.

The practice of dual compensation, or recognition of dual allegiance to public and private organizations, arose in part from the lack of men and women in government service trained in industry operations, familiar with the influential industry leaders, and capable of swiftly grasping the peculiar wartime problems in developing programs of economic mobilization and control. The policy of appointing outsiders who retained their financial or business connections had definite drawbacks. It gave substance to charges by other businessmen of special privilege and big-business domination, and lent support to demands for representation of other groups.

It should be added that use of consultants and experts drawn from business or other walks of life, for service either "without compensation" (WOC) or paid "when actually employed" (WAE), is under law an entirely normal thing in the federal government. Those so serving are legally under the very vague and equally antique "conflict of interest" statutes,[4] but these provisions do not create clean categories. They neither meet their purpose adequately nor furnish guidance on when and when not to bring interest representatives into government. The lack of clearer criteria caused political embarrassment to the Eisenhower Administration.

Problems of dual allegiance. In World War II, Julius A. Krug, then director of the War Production Board's Office of War Utilities, and Ralph Davies, deputy of the Petroleum Administrator for War, attempted to meet the charges of privilege and favoritism by a so-called "melting-pot" policy. It consisted of recruiting men from all branches and interests in the electric power and petroleum industries—publicly and privately owned enterprises, integrated and independent companies, state regulatory commissions, and so on. The first two administrators of the Office of Price Administration, who maintained a policy of personal disinterestedness of top price executives, were pilloried before Congress and the public for relying in too great measure upon economics professors in administering price control and rationing. The melting-pot policy, if it did not eliminate charges of special-interest domination, was rationalized by the respective administrators on the ground that it gave them the benefit of variety of training, experience, and ability in policy formulation and execution.

The concept of coordination as maintaining a variety and balance of diverse personalities and viewpoints within organizations is a familiar one in administrative theory.[5] Conceived in terms of competition in ideas and incentives for keeping the top administrator informed about what is going on in his organization, such a policy encourages vigor and initiative all down the line. The condition of its effectiveness in a cooperative system is, however, that the participants accept as pre-eminent the common purpose of the organization and that the divergences in understanding and interpretation of that purpose do not undermine their belief in its reality. While functional specialization is certainly compatible with organizational unity, it is also well recognized that the widest disparity of individual motives may

---

4 18 United States Code 281, 283, 284, 434, 1914; 5 United States Code 99.

5 *Cf.* Chapter 2, "The Study of Public Administration," sec. 4, "The Frontiers of Research."

still contribute to cooperative effort. A general statement of objectives permits wide differences in interpretation as to the best means for accomplishing them. However, particular individuals or staff units should not be given reason to conclude that other individuals or staff sectors holding conflicting views on policy have an inside track in policy councils.

A sound recruitment policy in any agency will consciously aim at securing a representative distribution or cross section of social experience in its staff. Such differences, so far as possible, should be kept on an individual basis, with a view to appealing to individual incentives and desires for rewards which will contribute toward attainment of the general goal. Introduction of conflicting goals imperils the realization of the highest value within the organization. From the standpoint of an individual who thinks of himself as representing an outside group and conscientiously strives to maintain two loyalties, the experience is apt to be extremely frustrating and unhappy, unless he happens to be an aggressive personality who finds self-expression in conflict, regardless of outcome. The outside group which favors "representation" but claims that agreement can be reached on methods of administration will soon be faced with two lessons of experience: First, it is bound to lose confidence in its representative when he is identified with the bureaucracy as a jobholder; second, the public employee who thinks of himself as a group representative will have the greatest difficulty in accepting the channels and levels of authority required by the organization.

Group representation through special staff units. Some agencies have deliberately incorporated the formal principle of interest representation by creating staff units on policy, linked to outside groups. Examples are labor, business, and consumer advisory boards. The gains expected from these arrangements by the sponsoring agency include sympathetic group attitudes, a safety valve for outside criticism, opportunities for influencing the positions that might be taken by important groups, and the likelihood of political support.

Such boards may establish some standards of policy acceptable to the agency head. These standards may improve the administrative feasibility of the policies adopted. At the same time, the boards and their staffs may psychologically separate themselves from the administrator and develop a corporate unity and loyalty of their own.

Balance sheet of experience. Objectively, staffing administrative agencies for "point of view" involves two logically contradictory criteria of selection and training. The responsibility of the administrator for achieving results under general policy calls for authority to appoint subordinates upon whose ability and judgment he can rely. At the same time, responsibility and loyalty of his administrative subordinates are to symbols or organizations outside the agency by which they are employed.

It may readily be admitted that administrative ingenuity should not be stultified by logical dilemmas. In the first place, when the factors of time and place are taken into account, it is conceivable that nine-tenths of the employee's job will never raise a conflict between his two loyalties. Secondly, the administrator may find ways of canalizing or utilizing the energies of interest representatives so as not to interfere with vital parts of his program. Thirdly, in many cases, the interests of outside groups may be complementary to his own, and mutual exploration of policy alternatives may remove barriers raised by institutional distance, misunderstanding, and errors in judgment.

The legitimate aspirations of labor, consumer, or citizen groups for more effective participation in administrative policy-making should not be directed toward securing positions as group representatives at operating or technical levels. Creation of representative staff units at the top-policy level, reporting directly to the administrator, may have some public-relations value to both the outside groups and the public agency. However, the advantages of inside information and symbolic cooperation with government that accrue to the outside group are probably outweighed by the implicit limitations upon freedom to criticize; the emotional and physical strains upon the group representative; and the unpleasantness of being open to charges from the group itself of bureaucratic sympathy by virtue of holding a government job. If the administrative job is worth being done, it would be best to place responsibility upon the administrator for making appointments on the basis of individual qualifications in relation to the job to be done; urge him to seek as varied as possible a basis of social experience, training, and personality in recruiting his staff; permit him to create the healthy and necessary unity of effort that arises from willing cooperation in an organization with high morale; expose him to outside policy pressures; and compel him to inform his public about what he is doing. It will pay, however, to protect him from ideological conflict within his own staff.

4. Interest Representation on Administrative Boards

Membership requirements. Practical politicians and political scientists are well aware of the opportunity for representation of group interests when public agencies are headed by boards and not by single administrators. Specifically, economic group representation may here be concealed by the qualification of appointees as party members—usually stated in terms of a limitation upon the appointing authority that no more than two members of a three-man board or three of a five-man board shall belong to the same political party. This leaves the chief executive ample discretion to nominate candidates acceptable to him, subject to the advice and approval of party organizations expressed informally as well as through one or both houses of the legislature. Analysis of the biographical history and administrative record of such appointees shows how many of them tend to favor particular group demands, but it may also reveal considerable independence of thought and refusal to follow lines of group cleavage under conditions of relative permanence of tenure.[6]

Specific representation for economic groups has been tried spasmodically in the establishment of regulatory tribunals.[7] Demands for it are associated with the idea that those responsible for wielding powers of such vital concern should have practical knowledge of the problems of the regulated groups. The legislative method is to insert a statutory provision that members of the board or commission shall be appointed as bankers, workers, businessmen, and farmers, or with experience in defined occupations. These provisions are found more frequently in state laws than in federal legislation, and there has been no general federal tendency toward adopting such requirements, for several reasons.

In the first place, the appointing chief executive can take the element of vocational experience into account without formal requirement of law. Moreover, legislators wish geographic and political affiliations to be considered as well. If the chief executive has a particular candidate in mind, he can usually find technical ways to meet the legal qualification. The legislature or the group interests therefore cannot ensure, as a matter of law, that their candidates will be selected. It is constitutionally doubtful, and undesirable from the angle of public policy as well, for the legislature to exercise the power of nominating the appointee. Hence, if an organized group does not succeed in tying the chief executive's hand by this method, it may prefer not to alienate him by a halfway step and rather approach him through informal and political channels. In the case of proposals for bipartisan representative boards, the group making the demand must anticipate counterdemands from other groups, with the implicit inference that a balance of power would be lodged in a public representative uncontrolled by any group. The consequences of permanently implanting such a conflict in administrative bodies should give pause to outside groups interested in effective and prompt procedural action.[8]

Nomination by interest groups. Another device, which may be either formal or informal, is to provide for appointment by the chief executive upon nomination by interest groups. This is the method by which most state professional examining boards are appointed. In a nonpolitical context, it amounts to permitting professional groups virtually to appoint their candidates and fix the technical standards of entrance to their trade or profession. The line between the political and nonpolitical is easily crossed,

---

[6] C. H. Pritchett's studies of the voting record of the Supreme Court led him to conclude that the major line of division between the justices is "the allowable extent of public controls versus private rights." This issue of principle transcends and cuts across lines of group conflict except insofar as some groups maintain a consistently antigovernmental or *status quo* position.

[7] *Cf.* Chapter 10, "Independent Regulatory Agencies."

[8] On this whole question, see Leiserson, Avery, *Administrative Regulation*, Chicago: University of Chicago Press, 1942.

however, and such agencies move carefully to secure legislative authorization for their tests and sanctions in granting or revoking certificates to practice.

In establishing public corporations the British have used variations of the device of formal nomination by group organizations to avoid "political" influences or control by government departments, and to secure the advantages of technical experience on the boards of directors. The governing board of the Port of London Authority is composed of eighteen members elected by shipowners, merchants, rivercraft owners and wharfingers, and ten members appointed by public authorities. Of the latter appointments, two are generally representatives of union labor. The Central Electricity Board of seven members is appointed by the Minister of Transport after consultation with such interest representatives as he thinks fit—that is to say, local government, electricity, commerce, industry, transport, agriculture, and labor. The London Passenger Transport Board is appointed by an *ad hoc* independent body of appointing trustees, composed of the chairman of the London County Council, the president of the Law Society, the president of the Institute of Chartered Accountants in England and Wales, the chairman of the Committee of London Clearing Banks, and a representative of the London and Home Counties Traffic Advisory Committee. There are two common elements in British methods of appointment through group organizations: (1) creation of a public agency to do a job without "political" interference; and (2) deliberate representation of many interests in order to prevent any one line of conflict from predominating, thus producing a situation in which managerial responsibility must be recognized.

Bipartisan and tripartite boards. The outstanding governmental function in which the representative board has been used time and again is the settlement of labor disputes. In spite of repeated disappointments, the demand for a bipartisan or tripartite board directly nominated by employer groups and unions, with or without participation of "the public," somehow always recurs. The reasons seem to lie in part in the complexities of employer-union relations, the facts of which are known better to the parties than to "outside" mediators or arbitrators; the disinclination to allow government agencies to administer any policy of compulsory arbitration—however named—that might control the terms of the labor bargain; the familiar custom and pattern in negotiation to be personally represented on the decision-making body when the policy settlement is unclear; and the desire of many labor leaders for status and prestige arising from participation in governmental policy-making.

Bipartisan boards, composed of an equal number of employer and union representatives, have functioned successfully for many years in the arbitration of collective bargaining demands. However, they operate quite differently when the problem is one of working out the details of applying an existing agreement, on the one hand, and when, on the other, the task is one of deciding general policy questions such as those of the proper level of wages or whether union membership should be a condition of employment. An analogy might be drawn in distinguishing between the problem of administering a provision that railroad freight rates shall apply fairly and equitably to different classes of shippers, and the problem of raising or lowering the general level of freight rates or changing the differentials between classes of shippers.

If the purpose of public policy is to throw primary responsibility for settling disputes back upon employers and unions, a bipartisan board may be appropriate. When the parties themselves have failed, as in disputes over proposed changes in labor agreements or negotiation of new agreements, another element is injected. It is the requirement that a public agency shall intervene, either to mediate the dispute by recommending formally to the parties a basis of settlement, or to decide its terms authoritatively. In these situations, representation of the disputants upon the public body tends to inhibit rather than promote a free formulation of the issues in terms from which agreement might be developed. Bipartisan or tripartite boards dealing with problems of changing general policy therefore invite continuance of settled lines of dispute, and tend to throw the burden of decision on the public or neutral members of the board. All this is well known. Yet because unions do not wish compulsory settlement of labor disputes, they recurrently urge bipartisan or tripartite representation on governmental labor boards.[9]

Test of interest compromise. The real test of the representative administrative board lies in its success in resolving policy problems by compromising the differences between the groups represented on it. The great compromise that the National War Labor Board brought about during World War II was the acquiescence of employers in the policy of maintenance of union membership and the cooperation of organized labor with wage stabilization. We must admire the accomplishment of the public members in holding the board together, and thereby maintaining an enormously important symbolic unity between labor and management during the war period. It may safely be stated, however, that it was only the exigencies of war that induced labor and industry to accept the wage stabilization program.

Students of the internal procedures within the National War Labor Board will notice the delays and backlogs of cases due to the refusal of employer and union members to accept policy decisions of the board as precedents in handling new cases. Here, once more, it is a matter of opinion whether the recognition of basic interests and the preservation of

9 *Cf.* U.S. Department of Labor, *Bulletins* No. 714 (1942) and No. 1009 (1950), and *Termination Report of the National War Labor Board*, Vol. 1, 1946. See also Economic Stabilization Agency, Office of Defense Mobilization, *Wage Stabilization Program, 1950-1953*, Vols. 1-2, 1953.

external unity were worth the price of administrative delays and suspension of the processes of collective bargaining. The contention that the board advanced collective bargaining and developed a legacy of policy which unions and employers might wish to preserve after the war went up in smoke within sixty days after Japan surrendered. Both parties seem quite united on keeping government out of labor disputes.

5. The Principle of Consultation

General theory of interest representation. At this point, the outlines of the general theory of interest representation may briefly be sketched. The underlying idea is best described by the phrase "economic federalism," in the sense of a division of authority and function between government and the broad economic groupings in which men and women spend most of their working hours. The ethical foundation of the concept is found in the importance of creating in the community as wide as possible a basis of training and experience in governmental affairs, and of the deeper unity arising from a commonly shared sense of contribution in solving social problems. The theory has appeal because of its justification of autonomous group life, and perhaps also because it is ambiguous enough to apply to three different forms of institutional arrangements, enabling its exponents to substitute one for another without being politically inconsistent. The three organizational concepts happen to be excellently illustrated in the writings of Britain's late Professor Harold J. Laski.

In World War I, during a period in his life of observation and speculation on a relatively abstract plane, Laski was greatly impressed with the importance of permitting voluntary groups such as unions and churches a high degree of freedom to select and pursue their objectives under organized government dominated by private-property attitudes.[10] Later, in his *Grammar of Politics*,[11] Laski rejected a constitutional structure based upon autonomous groups wielding powers of both economic and political decision. He substituted for this form of federalism a concept of group representation and consultation at policy levels of public administration, wisely allowing such details as the degree of policy-making authority and the selection of representatives to vary with the nature of the administrative problem. During the ensuing twenty years, Laski reflected on both the menace of fascism and the internal divisions within the Western democracies that inhibited the formation of an aggressively democratic program. After entering active politics, he came to emphasize the importance of a unifying democratic faith. The contribution of economic groupings to

---

[10] *Foundations of Sovereignty,* "Administrative Areas" and "The Pluralistic State," especially p. 75 *ff.,* New York: Harcourt, Brace, 1921. For a less personalistic, normative account of the relations between interest groups, political parties, and public bureaucracies, see Leiserson, Avery, *Parties and Politics,* especially secs. 10-12, 35-40, 46 and 50, New York: Knopf, 1958.

[11] Ch. 2, and p. 282-85, 384-87, New Haven: Yale University Press, 1925.

such a faith cannot be a matter of autonomous choice. It must be made in cooperation with government through a uniting symbol of the most inclusive good—namely, the program of a freely elected people's party.[12]

Basic distinctions in group representation. We can now see that the concept of economic group representation allows distinctions as to: (1) the level of policy determination—that is to say, the field and scope of governmental jurisdiction in which general decisions of economic policy should be made and local or functional differentiations permitted; [13] (2) the recognition of power groups and other interests in general policy formation; and (3) the method of organizing the process by which interest participation should be guaranteed. The problem involved in the first distinction is clearly one of paramount political and legislative policy. Any attempt to solve such questions by the exercise of administrative power simply throws the administrative agency into the middle of political controversy that a higher political authority should decide.

The problem arising from the second distinction refers in part to the constitutional guarantees and rights of free association, petition, and assembly. However, it blends into the administrative sphere when an agency is given discretion to select and define the group categories of organizations whose interests it desires to take into account. This problem may be summed up by saying that powerful group organizations can usually get their views presented. The difficulty of administrators is to maintain a clear understanding that their public responsibility is broader than their allegiance to any one group. Their responsibility requires consideration of general governmental policy and the interests of the community as a whole.

Organization of interest participation. This chapter has in general dealt with the third problem, which can be restated as the question of how to take into account the views of all relevant group interests in administrative policy-formation. We have analyzed several organizational devices and found each less than satisfactory. This is due to two factors. First, although administrative discretion affords an opportunity for groups to press for favorable determination of policy questions that are not legislatively settled, most groups fail to realize that an administrative agency cannot attempt to decide larger controversial issues without risking its own security through political conflict.[14] Second, interest groups often

---

12 *Faith, Reason and Civilization,* New York: Viking, 1944.

13 Paul Appleby has pointed out that from a management standpoint it is nonsense to decentralize until central policy integration has been attained. *Op. cit.* above in note 3, p. 101-102.

14 The right distinction is that administrators are proper sources of recommendations on forward-looking policy changes and should contribute actively to their decision, but should not try to decide in these matters themselves. Two excellent reviews of recent uses of advisory committees are: Brown, David S., "The Public Advisory Board as an Instrument of Government," *Public Administration Review,* 1955, Vol. 15, p. 196 *ff.;* Beer, Samuel H., "Group Representation in Britain and the United States," *Annals of the American Academy of Political and Social Science,* 1958, Vol. 319, p. 130 *ff.*

fail to recognize that they may want fairness and impartiality in administration even more than they want a share of official responsibility for policy determination.

The vital problem of how to bring interest-group influences to bear upon the process of administrative policy formation is not a simple matter of calling conferences and holding hearings. The sense of participation is essential to social or public morale, but is not automatically secured by formal arrangement. It must be developed and learned by creating a set of understood conditions, special skills, and mutual responsibilities on the part of the group members, their leaders, the administrator, and his staff. When these specifications have been met and the participants have learned how to promote their separate interests by working together, some form of the advisory committee will be found most acceptable to all. The reason is obvious. If we assume that consent is necessary to the administrator and that group interests wish to be freely and independently represented, the incentive should be placed upon the administrator to win group assent, and the group representatives should be free to withdraw and to criticize.

Foundations of interest consultation. There is some evidence to suggest that the principle of consultation may possess superiority over other forms of "shared participation" in public policy-making. As a cooperative arrangement, consultation places priority of importance upon: (1) mutual respect for the responsibilities of administrators and group leaders; (2) working with others rather than allowing one group to put something over on the others that they don't have to take; (3) fair dealing by making information available on purposes and methods of administration within the defined scope of the plan; and (4) providing opportunity for criticism and suggestions. The principle of consultation on the administrative level clearly will not appeal to those who assume that their views must be adopted or they won't play. It will work only under conditions where the participants assume that a process of expert investigation and open discussion is the proper way to discover the best means of realizing an agreed-upon public purpose.

An interest representative who wants to influence the formulation of that purpose is simply expressing his legitimate preference for participation in political conflict rather than for reducing political decisions from debatable hypotheses to administrative operations. It is confusion confounded to carry such conflict into the administrative process and to make administrative organization the arena for continuing political battles. Unless we decide to delegate governmental powers to a single political group which can only be overthrown by violence, we must assume that tentative solutions to our social and economic conflicts can be reached from time to time by those skilled in winning the people's votes, who will turn over to those trained in administration the task of seeing to it that the terms of political settlements are made to work.

Chapter 15 •

Legislative Control

1. Means and Conditions of Control

Constitutional framework for legislative-administrative relations. In all democratic regimes, a fundamental constitutional problem consists in the definition of the relations between the representative body and the executive. If the parliament is weak and ineffective, irresponsible power may gravitate to the executive agencies. On the other hand, if the executive possesses inadequate power, public policy may be faltering and hesitant, and government may be erratic and unstable. The question of the most appropriate balance between the popular assembly and the executive agencies invariably plagues constitution-makers. The place and power of the legislative body should suffice to permit the authoritative expression of the popular will as well as the exercise of suitable restraints on administrative action. Simultaneously, the executive must be so situated as to be able to meet the necessities of regularity, uniformity, consistency, and firmness of public policy.

The American Constitution resolves the problem of legislative-administrative relations by a separation of powers. That arrangement makes Congress and the chief executive independent of each other in tenure of office and, to a degree, in powers. To the representative body is denied the simple means of control of administration that would come with the power to terminate the services of the principal administrative officers. To the executive is denied the whiphand over the legislature that might come with the power of dissolution. The constitutional system assures rivalry, and therefore friction, between executive and legislature. The Constitution also, by the system of checks and balances, makes Congress and the President dependent each upon the other and thereby binds both together in inescapable, though often unhappy, collaboration.

The consequences of this system of separated powers permeate the entire administrative structure and account for many of the peculiar characteristics of public administration. In essence, Congress and the President tend to be rivals for the control of the administrative apparatus, and the administrative agencies are caught between their competing claims. Members of Congress often declaim in tones of irritation that the bureaucrats ought to remember their responsibility to the elected representatives of the people. Yet the President is also chosen by the people and is vested with powers of direction; the bureaucrat knows that he is, through the chain of command, accountable to the President. Although it rarely arises in such bald form, the question may distill down in individual cases to whether the President or Congress shall direct the administrative agencies in the execution of the laws. Supposedly an administrative agency may not serve two masters, but that maxim is belied by the everyday workings of the American administrative system.

In its relations with administration, Congress may seek to direct future action or it may review past action. The means for the accomplishment of these purposes are formal or informal. Congress may, for example, enact a statute; or it may, by the tenor of its debate, give an unmistakable indication of its desires about the exercise of administrative discretion. The informal influence of Congress rests ultimately on the possibility of the exertion of its formal power. An individual exercise of formal authority may involve direction of future action, review of past action, or both. A statute may, for example, lay down instructions for future action, but it may have developed from a committee review of the past performance of the agency affected.

Formal means of legislative control. The principal formal means in the hands of Congress for control of the administration are the powers (a) of enacting, amending, and repealing legislation, (b) of appropriation, and (c) of investigation. In addition, the Senate has the right to review presidential appointments, except those to "inferior offices," which are vested solely in the President or the heads of the departments. Moreover, the Senate's role in the ratification of treaties contributes to its influence over the management of foreign policy.

The power to legislate constitutes the basic means of congressional control over administration. Acts of Congress fix the scope of power of administrative agencies. They may also prescribe the manner of the exercise of that power and the internal organization of the agency concerned. Moreover, authority granted may be withdrawn. Administrators must proceed on the assumption that the legislation they administer may be repealed or modified, a factor which may condition administrative action.

The form a statute takes may give Congress especially effective control over administration. Legislation enacted to be in effect only for one year or some other determinate period assures congressional review of administrative policy and performance when an extension of power is sought. For months preceding the renewal of such an act, its administrators walk warily, perhaps fearing to take steps of urgent importance lest some group in Congress be annoyed. They must wage battle for renewal when the expiration dates of such statutes approach, and the difficulty of obtaining positive action from Congress gives to opponents of a policy based on short-term legislation tactical advantages they would not enjoy if they had to seek outright repeal. For example, both the reciprocal trade-agreement program and the mutual security program have rested on limited-term legislation.

Enactment of the annual appropriation bills provides the occasion for the most comprehensive and systematic review of administrative operations. Once a year administrators must appear before the subcommittees of the Appropriations Committees in House and Senate to explain and justify in detail their requests for money. They must answer questions— some penetrating, some sympathetic, some unfriendly—about their past operations. In effect, once a year they are on the carpet and must be prepared to defend their work against whatever criticism the members of the Appropriations Committees feel disposed to make. Within the framework of existing substantive legislation, the appropriation acts set the limits of operation for the fiscal year to which they apply. Moreover, in the course of committee hearings, legislative instructions are often given to administrators which, while not written into the appropriation act, are regarded as binding.[1]

Another weapon in the congressional armory is the power of investigation. It may be used to influence administration by focusing public attention upon practices whose revelation on the front pages suffices to induce corrective action. It may also be used to harass administrators out of favor with the congressional committee either on personal or policy grounds. In some instances, investigations are conducted by select committees acting under resolutions that define the field of investigation and grant committees power to compel the attendance of witnesses and the production of re'evant records and papers. In others, a standing committee decides to conduct an inquiry and requests the appearance of administrators.[2] In some instances, the inquiry is conducted with the assistance of a competent staff, which does the spadework necessary to prepare for an informative public hearing. In others, committee members depend on their personal knowledge for an offhand interrogation of witnesses. In motive the inquiry may be a sincere effort to promote the public good. Or it may be simply designed to discredit individuals or programs in an irresponsible manner.[3]

---

[1] Consult the excellent analysis by Macmahon, Arthur W., "Congressional Oversight of Administration: The Power of the Purse," *Political Science Quarterly*, 1943, Vol. 58, p. 161 *ff.*, 380 *ff.* See also Huzar, E., *The Purse and the Sword*, Ithaca: Cornell University Press, 1950.

[2] The Legislative Reorganization Act of 1946 makes it the duty of each standing committee of the Senate and House to "exercise continuous watchfulness of the execution by the administrative agencies concerned of any laws, the subject matter of which is within the jurisdiction of such committee."

[3] See Dimock, Marshall E., *Congressional Investigating Committees*, Baltimore: Johns Hopkins Press, 1929; McGeary, M. N., *The Development of Congressional Investigative Power*, New York: Columbia University Press, 1940; Morstein Marx, Fritz, "Congressional Investigations: Significance for the Administrative Process," *University of Chicago Law Review*, 1951, Vol. 18, p. 503 *ff.*

Legislative veto. Under some statutes, Congress reserves the right to review particular administrative actions before they may become effective. The legislative veto of administrative action first took finished form in the Reorganization Act of 1939. This act authorized the President to regroup agencies and functions within the executive branch, subject to congressional disapproval by concurrent resolution within 60 days.

Under some such acts either the Senate or the House may exercise the veto. For example, the Rubber Producing Facilities Disposal Act of 1953 permitted either house to disapprove proposed contracts for sale of synthetic rubber plants within 60 days after submission of the contract to Congress. In other instances, review is vested in a committee. Thus, the Defense Land Transfer Act of 1951 required the military departments to obtain committee approval of purchases of land costing $25,000 or more,[4] among other things. On occasion, the President has been able to overcome such clauses by vetoing the law that imposed them.

Informal means of legislative control. Formal actions by Congress as a whole or by its committees affecting administration are supplemented by informal exertions of influence. So diverse are these informal means of control that they are not susceptible of ready classification. Usually, however, the possession of a formal power carries with it opportunities for informal influence.

For example, the consideration of amendments to legislation governing an agency may induce alterations in administrative practice even though the proposal does not find its way to the statute book. Beyond such leverage associated with specific congressional functions, individual Representatives and Senators are probably the most active and influential lobbyists before administrative agencies. Their views often have an impact on individual cases or on administrative decisions of broader application.

Dispersion of power within Congress. The structure of authority within Congress profoundly conditions the exercise of its powers in relation to administration. Talk of Congress may evoke in the mind the image of an assembly that debates, deliberates, and decides. Yet Congress as a whole can master and decide only a few great issues, a fact that must be remembered if one is to comprehend the interplay between legislature and administration. So great is the volume of legislative business and such are our parliamentary practices that we have in reality not one legislative body but scores of small legislative bodies. When we seek to understand the relations of Congress with the executive branch, we must speak, not of either, but of this Senator, or that Representative, or this committee, or that bloc and the administrative establishment. The actions of Congress are in the great majority of instances those of a single member, or two, or

---

[4] For a thorough analysis, see Cooper, Joseph, "The Legislative Veto: Its Promise and Its Perils," *Public Policy,* 1957, Vol. 7, p. 128 *ff.*

a handful—actions which their colleagues ratify or to which they raise no objection.

The committee system accords great power to a few individuals in Congress. Our Congress does not have the great fear of committees that some representative bodies manifest. Committees are not regarded with jealousy as groups that grasp and exercise the power of the entire body, but as the normal media for doing business. Consequently, committee chairmen in particular are very powerful. Their power is greater for obstruction than for initiation; nonetheless it is formidable. If a measure goes through the committee, its chances of adoption are good. If the committee is hostile, the measure is almost certain to die, in spite of the occasional invocation of the discharge rule to compel the committee to report the bill.

Diversity of outlook of congressional power centers. Power is not only dispersed within the representative body; beyond that, the individuals of influence also are not necessarily in agreement with each other or with the dominant views of the majority party. The choice of committee chairmen is ordinarily determined by seniority of service, and the secret of success in Congress lies in a combination of horse-sense, luck, and longevity. A committee chairman, though belonging to the party headed by the President, may therefore be completely at outs with the general policy of the government. Thus, in a critical period in World War II, the chairman of the Senate Military Affairs Committee was quite hostile toward the principal phases of our defense policy. The major parties in House and Senate have discovered no generally effective way to bring such dissenters into line with the general party program or prevent their selection for committee posts. Nor has the House or Senate found a way to discipline the few irresponsible members who bring the lawmaking body as a whole into disrepute by stupid or demagogic actions.

Legislative usages ensure that divergences of view exist between the executive branch and at least some of the principal centers of power in Congress. The rule of seniority tends to give committee chairmanships and other positions of influence to members from sections most faithful to one party. Members from such areas, Democratic or Republican, are likely to have a different outlook on public policy than has the President, who must orient his policy toward the middle of the road or politically doubtful areas. But the actual pattern of power in Congress is both complicated and kaleidoscopic. Only to authors of textbooks on civics are our legislatures simple affairs. The student of comparative institutions finds in them elements of an English municipal council, with its close committee relations with administrative agencies; the Chamber of Deputies of the French Republic, with its individualism and shifting majorities; the House of Commons, with its party solidarity—all interlarded with a *liberum veto* of an indigenous variety.[5]

Because of the internal workings of Congress, the actual pattern of relations between Congress and the executive branch is incredibly complex. For the purposes of the present analysis, it is essential to note the power of the individual and of the small group within Congress with respect to the great mass of congressional business, and the diversity of policy views among these centers of power.

2. Contradiction of Integration

Legislative encouragement of administrative balkanization. A basic concept of administrative speculation of the past thirty years is that of integration. The idea has organizational implications, but it also includes the notion that the chief executive must so direct the administrative agencies that interagency conflict of objectives is minimized. Different agencies should administer related programs in a complementary fashion and will do so only by conscious top direction. The administrative structure is unified under the chief executive. The general concept of integration also carries with it the notion of unified legislative programs for administrative agencies. Departments should move forward in the same direction as well as be managed in their current operations in a coordinated manner. Examples are legion. One agency should not promote inflationary spending while another promotes deflationary taxation. Another should not try to drain land for agricultural use while still another attempts to preserve the same swamps as game habitats.

Congress, in its relations with the executive branch, tends to atomize rather than integrate the administrative structure and public policy. Factors of prime importance in this tendency are the feeble sense of collective responsibility within the administration and the complementary dispersion of power within the legislative body. Each department head must stand on his own feet. Important blocs in Congress may conduct guerilla warfare against him. Ordinarily, he must fight his own battle. His colleagues do not rally to his cause; they are not endangered. If he is in the good graces of Congress at the moment, he must shape his policy on the supposition that if he should run counter to the interests of the legislators most concerned with his program, he would have to fight for himself. The President will often stand aloof, for in the presidential system there is an element reminiscent of constitutional monarchy—the President must to some extent stand above the political fray.

The fact of individual responsibility is of profound administrative signifi-

---

[5] One of the best single volumes on Congress is Roland Young's *The American Congress,* New York: Harper, 1958.

cance. It throws the agency head into the arms of the congressional committees and blocs having a particular interest in the activities of his agency, and puts him at the mercies of whatever groups are involved. Administrative departments, both because of their internal drives and external affiliations, tend to be particularistic. Integration must proceed from the President, and, to be effective, it must curb the departments and the interests allied with them.

Under presidential leadership, a great deal of administrative unification may be accomplished on so-called noncontroversial matters. On questions of basic importance, however, the agency must sooner or later weigh the advantages of faithfully going down the line of presidential policy against the disadvantages of antagonizing a small but powerful group in Congress. Thus, a Secretary of Agriculture who recognized that the consumer of food has an interest in its price would probably be reprimanded from the floor of Congress and be given rough treatment by the producer-minded committees on agriculture. So he might merely pay lip service to an integrated economic policy.

Or, let us consider the various efforts by the President to unify operations in the development and control of water resources. The Bureau of Reclamation of the Interior Department and the Army Corps of Engineers are great competitors in this field. Each has its allies in Congress. Only so far and no farther can the President go in coordinating the two agencies, because the friends of each unite to deny funds to the President to employ staff for coordinating purposes or to obstruct his efforts in other ways. Under these conditions, the sense of collective responsibility—the feeling that ours is a government rather than a fortuitous grouping of departments—does not make itself strongly felt. Yet such a consciousness is requisite for the development of the most effective coordination and integration of administrative operations.

Legislative challenge to hierarchy. The centrifugal tendencies among administrative departments thus are reinforced by the dispersion of congressional authority among many working centers. However, the splintering effects of our system of congressional-executive relationships extend further down into the administrative machine. Direct dealings between Congress and the chiefs of departmental subdivisions often weaken the position of department heads. Hierarchical control within the departments is modified by a variety of practices. Probably one of the most significant is the custom in congressional criticism of placing the finger of responsibility on bureau chiefs and other subordinates of department heads.

Not infrequently speeches of Congressmen or their press conferences ring with denunciations of these subordinate departmental officials. Or, such officials receive congressional praise for their wise and statesmanlike management of affairs. The practice in either instance has the same effect—an erosion of intradepartmental controls. The general problem is well illustrated in a negative way by the reply of the Chief of Naval Operations to a question by the Senate Naval Affairs Committee on the *Greer* incident, a naval episode in the preliminaries to World War II, in 1941:

Q. Are there any reasons why the commanding officer and other officers and men of the *Greer* should not appear before the committee? If so, what are those reasons?

A. Yes. Testimony of such officers would be almost certain to disclose vital military secrets which would endanger other naval vessels. In addition, to establish a precedent or to have naval officers at sea feel that whenever they take action they would or might be called before a congressional investigating committee to explain and justify their action, would be prejudicial to the conduct of operations on the high seas.[6]

Legislative dealings with subordinate personnel. Direct congressional dealings with subordinates in the review of appropriation requests have something of the same effect. The department head may put in a brief appearance at the beginning of the hearings. However, members of Congress prefer to talk with the men down the line who actually do the work, and perhaps in the course of the interrogation give them instructions on how the job ought or ought not to be done in the future.

A bureau chief is "strong" or "weak" in dealing with Congress—"on the Hill." If "strong," he may be brought into line in an integrated departmental program only with difficulty. Bureau chiefs may become quite independent of the heads of their agencies insofar as broad policy is concerned. This independence is usually associated with their status "on the Hill" or with outside interest groups. Likewise, the manner in which appropriations are sometimes made may have a similar effect. The appropriation may be made to a particular bureau rather than to the department. Under these conditions, departmental—and occasionally presidential— direction may be met by the reply: "But we are responsible to Congress for the manner in which this program is carried out."

The close connections between members of Congress and bureau chiefs frequently promote stability and continuity in policy and are by no means invariably detrimental to the general welfare. These relations, however, make it difficult for the President or Congress to hold department heads accountable for the management of their affairs. Bureau chiefs and senior legislators are the cream of the career crop in the federal government. Both groups are likely to regard Presidents and department heads as transient trespassers. Probably the greatest resistance to direction by department heads is to be found in the highly professionalized services— in particular, the military services.

Congressional supervision of departments occasionally extends to mass examination of the qualifications, antecedents, and affiliations of subordinate personnel. Such inquiries may be quite impersonal witch-hunting

---

[6] *Congressional Record*, Vol. 87, p. 8314.

expeditions, with no specific animosity toward any particular employee. In some instances, congressional reaction reaches the point of formal measures to ensure the discharge of designated individuals.[7] These practices have an insidious effect on the work of subordinate personnel. An employee's spine may become spaghettilike when there exists the possibility of his being, in effect, blacklisted for federal employment through denunciation by individual lawmakers simply for doing his duty.

Subtler legislative influences. All these interferences with hierarchical control have been described in a manner which colors the exposition to a degree with exaggeration. In reality, the tendencies are more subtle and more difficult to identify than our discussion might lead us to believe. The significance of these practices may be best comprehended by comparison with the customs of British cabinet government.

The responsible minister is the man who must answer on the floor of Parliament for the misdeeds of his department. He cannot dodge the brickbats, and, in compensation, he has a monopoly of the bouquets. He can be held accountable only if he alone can hold his subordinates accountable. He therefore must make, or appear to make, the policy decisions. The concentration of criticism upon the responsible minister has a most pervasive intradepartmental effect in tightening up the internal lines of control, supervision, and communication.[8] All this, of course, is not the same as saying that the United States should have a cabinet government. It is only a means of illuminating by contrast the character of the influences at work under a system of separation of powers.

Grants of organizational independence. In some types of situations,

---

[7] See Cushman, Robert E., "The Purge of Federal Employees Accused of Disloyalty," *Public Administration Review,* 1943, Vol. 3, p. 297 *ff*.; Schuman, Frederick L., " 'Bill of Attainder' in the Seventy-Eighth Congress," *American Political Science Review,* 1943, Vol. 37, p. 819 *ff*. Section 304 of the Urgent Deficiency Appropriation Act of 1943 provided: "No part of any appropriation, allocation, or fund (1) which is made available under or pursuant to this act, or (2) which is now, or which is hereafter made, available under or pursuant to any other act, to any department, agency, or instrumentality of the United States, shall be used, after November 15, 1943, to pay any part of the salary, or other compensation for the personal services, of Goodwin B. Watson, William E. Dodd, Jr., and Robert Morss Lovett, unless prior to such date such person has been appointed by the President, by and with the advice and consent of the Senate. . . ." With the approval of their respective superiors, these three men continued to perform their duties after November 15, 1943, and sued to collect their salaries. The Court of Claims upheld their claim for compensation. The opinion of the court, delivered by the Chief Judge and concurred in by one judge, held that the act did not operate to remove the plaintiffs from office and that they were entitled to collect. In separate opinions concurring in the result, the other judges of the court went further and asserted that the congressional action was unconstitutional. Different judges, however, had different reasons for considering the provision invalid. The Supreme Court held Sec. 304 void; U. S. v. Lovett, Watson, and Dodd, 328 U. S. 303, June 3, 1946.

[8] The focus of accountability upon the political head of the department also tends to protect subordinate personnel from partisan retribution after changes in party control of the government. The heads of some federal agencies recognize this fact when they insist that they, rather than their career subordinates, appear before congressional committees in situations requiring advocacy of controversial policy or a defense of agency actions.

action by Congress has more direct effects in the atomization of administration than the more or less subtle influences described. Examples frequently occur in connection with organization. Thus, legislation which establishes a function independent of the department to which it might fall in the normal course has long-term administrative consequences. The new agency, uninfluenced by such forces of integration as flow from incorporation into a department, is left free to pursue its own inclinations. More important, it is likely to be politically weak, especially dependent on interest-group support, and unable to take a strong stand in its dealings with legislative blocs. It may become something of an administrative orphan, buffeted about by the political storms.

In the independent regulatory commission there occurs the most striking splintering of administration by legislative action. In a deliberate effort to make them independent of the chief executive, such agencies are declared to be "responsible" to Congress. The fact of the matter is that they are responsible to no one. They may keep their ears close to congressional committees, but Congress is not organized to enforce a continuing responsibility.

The chances are that a regulatory commission dealing with a single industry will be more nearly responsible to the industry than to the legislature. Deprived of the influences on policy that flow from give-and-take with other departments and from the directions of the chief executive, the independent commission gravitates toward an industry point of view. More or less from necessity, it seeks to retain the confidence of the regulated industry. Indeed, the theory on which such commissions are based makes it impracticable for them to collaborate wtih the chief executive or other executive agencies in the development of a unified policy. Their quasi-judicial procedure renders it improper for them to commit themselves to a general policy lest they thereby prejudice themselves in the determination of particular cases.

All in all, the legislative forces playing on the administrative structure contribute to disintegration in management. In effect, legislators seek to exercise piecemeal the function of direction over administration. Legislators who are jealous of chief executives, either in particular or in general, find this a congenial role. In reality, however, legislative control is most effective when all administration is sufficiently integrated. In appropriations, for example, lawmaking bodies are most effective when the chief executive presents a well-considered and carefully pruned budget. Under such conditions, the estimates become a tool of legislative oversight.

In other areas, legislative influences on administration are generated in no slight measure from the weakness of the chief executive. The power of the chief executive is usually described in awesome terms. In actual fact, the administrative apparatus at his command to aid him in knowing what is going on below his level and in guiding operations is quite inadequate.

This is in part the result of legislative jealousy of the executive, but whatever the origin, the lawmaking branch moves in to occupy the administrative vacuum. That vacuum has a far more impelling attractiveness to legislators when the President is weak than when he has an aggressive sense of policy direction.

3. Diffusion of Initiative and Responsibility

Embarrassments and frailties of executive initiative. Legislation fixes the scope of administrative power and to a large degree the manner of its exercise. Yet laws must be constantly adjusted to meet changed conditions and to reflect experience in their application. The administration in power must inevitably have an important share in the formulation of legislation. In the United States, executive-legislative relationships make inadequate provisions for the accomplishment of this need, with the consequence that initiative is diffused and the location of accountability for inaction uncertain.

Administrators participate in the formulation of legislation, but their activities are to a degree surreptitious and always subject to the accusation of constitutional immorality. If the chief executive presses for legislation proposed by him, he is charged in many instances with attempting to coerce a coequal governmental organ and leading the nation along the road to dictatorship. He may find it advisable to refrain from action when he should exercise strong leadership. On the other hand, because he will risk little if Congress rejects his proposal, he may urge legislation which he knows Congress will not enact. Thereby he gains credit with some sectors of the population. Similarly, he may ease his lot by placing a problem before Congress and leaving to that body the unhappy choice of means to solve it. Or he may for a long time neglect an urgent problem and present to Congress no proposed solution. Nor is the legislature able to develop and put into effect a comprehensive legislative program on its own initiative.

Obstacles to administrative program unity. The circumstances that contribute to disintegration within the administration and to the dispersion of power within Congress also lead to a diffusion of policy initiative within the administration. Even the most diligent efforts by the chief executive to whip together a coherent program of legislation often come to naught as they collide with the strong ties between particular departments, interest groups, and blocs within Congress. Each department head prefers to be free to promote his own legislative objectives in Congress. In turn he is encouraged in this preference by congressional protagonists of his agency.

Freedom of departmental initiative in appropriation matters is limited by the Budget and Accounting Act of 1921, which prohibits federal agencies from seeking funds in sums larger than those recommended by the President in his annual budget or any supplement. Administrative agencies, however, can usually manage to get their wishes on record through the interposition of friendly Congressmen. For instance, on questioning by a member of the House Appropriations Committee, an agency head may show himself unable to explain the cuts by the Bureau of the Budget in his request for funds, but volunteer to give his "personal opinion on these matters." When asked specifically, he might say: "I would like to see, if it were left to me personally, full restoration of the amount asked for in the first instance." That would be "just" his "personal viewpoint," to be differentiated from the President's budget request.[9] In other instances, the battle to upset the President's budgetary recommendations may be carried on by private organizations, working in closest contact with the administrative agencies concerned.

In matters other than appropriations, federal agencies are subject to the requirement that they clear with the Bureau of the Budget proposed legislation and comments on legislative proposals. The clearance process serves the purpose of determining whether the views of the agency are in accord with the program of the President. Formal agency statements to Congress are supposed to include an indication of the relationship of the matter in question to the President's program. The procedure results in a modification of some legislative ambitions of individual agencies and an early death to many of their proposals.[10] Yet the practice of coordination of such legislative urges into a systematic and consistent program is only in a relatively embryonic form. Further development will require a much more tightly knit management of the executive branch than has been the custom. Moreover, there is some doubt whether such a condition can be brought about until Congress itself ceases to encourage autonomous departmental initiative in legislation.

Consequences of inadequate legislative programming. Absence of cohesion in the legislative program of the chief executive—absence in fact of a program clearly designated as such—contributes mightily to confusion in the public mind, to submission of ill-considered legislative proposals, and to poor administration. Legislative schemes emerging from the departments are often ill-conceived and inadequately thought through. Not infrequently the scheme worked out in a single department raises a variety of questions about its relationship to other governmental activities. In fact, Congress has to devote a great deal of its energies to the settlement of interagency disputes on issues of no overwhelming public importance which might very well be settled within the administrative establishment.

---

[9] In a contrasting situation in 1958, General Nathan F. Twining, as Chairman of the Joint Chiefs of Staff, declined to answer a question whether he regarded as "adequate" the President's military budget which he was defending. "You can say it is inadequate and turn your suit in," he explained.

[10] See the testimony of F. J. Bailey, Chief of the Division of Legislative Reference, Bureau of the Budget, in House Committee on the Civil Service, *Hearings* pursuant to H. Res. 16, pt. 2, p. 359 *ff.*, 78th Cong., 1st Sess., 1943. See also Neustadt, Richard E., "Presidency and Legislation: The Growth of Central Clearance," *American Political Science Review,* 1954, Vol. 48, p. 641 *ff.*

Our ineffective linking of the administrative and legislative processes has important consequences in the operation of the executive branch. Perhaps one of the most significant is the necessity of operating under inadequate or inappropriate legislation which hampers or limits administration or makes it unduly costly. Government agencies hesitate to seek modifications from Congress. They will rather indulge in improvisations and patiently endure the oddest kinds of legal limitation. The reason is obvious. They never know what will emerge from the legislative mill once it begins to turn. Except for the most important questions on which broad public discussion and understanding may be brought to bear, the administrative tendency is to limp along on the existing legal basis, no matter how unsatisfactory it may be. It is regarded as better than to arouse sleeping dogs.

Incongruity between power and responsibility. The basic fact is that we have an institutional system which does not assure that administration will have power commensurate with its responsibility. Take, for instance, the following remarks of Senator Connally in 1940 during the consideration of a proposal to establish a joint congressional committee on national defense, whose consent would have been required before the President might make expenditures from an emergency fund for national defense:

> I want to perform my responsibility in this crisis or emergency. I want to fill the place in my country that my countrymen think I should fill, and perform whatever duty is laid upon me; but I do not want to take over somebody else's function or somebody else's responsibility. Give the President this $100,000,000. He has the responsibility; but if we hamper him, if we impede him, if we embarrass him with a smelling committee, we lessen his responsibilities. He can very easily say, "I undertook to discharge this function, but everytime I sought to discharge it, I had to run up to the Capitol and talk to some Members of the House and some Senators who could not make up their minds, who delayed, who hindered, and who undertook to interject into the theories of the War and Navy Department policies which I did not regard as wise or sound." [11]

Questions of like character are implicit in almost every important legislative proposal. Perhaps one of the reasons for the frequent incongruity between power and responsibility is that Congress has no routine means by which it can hold the executive branch accountable for the exercise of its power. A chief executive cannot say to Congress: "I refuse to accept responsibility for results on the terms imposed by Congress. I resign and yield the control of government to the opposition." Actions of Congress— keeping in mind that Congress for all practical purposes means this bloc, this committee, and even this member—thus are not fraught with the danger that its chickens will come home to roost.

Different constituencies, different standards of performance. The administrator and the legislator move in different environments and are subjected to different influences. The administrator often derives moral satisfaction

---

[11] *Congressional Record,* Vol. 86, p. 6593.

from the fact that he looks at public issues in a context different from that in which they are viewed by the legislator. He—so the theory runs—considers issues in terms of the national welfare, while the legislator views them as they bear on his state or district. In this contrast, which contains at least a grain of truth, the administrator has no cause for self-congratulation. The difference arises from the institutional structure. The voters elect their representatives to look out for their interests. A Senator from Nevada cannot very well be a statesman on the silver issue, just as a Representative from a coal-mining district cannot for long neglect the interests of his constituents. Moreover, administrators themselves have their prejudices. The Department of Agriculture or the Department of Labor and those who manage them are not free from bias in the definition of the national interest.

The interaction between legislature and administration, with the accompanying division of power, makes it quite difficult to place responsibility for action or inaction. The legislator can tell his constituents that he does his best to keep the bureaucrats from doing so many foolish things. The administrator can assert that he is doing as well as he can with the obstacles placed in his path by Congress. And both may be right.

From the newspapers we may gain the impression that legislators are an irresponsible lot, solely concerned with promoting the selfish causes of their own districts. The picture is far from correct. Every Congress has many members who labor earnestly, diligently, soberly, and steadily to promote the general welfare, as they see it. Their activities are far overshadowed in the press by the reports of the animadversions of their more picturesque or picaresque colleagues. The heavy routine work of the legislator does not produce headlines. Wild charges do. Thus, criticism by Congress of the executive branch takes on a fantastic character. Since such criticism is not in face-to-face debate, the most fabulous allegations may be made with no one to question them.

The continuing and inevitable attempts of Congress to manage the business of administration diffuse responsibility and confuse the public. In strict administrative theory, there is usually nothing but condemnation for the interferences of Congress with administration—interventions which are mostly in terms of particular cases or local interests rather than of general principle. Congress—the textbooks argue—should limit itself to action on general rules; then the individual cases would take care of themselves. In some respects, however, the very fact that lawmakers do criticize and intervene in specific cases and local situations makes their attacks a valuable corrective to administrative pursuit of general rules.

It is sometimes forgotten that ours is after all a huge country with citizens living and working under an infinite variety of conditions. There is in administration an almost inevitable tendency to reduce action to general rules and to treat all individual situations as if they were alike. Legislators, in their capacity as ambassadors for their constituents, intercede in individual situations and demand adaptation of administrative practices to fit the situation. It is not enough to dismiss this function of legislators by saying that they intervene regardless of the justice of the cause of their constituent. Generally they have a higher sense of responsibility than that; and because they cannot be ignored, they may and often do bring about many correctives of administrative action. Wisdom in government is not so much the formulation of just, general rules as the making of judicious exceptions.[12]

4. Quest for Accountability

Selecting department heads. Legislative supremacy means that the law-making body has power both to choose the principal executive officers and to terminate their services. The American constitutional system does not formally provide for legislative supremacy. The selection and tenure of the President are not determined by legislative action, although by virtue of their role in party affairs Senators and Representatives may make themselves felt in the choice of presidential nominees. On the other hand, the President as party leader is not without influence in the selection of members of the House and Senate.

Nevertheless, once elected, neither the President nor Congress can formally influence the tenure of office of the other. The status of subordinate executive officers is different from that of the President. There is a continuing effort by Congress to exert control over their appointment and tenure. These efforts are based in part on the formal powers of Congress—such as the power of the Senate to confirm presidential nominations to certain offices. In most instances, however, the legislature seeks to determine the top personnel of the executive branch by indirection. The President also has to choose. When two governmental organs attempt to select the holders of the same offices, conflict is inevitable.

The power to designate and discharge the principal executive officers is probably the most effective means of controlling administration. Both the chief executive and the legislature have a variety of devices for determining what is to be done and how it is to be done. However, it is far easier to guide the general direction of administrative business by the choice of chief officers whose viewpoints are of the desired type. Congress wants to influence these choices. Its efforts subside and flare up from time to time as the general temperature of attitudes toward the chief executive fluctuates.

In a broad sense, our principal executive and administrative officers must retain the confidence of Congress just as the ministers in a responsible cabinet system must have the confidence of Parliament to remain in office.

---

[12] For the problems touched on here, see Herring, Pendleton, *Presidential Leadership*, New York: Farrar & Rinehart, 1940; Laski, Harold J., *The American Presidency*, New York: Harper, 1940; Hyneman, Charles S., *Bureaucracy in a Democracy*, New York: Harper, 1950.

Ours, of course, is not a responsible cabinet system, nor is it equipped with the parliamentary procedures for expressing confidence or lack of confidence. Nevertheless, considerations of legislative confidence play a significant part in the selection and continuance in office of personnel at the top levels of the departments.

In the selection of agency heads, a long tradition concedes to the President fairly final discretion in the choice of the members of his Cabinet. Spectacular instances of senatorial refusal to assent to such presidential appointments merely confirm the general rule of presidential finality. Yet in making even these appointments, the President must be mindful of the probable attitudes of Congress toward prospective appointees.

Lower-level appointments. Legislative influence on appointments below the level of the Cabinet is on the whole more potent and more pervasive. The interest of Senators in appointments to positions in the "little cabinet" and to top positions in agencies not of Cabinet status has traditionally been of a patronage character. The desire has been to place in these positions persons who have rendered service to the party, and the actions of Presidents are ordinarily colored by the same inclinations. Hence, the usual problem of reconciling senatorial and presidential preferences has been simply that of allocating positions among the various factions of the party in a manner to provoke the minimum dissatisfaction.

When tension over issues is high, however, senatorial influence may be exerted to prevent the appointment of candidates with policy views contrary to those held by the dominant coalition in the Senate. On occasion, this is accomplished by the senatorial rejection of a presidential nomination. In other instances, nominations may be withdrawn by the White House when the temper of the Senate turns out to be clearly hostile. That such instances occur so rarely is an indication of the effectiveness of senatorial influence in screening out possibilities unacceptable to the Senate prior to nomination. In addition, at times control of top personnel is, in effect, achieved by legislative actions that transfer or reassign functions and thereby deprive particular individuals of control over particular activities.

Attempted extension of senatorial confirmation. Control by Senators and Representatives of appointments further down the administrative hierarchy has differed from time to time with the waxing and waning of the spoils system. Our traditions have accorded great influence to Senators and Representatives in appointments to the public service. During this century, however, with the strengthening of the merit system, large blocks of employees have been removed from the realm of congressional patronage.[13]

Apart from informal "clearance" of appointments with Representatives

---

[13] See the excellent study by Fowler, Dorothy Canfield, "Congressional Dictation of Local Appointments," *Journal of Politics,* 1945, Vol. 7, p. 25 *ff.*

and Senators, Congress on occasion attempts to broaden its formal control by the extension of senatorial confirmation to large numbers of lower positions. Thus, under various work relief appropriation acts from 1935 to 1942, senatorial confirmation was required for federal appointments as state and regional administrators receiving more than $5,000 annually. Scattered statutory provisions of similar purport were placed in various war agency appropriation acts. One act applying to the War Manpower Commission stipulated, for example, that no one might be appointed at a salary of over $4,500 save by the President with the advice and consent of the Senate. The actual administrative consequences of the requirement of confirmation have never been carefully analyzed. Certainly, in some situations the result is that a Senator may have at least a veto over important administrative actions within his state.

The debate in 1943 over a proposal to extend the confirmation requirement to all employees receiving in excess of $4,500 a year illuminates the theoretical problems of administration involved in legislative control of appointments. Some Senators indicated a desire to prevent abuses such as the payment of excessive salaries to unqualified individuals. Others thought that by having a hand in the selection of subordinate personnel, the Senate might gain a greater voice in the policies of administrative agencies. Senator Vandenburg asserted that "this is one of the few ways in which Congress can reach back into the implementing of its delegated powers, and have something to say and do by way of limitation of the sprawling bureaucracy which is the curse of our present-day democracy." On the other hand, the President asserted that the bill "presupposes congressional responsibility for the operations of executive agencies." If the power of appointment of subordinate personnel were divided between the Senate and department heads, he saw a dissipation of responsibility for the success of an agency's program.[14]

Removal power. Control of personnel includes the power to remove as well as to influence selection. Congress has no ready and easy method by which it can remove officials whose attitudes or policies are not to its liking. The power of impeachment is a blunderbuss of no utility. The power to specify that no funds shall be available for the employment of particular individuals has been used in scattered instances against relatively unimportant employees of the executive branch. But there is no clean-cut method by which the legislature can simply say, "We have nothing against you personally. Nor do we question your competence or your Americanism. Our views on what the policy of your department should be are not the same as yours. You are fired." The lack of workable means for the removal by Congress of executive officers is, of course, merely the corollary of independence of the chief executive—the glory or the fatal defect of

---

[14] See the analysis by Macmahon, Arthur W., "Senatorial Confirmation," *Public Administration Review,* 1943, Vol. 3, p. 281 *ff.*

the American system of government, depending on the point of view.[15]

Nevertheless, a determined legislature can virtually drive a man from office, although not without considerable vituperation and recrimination. Exposure of corruption and the consequent forced resignation of an executive officer occasionally occur. Resignations on account of incompatability either of personality or policy between Congress and an individual officer are better indications of the fundamental legislative as well as executive tendency to seek relationships of confidence. Occasionally congressional investigations appear to have as their primary objective the removal of an executive officer. That is, the investigation is certainly not designed to develop legislation; nor is it motivated by a search for corruption. It aims to oust an individual whose views arouse the animosity of the legislators spearheading the investigation.

By its control over appropriations, the lawmaking body can make an official quite uncomfortable. In some instances, arbitrary cuts in budget estimates are made because of congressional dislike of an individual, disagreement with his policies, or other related reasons. The pressure is thus on him to resign lest by continuance in office he will damage the agency which he heads or serves. In other cases, by persistent criticism from the floor, by frequent adoption of limiting legislation, and by similar means an official may be thoroughly persuaded that his period of usefulness is ended. Congress is most effective in its efforts to terminate the services of a particular individual when it has support in the press and the public generally. A common pattern of behavior is that the executive branch attempts to weather the congressional storm. Then, perhaps in the wake of a "moral" victory, a resignation occurs after things have quieted down. The formality of executive independence is preserved but the actuality of legislative discharge prevails.

No matter who is President or what the conditions of the time are, Congress exerts influence over the selection of the principal administrative officers. Harmonious relations between the chief executive and the legislature do not indicate the absence of congressional participation in appointments. This general condition may reflect careful consideration of congressional wishes. Legislative attitudes only become more apparent when differences of policy exist between the President and Congress.

5. Drives Toward Reform

Case for cabinet government. Of prescriptions to cure the ills of Congress there is no dearth. Hopeful souls come forward at moments when

---

[15] When the Senate declines to confirm a reappointment, its action may closely resemble a discharge from office. Thus, in 1948 the Senate, under the spur of the natural gas industry, refused to confirm Leland Olds, an advocate of strict regulation, for a third term as a member of the Federal Power Commission. See Harris, Joseph P., *The Advice and Consent of the Senate,* Berkeley: University of California Press, 1953.

they can gain a hearing and attempt to market their cures for Congress. A massive sales resistance usually meets their offerings, which are often based on faulty diagnoses. The principal error in diagnosis made by reformers is that they approach Congress in isolation from the rest of the government. The basic issues involve the structure of the entire government rather than Congress alone. They are almost invariably associated with the fundamental principle of separation of powers.

Outright adoption of the principle of cabinet responsibility has been strongly urged by a few students of government, but sentiment in support of such a move is not nearly so strong as it once was. The British system in its current usages has come to be recognized as something radically different from the older conceptions of that system. Furthermore, the manner in which it would operate under American conditions is quite unpredictable.[16]

The transplantation of the cabinet system would deprive us of the strength that inheres in the presidency, and might produce the instability associated with the French parliamentary system rather than arrangements similar to those of Great Britain and the Dominions. Moreover, it would necessitate a drastic revision of the working relationship between our two legislative chambers and the consequent decline of the strength accorded in our federal system to the states with small populations. Whatever our prognosis of the results of adopting the cabinet system may be, the likelihood of such action is remote. We must work out our constitutional problems within the framework of the system of separation of powers.

The drive for congressional reform has its peaks and its valleys. The policies of the Roosevelt administrations in depression and war stimulated unusual agitation among both members of Congress and citizens for a thoroughgoing reconsideration of the function and role of Congress. With proposals for the purely internal reorganization of the legislative process, we have no concern here. However, the various suggestions for alteration of the relationships between the legislative and executive branches are of interest in throwing light on the general problem dealt with in this chapter.

Merits of a question period. Estes Kefauver, when he was a member of the House, attracted considerable attention by his proposal to introduce a "question period," modeled on Britsh practice, when heads of executive agencies would appear before the House of Representatives to reply to questions of which they had received advance notice. Such an arrangement would permit members of the Cabinet and the heads of other agencies to answer criticisms and explain policies. Appearance of executive officers before the entire House would limit the monopoly of information which committees tend to have of subjects within their jurisdiction. This might

---

[16] For critical observations, see Price, Don K., "The Parliamentary and Presidential Systems," *Public Administration Review*, 1943, Vol. 3, p. 317 *ff.*

somewhat weaken the committees. It is not without significance that many of the "older heads" within the House—those who hold committee chairmanships and other positions of leadership—were strongly opposed to the Kefauver proposal. Conversely, the chief proponents of such measures tend to be newer members of Congress, who have little opportunity to utilize their talents because of their lack of seniority.

Legislative committee meetings with administrators. A variety of other schemes are suggested from time to time to produce a closer liaison between Congress and the administrative departments. Thus, it is proposed that individual legislators meet at frequent intervals with their opposite numbers in the executive branch to consider forthcoming problems, to inform Congress, and to bring the views of Congress to the executive officer concerned. This kind of arrangement is occasionally formalized by particular committees.[17]

While closer relationships between executive officials and legislative committees are in some ways advantageous, they also may contribute to the disintegration of administration. Congressional committees tend to be enthusiasts for the matters with which they deal. The public interest is not necessarily better promoted by giving, for example, the committees on agriculture in either chamber a stronger voice in the management of the Department of Agriculture than they now have.

Legislative staffs. Better staffing of Congress is another favorite attack on the problem. This is to serve two purposes: to aid the legislator in handling his legislative business and his constitutents' business as well. A more or less professionalized class of congressional secretaries has been developed consisting of men and women who "know" Washington and who run the errands that inevitably are the lot of legislators, not always unsolicited. More significant issues are raised by the need for assistance to the legislator in his legislative business.

In the staffing of congressional committees it is sometimes assumed that by this means the legislature can do directly many things which the executive branch should do. We can make ourselves felt—so the speculation runs—if we have staff to help us dig into the bureaucracies. When intelligently used, expert staff can make Congress much more effective. However, by overstaffing Congress we run the danger of merely setting up another bureaucracy "on the Hill" to do a job which, if it is not already being done elsewhere, ought to be. The contribution of the lawmaker in the governmental process is not in the exercise of professional expertness. If he merely

---

[17] Because of the delicacy of questions of foreign relations and the special problems of maintaining domestic support for external policy, systematic arrangements have evolved for consultation between the relevant committees and State Department personnel. See Galloway, George B., *The Legislative Process in Congress*, p. 144 *ff.*, New York: Crowell, 1955. In the field of atomic energy also, especially close committee-agency relations prevail between the Joint Committee on Atomic Energy and the Atomic Energy Commission, though these are not always harmonious.

mouths what his experts tell him, we lose important values of representative government.

Making legislative work manageable. These remarks suggest that one of the most important currents of reform is that of drawing the line between what the legislative body ought to do and what it ought to demand that the executive branch do well. No matter how much staff it builds up, Congress cannot make all the decisions of government, save for a change of the nature of the system. To make its job manageable, Congress needs to slough off a mass of minutiae which now absorbs its time and energies. One means by which it might shift a great volume of work to the executive branch would be through adoption of the British provisional order system—that is, rules and regulations made by the executive agencies would become effective within a specified time unless Congress decided to the contrary.

The most notable example of the use of this technique in the United States was under the Reorganization Acts of 1939 and 1945, which empowered the President to submit so-called reorganization plans to become effective unless disapproved by concurrent resolution. Over many subjects, this arrangement would actually reserve for Congress more substantial control than it now possesses, especially under legislation empowering an agency to regulate an industry in "the public interest." In the exercise of such powers, executive officers would also often be much more comfortable if their actions were subject to general congressional review. The endless criticism for exceeding legislative grants of power might be effectively terminated, and policy questions which probably ought to have congressional approval would not be settled finally by the executive branch, as they now are.

Many variations of the foregoing proposals have been made,[18] and the entire range of possibilities was explored by a joint committee set up by Congress late in 1944.[19] There are those who believe that adoption of one or more of these schemes would ensure peace and harmony in executive-legislative relationships. Such a celestial state of affairs will probably never come about because executive-legislative differences often boil down to the

---

[18] See the useful survey in *The Reorganization of Congress, A Report of the Committee on Congress of the American Political Science Association*, Washington: Public Affairs Press, 1945.

[19] See Joint Committee on the Organization of Congress, *First Progress Report*, Sen. Doc. No. 36, 79th Cong., 1st Sess. The hearings before the joint committee constitute a valuable source of information about the workings of Congress; *Hearings before the Joint Committee on the Organization of Congress* pursuant to H. Con. Res. No. 18, 1945, 79th Cong., 1st Sess. The committee's final report appeared as House Report No. 1675, 79th Cong., 2d Sess., March 4, 1946. See the later review in *Hearings before the Senate Committee on Expenditures in the Executive Departments on Evaluation of the Effects of Laws Enacted to Reorganize the Legislative Branch of the Government*, 82d Cong., 1951. Another approach aims at a strengthening of the national organs and the program commitments of the two major parties; see Committee on Political Parties of the American Political Science Association, *Toward a More Responsible Two-Party System*, Supplement to Vol. 44 (No. 3) of *American Political Science Review*, September 1950.

issue of who will rule. That issue cannot be settled without doing violence to the theory of separation of powers, which presupposes that Congress and the President share the power to rule. Friction is inevitable and, we might add, probably desirable within proper bounds. Nevertheless, much senseless controversy could be eliminated if administrators exerted more persistent and more intelligent efforts to keep legislators informed of the affairs of state and, in turn, to inform themselves of the views of legislators.

PART III

WORKING METHODS

Chapter 16 •

The Formulation of Administrative Policy

1. Policy Formation and Policy Sanction

Realm of administrative policy. The primary organ of policy sanction is the legislature. In the main, it lays down policy in general terms. For purposes of effective government such general policy, usually expressed in statutes, must be made more specific. This is done by administrative policy formulation as a means of giving more precise expression to statutory directions addressed to the executive branch.

Administrative policy may consist of the determination of a long-range work program, such as the number of applications to be processed, inspections to be made, and projects to be completed during a given time period. It may also mean establishing a criterion or standard for the guidance of subordinate officials in making decisions on recurrent matters in the course of day-to-day operations. Or it may mean a highly specific decision—for instance, whether a precedent-setting letter should be sent out or an important appointment made. In the broadest sense, however, a policy question is one which requires an authoritative determination as to whether or not a new program or a change in an existing plan of action should be undertaken.

Depth of policy-making process. Formal determination—or final approval—of a proposal setting forth what should be done occupies a very small segment of time in the process of policy-making. This is true especially in the case of administrative operations, unless the top administrator undertakes personally to review the basis of all decisions he is called upon to make, which would create an impossible bottleneck at his desk. On the other hand, one mark of a good executive is his ability to decide quickly whether more staff work or more thorough planning needs to be done before he can intelligently consider a proposed action. Policy questions that raise issues about his basic program objectives or the kind of structural arrangements and administrative coordination he wants in his organization will require more of his time than operating decisions, the bulk of which he must delegate to his immediate line subordinates.

On either type of policy question, however, regardless of the time ele-

337

ment involved, the final formal decision is preceded by an evolutionary stage of formulation. This begins with the spotting of some concrete needs and identification of the problem, bringing forth investigation and analysis. It is carried forward to the point of corrective recommendations, leading in turn to formal initiation of the proposed action for review and approval or rejection in terms of its implications for existing practices and relationships. Ultimate determination is succeeded by the stage of execution, which includes frequently a designation of the individual responsible and nearly always a description of the procedures to be followed for applying the controlling policy or general plan of action in particular cases.

Prompting role of management. Once the main lines of program objective, structural grouping, and functional coördination have been laid down, neither formulation nor execution of policy as a matter of practice is kept sharply apart from the other. Policy issues are continually arising out of problems of execution, and solutions may be initiated at any of its phases. New facts, different situations, and changing pressures are constantly coming up, which necessitate decisions by operating officials or else require requests for policy clearance or approval of proposed action on a higher level. A well-managed agency properly encourages suggestions from below, with the promise of money awards, or other recognition if a suggestion leads to improvements. However, such suggestions must be analyzed and reviewed in the wider policy perspective to determine whether the proposed measure falls within existing policy or whether the policy itself should be modified.

One task of management, therefore, is to establish appropriate methods for identifying existing or potential problems, and to provide channels for sifting and expediting consideration of policy issues at the most suitable agency levels. The determination having been made, it is equally important that its substance and its rationale be quickly disseminated to the whole staff and to the public affected by it. The ease and effectiveness with which an agency educates itself and its public on its own policies and any changes in them, determines in large measure its ability to dispose of its work with corresponding ease and effectiveness at operating levels.

Legislative basis of administrative policy. On a broader scale, the same process that goes on in administration organizations occurs in legislative policy-making, except that most of the issues do not arise out of the daily operations that make up the legislature's own business. In a loose sense, the legislative body acts as something like a board of directors for all administrative agencies, but policy determination is divided between it and another political organ, the chief executive. Both, separately or jointly, determine policy that is binding upon administrative agencies.

This division seems to assume two principal channels for policy formulation: one from the people through their elected representatives; the other from administrative officials to the chief executive. The interaction between these two processes would be relatively simple if the legislature confined its role in policy formulation to approving or disapproving policy proposals submitted to it by the chief executive, whether through statutory enactments or through the positive or negative exercise of its power to appropriate the funds estimated to be necessary for the achievement of stated public purposes. English-speaking countries, however, have rejected such simplicity after a historic struggle for control of the royal or executive prerogative. As a result, the legislature established its constitutional power not only to decide whether money should be spent for a public purpose, but also to take the initiative in policy-making and extend it to defining the method, principles, and organization by which that purpose should be attained.

Main division of responsibility. Nevertheless, the scope of governmental functions under modern industrial and technological conditions is so vast that legislative bodies from sheer necessity have delegated more and more responsibility for the content of policy proposals to administrative agencies. In these agencies, more technically competent, comprehensive, and balanced consideration of the issues is possible than in the atmosphere and procedures of legislative assemblies. The magnitude and pressure of public business upon legislatures has forced them to relinquish much of their initiating and planning function to the chief executive, which has enhanced the importance of legislative review and approval of administrative proposals. Such legislative review and approval are most effectively exercised in the creation or modification of administrative powers and authorizations, whereby administrative policy is controlled prospectively—in the first instance by substantive legislation, in the second by appropriation of funds.

The distinction between legislative and administrative policy does not turn so much upon an inherent difference in the content of policy as upon the extent to which the proposed innovation or plan of action involves a fundamental change in public policy. The new program or policy will require legislative authorization primarily as it calls for amendment or revision of either statutory provisions or established practices or expectancies around which public feelings or economic interests have become consolidated. No satisfactory substitute has been found for the educational value of open investigation and debate, for the safeguards implicit in public hearings, and for the stability gained by survival of the legislative test and the embodiment of policy in the form of law. The great hazards in the legislative process are the distorting influences of partisan forces seeking narrow objectives through piecemeal amendment, regardless— and sometimes at the price—of the over-all plan.

Coordinate tasks of legislature and chief executive. It is often claimed that the chief executive is in a better position than the lawmaking body to secure expert consideration of policy questions in the light of the complexities and conflicts that have to be reconciled. However, he has his own problems of maintaining personal relationships with the leaders of his party in the legislature, appraising the popularity of policy proposals in terms of votes, and ensuring cohesion of his party organization. Given the multiplicity of policy initiators in the legislature, it is clear nevertheless that he has an important and legitimate function on behalf of the whole people to state authoritatively his opinion on the substance of proposed policy. He is best placed to answer the pivotal question of how far policy should be formulated on the basis of considerations deemed important by the experts in getting votes—the politicians—and how much weight should be given the factors deemed important by the experts in getting the job done—the administrators.

Put in another way, our constitutional system assumes the desirability of divided responsibility and rivalry between chief executive and legislature. As a consequence, the chief executive bears a large part of the burden of formulating and explaining the need for public policies and for focusing the legislature's attention upon the issues which it should decide, as distinct from those decisions which should be left to administrative judgment and competence.

2. Fact-Finding and Discretion in Administrative Policy

Delegation of policy determination. Much discussion and analysis, particularly in legal literature,[1] has been devoted to the legislative delegation of rule-making power to the discretionary judgment of administrative officials. Turning aside the technical legal arguments we must start from the basic premise that a legislative body cannot administer. The practical question, therefore, is the extent to which it is desirable for the statute to prescribe in detail the methods of achieving its purpose. In other words, how free a choice of means should be given the administrator?

The Supreme Court has made it clear that if the legislature has the authority to adopt a given program of action or plan of regulation, it may prescribe the method of achieving that program in either general or specific terms. In doing so, it is subject to only two major conditions: first, responsibility for achieving the public purpose or program should be vested in public officials; second, the statutory statement of the public purpose should be expressed in terms that are sufficiently clear to afford a criterion by which the courts may judge whether the administrative policy has a reasonable relationship to the basic statutory purpose. Assuming the constitutionality of the legislative purpose, the problem of administrative policy-makers is to determine whether the conditions exist

---

[1] *Cf.* Chapter 3, "Bureaucracy—Fact and Fiction," Sec. 4, "The Battle against Regimentation"; Chapter 10, "Independent Regulatory Agencies"; and especially Chapter 23, "The Judicial Test."

under which the adopted policy should be applied and what should be done to give it effect. In these terms, the proper criterion for appraising administrative discretion is the general objectivity of official judgment and the basic accuracy of the information upon which such determinations are based.

Congress, the statute itself, and functional groups exert pressures which in their combined effects upon administrators tend to force them to seek as complete a finding of the facts, as rigorous an analysis of the relevant issues, and as precise a statement of the assumptions and reasoning upon which the administrative approach should be based, as can be obtained from their staffs. Assuming that as a rule the top officials of an agency are intent upon performing their tasks as fairly and effectively as they know how, the principal limitation upon the quality of administrative policy is the scope and reliability of the means for analyzing the necessary information. The question, therefore, is how the administrator can guard himself against the pitfalls of subjective preferences, based upon superficial or narrow assumptions as to what information is relevant and what issues are important.

Administrative contacts with private fact-finding groups. One thing the administrator may do is encourage the establishment of contacts with private fact-finding groups outside of government. Outstanding examples are the informal relationships between the Bureau of Agricultural Economics and the farmer organizations; the Bureau of Labor Statistics and the labor organizations; the Interstate Commerce Commission and the Bureau of Railway Economics of the Association of American Railroads; the Office of Education and the National Education Association; the Office of Business Economics and trade associations; the Census Bureau and the American Statistical Association; the Children's Bureau and the local councils of private welfare agencies; the United States Public Health Service and the American Medical Association.

Collaborative relationships in the planning and conduct of research programs are unquestionably helpful to both private and public agencies, sometimes developing into well-understood divisions of labor. The mutual interest of these different bodies in the problems of the same economic segment or the same area of professional concern arises out of essentially similar general views on public policy. Administrative policy-makers should therefore be on their guard lest the factors of propinquity bring about a public distrust of the reliability of the agency's official judgments, decisions, or publications.

Interagency use of staff resources. A second way of improving staff sources of information is to further the formation of technical relations and associations with officials of other agencies engaged in the same type of work. In the federal government, the interagency advisory group of the Civil Service Commission holds periodic office meetings of departmental personnel officers. The executive officers' group is another governmentwide organization, for which the Bureau of the Budget has served as a secretariat. Still another illustration is the Office of Statistical Standards in the Bureau of the Budget. This unit performs a semiofficial service for agency statisticians by establishing interagency coordinating committees to handle technical problems of program and method.

Arrangements such as these are valuable. They widen technical points of view. They increase professional experience through exchange of viewpoints and information. And they develop support for interdepartmental programs and techniques having general policy significance, as distinct from purely jurisdictional bureau-centered interest.

Governmentwide clearance of policy proposals. A third way of placing an agency in official touch with external sources of information is exemplified in the federal government by the procedure of formal consultation and clearance of legislative matters through the Office of Legislative Reference in the Bureau of the Budget. Any recommendation for legislative enactment or report by an agency upon pending legislation must be put before the bureau before submission to Congress. The bureau determines what other agencies are affected by the subject matter, supplies them with a copy of the pertinent materials, and requests a statement of their views on it. Having secured the views of all agencies concerned, the bureau ascertains the relationship of the legislation to the program of the President, and communicates its finding to the initiating agency, which in its report to Congress must include a statement of the advice received from the Budget Bureau.

This channel, of course, is not a means of broadening the span of attention of a very large proportion of the staff of a department. Formal clearance procedure represents a very late stage in the interdepartmental negotiation or exchange of views. Consideration of legislative proposals in administrative circles begins at a very early stage. Many pieces of legislation in recent years have been the result of a vast measure of informal preliminary discussion, prior to the initiation of final proposals through formal channels. Yet the existence of clearance requirements is a real incentive to interdepartmental consultation.

Insuring objectivity in staff recommendations. Personal and professional contacts and associations across departmental lines, together with similar staff contact between the executive and the legislative branches, are an important means of broadening the general outlook on policy questions. Top administrators also have a strong interest in this matter. The problem is particularly compelling when the administrator acts in a quasi-judicial capacity, in which he must find out what questions really are at issue and arrive at judgments about what should be done on the facts of specific cases. Such narrowing of the area of decision in specific cases from general arguments to definable factors or determinants of judgment is an outstanding feature of the entire administrative process. It accounts for much of the emphasis on the part of regulatory tribunals and agencies upon a "fair hearing," decision "on the record," and "substantiality" of evidence.

The problem is not restricted to quasi-judicial processes in the specific sense, however. Even ordinary administrative orders and acts must be based on a careful scrutiny of all the relevant facts. Moreover, all rules and regulations prescribing rights or obligations of individuals must be drafted on rigorously analyzed assumptions as to the type of situation that is anticipated or planned for. Generalized language is necessary, but trained analysis in advance of formal promulgation insures application of the rules within concrete and often quite precise limits.[2]

In order to create an administrative pattern in which this type of analysis operates continuously and as a matter of course, the administrator must establish machinery for institutional planning and for review of lower-level decisions or recommendations. This is first of all a matter of personal understanding and cooperation between the first echelon of subordinates and the top administrative authority, whether it be a board or an individual. Once the personal relationships at the top have been established, however, administrative planning is properly distinguishable from the review process.

Effects of planning and review. In formulating new goals of administrative effort, planning draws upon all resources in the organization, regardless of lines of responsibility. The function of review is closely associated with existing lines of command, and with the responsibilities of supervisors in scrutinizing the quality and quantity of their subordinates' day-to-day work. In complex organizations, the two functions may be brought together at the top in one review group. This will stimulate self-analysis and improvement in performance standards as well as in reporting methods on the part of operating divisions. Both planning and review presuppose thorough fact-finding as a basis for administrative decision.[3] On any problem of policy formulation, they rival and supplement each other by emphasizing different facts and different approaches to the same problem for attention at the top. Administrative planning should be closely tied into budget formulation, from whose planning phases it is indistinguishable.

It should be clear, then, that the administrative approach to the problem presented by legislative delegation of discretion to achieve a broad objective of public policy does not assume an unfettered choice of means.

---

[2] This process appears to conform to the "utilitarian" method and standard of arriving at ethical judgments, which has been applied to administrative theory by Leys, Wayne A. R., *Ethics for Policy Decisions—The Art of Asking Deliberative Questions,* New York: Prentice-Hall, 1952.

[3] In the words of Follett, Mary P., *Dynamic Administration,* p. 305, New York: Harper, 1942: "I have given four principles of organization. The underpinning of these is information, based upon research."

For example, the annual legislative review of appropriation requests provides a check. The technical nature of the particular issues imposes certain limitations. The sources of information and the devices of co-ordination available to top executives through budgetary and management channels, functioning under governmentwide standards, establish another set of brakes. The promotion of criteria of technical competence through interagency relationships, formal and informal, are further important controls of a professional character. Finally, the evolution of procedures for ensuring accurate and fair determination of the facts deserves mention, although these procedures suffer from the narrowness of statutory and technical perspectives rather than from a plenitude of "uncontrolled" power.[4]

A perhaps more understandable source of criticism of administrative policy-making arises from less objective factors. It stems from legislative and public distrust of the social ideals and political preferences that are imputed to certain administrators or to members of their staff to whom special influence is attributed by outsiders. This problem is important enough to deserve special attention.

3. Ideology and Administrative Policy

Sources of ideology. The word "ideology," as applied to an individual, is a synonym for his social philosophy. As an individual proceeds toward an integrated personality, he develops a more or less articulate social outlook, a world view, which is the result of many factors—his family background, his educational experience, his occupational status, his human wants, his cultural interests, his emotional preferences, and—last but not least—his intellectual choices. The individual's self-awareness in terms of these personality elements, together with the formulation of his own objectives and criteria of meaningful living, constitute his social philosophy.

In this sense everyone has an ideology, with infinite variations in comprehensiveness, hidden contradictions, and degrees of effective adjustment. If he is unwilling or unable to work out his own independent position, he finds several ideologies or systems of social interpretation—such as Americanism, individualism, liberalism, socialism—competing against one another for his attention as the most satisfactory method of explaining the facts of a complex world. The danger of all ideologies is that they may become substitutes instead of instruments for thinking. Since some explanation is essential to his sense of personal security and adjustment, the individual is apt to develop deep-seated emotional attachments to his own interpretation. Conversely, he may come to exhibit violent resentments

---

[4] Freeman, J. Leiper, *The Political Process,* New York: Doubleday, 1955; Schubert, Glendon A., "The Public Interest in Administrative Decision-Making," *American Political Science Review,* 1957, Vol. 51, p. 346 *ff.*

of "alien" ideologies which threaten the security or stability of his own conception of a desirable world.

Ideology of political office. In democratic politics, there is a rough connection between the personal ideology of the elective official and the means of holding him to account for his acts. The political officeholder's ideological problem consists of his ability to identify his preferences—or, if comprehensively thought through, his philosophy—with the objectives that a majority of the voters in his constituency will support at the next election. In administration, however, this type of ability is in demand only at the top-policy level, where a relatively thin layer of political office-holders is superimposed upon the permanent staff to bring about changes in policy when control of government changes hands.

The man at the head of an agency with the ability to gauge public opinion and to attract popular support must learn how to use his permanent staff, who possess vastly more technical information and experience than he. His administrative job is to guide and lead his managers and technicians in the direction in which he wants them to go.

Administrative ideology. In contrast to the qualifications of a political officeholder, those of the permanent administrative officer are experience, training, and ability to get a job done—that is, to plan and direct the performance of a program of work within policies and under conditions more or less broadly defined by law. Legal authorization implies that the function or program is of continuing value or service to the public, regardless of changes in political office. While statutory policies and conditions should be adjusted in the light of experience to changing public opinion, the rate of legal adjustment and administrative change is relatively slow.

Hence administrative employees, including those attached to top levels, are always faced with a possible conflict between their own preferences and the opinions of the public, the legislature in whole or in part, the chief executive, and the political superiors, to whom they are responsible. A great deal of latitude in expression of personal views may and should be permitted, insofar as raising policy questions is concerned. However, once the decision has been made, the subordinate must be held responsible by the superior for performing his duties along the lines of the policy laid down. The ideological problem of permanent public servants therefore consists not only in the barriers and resistances imposed by layers of authority above them, but also in their acceptance of the frustrations implicit in the slowness with which constitutional democracy moves.

Intellectual flexibility and emotional stability. These conditions impose two important qualifications upon permanent administrative officials who by virtue of their positions or abilities recommend, review, or on their own level approve policy decisions. One is intellectual flexibility; the other is emotional stability. The stresses and strains involved in making the necessary personal adjustments are so great that there is a strong tendency, particularly on the part of personnel "down the line," to escape them completely by shunning policy questions. This tendency may be reflected in a negative attitude toward new suggestions or unfamiliar ideas. Or, it may result in a refusal to take a position, except in accordance with established routines or express instructions from a superior. Moreover, those who do succeed in adjusting themselves to the requirement of flexibility are in danger of falling into opportunism and of abdicating their personal conviction.

The question is one of great difficulty because of the strains imposed upon both intermediate planning and supervising staffs and the top administrators. The latter, in their preoccupation with personalties and political considerations, tend to dismiss the importance of technical disagreements. In short, though the administrator may want to encourage initiative, he may reap conflict in his organzation. Under these conditions, he often prefers that policy decision which offers the best chance of enabling the organization to stick together—the"good of the service" doctrine.

Effects of ideological orientation. At its lowest extreme, the need for organizational solidarity may stifle all initiative, apart from uniformity with the "party line" of the group closest to the agency head. In its higher manifestations, organizational unity encourages objectivity of judgment and the raising of policy questions on the assurance that settled policy will be fully carried out. As a corollary, this solidarity proscribes special favors for special groups or individuals inside and outside the organization. At the same time, such a drive for unity places a large responsibility for policy coordination upon the agency head and his immediate associates, because once their authority has been divided up, differences over policy questions among them must be disposed of in terms of the prestige, self-respect, and pride of every member of the divisions involved.[5]

Administrative ideology, therefore, presents a very complex problem in social psychology. Immediately and concretely, administrative policy is to a large degree a matter of personality and personal relationships between the agency head, his immediate staff, and the first level of operating subordinates. *Ex officio,* so to speak, the understandings and commitments of this group determine much of the course of administrative policy. In personnel changes at these levels may be sought the significant clues to shifts in the direction of policy. However, the ability of top management to do its job in achieving the purpose of the organization as a whole depends in turn on the sense of contribution, accomplishment, and participation sustained in the working groups all the way down the hierarchy. In the face of the explosive problems generated by social idealism, personal will-to-power, and simple demands for a sense of job satisfaction by men

---

[5] For a systematic analysis of these personal adjustment problems in the language of role-system and group-equilibrium theory, see Simon, Herbert A., and Others, *Public Administration,* chs. 3–5, 23, New York: Knopf, 1950.

working in groups, it is not surprising that outsiders get the impression of powerful, anonymous influences which are feared because they are not understood.

4. External Influences and Administrative Policy

Impact of interest groups. Legislative relationships are, of course, not the only external influences which administrative policy-making must take into account. Organized pressure groups are well aware of—and sometimes responsible for—the delegation of discretionary powers to governmental agencies. These groups maintain an ever-watchful eye upon administrative decisions affecting their own purposes and programs.[6]

Their influence is exercised through requests for information; demands to be heard at formal hearings; prospects for an extremely unfavorable atmosphere of publicity for the agency; and refusals to cooperate with administrative officials. Over and above pressure tactics, however, group organizations have secured considerable recognition for a valuable consultative role through which, in various forms, they may participate in the formulation of administrative policy.

Public relations. Public relations, not only with legislative bodies and organized groups but also by informing the press and the general public of the work and accomplishments of an agency, have been accepted in recent years as an essential element in administrative policy.[7] While the general function of a public-relations officer is one of public information, his influence extends to the problem of how a complicated, technical policy decision can best be explained to the lay public. Sometimes he may have to propose the modification of a policy in order to secure better understanding and a more favorable public attitude toward the agency.

Beyond its decisions in particular cases, the long-run task of an administrative agency is a public-relations problem. The job is to transform a public policy, which originally is only a string of words in the statute book or in a directive, from a purely verbal expression into a pattern of public acceptance. Such acceptance implies a public expectation of a "legitimate" mode of action by the officials responsible for putting the policy into effect. In this broadest sense of public relations, the stature of an administrative agency—particularly in the regulatory field—will depend in large measure upon its success in establishing a favorable reaction to its basic policies and its normal methods of operation.

---

[6] *Cf.* Chapter 14, "Interest Groups in Administration." For challenging interpretations of public administration as a product of the distribution of power in society, and of policy as bureaucratic efforts to survive, see Bendix, Reinhard, "Bureaucracy and the Problem of Power," *Public Administration Review,* 1945, Vol. 5, p. 194 *ff.*; Long, Norton E., "Power and Administration," *ibid.,* 1949, Vol. 9, p. 257 *ff.*; Selznick, Philip, *TVA and the Grassroots,* Berkeley: University of California Press, 1949.

[7] *Cf.* McCamy, James L., *Government Publicity,* Chicago: University of Chicago Press, 1939; Pimlott, J. A. R., *Public Relations and American Democracy,* Princeton: Princeton University Press, 1951.

Issues of legality. Because government agencies function under law and are controlled through forms of law imposed by the courts, legal considerations are an important factor in administrative policy-making. Many agencies have a continuing problem, however, in clarifying for themselves the proper role of legal advice. The term "administrative law" may be said to include the legal rules controlling administration, the written letter of the polices developed for or by administration, and the procedural forms through which administrative acts secure legal effect. One or the other of these highly important aspects of the administrative process has upon occasion been used to justify the notion that legal considerations —that is, those proposed by lawyers—should dominate in the determination of substantive policy and likewise in the entire process of administrative investigation and review.[8]

To require legal consultation may not appear to be an onerous obligation. However, when it is construed by either the operators in the line of command or the lawyers, or by both, as a division of administrative responsibility, a truly perplexing situation arises. Similarly, at higher policy levels operating executives tend to resent the views of the chief legal counsel on policy proposals unless these center on questions of authority; adequacy of analysis of the legal issues; accuracy of the facts upon which the proposed determination is based; and propriety of the form and procedure in which action is to be taken.

Of these four categories, questions of authority are perhaps the least numerous, though the most irritating. In administration, the most sought-after advice relates to the questions: "What should be done?" and "How can this be done?" It is a great temptation for the lawyer, particularly if he is able and aggressive, to overextend his sphere in initiating policy on administrative matters. In most situations he will contribute to internal administrative unity and improved public relations if he raises his policy ideas and legal questions reasonably close to the final point of determination. In so doing, he will make his influence less questionable and secure more respect for the considerations that fall into his primary responsibility for litigation before the courts and for proper deference to the citizen's procedural interests.

Dynamics of administrative policy-making. All of these factors are dependent upon one another. In more than one way they are involved in most policy determinations, with their importance varying from problem to problem. Giving each factor its proper weight is the function of administrative judgment. Policy decision in administration is not an isolated act of top officials; it is not a legalistic interpretation of an hypothetical legislative intent; nor is it the exercise of unfettered power to steer a course according to the administrator's political preferences or social prejudices.

---

[8] *Cf.* in general Morstein Marx, Fritz, "The Lawyer's Role in Public Administration," *Yale Law Journal*, 1946, Vol. 55, p. 498 *ff.*

Rather, it is the result of an interplay of many forces and many brains, brought to a focus by the coordinating direction from the administrator and his closest aides. His is the responsibility for reconciling political and legal factors with the factual analyses and technical recommendations of his staff.

The dynamics of administrative policy-making are therefore not readily captured in any simple pattern of thought.[9] The least realistic view is that of administrative policy emerging straight from the administrator's autonomous decision. The gifted executive, it is true, will be able to sense the need for policy shifts as well as the weaknesses in existing policy through his grasp of the work of his organization. Even then, however, he will combat any tendency on his part to come forth spontaneously with specific remedies. Instead, he will be guided by personal "hunch" to probe into the matter with his immediate associates, and on this basis determine specific assignments of study and analysis by appropriate staff units or line officials. Their preliminary work in turn will furnish the basis upon which the particular problem can be discussed a second time with better insight on the top level.

Field office initiative. Far more often are policy proposals initiated, not by the administrator himself, but by those much further down the line, who see the issues in concrete terms in the course of their day-by-day activities. A field office chief, for instance, may grow aware of the inadequacy of a given policy. He may have informal ways of checking his own reactions with those of other field officers in his region. He is also in a position to take into account public attitudes in his area expressed to him in various ways, including occasional lunches with local spokesmen of his agency's clientele and other more broadly interested groups. Through his reporting relationships with the regional director, he has an opportunity for enlisting the latter's interest. Again, a broadening of relevant considerations is apt to occur when the emerging proposal and the substantiating facts are mulled over in the regional office, or perhaps are placed on the agenda of some periodic meeting of all field officers held by the regional head. As the matter moves up the line, it is likely to reach the departmental level in the context of an individual bureau, responsible for defined aspects of the agency's program. Ordinarily, the bureau chief will first assure himself of the thoughts of his own key people. Only thereafter will he draw other bureaus or staff units into consultation.[10]

Perhaps the bureau chief will have sufficient standing before the legis-

[9] Compare the strongly empirical case-study approach of the Inter-University Case Program, reflected in Stein, Harold, ed., *Public Administration and Policy Development*, New York: Harcourt, Brace, 1952, with the highly conceptualized frame of reference of Snyder, Richard C., "A Decision-Making Approach to the Study of Political Phenomena," in Young, Roland, ed., *Approaches to the Study of Politics*, p. 3 ff., Evanston: Northwestern University Press, 1958.

[10] *Cf.* Chapter 12, "Field Organization."

lature to take the initiative in sounding out some of the more important figures on the legislative committee that is primarily concerned with the agency's activities. He may thus be able to ascertain in advance the drift of legislative attitude. He may also seek the views of interest-group head-quarters, either through formal consultation or in off-the-record conversations. In all of these stages there occurs an enlargement of knowledge and a sounder appreciation of the realities surrounding the policy proposal. Such realities may well include gradually sharpening disagreements among different interest groups, among different bureaus, among different legislators, and among different staff officers.

Administrative gains to be secured by action on the proposal would have to be balanced carefully against the potentialities for internal and external conflict. In many instances, no doubt, the proposal is shelved before it goes any further. In other instances, the sponsoring bureau chief will grow convinced that a fuller examination of the facts and of possible alternatives to the proposal is required. Such examination may involve more extensive exploration by a particular staff unit in the agency, perhaps in cooperation with expert staffs in other agencies and on the level of the chief executive, or with private groups having research facilities or other resources of their own. In still other cases, the matter will become the subject of an opinion of the legal counsel of the agency—negative or positive; and if the latter, with or without significant qualifications.

Top consideration. All of this is merely the preliminary stage of preparing the ground for action on the administrator's level. When and if the matter comes up before him, it will usually be clear whether legislative changes must be sought or whether the issue can be disposed of through order of the chief executive or by the agency itself under its statutory authorization. The administrator must assure himself of the comprehensiveness of vision that should support the proposal. His immediate staff aides will help him to determine whether the recommendation makes due allowance for an agencywide or even governmentwide point of view, or whether it tends to overplay the institutional interest of one particular bureau or one particular function entrusted to the agency. He may decide to yield in this individual instance to what he must recognize to be an act of bureau self-promotion—simply because he is aware of the political strength of the sponsoring bureau in terms of its outside support. In any event he will have to alert his public-relations staff for the impending action.

Then, before he takes action, he may want to bring together once more the leaders of interest groups, perhaps in order to achieve a more satisfactory compromise among them or to win additional support through measured concessions to opposing interests. If he does, he may on occasion find it desirable to drop the proposal because of growing fear of public controversy. Conversely, it is also conceivable that the administrator will veto the proposal, notwithstanding a climate of wider support, for reasons of personal conviction or personal working relationships with individual legislators, other agency heads, or important interest groups. Furthermore, his thinking will be affected by his own anticipation of the reaction or the needs of the chief executive.

If the policy proposal requires for enactment an order of the chief executive, the administrator must give thought to the kinds of resistance or opposition he may run into when the drafted order enters the process of top-level clearance. In the face of a serious chance of conflict on this level, he would have to raise the question of whether he should first discuss the matter with the chief executive or present it in a cabinet meeting. Here again, reconciliation and adjustment will have to be worked out; and the ultimate product of the long chain of transactions may look quite different from anything the field office chief had in mind when he made himself the snowball that set off the avalanche.

This much is clear, however. Administrative policy-making is ordinarily not reduced to any single action either of a homogeneous bureaucracy or of the responsible administrator. It is more in the nature of a gradually developing conglomeration of agreements among a large variety of groups— agreements sufficiently widespread and substantial to outweigh remaining unresolved conflicts. It is a process that necessarily in most instances moves slowly, but proportionately moves more surely. It is also one that operates at a relatively high rate of mortality of policy proposals. With all that, it is no less an approximation of consensus than is the legislative process, and it is subject to the same irritations and handicaps.

Chapter 17 •

Government by Procedure

1. The Nature of Procedure: Functions and Limitations

Meaning of procedure. As this is written, the college is in the turmoil of autumn registration. One *expects* turmoil during registration period. Normal routines are disturbed: there is much waiting in line, puzzling over formidable prose in catalogs and instruction sheets, filling out baffling forms of varied color and shape, seeking proper signatures, searching for strange buildings and new classrooms. There is inevitably some feeling that time is being wasted and energy squandered, a certain amount of indecision and frustration, and even strong emotion. Gradually the turmoil subsides and new routines are established; professors and students "get used to" each other and the new situation. Yet some decisions made during the registration period will prove to have been incorrect or ill-advised. And some of the decisions made will prove to have determined in an important way, for good or ill, the future life-pattern of the student— or for that matter, of the professor.

In the experience of registration week will be found, upon reflection, an example of most of the matters discussed in this chapter. What is being discussed, in short, is not necessarily something in a remote and unknown government office, but something that is to some degree the common experience of all who live in a modern society. All of us need sensitivity to the procedural side of human organization. But before proceeding to definitions and general analysis, it may be useful to think a bit about the experience of registration. There is, first of all, an established pattern, that of the preceding period. People then "knew what to do." There was familiarity with schedules, places, pieces of paper, faces, and individual behaviors. The end of the term and the registration period are from one point of view "revolutionary": the aim is to destroy one pattern and to establish another. However, there is an underlying continuity also. Not *all* patterns change by any means, and there is an important continuity of objectives: "higher education" is pursued through trigonometry, say, instead of Spanish.

Someone must give some thought to how best to achieve "revolution" and continuity simultaneously. If the planning has been intelligent and knowledgeable, the registration period will proceed with a relatively small loss of time and energy, with minimum frustration and anger, and with a maximum of decisions that will benefit the students, the faculty, the college, and society. Procedure pertains to the customary or routine aspects of organizational activity, but also to the means by which these are changed—in short, to procedures to change procedures.

Let us now try a definition: *Administrative procedure is the prescribed or customary way of working together in the conduct of the affairs of an organization.* Attention is called to three important features. The first is the repetition of business in a prescribed or customary manner. The second is the coordination of the various activities into a larger pattern. The third is given by the existence of goals or purposes: the functions and limitations of procedures are to be considered always with one eye upon achievement of goals.

Role of procedure. The psychologist William James once referred to habit as "the great flywheel of society." Analogously, procedure may be thought of, first of all, as the flywheel of organization and administration. We should think of procedure as the routine relationships and activities—between one individual and another; between one organizational unit and another; between one process and another; between one skill or technique and another; between one function and another; between one place and another; between the organization and the public; and between all combinations and permutations of these. It is by means of procedure that the day-to-day work of government is done—mail sorted, routed, and delivered; deeds recorded; accounts audited; licenses issued; cases prosecuted; protests heard; food inspected; budgets reviewed; tax returns verified; data collected; supplies purchased; property assessed; inquiries answered; orders issued; investigations made; and so forth endlessly.

Procedure, properly applied, allows specialization to be carried to its optimum degree and effects the most efficient division of labor. Procedure not only divides labor; it also divides—and fixes—responsibility. Procedure is a means of maintaining order and of achieving regularity, continuity, predictability, control, and accountability. It is a means of maximizing control of an organization's members, of assuring that their official actions contribute—and, possibly, that their private aims conform—to the organization's objectives.

Procedure is not a unique feature of *public* administration. Many procedures are equally usable by private administration or public administration. Private as well as public "red tape" can be time-consuming and annoying to those affected, as anyone can testify who has tried to exchange a purchase without a sales slip or to cash a check without "proper identification."[1]

---

[1] For an interesting and amusing comparison of public and private "red tape," see Appleby, Paul H., *Big Democracy,* ch. 6, New York: Knopf, 1945.

Procedures as laws of activity. From one point of view, an organization's procedures may be regarded as a body of "law" applying primarily to its members, but also in varying degree and manner—depending upon the organization's authority and activities—to persons outside. More than analogy is involved. To the extent that procedures are prescribed by constitution, statute, and court decision, they are law in the full legal sense, enforceable as such. Most procedures, however, are only modes of conduct devised by the organization to regulate the working relations of its members. While these modes of conduct must be consonant with law, and while in the case of public agencies their ultimate purpose may be to give effect to law, they are not generally law in the technical sense. The sanctions for their enforcement are primarily administrative.

As with law, procedure may be either written or unwritten. Large and well-developed agencies have specialized organizational units for analyzing and changing procedure; these put forth a large volume of written procedural instructions. Small and rudimentary organizations may rely heavily upon unwritten custom. In any organization, large or small, custom and current conceptions of administrative right and wrong are very important. Some written procedures, as some laws and ordinances, are honored chiefly in the breach, though they have been prepared in the proper manner and duly signed by the highest authority. They may be so poorly written that they are not read or understood; or so unrealistic that they are not taken seriously; or they may be contrary to prevailing notions of administrative morality and incapable of enforcement. Conversely, some procedures may become well developed by custom and be followed religiously without being committed to paper—either because it is not necessary or because to do so would not be politic. "Standard operating procedure" is not necessarily set forth in a manual.

Again as with law, procedure is laid down at various levels. An organization may prescribe procedures applying to itself as a whole or to any or most of its component parts. Component parts generally may adopt any procedures that are reasonable and not in conflict with law or with procedures set forth by a superior organization unit. The structure of procedures in a large organization thus resembles a child's set of nested blocks. Accordingly, the "man at the bottom" operates under several, perhaps many, layers of procedure. Lest this be regarded as cruel, let it be said that unless he is an oversensitive individual, he is likely to become accustomed to his burden, and even to cherish it as something peculiarly his own.

Procedure as physiology of organization. From another point of view, procedure may be looked upon as the "physiology" of organization. As such it is not separable—except in concept—from considerations of formal organizational structure. Anatomy and physiology are but different aspects of the same thing: structure is meaningless without functions, and function is impossible without structure. Organizational structures are definable in terms of procedures—"shall be the function of," "shall report to," "are responsible for." And in turn, procedures are geared to organizational structure—"upon receipt from the Administrative Division," "shall forward to the appropriate district office," and so forth.

Organizations are structures of relationships between skills. Procedure brings the structures to life. For highly developed professional or scientific skills, procedure performs the function of uniting them with an organization and its purposes. It does not, however, substantially affect or reach into the skills or techniques of professional and scientific personnel. The preparation of a legal argument, the treatment of a plant disease, or the analysis of food for mineral traces are governed for the most part by rules outside the realm of administration. In descending the scale of specialized skills, however, this tends to be less and less true. Eventually a point is reached at which "administrative" procedure merges with whatever specialized function the individual may perform. Such operations as sorting, packaging, and loading are subject in their entirety to well-developed techniques of procedure analysis and improvement.

Procedure as institutional habit. In still another aspect, the procedures of an organization may be viewed as its "habits." Habits are the repetitive acts that in large measure express and affect the personality and character of an individual. Procedures are the repetitive acts that in large measure manifest and shape the personality and character of an organization. Both habits and procedures routinize and stabilize day-to-day existence, contribute to the achievement of immediate goals, and release energies to deal with what is novel or "higher."

As it has its characteristic merits, habit has its characteristic disadvantages, and it is here that the chief limitations of procedure emerge. For not only are procedures analogous to habits; beyond that, to an individual participant a procedure becomes largely a habit or series of habits, physiologically no different from habits developed in private life. Thus a clerk whose role in a procedure is to sort and route certain documents develops patterns of mental and muscular coordination that become second nature.

The disadvantages of habit lie in its propensity to engross the whole individual. The repetitive acts yield psychological and physiological satisfactions, and the habits become ends in themselves and substitutes for thought instead of aids to thought. A "cake of custom" develops and hardens, hindering adaptation to changed circumstances. It is a common experience to encounter a human being or an organization that is now an animated antique because habits or procedures were allowed to become ends in themselves instead of means to ends.

2. Procedures and Public Administration

Rule of law. Although procedure has generic qualities that do not differ whether the organization is public or private, the objectives of public administration and the conditions under which it is carried on create special procedural functions and problems. American public administration aims at the accomplishment of broad, diverse, and often intangible objectives, while working within the framework of one of the most complex legal systems of any modern state. It does this over great spaces—working with a large and heterogeneous population, and in interrelation with an economic system of unparal'eled intricacy.

The broad, diverse, and often intangible objectives of public administration are in large degree set forth in the statutes creating and instructing particular agencies. However, in pursuing the objectives laid down in its basic statute, an agency is motivated and guided not only by the statute itself. As a governmental entity, its actions are conditioned by many other legal provisions which in one way or another apply to it. These provisions are many because the constitutional-legal system of American public administration is of great complexity.

The fundamental significance of our complex legal system for actions that affect the public lies primarily in the idea of the "rule of law"— the idea that governmental actions may not be arbitrary but must proceed from and be consonant with law. This general idea has been imbedded in the traditions of Western civilization for many centuries and is by no means a unique possession of America. However, a number of factors have combined here to give it an elaborate institutional embodiment—so elaborate that, paradoxically, sometimes the ends of justice may seem obstructed by it. The relationship of public administration to the rule of law is the subject of many volumes. It is not the present subject of discussion.[2] Here, it is sufficient to note some of the chief features in the pattern of conformity required of public administration, and the role of procedure in achieving that pattern.

Every administrative act—national, state, or local—must conform to the Constitution of the United States as interpreted by the courts, ultimately the Supreme Court. State and local administrative acts must, in addition, accord with the constitution of the state and the organic law of the community concerned. Not only must administrative acts be in harmony with constitutional provisions; they must also be in accord with the laws that have been enacted under the constitution concerned.

Safeguarding liberty and equality. The Constitution of the United States and those of the various states, and many of the federal and state laws, contain provisions designed to safeguard citizens from unjust and arbitrary actions—that is, to assure the "rule of law" in its moral content, in its substance. What is the moral content, the substantive meaning, of the rule of law? A brief answer may be made: liberty and equality. As to liberty, federal and state constitutions and laws are studded with provisions seeking to guarantee that certain impositions shall not be made upon individuals by

[2] See Chapter 23, "The Judicial Test."

governmental action, or that, if they do happen, they shall happen only in a certain prescribed manner, by "due process of law." Examples are the provisions guaranteeing freedom of expression, or the rules of court procedure designed to safeguard the rights of those accused of crimes. As to equality, constitutions and laws are likewise replete with provisions seeking to make sure that all persons shall be treated equally by government; or that if classifications are established these shall be reasonable, with treatment equal within classes. Thus there are provisions securing for everyone "equal protection of the laws."

The ways in which procedure serves to ensure that the requirements of the "rule of law" are met are manifold. Probably most prominent are consultation and review in their various forms. Consultation—intra-agency, interagency, and extragovernmental—in proper procedural form goes far to make certain that regulations and decisions are both legal and proper. Procedures for administrative review of protested actions have been improved; this helps to lessen appeals to the courts. Procedures for internal review of correspondence, orders, and other official documents often take an undue toll of time and temper of personnel. Yet, adequately safeguarded by limitations on types of review and on time for review, "clearance" performs an invaluable function in contributing to administrative legality and propriety.

Legislative prescription of procedure. In seeking to assure that administrative procedures are consonant with and adapted to serve the ends of constitutional government, American legislative bodies often prescribe procedures in great detail, rather than leave the matter to the discretion of administrators. Legislation may, for example, direct that an agency issue orders only after consulting with the affected individual or group, or provide a review for certain types of contested decisions. Of necessity, however, such procedural instructions are set forth in phraseology less subtle than the facts that confront the agency. There is inevitably a large area in which the agency is "on its own" in devising procedures for achieving its particular objectives.

In the case of regulatory agencies, the creation of procedures is of special significance because the procedures followed affect the "substance" of law in spelling out the rights and duties of individuals. Often, in fact, it is only through procedures that the intent of the basic statute with respect to particular conditions is manifested. In the statutes governing regulatory agencies, even when carefully drawn, we find rather broad criteria of action, such as "public convenience and necessity," "fair and equitable," or "unfair methods of competition." Criteria like these are translated by administrative determination into specific substantive rules or decisions—that is to say, rules or decisions to the effect that certain categories of persons or enterprises may or must take or refrain from specified actions.

In translating the general criterion into the particular rule or decision, procedures must be carefully devised to ensure reasonableness, fairness, and consistency. Or, from another point of view, they must ensure that all rules and decisions are within the intent of the legislature and will be upheld if challenged in the courts. The "meaning" of a regulatory statute as it is applied depends upon procedural rules relating to the collection of data or evidence, review of proposed regulations, appeals from decisions, and so forth. In a society in which rules are regarded as important, "substantive" issues are often masked as "procedural" issues, and argued and decided in such terms.

In addition to laying down procedures designed to maintain the "rule of law," legislative bodies often prescribe such procedures for somewhat different purposes. Conceiving their role as that of a "board of directors" for the public's business, they attempt to control the management of that business by defining the manner in which it shall be carried on, particularly in matters relating to personnel and expenditure of funds. In part this may be ascribed to the fact that under the American constitutional system, legislative bodies try to compensate for their very limited ability to choose or remove a chief executive. They are therefore prone to supervise executive actions in as great detail as possible. In part, also, it may be ascribed to the special honesty, publicity, and propriety expected in the conduct of public business. As a nation, Americans have a double standard of administrative virtue, one for private organizations and one for public. As a result, legislators—and sometimes administrators—in a well-meant attempt to "keep out of trouble" tend to create substantive vices by excesses of procedural virtue.

Protecting administrative morality. Dishonesty in public places is news. Since through magnification in the press even the merest peccadillos may come to influence policy (and even perhaps political or organizational survival), public financial and personnel procedures are hedged about by a great mass of stipulations designed to attain, not speed and efficiency in the public's business, but honesty to the letter and accuracy to the cent.[3] The same is true of procurement of supplies, which is potentially and sometimes actually subject to serious abuse. To prevent dishonesty, elaborate safeguards have been erected. Thus governmental agencies may be induced to regard purchasing of supplies as a routine clerical operation that can be performed by anyone who has mastered the many relevant laws, regulations, and forms, rather than a business calling for skill in the economics of supply.

The criteria of success in this case are apt to relate more to the correctness of the paperwork or the absence of "exceptions" taken by the supervisory authority, and less to cost and quality. Of course, honesty is important. It is a prime question, however, whether there is not a basic deficiency in laws and rules that fail to encourage an efficient stewardship

---

[3] A lively discussion of limitations of this type will be found in Juran, J. M., *Bureaucracy: A Challenge to Better Management*, ch. 5, New York: Harper, 1944.

of the public interest, but on the contrary lend an aura of respectability to limited vision and dullness.

Aims of procedure. Clearly, the public character of public administration generates special problems in the creation and revision of procedures. At the bare minimum, administrative procedures must be above a legitimate charge of unconstitutionality or illegality. If they are good procedures, they will do much more. They will aim to conform to the spirit as well as the letter of our basic guarantees of freedom and equality. They will seek, under unusually difficult circumstances, to reconcile honesty with speed and efficiency. They will go beyond the requirements of law in providing for prompt and courteous treatment of the citizen.

The public official is like the preacher's wife in that higher than usual standards of morality, propriety, and courtesy are deemed to apply to both. In an economic sense, there may be no distinction between the sources of public and private salaries, but the Taxpayers League will never believe it.

3. Types of Administrative Procedures

Classes of procedures. A Linnaeus who will analyze and classify the flora of the procedural realm has yet to appear. For some reason, formal analysis in this realm has lagged behind that in the realm of organization. Perhaps this indicates only that no constructive purpose would be served by classification. Perhaps it indicates lack of courage and industry, for procedural issuances exhibit a forbidding tropical exuberance and diversity.

Administrative procedures can obviously be classified upon a purely formal basis in several ways—for instance, whether written or unwritten, whether issued centrally or by field offices, and so on. However, the formal classification that seems most significant, in terms of the sources and uses of administrative procedures, is one that distinguishes between procedures designed to keep the organization operating as an organization, and those designed to accomplish the particular objectives of the organization. The former are internal and purely "institutional." They are not issued to the public. The latter, being concerned with the specific job of the organization, vary greatly. They are of two main types: those affecting a public and issued publicly, and those issued and applying internally only.

Institutional procedures. Institutional administrative procedures in our sense are those pertaining to a staff, housekeeping, service, or auxiliary function. As noted earlier, such procedures for public agencies are in a large—and even undesirably large—measure prescribed by statute, though in practice the procedures of various agencies operating under the same statutory prescriptions may vary considerably. Some of the institutional procedures of each agency are also likely to emanate from a central unit operating upon a governmentwide basis—in the federal government the Civil Service Commission, the Bureau of the Budget, the Treasury, or the

General Accounting Office. Among the matters usually covered by institutional procedures are: mail and communications; meetings and conferences; travel; internal reporting; preparation, issuance, and distribution of documents; space; library service; files and records; clerical services; procurement; clearance and review; budgetary and fiscal administration; and personnel administration in all its aspects—recruitment, classification, leave and attendance, compensation and promotions, and so forth.[4]

The range and complexity of these procedures may well be illustrated by the travel regulations. In the federal government, the travel regulations prescribed for all agencies run to many thousands of words. They deal in great detail with such matters as receiving authority to travel; permissible accommodations; special conveyances; use of telephone and telegraph; calculation of per diem allowance; and use of various forms, a minimum of three in any case—travel authorization form, travel request form, expense voucher form.

Working procedures. Procedures designed to accomplish an agency's particular objectives are divisible into those publicly and those not publicly issued. Procedures that are issued publicly constitute a set of "ground rules" for the agency and any individual affected by the basic statute. They represent the agency's sense of the procedural requirements of the law, perhaps after judicial test, and also its conception of what is customary, fair, and expedient where the law is not explicit. In general, publicly issued procedural materials indicate the manner in which agencies will reach and apply substantive decisions; set forth the part the affected persons may take or are required to take in connection with substantive determinations; and stipulate the remedies and appeals, short of the courts, available to affected persons. Requirements of this kind in federal administration are governed, for the most part, by the Administrative Procedure Act of 1946. Specifically, such procedural issuances deal with consultations and conferences with interest groups; adversary proceedings; investigations; examinations; petitions; reports and records as a basis for findings; hearings; official notice; written evidence; oral argument; briefs and pleadings; depositions; subpoenas; and administrative review. They often contain forms to be filled out and utilized. Ideally, they should tell all persons affected "what, where, when, and how" in simple language. For the federal government, issuances of this kind are promulgated in the *Federal Register*.

Mention of "substantive" decisions or determinations requires a word of explanation. Many of the regulations, orders, and decisions issued by public agencies are primarily substantive rather than procedural. That is to say, they purport to state the intent or substance of the law, as applied to a given set of facts. Such are decisions of public utility commissions or "cease and desist" orders issued by the Federal Trade Commission. Often the dividing

---

[4] See Chapter 24, "Personnel Standards."

line between substantive and procedural issuances is not at all distinct. In some, procedural and substantive provisions are actually commingled. Thus Treasury regulations under a particular tax law may contain, without formal distinction between them, procedural instructions and substantive provisions supplementing specific sections of the law.[5]

When publicly issued procedures are in the nature of "ground rules," they give the key to the most important category of internally issued procedures designed to achieve an agency's objectives. For each important procedural issuance affecting persons outside an organization, there is likely to be issued another procedural document to persons within the organization, explaining in greater detail the part that they must play in the total operation. For example, if a statement or affidavit is required of an individual affected by the enforcement of the law, it is necessary to specify the manner of handling this document within the organization—the officers or organization units responsible, time limitations for each decision or process, criteria to be applied, and methods of disposition.

The publicly issued procedural regulation and its internal counterpart may be illustrated by considering the industry advisory committees established by some agencies. The publicly issued regulation will deal with such matters as general functions and powers of the committees; eligibility for membership and appointment of members; committee officers and finances; meetings and recommendations. The internal regulation will cover such matters as purpose of committees; when to establish committees; selection of committee members; securing official approval of committees; invitations and declinations; public announcements; resignations and removals; alternates; and so forth.

Diversity of procedures. Internally issued procedures designed to achieve an agency's objectives exhibit great diversity. For each agency they are distinctive because the agency itself is distinctive—in its organizational structure, its purposes, its location, its legal and administrative tools, its size, its clientele, its techniques, or its personnel. Procedure, as the structure of working relations between all the components of an organization, must vary with the individuality of the organization.

As diversity is the distinguishing feature of this category of administrative procedure, it is better to illustrate its manifold nature than to attempt classification. Let us consider, then, the differences between the procedures of two federal units—the Institute of Home Economics and the Bureau of Old-Age and Survivors Insurance.

Two illustrations. The former is a comparatively small constituent unit of the large Agricultural Research Service, which in turn is a constituent unit of the Department of Agriculture. The work of the Institute is carried

---

[5] It should be noted that "administrative procedure" is sometimes given a much narrower meaning, as referring only to the procedures of regulatory agencies in applying their statutes to affected persons.

on from Washington through three Divisions, namely, Clothing and Housing, Household Economics, and Human Nutrition. As suggested by the titles, the Institute provides a program of research and education with respect to household management, broadly speaking. In its research work, the Institute has relationships with other constituents of the Agricultural Research Service, with other constituents of the Department of Agriculture such as the Agricultural Marketing Service, and with other federal agencies such as the Bureau of Labor Statistics, and the Public Health Service. In its educational program it has relationships with the Extension Service of the Department of Agriculture and, to a lesser extent, with other federal agencies such as the Office of Education. In short, the Institute is small in size, concentrated in space, simple in organization, and limited in function. Its "institutional" procedures are for the most part specified for it by the several organizational layers above it; and its "working" procedures concern such matters as initiation and approval of projects; relationships among its three functional divisions; presentation, review, and publication of research findings; and relationships with the various agencies with which it cooperates on research or education.

The Bureau of Old-Age and Survivors Insurance is a constituent unit of the Social Security Administration, which in turn is a constituent unit of the Department of Health, Education, and Welfare. The Bureau administers a body of law establishing a national system of old-age, survivors', and disability insurance, and in so doing has important relationships concerning taxes and finance with the Treasury Department, and very complex relationships with state agencies dealing with social insurance. The Bureau is responsible for administering its more than 75,000,000 accounts, maintaining records of earnings, determining survivor rights, and so forth. This is an "operating" program, reaching into every corner of the country, and reaching nearly half of the total population. To perform its functions, the Bureau maintains not only six area offices, but over 560 district offices. In addition, there are large establishments for the maintenance of records on the millions of clients. In short, the Bureau has functions that are fairly narrow in range but of great depth and complexity; it has very broad geographical range; and it has a large number of officers and employees.

The typical procedures of this Bureau concern such matters as the assigning of account numbers; investigating and developing accurate wage data when such information has been incompletely or incorrectly reported by employers; verifying and posting wage reports; accepting and adjudicating claims; making insurance payments; and so forth. The performance of these operations upon so vast a scale necessitates procedures that are not only elaborate but also meticulous in the extreme, making use of the most advanced office equipment and recording and sorting devices.

If nothing else, our discussion of types of administrative procedures will have conveyed the impression that the species of procedure are not distinct and neatly labeled.[6] Perhaps this conclusion need not cause concern, inasmuch as the science of biology is itself without an unexceptionable concept of species!

4. Creation and Criteria

Procedure-making compared with policy-making. In the broad view, administrative procedures are conceived and developed in a manner similar to that of administrative policies.[7] This is natural, because the two are intimately related. Procedures should exist only to give effect (directly or indirectly) to policies; and a wise policy decision cannot be made without thorough consideration of the procedural implications of alternatives. As in the case of policy decisions, the top executive, the operating officials, staff personnel, legislative bodies, lawyers and courts, and outside interest groups all affect the formulation of an agency's procedures.

Compared with the formulation of administrative policy, however, there are significant differences in the roles played by the various participants. The top executive's role is proportionately less. His energies will be largely absorbed in activities related to the formulation of the agency's policies. Unless the procedure affects all or a substantial element of the organization, or has important policy or public-relations aspects, no extensive part is likely to be played by the executive head, except when formal clearance discloses disagreements. Similarly with line or operating officials generally. Their day-by-day business will account for most of their time and thought, and few of them will venture forth into the technicalities of improved procedures—however much they may be irritated by the inadequacies of present procedures. Yet, seldom will a procedural change be made without consultation with or even the cooperation and consent of the operating officials whose work the change affects. The question whether and in what cases they should be allowed to interpose vetoes to procedural changes is a fertile source of internal conflict. Operating officials often do veto procedural changes, by virtue of higher authority or by *sub rosa* methods. In any organization there is covert or perhaps open competition for position or influence, and victory and defeat in this competition are often manifested in procedural change—or lack of change.

As with the top executive and line officials, so with the legislature and interest groups—they claim a smaller share in the formation of procedures than they do in the formation of policies. Legislatures, as we saw, prescribe

---

6 The nomenclature of printed procedural materials is often inconsistent and confusing. Procedural materials are usually issued in serial form, in which case they are known as "regulations" or "orders"; or in code form, in which case items are designated by volume, part, chapter, and so on. There is no general distinction between categories, such as "regulations," "rules," or "orders." Each agency or jurisdiction uses the terms in accordance with its history and tastes, distinguishing between various types of regulations or orders by adjectives—for instance, different series of regulations may be designated as "administrative," "general," "divisional," and so on.

7 See Chapter 16, "The Formulation of Administrative Policy."

a considerable volume of managerial and housekeeping procedure. Some of the individual agency's main procedures, too, are likely to be laid down by statute—for instance, that a review division shall handle certain types of cases, or that outside interests shall be consulted upon an organized basis; but there is a great bulk of procedural detail to be filled in. Interest groups impinge upon the procedure-making process at several points. They may be consulted formally on proposed procedure or its revision; or they may exercise some informal influence, by virtue of personal relations between their members and agency officers or procedure-making personnel. Interest groups make their concern with procedure felt most effectively, however, when they can prevail upon the legislative body to change an agency's procedures—perhaps over the agency's objections.

The place occupied by the lawyer in procedure-making is of great importance, particularly in regulatory agencies. Also, his role is often in dispute. In the opinion of most students of public administration, it should be advisory only, similar to his role in policy development, even in the preparation of procedural materials that affect the rights and duties of individuals. Not legal learning alone, but knowledge of the facts and simplicity of phrase are of the essence. Certainly, however, the lawyer has a legitimate advisory function in laying out procedures that must meet the test of "due process of law."

Procedure-making units. So much for the broad picture, but what of procedure-making organs, the problems they face, the methods and criteria they use? Of necessity, the answers to these questions must touch upon many important subjects.

Procedure-making organs are of various kinds; and they exist under a wide variety of designations, depending upon the organization and customs of the agency of which they are a part. Generally speaking, procedure-making organs are attached in a staff capacity to the top executive or a subordinate line official, integrated with a budget office or an administrative management division, or associated with or located in a planning organ. A procedure-making organ may operate on a government-wide basis in its administrative jurisdiction. Thus the Civil Service Commission and the Bureau of the Budget, as indicated above, perform some procedure-making functions for federal administration generally.

In addition to special procedure-making units operating at different organizational levels of authority, there is frequently, particularly in large organizations, specialization in types of procedural work. Usually the unit dealing with institutional procedures is separate from that dealing with the agency's substantive procedures. Units for work simplification or standardization of procedures in such fields as personnel may be separate from either. Wherever they are located and whatever their functions, it is important that the procedure-making organs have authority equal to their tasks—and not only formal authority, but that firmer authority which stems from the interest and support of top management and from adequate professional skill. These last are two of the three most significant ingredients of good procedural work; the third is the interest and cooperation of the working force, particularly the line executives.

Two emphases run through procedural work. One is upon creating wholly new procedures, the other upon improving existing procedures. In either case, a "new" procedure must be tested and installed.

Art of making procedures. He who creates new procedures must first of all apply himself diligently to six questions: What? Why? Who? How? When? Where? Incisiveness and imagination are necessary. What does the statute say? Where the statute is not clear, what is the best interpretation? What procedural clues are offered by similar organizations doing similar tasks? Can the job be done effectively with the present organization or should change be recommended? If a particular method appears efficient, can it be reconciled with statutory requirements? Is the job one that can be done best by using ten skilled or fifteen unskilled employees? Such are some of the questions for which answers must be found.

Intimate knowledge of the facts is essential, but hardly less important is "writing up" the procedure. For this, some of the art of the playwright is necessary, for good written procedures are rather like the script of a good play. The "characters" must be introduced and identified; they should have an organic role in the production. Entrances and exits must be planned with purpose, stage directions must be given, and so forth. Procedural materials should be brief, clear, and concise. All the tricks in the writing and printing trades should be employed, for to learn their lines quickly the players must be induced to read them. Unfortunately, procedural manuals are frequently as dry and forbidding as the Sahara.[8]

Procedures must be installed. Even the best-written materials do not suffice of themselves. Educational campaigns must be undertaken, incentives offered, sanctions devised, methods for apprehending violators worked out, test runs made to discover "bugs," and followup inspections planned. All possible devices for breaking old habits and creating new ones must be used.[9]

The job of probing and bettering procedures is in part the same as that of creating procedures, in part different. It involves preliminary fact-

---

[8] On the subject of writing clearly and effectively, with special reference to "official English," see: Gowers, Ernest A., *The Complete Plain Words*, London: H. M. Stationery Office, 1954 (a combination of two earlier publications, "Plain Words" and "The ABC of Plain Words"); and Flesch, Rudolf F., *The Art of Readable Writing*, New York: Harper, 1949. Much pertaining to procedural change will also be found in Redfield, Charles E., *Communication in Management: The Theory and Practice of Administrative Communication*, Chicago: University of Chicago Press, 2nd ed., 1958.

[9] See Lippitt, Ronald, Watson, Jeanne, and Westley, Bruce, *The Dynamics of Planned Change*, New York: Harcourt, Brace, 1958. This discusses "planned change" generally, from a social-psychological perspective. It is an excellent work on the theory involved in change, and its bibliographies open routes to further exploration.

finding and planning; analysis of existing procedure; development of the proposed new procedure; and testing, installing, and following up the changed procedure. Determination must be made, first of all, of areas likely to be productive of results. Such phenomena as mushroom growth of activities, inexperienced personnel, or consolidation of units within an organization indicate areas most likely to need analysis and change. Next comes reconnaissance into the existing situation, followed by "softening up," by whatever strategems and demonstrations of shortcomings that can be employed. Then corrective action may be initiated.

Work simplification and procedural standardization. There are two well-recognized types of programs in the field of procedure improvement. One is work simplification, which has as its chief tools the work distribution chart, the process chart, and the workload chart. The work distribution chart is prepared from an inventory of the work of each member of an organization unit or participant in a particular procedure. It shows in tabular form the activities of all employees and the time they spend on their work. The process chart or flow chart traces step-by-step "what happens" for a given procedure—what is done, who does it, time consumed, and space and time between each step. The workload chart or work count aims to answer the question of "how much." What is counted and the method of counting depend upon what is being studied. The uses of these charts lie in dividing, relating, and scheduling work; finding bottlenecks; stimulating competitive interests in performance; assessing personnel needs; and appraising the value of particular processes. Using these three tools of analysis and sometimes others, work simplification programs perform the function of modernizing and streamlining procedures.

Procedure standardization differs from work simplification chiefly in emphasis, though it may make use of the same tools. It seeks to discover and install the one most economical and efficient procedure for doing common or interrelated work of certain kinds. In order to merit a standardization study, an operation must be fairly basic; it must cut across much or all of the organization, and it must involve a reasonably large number of participants. The values of procedure standardization lie in such matters as clarifying policy intent; publicizing and generalizing all useful information that was formerly the possession of a few employees; standardizing costs and man-hour requirements; and training new personnel by the use of procedural manuals.

Problems of procedure-making. The central problem in procedure-making of any kind is how to combine experience in procedure *per se* with knowledge about and an adequate "feeling" for the operations that particular procedures govern. To hard-working operating officials, the "procedural analyst" may seem an uninformed busybody—he cannot possibly know as much about the operation as those on the job; it's none of his business anyway; and if he really wants to be helpful—as he says he does!—let him pitch in and help with the work that's piling up. To the inquiring procedural analyst, in turn, operating officials may seem short-sighted, self-centered, narrow-minded—each interested only in his task of the moment and lacking in organizational perspective. Failure to solve satisfactorily this central problem of combining diverse outlooks has two results. Either the procedure-making organ, if bolstered by formal authority, promulgates procedures that are useless and often disregarded; or no procedural changes are made, except through tedious evolution or violent revolution.

Let it be admitted that the task of the procedural analyst is frequently difficult and thankless. Interest in procedures is a rather rare and precious quality, likely to mark him as suspect at the outset. Interference with established habits evokes deep and often sharp psychological reactions. The innate aversion to change is often reinforced by fear of loss of employment or of harder work if the *status quo* is disturbed. By humorous legend, the "efficiency expert" is peculiarly liable to accidents, such as falling down an elevator shaft or into an acid vat!

On the other hand, let it also be admitted that the Bright-Eyed Young Chap from upstairs is frequently a sore trial to anyone who has already missed the deadline on his current assignment. And after all, we cannot deny the kernel of wisdom in the belief that "there is much to be said for a poor procedure if people are used to it." A change in procedure may or may not pay off over the long haul, but the immediate results, as the man on the job knows, are almost certain to be confusion, unhappiness, questioning, and complaint.

What is "good" procedure? Reference has been made in our discussion to "good" procedure as distinguished from poor. But what is "good" procedure? No simple answer is possible. Or rather, a simple answer is possible but not very helpful: good procedure is that which is well adapted to achieve the desired ends. The trouble arises both in defining the "desired ends" and in determining whether the procedure really is well adapted to achieving them once they have been agreed upon.

The ends sought by administration are not easily stated. They are often complex and intangible, and it is frequently difficult to determine which of them is to be served by a procedure, and in what proportions. After decision upon ends, the relative "efficiency and economy" of alternative procedures must be measured. Efficiency and economy are not readily applied criteria; they vary in their implications according to the goal in view. Progress has been made in recent years in achieving objective standards of measurement in some fields of administrative performance. However, the tools are still relatively crude and inadequate. Thus, a new procedure saves paper and filing facilities; yet can we be sure that the operating official is not right when he says that the saving is but a straw in the balance, compared to the objectives served by more complete records? Or a new procedure establishes the optimum specialization of the functions of three clerks, as determined by work counts and time-and-motion studies; yet can we be sure that fatigue and staleness will not outweigh the gain within a month? Suppose that under the new arrangement the three clerks are not as "happy" as before. Is the happiness of employees a legitimate consideration in democratic administration? Even on a practical basis, are we sure that happiness won't "pay off" over the long run in loyalty and morale?

The "grammar" of procedure—its routine steps and its customary tools —is easy to learn. But knowledge of grammar is at most a first step in producing literature. And the art of procedural analysis still transcends the science.[10]

5. Living Among Procedures

Procedural pathology—"red tape." It might be said that our age needs (among many other things!) a technology to shorten queues and a philosophy for the person who, nevertheless, finds himself standing in one. We need, that is, ways of reducing red tape, but also an appreciation of the fact that red tape is an inevitable part of life in a complicated society. "Civilization equals complexity and complexity equals red tape." This is oversimplification, but contains an important core of truth.

Certainly there is a "pathology" of procedure. For example, in a sizeable organization some are likely to feel, rightly or wrongly, that they are the victims of "the system." Instead of trying to change the system, they develop a tactic of passive resistance, pulling only enough to keep the traces taut. Others make a false virtue of what seems a necessity by developing a cult of procedure. Unsure of their position, uninformed about the significance of their function in the whole procedural system, they magnify

---

[10] Much of the material dealing with procedural analysis has been prepared for agency use only; other material, though more widely circulated, tends to be "fugitive" and is available only in specialized libraries. Among the more recent items the following may be cited: Pfiffner, John M., and Lane, S. Owen, *A Manual for Administrative Analysis*, ch. 8, Dubuque, Iowa: William C. Brown, 1951; Hinojosa Petit, Jose Antonio, *A Work Simplification Method*, Brussels: International Institute of Administrative Sciences, 1953; Management Staff, Department of State, *Guide to Work Simplification in the Foreign Service*, Washington: Department of State, 1952; Bureau of the Budget, *Production Planning and Control in Office Operations*, Washington: Bureau of the Budget, 1949; Department of the Air Force, *Work Simplification: Fundamentals and Techniques for More Effective Use of Manpower, Equipment, Materials, Space*, Washington: Department of the Air Force, 1954.

Obviously, while pursuing the subject of procedural improvement one quickly invades other areas of administration; what is presented here is not so much a sharply distinguishable phenomenon as a point of view. One area or style of administrative study, which was developed during World War II and has gained important stature since, is "operations research" or "operations analysis," which may be characterized as the application of certain types of mathematical and scientific thought to certain types of problems in administration or "operations." Obviously, this development pertains to procedural analysis, but the extent to which it will change familiar categories and techniques remains to be seen. See American Management Association, *Operations Research: A Basic Approach*, New York, 1956; Churchman, C. West, and Others, *Introduction to Operations Research*, New York: Wiley, 1957.

their task far beyond its intrinsic importance. Their own procedural role becomes a Thing-in-Itself, a monstrous defense mechanism. Procedure is turned into a weapon to ward off the criticism of outsiders—ignorant intruders who do not recognize the pre-eminence of procedure. Woe betide the soul, inside the organization or out, who slights or fails to live by procedure!

Still others, at once sophisticated about procedure and indifferent to the ends it is designed to serve, will use it as an army uses fortifications, either as a base for attack or a line for defense. If action or inaction serves their interests, they will find a way either to fit it within the letter of the procedures or to circumvent or violate the rules. But if they are faced with an action they personally find disagreeable, even the minutiae of procedure will be used to obstruct such action. Needless to say, even the "good" administrator, acting from healthy instinct, will occasionally bend or ignore the written rules!

Need for a balanced view. On the other hand, there is procedural health as well as procedural pathology, and a balanced view should be cultivated. Too, it should be recognized that pathology affects the private organization as well as the public, though the mass media of communication tend to obscure this fact. In the stereotypes that the cartoonist has created, the public bureaucrat is often a malignant creature who spins red tape to accomplish his own evil ends, or a stupid person who creates red tape as the result of his stupidity.

Some of the reasons why these stereotypes have found such widespread acceptance should now be clear.[11] In the management of its affairs, public administration is held by the will of the people to guarantee full honesty and accountability, not solely efficiency and economy as these qualities are understood in private affairs. In its regulatory activities, public administration is governed by legal rules and institutions designed to guarantee the rights of the citizen against unwarranted governmental interference. Certainly we cannot expect particular speed and dispatch of public administration when it is subject to a body of law meant to prevent too great speed and dispatch. Perhaps speed and dispatch need more emphasis as against guarantees of rights. Or perhaps, under modern conditions, rights can be better guaranteed with more speed and dispatch in the public's affairs. But let the issues be clear.

One whose blood pressure rises dangerously upon encountering "red tape" in administration, whether public or private, can with therapeutic benefits pursue several lines of thought. He can reflect upon the wisdom of General Marshall's dictum that "if you cut red tape you must be damn sure of what you are doing." After all, one man's red tape is another man's system. Only when all the facts are known can condemnation be

---

[11] There are other reasons, such as the fact that under popular rule the "outs" castigate the "ins"—and a bureaucrat is by definition "in."

fairly entered and a change be recommended that is likely to be beneficial. Rarely does an isolated encounter with a personally irritating procedure yield the knowledge necessary for a just condemnation. Or he can reflect that red tape constitutes a protection against precipitate and arbitrary action to his detriment, and that this must be weighed against any possible annoyance. Or he may elect to act upon the half-truth that red tape, like caries or cancer, is an affliction of civilization, and, Thoreau-like, retreat to his own Walden Pond. But none of this absolves an administrative agency from responsibility if it fails to ask itself, time and again: "Is our way of doing business good enough, at *this* time, for the tasks we have *now*?"

Chapter 18 •

The Tasks of Middle Management

1. The Twofold Function of Middle Management

Importance of successive points of control. In order to bring executive direction to bear upon the general flow of operations in which the end product of public service takes shape, administrative agencies—like all large-scale enterprise—resort to hierarchical structure.[1] The essential function of hierarchy is to provide an integrated scheme of successive control points for the attainment of efficiency, consistency, and continuity in the performance of the organization's work. In linking these control points in descending order, from the head of the organization to progressively lower subordinates down to the first-line supervisor, one arrives at a "chain of command."

Too often we speak of hierarchy as if it were a physical structure separate from the human element. Actually it is a pattern of relationships—each member of the hierarchy responding to his superior and in turn influencing his subordinates, with countless variables entering into the picture.[2] Nor must it be assumed that hierarchy is principally a device for superimposing top determinations upon the whole organization. Hierarchy does create a desirable pull toward the center, preventing the organization from falling apart. However, the chief test of its effectiveness lies in appropriate devolution of responsibility so as to allow the organization to work under its own "steam." To the same degree that hierarchy reinforces accountability and responsiveness toward the top, it should also relieve those at the top of unnecessary burdens. This can be done only by adequate delegation of authority. Devolution of responsibility without commensurate delegation of authority is an empty gesture, bound to lead nowhere.

Small-scale organization has only two vulnerable areas—the character of its leadership and the productivity of its working force. In large-scale organization, the number of vulnerable areas is much greater because of the multitude of control points between top management and the rank and

---

[1] See Chapter 7, "Concepts of Organization."
[2] See Chapter 13, "Informal Organization."

file of employees. It is therefore hardly an exaggeration to say that one of the most critical sectors of management in large-scale organizations lies in the intermediate ranges of command. The whole concept of "channels of authority" underscores the importance of those points of internal direction and control which are lodged between the responsible head of the organization and its working force at the base of operations. The distribution of these intermediate points of direction and control indicates the field of middle management.

Middle management—stepchild of administrative research. Considering the significance of middle management for the success of any large-scale organization, it is surprising to notice how little emphasis it has found in the American literature on administration, both public and private. Much more attention has been devoted to the functions of the top executive [3] and to his staff facilities.[4] The explanation for the relative failure to deal more explicitly with the particular problems surrounding middle management lies largely in two historic factors.

In the first place, the movement toward administrative reform since the early twentieth century logically saw its main goal in the invigoration of the office of the chief executive. In stressing his responsibility for the entire executive branch, the reform movement chose the most promising lever for achieving better management throughout the administrative structure. Beginning with the novel idea of linking budgetary planning and control with the chief executive, his "arms of management" were consciously designed to make responsible direction truly effective. The same occurred later on the departmental level.[5]

Exercise of such staff functions called for personnel of professional competence and specialized background. As a consequence, the particular knowledge and training required to perform staff or auxiliary services have been in the forefront of academic and practical interest, deflecting consideration from the no less important needs of middle management. Judging only by the dominant themes running through the bulk of administrative research and writing, we might easily be led to the inference that middle managers are an uninspired lot, stung into action solely by the indefatigable prodding of shock brigades of specialists descending upon them from the higher realm of knowledge—administrative planning, budgeting, organization and methods analysis, and personnel work.

The second historic factor that has contributed to the relative neglect of middle management is its lack of homogeneity and cohesiveness as an occupational grouping. Most of the staff and auxiliary services have de-

---

[3] See Chapter 8, "The Chief Executive."
[4] See Chapter 8, "The Chief Executive," sec. 5, "Arms of Modern Management"; Chapter 9, "The Departmental System," sec. 2, "Interdepartmental Coordination."
[5] See Chapter 9, "The Departmental System," sec. 3, "The Secretary's Business."

veloped into fairly well-defined careers. A training specialist, for instance, is readily identified by his specialization. There is no such distinct career in middle management. Broadly speaking, middle managers are the natural offspring of a vast variety of functions. These functions, not the essence of middle management itself, are the fields of their specialized competence. Ordinarily they are middle managers not because they have displayed specific managerial talent as such, but because they became "indispensable men" in the administration of a particular function administered by their agency.

Recognition of middle management as a career? As late as 1941, the President's Committee on Civil Service Improvement, under the chairmanship of Justice Reed, pointed out that middle management, though having responsibilities, had no standing as a specific category within the federal service for purposes of systematic training and selection. Focusing especially on the higher middle and top grades of the classified service, the committee observed that these officials "perform the most difficult and responsible office work along specialized lines requiring extended training and experience." [6] As the committee put it,[7] those occupying such advanced permanent positions:

> ... perform the function of overhead management, direction, and supervision in every branch of the Federal Government. This is the principal duty of bureau chiefs and assistant bureau chiefs, of directors of divisions and assistant directors, of heads of institutions, of the executive officers of commissions and their associates, and of a growing number of administrative assistants and assistants to executives in high position. It is also one of the duties of the President and heads of departments and agencies, secretaries, commissioners, administrators and others; but these high officials have policy-determining duties and political responsibilities as well, which are absent from the permanent branch of administration. In its elementary forms the same function may be said to reach down to the first-line supervisors who must plan, direct, and coordinate the work of the rank and file.

While the Reed Committee did not differentiate sharply between staff and line positions, dealing rather with the more advanced classified grades in general, it necessarily included in its inquiry the main body of middle managers. The committee felt that better awareness of the distinctive requirements of these grades, especially from the point of view of selection and preparation, would yield measurable profit. Summarizing its recommendations, it stated:

> In general terms, we think it would be helpful if the positions involving administrative duties were identified and carefully described in each department and agency, and if each department and agency made and kept current a list or inventory of persons who had demonstrated that they

---

[6] President's Committee on Civil Service Improvement, *Report,* p. 56, House Doc. No. 118, 77th Cong., 1st Sess., Washington, 1941.
[7] *Ibid.*

possessed administrative skill, with the personal and official history, present classification and other relevant data. We also believe that the continuous search for good prospective material for administration should be more definitely recognized in some departments and agencies as a joint responsibility of supervisors and personnel officers. Finally, we think that the machinery is now for the first time available to permit a desirable extension of the program of training and testing which is already in operation in most departments.[8]

No doubt a more methodical approach would go far toward promoting the characteristic qualifications called for in administrative work, especially in middle management. This is not merely a matter of greater competence. It also carries over into the general orientation and outlook of middle managers. Hence the Reed Committee quite properly concerned itself with the broader question of occupational attitudes. What it had to say on this point could hardly occasion surprise. To quote again:

> Government departments and agencies, their divisions and their sub-divisions, suffer from an insularity which hampers their effective coordination as parts of a single whole. Indifference, jealousy, competition, and sometimes even sabotage develop in the effort of each small unit to protect itself and its staff. There is too little recognition of a common responsibility to a common and single employer, the American people as represented by the Congress and the President.[9]

Such insularity is in part the familiar result of both the size and the functionalization of large-scale organization. Put at a particular place in a complex structure of vast dimensions, the middle manager is apt to identify himself with the more tangible realities and objectives of his "shop." In part, however, his insular point of view derives from the fact that he has difficulty in seeing himself as a member of an occupational group with a larger loyalty. He is simply the product of the particular function within which he rose. Lack of a uniting bond among the middle managers keeps him enslaved to the individual function in which he has his roots. Recognition of middle management as a career grouping would tend to draw its mentality from the particular to the general, away from the specialized activities from which it springs. Being part of a distinctive grouping would deepen the middle manager's consciousness of his general role, especially if it were combined with a governmentwide scheme of transfers between functions and departments. He thus would gain a wider field of vision and greater capacity for responding to the necessities of coordination.

Middle management and top direction. Good staff work implies not only knowledge and experience but also a high degree of sensitivity to the needs of those in command—the top executive and line officials. In much the same way, effective middle management, aside from mastery of the functional field in which it operates, requires receptivity to higher execu-

---

[8] *Ibid.*, p. 57. See also Chapter 2, "The Study of Public Administration," sec. 3, "Training for Public Administration."
[9] *Ibid.*, p. 61.

tive direction as well as capacity for "getting things done." The outstanding factor about top-level direction is that it must encompass the organization as a whole and deal with each issue in terms of the whole. As the principal support of top-level direction, middle management therefore has to infuse the generality of organizationwide purposes into its individual operations. On this score it can succeed only insofar as it captures in its own thinking the broad-range ends of the organization at large. Conversely, it is bound to fail in exact proportion to the insularity of its outlook. If the middle manager does not bring to bear upon his own province the generality of organization ends, relating his day-by-day actions to the total administrative process, he ignores his basic duty. More mindful of his immediate sphere, he becomes a counterinfluence to higher executive direction rather than its reenforcement. This may be deliberate in certain instances, especially when a middle manager is at odds with the higher powers, but feels safe because of his alliance with political or economic groups outside the organization.[10] As a rule he succumbs to the enticements of autonomy unconsciously. Top management is far away. It is referred to not as "we" but as "they"—"we" do things our own way; "they" come in to tell us, though having not the faintest idea of "our" troubles and "our" business.

The strength of middle management rests in the fact that it thoroughly knows its own "shop." This knowledge is the middle manager's stock-in-trade and his legitimate pride. Outsiders—say, methods specialists from the Management Division—are likely to be glared at when they demonstrate that through a survey they have come to know the "shop" as well, if not better. Operators naturally do not take too well to the idea that anyone might know as much about operations as they do. However, the virtue of the middle manager's intimate familiarity with his own segment of the organization has its corresponding vice. The vice of the virtue lies in a proportionately dimmer perception of what the organization is trying to accomplish as a whole. Such dimmed perception inevitably affects the role of middle management as caretaker of the executive function on the subordinate levels of authority.

However urgent to the progress of operations, middle management must find time to face upward. As an informed student of federal administration has expressed it, "the drag of inadequacy is always downward. The need in administration is always for the reverse: for a secretary to project his thinking to the governmental level, for a bureau chief to try to see the problems of the department, for the division chief to comprehend the work of the entire bureau." [11] No doubt one of the most pressing needs in administration is that for increasingly broader consideration as matters

---

[10] See Chapter 13, "Informal Organization," sec. 2, "Elements of Informal Organization."

[11] Appleby, Paul H., *Big Democracy*, p. 45, New York: Knopf, 1945. See also Chapter 9, "The Departmental System," sec. 4, "The Bureau Pattern."

move upward from the bottom to the top. To this end, however, top management, expecting support from the middle manager, must contribute by conveying to him a sense of organizationwide objectives. Effective communication of top-level policy is one means. Another is the interest that top management shows in the way operations are going.

The communication system on which the organization relies is therefore a matter of crucial significance for the entire conduct of middle management.[12] A top management that wraps itself in silence resembles a head after decapitation. Top-level action by itself is an entirely insufficient agent of communication. In the first place, such action is by no means always conspicuous throughout the organization. The large body of personnel in the organization may live through many a day before the first concrete ripples come down to it. Secondly, the bare policy pronouncement and the letter of administrative orders and instructions are inadequate for full understanding of institutional goals. Middle managers need to know the motivations, intentions, and reasons that go into directives handed down to them. Without being posted on the course steered by top management, middle managers are likely to lose themselves in smaller problems, magnified to the point of distortion. The result is functional isolation and separatism—the occupational diseases of large-scale enterprise. At the same time, ignorance of top-level objectives encourages middle managers to pass too many matters to the higher level, causing dangerous congestion in the upper ranges of the organization.

Middle management and control of operations. At the base of administrative operations, management is concentrated in the first-line supervisor. Working with his small crew of perhaps no more than ten employees, he functions very much like the foreman in industry—organizing his team, maintaining the pace of work, securing the necessary quality of output, developing the skill of those working for him, showing them how to do their job and how to do it better. Although supervision on his level will be treated more specifically in another chapter,[13] it is clear that in a more general sense supervision runs through the entire organization, each superior supervising his immediate subordinates.

By and large, supervision becomes more specific as we proceed downward in the hierarchy. At the top, it tends to be rather general, in part because of the plausible assumption of higher competence for independent work, in part because the nature of the work on these levels renders specific surveillance unfeasible and ineffectual. Here the record of achievement or failure must be extensively relied upon as a substitute for the eyes of the supervisor. In the lower ranges of the organization, supervision is apt to be closer as it increasingly relates to more repetitive and less complex

---

[12] See also Chapter 16, "The Formulation of Administrative Policy," sec. 1, "Policy Formation and Policy Sanction."

[13] See Chapter 19, "The Art of Supervision."

transactions. The burdens of specific supervision—typical of middle management in general—therefore increase from level to level downward.

Control of operations, even under exceptionally favorable circumstances, is never a purely mechanical process. Human beings do not function like machines. Attainment of a reasonably standardized group product hence requires considerable leeway in direction. A great number of factors enter into any kind of organized group action. Only when the middle manager is placed in a position to influence these factors without undue restraint can he be expected to live up to his task. It follows that appropriate delegation of authority is a basic condition to successful guidance of operations.

Most middle managers feel that the scope of their authority is inadequate to their responsibility. How much justification there is for these complaints we shall examine in a subsequent section of this chapter. Here it may suffice to observe that nowhere is the urge to "be left alone" as great as in line operations. This is not surprising. Face to face with the task to "get the job done," under continuous pressure from above for speed and action, and hungry for the emotional thrill of "getting results," the middle manager is prone to wish for more power to his elbow. His eyes focus only on a defined sector of operations, only on part of the organization. But within that sector he is supreme, or has reason to think of himself as supreme. And he longs for the totality of authority that would make him fully master.

The doer's kingdom. However small, this is his world. To him, it is a complete world, just as complete in itself as the job to be done. Here he is the boss; it is he who is answerable for the state of business in his sector; it is he who earns the credit for accomplishment. The head of his agency and the galaxy of staff people higher up may fancy themselves to throne above the whole organization and deal with it in its entirety. However, only the line operator "hears the thing tick." Only he sees directly the concrete product of operations. Only he has the satisfaction of carrying his forces forward—through his leadership, his grasp of the situation, and what he personally is able to do about the situation. Looking for drama in administration? You find it most easily in the line.

A lot has been said about managerial "know how" of late. "Know how" is for the most part the property of middle management. "Know how" arises principally from trying—shrewd experimentation, ingenious improvisation, swift adjustment, and that kind of resilient initiative which is always willing to try all over again. Much of the glory of "know how" is the middle manager's. He is the one who performs the feat of bringing together the manpower and the administrative tools allowed him by his budget so that tangible values of performance come forth. He builds the human relationships into purposeful and productive effort. He also feels the first repercussions of lowered morale, and is the first called into the breach to furnish personal inspiration in order to raise the spirit of his force.

Control of operations extends all the way from the planning stage to the completion point. It entails the programming of activities to meet specified goals; the scheduling of sequences of steps in order to relate the use of manpower to the time factor; the spelling-out of particular assignments; the definition of standards of performance; the establishment of recording and reporting requirements; the designation of the most appropriate methods and techniques; the determination of the most expeditious flow of work; the identification of the mechanics for checking progress and quality; and the review of the end product. Usually all of these elements blend into one another. Yet each has its part to play in middle management, and each may require much thought and great care, especially when novel functions or undertakings are involved for which past experience does not provide a dependable guide. In such instances, the resourcefulness of line officials will often be put to an exacting test.

In its control of operations, middle management is in the main concerned with the tactics of administration, leaving the final decisions of a strategic character to the top level of the organization. The middle manager's tactical responsibilities compel him to face downward, toward the detailed transactions at the base of the hierarchical structure. At the same time, as we have noted earlier, he must view himself as the agent of top management, as a manifestation of the executive function. This makes it necessary for him simultaneously to look for the signals from above. In a very real sense, therefore, his attention is persistently drawn in two opposite directions. As there are pressures on him from the top, so there are pressures from the bottom. The impact of these opposite pressures would tax any man's equanimity. It is thus not startling that middle managers frequently give the impression of being either hardboiled or militantly defensive. They can hardly help it.

2. Supporting Top Direction

Effectiveness of downward communication. In order to achieve a secure alignment with middle management, top direction must "explain itself" as fully as it can. As has been suggested earlier, this puts in bold relief the need for effective downward communication. Communication has two separable though interrelated aspects—content and form. The former reaches into such matters as clarity, volume, and frequency. The latter runs through the entire process of communication.

As for content, unprecise, cryptic, or fragmentary communication of top-level objectives and policies may have different reasons. In many cases it is not simply the result of casualness, inattention, or sloppy phrasing. The head of an agency and his intimate associates may be quite clear about particular ends and yet may hesitate greatly to make these ends a subject of organizationwide pronouncement. The matter may be delicate; it may imply an admission of partial failure; it may require the equivalent of talking "among ourselves" in the family circle.

Large-scale organization meets peculiar limitations on this score. Its size increases the chance of unwelcome leakages. With so many people involved in the echelons of middle management alone—quite aside from the much larger body of first-line supervisors—can the executive be sure of confidential treatment? Can he safely assume a sufficient degree of loyalty everywhere? Is it at least possible to take for granted sympathetic appreciation of the difficulties he confronts in striving for sensible solutions, especially when these must aim at the organization as a whole?

Here, then, is one of the fundamental reasons why downward communication so often seems to withhold as much as it conveys. It throws a sharp light on the importance of widespread personal identification with the aims of the organization. No agency can think or talk within its "four walls" when its personnel lacks what is perhaps best termed a "sense of institution." This is not to minimize the stimulating effect of constructive argument over issues and problems.[14] However, only high *esprit de corps* can provide a hospitable climate for creative disagreement within the scope of a common allegiance.[15]

Economy of communication. Downward communication may be a meager trickle from sheer timidity, but it may also suffer from torrential abundance. The policy announcement is followed by an interminable series of clarifications, or the administrative order carries in its wake a whole string of implementing instructions, one more detailed than the other. The essential economy of communication lies between these two extremes. But is enough attention being paid to attaining such economy? Most middle managers consider themselves victims of either too little or too much. They may not always be the best judges of the "golden mean," but all too often they can make a good case to demonstrate that they are "left high and dry" or altogether "snowed under."

Despite technical advances such as the introduction of teletype conferences, communication as an art has changed amazingly little. For most uses, the "memo" reigns supreme, and usually in so many copies, for distribution. The incredible investment of time that goes into the manufacture and the consumption of administrative communications must often be entirely out of proportion to the effects intended. High-grade staff people processing the raw materials for official "issuances," lawyers scanning

---

[14] For the special problems that under auspices of interest representation affect the desirable administrative "freedom of thought," see Chapter 14, "Interest Groups in Administration," sec. 3, "Staffing for Point of View."

[15] On this question, see also Chapter 13, "Informal Organization," sec. 2, "Elements of Informal Organization."

"rough copies" with the eagle eye characteristic of their craft, draftsmen adding their flourishes, busy executives adorning the margin with their "queries," and solemn men bickering at the conference table over commas and periods—all of this is part of the tortuous gestation. Then the duplicating machines start humming, and the cloudburst comes down. "Did you read the latest one on paper salvage?" "Heavens, no! My girl just puts everything into the file."

A wide field exists for the imaginative communication-engineer to devise ways of cutting down the volume of waste motion in conveying information. In addition, there is the possibility of getting down closer to basic English.[16] Finally, establishment of agencywide issuance control has paid its way because of both its brake effect and the great convenience of locating quickly particular kinds of communications identified by series— directives, orders, instructions, informational bulletins. It remains a fact, however, that most systems of administrative communication fail to provide an even coverage of significant information. Priorities are ill-defined, and the trivial tends to drown the essential. With "all the stuff that comes down," the middle manager may still know very little about executive thinking at the top. And though he tries to keep abreast of developments, he may fall into the defensive habit of reading only when he "has the time for it." Judging by the evidence, top-level issuances ordinarily enter the mind of an organization only slowly, and by no means uniformly.

Two-way traffic of thought. Fortunately, communication to enable middle management to operate as the hands of top-level direction is today rarely a one-way affair. It travels increasingly on two-way roads. Downward communication reaches the ear of the middle manager most clearly when its substance relates to his own thinking—when he finds part of his own mind in it. Communication of policy gains in effectiveness in proportion to the scope of active participation of middle management in the policy-making process.

To a certain extent, of course, the middle manager is always a policy-maker. Not only does he take part in policy formulation by translating strategy into tactics, by tracing out top determinations into line activities, by framing operating policies under his own responsibility. He is also a policy-maker indirectly—by reporting inadequacies in current policies, and emerging problems and issues that warrant top-level consideration.[17] However, this role in policy formulation is intermittent and incidental.

---

[16] Mention should be made particularly of the campaign for increased readability of written communications carried forward by government here and abroad; see, for instance, Gowers, Ernest A., *The Complete Plain Words*, London: H. M. Stationery Office, 1954; General Services Administration, National Archives and Records Services, *Plain Letters*, Washington, 1955. See also Chapter 17, "Government by Procedure," sec. 4, "Creation and Criteria."

[17] For a discussion of the dynamics of administrative policy-making, see Chapter 16, "The Formulation of Administrative Policy," sec. 4, "External Influences in Administrative Policy."

His participation in the policy-making process should be continuous. One means is the regular staff meeting, when it brings together representatives of top management and middle management.[18] More important than devices such as the staff meeting is the habit of up-and-down and across-the-board consultation. This is something that only top management is in a position to instill in all parts of the organization. A feeble or small-minded top management, offended by any "criticism" from within, is obviously unable to foster such habits of consultation, however much lip service it may pay the abstract principle. Helpful suggestions and new ideas will not come forth when they fail to find eager takers.

In the operation of a department, for instance, it will be profitable for the head to meet once a week with a circle of key officers, including the top level of middle management, the bureau chiefs; spend at least an hour or two each month with the officials on the next lower levels—division and section chiefs—in order to focus attention on matters of common significance; and get together once a year with all his field-office managers, and more often with smaller groups of them, perhaps region by region, as well as with the regional directors.[19] This would not dispose of the customary media of circulating information—bulletins, periodic project and activity lists, weekly field letters. Needless to say, observing the proprieties of a conference schedule is one thing, but knowing how to reap benefits from it is something different.

It is probably true that the resources of ability available within large-scale enterprise are far from being fully utilized. The effect is like making a high-priced engineer count building permits. He gets disgusted and indifferent to the interests of his employer; and the employer wastes four-fifths of the engineer's salary because counting building permits, if it has to be done at all, could be done by the lowest-paid employee. Strangely, the loss in both efficiency and economy that results from leaving untapped much of the latent ability in an organization is frequently caused deliberately. Too many top executives continue to believe that middle management's participation in policy planning undermines their "authority." This conclusion is contradicted by the record of "multiple management"—a catch-phrase made famous by Baltimore's businessman Charles P. McCormick.[20] In his company—an example followed by hundreds of other firms—McCormick provided for special "boards" to feed ideas upward.

Taking orders. Middle management is in the "chain of command"—

---

[18] For mention of the staff meeting as a device for organizing administrative analysis, see Chapter 20, "Applying Management Knowledge," sec. 2, "Organization for Administrative Improvement."

[19] Cf. also Chapter 12, "Field Organization," sec. 3, "Field-Headquarters Relations."

[20] See his *Multiple Management,* New York: Harper, 1938, and *The Power of People: Multiple Management Up To Date,* New York: Harper, 1949. See also Craf, John R., *Junior Boards of Executives: A Management Training Procedure,* New York: Harper, 1958.

in fact it represents most of the length of this chain. Looking upon his "shop," the middle manager exercises his formal authority in large measure by giving orders. Simultaneously, however, he is subject to the formal authority of his superiors. If the familiar saying about learning to obey in order to learn to command settled everything, the middle manager, usually rising from below, would not only be an ideal commander but also excel at taking orders.

Taking orders is in many ways merely the reverse of familiarity and self-identification with institutional purposes and objectives. With self-identification, the order from higher authority is essentially an affirmative gesture, a signal to go ahead, more of a timing device than an indication of aims or direction. It is a different proposition, and one causing varying degrees of strain, to execute orders when top management is overbearing; or has embarked upon a dubious course without attempting to take the middle managers into its confidence; or appears to subordinate long-range objectives to opportunistic maneuvering.

This kind of emotional conflict illuminates again the narrow foundation on which formal authority rests.[21] No order executes itself. It moves down the chain of command only so far as its motion is sustained by the impetus furnished on each level of leadership. To be sure, compliance is bolstered by discipline and by machinery for the enforcement of discipline.[22] But disciplinary pressure is a far cry from free individual self-exertion. In the face of disciplinary threats, all one needs to do is turn on a show of compliance. "Getting by" is enough not to "get caught." Or one may "lie low," inching ahead reluctantly only when prodded. Or one may flatly refuse to budge, though always duly covered by some good excuse. Orders can be "misunderstood." "Buck-passing" is another possibility. Conceding that there are practical limits to passive resistance, we are once more reminded that faithful execution of orders in the last analysis springs from widespread acceptance of institutional ends, supported by a well-understood ideology of service.

At the same time, ability to take orders does not imply blind subservience. The middle manager for whom "orders are orders" may get his agency into serious trouble when he fails to speak up on obstacles which only he can spot from the vantage point of his line experience. He simply does not do his job if he dispenses with his personal judgment. Orders are indeed susceptible of misunderstanding. They may overshoot the mark. They may be overtaken by rapidly changing conditions. Then it is plainly in the interest of the whole organization immediately to inform the supreme command. On the other hand, everything would soon stall if middle management made it a general practice to refer each order to the

---

[21] See Chapter 13, "Informal Organization," sec. 2, "Elements of Informal Organization."

[22] See Chapter 21, "Morale and Discipline."

next higher level for elaboration. Here, too, and in the interpretation of orders for the lower levels, the middle manager needs to show alert judgment. He will err rarely when the broad picture of administrative strategy and the "way we operate" are clearly understood by all concerned.

Tribulations of the operator. In the conduct of line business, the middle manager carries a large responsibility. He has to "get the work out," all of it—and fast. Yet, especially in the realm of public administration, his hands are tied in many ways, though often in the name of good management.

He does not freely pick his subordinates; they are handed him through certification from an eligibility register by the central personnel agency, and his actual choice from such a register is generally limited by the "rule of three"—the top three names being "certified" to him from the register. He is not allowed to grade them up or down; that is a matter of formal evaluation known as reclassification, and his own judgment may be the least important factor. He is, of course, unable simply to fire an employee he cannot work with; he must state a "cause" in writing, and the matter may not rest at that, for it is not unusual among governmental jurisdictions to allow a dismissed employee to carry his case before the civil service commission.[23] These restrictions are not devoid of reasons that no one would want to brush aside lightly.[24] They are nonetheless very real impairments of the middle manager's freedom.

If we turn to governmentwide regulations on budgeting, auditing, accounting, procurement, and a host of housekeeping functions, the task of middle management grows increasingly befuddling. Like poison ivy climbing all over the cottage, the prohibitions seem to outdo the incentives. In the end, the middle manager's perspective may become badly distorted. He may feel that it is less serious for his "shop" to fall behind in its work than to get "fouled up" by governmentwide prescriptions about the handling of vouchers, for instance.

A good case can be made for the contention that American public administration has become top-heavy with central controls. Certainly this is a question to which careful research might be devoted with great benefit. Meanwhile, the line operator has to "sweat it out." We need little imagination to visualize the many instances in which he feels arrested in the application of straight common sense by hard and fast rules that to him have no rhyme or reason whatsoever.

Thinking in larger terms. Conditions conducive to self-identification with larger purposes, as we observed earlier, are vital to productive middle management. These can counteract the operator's concern with the particular province of his responsibility. His world, being the foundation of

---

23 This is not generally true of the federal government.
24 For a fuller discussion of public personnel administration in the context of administrative responsibility, see Chapter 24, "Personnel Standards."

his status within the organization, has a strong claim on his mind. This attitude makes him seek expansion—bigger and better programs, bigger and better appropriations, bigger and better staffs—because to him his jurisdiction is the most important one, the hub of the entire enterprise.

Indeed, the tug-of-war between the particular and the general runs through the whole of the executive branch. When, for example, a department considers itself always right, its officialdom may show high morale and great *élan,* but to the same extent the department is severely handicapped for open-minded interdepartmental cooperation. One aspect of normalcy in administration is rivalry between agencies themselves. Nor is this all. Department heads often display a keen competitive sense also in relation to the chief executive.

On the levels of middle management, the innate particularism can be mitigated only by a systematically cultivated inclination to think in larger terms. Top leadership may do much to widen the horizon of the line official. But appropriate indoctrination has best effects when it is governmentwide. We could place much more stress on middle management as a unified career group, and develop more effective arrangements to move middle managers about within their department and interdepartmentally, so as to encourage an administrative doctrine that would assure primacy to a comprehensive view of the public interest.

3. Running the Show

Problems of delegation. Top management expects of the line official that in due time he will be able to report, "Mission accomplished." In carrying out his mission, he must think and plan for himself. No detailed instruction coming from above can ever take the place of his own experience, ingenuity, and foresight. In fact, he is the chosen instrument to settle the details, thus freeing the leadership of his agency for policy consideration. To do his job he needs a considerable degree of leeway of action. No one would quarrel with the axiom that the authority delegated to him should measure up to the breadth of his responsibility for results. However, it is a different matter to transform the axiom into reality.

Generally speaking, delegation of authority has been hesitant and grudging. This can be explained in part by the direct and personal way in which American legislatures have sought to exact accountability from politically responsible administrators. It has produced a general inclination to hold the reins of top control more tightly than is ideal for good management. Part of the explanation lies in the traditions of the "spoils system" of an earlier day when line officials could not be trusted to stand on their own feet administratively. Still another part of the explanation must be found in the same tendencies that have retarded adequate decentralization of activities to the field.[25] For greatest efficiency, delegation of authority to middle management, by and large, could go much farther.

Even where delegation of authority is reasonably adequate, we often find unnecessarily extensive requirements for higher approval of whole categories of more important decisions. These requirements throw great burdens on the administrative process and are hardly conducive to the formation of a strong sense of responsibility. It is sounder to rely on periodic reports which make the danger of overworked delegation automatically visible, both to top management and to the operating officials themselves. Appraisal of the outcome of delegated administrative action in success or failure is superior to cumbersome mechanics of higher review of each proposed action.

Reinforcing the line sector. It is the hallmark of effective middle management to be able to stand on its own feet, knowing at the same time where to get help when help is needed. Much help—in advice and in temporarily borrowed skill or manpower—will be secured by the simple method of drawing upon the "crowd across the hall" or by pooling resources with it. Indeed, large-scale enterprise cannot achieve unity of action without a constant process of using cross connections—drawing into both planning and operations all the thought, information, and experience available within the entire organization. As a student of middle management has said, "The organization of crosswise relationships is one of the foremost problems of today and tomorrow."[26]

The wide-awake operator knows many turns for bringing these crosswise relationships into play—down to sources of "grapevine" and the unhurried conversation in the executive dining room. Line officials see eye to eye on many things and usually share their worries without reserve. They feel differently toward staff people from the top offices. Yet prudent use of staff specialists pays the middle manager high dividends, and he knows it. Growth of management staffs within the line organization itself has made him more willing to ask for assistance from "the experts" than he used to be. Higher-level staffs, though indispensable to him on major problems,[27] are still suspect for their skill in ferreting out hidden issues that call for much explaining by the middle manager—and occasionally make him look very sheepish.

Ideally, staff talent should be evenly distributed throughout the department. This would also allay the fears of middle managers that staff personnel called in for help might in effect lay down the law for the operators to live with, and then nimbly depart from the scene. Theoretically staff personnel are outside the chain of command. As a statement on organiza-

---

[25] See Chapter 12, "Field Organization," sec. 2, "Centralization and Decentralization."

[26] Niles, Mary C. H., *Middle Management*, p. 52, New York: Harper, rev. ed., 1949.

[27] See Chapter 20, "Applying Management Knowledge."

tion and methods work issued by the British Treasury has formulated it, departmental organization and methods branches "will operate by advice tendered and not by instructions issued." Of course, such advice may in concrete circumstances be equal to command.

Organizing for work. Line officials, like everyone else, may pride themselves on organizing their "shop" without ever stopping to think about organizing their own job.[28] One ailment widespread among operators is a pernicious preoccupation with lesser details—"the petty done, the undone vast." In administration, detail is seldom trivial; but it is also true that the competent middle manager must possess a sure feeling for the significant detail which alone justifies his personal attention. A kindred ailment is the abandon with which some line officials throw themselves into the routine technicalities of operating processes. They keep themselves so busy that no minute is left for the contemplative pause. In the end they have run so dry that the thought of thinking drives them frantic; so they have to go on being busy.

Generally it is simply an indication of a bad job of self-organization to be always pressed for time. This is especially serious in middle management because line officials stand or fall with their capacity for dealing personally with groups of human beings who look to them for guidance and stimulation. Time is of the essence in all human relationships—time for conferences, time for complaints, time for advice, time for instruction, time for a joke or a few friendly words wherever the opportunity presents itself.

A line official must be able not merely to project his influence upon the entire range of operations in his charge but also to detach himself mentally from the day-by-day activities, at least at sufficiently frequent intervals. Only with such detachment can he be a reliable overseer of the "whole show." Only by figuratively stepping back during his quieter hours can he preserve his perspective. Even if he holds that thinking is none of his business, the pressures on him will compel him to pick one or two understudies and to build up his key men. He will have to learn how to anticipate program changes and emerging problems. He will have to fit his own way of operating into the working methods of his immediate superior and the mode of business prevalent in those units which with his unit form a tactical entity. If he is far enough down in the chain of command, he must not only be readily accessible to all his first-line supervisors but also look over their shoulders to find out how they are doing.

Whatever his location in the hierarchy, he must be alert to opportunities for developing talent among his subordinates and be sufficiently unselfish to let promising men and women go on to higher responsibilities outside his "shop." One of the greatest qualities of middle management lies in training employees for advancement and selection for governmentwide or

---

[28] Cf. Niles, *op. cit.* above in note 26, ch. 11.

departmental "executive development" programs or other specialized training courses, including academic study.[29]

Reporting schemes. In the two-way traffic of information and thought, the upward flow of reports and recommendations is at least as significant as downward communication. Line reporting brings top management "down to earth." No fine-spun plan is worth a tinker's dam unless it holds up in the stress of operations. Without realistic line reporting, top-level direction would grope in darkness. Equally important is the contribution of reports on operations to the maintenance of internal control.

All programming and scheduling must be buttressed by reporting requirements. But reporting can run wild. In not a few administrative agencies, everybody seems to need to know everything, and in the ensuing flood of information everybody is drowned alike.

In the first place, in order to be of use for executive control, raw information must continually be translated into control information—by digesting, abstracting, and underscoring of relevant points. Secondly, informational priorities must be clearly expressed in designing the reporting system. Thirdly, time and again the question must be raised whether each periodic report actually meets concrete needs. Reporting requirements, once established, have great survival power, notwithstanding the disappearance of original demand.

Keeping records. Administration can mean many things, but it is always a lot of paperwork. Federal records now in existence are estimated to amount to some 25,000,000 cubic feet, with an annual accumulation of more than 1,000,000. Most of this is made up of operating records. Today, however, resort to documentation of past undertakings and full-fledged record reference—like library reference—have become essential to policy determination and top-staff activity.[30] Record management as a specialized service has made marked strides. It exerts a highly beneficial influence in strengthening the memory of an organization and in keeping its officials from improvising anew for each day or running their business "by ear."

Bodies of records may look like so much besmudged and dust-covered paper. Actually they are repositories of information, and should be treated as such. Documentation of policy decisions and study projects as well as of administrative transactions is an aid not only in achieving responsibility— the record tells—but also in making "know how" less fugitive and more of

---

[29] *Cf.* Dooher, M. Joseph, and Marting, Elizabeth, eds., *Selection of Management Personnel,* New York: American Management Association, 1957, 2 vols.

[30] *Cf.* Chatfield, Helen L., "The Problem of Records from the Standpoint of Management," *American Archivist,* 1940, Vol. 3, p. 93 *ff.;* Brooks, Philip C., *Public Records Management,* Chicago: Public Administration Service, Publication No. 19, 1949; Morstein Marx, Fritz, "The Role of Records in Administration," *American Archivist,* 1947, Vol. 10, p. 241 *ff.;* Odell, Margaret K., and Strong, Earl P., *Records Management and Filing Operations,* New York: McGraw-Hill, 1947; Schellenberg, T. R., *Modern Archives: Principles and Techniques,* Chicago: University of Chicago Press, 1956.

an institutional property. When the working files on each level of middle management are reasonably complete and in good order, it is much easier to move line officials around because the successor can find his way without asking innumerable questions or figuring out each thing again. Orderliness of control is in large part dependent on orderliness of documentation. No middle manager is truly up to his job if he fails to assure himself of good record administration.

Chapter 19 •

The Art of Supervision

1. What Is Supervision?

Formal authority for direction of others. From the viewpoint of management, the supervisor is that person in the organization to whom authority for the direction of the work of others has been assigned. Coherence in any organization is achieved by this top-to-bottom chain of supervision. From the viewpoint of the worker, however, the supervisor is frequently regarded as the organization itself. This dual role has always been important, but only recently have the conditions for the supervisor's optimum performance of his function been the subject of widespread research.

Supervision in its purest form occurs at the first or lowest level of the organization. In governmental parlance, this level is referred to as that of the first-line supervisor. In industry, the leadman or foreman occupies essentially the same position, and in the army the corporal or perhaps the sergeant. Most of our discussion here deals with the first-line supervisor.[1]

While the supervisor has a definite hierarchical position, supervision itself occurs wherever there are groups of workers, high or low in the organization, in or outside the "chain of command." Supervision may not always emanate from the organizationally designated superior, and workers may receive direction from more than one source. The staff employee or specialist may wield real influence by the force of his personality, the excellence of his suggestions, or some other means. The fact, however, that the supervisor directs with authority and is responsible to management for the results of that direction places him in a different role from all others in the organization who in one way or another influence employee behavior.

Coordination of influences. That the work of an employee is influenced from many sources has long been recognized. The problem of the most desirable nature of such multiple direction has not been resolved, but modern management holds to the concept of unity of command. Under this concept, influences outside the chain of command are best exerted

---

[1] The author is deeply indebted to Dr. Beatrice G. Markey, Assistant Professor, School of Public Administration, University of Southern California, for her assistance in revising this chapter.

through the immediate supervisor, who has authority to coordinate the organizational demands upon the workers.

Frederick W. Taylor, "father" of scientific management, felt that the highest production could be achieved if each special aspect of the worker's task was commanded by a specialist in that phase of the work. This was his case for the "functional foreman." Modern management, on the other hand, while recognizing the existence of multiple direction of tasks, generally holds one supervisor responsible for ultimate performance and devolves upon that supervisor the resolution of any conflicting directions from the several specialists within the organization.

Management responsibility. Because of disproportionate emphasis on production and efficiency, the supervisor's role was imperfectly understood in the past. There was more concern in organizations for the "what" than for the "how." Only recently has the role of the supervisor in the direction and guidance of the workers come to be seen as an integral part of the management process. It is being more completely understood on the basis of organizational study, aimed at exploration and explanation of what actually takes place in organizations and what are the factors that enhance or impede job performance.

The supervisor is now being viewed as "a member of the management team," [2] whose knowledge of both the work processes and the workers supplies important information for management. Management is increasingly being apprised of the advantages of accepting the supervisor into its circle, and supervisors are becoming more and more aware of their added responsibilities both on the job and off as representatives of management. The literature of management speaks of "the organizational climate" [3] and its effect on supervisory performance, of the importance of "team cooperation" and good public relations as necessary requisites of of the supervisor's job.

Management literature dealing with the role of the supervisor has increased a hundredfold in the last decade or so,[4] and both government and private industry carry on studies to determine the essential factors of good supervision.[5] As a result of these studies, advanced management today

---

[2] This is not peculiar to the literature on American management. The changing role of the foreman and the training problems attendant upon the changed relationship have also been recognized in Great Britain.

[3] For the effect of the organizational climate on supervisory training, see Fleishman, Edwin A., Harris, Edwin F., and Burtt, Harold E., *Leadership and Supervision in Industry,* Monograph No. 33, Bureau of Educational Research, Columbus: Ohio State University, 1955.

[4] The most complete work on the subject of supervision is Pfiffner, John M., *The Supervision of Personnel,* Englewood Cliffs, N. J.: Prentice-Hall, 2nd ed., 1958. A management report by the United States Civil Service Commission, *Leadership and Supervision,* December 1955, lists 158 works on various phases of supervision.

[5] Outstanding among these studies are those sponsored by the Office of Naval Research in the leading universities of the United States as well as the studies conducted by the Air Research and Development Command and the Institute for Social Research at the University of Michigan.

considers a knowledge of human relations a tool for the supervisory job which, as with other tools, it is the responsibility of management to provide. The supervisor is neither expected to come to the organization fully equipped to perform his role as leader of the work group, nor is he required to accept full responsibility for his own development. With the fuller understanding of the role of the supervisor in management has come greater emphasis on supervisory training.

Many factors have contributed to the changed role of the supervisor. The social sciences have explored the nature of job satisfaction. Worker organizations have pressed for a greater share in the production process. Technological advances have reduced individual job satisfaction while at the same time increasing the need for teamwork in the complex tasks of modern production. The extent of the changes in the role of the supervisor may be indicated by saying that in those organizations where thought is being given to the supervisory role, the supervisor has ceased to be another worker—one who merely passes on the word from on high and the complaints from below.

Scope of supervision. The supervisor is the person who knows both the work to be done and the policies and procedures set down by management, and who can motivate the work group to perform its tasks within the framework of these policies and procedures. His job may thus be described as (1) substantive or technical—relating to the work to be done; (2) institutional or adjective—relating to the policies and procedures according to which the work must be done; and (3) personal—relating to the handling of workers.[6]

The actual content of the supervisor's technical responsibilities will vary greatly depending on the product, the work process, and the work situation. In mass-production industries, the leadman may have almost no direct technical responsibility, except for quantity of output. Method is determined higher up, and equipment and materials provided. Quality control is also out of his hands, because it is the immediate concern of an inspector. In less systematized and routinized operations—office work, for example— any or all of these problems may well remain in the supervisor's hands. They demand therefore competence in planning the work, setting standards of quantity and quality, and making specific work assignments. With the help of a specialist, the "safety engineer," the supervisor may have the duty of encouraging safe work habits and enforcing safety rules. Further, the supervisor may have to provide tools and equipment, as well as equipment maintenance, or he may have only the partial responsibility for the custody

---

[6] For the relationship between the first two aspects of the supervisory job and the personal aspect—supervisors whom higher management considered to be "promotable," or "satisfactory plus," were also regarded as good at handling people by their employees, who stated that they felt free to discuss both job and personal problems with their supervisor—see Mann, Floyd, and Dent, James, *Appraisal of Supervisors*, p. 10-11, Ann Arbor: University of Michigan Research Center, 1954.

of the machines. To be sure, the supervisor must "know the work." But it does not necessarily follow, as is sometimes contended, that the supervisor must be an expert in the field. It is possible for a good supervisor to move over from one type of work to another, especially when he is picked for his leadership potential rather than for his expertness.

The institutional side of the supervisor's duties involves the policies, procedures, and practices of his agency or company. The supervisor must conform to the organization's ways of doing things. Personnel policies and procedures form a large part of this institutional responsibility. The supervisor may have authority to select, place, and evaluate employees, or any or all of these functions may be carried on by the personnel specialist. The latter arrangement is apt to be the case in civil service systems. The supervisor's choice of a worker, for example, may only be in terms of accepting or refusing to accept the worker selected by others. In any case, how the supervisor carries on these personnel operations is usually prescribed for him. He merely needs to know the forms and procedures, the rules and regulations in order to get along. This is particularly true in public administration. In many instances, indeed, institutional regulations interfere with good supervision. This is especially true in discipline cases, where the organization's rules are further complicated by union regulations. Attendance, punctuality, and personal conduct of the worker in conformity with "company rules," as well as the conservation and salvage of equipment and supplies, may all be spelled out in regulations.

To sum up, the supervisor must know the kind of work that is done by his unit and the policies and procedures of his agency, but neither the work nor the rules are the key to supervision. The critical knowledge and the indispensable skill for effective supervision is nothing less than personal leadership. This is the more distinctive phase of supervision—the human side.

2. Supervisory Skills

Identification of supervisory skills. Much of the research in the field of supervision centers around identification of the necessary skills for supervision in terms of the three areas of job relationships mentioned in the previous section. Some social research in group interaction closely relates supervisory skills to group acceptance. These studies speak of the importance of "interpersonal perception," and the degree to which it enhances job productivity. Thus the perception of a group member viewing the supervisor as friendly and helpful has an influence on work relations in a positive manner, as against perceptions of hostility or indifference between the leader of the group and the key members.[7]

---

[7] Illustrative is Fiedler, Fred E., *Leader Attitudes and Group Effectiveness,* Urbana: University of Illinois Press, 1958.

In the writings on management, the supervisory skills are identified as functions either of a "task nature" or of a "social nature." The prime question is whether or not these two facts of the supervisory skills can be combined in the same person.

In a different way, the supervisory skills have been categorized as those of job competence, those necessary for the transfer of job competence to the workers supervised, and those personal qualities necessary to help the workers to achieve job satisfaction within the framework of the organization's goals. These skills the supervisor needs in order to organize and coordinate the work and to develop and guide his employees.

Record of Training Within Industry Program. These required skills of supervision were given a central place by the Training Within Industry Program of the War Manpower Commission in World War II. During the war, when there was heavy pressure on learning fast, the essentials of learning the supervisor's job were stripped down to a minimum of three: JIT—Job Instruction Training; JMT—Job Methods Training; and JRT—Job Relations Training. Literally, hundreds of thousands of foremen were trained in three basic supervisory skills: (1) how to instruct a worker to do a job; (2) how to lay out methods and improve work processes; and (3) how to deal personally with workers. The program was based on the assumption that this was the irreducible minimum of supervisory skills.

The program was intended as a means whereby government could assist industry to meet the need for an enormous increase in supervisory personnel. Under auspices of the Training Within Industry (TWI) Service of the War Manpower Commission, headed by industrial experts of long experience, a nationwide effort was launched which extended to thousands of factories and offices throughout the country. These installed TWI's short, intensive training programs in job instruction, job methods, and job relations. By 1944, well over a million supervisors in war production industries had taken one or more of these courses.

Although the number of participants proves little, startling results were achieved by this emphasis on the skills of supervision. Two out of every three plants served by TWI reported production increases up to 25 per cent, and the other third found that better supervision raised output from 25 to no less than 500 per cent. Comparable savings in manpower and in the time needed to break in new workers, in reduced cost of scrap and waste, and in fewer accidents were reported. In some plants, absenteeism was cut in half, and the rate of turnover showed a constant decrease.[8] Following successful use in industry, experiments were carried on to determine whether the TWI program would be equally effective in governmental

---

[8] Similar results were reported in Great Britain, where the TWI program was introduced in 1944 by F. H. Perkins of the Ministry of Education, following a six-months' study of the program in the United States. See Tickner, F. J., *Modern Staff Training,* London: University of London Press, 1952.

agencies. The use of this program in government demonstrated that although the work and the environment may vary widely, the skills involved in supervising jobs are identical in most supervisor-employee situations.

There were several reasons for the popularity and effectiveness of the TWI program. First, the period needed for training was short. Five two-hour sessions for each of the three phases of the program acquainted the supervisor with the essentials and gave him some experience in practice and observation. Second, there was no lengthy text; the material which the supervisor needed to assist him in application of the principles learned was provided on a small blue card which he could carry in his wallet. Third, the training was given by members of the establishment in which the supervisor worked, and the interest of management engendered by the program was reflected in the interest of the supervisors. In order to make the TWI formula available to federal agencies, the United States Civil Service Commission set up a staff to train management personnel to administer the program to supervisors. The light which it shed on the role of the supervisor makes the TWI program of lasting interest. The basic elements of each of the three phases of the program deserve review.

Elements of job instruction. In Job Instruction Training (JIT) the supervisor is shown how to explain a new job to an employee, how to demonstrate it so that the employee can follow each step, and how to coach the employee while he practices the operation for mastery of each of the steps. Pitfalls in the instruction process are not only pointed out to the supervisor, but he is instructed in techniques that help him avoid giving the employee more than he can absorb at one time or using technical language that the learner cannot comprehend. The supervisor finds that instructing has two steps: (1) getting ready to instruct, and (2) actual instruction.

Each member of the group takes his turn in presenting an actual demonstration of the methods by using a job operation in his own office or shop. Before he can do this, he must break down the job into a sequence of steps and decide what key points the learner must know. In the demonstration before the group, the supervisor uses the job breakdown that he himself has prepared and follows a four-step method to instruct another member, who acts as a learner. The group then discusses the demonstration, criticizes the presentation, and suggests improvements.

Job methods training. Job Methods Training (JMT) assists the supervisor to overcome the strongest single impediment to management progress —the dead weight of tradition or the habit of doing things the way they have always been done. Habits are powerful, and the habitual method may survive simply because we are used to it, not because it is the best method. The only way that organizations can rid themselves of outmoded procedures, unnecessary operations, and wasteful duplications of effort is to subject every activity periodically to searching re-examination.

After being given a sound conception of the methods applied to an actual operation, each supervisor is required to analyze a job in his unit and to make concrete recommendations for changing the job to bring about more effective use of manpower, materials, and equipment. Each supervisor demonstrates how he analyzed the present operation and how he questioned every detail. He then explains the new method he has developed to eliminate unnecessary operations, showing how he combines, rearranges, and simplifies the details to make the job easier, faster, and more economical. The objective of the JMT program is to encourage constant reappraisal of existing methods. It can be articulated with employee suggestion systems, with employee "councils," and with agency planning and procedure work. With JMT as a basis for work evaluation, a flow of ideas for new and better ways of doing old jobs is stimulated.

The great virtue of JMT is that it opens up to every supervisor the opportunity to be creative about his work. In this natural tendency of human beings, management possesses an inexhaustible spring of improvement that is still virtually untapped. Although management may recognize the necessity for revising its procedures to effect modifications and shortcuts, too often it turns this task over to specialized planning staffs or methods engineers and overlooks the potential flow of ideas that could come from the mass of employees on the job. JMT does not make methods engineers, nor is it intended to do so. It does put into the supervisor's hands a tool that will enable him to examine operations critically and to work out improvements logically and effectively.

Management is incapable of streamlining all jobs in the organization without the vigorous assistance of the supervisor. The supervisor works closely with employees in the details of processes and projects and has intimate knowledge of a multitude of operations that in the aggregate make up the program of the agency. Many times, the supervisor is the only manager or representative of management who knows enough about the technical aspects of his unit to have intelligent views about it. Job Methods Training had such an immediate positive effect on the attitude of supervisors toward their own jobs that in some agencies the individual employee was also given the training. The results were gratifying. Besides demonstrating that the program is easily within the capacity of the average employee, this extension to the lowest level in the organization gave recognition to the fact that suggestions from everywhere are desired by alert top management. The natural reluctance which each of us has toward criticism of our superiors is overcome when such criticism is asked for.

Job relations training. The aim of Job Relations Training (JRT), the third phase of the TWI program, was to transmit to the supervisor "the foundation of good relations," the general knowledge essential to dealing with all employees, and to acquaint him with some of the techniques basic to the handling of individual problems. Special problems arise in any supervisory situation, because employees are not a "great grey mass," but individuals, each with his own reactions, emotions, backgrounds, and abilities. For many supervisors, the most difficult part of their job is to acquire the knack of dealing with employees. Supervisors do not need a course in applied psychology to get results through other people, but they do need an understanding of the fundamentals that lie behind employee attitudes. They also need a workable method of applying those fundamentals.

The training methods for JRT were much the same as for the two other phases of the TWI program. The technique of maintaining good relations is demonstrated to the group of participants, using actual cases from job situations. Each supervisor then brings in a case from his own unit and presents an application of the JRT method. The group helps him to establish what his real objective is, what facts need to be secured, what possible actions he could take, and the probable effect of each action. No final judgment is passed on the supervisor's solution. The purpose of the training is to give him skill in arriving at decisions, not to hand him a set of ready-made decisions. The training supplies the supervisor with an understanding of job attitudes and the methods of handling employee relations problems.

Any approach to the problems arising out of human relationships must be made inevitably on the basis of the individual case. Each individual brings to a job his own individual attitudes, his hopes and ambitions, his aptitudes and his interests. A given situation will affect each individual according to his own point of view. The same situation may affect him in an entirely different way on another occasion. Furthermore, all of us have other things burdening us besides our jobs—our health, our family, and our future, to name but a few. Any of these can well interfere with our state of mind. The average supervisor, though not in need of being a trained psychologist, will make sound, or at least sounder, decisions when given a technique of unearthing the facts underlying employee attitudes. If he uses job-relations techniques, his decisions will be better because he will try to learn all the facts in each case—not merely those which appear on the surface—and because he will not consider the case closed until the decision has been fully thought through.

Proficiency in the art of leadership is important, no matter how well the supervisor masters the points of the JRT program. Perhaps an outstanding leader must be born, but skill in leadership can certainly be improved, as JRT has demonstrated. Application of its fundamental propositions does have an important bearing on human relations on the job.

Research in supervisory skills and its application. Since the development of the TWI program, research in supervisory skills has been mainly in the field of identification of specific methods of supervision and of relating these to productivity and employee satisfaction. Some of the research has attempted to establish a relationship between the personal qualities of leadership and the degree to which the skills not inborn can be provided within the job situation. One of the studies concerns itself with the relationship of sociometric distance between the supervisor and his key worker to job performance of the entire group. This study established the fact that when the supervisor, for example, has a high degree of innate psychological distance which would prevent his establishing close working relationships with his workers, he can achieve the optimum working relationship by a high "sociometric preference" for his key worker.[9]

This type of research has to do with "treating people like individuals," one of the key concepts of the JRT phase of the TWI program. Likewise, advancements in instructional methods and employee participation in the learning of job skills may be considered to be outgrowths of Job Instruction Training. The need to integrate manpower, materials, and machinery later led to more sophisticated studies of systems analysis, methods analysis, and even of operations research. The highly condensed solutions of JIT, JMT, and JRT are, by themselves, merely shots in the arm. The supervisor must be provided with a plan for developing skill on the job. Follow-up is highly important, for continued use and perfection of his skills must be the watchword if the supervisor is to become adept at his trade.

Management must accept the implications of this kind of training by re-examining its policies and operations to see if they conflict with the tasks of the first-line supervisor. It is unreasonable to hope that he will maintain much enthusiasm for improving job methods in the face of hostility of his own supervisor every time he makes a suggestion. A supervisor will not be convinced very long that his superiors actually want to treat employees fairly and intelligently, if he himself is suffering from unfair or unintelligent treatment. He will relax his efforts if his superiors ignore the need for good employee relations in formulating or enforcing personnel policies.[10] Again, the supervisor may become fully convinced that it is part of his job to improve his employees' efficiency through training on the job, but this conviction will not be sustained if no continued interest is taken higher up in his own improvement. This is another way of saying that programs designed primarily for first-line supervisors enunciate ideas that are applicable anywhere in the organizational hierarchy right up to the head of the agency.

All of the three phases of the TWI program were utilized not only by the federal government but by states, counties, and cities as well.[11] Many of these jurisdictions took advantage of TWI trainers to secure supervisory instruction within their own jurisdictions. Others used materials developed

---

[9] Fiedler, Fred E., *op. cit.* above in note 7.

[10] In order for human relations training to be effective, top leadership must live it "in their own behavior where all can see it." Pfiffner, John M., and Mason, Frank V. K., "Personnel Management at the Grass Roots," *Personnel Administration,* May-June 1957, Vol. 20 (No. 3), p. 33.

[11] An excellent account of the program is offered in War Manpower Commission, Bureau of Training, Training Within Industry Service, *The Training Within Industry Report, 1940-45,* Washington: Government Printing Office, 1945.

by the work improvement program of the United States Civil Service Commission, and still others used the foundation of the TWI program to develop training materials particularly suited to their own organizational situation.[12]

Other developments. Additional aids to supervisory development have come into recent prominence. One of these is work simplification. It is built around three problems: (1) the distribution of work; (2) the sequence of work; and (3) the volume of work. For each problem there is an elementary aid: (1) the work-distribution chart; (2) the process chart; and (3) the work count, or work measurement. The supervisor can be trained in the use of these three devices in order to solve each of these problems as they arise.[13]

The use of the conference as a supervisory training medium is probably more widespread than any other single aid. In addition to the opportunity which conference participation gives the supervisor to exchange ideas and techniques with other supervisors, this training device usually provides some practice in conference leadership. Such leadership training has been found of assistance to the supervisor in presenting ideas to his subordinates and in counseling them. As a device whereby management at all levels can turn its attention at the same time to the same problem, the conference has been developed into the "management round table." Weekly guide sheets are issued by a training section, and each supervisor in the organization meets with his subordinates for discussion of a chosen topic. The conference chain is completed at the level of the first-line supervisor, who may be asked to take his turn as chairman or as conferee. Each conference group fills out a "record of meeting card," which goes up and down the hierarchy through the chairman of each group. On this card are noted questions which the group desires answered, suggestions to other groups, and suggestions for management improvement or other conference topics. These cards eventually return to the training section, which takes responsibility for disseminating the requested information.

As the case was the core around which JRT was built, so the case method has long been a conspicuous part of professional training in law, medicine, social work, and other fields. Although the case method will vary in form, depending on the field of its application, it provides essentially a study of actual occurrences in the past in preparation for the solution of similar

---

[12] In addition to those materials developed by various federal agencies, excellent materials for assistance to supervisors were prepared by many state and local personnel boards and civil service commissions. Illustrative are the 25 pamphlets on different aspects of management problems prepared by the Air Force, available for a small fee. See U. S. Air Force, *Management Course for Air Force Supervisors,* Washington: Government Printing Office, 1955.

[13] *Cf.* United States Bureau of the Budget, *Trainer's Guide to the Work Simplification Training Sessions; Specifications for Agency Work Simplification; Supervisor's Guide to the Work Distribution Chart; Supervisor's Guide to the Process Chart; Supervisor's Guide to the Work Count,* all Washington: Government Printing Office, 1945. The essence of these materials is also available in Publication No. 91, Chicago: Public Administration Service, 1945.

problems in the future.[14] Use of the case method for supervisory training gives the supervisor practice not only in observation of the behavior of his subordinates but also in recording his observations. He also learns to study the observations of others for their general applicability to his field of interest.

The incident technique is a modification of the case method as an instructional device, but disarms the objection to the case method—namely, that busy supervisors don't have time to read cases. The incident process, as devised by Paul and Faith Pigors, permits the development of the facts of the case through a resource person who answers questions of the conferees. On this basis, the problem is identified, the decision made and tested, and the facts isolated which substantiate or refute the decision.[15]

Assistance by specialists. These devices are only a few of the many being developed by managers, training officers, and training divisions to assist the supervisor in the performance of his task. Today the supervisor has the help of many specialists in the fulfillment of his responsibilities, especially a training officer or a training division. In some of the large companies, the supervisor's instruction is aided through preparation for the individual worker of detailed pictures of the operation being performed. The employee can run the pictures back and forth through an individual projector located at his work place, and he can also operate the sound track which supplements supervisory instructions of the task.

In the general handling of personnel matters, the supervisor likewise has many things done for him by a recruiting officer, an employment officer, and other specialists in personnel matters. To assist him to develop new methods, usually a planning staff is at hand, often stimulating him to improve old methods and work procedures. An employee counselor or employee relations officer in many jurisdictions helps him in the handling of problems of morale and any unusual cases of employee adjustment. The supervisor does not have to perform his job alone; but the burden continues to be his, for in the concrete situation all of this is his job.

3. Problems of Supervision

Variations in supervisory situations. Some of the problems of supervision have been indicated in the preceding sections of this chapter. Here we shall attempt to pinpoint the general nature of these problems and indicate some of the thinking that has been done in regard to them. The basic problems of supervision relate to (1) the determination of the qualities of supervision

---

[14] For the development of the case method in public personnel administration, see Reining, Henry, Jr., "Case Method and Public Personnel Administration," *Public Personnel Review,* July 1951, Vol. 12 (No. 3), p. 151 *ff.,* with references to the use of the case method in many other disciplines.

[15] A director's manual for the use of this process has been made available by the authors. Pigors, Paul and Faith, *Director's Manual: The Incident Process,* Washington: Bureau of National Affairs, 1955.

needed in different situations; (2) the finding and retention of capable supervisors and the extent to which their selection is related to an understanding by management of the supervisor's job and the qualities required; and (3) the relationship of the "institutional climate" to effective supervision.

Specific qualifications for supervisory responsibility vary with the people supervised and with the kind of work. The supervisor whose range of duties is narrow probably need not be as specifically qualified as the supervisor whose responsibilities are comprehensive in terms of the work of his unit. The supervisor who is bolstered by a training assistant, personnel officer, and employee counselor probably need not be as broadly trained as one who has to work on his own without such services. The level of supervision also will determine the relationship of the amount of detailed knowledge to the mental ability needed in the supervisor. Generally, the first-line supervisor will have less need for high intellectual ability than for detailed knowledge of the work to be done.

The kind of people supervised affects the specific abilities in dealing with them which the effective supervisor requires. Recent work in the field of research management points up the problems arising in the supervision of highly skilled technicians or highly educated professional employees. In addition to the "prima donna" temperaments likely to be displayed, the more important question arises of the optimum arrangements for supervision calling for careful planning and integration of the work done with organization goals and policies.

Variation in required qualities according to the situation supervised raises problems also in the field of supervisory rating. How does one rate a supervisor of a stenographic pool and a supervisor of a research unit of scientists in terms that will reflect equally the possession of the basic skills of supervision? In like manner, what similar means do these two supervisors use to rate their subordinates? The near abandonment of the formal rating system and the increasing emphasis on the use of rating procedure as a means of employee guidance instead of evaluation show how difficult it is to apply ratings with uniform meanings throughout an agency or a jurisdiction.

Criteria for selecting supervisors. All too often in the past, because of the emphasis on production rather than on the producers, the best worker in the shop or office was appointed as the foreman or supervisor. In addition, large industrial organizations and governmental agencies with involved procedures were prone to promote "the old hand" because he "knows the ropes." Both of these qualities have great value in a supervisor. But when used alone as bases for supervisory selection, they ignore the key to the supervisor's job—the personal qualifications that enable him to work with others and to make them work better. Seniority, alone, is one of the worst possible bases for picking supervisors. Someone has very pointedly remarked that twenty years of experience may be simply one year's experience repeated twenty times.

Ability to do skilfully the work supervised is helpful because it enables the supervisor to answer questions by his own example. Furthermore, it enables him to lay out the work in such a way that one worker is not overburdened and another underemployed. Skill in the task is also of assistance in judging the results of the work of subordinates. However, too great an expertness in the work is not desirable, especially if it tends to make the supervisor the best worker of the unit, rather than its supervisor. More important than expert job knowledge is a sense of system and method that enables the supervisor to organize and coordinate the work of his subordinates.

Personal qualifications. Professor John M. Pfiffner has identified the main personal qualifications of importance to the supervisory function as follows: (1) liking for people; (2) emotional stability; (3) integrity; (4) courage and fortitude; (5) enthusiasm for the work; (6) high ethical standards; and (7) curiosity and intellectual ability. No doubt, the best supervisory material comes from among those who like people, who enjoy working with others, who have the ability to attract others to themselves, who can motivate them positively and unite them in their work. Without emotional stability, the supervisor will not be able to control himself. If he cannot control himself at all times, if he is apt to speak to an employee in anger, he is not a good supervisor. Integrity implies an objective attitude which grows out of a knowledge of one's strength and weakness. Such a knowledge permits the supervisor to be level-headed toward others, especially in the handling of grievances.

Along with emotional balance, there should be balance in other traits as well. It seems fairly well established in psychological testing that good supervisory material is more dominant than recessive, more extroverted than introverted, more self-sufficient than dependent on others. But any of these traits, when carried to an extreme, is harmful. An individual who must dominate in every situation certainly is not good supervisory material. Neither is the individual who is so completely extroverted that he is not aware of the reactions of others. A man so well integrated and stable that nothing can ruffle him is by that very fact often deprived of motivating power and of the drive that may lead him or others far. Likewise, the supervisor who carries self-sufficiency to the extreme, never seeking advice from others, is apt to become an autocrat in his actions. Getting down to physical characteristics, it does help if the supervisor "cuts a good figure"—if he has the physical presence to command the attention of others.

Courage and fortitude make the supervisor fully assume responsibility in all cases where he should. Otherwise he will not have the stamina to take action decisively, to "walk toward danger," to say "no" when he should, to confess mistakes frankly. However, boldness must be balanced with caution, bravery with tact. Otherwise, the supervisor will "stick his neck out" until someone hacks it off. Again, without enthusiasm for his work, the supervisor finds it difficult to engender enthusiasm in others. He should love his job and be absorbed in it. Then he engenders enthusiasm by his own example. If he is career-minded, he will foster what has been called "clan pride" or *esprit de corps,* thus furnishing a subtle but effective motivation that is an all-important morale factor.

Ethical considerations are important. Whether it be petty pilfering of the stamp box, abusing the expense account for personal purposes, being careless about one's credit rating, piling up traffic offenses, or the wrong kinds of amorous involvements—any of these actions reflects on the respect and dignity that must attend the supervisor if he is to do his best at his job. Supervision requires a natural assumption of responsibility and a natural desire to set a good example. Default may well impair the value of such example. Not the least qualification is an inquiring mind, with an appetite for unsolved problems. The supervisor must not be submerged in the details of the work of his unit, but be detached enough to see the problems beneath. Furthermore, he needs to be sufficiently superior in intellect to be able to have an effective approach to problems and to be a good problem-solver. He needs the ability to separate essentials from nonessentials. He should be capable of making decisions in a deliberate manner, and not "by the seat of his pants."

How to pick supervisors. How to find qualified supervisory material is a critical problem. The only adequate answer is to have a plan well prepared in advance. Although this is the responsibility of top management, unless the workers also know the plan, they cannot have adequate incentive and direction to achieve advancement. In many work situations today, the system for picking supervisors is still the very informal and almost entirely unplanned one of observing workers on the job. When a likely candidate for a supervisory post is spotted, his name is recorded in the mind or perhaps the notebook of the boss, depending on how systematic he is. When an opportunity comes up, the various candidates are interviewed and their work records compared; then one is chosen. This system, informal as it may seem to be, can be a good one if definite standards are kept in mind. Some practices have been found to aid in the effectiveness of such a system.

For one, keeping pertinent information for each worker in a personnel folder will reduce the chances of an ill-considered choice. Such information may include records of work performance, but also document his behavior under tension, how he gets along with others, whether he is ambitious, whether he has made any suggestions for improvement of the work, and how he conducts himself off the job. The personal interview is another frequently used technique, particularly if the superior making the selection of the supervisor is two or three levels removed from the candidate and does not know his work intimately. Although the interview is generally useful in the determination of personal traits, it does not have sufficient validity to contradict the record of work experience or the recommendations of former superiors. These in particular should be given weight, but caution should also be exercised. The superior's recommendation is only as good as the superior himself. If he is one who, for his own self-protection, selects the worker who is aggressive and pushes himself forward, or if he notices only the people who are pleasant and innocuous, his recommendation would be misleading to that extent. By and large, however, it is to be doubted whether the superior's recommendation should ever be ignored.

Written tests can be helpful indicators in the selection of supervisors, provided their use is restricted to those factors which can be readily determined by such means—that is, general intelligence and subject-matter knowledge. It has been demonstrated that the intelligence test is a fairly good indicator of supervisory talent, provided complete reliance is not placed upon it and further screening takes place. The supervisor cannot be effective unless he is superior in intelligence or, as a bare minimum, is as intelligent as the average worker under him. A grave question arises, however, as to whether inventories of personal traits or basic interests may be used with the same complete assurance in a competitive situation. On the other hand, the competitive promotional examination can be a useful instrument; it is used by state and local governments in certain jurisdictions. However, it does not accomplish its purpose unless those persons identified in other ways as potential supervisory material are induced to take the examination. The mere posting of the opportunity to take a competitive examination would not insure the full usefulness of this device.

Election of supervisors by their fellow workers has been tried in a number of places and found to be none too successful. It is doubtful whether the most popular member of a group is always the best supervisor, although supervisors should conduct themselves in such a way that they would be the choice of the workers. A much better device is an understudy system. This gives workers with identifiable supervisory talent the opportunity to demonstrate their ability as supervisors. During a probationary period, when the candidate is acting as understudy, he should be given training to qualify him fully for his job. His performance both as acting supervisor during periods when the boss is away and as trainee will allow a fairly definitive rating of his promise.

Institutional climate. The character of supervision in any given organization is neither merely a reflection of a particular function or activity that is being supervised nor principally the result of the personal qualifications of the supervisor, important as these are. The policies imposed upon the first-line supervisor by top management and the attitudes of executives and managers on the intermediate levels above him affect his work to a great extent. These factors governing the "institutional climate" play a definite role in the character of supervision.

Of major importance in the "institutional climate" is the extent to which supervisors are permitted to participate in policy-making. If the agency head sees to it that managers on the intermediate levels down to the first-line supervisor meet regularly with their work associates to discuss the objectives of the organization in application to their area of responsibility, supervisors will have an opportunity to contribute to the making of policy. The "institutional climate" will more than likely be one in which the supervisor can do his best job, where his discretion is not sharply limited and interfering pressures are minimized. Pressures arising from uncoordinated functional specialization in the organization are lessened when all levels participate in policy-making. Other pressures resulting from legal restrictions on the exercise of supervisory control, especially in matters of discipline, are more uniformly coped with in the organization when higher levels of management "back up" the supervisor on the strength of the facts.

Another significant aspect of "institutional climate" is reflected in the degree to which it is possible for the supervisor to secure voluntary and spontaneous work response. Usually, the good supervisor is able to inspire in the employee loyalty to the organization, but the development of such loyalty becomes an impossible task when the environment is frigid and repulsive to the worker. This leads to the question of democracy versus hierarchy, the manner in which top management interprets the authority of the supervisor as a command function or as a leadership function.[16] When top management accepts the fact that authority arises out of "the law of the situation"—to use Mary Parker Follett's phrase—and thus springs from the intrinsic competence, worthiness, and strength of the individual in authority, the "institutional climate" will be conducive to effective supervision.

The "institutional climate" is further set by the manner in which management makes the workers aware of their obligations to the organization. Fair dealing and justice sometimes require painful measures for the good of the employees themselves. Democracy in administration cannot survive in the ways of a submissive supervisor, who dares not take action for fear of worker resentment. The spirit and practice of supervision can be democratic without infringing upon the essentials of manual-prescribed discipline. Democratic supervision requires a certain definiteness in the handling of human situations, in accordance with the laws and regulations. None can deny that even supervisors in the first line are the fingers on the hands of management; they are first-line executives as well. The supervisor

---

[16] See Chapter 21, "Morale and Discipline."

is apt to regard himself as a manager and an executive when his place is clearly indicated to him by top management and when top management is sympathetic to the worker. If the "institutional climate" is such that the worker is suppressed or exploited by management, the sympathetic supervisor is prone to side with the workers in a controversy with management.

Summary. Many of the problems of supervision that affect the practice of that art can be telescoped into one question—that of the short-run versus the long-run point of view. Management may insist on immediate peak production at any given level of work without taking time and money for training the worker or without giving him an opportunity to train and develop himself. Such a policy has far-reaching implications for the supervisor's role, for then the job contends against the individual's personal development.

In the past, government has generally done less than enough to provide training and educational opportunity by placing immediate efficiency ahead of long-run self-development. Today, however, governments are more and more accepting a training responsibility both to transmit skills and to deal with the human resources of the organization. A workable long-run arrangement requires that every individual be given an opportunity to find the type of work for which he has the greatest aptitude, and then be helped actively to develop himself to capacity. In broadest terms, this is the question of how much of each day is going to be given to planning for future days, and how much time should go into training to increase efficiency and productivity for the future. The balance may vary with different situations, but there must be a balance. The federal training legislation of 1958 may help to bring forth a better balance.

Do we make the most of supervision? The answer is that we do not, by any means, neither in business nor in government. By developing civil service systems and higher staff services, such as personnel, budgeting, and management planning, government has tried in a sense to make up for deficiencies in supervision. Today management is finding it increasingly to its interest to re-evaluate the role of the supervisor in the organization in an attempt to enhance rather than to thwart the potentialities of supervision.

Chapter 20 •

Applying Management Knowledge

1. Evolutionary Currents

Beginnings of the analytical approach. As we have seen earlier,[1] the analytical approach to American public administration had its origin in the establishment of the New York Bureau of Municipal Research in 1906. The methodically planned and systematically executed surveys undertaken by that bureau led to many striking improvements in the government of the city. The success of those surveys won almost instantaneous recognition for the analytical approach that supported them. Other communities called on the New York Bureau for help. Surveys were made of cities, counties, and states. Citizens saw that facts were more powerful than partisan assertions. As a result, bureaus of governmental research sprang up in many places, often staffed by men trained at the New York Bureau.

These research agencies helped political leaders to carry forward many basic reforms—elimination of the spoils system; municipal home rule; election reforms; and direct popular control through referendum and recall of officials. New programs were added, such as the short ballot; strengthening the chief executive; elimination of administration by legislative committees and independent boards; establishment of budget, accounting, and audit systems; departmental reorganization; scientific tax assessment; centralized purchasing; and judicial reform. The National Municipal League, established in 1894, gained in influence as it incorporated many of these features in its model city charter and provided a clearing house of best practices for citizen groups.

These governmental research bureaus and similar bodies carry on today. However, as the value of the methods of private research agencies became evident, governments also began to undertake such research. California long stood at the head of the list with the Los Angeles City Bureau of Budget and Efficiency and the Los Angeles County Bureau of Efficiency (later called Bureau of Administrative Research). The Division of Investigation of the City of New York and the Commission on Publicity and

---

[1] See Chapter 2, "The Study of Public Administration."

406

Efficiency of Toledo were early prototypes. In the federal government, the Bureau of Efficiency did useful work for almost twenty years, but was abolished in 1933. All of these endeavors advanced the cause of objective search for the facts.

Growth of systematic inquiry. The Commission on Economy and Efficiency, appointed in 1910 by President Taft, was in large part an outgrowth of the work of the governmental research bureaus. The commission presented a series of reports on the necessity for a national budget system, better departmental working methods, and other administrative reforms in the federal government. Although no immediate action was taken by Congress, the studies paved the way for later improvement, and the ideas they set forth lived on. Similar work was put under way in New York State under Governor Charles E. Hughes. Ultimately, a thoroughgoing reorganization of the state government grew out of the proposals of the New York Constitutional Convention of 1915. Special commissions of inquiry appointed by state and local chief executives appeared with increasing frequency as the years went by. Likewise, legislative committees undertook inquiries of their own. One of the most noteworthy was the Special Joint Committee on Taxation and Retrenchment in New York State, which began its work in 1921 under the chairmanship of Frederick Davenport. Both congressional committees and presidents have given increasing attention to organizational and administrative problems.[2] In 1937, comprehensive reports on these subjects were submitted by the President's Committee on Administrative Management[3] and by the Brookings Institution,[4] the latter employed by the Select Committee to Investigate the Executive Agencies of the Government. During World War II, the so-called Truman and Ramspeck committees made noteworthy investigations of specific aspects of administration. In recent years the Senate and House Committees on Government Operations have engaged in studies of organization and administration of federal agencies.

Although these congressional inquiries resulted in the tightening of administrative operations and the elimination of instances of inefficiency, few tangible gains in administrative organization have emerged from direct action by Congress. On the other hand, the work of the President's Committee on Administrative Management was outstanding. Its reports prepared the way for important organizational improvements effected on the eve of World War II. Since that war, systematic inquiry has increased at all levels of government—federal, state, and local. At the federal level,

---

[2] For a historical survey, see Meriam, Lewis, and Schmeckebier, Laurence F., *Reorganization of the National Government,* p. 181 *ff.,* Washington: Brookings Institution, 1939. See also Kraines, Oscar, *Congress and the Challenge of Big Government,* New York: Bookman Associates, 1958.

[3] See its *Report with Special Studies,* Washington: Government Printing Office, 1937.

[4] Senate Report No. 1275, 75th Cong., 1st Sess., Washington, 1937.

major efforts were carried forth by the two "Hoover Commissions," created by Congress in 1947 and in 1953. To avoid political difficulties, both commissions were organized on a bipartisan basis, with representation from Congress, the executive branch, and the public. "Task forces" of experts were appointed by both commissions to explore almost every main field of governmental activity. The first commission and its task forces produced some 5,000,000 words of text and 273 recommendations, comprising no doubt the most extensive study of government ever undertaken. A Citizen's Committee for the Hoover Report undertook the task of educating the general public on the significance of proposed reform measures. Many changes were initiated through orders by department heads and their subordinates, through administrative instructions of the President, through reorganization plans submitted by the President to Congress, and through new legislation.

While the two Hoover Commissions turned the spotlight on governmental problems on the federal level, as early as 1950 over 23 states and two territories had established agencies to study the organization and operation of their governments.[5] The contagion of these examples also moved into the municipalities. The mayor of New York City established a committee on management problems. As another illustration, in 1958 the city of Seattle engaged the services of a management consulting firm to do a comprehensive survey of its administrative operations. At the local level, however, the focus is chiefly on the increasing difficulties of providing effective public services in metropolitan areas. Major surveys have been made in St. Louis, Dayton, Philadelphia, San Diego, and Dade County, Florida. One of the most comprehensive surveys is that by the Cleveland Metropolitan Services Commission.

Academic support. Such efforts from an early date have required men and women trained in public administration and management improvement. The staff of the New York Bureau of Municipal Research had been in great demand in many places. To meet this demand, the bureau in 1911 set up a Training School for Public Service. The program acquired characteristic features of graduate training under Charles A. Beard and later under William E. Mosher. About the same time, the universities began to be interested not only in governmental research, but also in the preparation of students for administrative posts. Early arrangements mostly took the form of adding courses in public administration to political science curricula or of establishing centers of governmental research or public affairs. The current trend is toward separate professional schools, some covering a number of fields. More than 100 universities offer programs in public administration. Typical of the varied approaches are those employed at the following universities: Alabama, American, Cali-

---

[5] See *Reorganizing State Government: A Report on Administrative Management in the States and a Review of Recent Trends in Reorganization*, Chicago: Council of State Governments, 1950.

fornia, Harvard, Kansas, Michigan, Minnesota, New York, Pennsylvania, Pittsburgh, Princeton, Southern California, and Texas. Some of these programs are at the undergraduate level, but increasingly the emphasis is on graduate education of a professional character. The doctorate in public administration is now awarded by several schools.

Syracuse University, an early pioneer, and Pittsburgh, which has recently entered the field in a broad way, provide an interesting contrast, although both of them place strong emphasis on administration. The Maxwell Graduate School of Citizenship and Public Affairs at Syracuse is a social science school, with public administration functioning as a branch of political science. The Graduate School of Public and International Affairs at Pittsburgh is a school organized on the basis of providing professional education for service in local, national, and international agencies and in related quasipublic undertakings. On the other hand, New York University has placed public administration and social work as units within a single school. California has its Bureau of Public Administration as an autonomous unit, separate from its Institute of International Relations and the political science department.

These schools, institutes, and bureaus have contributed significantly to administrative improvement of local, state, national, and international agencies. In addition to offering training in governmental research and administrative management, they have made surveys, loaned staff for the conduct of studies, and provided information and consultation. Moreover, the increasing attention given by universities to the social and behavioral sciences is making a significant contribution to improved public management. One example is the research in human relations and management conducted by the Institute of Social Research at the University of Michigan, which includes the Survey Research Center and the Research Center for Group Dynamics. Its studies of worker satisfaction, productivity, and effectiveness of organization are especially noteworthy.[6] The Stanford Research Institute has also engaged in projects in human relations, motivation, and related aspects of organization to which the applied psychologist can make a contribution. Other examples of efforts to explore these new dimensions of administration are Yale's Labor and Management Center, Cornell's School of Industrial and Labor Relations, Pittsburgh's Administrative Science Center, and Michigan State's Institute for Community Development and Services.

Universities also are beginning to provide special short-term training programs for the higher-level government career executives—such as Wayne State, Chicago, New York, and California. The Brookings Institution, with foundation support, has initiated a conference program for further

---

[6] For reference to these studies and an illustration of research methods and content of a typical study, see Weiss, Robert S., *Process of Organization*, Ann Arbor: Survey Research Center, Institute for Social Research, University of Michigan, Publication No. 17, 1956.

development of federal career executives. The University of Chicago, again with foundation support, has begun to evaluate its program by trying to determine whether it is possible to increase the participant's capacity for "executive judgment." Another indication of the responsiveness of the universities to public needs is the growth of short-term programs geared to meet the needs of technical administrators running the various programs of government—health, public works, social welfare, police, and the like. Moreover, as a result of demand by governmental agencies, short-term institutes and workshops for practitioners are being offered by universities which give attention to administrative rather than technical matters. An example is the Upper Midwest Seminar in Public Health Administration given by the faculty of the University of Minnesota for state, city, and federal health administrators. In general, closer relationships between schools of public administration and other schools—such as those for engineering, social work, agriculture, education, military training, and business—would be mutually beneficial. Students in these fields interested in executive positions need an administrative capstone to their technical education.

Professional associations. Reflecting an increasingly professional attitude toward public administration, public officials have grouped together in organizations for the exchange of experience and information. Even before 1900, a number of such bodies were making contributions to better government—the American Public Health Association, the International Association of Chiefs of Police, the American Society for Municipal Improvements, and others. Another early development was the formation of state leagues of municipalities, which aroused interest in improving municipal practices and presented the needs of the cities to state legislatures. The work of such associations was given great impetus in the early 1930's by the foundation of Public Administration Clearing House in Chicago. It arranged for headquarters of a dozen or more of the principal organizations of public authorities and officials under one roof, commonly known as the "1313 Group" (1313 East 60th Street). Its members—typified by the Council of State Governments, the American Municipal Association, the American Society for Public Administration, the International City Managers Association, the Municipal Finance Officers Association, the Public Personnel Association, the American Public Welfare Association, and the American Public Works Association—are today enlisting thousands of officials in the cause of sound administration through conferences, professional journals, and dissemination of research. Other such associations are found in many professional and special fields at local, state, national, and international levels. There are more than 500 national organizations alone.[7]

---

[7] *Public Administration Organizations: A Directory of Unofficial Organizations in the Field of Public Administration in the United States and Canada,* Chicago: Public Administration Clearing House, 1954.

Public Administration Service (PAS) is especially significant for its contribution to improved administration. The work of the Research Committee of the International City Managers Association in 1930-33 in establishing and installing municipal standards and tested practices produced increasing demand for expert consulting assistance by cities and other public bodies. To fill this demand, and also to provide a home for the publications work previously performed by Municipal Administration Service, the "1313 Group" of organizations created PAS in 1933. With the termination of Public Administration Clearing House in 1957, PAS took over the common services to the other "1313" organizations.

Special mention is warranted of the American Society for Public Administration. With a membership of over 6,000, this association provides a common ground for public officials, academicians, researchers, and staffs of agencies concerned with public affairs to learn from each other and to promote better management in all sectors of the public service.

Role of the foundations. Most of the developments sketched thus far, and other studies too numerous to mention, have been made possible by foundation support. The Laura Spelman Memorial; the Rockefeller, Ford, and Falk Foundations; the Carnegie Corporation; and many others, have allocated millions of dollars for research, surveys, demonstrations, education, and services in public administration. Foundations have financed many projects of the New York Bureau of Municipal Research (since 1932 the Institute of Public Administration), much of the research of the Brookings Institution, basic studies like those carried on by President Hoover's Committee on Social Trends, the work of the Commission of Inquiry on Public Service Personnel and of the Committee on Public Administration of the Social Science Research Council, and projects of the "1313" organizations as well as of universities.[8] It was through an allocation by the Ford Foundation that the American Society for Public Administration was able to expand its activities significantly.

Foundation support has made possible metropolitan surveys, executive development programs, international study projects, the inter-university case programs, and special studies such as the survey of needed research activities in the personnel field by the Public Personnel Association.[9] But compared with the funds allocated to scientific, business, health, and other special fields, the total available for research in the vital field of public administration has remained meager.

Stimulus from private management. Even before the search for better administrative methods was under way in government, pioneers in industry had developed a fruitful technique of studying production problems, eventually to be known as "scientific management." Faced with the fact

---

[8] See Anderson, William, and Gaus, John M., *Research in Public Administration,* Chicago: Public Administration Service, 1945.

[9] Goode, Cecil E., *Public Research Frontiers,* Chicago: Public Personnel Association, 1958.

that employers were unable to adjust to the great industrial expansion after the Civil War, these pioneers began to study the methods by which production was controlled. Historically the movement began in 1886, when Henry R. Towne read his paper entitled "The Engineer as Economist" before the American Society of Mechanical Engineers. Towne proposed that an engineer should not only be interested in the invention, design, and installation of a machine, but also in devising means for the most effective operation in the shop. This idea of bringing the engineer into the problems of production suggested an entirely new relationship between employers and specialists. Its full implications were not explored by the society that Towne had addressed, which confined itself to discussing devices and methods of improvement in industry suggested by the experience of its members, such as piece rates.

Meanwhile, Frederick W. Taylor—as worker and later as foreman—was observing the causes of waste, breakdown in production, inefficiency in the use of materials and machines, conflict between workers and employers, and almost total lack of planning. Taylor began his inquiries by examining the daily problems of the shop. He experimented with all the variables connected with a certain operation, machine, or material until he found the best method of doing the job. He discovered that the study of one phase of operations led to another—to the relations of labor and management, and finally to the problems of basic organization. Taylor's ideas were presented in his *Principles of Scientific Management,* published in 1911,[10] and awakened worldwide interest in management circles. Further stimulation for the study of production costs resulted from hearings before the Interstate Commerce Commission in 1910-11, which put in question the operating methods of a railroad. Some of Taylor's associates, among them Henry L. Gantt and Frank B. Gilbreth, were called to testify on the new approach to management. It was at this time that the term "scientific management" was coined and first used publicly.

While the Taylor movement focused on the managerial problem of the shop, Henri Fayol in France set forth his managerial views from the angle of a key executive, rather than within the confines of a shop operation. His views extended the managerial focus to the problems of planning, organizing, coordinating, directing, and evaluating, all centered on the whole enterprise, not one of its parts. The broader concepts of Fayol underpin executive development in the United States today. Fayol's plea in 1911 for a profession of management is now a reality.

Much of today's concern with the worker and the executive as human beings is traceable to the research results of the "Hawthorne experiments" of the Harvard Graduate School of Business Administration conducted at the Western Electric Company in 1924. The discovery that working

---

[10] Republished New York: Harper, 1934.

conditions were less important than the worker's feelings of importance, status, and belonging started a new line of managerial probing in human relations. The studies of the Institute of Social Research of the University of Michigan have shown, for instance, that high productivity is closely related to employee-minded supervision, and that the human aspects of organization need to be blended with scientific management or the analytical approach.

In addition, the formation of management societies helped to raise professional standards and to disseminate information on new techniques to a much broader audience. Among the early bodies were the American Society of Civil Engineers, the Society for the Advancement of Management, and the National Office Management Association. The role of the American Management Association in research, documentation, dissemination, and training has done much to promote the wider understanding and application of effective management practice. The Systems and Procedures Association puts full attention on methods of management improvement. The management movement has extended throughout the world. The productivity programs initiated by the federal government after World War II in aiding other countries, and carried forward by the European Productivity Agency and various national bodies with similar aims, are especially notable. International interests are joined together through CIOS (Comité Internationale d'Organization Scientifique). No less important has been the expansion in recent years of business school curricula at many universities, with the result that one of every seven degree candidates in the United States is in the field of business administration. The research publications and journals of the business schools as well as the manuals published by management training staffs of industry provide valuable sources for government staffs. All of these developments have left an imprint on public administration. Increasingly, the common elements of administration, regardless of field or subject, are becoming evident and subject to common research. As an example, the Administrative Science Center at the University of Pittsburgh is studying the common elements of all fields as well as the basic theory of administration.

Streams of analytical methodology. Government has thus had three principal streams of administrative research and methodology on which to draw: (1) governmental research, (2) scientific management in industry, and (3) the behavioral approach, oriented toward human relations.

Perhaps the relatively slow adaptation of scientific management techniques was due to their inapplicability to many functions of government. In recent years, as scientific management has concerned itself more with problems of planning, organization, personnel, and administration, it has more to offer to government. The applicability of the newer insights in such fields as human relations and social science research has been avidly examined in government, including the military services. A common element in these advances has been the spirit of objective study.

2. Government Response

President's Committee on Administrative Management. Present-day approaches to the improvement of organization and management in the federal government stem directly from the work of the President's Committee on Administrative Management (1936-37). The pressure upon an overburdened President and the confusion of a rapidly mushrooming government precipitated the creation of that committee, consisting of Louis Brownlow as chairman, Dr. Luther Gulick, and Professor Charles E. Merriam. In contrast with the six major attempts in 40 years to cope with federal executive organization and management, a large number of the committee's recommendations were put into effect. Of greatest importance perhaps was the consolidation in 1939 of the Bureau of the Budget, the National Resources Planning Board, and the White House staff to form the Executive Office of the President. Included were six "anonymous assistants" to the President, of which one was designated Liaison Officer for Personnel Management.

For the first time, the President had in his own office expert staff to assist in providing essential information and help in handling his executive functions. Although all components of the Executive Office were in some degree concerned with the administrative management of the executive branch, it was the creation of the Division of Administrative Management under an assistant director of the Bureau of the Budget that gave the President certain specific tools.

Division of Administrative Management. A staff instruction of this division defined its functions as follows:

> The Division is generally responsible, as a part of the Bureau of the Budget, for assisting the President in bringing about better organization and management of the Federal Government . . . through . . . a better distribution of functions within and among Federal agencies, helping with the establishment of new agencies and liquidating old ones, assisting individual agencies on administrative problems, strengthening agency staff services, improving Governmentwide business practices and procedures, and reviewing the administrative aspects of proposed legislation and executive orders. A major emphasis is the development of programs which are of help to . . . agencies in solving their own problems.

One of the first steps taken by the Division of Administrative Management was to encourage and assist in the establishment of effective administrative planning, budgeting, programming, and personnel units within each agency. The ensuing network of staff connections gave impetus to improved administration and to strengthening executive leadership and management at all levels. The division applied itself in several principal directions: (1) assistance to the President in further studies of governmental organization and the drafting of reorganization plans, executive orders, and legislation; (2) conduct of departmental surveys at the request of the President as a demonstration of what the agencies should do for themselves; (3) activation in cooperation with the Treasury and the General Accounting Office of a program to improve the government's accounting and financial reporting procedures; (4) conduct of studies necessary to develop and later to liquidate the country's civilian war agencies and to improve the organization of the military services, including civilian-military relationships; (5) simplification and standardization of governmentwide procedures; (6) development, and promotion of agency use, of a wide range of administrative improvement techniques, and (7) assistance in the design of the organization and administrative arrangements for the government's international programs and those of other international bodies.

As a means of promoting better practices throughout the government, the division developed specialized management guides and programs for the widest possible use. Techniques were designed and documented in manual form, mostly for sale by the Government Printing Office. Emphasis was on such fields as work simplification, organizational analysis, form design, work measurement, production planning, property and supply control, and printing services. Agencies, in turn, took these techniques, refined them and put them to work, adding others like cost accounting, internal audits, and employee suggestion systems. More recently, the division's successor, the Office of Management and Organization, has placed emphasis on quantitative techniques, enhanced by automation and computers, such as automatic data processing. All of these tasks have required talented and trained personnel. Faculty and students from the colleges and universities, private governmental research staff, and management engineering experts were recruited for this purpose. With the aid of manuals or other materials assembled by the Bureau of the Budget and agency management staffs, thousands of civil servants were trained in the new management techniques. Most noteworthy were the Bureau of the Budget's training conferences in organization and methods work conducted for departmental officers. As another approach, the executive officers of the departments were brought together in monthly meetings.

Effects of the Hoover Commissions. These developments furnished a base for the proposals of the two Commissions on Organization of the Executive Branch of the Government, known as the Hoover Commissions (1947-49 and 1953-55). The Bureau of the Budget, with the personal backing of the President, capitalized on the fresh momentum for improvement and did the staff work for the President's management program and for his Advisory Committee on Management.[11] The President's manage-

---

[11] See President's Advisory Committee on Management, *Report to the President,* Washington: Government Printing Office, December 1952.

ment program had three objectives. The first was to create a clear line of authority from the President to agency heads, and from agency heads to their subordinates. The concept usually called "executive responsibility and accountability" was not a new one, but now something was done about it. The heads of most departments were given full authority over their subordinate bureaus by reorganization plans, and their positions were strengthened by authorizing additional top support, especially an Assistant Secretary for Administration or a Director of Administration, both intended to be career officers.

Other steps were designed to improve the common activities of government, such as financial management, work programming, performance budgeting, executive development, record and property administration, employee incentives, and supervision. Another category of actions was aimed at stimulating each agency to improve its individual management practices.

State and municipal progress. As mentioned in the opening section, commensurate activities have taken place at state and local levels. State reorganizations were usually patterned after those of the federal government. With the proliferation of governmental activities at the state level, there emerged the need for a strong executive with strengthened staff facilities. The use of administrative management and planning staffs has become prevalent among the states. New York, Pennsylvania, and California are good examples. In New York State fifteen agencies maintain planning units, in addition to the central one in the Division of the Budget, with activities such as organizational analysis, program planning, work measurement, reports control, operations review, and progress reporting. New York State likewise is attempting to strengthen departmental management by establishing administrative positions directly below the commissioner level, with responsibilities for budgetary and administrative planning. Pennsylvania also possesses administrative management units, with a Bureau of Management Methods located in the Office of Administration under the governor, which gives special attention to the training of organization and method analysts from all departments. California has administrative planning units at all of its governmental levels—state, county, and city. The California Department of Finance, for example, employs a substantial staff of specialists in the chief techniques of management analysis, who work closely with the budget staff.

The State of Minnesota in 1955 added a new technique to administrative improvement. The support of all state employees was enlisted in a do-it-yourself improvement project, called "Minnesota Self-Survey." Over 500 administrators, government employees, legislators, and citizens, organized into 43 task groups under the Commissioner of Administration, undertook to discover new opportunities for economy and efficiency. The self-survey idea was born out of negotiations with employee representatives over a new salary schedule, when it was discovered that insufficient money was available to cover the salaries. A by-product of the "little Hoover commissions" and other state reorganization activities was the growth of state services to local jurisdictions. These services usually aim at standardized financial procedures, improvement in local personnel practices, expansion of training programs, and provision of technical advice and assistance. In New Jersey, for example, a Department of Local Government offers advice and instruction to local officials. California, Minnesota, Rhode Island, Tennessee, and Wisconsin perform civil service activities for local jurisdictions on local option without cost. States have supplied other types of assistance, which include preparation of manuals of operation, conduct of administrative surveys and measurement studies, consultation on reorganization, and the exchange of information.

It is not meant to imply that improvement in local government has taken second place to state action. On the whole, the more progressive cities have been far in the lead in modernizing administration. New York City, for example, has successfully utilized administrative planning, in its departments as well as in its central budget office. Kansas City, Missouri, not only maintains a permanent staff for this purpose but also has provided field work experience for graduate students in public administration. Phoenix, Arizona, has found it profitable to create an administrative research arm to serve top officials in the improvement of municipal administration. Richmond, Virginia, and San Diego, California, also have staffs for administrative improvement. Municipal training has made great strides under the influence of state municipal leagues, the Institute of Municipal Training, professional associations, university schools of public administration and institutes of local government, and similar bodies. Michigan, California, and New York offer programs for local personnel officers. Louisiana, Connecticut, and Florida provide short courses for municipal finance officers. Only among the counties is there little to report, except where city-county consolidation has been achieved or where it has been possible to adopt a county charter providing for a strong executive.

International developments. While this was taking place in the United States, there were similar stirrings abroad. The United Nations and related international organizations stimulated educational exchange and consideration of common administrative problems. Technical cooperation programs gave a worldwide impetus to systematic methods of improving governmental organization and management. Though called "rationalization" in Europe and "planification" in Latin America, many of the activities parallel those of the United States. There is an ever-increasing development of administrative planning facilities, schools, institutes, associations, journals, and training programs. The Division of Organization and Methods in the British Treasury paralleled the establishment of the Division of Administrative Management in the Bureau of the Budget.

The concept of "O and M" caught hold, and units with this title are now found in many countries. The "O and M" Office in India is attached to the Cabinet Secretariat. Brazil has long been a pioneer in this field with its *Departamento Administrativo do Serviço Público* (DASP).

Improvement in organization and management within national governments has been partly a result of activities of the International Institute of Administrative Sciences (IIAS) in Brussels. Its triennial congresses and annual round tables cover many aspects of administrative organization and practice. Having official contact with 63 countries, IIAS is an important center for international exchange and documentation on administrative matters. Its quarterly journal, the *International Review of Administrative Sciences,* provides a guide to developments in administration throughout the world. Its Committee on Administrative Practices, created in 1947, has provided a channel of exchange and promotion of improved methods. Several bulletins have been prepared by IIAS with funds from the United Nations, among them guides for the conduct of management work.[12] The national sections of IIAS allow public officials and university representatives to keep abreast of new aspects of public administration. In the United States, the International Section of the American Society for Public Administration serves as the national section. The American Society for Public Administration has appointed a special committee in comparative administration. Such universities as Indiana and Yale are carrying forward programs of comparative study, and the Graduate School of Public and International Affairs at the University of Pittsburgh has set up its curriculum on an intercultural basis with emphasis on comparative analysis.

Because one of the main obstacles in many countries to achieving economic and social objectives lies in weak public management, technical cooperation in public administration has become a major element in the programs of both the United States and the United Nations. American resident consultants are lodged in almost 50 countries. Over 700 government officials from about 50 countries have been brought each year to the United States for training in public administration. Seventeen American universities are working through arrangements by the Public Administration Division of the International Cooperation Administration in direct association with a university overseas to strengthen local institutions in

---

[12] Titles include: *Issues and Problems in the Administrative Organization of National Governments,* by Arnold Miles and Alan L. Dean; *Central O and M Offices,* by Arnold Miles; *Improvement of Organization and Management in Public Administration,* by Thomas D. Kingdom; *Handbook of Organization and Methods Techniques,* by Hugh O. Dovey; *Presenting O and M Recommendations,* by K. S. Jefferies; *Administrative Manuals,* by K. E. Grainger; *National Organization for the Conduct of Economic Development Programs,* by Donald C. Stone and Others. These and other bulletins as well as the *International Review of Administrative Sciences* can be obtained from the International Institute of Administrative Sciences, 205 rue Belliard, Brussels, Belgium.

teaching and research. The United Nations Technical Assistance Program also provides expert consultants for cooperating countries, and training in the United States and abroad. Training projects include a School for Public Administration in Brazil, an Advanced School of Public Administration for the Central American Republics, an Institute of Public Administration in Egypt, and an Institute of Management and Administration in Burma.[13] Comparable projects have been carried on by such organizations as the Pan American Sanitary Bureau, the World Health Organization, the European Productivity Agency, and the United Nations Educational, Scientific, and Cultural Organization (UNESCO). In 1956, UNESCO commissioned the International Institute of Administrative Sciences to prepare a monograph on the teaching of administrative science throughout the world.

The overseas program of the Ford Foundation illustrates another important force. It has financed special projects, such as the public administration program at the University of Bologna in Italy, governmental improvement in Burma, and community development in India. Through use of regional resident representatives, it is also able to stimulate constructive approaches to administrative problems. In 1958, representatives of eleven Far Eastern governments convened in the Philippines in a regional conference on public administration, especially the administration of economic planning. The conferees created the Eastern Regional Organization for Public Administration, with a "research, documentation, and diffusion service" to be located in Vietnam. The training service of the organization was located in India.

3. Organization for Administrative Improvement

Common effort. The main lesson to be learned from the record is that success requires the combined efforts of all personnel, not only the work of a few dedicated staff assistants. This means active support from both the top executive, whether he be president, governor, mayor, city manager, or department head, and all the subordinate echelons. Lip service is not enough—it must be perfectly clear to each and every employee at every level of organization that his chief really cares about getting a better job done.

Thus the concept of administrative improvement calls for an organizational pattern that imparts to every place in the governmental structure both determination and capacity. This means a declaration of policy at the top, full and clear responsibility and accountability at each supervisory level, and provision of qualified management staff in all sizable organizational units.

---

[13] For a review of these training projects, see *Training in Public Administration,* United Nations Technical Assistance Administration, New York, 1958.

Alternative approaches. The chief executive or the head of a department, bureau, or division may approach the task of administrative improvement from a number of angles. Whatever the angle, the task divides itself essentially into attention to what is being done, who does it, and how it is done. Obviously, the governmental executive can do only a small part of the job personally. If he is to achieve results, he will need to supply himself with several types of aides and utilize a variety of methods. The first step is to delegate responsibility for improvement to subordinate operating officials. But he also needs a "general staff"—formed by the programming, budgeting, management, and personnel officers—in analyzing and disposing of major questions of program, organization, and procedure. He may further employ outside consultants to work on complicated and delicate administrative problems. Occasionally, it is useful for him to appoint committees of line subordinates or staff officials to develop recommendations on a particular problem. Staff meetings may also bring administrative problems on the table for discussion.

None of these alternatives limits the choice of the administrator. Each supplements the other. Each warrants consideration in the whole picture. Each plays a part in the broader context.

Personal action by the administrator. In the course of a day's work, the skilled administrator has many opportunities to remedy existing difficulties or prevent future trouble. But a steady flow of information and proposals coming to him from his staff officers and from operating officials is essential. It is he who must provide a fertile environment for constructive action by those subordinates. Generally, the administrator's principal contribution will be the giving of considered assent to changes that have come up to him for approval.[14]

In large organizations, the executive's actions for improvement may express themselves in organizational patterns and administrative machinery. For example, the Treasury Department in 1954 prepared a pamphlet called *Machinery for Management Improvement,* which the Secretary disseminated widely to the supervisory staff. This pamphlet described the organization and methods available for evaluating activities and improving management and made it the responsibility of the bureau heads to furnish leadership. Each bureau head was to "designate one person to assist him in carrying out his responsibilities for planning, coordinating, and reviewing the program." The pamphlet also described the various tools available to supervisory staff, such as periodic inspection and internal audits, administrative surveys, management improvement projects, procedure analysis, work measurement, and printing controls.

---

[14] For a fuller discussion, see Stone, Donald C., "Notes on the Governmental Executive: His Role and His Methods," *Public Administrative Review,* 1945, Vol. 5, p. 210 *ff.* This paper is also available in *New Horizons in Public Administration,* University, Ala.: University of Alabama Press, 1945.

These illustrations indicate the wide range of tools available today in management improvement.

Role of the administrative general staff. The general staff officers or units inevitably bear the brunt in analyzing complex problems of organization and procedure and in developing solutions. As one example, in setting up the general staff organization for the Economic Cooperation Administration (and its successor, the Mutual Security Agency), four divisions under the general coordination of a director of administration were provided: Organization and Planning, Budget, Personnel, and Administrative Services. All four worked as a team. A principal task of the director of administration was to effect close relationships with the administrator of the agency, the deputy administrator, and the heads of operating units. The term "administrative general staff" refers here to those staff officers or units that share with the agency executive his problems of management and deal with matters that he must resolve as the head of the organization. These general-staff units, as the programming, analyzing, and coordinating arms of the administrator, have a vital role to play in bringing about improvement in the agency's internal arrangements.

The budget office, for instance, deals with two general classes of problems in the formulation of work plans with the operating bureaus or divisions: first, the character and extent of operations that are proposed— that is to say, the program; second, the organization and methods to carry out the program. When the budget staff has true understanding of administrative matters, it will be able to raise the general level of management. Because of this interrelationship of budgeting and administrative planning, the two are often combined under the same head. The personnel office, too, can be a potent factor in improving administration. Staffing the organization with qualified personnel is the starting point, but also important is the opportunity the personnel office has of uncovering organizational and operating difficulties in the course of its daily contacts with officials and employees.

Administrative management offices. An administrative management office for the diagnosis and remedy of ills of organization and method is an essential part of the general staff group previously discussed. Such units are now found at all levels of government—federal, state, and local. In the larger jurisdictions, it is rather common to have a central management unit for the governmentwide or otherwise more significant types of problems, including arrangements and procedures involving two or more agencies. Central units in larger jurisdictions also act as stimulators of managerial improvement within the departments, but leave the detailed administrative analysis to the departments themselves. The Budget Division of New York State, as such a central organism, seeks to appraise policies, programs, organizations, and operations in terms of their suitability, efficiency, cost, and accomplishments. It does not write manuals of procedure, simplify work, or cut red tape; that is the job of administrative planners within the departments.

Within departments, one type of unit stresses the "program approach," by assisting in the formulation of goals and objectives and in the preparation of manuals of operations, progress reporting systems, and the like. Examples of the program approach are found in the Forest Service and the Soil Conservation Service, where administrative planning is intimately bound up with program activities. Another approach might be called the "direct efficiency approach." It stresses improvement through such means as work simplification, form design, record management, correspondence control, and mechanization studies, to streamline operations and to save time and money.

Some agencies with mass volume of paper processing—like the Bureau of Old-Age and Survivors Insurance—have emphasized work planning. Within the Department of Defense, emphasis has been put on relating administrative planning activities to financial operations, under the controllership concept. The following excerpt from the Controller's Guide of the Department of the Army is illustrative:

> The Controller is a member of the Commander's general staff; or if there is no general staff, he is one of the Commander's principal assistants. He assists the Commander in directing financial management, progress and statistical reporting and analysis, and management engineering activities. He is responsible for exercising staff and technical supervision over these functions throughout the installation. In fact, his broadest objective is to indoctrinate other staff members in the principles and techniques of good management so that he will not become unduly involved in the individual problems of installation units.

Units concerned with management improvement under this type of organization find themselves handicapped when being attached to an office that is fiscally oriented and viewed as a checking or controlling device. The same difficulty arises when the administrative management function is placed in a department of finance or submerged in a budget office dominated by the economy outlook.

Tasks of line operators and supervisors. Line operators and supervisors have a primary responsibility for administrative improvement.[15] Preoccupation with the work of management staffs has generally led observers to overlook this fact. The operator is the one who is apt to know first that things are not going well, and who must make any new solution work. The question may well be raised: Where does the role of the operator break off and that of the general staff begin? There is no clear-cut answer. The operator who has many organizational or procedural problems will—or should—have an assistant or a staff unit of his own to work on them. But those questions which cannot be settled

---

[15] See Chapter 19, "The Art of Supervision."

within his own division will usually rise in the organization. Here the higher management staff enters the picture. By providing useful service to the operators, the central staff will create a good market for its special competence and will not have to rely primarily upon orders from the top. It is best not to look at administrative management units or any of the other general-staff offices as control centers or to require a large mass of detail to be cleared through them. In fact, a check-and-review approach will defeat general-staff work.

Role of the rank and file. What has been said about the operator and supervisor in management improvement applies also to the body of employees. Employees know when things go wrong. Unless their ideas and suggestions are captured, the organization will lose one of its prime sources of help. Employee suggestions will not be made, nor will teamwork develop among employees in improving operations, if supervisors fail to furnish incentive.

Most first-line supervisors do not have time to explore and experiment in these fields on their own. Yet they need to have a grasp of some of the elementary aspects of analysis and some of the specific work-simplification techniques suitable for their own tasks. To meet this need, agencies have developed special training programs.[16]

Use of outside consultants. Government agencies often are confronted with administrative problems that require intensive study beyond what can be done by the regular staff. In such situations, the utilization of outside experts who have been schooled in solving similar problems in many jurisdictions is essential. Well known are the surveys for governmental reorganization made by the Institute of Public Administration, Public Administration Service, the Brookings Institution, the Governmental Affairs Institute, and private consulting firms.

Concentrating initially at state and local levels, Public Administration Service has applied on a broad scale the idea of quiet assistance to officials in the development and installation of improved organization and methods. This approach has proved more effective in most cases than the preparation of lengthy survey reports, which often end up gathering dust in bookcases. In recent years most of the projects of PAS have consisted of services to governments in Asia, Latin America, and Africa, thus contributing to the worldwide advances in public administration. In many areas, local and state officials obtain help in solving their problems from municipal and university research bureaus. The bureaus of public administration of the Universities of Alabama, California, and Virginia, for instance, have been called on extensively by public authorities for such assistance. The Pennsylvania Economy League has rendered a unique advisory service to local and state governments.

---

[16] For a fuller discussion of some of these, see Chapter 19, "The Art of Supervision," sec. 2, "Supervisory Skills."

Use of committees. Committees of subordinates have long been employed by administrators for solving administrative problems. Special committees are not only a useful means of developing new ideas, but are often helpful when it comes to putting the ideas into effect. But there are dangers as well as advantages. Committee members may already be overburdened to a point that the proposed course of action is apt to be thought out no more thoroughly than an off-the-cuff decision by the administrator.

Sometimes committees are appointed to meet situations in which the members have vested interests, so that no neutral viewpoint can be brought to bear on them. Moreover, the designation of a committee is often an effort to compensate for the failure of an operating official or for inadequate staff work. Committees are most fruitful when an administrative assistant of the administrator or a member of the general staff acts as chairman or aids the committee by collection of information and preparation of draft reports.

Staff meetings. Meetings of the administrator with his principal assistants can be of great value in administrative improvement. Such meetings are in general more productive as a forum for the recognition of deficiencies and for bringing about agreement on a course of action than in evolving specific solutions. By careful planning, the administrator can center attention upon important points.

Staff meetings are successful usually when problems of interest to all are on the agenda, such as methods of better work-programming and budgeting throughout the agency. In addition, regular meetings do give the governmental executive an opportunity to develop team spirit and to bring about a union of minds among his key men. This is essential to an institutional environment productive of management improvement.

4. Survey and Analysis Techniques

Mission of the administrator. Experience in government as in industry has shown clearly that we cannot expect better management than is supported by the quality of personnel in administrative posts. There is the famous illustration of one state which adopted a comprehensive reorganization plan, but continued to function as before. Nothing is accomplished except as ideas or plans are translated into action. Action requires administration. One of the mistakes of the early government reformers in the United States was the assumption that once a good structure had been established and competent officials placed in office, all would work smoothly from then on. How different is the fact! Administration is dynamic; organizational arrangements and relationships are continually in flux. Structure must be adjusted to meet changes in program, policy, product, methods, and human beings. When the administrator has been roused by observed inadequacies to consider remedies, how does he proceed? He will want to use critical, evaluative, and systematic introspection with regard to what his organization is doing and how it is doing it.

Such introspection must rely on what is called the survey method. Put another way, all administrative review and improvement of operations is dependent upon some fact-finding method. If the administrator suspects that the state of morale of his employees is low he should first ascertain why. If he discovers that work is piling up, he must locate the cause of the backlog. Whether the fact-finding method is used by the administrator himself, a committee, the staff meeting, line supervisors, general-staff experts, or outside consultants is relatively unimportant. Irrespective of who collects the facts, the method is common to each approach. The process must be planned. It must be organized and must lead to analysis. Conclusions must be reached, and a new policy or a plan of action for better organization or method must be developed. The proposals should finally be tested and installed. The basic fact-gathering device is the administrative survey.[17]

Types of administrative surveys. The plan for the administrative survey will depend upon its scope and the type of fact-finding to be undertaken. It may require several analytical techniques, depending upon the purpose of the appraisal. Three types merit attention here.

1. The *reconnaissance survey* is a diagnostic device to identify administrative difficulties, as a preliminary to all other types of surveys. The object is to arrive at an early conclusion about whether action can be taken immediately, and of what sort. The interview is the principal method employed. Pertinent workload and production figures, written statements of functions and operating methods, organization charts, record forms, and available statistical data may be compiled during the interview process. In the collection and analysis of material, it must be recognized that basic problems, not details, are sought to be identified.

2. The *over-all survey* is analogous to a complete check-up of a complex machine. It deals with all the elements of concern to management, from policy through organization and staffing down to detailed procedure.

3. The *special-purpose survey* may be based in scope upon the results of a reconnaissance survey, or it may be decided upon in advance, prior to any fact-finding. Usually it will involve either an organizational survey, a survey of some specific function, or a procedure survey.

Reconnaissance. As a preliminary to an intensive survey, reconnaissance should lead to a detailed plan of action as quickly as possible, generally starting with some previous indication of the field of attention and the reasons prompting a survey. Steps are then taken to obtain a more specific picture of what is to be covered and to be resolved.

---

[17] For more extended treatment of this subject, see Pfiffner, John M., and Lane, Owen S., *A Manual for Administrative Analysis,* Dubuque: Brown Co., 1951.

Whether two hours or two weeks are to be spent on such a preview, the objective is to make a general appraisal of the operation to be analyzed. This may include any or all of the following: identifying the nature and extent of activities; noting possible variations of activities from appropriation purposes; establishing principal manpower demands; making an estimate of the effectiveness of personnel utilization; appraising management practices, such as administrative reporting, work measurement, cost accounting, inspections, and program planning; spotting possible organizational or procedural weaknesses; observing the quality of executive leadership; and taking a look at headquarters-field relationships, the adequacy of the physical plant, the degree of mechanization of clerical processes, the extent of the backlog of work, and the state of employee relations.

When reconnaissance is the beginning and the end of an administrative analysis, much the same process is followed, but final judgments are made and recommendations are developed on the spot. It then becomes necessary to capitalize on the knowledge immediately available. Because intensive study is precluded, the recommendations should usually define the basic requirements, rather than the details, of administrative reorganization or managerial improvement.

Planning the survey. In an intensive survey, whatever its type, the basic elements remain more or less constant. The first step is the development of a precise plan of work, including the organization and scheduling of the study. This crystallizes the problems to be resolved. Setting up an orderly work schedule and outlining the steps to be taken also expedites the conduct of the study. Moreover, the work plan can be a great aid for further studies of the same general character.

The project outline should include a brief statement of the problem to be analyzed, the objectives of the study, and the scope of the work to be undertaken. Issues or problems likely to be encountered should be listed as precisely as possible. The individual steps to be taken in making the study should be set out. Sources, documents, and authorities to be consulted should be enumerated. A detailed schedule of the staff requirements should be worked out, including the length of time each member will be needed. The approximate date of completion of each major step in the project and of the project as a whole should be estimated as closely as possible.

In selecting staff for administrative analysis, it is important that there be balance among the types of skills drawn upon, and that the entire staff—including those co-opted from outside the agency—be subject to the controls of the leader of the survey group. Advance arrangements with those responsible for the operations to be surveyed ease the work and the working relationships of the project staff. Ready access should exist to the top official who is in a position to secure acceptance of recommendations. The project leader will find it desirable to arrange for staff assistance by the budget officer, the personnel officer, or other key staff. It is wise to explain the project to top officials, and if possible to all employees, in order to ensure their understanding and participation.

Review of written materials. When the fact-gathering stage is reached, the choice among approaches and devices is almost limitless. It is at this point that the analyst must use judgment and skill in determining those most appropriate to his purposes and combining or adapting them in a suitable fashion. Generally, the starting point will be a review of written materials, including statutes and orders, which give the historical background. The survey staff must also secure the benefit of any previous studies. The more can be learned about the business of the agency or the unit in advance, either through review of materials or conversations with those familiar with the situation, the more effective will be the subsequent steps.

Study of constitutions, statutes, charters, court decisions, executive orders, instructions, and other regulations will be of particular significance if inadequacies or inconsistencies in the agency's basic mandate are the primary concern, or if it is known what changes are to be made and the job is to revise the legal documents accordingly. Reports and administrative documents, legislative hearings and debates, minutes of commission or board meetings, newspaper accounts, and published treatises and historical records as well, provide an understanding of what brought about a particular organizational arrangement or method of operation. Such materials will usually supply only part of the story, however, since much of what went on before may never have been recorded, and available documents not infrequently fail to tell the most revealing chapters.

Materials reflecting the main outlines of the current administrative picture should always be given a careful review at the outset of a survey. These include financial and activity reports, budget justifications and hearings, work programs, and organization charts and manuals. Such records as job-classification sheets and other personnel data may also be helpful.

Questionnaires and check lists. When secondary sources of information have been exhausted and the analyst is laying plans for collection of detailed firsthand data, the questionnaire or check-list approach is likely to come to mind. This is a useful method of producing information quickly from a large group of people in a standardized pattern. It also provides a ready check of one answer against another.

A questionnaire submitted to officials in advance will prove helpful in directing their attention to relevant topics. It will also secure greater co-operation by permitting advance consideration of the questioner's needs. The framing of significant questions in advance and in detail, however, requires an appreciable foundation of information on the agency and on the problems being covered, as well as on the techniques of using questionnaires.

Interviews. Although much has been written about interviewing, little is available on the use of the interview as a technique in administrative analysis.[18] Careful scheduling and conduct of interviews can readily provide information, insight, and ideas that are otherwise unobtainable. When good coverage through interviews has been obtained, the risk of findings and recommendations being sidetracked on questions of fact is substantially eliminated. The analyst skilled in interviewing can also size up psychological factors, disarm resistance to change, and build up potential support for forthcoming proposals. Interviews can also be used to trace through a procedure by asking each person who successively participates in that procedure what he does and how, or by retracing a specific completed action by asking each person what happened at his point of the operation. In the course of interviews, the skilled analyst looks at working papers, observes the actual operations, and brings into play other aids to analysis. He will also compensate for weaknesses in this kind of testimony as he recognizes or suspects them.

If the required information is actually to be assembled, a check list of points should be prepared and a line of questioning planned. The interviewer should also be forearmed with knowledge about those he is to question so that he will not be in the dark in his approach. Close attention needs to be given to the atmosphere engendered in the first conversation. Helpful hints to the interviewer would include these: Try to see each individual privately; encourage him to talk; be sympathetic and a good listener; don't try to give offhand advice; make an effort to get operators to define their problems and to state what they think should be done about them. But the interview is more than an assembling of opinions; it is aimed at getting facts through conversations. Complete notes, including headings for future reference, should be made after the interview on the basis of the project outline.

Observation of operations. Direct observation of what is happening is one of the more obvious but often neglected means of analysis. Observation enables the analyst to see operations in relation to each other—a street-paving crew at work, or a group of file clerks classifying, sorting, storing, and pulling papers. A walk through an organization with a knowledgeable guide can be a big help in judging performance prima facie, and in acquiring a general awareness of employee opinion and the relationships between supervisors and the rank and file—in other words, in getting the feel of the place.

In any survey, observation is essential to an appraisal of the physical layout and the use of working tools. It is a major element in any motion study in which an individual operation is viewed again and again to break it down into a phase sequence of action or inaction. Sometimes the motion-picture camera is used so that the operation can be reviewed

---

[18] See Pfiffner and Lane, *op. cit.* above in note 17, p. 6-7.

repeatedly in slow motion. Understanding through observation becomes increasingly difficult when an individual's activities are diversified or variable or when activities are incompletely reflected in actions or words. Looking or listening will not help when the object of study is a man sitting at his desk formulating a policy. Even though he sees and hears, the skilled analyst also recognizes that in many situations he may misunderstand or misinterpret elements of the transaction unless he uses other analytical tools as well.

Review of communications. Many devices have been worked out for breaking down the flow, distribution, and accumulation of work.[19] One of the best is the review of working papers, either in storage or as they flow through a distribution center, perhaps the mail room. An examination of papers may also be of help in identifying the level of difficulty of different types of work. It can reinforce findings and nail down recommendations. It can help the analyst to avoid the overgeneralizations, misinterpretations, or omissions that may come from sole reliance on secondary sources or personal interviews. Working papers also may be analyzed in order to simplify communication. Opportunities for form letters, check lists, and other time-saving devices can be located after such a study.

On the other hand, reading of file materials or correspondence can prove to be an inordinately time-consuming method of administrative analysis. For many activities, moreover, working papers provide an inadequate reflection of the operation. Working papers may contain only the end product or otherwise fail to reflect fully what is done and why.

Work load and work-measurement data. The gathering and interpretation of statistics play an important part in administrative analysis, particularly in connection with measuring the work passing through organization units, in evaluating the effort required to perform tasks in a certain way, and in arriving at a conclusion about the efficiency of operations. Work count, work measurement, and cost-analysis techniques all belong here.[20] By drawing together significant figures it is possible to isolate and identify administrative bottlenecks upon which attention should be concentrated; point up defects in the existing allocation of functions; reveal periodic peaks and valleys in workload, which can be eliminated by rescheduling or by rearranging work assignments; disclose lack of balance in the distribution of work; discover unnecessary operations; and frequently support recommendations by showing savings in time, money, or work requirements.

---

[19] See Redfield, Charles E., *Communication in Management*, Chicago: University of Chicago Press, rev. ed., 1958.

[20] The Bureau of the Budget has prepared working guides and discussion materials on work measurement: *A Work Measurement System: Development and Use* (a case study); *Techniques for the Development of a Work Measurement System;* and *Work Measurement in Performance Budgeting and Management Improvement,* all March 1950.

In addition, administrative results often can be tested against statistically developed standards of performance and accomplishment. Many functions of municipal government have been closely related to standards of cost accounting or work measurement. The movement toward performance budgeting is now leading to increased attention to work measurement and cost analyses in state and federal operations.

Charting devices. Much help is available to the analyst in the charts, pictures, and diagrams that have been developed for recording of data and speeding up the process of communicating ideas.[21] To show a succession of operations, a wide variety of charting devices has been evolved.

The organization chart is commonly used to show the basic allocation of functions, the hierarchy of responsibilities, and at times the number and classes of employees performing each main function. The work distribution chart pictures detailed individual work assignments of the first-line operating unit. There is the work-flow chart, portraying the general sequence of major activities through the organization. The process chart gives a picture of the detailed, consecutive individual operations, transportations, storages, delays, and inspections by which a job is done. The right-and-left-hand chart or the simo-motion chart can be used when a breakdown of the work movements of one individual is desired. In analyzing working arrangements and the utility and layout of facilities, pictorial diagrams can vividly present the individual or group operations. Space analysis becomes much easier with a layout diagram. Lines showing the flow of work or the number and types of personal contacts in a given time period reflect clearly any defects in existing physical arrangement.

Reports. Throughout the course of analysis, facts are mentally organized and related to one another, to past experience, and to previously accumulated knowledge. In any substantial fact-gathering, however, some systematic recording of data is necessary for the development of findings and recommendations or the communication of ideas. Data must be organized to fit the audience if recommendations are to be accepted or effected. Will the top executive or line operator absorb and understand proposals most easily through conversation, charts, pictures, a brief written summary, or a lengthy report? Does he like to get right down to proposed changes or does he prefer first to think through the facts or consider the existing defects? The answers to such questions should determine presentation methods. In addition, questions of timing will have a bearing on the way in which the materials are brought together. Should conclusions and recommendations be presented as they are developed, and agreements be reached stage by stage, or should the story be presented as a whole at the end of

---

[21] See, for example, the Budget Bureau's management bulletin on *Process Charting*, November 1945.

the project? If the latter, should the report be offered as a finished product or should there be submission of a tentative report subject to revision after discussion?

In submitting the report, plans need to be thought out for the implementation of the proposals. This may require establishing a special unit within the organization surveyed to carry forward the recommendations; or seeing to it that special staff is employed to do the job; or temporarily transferring some of the analysts who did the study to the agency or unit studied. Whenever possible, it is desirable so to arrange matters that the proposals will be adopted by the line operator as his own. Maximum effect cannot be derived as long as the product remains that of an outsider.

Qualifications for analysis. Three types of abilities and backgrounds are important in the formulation of sound administrative proposals. The first is an understanding of administration—of the kinds of things that give trouble, points of friction, bottlenecks, the telltale evidences of an effectively or ineffectively operating organization, and the arrangements that generally work out well.

Skill in the actual process of observation and analysis is the second essential. This is partly an innate ability and partly a matter of training and experience. The third personal characteristic required is judgment. The individual must be objective in his view of life around him or of the particular situation with which he is dealing. He must have the ability to see both the forest and the trees. He must also have a flair for developing practical solutions and getting them across.

Skill in human relations. Underlying all such personal requirements is the need for skill in human relations. The analyst is constantly searching for operating arrangements in which individuals are able to act more easily and effectively. It may even be said that administrative analysis is, in large part, psychological analysis.

Psychological factors enter into the survey process all along the line. Fact-gathering involves face-to-face contacts. There must be cultivation of good relations to build up useful sources of information and ideas. The productivity of interviews will depend to a degree upon how well one responds to the reactions and attitudes of those interviewed. Discussion of ideas or proposals couched in the language in which an individual thinks and feels may transform his opposition or indifference into cooperation or, at least, receptivity. Finally, recommendations may have to be made in the light of major personality factors in the organization.

The competent top administrator, the supervisors at the various levels in the hierarchy, and the administrative general-staff personnel are all in need of these abilities. The latter will find competence in administrative analysis their principal stock-in-trade. Their whole day is devoted to observing, diagnosing, evaluating, stimulating, and recommending. As they become masters of the techniques, they will be able effectively to accomplish in a week—and perhaps in a more thoroughgoing fashion—what would take the unskilled analyst months.

5. Other Tools for Administrative Improvement

Program planning. Though the survey is a basic technique in administrative improvement, other tools are used to great advantage, such as program planning, work simplification programs for the supervisors, internal audits, reporting systems, and the analysis of attitudes and group behavior. The quantitative and mechanized approaches of operations research and automatic data processing have also proved useful.

Program planning is essential but nevertheless still quite underdeveloped. It is the translation of objectives and policies into activities, operations, projects, and other work elements for specified time intervals. In the field of public health, for instance, considerable advances have resulted from careful study of needs, clearly defined objectives, well-considered means of achieving those objectives, and critical analysis of the results obtained. Program planning provides a basis for the development of organization and staff requirements, budgets, and supply and plant needs.

Work simplification. As mentioned earlier,[22] certain elementary techniques have been developed which can be taught to supervisors so that they can bring about improvements in work assignments and methods. During World War II, the Quartermaster Corps Control Division in the Army Service Forces adapted process charting and layout-flow charting to the simplification of office work and introduced the gang-process chart as a device for analyzing material-handling problems. With mass employee participation, the Quartermaster Corps saved 26.4 per cent of all manpower covered by the program for other assignments in the expanding war effort. The Bureau of the Budget added to the process chart the work-distribution chart and the work count, and packaged them in such a manner that busy first-line supervisors could be instructed in the use of these elementary devices in a few short sessions. In the Office of Price Administration, for example, savings of nearly $2 million were reported after the application of this program.[23]

Work simplification requires for its most beneficial use an interested middle management and a central unit to cope with problems supervisors turn up that are beyond the scope of their authority.

Employee-initiated action. Administrative surveys are initiated by top management, and even work-simplification programs focus on super-

---

[22] See Chapter 19, "The Art of Supervision," sec. 2, "Supervisory Skills."
[23] The Budget Bureau's work-simplification training program, including the visual aids used, has been published by Public Administration Service as Publication No. 91, Chicago, 1945, and also by the Government Printing Office.

visors. What of the rank and file? Employee suggestion systems have been instituted in many governmental units to encourage employee initiative in management improvements. Employees are provided with forms on which they outline a proposed improvement. Federal legislation has provided awards or salary increases, both for usable suggestions and for superior accomplishment, by individuals or groups. Annually, awards have been paid to thousands of employees whose contributions resulted in savings to the federal government running into the millions.

The significance of employee-initiated action is not limited to cash savings. It rests also in the highly intangible but fundamental factor of improved morale. As each employee considers his work on his own initiative, he tends to take greater interest in his job. This feeling is increased as employees are permitted to share in management discussions. Shop committees and labor-management committees composed of supervisors and employees have brought about better common understanding of problems arising on either side. Depending upon the interest of management, they have contributed to effective settlement of many issues.

Administrative audits. The administrative audit provides an inspection of an organization at regular intervals to appraise the efficiency and economy of its operations. This is often an expansion of internal audit practice, which historically stressed the review of financial transactions and the accountability of funds and property.

When practiced properly, the techniques utilized in administrative audits resemble more closely the administrative survey. A drawback is that auditors rather than administrative generalists trained in analysis are frequently utilized, with the result that subjects are covered beyond the auditors' field of competence. An accounting and auditing office does better work when it keeps to its own field of specialization.

Analysis of attitudes and group behavior. Sample surveys and behavioral research provide new means of improving organization and management. Significant analyses are being made of perceptions, values, attitudes, and motivations in public administration as well as in private management. Such data make it possible to determine the suitability of policies and goals, the appropriateness of organizational arrangements, the effectiveness of supervision, and the requisites for full performance.

The Institute for Social Research at the University of Michigan has been pioneering in the development of these devices. Administrators as well as management staffs need to have better grounding in the human relations aspects of organization and the use of soundly conceived techniques. These staffs need to include social scientists skilled in their use.

· **Operations research and automatic data-processing systems.** An important contribution to administrative improvement is being made by operations research. It makes considerable application of mathematical and statistical theory to decision-making, particularly probability and game theory, and of linear and mathematical programming.[24] While still in an early stage, these techniques offer much promise. Another managerial tool is the automatic data-processing system. Such systems can perform a wide variety of work in a mere fraction of the time it would take individual employees with ordinary calculating machines. Federal, state, and local jurisdictions are using electronic machines in payroll operations, traffic analysis, inventory controls, cost analysis, and military planning of requirements and demand.[25]

An inter agency committee in the federal government, sponsored by the Bureau of the Budget, has developed a series of aids in installing automatic data-processing systems, including feasibility studies. The extensive planning for automatic data-processing in the Defense Department has led to the creation of a council for data-system policy, with a research staff, to promote the development of common policies and joint programs for the use of the equipment. However, innovation for innovation's sake should be guarded against. Techniques should be adapted to specific situations.

---

[24] Cf. Churchman, C. West, and Others, *Introduction to Operations Research*, New York: Wiley, 1957; Davidson, Donald, and Suppes, Patrick, *Decision-Making: An Experimental Approach*, Stanford: Stanford University Press, 1957.

[25] Cf. Hattery, Lowell H., and Bush, George P., eds., *Electronics in Management*, Washington: University Press, 1956; Chapin, Ned, *An Introduction to Automatic Computers*, New York: Nostrand, 1957; Canning, Richard G., *Electronic Data Processing for Business and Industry*, New York: Wiley, 1956.

Chapter 21 •

Morale and Discipline

1. The Meaning of Morale

Morale defined. Thirty years ago Leonard D. White wrote: "Morale is both an index of a sound employment situation and a positive means of building an efficient organization. It reflects a social-psychological situation, a state of mind in which men and women voluntarily seek to develop and apply their full powers to the task upon which they are engaged, by reason of the intellectual or moral satisfaction which they derive from their own self-realization, their achievements in their chosen field, and their pride in the service." [1] If one were to enlarge upon this definition, it might be possible to introduce additional factors in the range of motivation, such as high pay or security of employment, on the one hand, and fairness in hiring and firing or a feeling of group identity, on the other.

Thus considered, morale is obviously the very essence of successful administration. Whether the undertaking administered be an army, a public agency, or a private enterprise, it is clear that if its leaders aspire to sustained accomplishment of defined results, they must seek to master the problem of morale both as a standard of appraising the effectiveness of their organization and as a means of maximizing its *esprit de corps*. Since Professor White set forth his definition, the elements of morale have been the subject of extensive exploration by both students and practitioners of administration.[2] Identification of the components of morale, however, is

---

[1] White, Leonard D., "Administration, Public," *Encyclopedia of Social Sciences,* Vol. 1, p. 446, New York: Macmillan, 1930.

[2] A cross section of the writings bearing on the subject of this chapter is supplied by the following: Argyris, Chris, *Personality and Organization: The Conflict Between System and the Individual,* New York: Harper, 1957; Weiss, Robert S., *Process of Organization,* Ann Arbor: Survey Research Center, Institute of Social Research, University of Michigan, Publication No. 17, 1956; Selznick, Philip, *Leadership in Organization: A Sociological Interpretation,* Evanston, Ill.: Row, Peterson, 1957; Tead, Ordway, *Human Nature and Management,* rev. ed. New York: McGraw-Hill, 1940, and *The Art of Administration,* New York: McGraw-Hill, 1951; Follett, Mary P., *Dynamic Administration,* ed. by Metcalf, Henry C., and Urwick, Lyndall, New York: Harper, 1942; Roethlisberger, Fritz J., *Management and Morale,* Cambridge: Harvard University Press, 1941; Roethlisberger, Fritz J., and Dickson, William J., *Management and the Worker,* Cambridge: Harvard University Press, 1943; Mayo, Elton, *The Social Problems of an Industrial Civilization,* Boston: Harvard School

still rather elusive, despite growing agreement upon several generalizations.

Components of morale. One of these generalizations is that the group climate must provide opportunity for individual self-expression or self-accommodation by the members of the group. Another is that the occupational context must furnish outlets for the individual's pride in his own workmanship. Still another, and more important, is that members of the group must find it easy to accept the purposes and values of the group as their own—that they have a sense of belonging to the group or of identity with it. These may be described as the individualistic bases of morale. Of equal importance are those bases from which the group derives its own collective individuality and vitality. The prestige of the organization supplies one such basis, especially when its rests, in turn, on value attitudes widely shared in the public. Another basis is personal opportunity for participation in the formulation and pursuit of group objectives.

The highest morale has an intellectual as well as an emotional quality. The intellectual quality results for the individual from being enabled both to appreciate the quality of leadership within the organization and to accept generally the product of the decision-making process. This implies an adequate flow of information and opportunities for sharing in institutional thinking. Some observers have laid great stress on a more static component—that of the security of the individual within the group. Security, however, is more accurately an effect, not a creator of group morale. Its overemphasis inevitably adulterates morale.

Not a few students have concluded that there are certain additional requirements for the maintenance of positive morale. They underscore the need for fundamental unity in the purposes of the group. There must be, they say, at least the absence of inconsistency in group purposes, since contradictions produce stresses and strains destructive of group identity. To be sure, disunity of purposes which engenders within the group a conscious and prolonged competition in the pursuit of irreconcilable objectives is hostile to morale. Yet the limits of tolerance may be fairly generous. The group thrives upon variety in points of view as well as upon unity. Of course, general agreement upon the master objective is desirable. However, constructive competition as to means, particularly as to those means which call for adaptation to time and circumstance, is a generator of morale —not its enemy. Homogeneity in the composition of the group, it is argued, is also essential. Staff homogeneity with respect to age, ability, energy, and permanence is deceptively attractive, but it also may cause undue narrowness. The search should rather be for that fine balance of staff composition which gives to the group the strength which comes from

of Business Administration, 1945; Niles, Mary C. H., *Middle Management*, rev. ed., New York: Harper, 1949; Vitalis, Morris S., *Motivation and Morale in Industry*, New York: Norton, 1953; Leavitt, Harold J., *Managerial Psychology: An Introduction to Individuals, Pairs, and Groups in Organization*, Chicago: University of Chicago Press, 1958.

seasoning and maturity and the momentum which comes from zest and youth.

Other writers have suggested that the group must have a conviction of success—that is, accomplishments must stand out in terms of group purposes and be obvious to outside observers as well as to the group itself. Such conditions are usually beyond the control of the group, however. On the other hand, the idea of success is frequently sustained by the conviction that one is doing what is worth doing or that the organization "is coming through fine." Still other students have contended that morale depends upon the degree of indoctrination which the group has absorbed. The validity of this contention is limited by the boundary between education and deception. Indoctrination is an instrument, the utility of which is linked to its educative quality and the soundness of the "doctrine" instilled. Indoctrination is one thing, the character of the doctrine is another.

True coin and counterfeit. Morale as relevant to democratic management is frequently confused with its counterfeits. The crowd has its moments of evanescent enthusiasm. The clan has its solid, introverted self-sufficiency. The clique has its conspiratorial intoxication. The caste, conscious of its exclusive membership, has its somber, pretentious symbols of unity. The gang has its exaggerated forms of self-importance.

These are not manifestations of morale that interest us here. Morale is significant to those concerned with administration only when it converts itself into a larger social utility. To serve such a function in administration, morale must be stripped of its parochial appeals. It cannot be allowed to build little islands of protected privilege, each a world by itself, unconcerned about how well the organization as a whole is making out. In the administrative environment, the significance of morale lies, first, in its barometric function—its function as a psychological index of the net quality of management; and, second, in its instrumental function—its contribution of emphasis to the values of creative group effort.

In this perspective, group morale involves commitment to desirable purposes, persistence against adversity, and capacity for constant renewal. Morale, as the spirit of the group, is a living thing. To be sustained, it must be constantly renewed by the vitality of day-to-day relationships and operations, by the example of those who respond to the larger social utility, by the stimulation that comes from sensitive administrative leadership. Devoid of these influences, the group learns much more readily the habits of smugness, complacency, and exclusiveness. It is always tempted by the familiarity, comfort, and ease of old ways—the dead level of mediocrity.

Democratic implications of morale. These generalizations about the nature of morale point clearly toward one major conclusion. For our purposes, morale is a democratic concept. Fascism, Nazism, and Shintoism at one time seemed to be effective "morale" builders. However, their "morale" was brittle, an unyielding spirit which was shattered when cracked. The product of superficial indoctrination and dead repetition, this type of "morale" was hammered into men's minds. It discouraged initiative, inventiveness, and imagination—except in its own service.

The essence of democratic morale is to be found in its accent on shared knowledge throughout the group. Democratic morale seeks to evoke a common spirit through the art of leadership, not by authority; through the inner unity of the group, not by its division into hierarchical levels; through the dynamic drive of the whole group, not by requirements imposed by command.

Doctrinal counterinfluences. There is still great need in the public service for the development of an understanding of morale in its positive forms. We have depended too long upon the lawyer and the engineer to provide the master theory of human relations in public administration. Fundamentally, their product has tended toward authoritarian dogma.

The lawyer is prone to construct an administrative universe out of a logic concerned with the right ordering of words on paper, a process to which human behavior and human motivation may appear irrelevant. The engineer looks to the efficient manipulation of materials—blocks of stone, bars of steel, and the more mysterious action and reaction of molecule and atom, light and sound. Human behavior may appear to him as an equilibrium of forces. He is apt to forget that in administration these forces are animate and impulsive. To both the lawyer as an artisan of words and the engineer as a manipulator of materials, authoritarian concepts of administration have appealed as necessary and virtuous. No less influential has been the elaboration of hierarchy as indispensable and immutable. Hierarchy is seen as the alternative to disorder. The natural place of hierarchy as one of the methods of group action has been exalted to a higher status—that of the central instrument of organization to which all other means are subordinate. To that extent, however, hierarchy may operate as an adulterant of morale.

In the theory of public administration, the derivatives of hierarchy take many forms. One of the most universal is the organization chart, with its illusion of symmetry and finality. But the organization chart has its counterpart in the written procedure and directive, spelling out in persuasive and impressive ritual the abstract implications of hierarchy and the inarticulate lesson of the organization chart. The language of the chart is usually the language of authority and command, rarely the language of leadership and collaboration. "Span of control," "chain of command," "final authority"—these are familiar figures of thought. Nor is this all. Devotion to the concept of hierarchy has also been expressed in the creation of additional pillars of authority—notably the staff office as a device of control to police the organization and to guard its procedural supports.

Impact of military and business prototypes. Still other influences have abetted the authoritarian tendency in administrative theory. One of these has been the borrowing from military administration, reflected most clearly in the structure and habits of agencies concerned with public safety. Moreover, the military tradition exerts its influence in many other administrative areas.

No less pervasive and influential in public administration has been the example of private enterprise. Here the concepts, forms, and usages of authoritarian management have often been justified on the assumption of their alleged relationship to the achievement of profit. Despite this fact, most of the pleas for acceptance of new methods in public administration still seek the endorsement of private-enterprise analogy. The dogmas of efficiency and economy, for example, are frequently invoked by the theorist and practitioner of public administration as the main rationalization, or at least the protective coloration, for almost every formula of improvement. In the development of a fruitful theory and a productive methodology for the stimulation of morale in the public service, the largest difficulty lies in the necessity for repudiation of the seductive but demoralizing nostrums of authority.

2. Building Group Morale

Basic premises. By comparison with the long-established claims of authority in the historical evolution of management, democracy is a comparatively new and a still timidly applied concept. But it is well to remember that the rise of democracy as a political force had the effect of opening the channels of self-expression to large groups that were hitherto bound by authoritarian controls. The enormous growth of America was due largely to the existence of conditions that released the innovative spirit in so many of its people.

Yet the ideas, attitudes, and customs of authority persist. Orthodox doctrine of military organization and discipline reflects a command system. Administration in industry, government, and education continues to lean heavily upon formal authority. Thus, as our life has become more highly organized into public and private groups, the shadow of authority has grown longer.

The more democratic life of America—as demonstrated by the analytical methods of the social scientist—has revealed the deeper resources of responsibility when men and women have an opportunity to be themselves and join with others in pursuit of common goals. We still have much to learn of the potentials of human beings and how to realize those potentials. As we move forward, administration must learn to substitute imagination, invention, understanding, and persuasion for unenlightened authority.

New methodology. A new theory, a new language pattern, a new intellectual climate, a new methodology will not be the full-blown product of today's labors. Instead, its realization will more probably flow from the slower currents of common practice in administration. But we are clearly beyond a promising beginning.

There is cumulative evidence to show that the practitioners of administration are growing increasingly conscious of the roots and the process of behavior and motivation. Consideration of the findings of the psychologist and the sociologist is becoming more frequent. In some part of the recently emerging doctrine of administration, the shift in emphasis from the language of authority to the language of human relationships is quite pronounced. For the most part, however, the inconsistency between the articulate premises of authority and the inarticulate premises of democratic management is not yet clearly seen. The forms and practices of democratic management have, instead, been engrafted with greater or lesser skill upon the forms and habits of authority.

Even under such limitations, the dynamics of morale, once partially released, will exert an educative force. But when the new patterns are applied uncritically, or for management's transient or self-serving purposes, they naturally are in the main unsuccessful and frequently self-defeating.

Teamwork. The methodology of morale includes a list of techniques of respectable length and depth. Most of these have been tested in the fires of application. Distinctly prominent are the several devices by which the concept of "the team" is gradually being substituted for the unmitigated concept of hierarchy. These devices are the most promising, although the most difficult to apply. Their great value lies in the fact that they strike at the basic causes of static morale. Without them, other devices are restricted to marginal influence upon morale improvement.

Methods for establishing "the team" as the action group in public administration are many and diversified. One complex of methods is designed to increase the forms and content of communication among all levels of the organization, emphasizing especially the two-way function of the channels of communication.[3] Staff indoctrination is thus perpetuated and transformed into group consultation. Lines of command become the machinery by which preliminary goals are set, revised, agreed upon, and made into group objectives and standards of accomplishment. Staff meetings—sterile institutions under the literal premises of hierarchy—become generators of high morale as both skill in performance and sincerity of purpose are nourished through their successful development. The written word in the process of communication is no less important. When the reports of progress and achievement and the assignments of general and specific tasks are consciously used as instruments of consultation by the whole group, their value to morale increases tremendously. But thought-

[3] See also Chapter 18, "The Tasks of Middle Management," sec. 2, "Supporting Top Direction."

less reliance on devices "that used to work," without regard for changing circumstances, is more likely to kill than to invigorate morale.

Teamwork implies assurance of basic fairness of treatment and elementary security of status for the members of the working force. The absence of general guaranties of "due process of law" in the sphere of public employment in the United States—part of an obsolete, but traditional judicial inference—can have serious consequences for the condition of morale in the civil service, especially when the administrative system is compelled to submit to various kinds of political witch-hunting.

Leadership. Another category of morale methods has for its common focus the subtle role of leadership in its various forms and grades of responsibility. These are in particular the executive task, the special contribution of middle management, and the crucial role of the first-line supervisor. The metamorphosis from authoritarian to democratic management depends almost exclusively upon the skill with which the commander transforms himself into the leader. All the pressures of convention and all the lines of least resistance move him toward the continued use of formal authority. Nevertheless, he must *want* to be the leader rather than the commander.

The role of leader is more difficult than any other. Except by the obsessed or the inspired, it is therefore reluctantly adopted. The leader has no vacation from his task, no gadgets to manipulate defensively, no alibis available. Despite his greater satisfactions with success, he must constantly refrain from creating a common dependence upon his methods of leadership. Otherwise he becomes the "big boss." The finding and training of leaders is, accordingly, one of the main burdens of those who aspire to promote the growth of democratic management.

The specific elements of leadership appropriate to democratic group performance have not received sufficient attention in management literature. Small practical beginnings have slowly spread into more confident application on a broader scale. Among these, the experiments undertaken by the Tennessee Valley Authority deserve pioneer status.

No less important are the methods of leadership training and selection of leaders. Effective leadership can usually be developed in any organization that attracts competent aspirants. Leaders that rise on the strength of their ability often show a realistic regard for the resources of good ideas and common sense available in the rank and file. Executive development programs, in government as well as in private enterprise, have contributed both to building a store of candidates for leadership and to raising the general level of morale.

Staff development. The following excerpts from the induction guide for new employees of the United States Civil Service Commission ("Working Together," revised May 1957) represent an example of documentation of the emerging tendencies for the promotion of self-development:

YOU AND THE CIVIL SERVICE COMMISSION

You are now an essential team member on the staff of the Commission and your work is necessary to the accomplishment of our goals. The business that we are engaged in is big and it is important. The Commission is charged by the Congress to carry out a number of personnel programs which apply to Federal employees all over the world.

Remember that in the Commission we are never just dealing with papers, as such. We are dealing with people. Everything you do, every paper you process, every case you work on, affects a person. The way you treat the assignments which you receive and the papers which come across your desk—in short, what you create on the job—you create for the American people. How well you serve them is, in the final reckoning, the measure of how well you serve yourself.

YOU AND YOUR SUPERVISOR

. . . your supervisor . . . is very important to you and is your first source of information and guidance. He will be able to answer your questions or to direct you to the right source. You and your supervisor have much in common. You are both in the public service, working together for the same employer—our Government. Both of you are here to get a job done. He does one part—you do another; *both parts are important and necessary.* You need each other's cooperation. He can't readily get his job done without you, nor can you get along very well on the job without him. He is ready and willing to help you. Your supervisor, your fellow workers and you are all working for one employer toward the same goal—the good of the service.

HOW ABOUT DEVELOPMENTAL OPPORTUNITIES?

The Commission has a Career Development Plan.
The three major goals of the Plan are:

1. *To increase individual and agency effectiveness* by improving each employee's performance in his present job.
2. *To provide a reservoir of skilled employees* to meet future professional, administrative, technical and clerical needs of the Commission.
3. *To increase job satisfaction among employees* by providing them with the opportunity to grow toward their occupational goals.

As this is a self-development plan, employees must volunteer to participate. Your supervisor will furnish you with a copy of the pamphlet which describes the plan.

EMPLOYEE ORGANIZATIONS

You have the right to organize or join unions or other employee organizations. You may not join an organization that asserts the right to strike against the Government and you may not belong to any organization which advocates the overthrow of the Government by force or violence.

Working together. No less productive of morale than are teamwork, leadership, and group development are the moves toward collaboration between public management and the organized rank and file. The weight of the old approach, as in private management,[4] has been toward the antithesis of collaboration. The tradition of authority and command in management has generated a reciprocal tradition—the grouping of employees into combative and hostile organizations. As the French example shows, the more the authority of the "state" as the "sovereign" employer is stressed in uncompromising terms, the more aggressive—and equally irresponsible—becomes the temper of government employee unions. The authoritarian attitude has met employee aspirations for joint consideration of management issues in the administrative process by many types of resistance and defense. In the name of the sovereignty of the state, techniques of paternalism have been widely used. And when these proved unavailing, public management has marked out narrow jurisdictional areas of employee consultation.

Government-employee organizations tried to defeat these tactics with countermeasures of open or concealed warfare. The result has been, generally, that morale was sacrificed upon the altar of authority. Slowly, however, the rank and file have pushed toward recognition of their interests. As concessions were won, collaboration brought forth some of the minimum conditions of democratic management. Particularly in the last two decades, the habits of hostility have been progressively abandoned.

Substantial headway has thus been made toward the removal of negative factors, but less advance has occurred in the building of machinery for fruitful employee partnership in public administration.[5] The state of development in the federal government is perhaps best shown by the following circular which the Special Assistant to the President for Personnel Management issued on June 3, 1958, to the heads of the executive agencies:

> Four years ago the Civil Service Commission issued, as Chapter A4 of the Federal Personnel Manual, guides for determining the nature and scope of agency personnel programs. The introduction to this chapter states the following principles:
>
> > "The economical and efficient operation of the Federal Government depends on the quality of its employees, their interest and devotion to their work, their working environment and the effectiveness of their leadership.
> > "In addition to fulfilling legal and administrative requirements, it is a fundamental obligation in personnel management to establish and

---

[4] For current tendencies, see Walters, J. E., *Personnel Relations: Their Application in a Democracy*, New York: Ronald Press, 1945; Knowles, William H., *Personnel Management: A Human Relations Approach*, New York: American Book Co., 1955; Roethlisberger, Fritz J., and Others, *Training for Human Relations: An Interim Report*, Cambridge, Mass.: Harvard University Press, 1954; Yoder, Dale, *Personnel Management and Industrial Relations*, 3rd ed., New York: Prentice-Hall, 1954.

[5] See also Chapter 24, "Personnel Standards."

maintain a situation in which employees, working together, will be stimulated to give their utmost in the service to the public.

"Essential to the effective operation of all personnel management activities are means for communication and employee participation in order to achieve effective interchange of information and ideas between individuals and groups at all levels."

The standards set forth in Chapter A4 have provided the basis for the establishment of sound personnel management programs by the departments and agencies of the Executive Branch. These standards require that agency personnel policies provide for (a) the solicitation and consideration of the views of supervisors and employees (including employee organizations) in the formulation and adjustment of personnel policy, (b) the development of a climate which encourages employees and their representatives to consult effectively with management, (c) protecting the right of employees to organize, join, or refrain from joining lawful organizations of their choice and cooperating with employee groups whose interests are identifiable with those of the agency, and (d) the establishment and maintenance of a simple, adequate method for handling grievances and appeals which recognizes the right of the employee to designate a representative of his choice in presenting his grievance. Specific standards for the formulation of agency grievance procedures are provided in Chapter E2 of the Federal Personnel Manual.

Substantial progress has been made by many Federal agencies in the field of employee-management relations since these guides were issued. Agencies have formulated and issued personnel policies consistent with the standards established. However, there is evidence that continued improvement is still needed, particularly in the area of working relationships between agencies and employee groups.

The establishment and maintenance of good employee-management relations requires cooperation and acceptance of responsibility by both parties for taking all available measures to remedy situations that need correction. It is essential that all agencies, in carrying out their personnel policies, adhere to the spirit as well as the letter of the standards established by the Commission. It is equally important that employee organizations accept their responsibility for consultation and action in good faith and for calling to the attention of appropriate administrative officials instances in which they believe the spirit and intent of the policy are not being followed. The degree to which there is acceptance of this mutual responsibility will determine the effectiveness and quality of our management-employee relations.

To be sure that all levels of management throughout the Executive Branch are accepting their responsibility for effective employee-management relations, the head of each department and agency in the Executive Branch is asked to evaluate the personnel management activities of his own agency with respect to employee-management relations, including relations with employee organizations. The Civil Service Commission is requested, as part of its regular inspection, to review the personnel policies and procedures adopted by each agency in accordance with Chapters A4 and E2 of the Federal Personnel Manual, and to report periodically to this office on their utilization and effectiveness.

Union attitudes. An illustration of employee thinking about conditions of good morale are the following excerpts from a statement published by the National Federation of Federal Employees, a body not affiliated with the American Federation of Labor and the Congress of Industrial Organizations:

HINTS FOR GOOD ADMINISTRATORS AND FOR GOOD FEDERAL EMPLOYEES [6]

Administrators	*Employees*
Promote your employees as rapidly as is justified and possible.	Boost your employer's stock.
Promote one of your own employees, an insider, to new and available jobs; do not bring in outsiders and place them above insiders of equal efficiency.	Work hard to improve your efficiency so as to become qualified for a better position.
Be economical, but remember the best economy is a staff of good workers, well paid, possessed of high morale, and effecting maximum production.	Help to get the job done with the greatest economy of materials, time, and energy.
Know your people personally, as many of them as possible. Take a personal interest in their welfare.	While no employer likes an apple polisher, the employee should go at least half way. Supervisors are human.
Take your employees into your confidence. Hold frequent conferences. Keep in touch with your personnel office.	When you have a grievance take it to the supervisor first. Give him a chance to straighten things out.
Make the most of yourself and your outfit. Folks like to work for a successful administrator, strong enough to get the job done, protect his employees, and advance his organization.	Give individual loyalty to employer and organization. Put all you've got into it, so it can really get the job done and advance.

The concept of morale as something toward which each government employee must make a personal contribution is also reflected in a pronouncement to its membership which the same rank-and file organization issued in 1956:

> The National Federation of Federal Employees deliberately chooses certain policies and follows certain courses of action, and carefully avoids others, because it has an acutely developed sense of public responsibility which demands that every objective of the organization shall serve the national interest as well as benefit the career employees themselves.
> This means that the NFFE recognizes that *public office is a public trust* and that every career Federal employee takes upon himself very special obligations.
> These obligations include:
> Service above and beyond the call of duty whenever and wherever that may be necessary.

---

[6] *Federal Employee*, 1945, Vol. 30 (No. 2), p. 8 (by permission of the editor).

An honest day's work every day.

The fullest possible measure of courteous, devoted and intelligently interested service to the public.

Adherence to the *spirit as well as to the letter* of the civil service rules and regulations—whether they refer to leave, to hours of duty, to conduct, to any and all phases of employment and the relationship of that employment to the Government and people of the United States.

The program of the National Federation of Federal Employees is directed toward the creation of a better public service. In the past we have had strong support from the American people for our objectives. That support has had a decisive influence upon our past progress.

Incentives. Much attention and experimentation have been given to a class of morale methods concerned with identifying and using systems of incentives and rewards. Conventionally, two types of incentives and rewards are recognized—the economic and the noneconomic. Extensive analysis, particularly in private management, has demonstrated the fact that in individual motivation, by and large, these two are not only inextricably mixed but that they also have approximately equal significance. In public employment, it has been usually assumed that nonfinancial incentives count more heavily than financial. Increased security, the prestige of public service, the evolution of career systems, and the use of objective standards for individual advancement have often been described as substitutes for the higher monetary awards in private industry.

The sharp limits drawn to the validity of this thesis have led to the introduction, in more recent years, of various additional financial and nonfinancial incentives for public employees. Salary increases for meritorious service and cash awards for constructive employee-suggestions have become regular features of administrative practice. Nonfinancial incentives have also been increasingly emphasized. Official recognition of distinguished service has been formalized in service awards and other documents and insignia. Most incentive systems, whether financial or nonfinancial, are still at a point of development well below their potential. They warrant fuller elaboration. In the federal government, the Civil Service Commission administers an incentive award system for all agencies and serves as a source of information in the establishment of departmental suggestion programs.

In the absence of more basic morale generators, incentive systems may serve largely to ameliorate the rigidities of administration "in channels" and to provide management with showcase demonstrations of democratic intentions. Under these conditions, they invite and receive the suspicion or indifference of the rank and file, rather than recognition as important parts of the work environment. In another setting, governed by good will without valor, incentive systems may represent superficial comprehension by management of the basic factors in human motivation. When offered as a deliberately contrived but measured concession to the ideal of democratic management, such systems invariably disappoint their creators. Only as a *bona fide* expression of genuine effort toward individual participation in attaining the goals of the organization are they worth the cost of installation and administration.[7]

Performance standards. Incentive systems point the way toward a more important method of morale improvement. The work group needs, and will invariably respond to, objective standards of performance. These must be standards acceptable to the group, not simply the *ex cathedra* standards of management. Here again, the process of creation has been slow.

Standards have been characteristically established by statistical averages, by the pace-setter in the group, by time studies, or by the standard of maximum profits. These are not the standards that increase morale. Standards useful to morale are those whose logic and reasonableness appeal to the group—those which have been developed in the work experience of the group. Standards imposed unilaterally from above invite sabotage of quality if not of quantity of performance.

Production standards, though frequently used as the main test of morale, are in fact deceptive instruments of diagnosis. Production is the resultant of many variables. Low production may be the sign of pathology in collaboration. But a complete diagnosis may require scrutiny of the total environment of the group. Effective therapy as a rule involves correction of the modes of organization and of the exercise of authority by supervisor and manager. Only such correction may release the creative potential of the group.

Essentiality of purpose. In public administration, the manager and the supervisor have at hand a morale potential greater than that tapped by any of the methods thus far mentioned. Theirs is the rare opportunity to use the direct relationships of the ends and purposes of society to the objectives of the groups they lead. Public service, in its central significance, is an indispensable means by which the community attains its aims.

Participation in a low-cost housing program, for instance, whose direct and indirect effects reach thousands of individuals has great importance for the general welfare. The same is true of participation in the administration of social security, in the protection of the rights of workers, in a program of service and information to American business, in the conduct of foreign affairs. All these undertakings are charged with such implications that when employees are aroused to the importance of what they do, the effect upon morale can be electrifying. As the Employee Handbook of the United States Department of Agriculture says in the Secretary's introduction: "Each one of us who has the privilege to work here can make a significant contribution to the life of farm families of America and the

---

[7] See Roethlisberger, *Management and Morale, op. cit.* above in note 2. See also Chapter 19, "The Art of Supervision."

entire agricultural industry by performing his task with inspiration and enthusiasm" (revision of April 1957).

Unfortunately, too many employees, public and private, are not helped to see beyond their own desks. Their activity becomes a dull routine; their self-reliance is smothered by hard layers of hierarchy. Thus is lost a great and ever-present morale potential.

3. The Modes of Discipline

Aims of discipline. The modes of discipline are best appraised in the perspective of democratic management. Thus viewed, they obviously represent techniques for handling the crises flowing from the breakdown of morale. Too often discipline is relied upon to bolster the edifice of command, to control the deviations from established authority, and to induce conformity as a substitute for reason. When the modes of discipline are employed for these purposes, the frequency of their use supplies an index to the state of morale. Conversely, self-enforcing discipline is a function of high morale.

However, even within the framework of democratic management, machinery of discipline has its place. As first aid to treat the failures of leadership or of individual performance, discipline may provide the starting point for constructive morale action. This means that the most important matter about discipline is the purpose and the manner of its use. Purpose raises the question of the major premise of discipline. Is it to preserve the structure of command? Or is it to contribute to the improvement of cooperation and morale? These are not so much inconsistent premises as they are competing emphases. The problem resolves itself into the question: Which is major; which is minor? The fact that the traditional pattern exalts the relation of discipline to command has compelled the growth of many ameliorative safeguards—formal statement of "cause" of disciplinary action, right of hearing, right of appeal. The more conventional literature of discipline puts stress on these safeguards without giving much consideration to the premise which makes the safeguards so necessary. The current task is to infuse into the subject the vitality of democratic morale.

A positive approach to discipline would treat it as the systematic development of the understandings, values, skills, and attitudes involved in the attainment of the goals acknowledged by the organization. Thus, discipline would assume an educative rather than a punitive function. Here we can perceive once more the sharp distinction between the democratic and the authoritarian versions of administration. High morale comes only from untiring and positive discipline in the arts and manners of teamwork. Discipline in this sense is a product of democratic leadership that concentrates on education, persuasion, and consultation rather than on authority and control. Then the disciplinary techniques of the reprimand, the demotion, the dismissal, together with efficiency rating, assume their proper and relatively minor roles of complementing the positive appeals of leadership.

Disciplinary restraints. In the public service, discipline is also represented in other institutional forms. Traditionally, these have taken the shape of more or less restrictive codes of behavior imposed upon the employee by statute or civil service rule, or by norms of conduct originating in an atmosphere of popular suspicion and antagonism toward government. Such codes are dubious instruments of discipline since their more drastic provisions have no roots in common points of view among those whom they are intended to control.

Legal devices to hold in check any bureaucratic partisanship in politics or to neutralize the influence of the government employee in his role of private citizen may have demoralizing effects. In the larger perspective, formal disciplinary clauses often fail in their positive purposes and simultaneously retard the growth of democratic morale. Far more important are the standards of self-restraint and propriety that emerge naturally in the consciousness of a career service and are consistently cultivated by its members as maxims of professional behavior.

Political aspects. Disciplinary rules in the United States usually prohibit public employees from playing a part in political campaigns and in party management, aside from defining the scope of their freedom to make political contributions. To some extent, these rules have a protective intent— to reduce political pressure on government personnel. However, injunction and protection may often overlap in strange ways.

As an example of the dilemmas posed by the traditional codes, the following statement by a member of the United States Civil Service Commission before a congressional committee on employee activities which "may in a sense be political" but are not prohibited by either the Hatch Act of 1939 or the civil service rules is instructive:

> The Hatch Act by a direct provision in section 9 (a) fully protects a Federal employee's right to vote as he may choose and to express his opinions on all political subjects and candidates. Section 18 of the act definitely provides that Federal employees may actively participate in wholly nonpartisan local elections and may work for or against any general question that is to be decided at the polls by the voters. In addition to these, it has been ruled that a Federal employee is permitted to engage in the following, notwithstanding the provisions of the Hatch Act and the civil service rules:
>
> Attend open political meetings as a spectator; make voluntary contributions to a political party general campaign fund; become a member and attend meetings of a political club; wear a campaign badge or button; display a candidate's campaign photograph in his home or automobile; sign a political party candidate's nominating petition as an individual.[8]

---

[8] House Committee on Appropriations, *Hearings* on the Independent Offices Appropriation Bill for 1947, p. 1111, 79th Cong., 2nd Sess., Washington, 1946.

Thus general rights, though restricted, shine through again in a reluctant catalog of interpretation.

Service ethics. The methods of emancipation from purely negative restraints imposed on government employees are to some degree already spelled out. They may be described in different main categories. The common objective—as has been suggested earlier—is the substitution of a body of service ethics, providing positive aims and group-supported standards of behavior, for the restrictive codes of control so widely relied upon in the past.

One method would be the official promulgation of basic postulates for public-service conduct. This method is best illustrated in the German constitutional development, especially in several of the provisions of both the Weimar Constitution of 1919 and of the Basic Law adopted after World War II. Equally explicit was the declaration of the Michigan Civil Service Act of 1937:

> Every state employee shall fulfill conscientiously, according to the constitution and the laws, the duties of the office conferred upon him and shall prove himself in his behavior inside and outside the office worthy of the esteem which his profession requires. In his official activity, the state employee shall pursue the common good and not only be impartial but so act as not to endanger his impartiality nor to give occasion for distrust of his impartiality.[9]

Postulates of such breadth and universal validity inspire creative response. They draw forth implicit sentiments of public service. Their essence is the establishment of goals and norms whose appropriateness is satisfactorily self-evident. Their appeal is to the professional spirit of the career man, whose alert judgment of right conduct springs from his sense of service.

There is, however, a corollary essential to the full realization of this method. The authors of such basic postulates of behavior must refrain from weakening the principal pronouncements by the inclusion or subsequent addition of wholly restrictive lists of imposed conditions. These serve only to rob the higher postulates of their full meaning and to limit the aspirations of the public servant.

Evocation of self-discipline. Another method is the promotion of career ethics in the many professional segments of the public service, including the administrative personnel in the more specific sense. The evocation of self-discipline in the form of professional codes of ethics is evident in many contemporary practices. Professional solidarity in its positive manifestations furnishes guides to willing deference to the public interest.

The International City Managers Association, for instance, has built a sound and widely applicable tradition in its many years of emphasis upon

---

[9] Sec. 23 of the act.

the professional standards to govern the official conduct of the city manager. The special significance of its approach as a method of positive discipline is in the manner of its origin and growth. These are standards of behavior created by the group, though not without the labor of leadership. In their final institutional form they represent an agreed-upon declaration of group aims.

4. Morale and Institutional Patterns

Organizational structure and concerted action. To point to the negative effects of hierarchy and of authoritarian administration is not to underestimate the needs for organization, for structure, and for clarity of command. On the contrary, what we seek is a new *perspective* on structure and its uses. As Paul Appleby has put it, "Getting agreement on action has its beginning in structure. Concerted action becomes possible only by organizing for action. . . . structure comes first and remains basic."[10] Thus the main difficulty lies in the exaggeration given in administrative literature to hierarchy and other embodiments of authority.

In Appleby's words:

> Administration is somehow a respectable word while "coordination" seems to be disreputable. Yet administration always proceeds through coordination. To coordinate is to bring into common action, and this is a reasonably adequate general definition of administration. Administration is thought of popularly in much too simple terms—as management and, increasing the distortion, in the military or authoritarian tradition. Psychologists and administrators alike have come increasingly to realize that management consists much less in giving orders than in inducing or in organizing to secure agreement. When the process is thus understood, orders are seen as the formulation of what has been or will be agreed to. . . . The tendency among the uninitiated is to feel that if someone would only issue the proper orders or if only someone were clothed with sufficient authority, there would be no need of coordination and everything would become a matter of "simple administration." [11]

All organization theory, in a larger sense, aims at the essential reconciliation of the demands of structure and command with the necessities of group participation and agreement. Structure is basic, but it tends to be static. Morale is indispensable, but it tends to be fluid. The correct balance between structure and morale, then, is that which provides form and direction to the dynamics of self-realization and group expression in the accomplishment of the purposes of the organization.

Balance of structure and morale. The reconciliation or balance between structure and morale is discovered only by constant re-examination of the precision with which existing organization reflects the needs of group

---

10 Appleby, Paul H., *Big Democracy*, p. 92, New York: Knopf, 1945.
11 *Ibid.*, p. 78 (by permission of the publisher).

purpose and group participation. This perpetual scrutiny of organization properly begins with a searching question: How effectively does current structure and hierarchy express the common objective?

Except perhaps for the very moment of its first creation, organization always lags behind the expression of evolving purposes. Invariably, therefore, the drag of unexamined structure is backward. Organization is forever out of date. Its rebuilding or adaptation is a constant necessity.

Organization in action. From this first inquiry, the continued reconsideration of structure proceeds to an appraisal of organization in action. Does it still truly provide the mechanics of consultation and communication which are essential to group morale? Have the arteries of participation hardened? Have the signs and facts of agreement diminished? Have the goals set become too easy of accomplishment and is their attainment no longer impressive to the group? Has leadership sunk to the plateau of amiable ratification of casual group proposals? These are the diagnostic questions in the reassessment of structure in action. The findings must be applied ever anew to the redefinition of organization forms.

Structure is progressively reconciled with morale when the process of reconsideration produces repeated emphasis upon participation, upon giving full play to the human resources of the organization. Participation is the bridge between the structure and the group. Its manifestations are productive to the degree to which they are at once purposeful and informal. Structure, then, in many ways needs to be consciously subordinated. It is most efficient when it gives direction unobtrusively, when the group feels its presence in substance, not in form.

Effects of specialization. Modern organization suffers from excessive accommodation to the dogma of specialization. Effective operation, particularly in the complex tasks of modern government, requires the proficiency and skill which come from specialization. However, specialization is apt to be separatist, to be narrowly conceived, to isolate its practitioners from all others.[12]

Thus organizational theory is confronted with the additional imperative to integrate and simultaneously identify the specialized parts with the whole. The reconciliation of structure with morale therefore imposes a further task upon the art of leadership. It is the conscious emphasis upon interrelationships, upon the processes of intercommunication—particularly the methods by which the specialized parts participate in the shaping of general objectives, the evaluation of general accomplishments, and the appropriate subordination of all the structural components to the overriding purpose of the organization as a whole.

Discipline as affirmative pressure. Structure and command, as we have seen, lean toward self-preservation and aggrandizement. In this inclina-

---

[12] *Cf.* Chapter 9 "The Departmental System," sec. 1, "General Features."

tion, discipline in its negative forms is most frequently invoked. Mitigation of such tendencies by awareness of the necessities of democratic morale is a further problem in organizational theory and practice.

The regressive uses of discipline are ubiquitous. Administrative architects who seek the optimum balance between structure and morale must accordingly look toward the identification and isolation of disciplinary elements. The whole range of disciplinary sanctions, from the reprimand to the dismissal, presents opportunities for reciprocity and accommodation, building toward a constructive joining of institutional interests. When rightly seized upon, these opportunities may provide the moment and the means for fruitful exercise of leadership and collaboration. Such objectives are realized only when discipline is viewed as one of the affirmative pressures toward common ends. In the hands of skillful leadership, the reprimand, for example, is not a coercive weapon but a tool for the promotion of mutual understanding, objective evaluation, and new direction.

Morale and structure are the complementary halves of administration. In the sphere of modern public administration, their unity can be as productive as the democratic idea itself.

RESPONSIBILITY AND ACCOUNTABILITY

Chapter 22 •

Essentials of Responsibility

1. Men and Institutions

Responsible men. Responsibility is at the roots of civilization and government. It is the derivative of centuries of human experience. It is based on the best in Hebrew-Greek-Christian thought as revived and reinterpreted in our culture since the beginning of modern times. Responsibility is a characteristic of both men and institutions. Indeed, it needs to permeate men and institutions alike if it is to exist at all. Responsible men create responsible institutions, and responsible institutions develop responsibility in men.

The concept of responsibility is ubiquitous. It is not an isolated phenomenon of politics. Responsibility is a determining factor in the character of property, the nature of the family, and the constitution of the state. It pervades our systems of ethics, law, politics, and religion. It is not something to be defined in a neat sentence—it is the horizon of mankind.

In the long journey toward that horizon, however, much ground has been covered. Some of the landmarks are worth noting. Responsibility, as we know it today, is a product of Western civilization. It has assumed progressively clearer meaning since the Renaissance and the Reformation. It is a matter of ideas, ideals, attitudes, and conscious obligation. It is also a matter of custom, convention, and law. We note a striking geographical coincidence between the development of cultural individualism and that of institutions of political responsibility. Representative assemblies, majority rule, minority rights, accountable officials, and government according to law are not to be found except where a high value is placed upon man's growth for his own sake and where men generally, more than a mere few, have come to accept responsibility.

Attributes of responsibility. What are the attributes of responsible men? We may name some of them. First, responsibility cannot exist unless there is capacity—in the political context, authority—of a discretionary character. Children once were said, perhaps hopefully, to reach "the age

457

of responsibility." Helpless infants are not responsible. Not until the child's powers have developed is he able to be responsible, or irresponsible. Before that time the concept is inapplicable. We look not to the helpless but to the powerful in society to play a responsible role. Discretion is also essential to responsibility, which is something more than enforceable accountability. A duty that contains no element of initiative, judgment, or choice for the one obliged to perform it may be a matter of accountability, but not of responsibility in the wider sense. In the Parable of the Talents, the servant who hid his talent in a napkin chose to meet a standard of accountability—he produced the talent on demand—when in fact he knew that he was vested with discretion and that he was expected to exercise his initiative in pursuing a policy of investment.

A second characteristic of responsible men is recognition of an obligation to meet a need that exceeds the individual's and to act according to a standard that is outside himself and beyond his control. Such recognition must be effective even though it may not necessarily be articulate. A responsible member of a family recognizes at least some family interests as superior to his personal interests. A member of a political party recognizes certain party interests as being above his own interests. A responsible public official recognizes a public interest as overriding any interest of his own or the interest of any group or class to which he may belong. The standard of responsibility is perhaps as important as the interest. Hitler's action in attempting to destroy Christianity in Germany was not a simple act of gratuitous malevolence. The action had a certain logic to it. As long as a standard of conduct existed that was outside his control, he might be held responsible in terms of that standard in the minds of some. To escape completely such judgment, he was driven to attempt to destroy the independent system of values. The existence of a state religion in authoritarian countries is no mere accident.

A third characteristic of responsible men is regard for consequences. We say that an automobile driver who recklessly endangers his life and the lives of others drives irresponsibly. He who has no regard for truth but makes wild statements is also said to speak irresponsibly. A political representative who votes in disregard of the effect of his decisions acts irresponsibly. Responsibility connotes a certain amount of rationalism and an element of prudence. A responsible leader may endanger his own life or the lives of his followers, but he will only do it for a considered reason, after some weighing of the objectives and some calculation of the risks. It is this element of responsibility in leadership that holds a group together. Men will not continue to support a program that an irresponsible leader deprives of promise of success. Another way of putting it is that responsibility contains a time perspective of more than the moment. The future is as important as the present. A responsible party leader does not jeopardize the welfare of his party. A responsible official does not endanger the security of the state. A responsible administrator does not imperil the vitality of his organization.

Responsible institutions. When the concept of responsibility is sufficiently strong to be reflected in men's lives, it is also to be found in the political institutions of representative government. In the United States, we take these institutions for granted and have forgotten their origin. Their common ancestry is worth noting.

All may be traced to the combined influence of Christian thought and Greek rationalism reconsidered in the perspective of the Reformation and Renaissance. Majority rule, minority rights, and individual rights rest squarely upon belief in the value of the individual human being, upon belief in the *equal* value of human beings. In the light of reason, justification of majority rule is a simple mathematical process. The coexistence of majority rule with minority rights and individual rights has in it not a little of the Grecian ideal of moderation and restraint. It also assumes sufficient unity and generosity to permit a reconciliation of majority, minority, and individual interests.

In the development of discrete institutions, formal procedures, and known rules of law we recognize the influence of rationalism. Good will is not enough. The problems to be dealt with are of a nature and volume to require concrete machinery. To assure responsible results, men steeped in Western culture have not been content to rely on mysticism, absolutism, or chance. With the rationalism of the observational-clinical-laboratory approach, they have preferred mechanics as a means of increasing the probability that responsible men will govern in a responsible way.

Interdependence of men and institutions. Some aspects of the interdependence of responsibility in men and in institutions may be seen in the family. Marriage is a responsible institution with duties and obligations—some of them established by laws. But it also gives the parties to the union wide discretion. Administrative supervision ends with the issuance of the marriage license. The obligations assumed and the standards accepted by the contracting parties are stated in very general terms. It is up to each party jointly to recognize and determine what the needs of the family require in personal terms and to make his or her contribution accordingly.

Families flourish because men and women do make the contribution needed. It is frequently much greater than they could be compelled to make, and it is not always an equal contribution. The interests of the family, future as well as present, are the governing considerations. Responsible men and women recognizing such needs, accepting obligations to meet them, and thinking about the future of the family make the family successful.

The traditions, the conventions, the social sanctions, and the laws which surround family life stimulate, influence, and restrain action. They outline the pattern and help to secure conformance to it. Both the pattern and the sanctions are essential. We must add, however, that they are not sufficient alone. Some families break up even though the institution of marriage in general does not collapse. Unless there is generally a reasonable development of the quality of responsibility to the people involved, any institution is ineffective. The position of the child in the family also emphasizes the relationship of institutional management to the personal quality of responsibility. Rearing a child is in part a matter of developing in him an effective sense and habit of responsibility. A general regime is set up for the child, and he is instructed about things to be done and things not to be done. Both father and mother try to hold him to account for his conduct.

But this is an exhausting and time-consuming process. A child's interests and energy quickly go beyond the limits of any scheme of detailed guidance. The parental council would have to be in continuous session to prescribe, proscribe, and prohibit; and more supervision than is feasible would be necessary. Parents cannot stand over the child with a stick all the time or wash behind his ears all his life. The only real solution for child as well as parents is for the child to assume increasing responsibility for his own conduct—responsibility that involves initiative, judgment, restraint, and recognition of obligations.

The growth of responsibility in the child is by no means spontaneous. It is in part a product of the efforts of the parents. In fact, it is a principal function of the institution of family life. The effort required to develop responsibility in a boy or girl probably varies greatly; but even the minimum effort is colossal. Success is the crowning achievement of the home, bolstered by school and church. An active system of expressing accountability is essential to success, but unless there is success in establishing the ideals, attitudes, and habits of responsibility, the home has failed.

Political implications of business practice. Responsibility is taught explicitly and also by inference. Specific concepts grip men's minds, and the implications of ways of living are equally influential. How can we explain the change in political responsibility that took place in the United States during the nineteenth century? At the beginning of that century, as we know, the leaders of society—that is, the leaders in business, agriculture, and the professions—were also the political leaders. They recognized public needs and stepped forward. Many of them devoted their thought, their energy, their money, and their lives to resolving public issues. These leaders were broadly active in public affairs. They took upon themselves the burden of political discussion and decision. By the end of the century, the situation had changed. Some businessmen continued to be publicly active in politics, but they were now a minority. Most business leaders had withdrawn from broad political responsibility. The professional politician had appeared, recognized as a broker, not to take the place left by the natural leaders of society, but to substitute for them, to fill the vacuum.

Why did so many men whose ability, achievements, wealth, and prestige qualified them for leadership choose not to exert such leadership? There are many explanations. Among them was the important influence of the pattern of business itself. The new business organizations and business practices were training men to narrow their responsibility as much as possible, even to escape responsibility entirely.

At the beginning of the nineteenth century, property was private in a personal sense. Business *property* was private, *business* was private. A man was engaged personally, either alone or with his partners, in a business enterprise. He was personally committed, personally accountable, personally responsible for the business enterprise. Joint stock companies were the exception.[1] In the orthodox view their usefulness was limited. Charters were a special privilege conferred by special legislative act, and they did not necessarily grant limited liability to corporate owners. Corporate purposes were narrowly limited, and corporate powers were narrowly construed.

By the end of the century the situation in the United States had completely changed. Businessmen who were fully responsible in their person and property for all their actions were a dead or dying species. Business was corporate. All corporations carried the privilege of limited liability. Moreover, the requirements of capital investment by the incorporators had been so far abandoned, and the capital structure had been permitted to become so complicated, that it was both possible and proper for businessmen to launch and operate an enterprise without any true personal liability. The restrictions on corporate purposes had been swept away, and the privilege of incorporation had become a right. Business had ceased to be private in any real sense, but it had certainly not become public. It was characteristically irresponsible. Businessmen who lived and worked in this system were schooled in the arts, the attitudes, and the habits of irresponsibility. Through the corporate charter they could secure capital with a negligible, if any, investment of their own. They could control a corporation which they did not own. They contracted for land, materials, and labor; and these contracts could either be lived up to or repudiated and litigated. The system of minimizing responsibility, coupled with the vast growth in size of business units, had an inevitably debilitating effect upon the quality of responsibility in the natural leaders of a society which was becoming increasingly industrial in character.

Automatism? It was easy to transfer these attitudes and habits of mini-

---

[1] *Cf.* Adam Smith's dictum that "The only trades which it seems possible for a joint stock company to carry on successfully without an exclusive privilege, are those of which all the operations are capable of being reduced to what is called a routine, or of such a uniformity of method as admits of little or no variation." *Wealth of Nations*, bk. V, ch. 1, pt. 3, art. I, "Of Public Works and Institutions which are Necessary for Facilitating Particular Branches of Commerce."

mizing responsibility from business to politics. In both fields, irresponsibility was doubtless fostered by the prevailing belief in the automatic qualities of the economic and political order. The vulgarized version of the doctrines of the classical economists seemed to encourage each entrepreneur to do the best he could for himself by whatever means he could find. Although the competition of numerous small and distinctly private business units had given way to the strife of corporate combinations, relatively irresponsible in character and ruthless in methods, it was still argued that the aggregate of this total effort was the public good. It was still assumed that there was an economic "system" which could stand any amount of pulling and hauling.

Similar reliance was placed upon the automatic qualities of the political order. Representative assemblies were firmly established. Almost universal manhood suffrage had been achieved, and the franchise was exercised through a long ballot at frequent elections. It was felt that this kind of democracy had so much inherent stability that any number of people could rock the boat with impunity, and that the efforts of special interests to secure privileges would balance. No one had to assume responsibility for operating or maintaining the ship of state. Darwin's theory of evolution and the popular inferences that were made from it no doubt encouraged the belief in social automatism. In America, furthermore, the expanding population, the exploitation of rich resources, and the process of industrial development provided what seemed to be tangible and convincing evidence of the durability of "progress." It was easy to believe in a scheme which did not require anyone in particular to play a responsible part in public affairs and which made it unnecessary to worry about the social consequence of individual action.

Two world wars, the intervening worldwide depression, the aftermath of continuing fluctuation between "limited war" and "cold war," and the emergence of an archaic type of intransigent nationalism hungry for the fruits of industrial civilization but too impatient to wait for them to grow— these painful experiences have taught mankind a hard lesson. Who now really thinks that the world order or any "system" will unguidedly produce either peace or prosperity? Who really believes in the automatism of any stereotyped concept of society? The events of the last half century challenge any superstitious belief in social automatism. It is now obvious that if the benefits inherent in world culture and world resources are to be realized, it is necessary to achieve a higher level of responsibility in men and in institutions than society has yet attained. The situation demands ability, initiative, and discretion, exercised to meet the needs of society and not merely the needs of an individual, a class, or even a single nation. The standards by which the adequacy of policies must be measured have risen. The consequences of action or inaction by any substantial group in society must be carefully considered. Responsibility is at an extraordinary premium for the present and the future.

2. Legislative Responsibility

Responsible legislators. In this chapter we are concerned particularly with political responsibility, even though it is obviously only a part of the wider phenomenon. What is the responsibility of legislators? Of elected executives? Of administrative officials? We will forego the pleasure of talking about the responsibility of judges.

Responsible government is impossible without responsible legislators and without a realistic system of legislative responsibility. The essential features of a system of responsibility are generally agreed upon and need only be mentioned here: frequent but not too frequent elections, honest elections, an adequate number of representatives but not too long a ballot, reasonable equality in representation as a basis for majority rule, and so on. Although the advent of the initiative, referendum, and recall may seem to complicate the system, it also highlights an important aspect of all responsible institutions.

Institutions which permit responsible political action necessarily provide for discretion, and discretion admits of abuse. If the ends of responsible government are to be achieved, the authorized discretion must be exercised with due regard for consequences, must be guided by the needs of the community, and must conform at the very minimum to the ethical and moral standards of the community. The usefulness of the initiative and referendum depends upon the restraint and the judgment with which they are exercised.

Persistent and irresponsible special interests could conceivably weaken the legislative process seriously by excessive use of the initiative. Although a highly developed sense of responsibility in the electorate would check and eventually shut off such tactics of pressure groups, the system of direct control calls for a sense of responsibility among special interests as well as in the general public. The referendum, too, can be abused by excess. With reasonable restraint in application, it becomes a valuable procedure for dealing with extraordinary situations. The recall is similarly a welcome addition to the scheme of responsibility which could be, but generally has not been, carried to extremes.

Realism in responsibility of legislators. The demand for responsibility in legislators goes much further than is indicated by electoral devices. It is obvious that representative government is a farce if the elections are dishonest. Honesty in elections, however, requires a great deal more than counting the ballots with due regard for mathematical accuracy. An election can perform its full function only when the campaign itself is reasonably honest. If the candidates for election disregard the truth and fill the air with unfounded assertions, fantastic charges, and malicious misrepresentations, they make it impossible to achieve responsible government through the electoral process.[2]

The need for honest discussion is equally great within the legislative assembly. Lawmaking bodies and the legislative process rest on the foundation of faith in reason. Discussion is an effective means of getting at the facts and of weighing them when all parties to the discussion act in good faith. However, unless the preponderant purpose of the legislators is to make debate a rational process, the issues can be so confused with half-truths or untruths as to render discussion ridiculous.

Majority rule is obviously a cornerstone of responsible government. The legislative process is intended to be a means of discovering or formulating a majority view, and a legislative decision should rest upon the support of the majority. Majority rule may be and frequently is defeated, however, by irresponsible legislators. Dilatory action may prevent effective discussion or make a decision impossible. Committees may refuse to report bills upon which a majority clearly wishes to act.

Although legislative rules generally permit the majority to compel committees to act, the procedure is so laborious as to be serviceable only in rare instances. A committee may also handle its hearings and taking of evidence in such an arbitrary and biased way that the lawmaking body never has a chance of considering the proposed measure on its merits. Committee members who are governed more by a special interest than by the general interest may destroy responsible government. Can a legislative chamber function effectively as a representative body when the committees are not fully responsible to the majority of the chamber?

Legislative irresponsibility? The British government is sometimes criticized on the grounds that the Cabinet—conceived as a committee—is not the servant of the House of Commons, but has become its master, and a despotic master at that. In American legislative assemblies, which typically work through committees, are the committees fully responsible to the assembly or have they become arbitrary and irresponsible rulers? In many instances they fall short of any reasonable standard of responsibility.

Let us consider the evidence, starting with committee hearings. Is the investigation an impartial and careful inquiry into the facts? Too frequently it is the cross-examination of witnesses by a hostile prosecutor, or the staging of a dramatic scene with a carefully selected professional cast. When we consider the methods—not to mention the manners—of some committees of Congress, we find it not so strange that civil servants may cringe at the thought of "going up on the Hill," and that legislative-executive

---

[2] Beginning in 1954, the Committee on Fair Campaign Practices has sought to pledge candidates to employ only fair campaign methods. Increasing numbers of candidates have subscribed to the Committee's code.

relations lack cordiality. The "third degree" is not a good way to find the truth or to make friends. It may force testimony which is desired; but if the victim lives and is interrogated again he will be forever after on guard.

The mysteries of a committee's deliberations perhaps defy analysis, but what about its decisions? One of the committee's functions in American practice is to "screen" legislation. This is an act of responsible discretion. But how is the screening done? Is it a rational process of sifting the significant from the trivial? Is it guided by a policy based on views of the majority of the committee? If there is a general policy, does it have the support of the majority of the legislative chamber or does it represent merely the views of a vested legislative interest? And if there is no guiding policy, what governs the screening process? Chance, whim, or the dictates of the chairman?

How many sessions of Congress pass without arbitrary action by some standing committee or by the House Rules Committee to prevent discussion and to defeat the determination of a policy by the majority? Not many. It is no defense against the charge of irresponsibility to argue that not a few members wish to be relieved of the necessity of confronting embarrassing issues. The evasion of responsibility can only weaken responsible government.

Suicidal tendencies. The responsibility with which a legislative chamber acts is the product in part of the way in which it is constituted, in part of the character of its members, and in part of its rules and organization. The strength of the seniority principle in controlling committee assignments, committee chairmanships, and positions of authority in the chamber is a serious cause of irresponsibility in American government. The methods by which the whole house can hold the committee to account for its action, or inaction, are generally inadequate.

Gerrymandering, whether by constitution or statute, is bad enough in most legislatures. When the lawmaking body by its rules and organization further skews the representative process through perpetuating an uncontrolled oligarchy of unrepresentative members, it allows a dangerous sapping of its own vitality. If the legislative branch is suffering a decline, as some think, the danger to its survival is not to be sought in an encroachment from outside by the executive branch. It is to be found rather in the suicidal tendencies within the legislature itself. No lawmaking body that fails to cherish the basic principles of responsible representation can hope to play an effective role in grappling with the complex issues which today confront government.

Responsibility and leadership. Discussions of the responsibility of legislators frequently center about their relations to their constituents. Should legislators lead or follow? If they lead, how far ahead should they lead? It is generally agreed that voters have a right to expect their representatives to be better informed and more farsighted than the general public. Hence the voter can without embarrassment change his mind about a policy as he grows wiser through experience. The legislator, however, is supposed to be sufficiently well informed that he makes fewer errors and foresees developments the average man could not anticipate. The legislator's foresight should be at least as good as the voter's hindsight.

The relationship between the representative and his constituents is not a matter of dealing with a monolithic mass of people. In even the most homogeneous district there is a wide variety of people and groups. The number of purely agricultural districts—which might be presumed to be most homogeneous—is dropping, and the diversification of agriculture is creating a variety of agricultural interests. Even in a purely agricultural district living off a single crop, interests of owners, tenants, laborers, primary processors of foods, merchants, and bankers have to be considered. People also vary in race, religion, and general outlook on life. In urban districts or in urban-rural districts the variety of interests is, of course, very great.

The variety of interests which a representative must consider is in one sense the essence of his problem, but it also provides a solution to the representative's dilemma. Some interests are avid and well organized. If he heeds only these, he may become their slave. Here is where his leadership can come to the fore. If he has not sufficient leadership to educate, organize, and appeal to the broader interests of his district, he is doomed to be the servant of special interests. But if he exercises real influence he may greatly broaden his base of support and play the part of a responsible leader in matters of public policy. The representative's relationship to the party organization, the political machine, or the "boss" presents a similar situation. It is sometimes said that a man has to have money, organization support, or both to be nominated and elected. It may be readily conceded that some men are completely dependent upon money or the machine for their political life, but it does not follow that everyone is so dependent. A political "nobody" naturally cannot become a Washington, a Jefferson, or a Roosevelt by simply announcing his candidacy. If a man has qualities of leadership, however, if he has the ability to exercise wise judgment in the public interest, if he has demonstrated this ability in previous activities, he will have a reasonable chance of being elected on his own merits. When a political "somebody" comes along who has real qualities of leadership, no machine and no amount of money ordinarily can beat him. The opposition also has to put up a strong candidate. When a candidate says that "no one" can be elected without money or machine support, he deserves being looked over.

This is not to say that money and the political machine may not tip the balance or even defeat the interest of a majority of the people. They often do. The point is rather that real leadership of responsible character is vital, and a man who has it is certain to be able to play a useful part in politics.

He may not always win, but he will always make his leadership felt and he will frequently represent the public.

Responsibility of the legislative body. The question of a representative's relation to his constituents is no more important than that of his relation to his colleagues, to the legislative body as a whole, and to the general public. As responsible government requires a man in authority to look beyond himself, his group, his class and his party, so it requires him to look beyond his constituency in considering public needs. His obligation to the total public overrides his obligation to any part of it. Public obligation is not set aside by a federal structure of government. The right of secession was denied in our constitutional history in a bloody Civil War. The principle of the higher loyalty to the broader unity is fundamental. The obligation is legal as well as ethical. But how can it be implemented?

Any representative can fulfill the obligation for himself. Many do so. The name of George W. Norris will long be remembered as that of a *national figure*. He was a responsible leader, a representative whose horizons and constituency were as broad as the nation. The Tennessee Valley Authority was not built in Norris' Nebraska. If a representative will not meet his broader obligations, what can be done about it? The remedy lies with his colleagues and in the rules, procedures, and organization which they establish. How long the more or less disfranchised rank and file of the House of Representatives will stand for being pushed around by the venerable oligarchs who rule them without representing them, no one knows. But they don't have to take it forever. The rules can be revised, and the committee system can be changed. The particularism which now makes both House and Senate a playground for special interests can be controlled.

This control is not an impossible task. It is not inevitable, for example, that committees on agriculture should be in the hands of the "farm bloc." If these committees contained a considerable number of members representing areas which are heavy consumers of agricultural products, would not the committees do a better job for Congress, for the public, and, in the long run, for the farmers? Reconciling the special interest with the general interest should begin not later than in the committee stage. In any reconsideration of means of improving the legislative process, it is essential not to overlook the basic importance of responsibility. Many things can be done to improve and expedite the work of Congress and of state legislatures. However, unless reforms include steps to strengthen the responsible qualities of legislative action, they will not be very effective. Representative committees under responsible, not dictatorial, chairmen, responsible to the entire legislative body under its own responsible leaders, could effect a revolution in the quality and vitality of American legislatures.

Power to make these changes rests with the lawmaking bodies themselves. The present leadership is opposed to change, and the present setup with the inertia of many years behind it protects them. But the legislative rank and file are not helpless. Responsibility carries with it the obligation to use granted powers only for the public good. There is in the history of responsible government a deep-seated "right of revolution." There is also a positive duty to revolt against any abuse of discretion or authority which obstructs the processes and the ends of responsible government. The objection may be raised that someone will get hurt in the course of a revolt against the present scheme of things. To be sure, someone will get hurt, but responsibility carries with it the obligation to risk some danger and to make some personal sacrifice if necessary. Responsible government can never continue very long unless the rank and file as well as the leaders of the moment show qualities of responsibility, and unless the former establish the most practical means possible of holding the latter responsible.

3. Executive Responsibility

Elected chief executives. The responsibility of legislators, who have the broadest authority and discretion in government, should properly be discussed first. Next in order comes that of the elected chief executives, such as the President and the governors.[3] They are participants in the legislative process. They are elected representatives of the public. They are also the chief channels through which the experience of government in operation can be brought together, interpreted, and reintroduced in the necessarily continuous process of policy formulation and administrative improvement. The elected chief executive is as significant an American contribution to the art of government as that of judicial review.

A salient feature of the elected chief executive is the breadth of responsibility which attaches to his office.[4] There has been public insistence and expectation that the chief executive take the broad view of public policy; that he hold the balance even among powerful special interests; and that he subordinate particular interests to the general interest. Presidents are

---

[3] For systematic discussion of the presidency and of the position of state governor, see such works as Brownlow, Louis, *The President and the Presidency,* Chicago: Public Administration Service, 1949; Corwin, Edward S., *The President: Office and Powers,* New York: New York University Press, 4th ed., 1957; Hyman, Sidney, *The American President,* New York: Harper, 1954; Berdahl, Clarence A., *War Powers of the Executive in the United States,* Urbana: University of Illinois, 1921; Hart, James, and Spicer, George W., "Executive Leadership in Administration," pt. II, in *Essays on the Law and Practice of Governmental Administration,* ed. by Haines, Charles G., and Dimock, Marshall E., Baltimore: Johns Hopkins Press, 1935; Lipson, Leslie, *The American Governor: From Figurehead to Leader,* Chicago: Chicago University Press, 1939; Ransone, Coleman B., *The Office of Governor in the United States,* University, Ala.: University of Alabama Press, 1956. *Cf.* also Chapter 8, "The Chief Executive."

[4] All responsibility of public officials is responsibility under the law, within the law. That goes without saying and need not be reiterated. It is, however, the initiative and the discretion which the law—constitutional and statutory, conventional and formal, written and unwritten—gives to the public official that make responsibility a subject of intrinsic interest and importance.

looked to for leadership in the entire process of making and administering a truly national policy; and, similarly, governors and mayors are expected to rise above any special interest.

The elected chief executive's is a responsible office which has tended to develop in men holding it a sense of responsibility. It has generally brought out the best in presidents, governors, and mayors. The tendency of men elected to it to rise to the high requirements set for them is one of the most encouraging features of American life. This tendency may also account in part for the growth in political power and prestige which our chief executives have experienced. Whatever the degree of change in the relative standing of legislative bodies and chief executives, it has certainly been affected by the different ways in which the two have faced up to the challenge of responsibility.

Responsibility of the chief executive. The chief executive's responsibility to the public and to the legislative body is peculiarly a matter of integration. He must take the lead in reconciling conflicts and inconsistencies in policy. He must secure some synthesis of the desires of his total constituency and the total experience of the administrative process. His responsibility to the public and the legislature also largely determines the nature of his responsibility to his subordinates—his administration. That responsibility has four principal features: (1) The chief executive must give his subordinates guidance on the general direction of public policy and the timing of action. (2) He must see that divergent tendencies within the administrative organization are reconciled and that an integrated program is developed. Differences of personality are at times an obvious problem, but much more fundamental and difficult are the issues of policy. (3) To meet these needs, he must be in touch with the entire administration, and he must utilize its experience and advice. That is to say, he has an obligation to his subordinates to be familiar with their experience and points of view bearing on important matters, whether or not he acts upon advice they give. (4) He must also see that there is an adequate pool of knowledge and effective cooperation among the key people of his administration. The pool of knowledge must be greater and the cooperation more extensive than the chief executive's own knowledge or capacity for supervision.

The process of exchanging information of mutual interest and of working together toward an over-all program and its consistent administration must go on throughout all levels and all parts of the executive branch. For the chief executive, all of these responsibilities are controlling, both in organizing and managing his administration, and in shaping his executive office.

The chief executive's responsibility for guidance on broad questions of policy is obvious. The process of formulating and perfecting public policy is partly a matter of reducing alternatives and of concentrating upon the more promising possibilities. However, for the most effective use of the resources of government the general direction must be determined. There should not be too much standing around at the crossroads. If these decisions are made promptly, political officials and civil servants can make their efforts count most effectively.

It may at times be desirable to advance along several parallel or even slightly divergent routes. Such progress requires supervision to make sure that divergence does not become too great and also that all forces converge upon the goal at the right time. If a choice between completely inconsistent proposals is delayed too long, either much of the subsequent work is bound to be wasted or all progress is certain to stop. Neither result is desirable, nor is the accompanying low morale. Of course, not all of the chief executive's decisions are necessarily difficult. If he is well informed both politically and administratively, the general course to be taken may be fairly clear. Even on the most difficult questions, however, he must make up his mind without unreasonable delay.

Executive restraint. How much responsibility has a chief executive for initiating policy himself? Obviously, if there is no other way to get things started, then he must crank the engine with his own hand. But his prime responsibility is to see that sufficient initiative is exercised within his administration, rather than to generate all the ideas himself. Some elected chief executives have personally identified themselves with many detailed policies in the early stages of development. As a general practice, this is probably inconsistent with the executive function.

In the game of government, the captain of the administrative team is supposed to play the full sixty minutes. If he runs with the ball on every play he may find himself completely tuckered out before the end of the first half, and he cannot be very effective from then on. For example, the President is not only a legislative leader, and the leader of the administration, but he is also chief of state.

There is a certain inconsistency between the President's several roles, though it is not a serious problem as long as he does not overplay any one part. He is much closer to his essential function when he takes public responsibility for reviewing and integrating proposals initiated within the administration than when he himself proposes and promotes. The emphasis in the chief executive's responsibility is upon integration. But there is a limit to which he can minimize his own role and personality, without weakening his leadership. He must make his personal leadership felt on the big issues.

Executive emphasis on teamwork. If the chief executive takes his responsibility as head of the administration seriously, it may not be necessary for him to make many public decisions of a controversial character. The best time to integrate policies is in their early stages of development, and on the lower echelons of government. As Mary Parker Follett so well understood, many conflicts—social as well as administrative—are unnecessary, and result from overlong delayed collaboration.[5] They are also the

---

[5] For a cross section of her writings, see Metcalf, Henry C., and Urwick, L., eds., *Dynamic Administration*, New York: Harper, 1942.

consequence of an inadequate pool of knowledge and of too limited perspective.

If the chief executive takes a lively interest in assuring that his associates in the government get together at the earliest feasible moment on matters of common importance, he tends to avoid many of the conflicts which would otherwise harass his administration. The policy of horizontal, voluntary coordination should be facilitated by the administrative structure itself. In this respect, federal administration and most of the state governments leave much to be desired. No better device has so far been discovered to secure cooperation within a government than a common superior officer who insists upon cooperation. There are too many programs of both federal and state governments which lack any effective common superior.

High officials—political leadership. The highest category of administrative officials includes those who also have, by the nature of their office and duties, political responsibility. A typical example is the head of an executive department. He stands between the chief executive and the lesser administrative officials whose positions are or should be nonpolitical in character. That pivotal position makes his office of peculiar importance in the total scheme of responsibility. It is the point at which politically responsible lay control of professional administration is to be made effective.

To handle his job, the department head needs to be a good administrator. But it is as important—perhaps even more important—that he be a good politician, in the broadest sense of the word. The department head's primary responsibility to the public, to the chief executive, and to his subordinates is for active political leadership. As we have noted, the chief executive must limit himself most of the time to general guidance, review, and integration in the development of policy. The department head, however, has no obligation to continue in office for a fixed period.[6] The measure of his success is how much he contributes, rather than how long he lasts. He is politically expendable. It is his function to take risks, to expose himself to hostile fire, and to withdraw or be carried off the field when he has performed his mission. The department head who always plays it safe, and who lets his chief run interference for him rather than get into the interference himself, is operating on the wrong level. He should apply at the nearest post office for an announcement of the next civil service examinations and get a job that really suits him.

When the chief executive is a strong political figure, there may be a tendency for his subordinates to let him do all the heavy political work. This starts a wholly undesirable trend. The chief executive develops more muscle from constant exercise and his lieutenants get weaker from lack of it, throwing still more work on their chief. One answer is for the depart-

---

[6] The positions of elected department heads, which exist in many state governments, would be an exception to this rule. On the appointive department head, see also Chapter 9, "The Departmental System."

ment heads to face up to their political responsibilities even if they have to risk their office by doing so. There ought to be a law against cabinet members owning real estate in or near the District of Columbia.

4. Administrative Implications

Politician and civil servant. Another phase of a department head's role is to take full responsibility for the acts of his subordinates. This does not apply, of course, to those of his associates who share with him a personal political function. Above all, he must always protect the civil servants from political pressures.

He is free to disregard the advice of his professional staff. He may modify their proposals or overrule them entirely. But he should never allow political pressures to get past him to the permanent personnel. If a political head of department cannot or will not take public responsibility for the work of his organization, he is not big enough for his job.

General interest versus special interest. A further aspect of the responsibility of officials who are immediately subordinate to the chief executive is their common obligation to work together in the development and administration of a coordinated program.[7] This is reciprocal to the chief executive's obligation to secure teamwork in his official family. It calls for a nice balancing of obligations. As head of the department, the administrator is responsible for the development and management of his department's program. He must see that the needs of the program receive adequate attention, and that the full implications of the operating experience are available in the revision and further development of the program.

This function not infrequently makes the political head of the departmental organization a spokesman for a particular interest of—or in—the government. He speaks for agriculture, or labor, or the Navy. It is thus easy for him to forget or minimize his still greater obligation to see that his particular program is developed and administered in accordance with the broadest interests of the government, and as part of its total program. Balancing the particular and the general requires fine discrimination and a high sense of responsibility.

Although the chief executive is responsible for making certain that the essential teamwork occurs among all agencies, he is to some extent at the mercy of his subordinates, notwithstanding his possession of the ultimate sanction of removal. He can punish public quarreling, but it is more difficult to prevent his desk from being loaded with conflicts which need never have arisen. And if subordinates involved in a conflict of policy go through the motions of collaboration but never progress toward common ground, it

---

[7] One of the best discussions of the essential role of the key administrator is to be found in Appleby, Paul H., *Big Democracy,* esp. chs. 4, 7-9, New York: Knopf, 1945.

is not easy for the chief executive to tell whether one of them is recalcitrant or all of them are simply standing pat.

Among the more painful difficulties of any administration are certain top officials who are uncritical and unrestrained advocates of the worthiest causes. They are quite unwilling to try to find means of achieving their ends which would be reconcilable with other equally important objectives. They mean well but they create more problems than saboteurs.[8]

Integrity and good faith. Certain responsibilities of political officials are duplicated at lower levels of the administrative hierarchy. Cross co-ordination is, of course, a responsibility at all echelons. Each key man has an obligation to keep his group posted on major developments or information that will make their work more intelligent. Similarly each has an obligation to bring to the attention of his superior all the facts or considerations which the latter will need later to make the most intelligent decisions possible or to take the action that may be required.[9]

"The truth, the whole truth, and nothing but the truth" *so long as it is relevant* probably sums up an administrative official's responsibility to his boss for information and advice. Summarization is necessary, but it must be accurate condensation. In handling questions of policy, an executive is dependent on his staff for advising him honestly and fully. The integrity of the entire organization depends upon their good faith in the discharge of this function. Mistakes and errors can be forgiven, but lack of good faith is inexcusable.

A corollary of integrity and good faith in dealing with the one *to* whom an administrative official is responsible is effective supervision in dealing with those *for* whom he is responsible. A large element in effective supervision is real contact. There must be a meeting of minds. There must be mutual confidence and understanding. When contact is lost either through infrequent association or loss of confidence and understanding, there is danger of arbitrary administration.

An official may not always be able to put his mind to the merits of every issue that comes before him. But he must be sure that someone whom he has tested and proved to be competent has put his mind to every issue. This assurance has to be kept current. The head of an office can lose contact at times with some of the business flowing through it, but he dare not lose contact with the men who handle that business.

Civil service—but not servility. A subordinate's responsibility includes the obligation to tell his boss things which the latter may not want to hear. But how far does the obligation go? You can wear out your welcome, and "vain repetitions" get you nowhere. Some judgment is required on how hard to press an unpleasant issue. One guide is the importance of the issue. If the matter is of some possible consequence, even the most timorous soul

---

[8] *Cf.* also Chapter 14, "Interest Groups in Administration."
[9] See also Chapter 16, "The Formulation of Administrative Policy."

must take himself in hand and make at least one serious effort to see that his superior is adequately informed. The fact that his responsibility is administrative rather than "political" in character does not give a civil servant the right to be a Caspar Milquetoast.[10]

The scope of initiative and discretion, of course, declines as we go down the administrative ladder. Responsibilities become duties. Accountability, not responsibility, governs.[11] This transition, however, is not uniform. Many civil servants far below the level of political responsibility have positions in which they may and must exert considerable influence upon policy and upon the administration of programs.[12] They have positions of a highly responsible character even though their responsibility is within the administrative family and not to the public or the legislative body directly. It is upon their integrity and their devotion to the loftiest traditions of responsible government that much of the success of modern administration must rest.

---

[10] The literature on administrative responsibility is growing. Reference may be made to the following writings: Gaus, John M., "The Responsibility of Public Administration," ch. 3, in Gaus, John M., and Others, *The Frontiers of Public Administration,* Chicago: University of Chicago Press, 1936; Dykstra, Clarence A., "The Quest for Responsibility," *American Political Science Review,* 1939, Vol. 33, p. 1 *ff.*; Friedrich, Carl J., "Public Policy and the Nature of Administrative Responsibility," p. 3 *ff.,* in Friedrich, Carl J., and Mason, Edward S., eds., *Public Policy,* Cambridge: Harvard University Press 1940; Morstein Marx, Fritz, "Administrative Responsibility," p. 218 *ff.,* in Morstein Marx, Fritz, ed., *Public Management in the New Democracy,* New York: Harper, 1940; Finer, Herman, "Administrative Responsibility in Democratic Government," *Public Administration Review,* 1941, Vol. 1, p. 335 *ff.*; Key, V. O., "Politics and Administration," p. 159 *ff.* in White, Leonard D., ed., *The Future of Government in the United States,* Chicago: University of Chicago Press, 1942.

Following the hearings of the Douglas Committee (Subcommittee of the Senate Committee on Labor and Public Welfare, *Establishment of a Commission in Ethics in Government, Hearings,* 82nd Cong. 1st Sess., 1951) and the publication of the Committee's report, *Ethical Standards in Government,* Washington: Government Printing Office, 1951, discussion of responsibility turned to some of the moral dilemmas that confront men and women in the public service. For example, see Appleby, Paul H., *Morality and Administration in Democratic Government,* Baton Rouge: Louisiana State University Press, 1952; Douglas, Paul H., *Ethics in Government,* Cambridge: Harvard University Press, 1952; Graham, George A., *Morality in American Politics,* New York: Random House, 1952; Leys, Wayne A. R., *Ethics for Policy Decisions: The Art of Asking Deliberative Questions,* New York: Prentice-Hall, 1952. See also the earlier article by Morstein Marx, Fritz, "Administrative Ethics and the Rule of Law," *American Political Science Review,* 1949, Vol. 43, p. 1119 *ff.*; and Maass, Arthur A., and Radway, Laurence, "Gauging Administrative Responsibility," *Public Administration Review,* 1949, Vol. 9, p. 185 *ff.*

A rewarding analysis of administrative responsiveness—as contrasted with responsibility—is provided in Keith-Lucas, Alan, *Decisions about People in Need,* Chapel Hill: University of North Carolina Press, 1957 (with bibliography). For discussion of this chapter's subject in a still wider frame of reference, see Redford, Emmette S., *Ideal and Practice in Public Administration,* University, Ala.: University of Alabama Press, 1958; Dimock, Marshall E., *A Philosophy of Administration Toward Creative Growth,* New York: Harper, 1958.

[11] The transitional area is surveyed in greater detail in the succeeding chapters of this book.

[12] This point has been developed earlier, especially in Chapter 4, "Democratic Administration."

Chapter 23 •

The Judicial Test

1. The Rule of Practicality

Propriety of administrative rule-making and adjudication. One of the surest ways to obscure the workings of American government is to insist on some facile generalization like "the legislature enacts general principles, the courts interpret them, and the executive branch administers them." The theory of the separation of powers was never fully applied to any government in the United States—federal, state or local. Yet it has misled many people into believing that it is somehow improper for an executive agency to issue regulations or to judge cases affecting private rights.

Before we discuss the way in which public administration enters into the formulation of general rules and the adjudication of cases, subject in both respects to review by the courts, one elementary fact about the American governmental system should be noted. On each level of government, the legislature generally acts only as a single body, the judiciary handles all sorts of cases without specializing very much on defined categories, but the executive branch is divided into departments and bureaus each of which does a particular kind of work. Specifically, when an issue comes to a legislative decision, every member of the lawmaking body has an equal vote with every other member on every type of question, irrespective of his individual range of pertinent information. Moreover, because of the sheer quantity of business, the legislature cannot undertake to prescribe in detail all the rules and regulations that need to be issued to give effect to the decision it has reached. Similarly, the courts hear cases involving all kinds of legal situations arising in all walks of life. Although the judicial branch may have any number of inferior courts, it is fundamentally not organized to decide a large volume of particular categories of specialized cases promptly, cheaply, and uniformly. Only by appropriate organization and specialization can the bulk and variety of government business be handled effectively.

The legislature decides the most important questions by statutes and by voting appropriations, but beyond the general disposition of the matter it must rely on executive officials to make the detailed decisions. At this point there is still a tremendous quantity of rules to be issued to implement the statutes and interpret their meaning. Similarly, each day in the process of administration questions come up that involve private rights. Administrative officers must decide most of these questions—partly because they can decide them quicker, cheaper, and more generally to the satisfaction of the public than any one else; and partly because the judiciary is better equipped for the decision of cases involving broad principles of justice.

In short, the functions of issuing rules and deciding cases are by no means exclusively legislative and judicial. Executive agencies must discharge them in the normal course of business. By doing so they manage, in a general sense, wide areas of our social and economic system. Because this chapter deals particularly with the administrative processes of issuing regulations and adjudicating cases, and with court review of these processes as well, it should be remarked at the beginning that it is quite normal for the quantity of administrative regulations to exceed the quantity of statutes, and for a great many more cases to be decided by administrative agencies than by the courts. It has never been the function of the judiciary to pass automatically on all regulations, or to reconsider all aspects of every administrative decision whenever a citizen believes that his interests have been affected by a government agency.

Test of social utility. Then what, in those respects, is the judiciary's function, and who decides what its function is? The last question should be answered first. The legislature by statute says how much rule-making power it wants to delegate to executive agencies, and also fixes the boundary between the process of administrative adjudication and the judicial function. The courts apply the Constitution and the statutes to these problems, and— subject to the guidance of law—may have the last word. The executive branch, whatever its political influence, has no authoritative voice in deciding how far its power runs.

A legislature may require specific types of administrative rules or decisions to be reviewed in every respect by the courts, and it sometimes does. A court may review a case or a regulation with so little respect for the original decision of an administrative agency that it usurps the agency's function, and this it often does, too. In either case, the administrative agency has no protection, except the fact that in the long run the increasing interdependence in society and the resulting expansion of governmental functions in themselves will convince the public of the need for flexible and specialized management that administrative organization alone can provide.

Only by administrative organization and management can we supply the initiative, the expertness, and the planned teamwork that are required to solve modern problems. The way in which executive agencies should organize their system of issuing regulations and deciding cases, and the line between their function and that of the judiciary, are matters to be settled not by automatic formulas or political slogans, but by the practical test of social utility.

Two illustrations. Let us consider one or two examples to illustrate the point. The Post Office Department will carry an ordinary letter if the sender puts a four-cent stamp on it, and it will carry a periodical at a reduced rate if the sender qualifies for second-class mailing privileges. If a letter has not been properly stamped, it is only sensible to have the postal clerk return it to the sender for postage, or put a postage-due stamp on it and collect from the addressee, according to the instructions the clerk gets from his department. However, the question of second-class mailing privileges, though hardly different in principle, is a question of vital concern to considerable economic interests, and the statutes say that a publisher must have a formal hearing before the Post Office Department can take those privileges away from him.

In both types of transactions the Post Office Department is performing the same service. In principle, there is no reason why a statute should not provide for a formal hearing whenever a postal clerk and a private citizen disagree over the weight of a letter. In practice, there is a perfectly good reason. People want their mail delivered, and realize that it would not make sense to encourage contentious proceedings that would hamper the service. Therefore, the less important question, and the question that can more easily be answered according to a definite standard, is entrusted to the discretion of an administrative subordinate, while the more important question of second-class mailing privileges is the subject of more formal procedure at a higher administrative level—and, if necessary, before a court of law.

For another example we might turn to the creation of an army. In the eighteenth century, the nation relied to a considerable extent on legislative and judicial machinery to do this job. The Militia Act of 1792 (1 Stat. 271) provided that all men be enrolled in the militia, and enjoined them to provide themselves with muskets and with musket-balls one-eighteenth of a pound in weight. Citizens who provided themselves with such arms were, the statute said, to "hold the same exempted from all suits, distresses, executions or sales, for debt or for the payment of taxes." The lack of necessary administrative machinery recommended by President Washington but neglected by Congress made this system a fiasco, as the War of 1812 demonstrated. The mid-nineteenth century system—during the Civil War— was a centralized system of conscription administered directly by the Army. The citizen could appeal only to the ordinary courts. The drafting of men during the Civil War was both scandalously arbitrary and inefficient.

In the twentieth century, we have done better by applying two related concepts: the creation of an organization—the Selective Service system— by cooperative arrangements among different levels of government, and the issuance of rules and the adjudication of individual cases by that organization. It would be hard to imagine how bad a system Selective Service would be if the functions of administration and adjudication were separated. If the Army itself drafted men, and the ordinary courts were the only place in which to get a hearing, the drafted men and their families would certainly consider themselves less fairly treated.

Extending the rule of law. In these two examples—the postal system and the armed forces—it is especially obvious that the process of administrative regulation and adjudication is not a perversion of the ordinary legislative and judicial methods, or a usurpation by executive agencies of functions ordinarily belonging to the legislature and the courts. On the contrary, it is simply a means by which an executive agency—either on its own initiative or in accordance with legislation—takes systematic precautions to safeguard private rights. As one authoritative study put it, the formal procedure of administrative rule-making and adjudication, "far from being an encroachment upon the rule of law, is an extension of it." [1] Administrative adjudication in agencies like the Social Security Administration and the Veterans Administration has a similar purpose—to make sure that governmental services or benefits are distributed fairly, which is a matter somewhat different from the determination of rights.

Although administrative rule-making and adjudication are added safeguards to fair play in the administration of some governmental services, they are a major part of the business of regulating private interests. Some activities which need to be controlled in the public interest are operated under systems of government ownership or management; others are in private ownership and subject to government regulation. Thus regulation, with administrative rule-making and adjudication, is an alternative to public ownership or direct public control.

Administrative regulation as alternative to public ownership. The nation might have considered authorizing the federal government to take over the railroads, if it could not have regulated them through the Interstate Commerce Commission; or the shipping lines, if it were not for the Federal Maritime Board; or the radio networks, but for the Federal Communications Commission; or the banking and exchange system, but for the Federal Reserve System, the Federal Home Loan Bank System, the Securities and

---

[1] Attorney General's Committee on Administrative Procedure, *Final Report*, p. 12, Senate Doc. No. 8, 77th Cong., 1st Sess., Washington, 1941. The body of specialized writings on administrative law, including comprehensive treatments, has greatly increased in the United States, although for the most part it is not as closely informed about the practical aspects of administrative activities as is true of its Continental European counterpart. For good guidance into the field of administrative law, the reader may turn to the systematic treatments by such well-known authorities as James Hart, Rinehart J. Swenson, and Walter Gellhorn. A comprehensive treatise (now in four volumes) is that by Kenneth C. Davis, perhaps the leading work on the "lawyer's law" of public administration.

Exchange Commission, and other agencies. Some agencies handle cases by direct executive action—the Home Owners Loan Corporation did not hold hearings before making a loan. Others are primarily regulatory agencies with highly developed processes of adjudication. In most of them, however, the functions of administration and adjudication are inseparable.

It is at least partly an historical accident that in the United States the federal government operates the postal service but not the telephone and telegraph systems; or that state governments operate certain hospitals and sanatoriums and not others; or that municipalities own airports but not railroad stations, or operate one utility—from abattoirs to waterworks—and leave another in private ownership. What may start as an historical accident usually becomes a firmly rooted tradition. Podunk is shocked to learn that Middletown is socialistic enough to own its electric-power plant, while Middletown is surprised to discover that Podunk violates American tradition by getting some of its beef from a municipal slaughterhouse. In much the same way Americans are generally surprised to learn that the British Post Office Department handles telegrams, while the British find it hard to understand that even well-to-do Americans may be educated from kindergarten to Ph.D. in governmental institutions.

When government undertakes to regulate great corporations instead of taking them over, it has two general alternatives, or a mixture of both. One is to proceed by first laying down statutory definitions of the standards which the corporations must follow, then by having an executive agency investigate their operations, and finally by having any violations prosecuted before the courts. The other alternative is to give an executive agency authority to issue detailed regulations, to conduct the necessary investigations, and to hear any cases involving violations. The latter alternative has been followed, not because government agencies grasped for power, but because the regulated interests greatly preferred it. A private corporation, like a government department, cannot operate if many of its decisions are likely to be litigated. If it has to be regulated, it would rather be regulated by having an administrative agency enter into a sort of operating partnership with it and take over certain defined controls, instead of having a prosecuting attorney dogging its footsteps.

This preference may be a surprise to the casual observer who takes the complaints of businessmen about government regulation to mean that they would rather be prosecuted in a court than regulated under an administrative procedure. As one Senator has put it, "One of the great difficulties of the Congress in attempting to avoid the detailed regulation of business, with indefinite power in a federal bureau, is the fact that in many cases the businessmen themselves seem to want that kind of regulation." [2]

---

[2] *Congressional Record,* Vol. 86, p. 10070 (August 8, 1940).

2. The Administrative Process and the Lawyers

Prevention over punishment. If we look in some detail at the methods of government regulation, we may see how much they are like the management of a broad field of activity by a corporation, and how much they have in common with those methods that are essential to the conduct of public administration in general. As with all types of administrative actions, one main way in which the work of regulatory agencies differs from that of the judiciary is that in the main they try to prevent mistakes rather than punish offenders.

A municipal building-inspection department does not wait to take steps against a landlord until the elevator collapses and kills some passengers; it inspects and certifies elevators to make sure they are safe. The Civil Aeronautics Administration does not merely wait to prosecute airplane pilots who through incompetence smash their planes; in a more practical fashion it examines and licenses those who present themselves as competent. The Federal Deposit Insurance Corporation does not merely adjust its premiums to take care of the number of bank failures; it inspects insured banks to make sure they are not going to fail. It is possible, of course, to study these administrative processes solely as degenerate offshoots of the judicial system. It would seem more realistic, however, to observe that each such activity is, in a broad sense, a part of the management of the real estate business, the air transport business, or the banking business.

Regulation as partnership in management. Likewise, the Securities and Exchange Commission, which has to approve registration statements before securities are offered on the market, must act more like a partner in the management of the issuing enterprise than like a court refereeing disputes. An investment firm must put its securities on the market promptly in order to make a profit, and any public question about their soundness would wreck the sale. For this reason it is no wonder that the securities market in general prefers to have questions about registration statements handled informally and privately by staff members of the commission, rather than aired and delayed in an open formal hearing.

Again, as with all administrative activity, the primary purpose of regulation is to protect the public interest. In order to do so, an administrative agency may make use of specialists who are also valuable to the regulated industry. The Department of Agriculture grades and inspects grain, and inspects perishable commodities and imported farm products. The work of its inspectors, scientists, and technicians—and its associated state and local institutions—makes up the national research program for agriculture. The merchant-marine inspectors of the United States Coast Guard inspect the construction, maintenance, and repair of vessels. An inspector in a shipyard who makes sure that work is up to specifications may save the shipbuilder and the ship buyer the cost of hiring men for some of the same work. And a marine inspector who crawls through the dirty boiler of a cargo vessel in order to tell the ship's engineers what repairs need to be made for the next voyage may be engaging in quasi-judicial activity, but the ship's officers look on him as an expert consultant, and if they think of anyone as "regulating" them they are likely to think of their company management.

In another way the processes of administrative regulation are more similar to those of management than to judicial proceedings. The administrative agency makes a continuous positive effort to prevent adjudicatory cases from occurring by using its field staff to educate the affected interests. It may take a positive lead in developing new techniques and new methods of management for the regulated interests. The United States Public Health Service, for example, is not merely concerned with the prosecution of offenders, but also with the development of new methods of sanitation. The Federal Home Loan Bank Board does not merely regulate local mortgage-credit institutions; it develops new credit opportunities for them, and instructs them in the organization of their business and the techniques of encouraging savings and home financing. Because such agencies specialize in a single field of activitiy, and have direct administrative control over their personnel, they can develop standard national policies for the regulated interests and help them improve their operations.

Some of the agencies in question have a still more positive function of over-all management. The Federal Maritime Board, for instance, is less concerned with regulating than with subsidizing and developing the American merchant marine. The Civil Aeronautics Administration decides which airlines can operate where, and sees that they have proper airport facilities, flight services, qualified crews, and safe equipment. The Federal Reserve System, similarly, has some functions of adjudication; yet its main function is the general direction of a crucial field of economic activity— banking and credit.

To be sure, some of the agencies which make rules and hear cases do not deal with a single type of business, but with a particular aspect of many types of business. The several regulatory agencies in the field of labor relations are examples. Other examples are revenue-collection agencies: the Internal Revenue Service and the Bureau of Customs. The Immigration and Naturalization Service is the federal administrative agency whose proceedings most closely resemble those of criminal courts.

Informal settlement versus formal adjudication. As most of the agencies with rule-making and adjudicatory functions are either service agencies in the main, or have responsibilities for promoting or even managing broad fields of economic interest, they should not be considered primarily as tribunals for handling complaints, prosecuting offenses, or settling disputes. Such business is generally only a by-product of their work, or rather it is only the way of disposing of their unsatisfactory commodities. For their basic product or objective is the cooperative management of a national activity, and any case in which the private parties concerned cannot be led to cooperate is a failure, not an accomplishment.

The figures cited by the Attorney General's Committee on Administrative Procedure illustrate this point.[3] The Interstate Commerce Commission arranged voluntary settlements in all but five of 3,500 demurrage complaints. The Department of Agriculture, administering twenty-odd regulatory statutes, had fewer formal hearings than one per day, and an exception was taken to an examiner's report less often than once a week. The National Labor Relations Board, in the first four years of its stormy career, had to issue formal complaints in only 8 per cent, and to make formal decisions in only 4 per cent, of its 12,227 unfair labor-practice cases. To look on regulatory agencies primarily as courts and to make them follow the same procedure would be to organize them not for their main purpose, but for the small proportion of cases in which their purpose could not be accomplished—as if business were to be organized mainly for the convenience of referees in bankruptcy, or hospitals for the convenience of undertakers.

Balance of public interest. In each field of activity a balance must be struck between the need for a formalized procedure—somewhat resembling that of the judicial system—in order to protect people from arbitrary action, and the need for administrative initiative, discretion, and dispatch, in order to further the interest of the people concerned and to protect them from frustrating formalities. The balance may vary from time to time. For example, because the Interstate Commerce Commission was too much like a tribunal to manage the national transportation system in wartime, the Office of Defense Transportation was created.

Those who mainly wish to protect private interests against interference will naturally—at least in the short run—want to tip the balance in favor of more formalized procedures. Those who mainly wish to accomplish broad social objectives and to integrate national policy will generally want to tip it in favor of more administrative discretion. The same issue may be debated, too, in another aspect: whether a regulatory function, especially in the federal government, should be lodged in an ordinary executive department—as are those in the field of agriculture—or in an independent commission—as are most of those that deal with business. However, any differences of opinion are less likely to be irreconcilable if we remember that the issuing of rules and the hearing of cases may be an essential part of an administrative function, and that some types of private interests may prefer to be regulated by an administrative agency that is also concerned with promoting their welfare, rather than to run the constant risk of court action. The modern maxim is to temper justice with subsidy.

"Snuffing the approach of tyranny." One of the great debates of contemporary public affairs is that of the traditional lawyers versus the ad-

---

[3] *Op. cit.* above in note 1, p. 35. *Cf.* also Chapter 10, "Independent Regulatory Agencies."

ministrative lawyers. The legal profession of the United States today—as Edmund Burke remarked of it in 1775—is "numerous and powerful" and its members "augur misgovernment at a distance, and snuff the approach of tyranny in every tainted breeze." [4] The controversial publications of the various schools of legal thought illuminate the subject of administrative adjudication and "delegated legislation" for the student. However, they keep the spotlight on the small minority of cases that come up for formal hearings—on that part of administration that follows, or may perhaps be made to follow, procedures similar to those of the judiciary. This preoccupation with the margin of the problem is typified by the terms "administrative process," "administrative procedure," and "administrative agency," which in most lawyers' studies of the subject are used to refer only to the agencies that issue rules and adjudicate private rights, and their methods of doing so.[5]

Because the debate is essentially on the margin of the problem, we find that even those writers who are the most vigorous critics of administrative regulation and adjudication may also give the clearest picture of the necessity for their existence. For example, one might turn to the works of Roscoe Pound, who was for many years the spokesman of the Committee on Administrative Law of the American Bar Association, and hence the leading critic of administrative procedures. Yet Dean Pound tells how the United States was "law ridden" in the nineteenth century; how the demands of an expanding law of public utilities and the requirements of social legislation led to the development of administrative procedures and regulatory agencies; how the judiciary reviewed the decisions of these agencies without giving any weight to their findings of fact, thus forcing them to follow rules of evidence suitable only for jury trials in common-law courts; and, in consequence, how the state legislatures and eventually Congress began to give more and more functions to administrative agencies and comparatively fewer to the courts. He mentions workmen's compensation, corporate reorganization, the adjustment of private water rights. Then, too, for the past sixty years "the judiciary has been falling into line and . . . powers which two generations ago would have been held purely judicial and jealously guarded from executive exercise . . . are now cheerfully conceded to boards and commissions." [6]

On the other hand, Dean Pound's writings and speeches over a period of years summed up the philosophical and technical criticisms of the

---

[4] "On Conciliation with the Colonies," *Speeches and Letters on American Affairs*, p. 95, New York: Dutton (Everyman's Library), 1931.

[5] This type of definition led the Attorney General's Committee on Administrative Procedure to speculate on how things would be managed "if administrative agencies did not exist in the Federal Government." *Op. cit.* above in note 1, p. 13. *Cf.* also Chapter 17, "Government by Procedure."

[6] *Administrative Law: Its Growth, Procedure, and Significance*, p. 31, Pittsburgh: University of Pittsburgh Press, 1942. This brief study ably summarizes Dean Pound's views on the subject.

professional lawyer against the administrative agencies. He has charged that the philosophies of Marx, Freud, and Einstein have led certain people "to believe in supermen administrators free from the checks of law or rights or judicial review." [7] This belief, he holds, has been responsible for basically unfair procedures in administrative hearings. The courts, he says, are headed by judges who are trained to conform to known standards and settled ideals; their decisions are exposed to the criticism of an informed profession; reports of the cases appear in the public records; and individual judgments are subject to review by a bench whose attitude is analytical. The administrative agencies, he argues, are under none of these safeguards. Moreover, they have an "obstinate tendency to decide without a hearing or without hearing one of the parties"; they make determinations on the basis of private consultations; they fail to disclose to affected parties the evidence on which their orders are based; and heads of administrative agencies act on abstracts of testimony prepared by irresponsible subordinates, without studying the original testimony.[8] These evils are all connected with the fact that the same agency is acting as prosecutor and judge in the same case.

Campaign for judicial justice. The followers of Dean Pound were inclined to believe that justice will most probably be attained in administrative procedures if they can be made to conform as closely as possible to judicial procedures; and that this can best be done by the adoption of uniform standards and forms of procedure, if indeed the function cannot be transferred outright to the courts themselves.[9] This type of criticism was parallel to the lawyers' attack in Great Britain at the same period, or a little earlier; it led to the appointment of the Committee on Minister's Powers, which gave an authoritative and detailed analysis of delegated legislation and administrative adjudication in the United Kingdom.

In the United States the professionally organized criticism brought about the passage of the Walter-Logan Bill in 1939 (H.R. 6324, 76th Congress, 3rd Session). This bill applied the lawyer's prescription to the reform of administrative regulation and adjudication with a vengeance. It laid down a single rigid method for the issuing of regulations, on no matter what subject; it provided for extensive judicial review of rules, even if they were not the subject of controversy; and it required that all adjudicatory decisions be reviewed by superior administrative authorities, whether anyone appealed or not. The President vetoed this bill; but taking account of the sentiment of Congress and the criticism by the bar,

---

[7] *Ibid.*, p. 22. See also Chapter 3, "Bureaucracy—Fact and Fiction," sec. 3, "The Charge of Despotism."

[8] *Ibid.*, p. 60-75.

[9] For a recent example, see *Report on Legal Services and Procedure,* prepared for the (second Hoover) Commission on Organization of the Executive Branch of the Government by the Task Force on Legal Services and Procedure, p. 138, Washington, 1955.

he asked the Attorney General to appoint a committee to study the possibility of "procedural reform in the field of administrative law." At about the same time, the Governor of New York appointed Robert M. Benjamin to conduct a similar study in that state. The Benjamin Report and the report of the Attorney General's Committee on Administrative Procedure jointly represent the best study of the problem. Although they criticized specific procedures and recommended specific reforms, they generally agreed that the courts could not do the job the administrative agencies were doing, and that the administrative agencies themselves could not do it if anyone made them imitate the courts.

In addition a series of works by lawyers undertook to refute the point of view of Dean Pound and the major drift of opinion of the American Bar Association. The experience of Judge Jerome Frank and Dean James M. Landis in the Securities and Exchange Commission, and of Professor Walter Gellhorn in the Attorney General's Committee and later in the Office of Price Administration, gave the flavor of administrative experience to their scholarly writing.[10] But the forces that had originally carried forward the case for the Walter-Logan Bill were not persuaded by the findings of the Attorney General's Committee or by the writings of these scholars who had contributed to its work. The campaign for general legislation was resumed in Congress at the end of World War II and resulted in the Administrative Procedure Act of 1946.

Afterthoughts. The Administrative Procedure Act set out to extend the scope of judicial review over administrative decisions; to require more uniform and formal procedures in both administrative adjudication and administrative regulation; and to create a corps of hearing examiners, with a somewhat separate status within the civil service, to provide a measure of independence in the process of adjudication.

At the time the Act was hailed by its advocates as a great reform. Others, among them some of the closest students of administrative law, predicted detrimental consequences from the sweeping and rigid terms of the new provisions. The practical development, however, has disappointed extreme expectations or fears on both sides.

On the other hand, the debate over the issues continues. It is partly recorded in the pertinent reports of the first and second Hoover Commissions, of the President's Conference on Administrative Procedure of 1953, and in the periodic reports of the Administrative Law Section of the American Bar Association. But with time the issues became less dogmatic. Political liberals, with an eye on the threat to individual rights implicit in the civil liberties cases and in the loyalty and security investiga-

---

[10] See Frank, Jerome, *If Men Were Angels,* New York: Harper, 1930; Landis, James M., *The Administrative Process,* New Haven: Yale University Press, 1938; Gellhorn. Walter, *Federal Administrative Proceedings,* Baltimore: Johns Hopkins Press, 1941.

tions, were less eager to defend administrative procedures against judicial review, and conservative lawyers were less certain that the courts were prepared to take over the function of administrative agencies.

The questions remained how best to reconcile the demands of justice and of administrative efficiency. To examine this question in a fuller context, we may look in a little more detail at three of the main problems of administrative adjudication: how to make sure that administrative hearings are conducted under fair procedures; how much opportunity to give the courts to review administrative decisions; and how to organize the administrative agencies for their function of adjudication.

3. Hearing Procedure

A single code of procedure? The most controversial general issue regarding the procedure of adjudication is whether, or how much, the various agencies should be required to conform to a single code of procedure, especially one modeled on the rules of the regular courts. This argument applies only to those types of business for which formal hearing procedures are appropriate. These, like the visible part of an iceberg, are a small fraction of the whole. Beneath the surface lies the great volume of administrative decision-making which affects private rights and interests, but which for one reason or another cannot be handled by formal adjudication. Some matters depend on technical tests or inspection—is the food free from bacteria, or will the steamboat boiler hold the required pressure? Others involve too little in economic interests to justify the expense of formal hearings—who should be granted a peddler's license by a village clerk? And still others require immediate decision in the interests of safety or national security.

But as governmental regulation and administrative decisions become more important both to great economic interests and to the welfare of individuals, it is desirable to formalize the processes of making decisions that affect private rights. The administrator wants to do so, both in order to do his job well and justly, and to protect himself against the demands of those who want special favors. The individuals or interests affected want him to do so, so they may be assured of fair treatment. And the legal profession is always alert to demand a formal procedure, naturally hoping to further both the ends of justice and the employment of its members. There is little difference of opinion on the broad objectives to be gained by formalization of procedure. The public ought to know the rules it is expected to obey and how an agency considers its cases; to be sure that all the facts in a case are fully and fairly presented, with each side knowing the full position of the other, and having an opportunity to refute it; and to be confident that no one has an opportunity to influence the decision by the exercise of influence or pressure.

At the same time, the quasi-judicial business of the administrative agencies is so varied, so specialized, and necessarily so mixed up with its service and promotional functions, that it has proved impossible to attain these general objectives by the enactment of a single code of detailed procedure. In the 1930's such a code was still the dream of many of the lawyers who were most dissatisfied with the methods or the objectives, or both, of the new agencies in Washington. The majority of the Attorney General's Committee on Administrative Procedure found that a single code would be impracticable. Indeed, it found "few instances of indifference on the part of the agencies to the basic values which underlie a fair hearing," but instead "a healthy self-criticism and considerable alertness to fulfill not only the letter of the judicial pronouncements but the basic implications of fairness in hearing."[11] As a result, it chose to recommend not a general code, but specific changes in the procedures of individual agencies.[12] Far from assuming that the remedy should always be to increase the formality of administrative hearings, the Committee blamed "lengthy hearings and incredibly voluminous records" for burdensome delays, and even suggested that some of the agencies might operate less formally by imitating the expeditious "pre-trial hearings" of some of the courts.

Changing points of view. With time, here again, the battle lines shifted considerably. In the Administrative Procedure Act of 1946, Congress had enacted general requirements of procedure. But experience under that act did little to persuade anyone that there was much to be gained by extending such requirements into a more sweeping and uniform code of procedure. Within a few years, Congress itself had enacted twelve statutes exempting various functions or agencies from the requirements of the act. The second Hoover Commission's Task Force on Legal Services and Procedure proposed an "administrative code," but the Commission refused to endorse this recommendation.[13]

Soon after, the American Bar Association put a special committee to work to draft a revision of the Administrative Procedure Act. Its draft of 1958 showed that the bar was much less inclined than it had been to push for large changes in the procedure of adjudication, and much more inclined to accept the delicate balance that had been achieved and to adjust it but in minor respects.[14] In part this change of position was, as we have

---

[11] *Op. cit.* above in note 1, p. 62.

[12] See the series of monographs on individual agencies issued by the Committee. Study of almost any two will show the reader how considerably the subject matter and the procedure differ from one agency to another.

[13] Indeed, more than half of the Commission's members disavowed the recommendations in its own report on amendments to the Administrative Procedure Act. See *Legal Services and Procedure,* a report to the Congress by the Commission on Organization of the Executive Branch of the Government, especially p. 50-51 and 95, Washington, 1955.

[14] A summary of this position is given in Ruth Smalley, "The Federal Administra-

already noted, the result of a political change. The New Deal agencies had come to be taken for granted; the administrative hearings that roused the passions of debaters were the loyalty and security hearings. So the conservatives were beginning to discover unforeseen values in the administrative process, while the liberals were gaining a new respect for the rigorous rules of judicial procedure.

Coincidentally with the shift in the political tides came a greater degree of realistic and mature understanding of the basic problems. This was, in good measure, a result of a generation of study and debate and a series of level-headed court decisions. Consequently, some of those who hoped for the reform of adjudicatory procedure changed their basic strategy. Instead of relying on the enactment of a detailed and uniform code, they began to emphasize staff work inside the executive branch, to induce agencies to improve their procedures. An Office of Administrative Procedure was created within the Department of Justice in 1956, in response to a recommendation made to the President in 1955 by the President's Conference on Administrative Procedure, which had devoted two years to its studies.[15] The office began its work as a staff agency relying on a cooperative approach, and not undertaking to exercise direct authority over the several agencies. But its position in the Department of Justice, and its opportunity to review and advise on new legislative proposals as well as on existing procedures, gave it a position of great potential influence within the government.

4. Judicial Review

Case for judicial review. The problem of judicial review has been magnified out of all importance, for in numerous types of cases that are handled by administrative agencies the citizen would get little or no tangible protection from appealing to the courts. Many administrative agencies, in matters of adjudication, deal with questions that have to be answered immediately in order to prevent hardship, or that individually do not justify the cost of legal proceedings. Thus an unsuccessful claimant for a small social security benefit will usually not hire a lawyer to contest a doubtful case, simply because the odds are not worth the cost. A grower will not take to court a decision by an examiner of the United States Department of Agriculture condemning a carload of perishable commodities, for his goods will decay before they could be introduced as evidence. A securities

tive Procedure Act: Its Accomplishments and Proposals for Amendments," *Federal Bar News*, May 1958, Vol. 5 (No. 5), p. 138 *ff.*

[15] Similar recommendations were made by the Attorney General's Committee on Administrative Procedure in 1939 and also by other groups. For a brief review of the Office of Administrative Procedure and its approach to its problems, see *Study of Administrative Organization, Procedure, and Practice,* Hearings before a Subcommittee of the House Committee on Government Operations, 85th Cong., 2nd Sess., 1958.

broker will find little satisfaction in appealing from an adverse decision of the Securities and Exchange Commission on the listing of a security, for the opportunity to sell it profitably may have gone.

To depend mainly on judicial review in these cases would be futile. The chief problem is how to organize on a fair basis the system of rendering the original decision. The volume of administrative decisions alone would make it unwise to rely too extensively on review by the courts. It is no more reasonable to ask the courts to decide anew any considerable portion of administrative decisions than to ask the Supreme Court to consider again most of the cases decided by lower courts.

What the courts can do, however, is to protect the fundamental rights of citizens to fair treatment in the hearing of their cases, and to maintain the basic political and constitutional relationship between the administrative agency and other branches of government. If the courts are to do this effectively, they must restrict themselves to two questions: first, the type of case which they will review at all; and second, the extent to which they will give weight to the original decision of the administrative agency.

In four general ways the federal courts have narrowed down the number of cases they will review, even though they have avoided a statement of principles and have carefully maintained their discretion to consider each case as it comes up. One such restriction is that the individual appealing from the administrative decision must have "legal standing"—that is, in general, he must be "adversely affected" by the decision. Another is that the administrative decision must be a final one. No one may come to the court with a case until he has done all he can to get a favorable decision from the administrative agency. Third, there is some question of whether courts will generally review an administrator's refusal to take action—such as refusal to issue a license—even though the Supreme Court in 1938 withdrew its earlier doctrine that "negative orders" were not reviewable. Fourth, courts will not review—sometimes by self-denial, sometimes because of statutory limitations—some types of decisions that seem particularly suited to administrative discretion. Examples are a decision that a contractor on a government project must pay certain wage rates, or decisions of the Veterans Administration with respect to certain classes of benefits to veterans.[16]

Scope of judicial review. Much more important, however, than the question of whether or not to review a case is the question of how far a court is to go in its review. For just as the administrative agency has no more extensive rule-making or quasi-legislative power than the legislature intended to give it, so it has only as much power to make decisions as the courts leave in its hands. An illustration of the way in which the judiciary may take over decisions that are the very heart of administration

---

[16] *Cf.* Attorney General's Committee on Administrative Procedure, *op. cit.* above in note 1, p. 84-86.

may be chosen from the annals of New York state government. In 1903, the Court of Appeals held that the duty of classification of positions—as competitive, noncompetitive, or exempt—under the civil service law was quasi-judicial in its nature, and could be reviewed by the courts by writ of certiorari, much like any decision of a lower court. After a few years the Court of Appeals came to the uncomfortable conclusion that it had— in its own words—"in effect assumed the functions of the Civil Service Commissioners, for every challenged decision of these officers was brought to this court as a question of law." [17] Accordingly, it reversed itself; decided that the function was not judicial or even quasi-judicial; held that such decisions could be reviewed only by writ of mandamus; and explained that, while clear failure or refusal of the Civil Service Commission to do its duty could be reviewed, the court would not reverse any decision, even though it might differ with its wisdom, if there was "a fair and reasonable ground for difference of opinion."

In short, since every act of a public official must be based on legal authorization, courts may stretch their logic a bit and make nearly any type of administrative decision all over again. The stretching would not be too difficult. It is a settled principle that the courts have the power to review questions of law, since otherwise the citizen would have no way to appeal against the actions of an official who plainly acted illegally. It is a commonplace among lawyers, however, that no clear distinction exists between questions of law and questions of fact, since their subject matter is basically the same. As one frequently quoted passage runs, "the knife of policy alone effects an artificial cleavage" between the two questions, and furthermore, "at the point where the court chooses to draw the line between public interest and private right." [18]

To illustrate this point, we may take the classic case of Miller v. Horton.[19] A public health official killed a horse that in his judgment had the glanders. The jury decided that the horse had not really had the glanders after all; that the official who thought it had was wrong; and that therefore he had not had legal authority to kill the horse and must pay for it. The law usually authorizes an official to act only in certain circumstances and for certain purposes. If a judge wants to reverse the official's decision on the facts of the situation, he can sometimes find the facts so thoroughly mixed up with the legal issues involved that a review ostensibly of the law will take care of the facts as well.

Legitimate judicial concerns. If the courts were generally preoccupied with private rights and careless of the public interest, logic alone would not

---

[17] Simons v. McGuire, 204 N.Y. 253, 257-258, 97 N.E. 526, 527 (1912), as quoted by Hart, James, "Judicial Review of Administrative Action: A Thesis," *George Washington Law Review*, 1941, Vol. 9, p. 501.

[18] Dickinson, John, *Administrative Justice and the Supremacy of Law*, p. 55, Cambridge: Harvard University Press, 1927.

[19] 152 Mass. 540, 26 N.E. 100, 10 L.R.A. 116, 23 Am. St. Rep. 850 (1891).

stop them from reducing the original administrative ruling to little more than a formal preliminary to the judicial decision. Fortunately, the courts in the main do no such thing. Their prevailing philosophy has followed the election returns in accepting the idea that considerations of public interest have greatly expanded as our economic system has increased its interdependences. Accordingly, when a court reviews an administrative adjudication, more often than not it adjusts the scope of its review to the extent to which fundamental principles appear to be involved, much as an executive gives his attention to the more significant problems of administration and leaves others to his subordinates.

Above all, a higher court will thoroughly review cases involving constitutional rights. It may consider all the aspects of such a case anew, giving comparatively little weight even in questions of fact to the original decision of an administrative agency. The next most intensive review will be given those cases in which the problem arises whether an agency acted outside its statutory authority. Even though such questions of law are entangled with questions of fact, the courts will certainly not hesitate to reverse an agency's decision when that decision was clearly beyond its legal power.

A part of the question of whether the agency acted legally or not is this: Did it follow a fair procedure? The courts are likely to insist rigorously on the fundamentals of fair play—the right to face and cross-examine witnesses for the other side, and so on. In recent years, the Supreme Court has been most concerned with this issue with respect to the security and loyalty hearings, especially with respect to the traditional right of a "defendant" to be fully informed about the details of the charges and the evidence, and to confront anyone who brings evidence against him. The pressure of the courts, and the professional conscience of leading lawyers, did much to bring about a recognition of the need for fairness of procedure in the enforcement of security regulations.[20]

In expressing their concern with the elements of justice, however, the courts have been discriminating in their rulings on procedure. They are not likely, in general, to insist that specialized agencies with expert trial examiners be bound by the elaborate rules of evidence that were developed to help a judge keep a jury of laymen from being bamboozled. American courts, it should be added, are still somewhat more inclined than English courts to assume that an administrative agency has acted fairly only if it has acted like a court. The Arlidge case [21] in Great Britain established the

---

[20] See *Report of the Special Committee on the Federal Loyalty-Security Program of the Association of the Bar of the City of New York*, Dodd, Mead & Co. New York, 1956; Cushman, Robert E., *Civil Liberties in the United States*, Ithaca: Cornell University Press, 1956.

[21] Local Government Board v. Arlidge, L. R. (1915), Appeal Cases, 120. For current British points of view, see the report of the Committee on Administrative Tribunals and Enquiries (chaired by Sir Oliver Franks), Cmd. 218, 1957.

principle that administrative agencies might conform to "methods of natural justice" without following "lawyer-like methods." In contrast to this, in the equally famous Morgan cases [22] in the United States, the Supreme Court, in regard to certain procedures, considered the function of the Secretary of Agriculture "a duty akin to that of a judge."

Legislative and judicial standards of review. The courts will rely most on the administrative agency's decision, and insist least on their own point of view, in questions that are clearly and solely questions of fact. In reviewing such questions, the courts have come more and more to the point of trying to decide, not whether the administrative agency made the correct decision—which could only mean the same decision the court would have made if it had been the agency—but whether the decision was made reasonably and on the basis of substantial evidence. Language to bring about this effect has been incorporated in legislation defining the extent of court review of the decisions of certain federal agencies: "findings of fact by the Commission, if supported by substantial evidence, shall be conclusive unless it shall clearly appear that the findings of the Commission are arbitrary and capricious." [23]

There was a great deal of legislative maneuvering over the exact language of this formula, until the "substantial evidence" rule was incorporated in the Administrative Procedure Act of 1946; yet in practice the exact words of the formula did not seem to matter very much. For instance, Congress declared the findings of the National Labor Relations Board conclusive if "supported by evidence," but the Supreme Court held that if the evidence was not substantial it was not evidence and the omission of the word "substantial" made no difference.[24] Those who wish to broaden the scope of judicial review still argue for different phraseology, but the question cannot be solved by the juggling of words. In recent years the judicial point of view, in practice, has generally been reasonably sympathetic toward the necessity of letting the administrative agencies do their jobs.

In general, court review of administrative decisions and orders is least useful on those aspects of a case that require discretion—the selection of one choice among several with nearly equal advantages—or call for technical or scientific qualifications. It is most useful, on the other hand, on those aspects of a case that involve the protection of definite individual rights or personal liberties against arbitrary, unreasonable, or careless official action. However, no line can be drawn in advance between the various aspects of any single case. Just as the judge may substitute his personal predilections for the scientific opinion of the expert, so the expert may come to believe that his science justifies exceeding his authority.

---

[22] Morgan v. United States, 298 U.S. 468 (1936); 304 U.S. 1 (1938); 304 U.S. 23 (1938).

[23] Communications Act of 1934 (48 Stat. 1094, 47 U.S.C. 402e).

[24] Consolidated Edison Co. v. N.L.R.B., 305 U.S. 197, 229 (1938).

In the long run, mutual respect by judges and administrators will help maintain a sense of jurisdictional differentiation between them, particularly if an aggressive and well-informed public opinion watches the entire process of adjudication.

5. The Organization of Adjudication

Prosecutor-and-judge agencies. Since practical limitations apply to the usefulness of judicial review in a dynamic administrative system, it is all the more important to organize properly the hearing activities of the government agencies concerned. This problem, it is true, has nothing to do with the great mass of business of most of the agencies, which is handled by informal settlement. Nor has it anything to do with the business of some of the agencies, which proceeds by such techniques as scientific inspection and makes little or no use of formal hearings. However, the agency that holds formal hearings must take care to organize itself so as to avoid the charge—and any basis for the suspicion—that its interest in initiating the case leads it to be unfair in the hearing.

This is the question of whether a single agency should be both prosecutor and judge in the same case. The question is partly fallacious, but nevertheless it has made many people doubt the fairness of administrative procedure. The element of fallacy in the question is that an agency is not a single person. The agency may be an extremely large organization— much larger than the whole government of the United States a century ago—and it is surely as possible to set up within it a system of checks and balances as it was to create such a system in our national government.

The agency may well be expected to have a bias in favor of a certain policy—the policy which it is instructed by statute to enforce. And if certain groups oppose that policy it is possible for the agency to develop a bias against those groups. Even judges, however, are not supposed to be completely neutral toward the laws they are enforcing, or toward those who fail to obey the laws. They are only supposed to reserve judgment on the question of whether any given individual has in fact disobeyed the laws. Still, administrative agencies are particularly likely to be directed to enforce laws that are vigorously opposed by one or another interest, and their unpopularity may sometimes be a measure of their effectiveness.

Alternative approaches. To guarantee fairness in the hearing of complex and difficult cases, it is generally agreed that administrative agencies should establish formal hearing units and give them a measure of independence from the divisions that investigate and initiate cases. The President's Committee on Administrative Management proposed a thorough system of separation of functions within the regulatory agencies in its report in 1937, which was based on the study of the independent regulatory commissions by Professor Robert E. Cushman. Taking into consideration the important policy relationships of the regulatory commissions and boards to the general program of the executive branch, that committee proposed that these commissions and boards be put into the executive departments, with a division into two sections—an administrative section to handle the rule-making and investigating phases of the work, and a judicial section, composed of members appointed by the President and confirmed by the Senate, to hear cases and appeals.[25] The debate over the proper organization of the function of administrative adjudication, in its broadest terms, then turned primarily on the question of whether adequate safeguards could be provided by some such internal separation of functions, or whether instead a separate system of specialized or administrative courts ought to be provided.

Let us look first at the proposals regarding such specialized courts. Superficially, the proposal for the creation of specialized courts to hear administrative cases or appeals seems to be a fundamental shift from the position of the traditional common-law attorney in the English-speaking countries. The classic statement of this position was put forward by A. V. Dicey, who held, in summary, that administrative law as he defined it does not exist in English-speaking countries. In his work on the law of the British Constitution,[26] Dicey emphasized that any citizen could go, as he still can go, to the regular courts if any official injured him by acting beyond his legal authority; and that under the continental system of administrative law the citizen is not able to do so.

What Dicey failed to see were the limitations of the common law court. Such a court may be too slow and too expensive to help the citizen. Or it may achieve nothing if the official act that damaged him was performed within the law. By contrast, an administrative court might give him quick and cheap relief. On points like these, Dicey's Continental European critics scored heavily, especially those who, like Duguit,[27] emphasized the service functions of public administration and the role of governmental authority in giving effect to democratic policies.

Continental administrative courts. English-speaking countries were reluctant to permit executive departments to hear and decide cases after the manner of a court. They showed even greater reluctance to evolve special-

---

[25] This is substantially the system that was adopted in 1950 in the field of maritime regulation, by the creation within the Department of Commerce of the Federal Maritime Board, made up of presidential appointees and independent of the Secretary of Commerce with respect to its regulatory functions, and the Maritime Administration as a regular bureau within the Department. For the views of the President's Committee, see its *Report with Special Studies,* Washington: Government Printing Office, 1937. One of these special studies was "The Problem of the Independent Regulatory Commissions," by Robert E. Cushman, from which the proposal of the committee on the subject was drawn. See also Cushman's more recent book, *The Independent Regulatory Commissions,* New York: Oxford University Press, 1941.

[26] Dicey, A. V., *Introduction to the Study of the Law of the Constitution,* 8th ed., New York: Macmillan, 1915.

[27] Duguit, Léon, *Law in the Modern State,* New York: Viking, 1919.

ized branches of the judiciary to handle the new types of cases that arose with the extension of government functions. These attitudes kept the United States and Great Britain, in some types of cases, from developing as effective machinery for protecting private rights as was brought into being by the administrative courts of Continental Europe.

The French established a system of administrative courts as a result of the decision, effected in their revolutionary constitution, to separate the powers of government with logical thoroughness. They carried their logic so far as to forbid the judiciary to interfere with administrative acts, and initially left the citizen with no recourse except appeal to the higher level of administration. The executive branch subsequently organized a formal system of inferior and superior councils to hear such appeals. These councils secured increasing independence as administrative courts, hearing all kinds of cases arising out of the relationship between public authorities and the citizens.

The system of administrative courts, with national variations, is common to almost all countries of Continental Europe. At the highest stage of its development, it had several fairly general characteristics.[28] It was a system of judge-made law, in that the administrative judges built up an expanding body of precedents in the process of interpreting statutes and deciding cases. There was a hierarchy of courts, with appeal from the lower to the higher. The procedure made it relatively easy and inexpensive for the average citizen to get a decision.

Drawn in many instances from the legally trained higher ranks of the career service, but acquiring judicial independence upon appointment, the judges were closely in touch with administrative developments, and in an excellent position to interpret the motivation and to control the discretion of officials. At the same time, they were sympathetic toward the public purposes of government agencies. Career administrators themselves were trained in public law as well as for management. For this reason, and because most administrative actions did not come before the less well-informed ordinary courts, government departments were not in need of large legal staffs who might—as in the United States—have carried on feuds with operating officials.

American proposals. The hope of establishing a more systematic body of administrative law in the United States has led various scholars to propose special courts of appeals for administrative cases.[29] This is not an

---

[28] For a summary description and citations to the literature on this subject, see Morstein Marx, Fritz, "Comparative Administrative Law: The Continental Alternative," *University of Pennsylvania Law Review*, 1942, Vol. 91, p. 118 *ff*. See also "Legal Redress of Administrative Wrongs," in the same author's *The Administrative State: An Introduction to Bureaucracy*, p. 138 *ff*., Chicago: University of Chicago Press, 1958.

[29] *Cf*., for example, Blachly, Frederick F., and Oatman, Miriam E., "A United States Court of Appeals for Administration," *Annals of the American Academy of Political and Social Science*, 1942, Vol. 221, p. 170 *ff*.

unprecedented proposal, as Congress has set up several constitutional curiosities called legislative courts (such as the Court of Claims) which hear appeals from administrative agencies. Quite a different proposal is that outlined in the report of the second Hoover Commission, and recommended in 1956 by the American Bar Association.[30] The commission recommended that an administrative court be established and that Congress transfer to it the functions performed in the executive branch by the Tax Court, the National Labor Relations Board, and various agencies in the field of regulation of trade. This court was to be within the judicial branch, and was meant to be only "an intermediate stage in the evolution of administrative adjudication and the transfer of judicial activities from the agencies to courts of general jurisdiction."

Among the opponents of such a scheme were various groups that did business with the regulatory agencies without the help of lawyers or legal training; these looked on the proposed change as a scheme to increase the business of lawyers. For example, the Tax Court remains in the executive branch mainly because accountants, who have always been permitted to practice before it, oppose its transfer to the judicial branch, where the normal rules of procedure would weaken their status in competition with the lawyers.[31] Another objection relates to economy in the use of personnel. Some functions that might be transferred to administrative courts, where cases would be heard by judges presumably with legal training, are now handled in agencies which can combine the hearing functions with various technical jobs and other assignments—especially when the functions are performed in out-of-the-way field stations.[32]

But a much more crucial and less obvious point is the difficulty of separating the function of adjudication from the functions of supervision, promotion, and regulation, without causing difficulties for the private interests as well as the governmental agency concerned. These difficulties might be avoided if a system of true administrative courts were set up within the executive departments. But if the function of adjudication were transferred to the judicial branch, the job of prosecuting or initiating cases would probably be transferred from a specialized regulatory agency to the Department of Justice. Then the regulatory agency would become little more than a research agency, with none of the effectiveness that it now has as a result of its combination of functions.[33] The organized bar

[30] *Op. cit.* above in note 13, p. 84 *ff.* For articles analyzing and criticizing this proposal, see the *George Washington Law Review*, June 1956, Vol. 24 (No. 6), and *Federal Bar Journal*, Oct.-Dec. 1956, Vol. 16 (No. 4).

[31] See Gribbon, Daniel M., "Should the Judicial Character of the Tax Court Be Recognized," *George Washington Law Review*, 1956, Vol. 24, p. 621 *ff.*

[32] See the discussion of the handling of applications for various uses of public lands in *Study of Administrative Organization, Procedure, and Practice, op. cit.* above in note 15, p. 40.

[33] For example, see the arguments in Freer, Robert E., "The Case Against the Trade Regulations Section of the Proposed Administrative Court," *George Washington Law Review*, 1956, Vol. 24, p. 637 *ff.*

is not as wholeheartedly in favor of the general transfer to the courts of all the adjudication now performed by administrative agencies as one might suppose from the public debates. On the one hand, many lawyers now practice before the administrative agencies; that is why the District of Columbia Bar often disagrees with the American Bar Association on this issue. On the other hand, many lawyers and judges are mainly interested in protecting the supremacy of the general standards of justice against erosion by specialists of all kinds—and they would distrust specialized courts, in this respect, almost as much as the administrative agencies that the courts would replace.

Independence of the hearing function. For whatever reason, the support for specialized administrative courts seemed to have become an academic rather than a practical issue. The decision had been made, in effect, to put trust in an internal separation of functions within the administrative agencies—the so-called "independent" commissions and boards, often considered agents of Congress, as well as those agencies under the President's unlimited direction.

The problem then becomes one of giving the proper degree of independence to the officers who conduct the administrative hearings and of assuring high standards in their selection. These have come to be known since the Administrative Procedure Act of 1946 as hearing examiners. The act gave the hearing examiners a measure of independence by making the Civil Service Commission responsible to an extraordinary degree for their selection and promotion, and for protecting them against dismissal except for good cause.

As the Civil Service Commission undertook to carry out these responsibilities, its most difficult problem was what to do with the incumbent hearing examiners. It appointed a special advisory committee to screen them and advise on their qualifications. The committee found about a fifth of them unqualified. The Commission at first requested their dismissal, but withdrew its request after a storm of protest and appointed all incumbents. For this it was roundly criticized, especially by the second Hoover Commission, but the Hoover Commission itself recommended that all incumbents with as much as a year's experience be continued in office under the new system which it proposed.

The system proposed by the second Hoover Commission was one in which responsibility for supervising the hearing examiners would be transferred from the Civil Service Commission to a new office within the judicial branch, a Chief Hearing Commissioner. But this proposal found little support; the contrary judgment of the President's Conference on Administrative Procedure in 1953 had apparently proved convincing. And the Civil Service Commission was left with the difficult problem of building up a strong, independent, and competent corps of hearing examiners. This was a difficult problem not mainly because the examiners suffered under the supervision of their administrative superiors but because, like their superiors in the public service, they were badly underpaid by comparison with those whom they were regulating.

Political factors. There is no essential reason why a system of administrative courts should be expected to take over the administrative functions of executive agencies or encroach on them by extending the scope of judicial review. However, the administrative courts grew up on the Continent in part because the ordinary judiciary was not permitted to check administration. To duplicate them here, where the courts have been accustomed to interfering too much, might give more opportunity for such interference.

It has often been remarked that a regulatory agency and the regulated interest may tend to work together very closely. Pressure of the political agency heads on their subordinates will often be in the direction of prosecuting only clear cases of violation in order to avoid the protests and political opposition that might be caused by questionable ones. The agency ordinarily has a strong motive for going easy on its "constituents," since it may need their support in obtaining appropriations or additional legislative authority. Moreover, agencies may have reason to fear that some of their regulatory functions will be taken from them and transferred to a competitor. It is possible that this fear adds to their desire to cultivate the support of the interests they are regulating.

The agency usually issues regulations as well as enforces them, and in preparing such regulations it generally consults closely with the interests concerned. Any unreasonable requirement will certainly cause a protest to Congress, which holds over the agency the threat of reduced appropriations or withdrawal of statutory authority. Thus we have a degree of responsibility to the legislature in the regulation of economic interests, whether the regulating agency is an independent commission or an executive department, in addition to the latter's responsibility to the President. Neither house of the lawmaking body as a whole can deal with protests, but committee hearings give legislators a much more effective opportunity to dig into the details of administration. The main shortcoming of the existing system is that—except in the event of disaster or crisis—it puts all the pressure in the direction of relaxing, rather than strengthening, the authority of the regulatory agency.

6. Conclusion

Benefits of administrative specialization. The essentials of justice in human relations are eternal. They involve basic questions of ethics and politics which do not change with scientific or industrial development. In order to safeguard human rights and human dignity, it is necessary to have not only an elected legislature with power to establish the basic rules of society, but also a judiciary whose concern with fundamental values will not be distorted by specialized interests.

However, as the legislature will best discharge its general function if it leaves technical rules to be established by responsible administrators, so the courts can most effectively protect human rights if the great volume of specialized cases is handled by administrative adjudication—subject to the power of the courts to enforce the principles of fair play.

Combining flexibility and principle. The role of government in modern society is too dynamic and too diversified for us to attain justice merely by conforming to traditional methods. Rigid judicial procedure would be intolerable in the wide fields of activity in which administrative agencies are today the copilots with private management.

Here is left one of the great challenges to public administration—to organize a system of administrative adjudication, closely associated with the execution of policy, that will combine the virtues of dispatch and flexibility with the degree of institutional independence and fair procedure necessary to safeguard individual rights.

Chapter 24 •

Personnel Standards

1. Responsibility and Competence

Ensuring responsive and resourceful administration. Responsible public management is not attained simply by subjecting administrative agencies to axioms of "government of laws." It requires corresponding modes of administrative behavior—a true service ideology. It also requires institutional safeguards of technical competence. The demand for a high caliber of public personnel aims at a working force of proved ability and at general standards of efficiency. Without such standards no government department could undertake effectively to shoulder its statutory responsibilities.

In this sense, personnel administration provides the very foundation of resourceful and responsive management. The rules and methods which govern the organization of the working force in public employment occupy a central place in the system of administrative responsibility. Civil service commissions and personnel officers concern themselves with a large variety of highly specialized activities, but all of these activities bear in one way or another upon the problem of providing a basis for responsible conduct of governmental business.

Management and the personnel function. As with comparable functions like budgeting and planning, it is characteristic of personnel administration that its contribution can rarely be measured objectively when it is at the level of greatest effectiveness, but its value is more easily determinable when it neglects its most important function. The paradox is simple to explain. The personnel director is essentially an adviser to management—from the top executive down to the first-line supervisor. As he performs this task, his contribution is commingled with that of general management. On the other hand, if the personnel office confines itself to its own operations, it can boast of the number of applicants recruited, of training classes held, of jobs classified, and point to similar activities that are capable of statistical treatment. These are all useful and necessary services, but such reporting fails to demonstrate the role of the personnel office in management decisions.

The growing significance of personnel administration results from the increase in the knowledge required to handle successfully the staffing needs and the human problems of large organizations. The specific techniques of personnel administration are highly important, but they achieve this importance only to the extent to which they contribute to productive working relations in an organization. Personnel administration aids the supervisor in accomplishing the goal of effective management and cooperative human relations by the assistance it can give him in meeting his responsibilities, even though his superiors have to set the objectives of institutional policy.[1]

Changing attitudes. In the years since 1883—the date of the adoption of civil service laws by both the federal government and New York State—personnel management in the public service has run the full gamut from blocking political interference to concern with efficiency as shown also by nongovernmental organizations. The early era's slogan was to "keep the spoilsmen out." The modern era is more concerned with such matters as recruiting, training, managerial selection and development, human relations, the organization of the personnel function, wage and salary systems, collaboration with organized employee groups, handling of grievances, fringe benefits, incentive awards, suggestion systems, and employee safety. No doubt the public service has unique elements, compared with business management. In government, personnel policies are heavily influenced by the potential reaction of the legislature and the public, and the legislature sets the pace on many fundamentals such as compensation, and also on restrictive employment practices such as residence requirements. But the broadened scope of personnel management and relatively full employment have meant decreasing pressure for the appointment of those with influence and a more limited attention to the deep-rooted preoccupation of the public service with examinations and the classification process. The change was well exemplified by a report of the California legislature, which praised the State Personnel Board's handling of the traditional functions but chided the Board for its lack of leadership in general personnel management. Practically all forward-looking government units in the United States now accept this new concept—the differences among them are in their ability, based on staff competence and budget, and in their wholeheartedness in living up to the implications.

---

[1] For general treatment of the governmental approach in this field, see Stahl, O. Glenn, *Public Personnel Administration,* New York: Harper, 1956; Powell, Norman J., *Personnel Administration in Government,* Englewood Cliffs, N.J.: Prentice-Hall, 1956; Van Riper, Paul P., *History of the United States Civil Service,* Evanston, Ill.: Row, Peterson, 1958. Civil service reform has been in the mainstream of good-government movements in the United States. The activity on this front began after the Civil War and is still going strong. The National Civil Service Reform League only recently dropped the word "Reform" from its name, possibly as a result of the changed connotation of the term. The student and the practitioner of public personnel administration should know the history of civil service reform. Special sources are: Foulke, William D., *Fighting the Spoilsman,* New York: Putnam, 1919; United States Civil Service Commission, *A History of the Federal Civil Service,* 1789-1939, Washington: Government Printing Office, 1939; and Stewart, Frank M., *The National Civil Service Reform League,* Austin: University of Texas, 1929.

The new concept and the physical growth of many federal agencies have resulted in greater participation of these agencies in the examining and classification processes and a remarkable expansion of their personnel divisions. In total, these now outnumber the Civil Service Commission's own staff, a ratio which is probably a good index of the attention being paid to the newer personnel functions. The growth of agency personnel activities has prompted the establishment of committees of agency personnel directors to meet regularly with the Civil Service Commission.

Not surprisingly, much attention has been paid to the place of the Civil Service Commission in the governmental structure. Fundamental points of controversy have been: (a) whether the commission should be independent or tied directly into the office of the mayor, governor, or president; (b) whether the commission should be only a part-time body, with its administrative functions under the exclusive direction of a director reporting to the chief executive; and (c) whether an independent commission, limited to traditional functions, should be placed side by side with a separate personnel office in charge of the newer functions and reporting directly to the chief executive. Thus far there is no single answer to these questions. But it is probable that desirable organizational relationships will not weigh as much as tradition, the institutional climate, the interest of the chief executive in management, and even personalities. The desire for change is often as much the result of dissatisfaction with key personalities as of real belief in the organizational alternatives suggested.

Conflicting influences. Personnel administration has not been fully accepted in a great number of organizations. Instead it is frequently considered a necessary evil. This situation arises from a number of reasons. Personnel directors in many places have no interest in the program objectives and problems of the organization; rather, they market a standard product which fits diverse situations poorly. Line administrators cannot be expected to be sympathetic to personnel policies when no effort is made to relate these policies to their operations. Also, personnel specialists offer little help on many problems which are close to a manager's heart—how to obtain increased motivation, attention to quality and quantity of work, and self-development in a system dominated by standard procedures. But line management is often guilty, too. It stresses the immediate solution and abandons the principle with its long-range effects. It complains about the personnel staff taking over line functions, while at the same time neglecting its responsibilities for employee utilization, appraisal, and stimulation. There seems only one way out of this impasse—by gaining greater breadth and depth in the professional work of personnel staffs and greater managerial competence in line management. Mutual recrimination may relieve potential ulcers but not management problems.[2]

---

[2] See also Chapter 21, "Morale and Discipline."

The relative prestige of government is an additional overriding problem. In few units of government is it sufficient to attract the ablest graduates of high schools and colleges. Low prestige has vicious effects on recruitment, on the morale of employees, and on their feeling of responsibility. On the other hand, in fields such as forestry and geology, its predominant position as employer has made government a more attractive place of employment. Despite pessimistic voices, however, the importance and challenge of government work have called forth a hard core of college graduates whose first interest is in public service.

Governmental personnel management is further affected by the ethics of the public servant and his feeling of responsibility for the general welfare, as distinguished from his own welfare or the welfare of other special groups. Democracy can survive internal strife if the public considers its servants to be responsive and honest. Conversely, decay in the public's confidence in its servants is a sure sign of general decay. Indeed, those who create public distrust of the public's civil servants are also battering at one of the foundation stones of government. Because of the importance of this matter, it is right and proper for government to insist on higher standards of public and private behavior among its employees than is necessary for industry. But it is also obvious that this principle can be used to destroy the self-respect of the civil servant by subjecting him to petty regulations and snooping, which are defended on the grounds of ethics. Christianity teaches that self-discipline is the best censor. All that is needed in addition are guidelines to the requirements of the public service and responsible leadership at the top.[3]

Developments in psychology and sociology have made a tremendous imprint on personnel management in both content and methods. Thus far, however, these developments have served mainly to increase the appreciation of the complexity of personnel problems and an awareness of the various forces—personal, environmental, and associational—that affect behavior in an organization. The skill needed to apply this new knowledge is still beyond the capacity of most personnel officers and line managers. At present, in addition to the need for further research, the problem is to develop the ability to use the new knowledge. In many cases, inept application of concepts as well as overenthusiastic claims for results may very well have retarded progress. Most of the personnel training now under way emphasizes the acquisition of new knowledge; but it either neglects the need for skill in applying it or assumes that those acquiring the knowledge will automatically know how to use it. The available evidence does not support such assumption.

Importance of good management. More significant than any of the points discussed thus far is the full recognition of the importance of good manage-

---

[3] See Chapter 22, "Essentials of Responsibility."

ment. As the Task Force Report on Personnel and Civil Service of the second Hoover Commission (1955) has said: "Increasing the supply of managerial talent . . . is the heart of the Federal personnel problem today, and this is the area where the greatest benefits are to be gained." Much has been and is being done by the federal government in response to this truth—an example not yet emulated by city and state governments. Major events in the federal government were the issuance of Executive Order No. 10758 on March 4, 1958, establishing a career executive program for top-level civil servants and, at the other end of the hierarchy, the junior management assistant and management intern examinations, first announced in 1948, together with the intern training programs established before World War II. In addition to departmental executive development programs, seminar conferences are provided by the Brookings Institution in Washington and the University of Chicago, both started in 1957 with grants from the Ford Foundation. New York University offers a similar program for New York City. Thus a beginning has been made in the formal training needed for the three-step scheme of quality recruitment into the service, identification of management ability after entrance, and development of those found promising.

The initial unfavorable reception of the career executive program illustrates very well some of the fundamental problems connected with management progress in government. Although a pallid imitation of the successful European efforts to identify and train an administrative group with high qualifications, this program was condemned by those who feared political interference in executive selection, criticized by others as an effort to establish an elite, and scorned by those who insist that all executive positions need different qualifications. Yet the record of all large-scale organizations indicates that a special effort is necessary to spot administrative talent in order to provide the training and mobility which are essential for a career service. Attack on the program for establishing an elite group is hardly justified in the case of the federal service, which has no rigid educational barriers, and in a country such as the United States where the economic obstacles to a college education are at a minimum. Only time will tell whether the extent of political interference is increased or decreased by such a program. By creating a high-level advisory board within the framework of the Civil Service Commission, the program supplies a barrier rather than an aid to political interference, whereas previously there were no institutional mechanisms to help thwart such interference in promotions to high-level jobs.

These developments in the improvement of management competence are in contrast to the situation before World War II. Then training in typing skills, training in letter writing, training of apprentices, and the development of better tests for clerks were at the focus of attention. It is no criticism of the importance of these efforts to say that, no matter how well done, their satisfactory performance is not of much benefit when the managers of these typists, letter writers, apprentices, and clerks are incompetent.

Rules—need and cost. The equalitarian tradition of the public service results in both strengths and weaknesses. It results in less human distance between the executive suite and the file room. It thereby promotes career development from the bottom to the top and an employee attitude fundamentally favorable to those in high places, rather than hostile towards them. But the tradition hinders the payment of rewards, financial and nonfinancial, proportionate to responsibilities. It also reduces the speed of advancement for even the most able. In many places this tradition helps produce a good system; but carried too far, as it often is, it produces complacency and mediocrity. Nowhere has the equalitarian tradition produced an outstanding system. In the case of the Tennessee Valley Authority, this scheme was replaced by a system that does encourage outstanding management and is equally democratic. It was based on the belief that all employees have the right to be developed to the limit of their ability, in contrast with the belief that all employees are equal in ability.

The formulation and application of rules and regulations stand in the center of public personnel administration. On the one extreme, the promulgation of many rules, each providing for every contingency and qualification, absorbs an increasing percentage of the time and efforts of personnel staffs. It often leads to greater reward for those with skill in interpretation or evasion than to those with skill in personnel administration. Yet the other extreme, of a few general rules, is not much more palatable. It causes injustices quickly noted by employees. It ignores one of the great lessons learned from social science research—that employees often prefer uniform treatment, even if the treatment is not generous, to unequal treatment, even if it often means generous treatment to some or many.

Civil service commissions have often shown restraint in enacting rules, but they have been pushed by legislative threat and the action of pressure groups. It is only recently that one sees corrective action, taken in a specific situation, used as a substitute for general rules which punish both the saint and the sinner. Incidentally, the rules issued by personnel staffs in large agencies may be as objectionable to operating officials as the rules of the central personnel agency. Happily, the development has been toward use of standards rather than of rules, and toward inspection and evaluation on the basis of situations found rather than toward undifferentiated application of general principles.

The examining process. Broadly speaking, the examining process includes recruitment, measurement, placement, transfer, and promotion. The technical and administrative problems which arise from the examining process are at the heart of any personnel program. In many cases training and supervision can do little to overcome basic inadequacies in those selected. A sound technical approach may also come to naught if procedures are slow and cumbersome and fail to take into account employee desires and management objectives.

In a period of relatively full employment, when government salaries and prestige are not particularly high, attracting potential applicants becomes a primary task. Perhaps the most remarkable development in public personnel administration in the last quarter-century is the complete change from the 1930's, when civil service commissions looked for methods of reducing the number of applicants, to the 1940's and 1950's, when they made every effort, and showed encouraging flexibility, to increase the number of applicants. Some of the methods now commonly used for this purpose are: (1) hiring students for summer employment in order to increase their knowledge of and interest in government employment; (2) periodic visits to school campuses to interest faculty members and students; (3) arranging examination schedules at times and places to meet the convenience of applicants and speeding up the examining process so that the delay between examination and notification of results is considerably reduced; (4) extensive use of operating officials in recruiting in order to get the benefit of their knowledge of work and career opportunities; and (5) broadening the recruiting base by more general entrance requirements so that a large group of applicants can be evaluated concurrently, stressing aptitude rather than experience or special knowledge.

All of these efforts have proved worthwhile when well administered. But it would be foolhardy to contend that they have produced the quality and quantity of employees needed by government in the face of competition from other employers, who offer in many cases more prestige and money. Security of employment, presumably an important motivation in the past, is not ranked high by a generation which has not seen long-run mass unemployment. Actually the only real motivations the government can appeal to are the importance of its work, the challenge of its problems, and the opportunity in the federal government of overseas service. But these motivations can be met by nongovernmental organizations in many occupational and professional fields.

Measurement in the examining process means the methods used to determine whether the applicant meets minimum standards and, if he does, his rank among competitors. Because measurement is the oldest civil service process, the changes in it tend to be small in any brief period of time except to the technicians engaged in it. The essay test has been pretty well displaced by the short-answer test, a change now sometimes publicly condemned. Much greater use is made of tests which measure aptitudes, learning ability and judgment, in contrast with previous tests to measure the ability to absorb textbook knowledge.[4]

---

[4] See in general Lawshe, C. H., Jr., *Principles of Personnel Testing,* New York: McGraw-Hill, 1948; Super, D. C., *Appraising Vocational Fitness by Means of Psychological Tests,* New York: Harper, 1949.

Types of testing. The interviewing process has been somewhat improved, although it still suffers from the basic defect that it involves extensive inferences from limited data obtained in an artificial situation by untrained observers.[5] The group oral-performance test is an interview in which several candidates are observed interacting with each other in discussing or handling a problem. It has extended the potential range of the interview and, at the same time, provided an economical method for underfinanced and overworked personnel agencies.

The rating of training and experience has gained some depth by the use of such factors as the variety and progress of experience, as well as the traditional factors of type and length of experience. The most important next step is to add information on the quality of actual performance, obtained through inquiry from present and former supervisors and colleagues. Although the value of such inquiries is dubious when the information is obtained impersonally by means of written documents, this method is a valuable if costly means of measurement when the information is assembled in a systematic manner by personal visits and is subjected to intensive analysis.

Performance tests require the typist to type, the welder to weld, and the truck driver to drive. They are appropriately considered valid when well done. These tests can be extended to draftsmen, architects, engineers, and writers. The group oral-performance test is available when the occupation for which it is used involves conferences and negotiations.

In addition to the group oral-performance test and inquiries from among associates, the only general new development in the field of measurement of personal characteristics is an increase in the use of psychiatric examinations for police applicants. This is a desirable development because of the nature of the patrolmen's duties and the limitations on other methods for achieving the same objective. Research is under way on simpler methods to measure these characteristics by means of written tests, but the current state is still rudimentary.

Placement, transfer, and promotion. The placement process consists of assigning the employee to a job and a supervisor where he will be most productive. Still in its early stages, this process as yet is given adequate attention only in those organizations which recognize that summer employment and internship can also be used, by rotation among several supervisors and types of work, to determine the assignment that will best fit the individual. Proper placement can contribute significantly to a reduction of turnover and an increase in productivity. Smaller organizations are obviously limited in what they can do in this field. Larger organizations tend to neglect it because they do not obtain the data that would demonstrate the value of efforts in this direction.

---

[5] *Cf.* United States Civil Service Commission, *Employment Interviewing,* Personnel Methods Series No. 5, Washington: Government Printing Office, 1956.

The transfer process is related to placement, but is broader in objectives. In addition to achieving placement objectives, transfer is highly desirable as a means for an employee to gain broader experience and different perspectives in order to aid his self-development. In many organizations a request for transfer is considered lese majesty rather than a necessary part of a positive personnel program. Transfer is also needed to correct placement errors and to adjust the work force to shifting workloads.

The promotion process is potentially one of the most valuable elements of personnel administration. But it has become as encrusted with rigidities in many places in the public service as in certain private industries, like the railroads. Promotion is a means for developing a career service, attracting and retaining the able, and rewarding those who produce and are interested in self-development. As often actually administered, however, it rewards the mediocre who stay long in one place and can master a small field with some adequacy. This results from narrow channels for promotion, and undue weight for length of service and for closely delimited practical knowledge, procedural and substantive. It should be emphasized that this unsatisfactory condition is as much the result of limited horizons of management, the influence of the products of the system, and their unwillingness or inability to resist pressures from among their employees, as it may have to be laid to the inadequacies of personnel staffs.

Generally speaking, in many places in the public service and in industry, personnel procedures are selected and used with little awareness of the fruits of scientific research bearing on selection methods—as if engineers were to pick materials for a bridge without knowing metallurgy and mathematics. Although this situation is slowly being corrected in government, partly with the help of the Public Personnel Association,[6] there remains a defensiveness among practitioners which can block the efforts of all but the most determined personnel director.

Overseas personnel administration. Personnel activities in support of the federal government's overseas operations represent one of the most challenging tasks today.[7] Recruiting for overseas work makes special demands because additional factors in the applicant have to be considered. Those who cannot adjust to the overseas environment must be eliminated because of the effect of such maladjustment on performance and on the role of the United States. Many individuals who get by in their native environment display their defects in a strange situation. Off-the-job behavior becomes as important as work performance when this behavior directly affects the standing of the United States. Also, the employee over-

---

[6] See, for instance, Goode, Cecil E., *Personnel Research Frontiers*, Chicago: Public Personnel Association, 1958.

[7] See Cleveland, H., and Mangone. G. J., eds., *The Art of Overseasmanship*, Syracuse: Syracuse University Press, 1957.

seas must show flexibility—flexibility in solving new problems, in adjusting to the lack of familiar equipment or assistance, and in teaching others, rather than doing the work himself. Moreover, the work must often be done within sight of those looking for an opportunity to criticize the American contribution.

The main task of training is to accustom the American to living in a different culture. Federal agencies have had many difficulties in getting the applicants needed. Life in Laos and Cambodia attracts few persons during a time of full employment at home. Uncertainties about programs and needs in the military, information, and technical assistance agencies have been deterrents. Those first attracted sometimes included escapists fleeing from work and personal problems. Problems connected with children and health have cut further into the available number. So has the lack of popular support in the United States for some of these programs.

Responsibility for thousands of non-Americans employed overseas by the United States has meant the need for learning about foreign labor laws, wage systems, and methods for training and supervision. Work standards and behavior are often different. The wise administrator learns about these differences and criticizes them only in his own home, but pays attention to them on the job. With time the United States is developing a body of men and women with extensive knowledge on how to operate effectively overseas.

Evaluation of performance. The hope for improved methods of evaluating employee performance is a powerful siren which leads many entrants into personnel work astray. Although the results are not so disastrous as in the case of the ship's grounding on the rocks in responding to the siren's call, they do lead to much frustration. That better methods for the evaluation of performance are central to a successful personnel program can be theoretically demonstrated beyond question. Such methods are needed to inform the employee of how he is doing and to help him improve his work; to serve as a basis for pay raises and promotions; and to identify training needs. As in the case of many management techniques, however, the gap between objective and fulfillment is great. Research evidence based on a study by the United States Public Health Service indicates that evaluations lead to tension rather than to composure. Moreover, many evaluations are more indicative of the value systems of the appraiser than of the performance of the employee. Many superiors know that day-by-day supervision is much more effective in letting the employee know how he is making out and in helping him to do better than a formal, periodic appraisal. Indeed, by their appraisals they show that other factors, in addition to work performance, should be considered in advancement. It is also obvious that appraisals improve if they are prepared for specific purposes. Finally, as in the case of all personnel techniques used by management, better results can be obtained when supervisors themselves are motivated to better performance by their superiors and are given adequate training.[8]

2. Classification and Pay

Purpose of classification. Classification is a tool of public personnel administration which, though not yet perfected, is of basic importance to governmental management. The first classification plan in the public service which approached present-day standards was developed in the city of Chicago shortly before World War I. The federal government's classification program was adopted by Congress in 1923. A substantial number of city and state governments have made progress in this field since that time. It is now generally accepted practice for a local or state government that enacts a civil service law to begin immediately with the preparation of a classification plan.[9]

The purpose of classification is to group positions that have similar duties and qualifications so that they may be conveniently treated jointly for all management requirements—recruitment, compensation, budgeting, training, and organizational planning. Generally, positions are grouped both vertically and horizontally: vertically into grades or levels in accordance with their responsibilities, career relationships, and pay; and horizontally in accordance with the kind of specialized work performed. A group of positions justifying similar treatment is a "class," and is identified by title.

Development of classification system. The development and installation of a classification system begins with an inventory of the individual positions. Sufficient information must be obtained through job analysis to make it possible to identify the common characteristics of positions and to sort the positions into classes. Further probing results in class specifications, which define the duties and requirements of each class and usually attempt by explicit statement to distinguish the class from related ones. The classes are then related to each other in an occupational structure, grouping like series of classes into larger families having homogeneous characteristics, and generally arranging the classes into hierarchies of levels or grades, to reflect increased responsibility and compensation. Individual positions are then assigned to their appropriate classes.

Determinations about the number and kinds of classes to be established, and their relationships to each other, should be influenced by management goals. Answers to such questions as the following should serve as guides: How will the work be organized and assigned? Will assignments be narrow

---

[8] *Cf.* United States Civil Service Commission, *Selecting Supervisors,* Personnel Methods Series No. 2, Washington: Government Printing Office, 1956. See also Chapter 19, "The Art of Supervision."

[9] For this section the author gratefully acknowledges the contribution of J. Kenneth Mulligan, Executive Vice Chairman, Interagency Advisory Group, United States Civil Service Commission. *Cf.* in general *Position Classification in the Public Service,* Chicago: Civil Service Assembly, 1941.

and specialized, or broad and flexible? What career ladders or promotional patterns are needed and desired? What classes should relate to each other for pay purposes? What are to be the employment policies for entrance levels? What kinds of transfer channels need to be open? How many pay levels are useful? Answers to these questions will vary among occupations and organizational units in the same agency as well as among agencies. They are illustrative of the management considerations that should guide the development of the classification plan.

At the conclusion of its development, a complete classification system will have several indispensable parts. One will be the definition of classes, the class specifications. These are a necessity, not only to guide the process of allocating individual positions, but also to indicate generally the content and characteristics of each class. Another will be a structure of related classes, or schematic outline, grouping them for their consideration in the development of career patterns, examination programs, and pay systems. There will also be a definite method for the continuous assignment of new positions to classes, and a review of the allocation of existing positions. Another feature of any successful system is a deliberately planned program for the creation of understanding about it among its users—management and employees.

Keeping classification current. Effective planning and administration of a classification system is based on the recognition of the dynamics of job assignments, job relationships, and improving techniques. The failure to provide for modifications in a system to account for these constantly occurring changes results in a static and obsolete pattern. The pace of technological change in the modern world means that the content and relationships of many occupations change rapidly—the fields of clerical machine operations, computers, and engineering furnish ready examples. In addition to technological change, other influences shape the structure of occupational relationships. The changing knowledge and skill content of occupations, reflected in diminished or extended educational or training demands, have their effect. Prestige factors relating to the activities of occupational associations or to the social recognition of particular occupations contribute to fluctuation in relationships. Long-term changes in supply and demand in various occupations need to be recognized.

This requires not only a flexible and creative attitude, but also constant review of the system. There is a natural inertia and resistance to change among those operating a classification system, caused by their constant need to explain and defend the system as it is operating at any given time, and the upsetting impact of change on the users of the system. It is also true that changes beneficial to one group usually can be interpreted as adversely affecting another. But unless necessary revisions are made when needed, the system will fail to accomplish its purpose.

Another problem in keeping the system current relates to the assignment of individual positions to classes. New assignments, changes in tasks, and changing abilities of individuals have their effects on the characteristics of individual positions. Although in the administration of most systems great stress has been put on the need to consider the individual and the job as separate entities, there is growing recognition that the man in the job frequently is a more meaningful and realistic concept for classification purposes. The characteristics of many positions change with the characteristics of the employee performing the duties. Generally, individual classification decisions are made through periodic reviews of positions by position classifiers, using job analysis, individual position descriptions, and surveys. In the early stage of the development of classification—and it can be said that many jurisdictions are still at this stage—great attention has been given to this work. Techniques have become elaborate, expensive, and highly specialized. Trends now developing are toward simplification, and toward greater reliance on the participation of nonspecialists in classification determinations. A corollary is the use of simplified job analysis and simplified classification specifications. The tendency in some jurisdictions to use broader classes also contributes to simplicity.

Despite several decades of experience and widespread application, progress in the development of techniques in position classification has not been notable. The key techniques used—job analysis and job evaluation—have not been significantly improved in recent years. Factor analysis has segmented the job into its characteristics as they relate to qualifications required, working conditions, controls, and other elements. This technique is widely practiced. Complementing it, classification or evaluation methods are being designed to measure parts of the job to arrive at a summarized judgment. Here too, the needs are simplicity, validity, and economy of application.

Classification and the career service. The implications of a classification plan for a career service and for the total personnel program are often overlooked. A good classification plan can be compared with a tree with a strong trunk, a few main branches, and with other branches extending from the main branches higher up. This is a symbol of unity and organic connections.

In a classification plan, the number of classes consisting of groups of positions designed for original recruitment—the trunk and the main branches—should be kept to a minimum. They should also be related to the educational system so that, for example, entrance classes are linked with high-school graduation, college graduation, and graduate and professional-school levels. To provide a larger number of special classes above these entrance classes would not close these special classes to even the best students simply because of their lack of occupational experience; they would rise to them from the entrance classes. Nor would it throw a heavy burden on the examining process by unduly multiplying the number of open competitive examinations which would have to be administered. But each special class should respond to a clearly justifiable need of management.

Compensation and classification. An overburdened and sometimes troublesome cliché in personnel administration is the statement that the classification and compensation systems should be independent of each other. There is certainly value in the principle that the day-to-day assignment of positions to classes should be accomplished without regard to the money values of the separate classes.

But this principle has validity and can be realistically applied only when careful attention has been given to pay problems in the arrangement of the classification structure. As employment, placement, and organizational policies influence the classification structure, so do compensation goals. Systems for attending to these matters all have common management objectives; in their development and application, the obvious relationships should be stressed rather than minimized. The relationships of classes in the classification structure, from which pay relationships are derived in the operation of the compensation system, must be designed and constantly reviewed to assure that they are realistic and consistent with the needs of management.

Pay policy. The initial question that confronts the administrator or the legislative body in the development of a pay plan is one of purpose and goals. In private business, pay determinations relate to such pragmatic considerations as ability to pay, profit margins, supply and demand of workers, and collective bargaining, the latter being a major factor today. Although a form of collective bargaining exists in many public jurisdictions, such as in the Tennessee Valley Authority and in many cities and states, its effects are significantly limited because of the concept of the state as "sovereign employer." [10] Furthermore, the absence of a "right to strike," which is the final weapon in industrial bargaining, means that the bargaining process in the public service is different.

Therefore, although agreement or acceptance play a part in the process of setting public pay, other considerations are more influential. The principle most widely adopted today is that the public employer should pay a rate comparable to the prevailing rate paid by private employers for similar work in the community, or within the geographical boundaries served by the public agency. This policy enables the public agency to compete equally in the labor market for workers; it also has the acceptable rationale that the government's pay policy will neither depress salaries in the area nor raise them beyond economic levels. Still other factors enter the picture. Many governmental occupations are not found in private life; these must be "fairly" related to others by job evaluation methods, taking

---

[10] See Spero, Sterling D., *Government as Employer,* New York: Ronald, 1948. See also Chapter 21, "Morale and Discipline."

career considerations into account. The theory that government should be the "model" employer, setting the pace for the general economy in pay and working conditions, is rarely employed today. Those who advocate its use claim that government needs the best workers, and seeks them through its selection and examining processes. Practical considerations which restrict the application of this theory include budgetary limitations and the problem of pay relationships between the top career personnel and elected or other political top officials. Usually pay levels set for the latter are the effective ceilings for subordinate career executives.

Authority for making general pay adjustments for the public employee usually rests in the legislative body, directly related as this authority is to the need for control over taxes and appropriations. The legislature may confine itself to a general review as the appropriating body, to the establishment of broad limits for the total pay range, or to consideration of periodic recommendations of the executive branch. In some states, the central personnel agency now has the authority to revise pay schedules—notably in California, Michigan, Pennsylvania, Minnesota, and Oregon. In New York, the legislature sets a band of rates, but the executive branch may move classes within this band, unrestricted by statutory definitions of classes or levels. Greater freedom for the executive branch exists in dealing with trades and crafts workers than in setting rates for white-collar employees. In the federal service, for example, pay for a third of the employees—those in trades, crafts, and manual labor occupations—is set by the employing agencies in accordance with prevailing rates. This is in response to the need for greater flexibility, accented by the continuous inflationary trend in salaries and wages.

Pay plans. The need for data on which to base rates has stimulated the practice of wage or salary surveys by public agencies. Systematic and refined procedures for analyzing the labor market have been developed. Key occupations are selected for the survey, samples are chosen to represent the kinds of employers and conditions of work that are believed to be representative, and statistical devices are employed to analyze data and to develop wage or salary structures.

Beyond the general pay policy, many detailed considerations are involved in the development of a pay plan. What should be the scope of the total range of rates? How many usable and discernable pay levels are needed and appropriate? Should there be a range of rates for each occupation, as a means of recognizing merit, seniority, and longevity? May these ranges overlap? The range of rates is usually determined pragmatically: at the bottom, by consideration of minimum wage legislation or by the desire to pay enough to permit a minimum standard of living; and at the top, by reference to controls established by the legislature or by inference from rates established for elected or other political top officials. The number of levels needed will vary among occupational fields, as will the need for, and the size of, rate ranges for individual occupations or classes. Dead-end occupations, and fields of work where performance can continue to improve with additional education and experience, require greater rate ranges than others; such occupations may similarly require an overlapping of rate ranges. Traditionally, new hiring occurs at the bottom of each rate range; but flexibility is being introduced to permit entrance within the range, depending on labor market conditions or on the quality of applicants.

Growing importance attaches to fringe benefits of monetary value—the "hidden" pay reflected in subsidies to retirement, insurance, leave, and related programs. These matters cannot be ignored in the development of a pay program. Today the public agency must take into account the value and cost of these fringe benefits as they compare with similar pay plans of competitors for qualified manpower.

3. Training

Training and management. There is today general acceptance of the importance of training in the public service. The old concept that those appointed to positions in government should be fully accomplished at the time of entry, and therefore not in need of further training, is now obsolete. Training implies orientation to the new job, development of knowledge and skill needed for the present work, and growth for future responsibilities.[11] As a statement issued in 1955 at the direction of the President puts it: "Training and development of employees is an essential aid to efficient operation of the Federal service and to attainment of its program goals. It is therefore the policy of the executive branch to plan and provide for training and development as an integral part of its responsibilities for the effective conduct of its affairs." This policy was confirmed by legislation enacted in 1958, which authorized generally the use of nongovernmental facilities, such as universities, as well as other arrangements for training federal employees.

The concept of training as an essential part of administration is gaining acceptance also in state and local governments. Instead of being an incidental activity, training has become an important aspect of public administration. Government agencies are giving more attention to developing the

---

[11] For this section the author is indebted to L. David Korb, Bureau of Programs and Standards, United States Civil Service Commission. For further reading, see Korb, L. David, *Training the Supervisor*, Washington: Government Printing Office, 1956; and Planty, Earl G., McCord, William S., and Efferson, Charles A., *Training Employees and Managers*, New York: Ronald, 1948. See also Chapter 2, "The Study of Public Administration," sec. 3, "Training for Public Administration."

Much useful information on careers for college and university graduates is presented in Sweeney, Stephen B., ed., *Education for Administrative Careers in Government*, Philadelphia: University of Pennsylvania Press, 1958; Westcott, Jay B., *Government Careers: Opportunities for College Graduates*, Syracuse: Syracuse University Press, 1957; United States Civil Service Commission, *Federal Careers: A Directory for College Students*, Washington: Government Printing Office, 1956.

present and potential skills of employees; they are using training specialists to plan and coordinate courses of instruction; and they are conducting a wide variety of training programs.

Training defined. Most training, and probably the most effective part, is informal: the day-to-day guidance and instruction given to employees, generally by supervisors.[12] This is the way most people learn their jobs. However, the success of this type of training is somewhat a matter of chance. A supervisor may know his job, but be unable to teach, to communicate what he knows to a subordinate; or a supervisor may be able to teach, but be limited in what he himself knows or be too busy. If an organization were to depend on informal training only, it could hardly expect to increase the skill and knowledge of its employees above the level of its supervisors.

Accordingly, if an organization is to reach greater effectiveness, it must supplement informal training with planned programs of employee development. From this point of view, we can define training as the conscious effort on the part of management to give assistance and direction to the employees in learning their jobs and in their occupational development. To meet the need for the most efficient utilization of employees, agencies must seek out competent individuals on their rolls and on an organized basis promote their development.

Training in public administration. Government employment covers nearly the full range of occupational skills and professional disciplines of our civilization. Most public jobs require some previous education or experience. For many positions, the education needed is generally the same as that for private employment: for example, engineering, accounting, law, economics, and medicine. The same is true for positions such as typist, clerk, automobile mechanic, and machinist. The administration of public activities represents partly a unique body of knowledge.

There is a great need for men and women who have the knowledge and ability to help with the management of public agencies. This need is met in part by executive development programs in government, and in part by special curricula in the social sciences as well as specifically in public administration offered by many universities, especially for those interested in government employment. The intent of this training is to provide the participants with a broad background useful in public administration, together with the analytical skills of an intellectual discipline, but not to prepare them as technical specialists.

An important part of training are the intern programs in government. These programs serve to identify and develop young people having management potential. A first large step in internship training in public administration was taken in 1934, when the privately supported National

---

[12] See Chapter 19, "The Art of Supervision."

Institute of Public Affairs undertook to bring to Washington on fellowships outstanding young college graduates. These were given a program of training that included orientation to governmental agencies, rotating work assignments in them, group training sessions, and advanced academic instruction. The program was successful; many of the graduates advanced rapidly into positions of responsibility in the federal government. The idea was next taken up by the United States Civil Service Commission and many federal and state agencies. Both the Commission and federal departments such as Agriculture, Commerce, Defense, Interior, and Labor now conduct intern programs. The State of New York fosters internship by paying one half of the tuition of interns who undertake advanced academic training. The colleges and universities, on their part, also cooperate. Harvard University, for example, offers Littauer fellowships in administration to outstanding government employees.

The proliferation of executive development programs, for government and industry, has been the most dramatic development in training. One of its causes is a reaction to the previous emphasis on technical and clerical training. Others are the increasing specialization, with the consequent difficulty of obtaining executives by natural progress, and—perhaps most important—the increase in the number of executives needed as administrative activities grow in size and complexity.

Principles and concepts. Increasing emphasis has been placed in recent years on careful planning and evaluation of training programs. There is less willingness today to accept either the idea that training is not needed, or its reverse, that training is good for its own sake. From this more critical appraisal of training activities a number of principles have emerged that serve to guide training in the public service. They are based on the experience of public and private organizations and on the results of research by social scientists in supervision, employee productivity, and organizational effectiveness.

The first principle is that the organization must know what it is training for—the objectives must be known. Unless a training program has been planned in terms of specific goals, it is not possible to organize instruction or to measure the extent of accomplishment. Next, the training needs of the employees have to be known. Training must be based on needs grounded in the work situation. The Navy Department, for example, found a need for more scientists trained in certain aspects of nuclear technology. It then set up special courses in radio-isotope techniques and reactor design to meet this need. Based on a similar lack of employees with certain specialized skills, the Geological Survey conducted a course in geological field mapping. The Rural Electrification Administration arranged a six-month course in telephone engineering. New York State conducted an intensive training program for bank examiners.

Once an organization has decided to set up a training program to meet certain needs, it proceeds to construct a course of instruction to meet these needs and, equally important, determines the training methods that will be most effective. The information to be taught or the skills to be developed have to be presented in an orderly sequence of instruction units. Instructional material must be developed according to established educational methods and according to the learning ability, knowledge, and interest of the employees to be trained. Moreover, training in the public service must be economical and job-related; and it must also prepare employees for advancement. The career development of employees meets future governmental needs for technical and management personnel. Programs in which the trainees are only passive beneficiaries do not produce the kind of resourceful employees and leaders that a public agency must have. Needless to say, training requires management support. It is interesting to note that organizations with important missions tend to be the most active in the support of training; examples are the Department of Agriculture, the Tennessee Valley Authority, the Atomic Energy Commission, and the Department of Defense. Another illustration is the training program for executives sponsored by the Michigan State Civil Service Commission in cooperation with the International City Managers Association. In many of these cases, the training is taken on the employee's own time and often at his expense—the agency stimulates the university to provide the training and encourages employees to attend. The agency often provides space for the program.

Lastly, there should be a continuing effort to improve training programs. This means a systematic effort to evaluate the effectiveness of training, both in terms of the quality and efficiency of the training itself and in terms of the ultimate criterion—improved employee effectiveness on the job. On this point, however, very little has been done, either in industry or in government. Most attempts at evaluation have been rather superficial, consisting mainly of statements by the participants that they enjoyed the training or of a test given at the completion of the course of instruction.

Types of training. Public jurisdictions engage in a wide variety of training activities. Orientation is the instruction given to a new employee to acquaint him with his organization and his job. Many federal and local agencies give him a handbook, which describes the agency's activities and its personnel policies. Some of the larger agencies periodically hold orientation courses for new employees. At these sessions, agency officials give brief talks on policies, history, and organization of the agency. The real job of orientation is usually done by the supervisor, who instructs and guides the new employee day by day. Again, a large number of agencies provide training to appropriate employees in correspondence procedures, letter and report writing, bookkeeping, machine operation, English usage, accounting, purchasing, telephone courtesy, and work simplification. But of all the training activities at the state and local levels, the most carefully organized is that given to policemen and firemen. Recently emphasis has also been given to training in advanced techniques and the development of administrative skills in these fields. Cities such as Peoria, Illinois, and Wichita, Kansas, for example, have conducted advanced training courses in police and fire administration. Many officials take part in special programs given by state universities, such as that of the Fire Extension Service of the University of Maryland.

One of the oldest forms of training is apprenticeship in the skilled trades. The Navy Department, for instance, has apprenticeship programs in some 60 trades, such as modelmaker, machinist, electrician, and carpenter. Training extends generally over a four-year period, with the apprentice spending one week each month in classroom work and the other three weeks in the shops, under the supervision of a journeyman mechanic. Although there has been a moderate decline in apprenticeship training in the public service, technical training has been on the increase. This type of training covers a wide range of fields, including accounting, hospital work, chemical laboratory work, highway construction, regulatory activities, and personnel administration. Much of this training has been provided in cooperation with schools, institutes, and universities. Considerable impetus at the local level has come through the George-Deen Act of 1936, under which federal funds are made available for the training of state and local employees. Many agencies also conduct supervisory training. The course of the Department of the Air Force consists of 25 conferences on the responsibilities of the supervisor, work improvement, employee training, and human relations. More advanced management development courses are often conducted in cooperation with universities. In administering such training programs, public jurisdictions have displayed considerable resourcefulness in the use of training methods and media. The conference method and also such techniques as role playing and case studies have been extensively employed in management development programs. There has also been much use of professional associations. Government employees have participated in institutes given by the American Society for Public Administration and the American Management Association; they attend national and international conferences; and they take part in group visits to other agencies and to industrial establishments.

Current trends. Several trends are evident in employee training in the public service. Increasing use is being made of professionally qualified training staffs to plan and administer training programs. Greater emphasis is being placed on programs built on specific training needs of employees. More stress is being put on long-range planning—on viewing the work of employees not only in terms of their present jobs, but in terms of a career system with organized ladders of advancement. Some effort is being made to tie together the various training activities of an organization into a unified approach, aimed at closer coordination of employee development with the mission of the organization.

Again, more attention is being given to evaluation of the effectiveness of training activities. There is closer cooperation with universities and professional organizations. More use is made of external facilities, and employing agencies are bearing a larger part of the cost of the advanced technical and professional training of their employees. Additional attention is being given to the training responsibilities of the supervisor, to guidance and counseling, and to planned learning on the job. Finally, there is an increasing awareness that attention to training, formal and informal, is a symbol of an organization's desire to keep up-to-date and a recognition of its responsibility for the utilization of employee capacities.

4. Employee Relations

Appeals and grievance systems. Employee relations are a subject of several dimensions.[13] To begin with one aspect, common to most civil service jurisdictions is a network of appeals and reviews, as built-in safety factors. Where the central personnel agency exercises directly day-to-day personnel functions, appeals are directed to that body. As the complexity of government and the number and size of administrative agencies have increased, a delegation of functions to these agencies has occurred. Hence they are usually responsible for considering the initial appeal, with the central personnel agency often exercising a review function.

In contrast to appeal systems established by legislative or executive authority, grievance systems are customarily set up by the agency head. Appeals usually relate to acts of omission or commission that have a personal adverse effect, such as downward classification, a finding of ineligibility on an examination, or a removal. Grievances usually relate to the complex of policies and practices of the employing agency known as "conditions of work." The latter encompass such disparate things as physical discomforts at work sites; lack of provision for certain services; dissatisfaction with supervisory application of agency policies on hours of work and assignments, with access to parking areas, or with cafeteria location or coffee breaks; charges of discrimination or favoritism in selection for training, desirable transfers, assignment to specific equipment and location of work place; disagreement with supervisor's leave practices on contested sick leave, lateness, or unauthorized absences; and severity of disciplinary action for alleged infractions of administrative requirements, misconduct, or other deficiencies.

---

[13] For this section the author is in debt to Jack Pockrass, Chief, Placement and Employee Relations, Directorate of Civilian Personnel, Department of the Air Force. *Cf.* in general Spero, *op. cit.* above in note 8. See also Chapter 21, "Morale and Discipline." For systematic treatments of civil service law, see Kaplan, H. Eliot, *The Law of Civil Service,* New York: Bender & Co., 1958; Field, Oliver P., *Civil Service Law,* Minneapolis: University of Minnesota Press, 1939.

Systematic resolution of individual or group grievances has developed as a self-serving activity of management. Gripes or grievances that rankle within individuals naturally create adverse attitudes toward supervisors, fellow employees, agency policy, or the work materials, equipment, and and processes. Such resentment of wrongs or inequities, whether real or fancied, can lead to disruption of work, lowered group morale, absenteeism, turnover, spoilage, accidents, slow-downs, or even more violent reactions. Many labor disputes have been brought on by apparently trivial matters that were ignored or suppressed. It is to management's benefit from the viewpoint of production and services that there be a fair procedure for "ventilating" and adjusting grievances. It is fairly uniform practice to have such differences first resolved informally between employee and supervisor, but with the employee being able to invoke the assistance of a personal representative, a shop steward, or an intermediary from the personnel office. Formal grievance systems come into play when there is no acceptable resolution at the person-to-person level. Management has found that providing for an equitable grievance system has additional benefits in helping to reduce pressures from external groups whose intercession is sought by employees, and to minimize the chance of litigation.

Employee interests and legal safeguards. The availability of grievance and appeal procedure is an essential in employee-management relationships. Yet such procedures have limited value unless there are safeguards against peremptory removals, with knowledge of the reasons so that there will be opportunity to defend oneself against charges. Because the federal service accounts for more than two million employees, it is perhaps useful to trace the significant developments relating to removal from that service. "Removal for cause" should be distinguished from "separation," the broad catch-all for departures for other reasons, such as disqualification, resignation, termination of appointment, reduction in force, and retirement. The Lloyd-La Follette Act provided that "No person in the classified civil service of the United States shall be removed or suspended without pay therefrom except for such cause as will promote the efficiency of such service and for reasons given in writing." It was not until enactment of the Veterans Preference Act of 1944 that additional protection was granted to veterans by the stipulation that such employees "shall have at least thirty days' advance written notice . . . stating any and all reasons, specifically and in detail." This legislation incorporated considerable procedural detail, and the Civil Service Commission, in acting on appeals under the act, had to adjudicate both compliance with procedural requirements and the substantive merits of the case.

The Korean conflict gave rise to statutory provisions designed to protect the security of the United States, especially by permitting summary suspension of government employees. The provision for summary suspension did retain the requirement of a written statement of charges, but subject to the potent limitation: " ... to the extent that ... the interests of national security permit ... stated as specifically as security considerations permit." Administrative appeal was not cut off, nor back pay if the employee was restored or reinstated; the law provided, however, that determination by the agency head concerned " ... shall be conclusive and final." This new authority was granted only to those agencies directly concerned with the emergency effort, to be exercised independently by each. Executive Order No. 9835 of March 21, 1947, established governmentwide standards for investigation and consideration of derogatory information about an individual federal employee's loyalty to the United States. This executive order was replaced by Executive Order No. 10450 on April 27, 1953. Its main criterion required the head of each agency to determine positively "whether retention of such person is clearly consistent with the interests of the national security."[14]

The administrative handling of loyalty and security cases has given rise to serious questions, but momentarily the most unfortunate outcome was the creation of an impression in the public's mind that a large number of federal employees might be disloyal. Actually, the number of those whose records disclosed them to be subversive or Communist was very small. After much of the excitement had died down, the Supreme Court, in Cole v. Young,[15] held that removal procedures under Executive Order No. 10450 are applicable only when the position occupied has been identified by the agency as being "sensitive." But there can be little doubt that the adverse publicity given to the loyalty and security cases created considerable insecurity among government employees. Even though the employee body was found to be more than $99\frac{44}{100}$ per cent pure as sound employment investments, the methods of handling the sniffing and sifting left much to be desired from the point of view of constructive employee-management relations.

Employee organizations. Although historically employee groups have tended to organize around grievances, the more knowledgeable, mature unions came to recognize the limited advantages of this approach. True, by union representation assistance is furnished to individual members in resolving their grievances. But employee unions that hope to influence management practices and to obtain substantial employee benefits deploy their resources most effectively by seeking beneficial legislation, by supporting litigation for reversal of unwanted governmental policies, or by negotiation with agency heads to secure policy concessions having agency-wide application. Gains along these lines attract membership, as con-

---

[14] See for references Tompkins, Dorothy C., *Loyalty-Security Programs for Federal Employees: A Selected Bibliography,* Berkeley: Bureau of Public Administration, University of California, 1955. For a comprehensive treatment, see Brown, Ralph S., Jr., *Loyalty and Security: Employment Tests in the United States,* New Haven: Yale University Press, 1958.

[15] 351 U.S. 536 (1955).

trasted with isolated grievances which win attention if the case is won but can also serve to alienate management as well as potential membership, depending on issues and tactics. A disciplined union can make continuing gains for its membership and the entire employee group by friendly working relationships with management. The effectiveness of a vocal, well-organized employee group in legislation is amply illustrated by the postal employee unions. They represent only a minority of federal employees, but pay legislation for the postal service frequently precedes similar and sometimes less generous legislation for the remaining classified employees. This is a clear object lesson to all employees. Even where national employee unions have not succeeded in obtaining passage of beneficial legislation, its introduction alone has sometimes accelerated certain administrative reforms. The legislative approach actually has the effect of bargaining tactics.

It is difficult to generalize on labor-management relations throughout the public service.[16] Each jurisdiction is a situation unto itself, with conditions ranging from completely negative attitudes by all levels of management to cooperative working relationships, with collective bargaining practices under law. The municipal civil service system in Philadelphia has entered into a collective bargaining agreement which recognizes one union as the sole bargaining authority for a sizable segment of the work force. At the same time, professional, supervisory, investigative, and uniformed personnel are not permitted to unionize. The practices of "check-off" and collection of contributions to a union health plan—common in industry but infrequent in the public service—are authorized in this agreement, as part of the "no-strike" pledge. New York City has also entered into labor agreements with the occupational and trade unions in the municipal service. In the federal government, one of the world's largest employers, policies differ by agencies. The more progressive practices are found in such organizations as the Tennessee Valley Authority, the Bonneville Power Administration, and the Government Printing Office, which utilizes independent wage-setting agreements for its organized employees. Federal agencies vary from the most conservative minimum compliance with appeals requirements to industrylike practices of negotiation and arbitration.

Federal employees live under specific statutory prohibition of the strike. The law is turned against the employment or retention in employment of any person "who participates in any strike or asserts the right to strike against the Government of the United States . . ." singly or by being a member of an organization that asserts such right. One should add, however, that there are widespread misconceptions about the "right to strike"

16 For relevant factors in private enterprise, see Blum, Milton L., *Industrial Psychology and Its Social Foundation*, New York: Harper, 1956; Finlay, William W., Sartain, A. Q., and Tate, W. H., *Human Behavior in Industry*, New York: McGraw-Hill, 1954; Tiffin, J., *Industrial Psychology*, 3rd ed., New York: Prentice-Hall, 1952; Haire, Mason, *Psychology in Management*, New York: McGraw-Hill, 1956.

in many civil service systems. The hundreds of strikes that have occurred in jurisdictions of all sizes belie any concept that "it can't be done." Strikes have happened in transportation, public utilities, and sanitation systems as well as in school, police, and fire departments. The challenge here is to establish adequate machinery for the resolution of problems so that a strike would have no point. In a letter to the National Federation of Federal Employees, President Franklin D. Roosevelt wrote in 1937:

> The desire of Government employees for fair and adequate pay, reasonable hours of work, safe and suitable working conditions, development of opportunities for advancement, facilities for fair and impartial consideration and review of grievances, and other objectives of a proper employee relations policy is basically no different from that of employees in private industry. Organization on their part to present their views on such matters is both natural and logical, but meticulous attention should be paid to the special relationships and obligations of public servants to the public itself and to the Government.

In still more positive forms, the President's Special Assistant for Personnel Management in 1958 drew the attention of the heads of the federal agencies to the importance of equitable management-employee relations in the government service.[17]

---

[17] For the text of this statement, see Chapter 21, "Morale and Discipline," sec. 2, "Building Group Morale."

Chapter 25 •

Fiscal Accountability

1. Fuel for the Engines of Administration

Administrative responsibility and fiscal accountability. As general terms, responsibility and accountability may seem to have almost identical meanings. In the realm of administration, both terms imply a relationship of subordination to the intentions of a higher principal. Thus we speak interchangeably of the municipal director of public welfare as being responsible to the city manager, and of the head of the state police as being accountable to the governor. However, under the political principle of "government of laws," the relationship of subordination to the intentions of a higher principal is institutional rather than personal; circumscribed by legal norms rather than by habits of dependence; sustained by free acceptance of its implications rather than by the claims of superior authority. Effective answerability is therefore less a response to specific demands made at will by a higher principal than it is the product of awareness of a common purpose. Responsibility is likely to suffer when its formalized elements—its "sanctions"—fail to bear closely on generally endorsed ends.

This becomes especially evident when we consider the evolution of those mechanisms by which government officials are made to answer for the use of public funds placed at their disposal for the accomplishment of defined objectives—accountability in its more immediate sense. The need for such accountability springs from the heart of popular government.[1] Legislative control of public administration would be only intermittent and intolerably clumsy as well if it were confined to the lawmaking function proper. For it is clear that sole reliance on the lawmaking function would reduce the writing of marching orders for the executive branch to statutory grants of authority or their repeal. Allocation of the fuel supply for the engines of administration on a year-by-year basis allows for much greater efficacy and flexibility of legislative determination. This method of control, combined with adequate examination of the actual use of the funds voted, is focused on the questions of the desirable—and possible—*volume* of services *within*

---

[1] *Cf.* also Chapter 15, "Legislative Control."

the framework of an agency's statutory mandate, and of priorities among alternatives.

The maxim of fiscal accountability on the part of public officials has never been seriously challenged. Indeed, it could not be challenged without a simultaneous onslaught on government itself. To develop the most appropriate *forms* of fiscal accountability has proved to be an entirely different matter. Here we have been faced with a dual dilemma. In the first place, both the legislative and the executive branches have found it difficult to keep at a safe distance from the Scylla of controls so unrefined as to be practically worthless and the Charybdis of devices so detailed as to be destructive of broader perspective. And secondly, we have not yet achieved the necessary synthesis between suitably precise requirements and unhampered pursuit of constructive administrative goals. Ironically, though not surprisingly, the highest sense of administrative responsibility has collided all too often with formal stipulations of fiscal accountability. Conversely, the more distrustful and exacting these stipulations have been, the less have they attained their aim.

Despite procedural rigidities of fiscal accountability, it is plain that of all the great powers of government the most elastic and the most generally congenial is the spending power. It is adaptable to the widest variety of objectives—to wage war, to buy peace, to regulate the acreage of agricultural crops, to build highways, to stabilize the price of peanut butter. It is susceptible of countless techniques of application—by adding to the public payroll, by contracts for the services of private enterprise, by grants-in-aid to states and cities, by outright gifts, by conditional loans. It is supported by the taxing and borrowing powers of the nation. It is subject to no constitutional restraints of consequence. And if there are economic limits on its exercise, they have not yet been measured. The disbursement of government funds is one of the great political harmonizers of divergent interests.

Multitude of voices. Although the American Constitution is explicit that "no money shall be drawn from the Treasury, but in consequence of appropriations made by law," [2] the practice of conflict, compromise, and cooperation under the separation of powers divides authority and influence over the disposition of funds among many hands. Congress receives financial requests from the President. It obtains assistance on ideas and factual information from the various federal agencies. And it has the benefit of the governmentwide vantage point of the Budget Bureau on the expenditure structure and of the Treasury Department's revenue forecasts. Yet it is free to disregard all such advice in any particular case.

Moreover, the legislature is importuned by lobbies, and must choose what answer to give to their demands. Its own members exhibit a spectroscopic array of opinions. Congressional rules of procedure afford few

---

[2] Art. I, sec. 9.

automatically effective self-disciplinary checks against divisive tendencies in fiscal policy. Last but not least, the scheme of congressional organization emphasizes the pluralism of power. Separate committees in the House and Senate are charged with jurisdiction over taxation and appropriations in the executive branch. Many other legislative committees concerned with particular subject-matter areas contend for a voice in financial decisions affecting their clienteles.

Within the administrative structure there is also diversity of purpose. A bureau chief may have plans for bettering his program by the enlargement of field-service facilities. A field-office manager may come forth with different proposals for implementing the program in his area. The department head, sympathetic but harassed with alternatives of action, may fail to grasp the implications. A bureau with related responsibilities in another department may keep its jealous eyes on the administrative rival to its own position. The Budget Bureau weighs all such proposals with a detached view of operations and under the institutional necessity of trimming most requests for money.

Pressures and restraints. Purposes and pressures are dynamic. Congress does not exhaust its power in a single exercise, although its action tends to culminate in the passage of legislation. Administrative agencies, on the other hand, are involved both before and after legislative action. In continuing cycles they prepare and urge their financial requests for the next fiscal year while the funds appropriated for the current fiscal year are being spent and the expenditures of the previous one are being reviewed and analyzed. Historically, objectives and methods of the spending process have not remained the same. Since the passage of the Budget and Accounting Act of 1921, the mechanisms for formulating and implementing an integrated financial program for the executive branch have been steadily elaborated.

The emerging machinery still leaves something to be desired. The elements of the system are only partially utilized by the direct participants in the fiscal process—legislative and administrative, staff and line. Congressional particularism is often hostile to a general approach that puts consistency and the broader public interest ahead of free barter over special interests.[3] On the administrative side, bureaus and departments have their traditions of autonomy as well as their own program interests, and cultivate their separate ties with legislative groups.

Line establishments do not readily defer to the restraints of coordinating bodies. Staff agencies, on the other hand, sometimes need to be reminded of the essential conditions of successful staff work. Yet, in spite of surviving shortcomings, the gains of recent years in the techniques of fiscal coordination are impressive, when contrasted with the splintering of re-

---

[3] See Chapter 15, "Legislative Control," sec. 1, "Means and Conditions of Control."

sponsibility that characterized nineteenth-century financial administration.

Pattern of legislative money grants. Annually Congress passes half a dozen or more general appropriation acts, each supplying funds for the coming fiscal year to a number of federal agencies. Ordinarily these acts are voted during the closing quarter of the fiscal year, which expires on June 30. In addition, several supplemental or deficiency bills are passed at irregular intervals throughout the year, disposing of the financial requests arising from needs not anticipated when the regular appropriation requests were formulated. Appropriations lay down the purposes to be served in all degrees of specificity. The degree of specificity may be larger for a small appropriation than for a big one.

Appropriations are authorizations to spend money. They are also statutory limitations. The appropriation acts must be passed in some form each year and are not likely to be vetoed. They are therefore very handy vehicles for the attachment of legal clauses, or "riders." Some riders grant new authority to relieve past inconveniences. Most of them embody additional restrictions, expressive of current legislative sentiment. Like barnacles once attached, such riders tend to become in effect permanent parts of the vessel, usually being carried forward from fiscal year to fiscal year. Each government agency has also its organic legislation, authorizing its existence and defining its powers. These laws establish limitations on the purposes and methods of expenditures. Another group of statutes lays down or authorizes uniform regulations of administrative practice covering all agencies unless specifically exempted—the salary limits of the classification act; governmentwide pay-raise legislation; the retirement acts; the standardized travel regulations; the requirements of publicity and competitive bidding on government contracts in order to eliminate discrimination and favoritism. A further set of legislative restrictions is meant to protect congressional prerogatives against executive encroachment. Finally, the Walsh-Healey Act, forbidding the letting of government contracts to firms that do not meet specified labor standards, is typical of a category of laws which limit administrative discretion in the interest of promoting an ulterior economic policy.

From another point of view, the character and impact of these restrictions vary considerably with the nature of the individual agency and the immediate objects of its expenditures. The overhead of salaries, office space, supplies, and travel is common to all agencies in some degree and makes up nearly the whole budget of regulatory agencies. Fiscal procedures and limitations governing these matters are widely standardized and minutely worked out. Different sets of safeguards are appropriate for payments of interest on the public debt; for loans to be made to business firms; for soil-conservation contracts with farmers; for veterans' benefits and pensions; for the construction of public works directly or on contract; for purchases of land; and for the procurement of industrial materials and manufactured goods. Superimposed on this class of limitations are variations in statutory restrictions based on the character of the agency—civilian or military, temporary or permanent—and on the degree of legislative confidence in its leadership as well as on the secrecy or emergency nature of its work.

The administrative spenders of public funds must proceed in the context of all these legislative directives. It is not necessary here to attempt a comprehensive appraisal of the immense and detailed content of this body of law. Suffice it to say that the whole edifice of fiscal law is an outgrowth of the constitutional separation of powers, and administrative agencies are accountable for giving the law full effect.

Forms of accountability. It is time now to raise more specifically the question of who is accountable to whom and for what. In formulating an answer, the four focal points of financial control should be borne in mind. These are: (1) the operating bureau or unit which actually spends the money; (2) the larger agency of which the unit is a part; (3) the central offices through which executive control is exercised and over-all staff or auxiliary services are rendered—the Budget Bureau and the Treasury; and (4) the congressional committees dealing with revenue and expenditure.

The major mechanisms of control must be separately recognized also. In broad outline these involve: (1) the justification of estimates; (2) the superintendence of the use of appropriated funds; (3) the devices for timing the rate of expenditures; and (4) the audit and settlement of accounts. Finally, we must take into consideration the sequence of successive steps in the processes of appropriation and expenditure, which ordinarily spread over a period of two to three years—from the first administrative forethought to the last spending act. It is convenient to treat these factors by following the various stages in the life history of appropriations and expenditures as they occur in order to bring out the relevance of each factor.

In doing so, the landmark quality of the Budget and Accounting Act of 1921 emerges most visibly. In a very real sense, the act represented the fruition of years of enlightened agitation and thought. It charted a new course in the progress of financial administration. Looking back in some respects to the original conception of Alexander Hamilton, it reversed the drift of events during an intervening century to the fundamental emphasis on the unifying and consciously planning potentialities of fiscal processes, centered in the constitutional responsibility of the chief executive. The act created one entirely new agency—the Budget Bureau, as a staff arm of the President—and reorganized an existing group of auditing and accounting offices into another new establishment, the General Accounting Office under a Comptroller General.

The subsequent development of these two agencies has had a profound influence on the further evolution of federal financial management. Let us begin with the phase of justification of agency estimates of expenditures. The full cycle begins with the operating units in the several departments and establishments and returns to them in the end.

2. Justification

Call for estimates. Each year, usually in June, the budget director issues a call to all federal agencies for their budget estimates covering the fiscal year to commence thirteen months thereafter—July 1. The call for estimates is in effect one method of achieving accountability. It places responsibility on the operating agencies for planning, formulating, and reviewing the work they see lying ahead of them, and for presenting justifications for funds to carry it on. The justifications must prove persuasive enough to induce the President to request, and Congress to approve, appropriations that will enable the projected activities to go forward. But to do their part, the agencies must know the general frame of reference within which to cast their budgetary planning. That frame of reference is provided in the President's budget policy, based on fiscal preferences of the administration in power, on economic assumptions with respect to such matters as purchasing power and price levels, on strategic planning concepts of national defense, and on other public needs. Crystallization of the President's budget policy takes place as early as in the spring, when, after discussion of the budgetary outlook in the cabinet, the President gives each of the larger agencies a planning figure as its budgetary ceiling. This relieves the President of undue pressure when in the fall the appropriation requests of the agencies come into the Budget Bureau for review.

The call for estimates is itself a substantial document.[4] It requires all agencies to submit to the Budget Bureau their estimates—the so-called language sheets, which set out the text of what the agency would like Congress to enact. It calls also for schedules of obligations—the so-called green sheets—showing the breakdown of expenditure, by main activities under each appropriation in relation to the program to be accomplished as well as in such terms as personnel, travel, printing, and the like. It asks, finally, for justifications of the estimates. These consist of descriptions of the agency's work program, together with supporting data indicating its financial needs. In order to assist the operating establishments in presenting their case with care, the call for estimates is accompanied by a series of instructions. The usual deadline for the submission of the materials requested is September 30. Only in exceptional circumstances can this deadline be extended without jeopardizing actions at a later stage which have a fixed calendar.

---

[4] *Cf.* Morstein Marx, Fritz, "The Bureau of the Budget: Its Evolution and Present Role," *American Political Science Review*, 1945, Vol. 39, p. 653 *ff.*, 869 *ff.*

The call for estimates is properly concerned with the application of objective criteria in the framing of justifications submitted by the agencies. Such objective criteria are especially important as a foundation for workload forecasts and operating standards of general validity. Usually, therefore, the call for estimates contains specific pointers about how to translate operating standards into workloads and costs. Increasingly, whenever relevant, estimates of requestetd appropriations are presented as so-called cost-type budgets.

Departmental consideration. Receipt of the call for estimates passes the ball to the departmental budget officer, whom each agency is required by the Budget and Accounting Act to designate as the center of its internal financial controls. The development of budget offices has proceeded unevenly among the federal agencies. The departmental budget officer in some cases is little more than a glorified bookkeeper attached to the office of the agency head. In other cases, the budget officer has become an important participant in the management and planning of the department. For this role he is equipped with his own staff to keep abreast of the work of his agency.

Many variations from agency to agency prevail in the internal procedures for assembling and reviewing the preliminary estimates secured from each of the operating units within the department. Then also, some anticipated operations lend themselves readily to objective measurement, while others must rest on little more than informed forecasts and realistic guesses by those who have been closest to the particular program during the preceding fiscal year. Comparative materials may also be drawn in, as in the case of field offices performing substantially similar functions. Patently, it is not enough for the budget officer to add up the sum of the operating requests thus assembled and report the total. Both before he relays the call for estimates to the bureaus and divisions and upon scrutinizing their requests, consultation with directing and planning officials at the top of his agency is needed. The several programs of the department must be correlated. Conflicts over activity priorities among departmental subdivisions must be resolved. Scales of values must be established for choosing among a multitude of competing alternatives. The terms of the justifications must be reviewed as well as the figures they accompany. Inconsistencies and ambiguities not only jeopardize favorable action at higher levels but also point up weaknesses in the agency's own managerial arrangements. The function of the budget officer here is that of probing and questioning—and drawing attention to issues that require remedial action on the operating or policy-making levels. Except within the limits of clearly expressed agency policy, he cannot safely attempt a resolution of the questions he raises without first assuring himself of the views and attitudes of the agency head or his deputies.

The measure of influence which this kind of departmental review year upon year exerts is a test of the strength and caliber of each agency's general management. In American administration, the tradition of bureau or divisional autonomy is strong. It may be fortified by outside links—personal relationships between the bureau chief and strategically placed members of Congress or a tightly organized special-interest clientele. Such relationships may render a particular bureau's estimates well-nigh untouchable. The first head of the National Park Service in the Interior Department—himself a commanding figure—kept that bureau in such a position. Occasionally the well-dramatized personality of a bureau chief, particularly one connected with an activity of such general public interest as crime detection, may have the same effect. The budget officer single-handedly cannot try to change the institutional "facts of life." Lack of interest and backing on the part of his agency head may stall him. Nevertheless, the trend of recent years has been to professionalize and invigorate the budget process. Pressure from the Budget Bureau has helped. Moreover, ordinarily too much is at stake for the future of the agency to allow the budgetary aspect to be slighted. When departmental review of estimates is undertaken intelligently, it affords one of the best occasions in the entire range of administrative management for program planning and reappraisal. This would be inconceivable without participation of the agency head. On him falls the main burden of public responsibility for the success of his department's program. Departmental consideration of the proposed program for the next fiscal year also supplies opportunity for experimentation with different methods of budgetary presentation.

Review of estimates within the agency may occur more than once. At a later stage, it is not infrequently necessary to repeat appraisal and reappraisal with a still sharper focus. The agency's estimates may even be returned by the Budget Bureau for reconsideration and reduction, perhaps to a specified lower figure if the ceiling has been exceeded without compelling reason or if there is a change in the President's budget policy, perhaps on urgent grounds of economic need. Then the agency will have to recommend the manner in which the reduction is to be absorbed.

Formulation of the executive budget. Up to this point, the process of justification has served to secure accountability for orderly planning and correlation of the various programs that each agency proposes to carry forward. Within the Budget Bureau, on the basis of policy guidance and technical instruction from its Office of Budget Review, all departmental estimates are examined in the five divisions. Their staff members are assigned on an agency basis so that over a period of years a considerable degree of specialized knowledge and practical familiarity with the operations and problems of each agency is developed by individual budget examiners. These may in fact have been informally consulted by the departmental budget officer while the estimates were being prepared under his guidance. Now the process reaches the stage of administrative hearings under the auspices of the Budget Bureau. These hearings are conducted by teams of examiners, each headed by a senior staff member. The individual department is represented not only by its top officials and its budget officer but also by those of its program chiefs whose areas are primarily concerned. The hearings are informal but searching. They may dwell on policy and program questions as well as operating problems and cost standards. They may be over in a few hours for a small establishment or take weeks for a large department. Particular attention is paid to issues requiring further exploration and to changes in financial requests over those for the current fiscal year.

In all these matters the members of the hearing groups have the benefit of specialized counsel from the staff offices of the Budget Bureau. The Office of Statistical Standards, with its coordinating functions in the wide area of data collection as an essential aspect of the administrative process, can contribute technical information and professional judgment on agency plans involving fact-finding projects. The Office of Legislative Reference, as a clearance facility for the adjustment of departmental intentions to the President's legislative program, is able to account for the status of pending measures. The Office of Management and Organization, through its studies of organizational matters and operating methods throughout the government, is likely to possess first-hand knowledge of the conditions of agency management, as is the Office of Accounting, with its concern for improved financial practices throughout the executive branch. The last two staff offices have gone far toward giving full expression to one of the most significant features of the Budget and Accounting Act—the integration of the budget process with the managerial concerns of the chief executive. The act expressly charged the Budget Bureau with the task of studying problems of governmental structure and operations in order to promote "economy and efficiency in the conduct of public service." It is difficult to overestimate the importance of this assignment. It gave a healthy emphasis to the positive core of budgeting as a means of developing a unified and comprehensive work plan for the government. Such a work plan does not result from a formalized adjudication of agency requests for funds. It can take shape only when there is mature appreciation of the living processes of administration as well as firm grasp of program interrelations. Conversely, the framing of a work plan for the government as a whole puts the spotlight on hidden managerial weaknesses and operating inefficiencies. These are not eliminated by pious admonitions alone. A workmanlike approach is required to show how to do it.

The business of the hearing groups, though removing the remaining doubts about facts or reasons, is merely preliminary to another step. This is the internal examination of the emerging picture, department by department, by the budget director assisted by an advisory review body of other top officials of the bureau. The members of this group as well as the budget director are familiar with both the basic position of the President and the views of the Council of Economic Advisers and the National Security Council, each part of the Executive Office of the President. The outcome of this review determines the array of surviving issues and general problems that can be settled only in conferences with the President. The President's decisions give the executive budget its final form. However, the principle of the executive budget means merely that Congress has the assurance of receiving a responsible and all-embracing proposal, framed with an eye to governmentwide rather than purely departmental interests. The last word is the legislature's.

Legislative action. The executive budget is placed before Congress early in January, accompanied by the President's budget message. This message contains the highlights of his financial program for the next fiscal year, including an informative discussion of its anticipated impact upon the economy and of the government's principal plans for action. It follows by a few days the President's annual message on the State of the Union, and is in turn succeeded by the President's Economic Report under the Employment Act of 1946.

The federal government today represents "the world's largest enterprise." It is therefore evident that its annual revenue program and the character of its yearly outlay have profound effects upon the whole economy. Modern economists such as the late John M. Keynes, William H. Beveridge, and Alvin H. Hansen have done much to make governments aware of the opportunities they have at their disposal for influencing the general level of economic activities through a carefully planned fiscal policy. Fiscal policy is made up of four basic components—taxation, borrowing, expenditure, and debt management. Constructive fiscal policy, as an increasingly important tool of public stewardship, must attempt to relate the government's budget to the nation's budget. The latter is in balance only when the anticipated receipts of consumers, business, and public authorities—federal, state, and local—equal their projected expenditures. Economists call these expenditures collectively the "gross national product." Fiscal policy can be effective only when it is bolstered by more than coherent revenue and expenditure planning. It may be contradicted by governmental pay policy. It may be defeated by tax measures that impair the formation and free play of venture capital. It may collapse when the government fails to take prompt action in order to prevent an inflationary spiral or an impending slump. In brief, it must have the support of other public policies, including those controlling the various types of economic regulation and the scope of spending operations such as national defense and social security. Only when fiscal policy is the reflection of a fully consistent working approach permeating all activities of government can it achieve its course-setting ends. For this, a realistically considered budget is a prerequisite.

Although the President's budget message outlines the major considerations that underlie the proposed expenditure structure, it has thus far been less revealing on the "background of thinking" [5] about the budget at large. Thus, in a departure from the theory of the executive budget, the "defense" of the President's estimates before the Appropriations Committees has been traditionally entrusted to the representatives of the individual agencies concerned. The Budget Bureau has no official share in the legislative process, except in the role of a watchful observer and an occasional source of additional information in response to committee requests.

Ordinarily the Appropriations Committee in either chamber, without any penetrating preliminary analysis of the executive budget as a whole, distributes its various segments among a group of subcommittees, each operating in considerable independence. The consequence of this procedure has been inadequate attention by Congress to the larger issues of federal budget policy. The relative autonomy of the subcommittees of the Appropriations Committees leads to a fragmentation in the legislative treatment of the executive budget. Submitted to Congress as the work plan of the government, it is analyzed principally in terms of the needs of particular departments. In order to overcome this distortion of perspective, Congress long ago consolidated the several appropriation committees in each chamber as a much-needed implementation of the Budget and Accounting Act. In actual fact, however, the diffusion of responsibility which the consolidation was intended to remove has come to life again in the present scheme of subcommittees.

Fragmentation of point of view toward the executive budget as a whole encourages an alignment between individual subcommittees, on the one hand, and their departmental clients as well as outside pressure groups linked to the departments, on the other. In addition, the degree of power exercised by the subcommittees plays into the hands of individual lawmakers who exert personal influence within their particular subcommittees. This often becomes conspicuous at a later stage when Senate and House conferees meet in order to iron out disagreements in their votes on appropriation bills.

Congressional reform ideas. Equally consequential is the institutional separation between the revenue-raising and the appropriating committees.

---

[5] Budget Director Harold D. Smith testifying before the Senate Appropriations Committee, *Hearings* on the Independent Offices Appropriation Bill for 1946, p. 307, 79th Cong., 1st Sess., Washington, 1945. More recently the Appropriations Committees have come to avail themselves of explanatory testimony by the Budget Director and the Secretary of the Treasury at the beginning of the committees' analysis. The complexities of budgetary planning in the military field, where vast-scale, long "lead" times for the introduction of new weapons and great uncertainties are inherent, are penetratingly analyzed in Mosher, Frederick C., *Program Budgeting: Theory and Practice,* Chicago: Public Administration Service, 1954. In this general field, a comparison with schematic thinking—such as Brownrigg, William, *The Human Enterprise Process and Its Administration,* University, Ala.: University of Alabama Press, 1954—is very instructive.

Neither feels called upon to give much consideration to the relationship between income and expenditures. One attempted remedy was that incorporated in the Legislative Reorganization Act of 1946—adoption each spring of annual budget totals proposed by joint action of the revenue and expenditure committees, before the detailed examination of departmental requests begins. Practically, this remedy came to naught after one trial, for reasons that some observers had foreseen.

In the first place, an automatic general ceiling is a crude device at best, allowing for no differentiation among varying levels of priority with respect to individual programs incorporated into the executive budget. Secondly, determination of annual totals after submission of the executive budget to the legislature raises a practical question of appropriate timing. Much of the effort embodied in the executive budget will be wasted if it is necessarily unrelated to ceiling figures adopted only after budget completion. The internal balance of the plan is in part conditioned on the size of outlays. On the other hand, it would hardly be a feasible procedure for Congress to commit itself to budget totals without having taken a good look at the individual programs to be financed. In a sense, no doubt, the idea of budget ceilings determined after completion of the government's annual work plan is a partial negation of the very theory of the executive budget. The President would ordinarily have reason, of course, to welcome a general expression of sentiment on the part of Congress before the executive budget is formulated. Yet there will be occasions when even in full knowledge of such sentiment he would consider it his duty to present facts and figures in justification of higher expenditures for vital programs on which he would want to argue his case. Lastly, a uniform reduction of all appropriations—with few exceptions—on a percentage basis destroys the opportunity for administrative reconsideration and adjustment in the volume and emphasis of individual programs and activities.

The Legislative Reorganization Act also placed desirable emphasis upon expansion of competent staff assistance to the Appropriations Committees. Inadequate staffing of Congress is an old and legitimate complaint.[6] Better-staffed Appropriations Committees are at the same time able to develop working contacts with their counterparts in the executive branch, especially the Budget Bureau. Cooperative arrangements might also temper unfavorable congressional attitudes toward the budget process. For instance, legislators have repeatedly urged the Budget Bureau to assume the role of a strong-minded and independent guardian of economy for economy's sake, while equally often censuring it for reduction of expenditures proposed by

---

[6] See Rogers, Lindsay, "The Staffing of Congress," *Political Science Quarterly,* 1941, Vol. 56, p. 1 *ff.*; Committee on Congress, American Political Science Association, *The Reorganization of Congress,* p. 22 *ff.,* 79, Washington, 1945. For the earlier evolution of the staffing practice of the House Appropriations Committee, see *Congressional Record,* 1943, Vol. 89, p. 10994 *ff.*

agencies that happened to be in the good graces of particular groups in Congress.[7]

3. Budgetary Coordination

Essence of coordination. On the administrative side, the budget process brings into being a proposed work plan for the government. Preparation of the executive budget is therefore a demonstration of coordinative procedure in action. Coordination is a fundamental element in institutional cooperation. In connection with our discussion of the morale factor we have noticed especially the democratic implications of effective coordination.[8] Perhaps it is useful at this point to take a closer look at the coordinative aspects of the budget process.

Much of the literature on management treats of coordination primarily as an integral part of the executive function. The coordinative needs of large-scale enterprise are supposed to be met in the main in the sweep of executive leadership and in the anonymous ministrations of higher staff offices. No one would want to minimize the contribution that wise top direction buttressed by astute staff work is able to make to the sense of unity so essential to any organization. But it is equally true that coordinative action springing from the center of formal authority can attain results only when there is widespread receptivity. Coordination becomes a sham when it attempts to operate by fiat. One may order men to work together, but the order of itself does not generate cooperative inclinations.

Moreover, in the organizational sense coordination is never consummated in a single act. To put it differently, it aspires to arrangements that will endure as long as they serve a given purpose. From this vantage point, coordination is not so much a function as it is a state of working relationships. The test of effective coordination is the pattern of relationships achieved rather than the existence of coordinative mechanisms or their actual utilization by higher authority. It follows that coordination would be futile if it were confined to "laying down the law." It must seek consensus. It must convey reasons. It must elicit identification with its objectives.

Stimulation of program thinking. The "tone" of administration is in part the product of the spirit of management that radiates from the top; in part—and not the smallest part by any means—it is the reflection of the

---

[7] For a discussion of the traditional principles of budgeting in their impact upon creative administrative management, see Smith, Harold D., "The Budget as an Instrument of Legislative Control and Executive Management," *Public Administration Review*, 1944, Vol. 4, p. 181 *ff*. Mention may be made in this connection of the searching analysis of the review approach of the Appropriations Committees by Macmahon, Arthur W., "Congressional Oversight of Administration: The Power of the Purse," *Political Science Quarterly*, 1943, Vol. 58, p. 161 *ff*., 380 *ff*.

[8] See Chapter 21, "Morale and Discipline," sec. 4, "Morale and Institutional Pattern."

point of view that prevails in the operating cadres of the organization. Here, especially in the crucial ranges of middle management,[9] we encounter a deepseated tendency toward a microcosmic outlook. Capsular thinking is encouraged by the institutional distance between the day-by-day routine in which the operator is enmeshed and the loftier visions that present themselves at the apex of the hierarchy. Even in the highest intermediate strata of the organization—on the bureau and divisional levels—attention is usually concentrated on the particular programs for which bureau and division chiefs are specifically responsible.[10] To them, the total agency program is far less tangible and immediate. In fact, they may doubt at times the existence of such a program.

Although doubts of this sort will usually be without foundation, the self-assertive qualities of the total program may be obvious only to the head of the agency and his entourage. Policy pronouncements will speak eloquently about the comprehensive program. Yet it is more likely than not that the average line official will scan each such pronouncement with only two questions in mind: What does it give me? What does it take from me? Stronger stimulation is required to make the line official aware of the departmentwide perspective. And if he does not share in the department-wide perspective, if he ignores it in his limited area, how can the entire agency program ever be a full-bodied reality? How can he be depended on to fit his actions into the broader framework of closely knit organizational interrelations? How can he be expected to serve as an instrument of co-ordination? The budget process is peculiarly well suited to operate as a corrective to such localized introversion and self-sufficiency.

Budgetary justification of proposed expenditures is essentially self-justification in terms of the larger enterprise. The fundamental point of reference is the need of the whole. The password of justification is the contribution that each individual unit within a particular agency is able to make to the whole agency program, and—on the higher level—each particular department to the whole governmental program. Indeed, only through an examination of these specific contributions in their relation to one another is it possible to spell out the total program in reasonably definite terms.

Coordination by consultation. A general indication of the main emphases that are to run through the work program of an agency for any given fiscal year rarely derives directly from financial considerations alone. Such an indication cannot come from the departmental budget officer. It calls for guidance from the policy-makers of the agency. Even these, however, have to seek an objective basis for the policy direction they must furnish the budget officer and the line officials with whom he has to "thrash things out."

[9] See Chapter 18, "The Tasks of Middle Management," sec. 2, "Supporting Top Direction."

[10] See Chapter 9, "The Departmental System," sec. 4, "The Bureau Pattern."

Before the agency head is in a position to commit himself in rough outline on the kind of expenditure structure that would best meet next year's needs, he must weigh many factors in the light of concrete data, confer with those on the second level of command, take counsel with his staff officers—and even check with political associates outside his organization.

Consultative procedure takes on a more specific form as the departmental budget officer, forearmed by the "general line" indicated at the top, starts out on his review meetings with the higher operating officials to appraise the merits of their estimates. Ordinarily, to the operating official this is merely the terminal phase of a process of joint consideration that may have occupied a good share of his time during the preceding weeks as the various units in his charge, departmental and in the field, argued their respective fund requests before him. The budget officer's labor is eased by the thoroughness with which conflicting demands and activity maladjustments have been eliminated during the estimate planning within each bureau and division. From the very moment that the first field-office manager of the particular bureau, far up in the Pacific Northwest, thoughtfully scratched his chin and began to ponder the prospect of the coming fiscal year, uncounted operators were prompted by the budget process not only to account for themselves but also to turn their eyes upon the organization at large. It thus became a matter of consequence to them to find out what and how others were doing in the individual "shops."

To this extent coordination by consultation is self-generative. One needs no orders to achieve a modified arrangement when he discovers that he is stumbling over the legs of someone else. Such modified arrangements usually can be worked out on the spot by give-and-take procedure. In other instances, when the matter is more complex and special assistance appears necessary, "loose ends" may be marked for a full-fledged survey to be undertaken by the departmental management staff. In either case, the foundation for curative action emerges in the meeting of minds across jurisdictional boundaries. The budget process is a continuing incentive for every one in every corner to take into account the need for a unified conception of the entire organization. As this conception grows in strength, operators are encouraged to develop an instinct for coordination.

Departmental synthesis. With all the full-throated eulogies of the executive function and all the enthusiastic dissertations on the role of central staff offices, large-scale enterprise would screech to an abrupt stop if suddenly deprived of the self-perpetuating qualities of intelligently steered line operations. It is not unrealistic to think of the departmental budget officer as a monitor of efficiency—which is in large part coordination. But no one, not even the top executive of an agency, is strong enough to swim against the stream of adverse administrative attitudes and traditions. Coordination, too, under auspices of the budget process, must face the institutional "facts of life." It cannot maintain itself in its own make-believe. Yet it is capable of turning into a pervasive influence and of steadily augmenting its momentum.

Budgetary coordination in the departmental sphere exerts its influence not so much because of any sanction of superior authority but because of its capacity for "making sense" to those affected by it. The sense it tries to transmit to operating officials who are fond of the self-contained life must attempt to fasten upon their own scale of values. That the "big boss" wants it thus and so will in itself have little appeal.

Where there is confusion among objectives and conflict among programs, with resulting antagonisms between individual line chiefs or between them and the top level, one cannot simply go in with a whip. However, one may fruitfully examine the deeper causes; attain agreement on the basic facts controlling the situation; request from each official involved his best thinking on a remedy; make each familiar with the other's point of view; work toward joint appraisal of all forthcoming proposals; attempt acceptance of a trial arrangement to be reconsidered at a later date; and cultivate the conviction that all are likely to gain and no one to lose when irritations are removed, working relationships placed above legitimate challenge, and operations geared to common goals. Departmental synthesis is approximated most closely when people understand and appreciate its benefits in terms that strike close to home.

Top-level coordination. The most persuasive argument for coordination that is brought forth in the budget process is the argument from incontrovertible evidence. The departmental budget officer may have one general view of coordinative necessities and the operator another. Who is to tell abstractly which is right? It is quite a different matter when the budget officer is able to say with his sweetest smile, "See here, Jim, what you want to take on is already being done by Bob." Or, "You feel it's essential that you go ahead with all of these new projects; but Bill and Harry are sensible enough to defer some of theirs, though they feel exactly like you." Or, "If we don't get more consistency and coherence into our whole program, how do you expect us to get by the Budget Bureau and the Appropriations Committees?"

This means, in effect, playing the ball back. Restraints are activated, but the operator's judgment on the best solution within the frame of governing circumstances remains controlling. And follow-up, next year at the latest, is easier. Fundamentally the same approach commends itself for the final review of the entire body of estimates by the Budget Bureau. The hearing procedure, it is true, does not lead to confronting the representatives of one department with those of another. However, the same result is attained when the bureau's officials have occasion to point to lack of broader balance, contradictions in policies, or ill-drawn borderlines between certain programs of one agency and others undertaken elsewhere.

Conferences between the budget director or his deputy and agency heads, individually or jointly, occur within the "budget season" or without. These conferences would not carry far if the budget director were unable to speak in the name of the President, thus simultaneously reducing the burdens on him. The legislative founders of the national budget system envisaged close contact between the President and his budget director [11]—a relationship that was greatly strengthened by the Budget Bureau's move, in 1939, from its previous physical location in the Treasury Department to the new Executive Office of the President.

Congressional voices have sometimes been raised in favor of a Budget Bureau that would growl always and bite often. More lasting—and more constructive—effects arise from the less dramatic pursuit of program integration and management improvement through counsel and recommendation. Only thus can a demoralization of departmental responsibility be avoided. Only thus can such responsibility be enlisted positively for the acknowledgment of governmentwide ends. Clearly, however, advice and suggestions from a central staff agency must extend to more than budgetary figures and fiscal mechanisms. The Budget Bureau's coordinative task calls for breadth of information, imaginative thinking, competence in analysis, and toughness of reasoning. These, not formal authority, are the salesmen of over-all coordination.

4. Budget Execution

Budget principles and the test of practice. When the appropriation acts have finally been passed and become law, another stage in the attainment of accountability in administration begins. This is the expenditure process —the execution of the budget. As was pointed out earlier, appropriations have the twofold aspect of conveying spending authorizations as well as imposing responsibility. Since for our discussion the latter object is uppermost in mind, the first inquiry may be directed to the suitability of the budget as enacted for accountability purposes. From such a point of view a number of qualities are desirable which in governmental practice— municipal, state, and federal—are commonly realized only partially. These qualities may be summarized as budgetary publicity, clarity, comprehensiveness, unity, specification, prior authorization, periodicity, and accuracy.[12] As fundamental requirements, they seem obvious enough. Yet none of them has been consistently satisfied.

---

[11] *Cf.* Morstein Marx, *loc. cit.* above in note 4, p. 664 *ff.*

[12] *Cf.* Smith, *loc. cit.* above in note 7. A broader treatment may be found in Burkhead, Jesse, *Government Budgeting*, New York: Wiley, 1956. See also Lawton, Frederick J., "Legislative-Executive Relationships in Budgeting as Viewed by the Executive," *Public Administration Review*, 1953, Vol. 13, p. 169 *ff.* For a comprehensive presentation of fiscal administration in the federal government prior to World War II, see Selko, Daniel T., *The Federal Financial System*, Washington: Brookings Institution, 1940. For critical analysis, see further Smithies, Arthur, *The Budgetary Process in the United States*, New York: McGraw-Hill, 1955; Colm, Gerhard, and Young, Marilyn, *The Federal Budget and the National Economy*, Washington: National Planning Association, 1955.

At first glance, it may appear axiomatic that funds ought not to be made available to any governmental agency without public notice of the fact. In time of peace it is doubtful whether any public purpose can be so cogent as to justify secrecy about the amounts of appropriations—even, for example, for making atomic bombs or for the use of the Central Intelligence Agency. It seems equally axiomatic that the budget should be understandable; but complications and ambiguities are hard to keep out of it. Despite the formal acceptance of performance budgeting—meant to relate funds to programs, as all good budgeting should—and despite the turn toward accrual accounting in the federal legislation of 1956 and 1958, aiming at close correlation of the actual use of funds and the bookkeeping about the status of amounts available, it takes more than a thousand quarto pages to present the federal budget to Congress, including summary tables for a quicker view of perspectives.[13] The appropriations are contained in separate acts interlarded with much extraneous material, and there are no underscorings in them for the lay reader. Much of this is understandable in terms of the variety of sources and uses of public funds, and the multiplicity of agencies participating in the spending process. More of it can be explained by the fact that it would be difficult to make comparisons if the manner of presentation were changed from one year to the next. Reviewing authorities, both administrative and legislative, have an understandable suspicion of innovations in the general setup. Moreover, rival services may have an interest in concealing the full scope of their programs from outside eyes.

Unless the budget comprehends all proposed expenditures, its usefulness for purposes of control and accountability is limited, and appraisals of its over-all fiscal effect must be qualified. Yet difficult questions arise in the effort to achieve the ideal of comprehensiveness. They are aggravated when large expenditures, as for the development of new weapons, must be authorized over a span of years ahead. The resolution of such problems, in conformity with the principles of budget clarity and comprehensiveness, may be found in the use of annexed or subsidiary budgets, while the main budget carries only the net deficit or surplus. Another type of difficulty was illustrated, prior to World War II, in the experiments with double budgets. One provided for what were thought of as the regular and continuing expenses of government—the "ordinary budget"—and the other showed separately the extraordinary expenses proposed for relief in a depression period and later for the defense effort. In justification of this dualism, it was urged that the "extraordinary budget" was intended to be in the nature of capital outlays to be amortized over a period of years. In the one case the expected upward swing of the economic cycle was viewed as the period

---

[13] Mention should also be made of the concise summarization of the total picture in the Budget Bureau's annual publication entitled *The Federal Budget in Brief*, available at small cost from the Superintendent of Documents, Government Printing Office, Washington 25, D.C.

of amortization; and in the other, a postwar period of peace of indefinite length. In both cases, the efforts at distinction proved rather impractical and were abandoned after trial. Yet there is a case for separating in the budget matters of longer-range investment and improvement outlay from current expense, as in the capital-budget practice of New York City.

A final and continuously troublesome question relates to the treatment of permanent and indefinite appropriations. A milestone in the efforts to overcome these difficulties was the Permanent Appropriations Repeal Act of 1934. However, instances recur where particular receipts of the government are earmarked for special-purpose spending in a manner that defeats the program-coordinating process implicit in the regular appropriating procedure.

Legislative controls. Although the federal budget is presented to Congress in one complete annual document, supplemental or deficiency estimates are often inescapable. While this should not obscure the substantial degree of achievement of the goal of unity in the presentation of estimates, it is true nevertheless—as has already been indicated—that the appropriations themselves do not emerge as one piece. A single Appropriations Committee in each house has jurisdiction over all expenditure requests, but it considers them in subcommittees which report on them successively. Moreover, there is never an effective legislative opportunity for viewing the prospective or actual total outgo until all the appropriation acts have been passed and the session is closed.[14] In the execution of the budget, in consequence, there is no over-all "master plan" to serve as a point of departure for governmental accounting.

The degree to which the budget and the individual appropriations should specify sums and purposes is perhaps the most controversial question of all. Presumably, while the estimates must present much detail, the appropriation acts ought to allow considerable flexibility for administrative discretion in order to meet changes in conditions. As will be demonstrated later,[15] efforts to tie administrative hands by extremes of budgetary specification have proved unproductive and even onerous. The length of time from the administrative development of estimates until expenditures are actually made is a virtual guarantee that some alterations in the original planning will be required. With respect to new programs particularly, a delicate balance has to be worked out in executive-congressional relationships between the need for furnishing as much detail as can fairly be foreseen and the later reappraisal if the estimates prove insufficient or wrongly projected. In addition, the relative equilibrium of political strength between Congress

---

[14] The annual *Midyear Budget Review,* issued by the Budget Bureau after the beginning of the new fiscal year, gives the essential data, including up-to-date forecasts revised in the light of later developments; but this, of course, follows legislative action. The *Midyear Review* is also available from the Superintendent of Documents.

[15] See below sec. 5, "Audit."

and the chief executive has been an important factor in determining the degree of specification imposed by the legislature.

The requirement of prior authorization is politically central. It can be disregarded by the executive branch only at its own peril. Still, history has shown that occasions present themselves when the risks have appeared to be warranted. Wilmerding has brought together many instances to illustrate that American government has not been slow to recognize the ancient maxim of public safety being the highest law, even when acted upon by the President on his personal initiative. To take a notable example, shortly after the outbreak of the Civil War, at a time when the allegiance of many federal officials was in question, President Lincoln directed the Secretary of the Treasury to advance two million dollars to private individuals of known loyalty to pay for such defense steps as might prove necessary. No disclosure of this move was made to the public or to Congress for over a year.[16] One parallel occurred in 1941 when fifty overaged destroyers were traded with Great Britain for sea and air bases without prior congressional authorization.

Any methodical administration of expenditures must make it possible from time to time to close the books on successive stages of operations. The rule that appropriations are made for a single fiscal year is generally observed. However, it is subject to exceptions. The principal example is the permanent indefinite appropriation for interest on the public debt. This is thought to be necessary to give the money markets adequate assurance on the public credit. Mention should also be made of the habit of re-appropriating unexpected balances—the exact amounts involved not being susceptible of ascertainment at the time of reappropriation. This practice serves again to blur the definiteness and periodicity of appropriations. Moreover, the general rule of making appropriations and considering deficits and surpluses annually should not blind us to the essentially arbitrary nature of using any such fixed period of time. Particularly when the budget is viewed more broadly as an instrument of national fiscal policy to be employed with conscious regard to its effects on the whole economy, the value of appraisals that would more closely relate to the span of business cycles of prosperity and depression becomes apparent.

Divergence over ultimate ends. The shortcomings in meeting the formal requirements of a properly developed budget system, listed at the outset of this section, point up a basic lesson. There is divergence over the ultimate ends to be served as well. The run of legislative responses to the play of economic and social forces is different, at least on particulars, from the executive response.

The aims of local and regional pressures are apt to find expression in legislative limitations on appropriations. Lacking a reconciliation of these

---

[16] Cf. Wilmerding, Lucius, Jr., *The Spending Power,* p. 14, New Haven: Yale University Press, 1943.

localized impulses at the stage of formulation of the budget, the processes of compromise implicit in the final passage of appropriation acts and their approval by the President are piecemeal. They override formal requirements. So also do the institutional jealousies that lead Congress to prefer an atomistic organization of the executive branch, and to be unsympathetic to administrative mechanisms for the integration of policy. In the rudimentary and inconsistent resolution of the conflicting claims of legislative control and executive management,[17] the basis for orderly fiscal administration is the surest victim.

Fund control. Responsibility for carrying out congressional directives in the expenditure process is fixed by means of the accounting system. The federal accounting machinery has to be geared to keep track of more than 350,000,000 government checks paid annually by the Treasurer of the United States. In the maintenance of this system the Treasury, the Budget Bureau, the spending agencies and the General Accounting Office all share in important ways—a fact that of itself underlines the need for effective correlation. From this need has grown the joint program for improving federal accounting, sponsored by the three main fiscal agencies in cooperation with the departments.

One element is fund control. This is the treatment of each item of appropriation, including many of the appropriation limitations, as a separate fund account, to be credited with the amount of the grant and charged with the expenditures applicable to it. As to limitations, if the Department of the Interior, for instance, is appropriated a sum with the stipulation that no more than a stated amount or percentage may be expended within the District of Columbia, the limitation can readily be set up as another account. But if the appropriation is to one of the department's bureaus like the Geological Survey, while the limitation is applicable to the total amount for the department, control is not so easy. It is the Budget Bureau's task to see that each agency has adequate procedures for fund control.

Fund accounts are established on the books of the Treasury for all appropriations, and in each agency for the appropriations made to it. On requisition by these agencies, advances chargeable to their appropriations are made to the chief disbursing officer of the Treasury or one of his agents. The former maintains a series of checking accounts with the Treasurer of the United States. The Treasurer in turn acts as a bank for payments and deposits. The chief disbursing officer and his agents issue checks against vouchers properly certified by designated officials in the spending agency so long as there is a credit balance in the applicable account. In this manner fund control prevents an overdrawing of appropriations.

Allotments. Fund control by itself is a control of the flow at the nozzle. It does not prevent the creation of obligations that will produce pressures

---

[17] *Cf.* Smith, *loc. cit.* above in note 7, and Lawton, *loc. cit.* above in note 12.

for deficiency appropriations. To forestall these pressures and assure that administration will keep within the fiscal bounds originally fixed, control is reinforced by allotments and apportionments, as two supplementary devices of accountability. A third device—centrally administered personnel ceilings —was used for several years after 1943 in federal management as an additional control. A scheme of financial reporting is the mechanism for bringing about a correlation of these devices.

Funds appropriated for the agency's work are divided up in fiscal terms by means of allotments. Subdivision can be carried to any desired degree of detail, and agency practice varies considerably. Allotments are ordinarily made to each of the component organizational units of the agency, down to a given level. In some circumstances they can also be made for the several projects to be carried on by such a unit, as for categories of loans or grants-in-aid, for example. They set the limits within which the unit is authorized to proceed in drawing on appropriated funds.

The importance of allotments differs in proportion to the scope of administrative discretion over the use of funds vested in the agency; it varies also with the size of the sum in the appropriation account. For purposes of the financial accountability of the agency, allotments are essentially a safeguard against the overobligation of appropriations that might occur because a number of hands are reaching into the same pocket at once.

Apportionments. Apportionments are designed to prevent these hands from reaching too deeply too soon, with the result that all of the year's funds are gone before all of the year's work is done. In the federal government, the Budget Bureau is charged with control of apportionments— for the most part quarterly amounts into which the annual appropriation must be divided in advance, and which set limits to the agency's spending during the quarter under each appropriation heading. The requirement of apportionments was originally imposed under the antideficiency legislation of 1905-1906, but lapsed in innocuous desuetude until the authority was centralized in the Budget Bureau by Executive Order No. 6166 of June 10, 1933, subsequently reaffirmed and elaborated by statute.

A classic example of the evil the old act was designed to combat occurred late in 1879, when the Postmaster General asked Congress for an additional sum of $2 million to supplement the appropriation of $5,900,000 for inland mail transportation on the "star routes." There had been no cut in his original estimate; the deficiency was needed to cover commitments, the department having let contracts requiring expenditure at a rate that would exhaust the appropriation by April. When called to explain, the Postmaster General replied that the department had not overexpended its appropriation and would not do so. If the deficiency were not forthcoming, the contracts would be annulled and the carriage of mails stopped. The country might be inconvenienced, but congressional authorizations would not be exceeded.[18]

The apportioning process is no mere matter of dividing by four. Areas of expansion and contraction in the agency's operations must be continuously reviwed. To this extent the justification process must be repeated in outline in order to project the agency's spending plans more realistically and with closer precision against the current record of performance. Apportionments may be reconsidered within the quarter as particular needs arise. On the other hand, the Budget Bureau may go further, as provided by law, to protect the government against overobligation or to keep in the Treasury funds that appear to be in excess of actual requirements for the developing program of an agency by establishing reserves against appropriations which are withheld from apportionment altogether.

Financial reporting. In connection with control over apportionments, and in order to provide current information on the status of obligations as well as expenditures, specific reporting machinery is needed. To this end the Budget Bureau and the Treasury developed a financial reporting system, applicable to all federal agencies and government corporations.

Perhaps the most important element is the monthly report from the operating establishments on the status of each of their appropriations, showing unobligated balances and unpaid obligations. The monthly status reports are a substantial help in backing up the apportionment procedure. They sound a warning signal when the rate of spending and obligating threatens to run away from the assumptions on which the apportionments are based. Moreover, the monthly status reports afford another means of comparing actual expenditures with agency estimates for the next fiscal year up to the very time that the projected executive budget is placed before the President.

5. Audit

Public finance and representative government. Since the seventeenth century it has been an article of faith among English-speaking peoples that legislative control of the purse-strings is the best practical guarantee of the maintenance of representative government. The taming of royal power in England was an institutional achievement of the legislature. Fiscal supremacy, buttressed by the twin rights to refuse to levy taxes and to refuse to

---

[18] See Wilmerding, *op. cit.* above in note 16, p. 137 *ff*. On the opposite situation— the administrative establishment of reserves—see a case study by Williams, J. D., *The Impounding of Funds by the Bureau of the Budget,* Inter-University Case Program Series, No. 28, University, Ala.: University of Alabama Press, 1955. Larger and more controversial cases have occurred when Congress has insisted on National Guard, naval, or Air Force appropriations beyond presidential requests; see Huntington, Samuel P., "Civilian Control and the Constitution," *American Political Science Review,* 1956, Vol. 50, p. 676, 692.

appropriate their proceeds when levied, was an important instrument in that achievement. From this example, the American colonists drew their basic lesson.

Colonial legislatures could not control their appointed governors themselves. But the lawmaking bodies used their powers over the sources and uses of funds to express their dissatisfaction with the agents and policies of the home government. Frequently they elected their own treasurers in order to ensure the sympathetic administration of their financial instructions.

The prestige of legislatures was high when the American Constitution was adopted. The colonists had reason to distrust every kind of executive authority they knew. The framers of the Constitution therefore put the ultimate authority over public finances squarely in the hands of the lawmakers, and allotted to the more popular chamber—the House of Representatives—the prerogative of introducing tax bills. To this day, in no field has Congress made less use of statutory delegation, and kept the detailed exercise of its power more jealously to itself, than in the field of taxation. The provisions of the Internal Revenue Code fill a very large volume.

External audit: England. Legislative control of actual expenditures after appropriations have been voted—keeping the spending of money within the scope of the grants authorized, checking the observance of limitations, and analyzing and appraising the results obtained—has proved to be quite another matter. This is a special case of a problem common to virtually all organizations, private and public: How to get those handling other people's money to do so in accordance with the instructions of a third party claiming superior authority. The solution in practice depends in part on the degree of confidence reposed in the agent, or on an act of faith in the face of an urgent, uncertain, or confidential need—as when the State Department is voted a secret contingent fund to be expended upon the sole certification of the Secretary of State. So the ethical standards and professional codes of those who handle or have access to the money are the first concern in an appraisal of the safety and adequacy of any system of fiscal accountability. But experience in the use of money belonging to others teaches the wisdom of tangible safeguards to reinforce moral precepts. The stakes are raised as the size of an organization and of the resources at its disposal grows, and as the degree of discretion vested in its officers increases. The problem is further complicated when the instructions of the superior authority are no longer the voice of a single ruler but instead the diverse wills and purposes of the many individuals who hold some portion of constitutional authority. So the second concern in a system of accountability is a dependable verification of the administrative records of what has been done with the money appropriated—an independent audit, in other words.

In government this is a question of constitutional arrangements, of the unity and strength of the governing institutions at the top. In the United

States, for instance, on the level of state and local governments, the popular election of several executive officials with financial powers—governors, comptrollers, auditors, treasurers, perhaps of different party affiliations at the same time—may effectively frustrate any possibility of getting a satisfactory external audit by or from any of them, or from the legislative body. A parliamentary system may ease the solution of this particular problem. In England, for example, the political unification of the executive and the legislative powers at the top, in the institution of cabinet government, had become so well established by the middle of the last century that a mutuality of interest developed in an external, independent audit of all financial transactions. This was provided for by the Exchequer and Audit Departments Act of 1866.

Under that law the position of Comptroller and Auditor General was created, an office to be held "during good behavior"—that is, on permanent tenure. With the help of a modest but expert staff, the incumbent annually examines the accounts of the Treasury and the other departments. He goes into such details as he finds necessary in view of the internal administrative checks in operation. He ascertains whether expenditures have been kept within parliamentary appropriations, and whether Treasury directions have been followed.[19] The Comptroller and Auditor General reports his findings to the Committee on Public Accounts of the House of Commons, whose chairman is a member of the legislative opposition. The committee first holds searching hearings over these reports, attended by the Comptroller and Auditor General and by representatives of the Treasury and the departments affected. Subsequently the committee reports its appraisal and the supporting data to the House of Commons. In case of legislative criticism, the Treasury must alter its practice or defend it publicly. Where expenditures in excess of appropriations have been made by a department, the Treasury must give its sanction by authorizing transfers of funds insofar as that is possible; if it is not, the Treasury must secure a ratification from the House of Commons in the form of a supplementary appropriation. If neither course prevails, the departmental accounting officer is held personally liable.

Under this system there is public assurance that financial policies and procedures will stand disinterested scrutiny, without calling in question the major substantive decisions for which the government assumes political responsibility. A roughly similar result is aimed at under modern practice by the independent audit of private corporations whose securities are publicly traded, in line with requirements of the stock exchanges and of the Securities and Exchange Commission. However, the position of minority

---

[19] *Cf.* Beer, Samuel H., *Treasury Control: The Coordination of Financial and Economic Policy in Great Britain,* rev ed., Oxford: Clarendon Press, 1957; Chubb, Basil, *The Control of Public Expenditure,* Oxford: Clarendon Press, 1952. See also the excellent (6th) report of the Select Committee on Estimates, House of Commons, *Treasury Control of Expenditure,* 1958.

investors in relation to corporate management is obviously much weaker than that of the House of Commons. As a result, the degree of disclosure to them—and the corresponding influence of possible publicity on corporate practices—is distinctly smaller.

Beginning of expenditure control in the United States. The separation of powers embodied in American government has so far precluded any such amicably efficacious arrangement for legislative control of public expenditures as we find in England. Once the appropriation acts have been passed, the use of funds is in administrative hands. To be sure, the process of administrative spending is one in which individual legislators often share as they pursue particular interests, such as an allocation for public works or the location of a field installation.[20] Yet no audit committee brings comprehensively before the lawmaking body its considered review of what has transpired.

This does not mean that the United States lacks a system of expenditure control and fiscal accountability. The roots of its system run back through time to the revolutionary governments preceding the adoption of the American Constitution. From 1789 to 1921—the year of the Budget and Accounting Act—Congress relied on two main devices of surveillance, supplemented occasionally by committee investigations. These were: (1) the language of the appropriation acts; and (2) a set of internal checks within the executive branch. The descriptive language set forth with more or less particularity the purposes of the individual appropriation. The internal administrative checks were designed to ensure that at each stage in the spending process a separate official was responsible for attesting the integrity of the transaction—too many officials in all, and too divergent in interests, to make collusion practicable.[21]

Specificity of appropriations. Reliance on qualifying language to govern administrative spending led to the doctrine of specific appropriations. The development of excessive specificity was an inevitable outgrowth and in the end proved self-defeating. The earliest appropriation for the support of the government, in 1789, was simple enough. In 123 words it disposed of $639,000 under four headings. The amounts were derived from estimates furnished by the Secretary of the Treasury, Alexander Hamilton. A little experience in the method of deficiency requests to cover objects thought to have been already provided for soon showed that there was no necessary restrictive connection between prior estimates of expenditure and the actual use made of available funds.

Under the sting of criticism from Gallatin and Jefferson, the Federalists gradually accepted a greater specification of objects. This was softened, however, by a delegation of power to the President to authorize certain

---

[20] See Chapter 15, "Legislative Control."

[21] The history of congressional efforts to control expenditures has been traced with insight and charm by Wilmerding, *op. cit.* above in note 16.

transfers between appropriation headings when Congress was not in session. As party control of the government shifted, so did the points of view. But the trend toward particularization continued. Nevertheless, within a generation theory and practice were no longer within speaking distance of each other.

Appropriations were specified in the minutest detail. However, by means of transfers, the carrying forward of unexpended balances, and the incurring of obligations in anticipation of deficiency appropriations—all in the teeth of statutes designed to prevent these practices—funds were found for expenditures the departments wanted to make beyond the original appropriations. John Randolph in 1806 expressed the feeling of congressional helplessness when, though in opposition, he refused to try to reduce the naval appropriation for contingent expenses: "If we cannot restrain the expenditures of the Navy Department within the sum annually fixed, after giving as much as is asked for, is it not the idlest thing to attempt to restrain them by giving less?" [22] We may also think of the anecdote related by Henry Clay in 1819 to show how institutional frustration turned into individual cynicism:

> Some years ago it had been the custom, now abolished, to use in this House a beverage in lieu of water for those members who preferred it. A member of the House said he was not in the habit of using this sort of substitute for one of nature's greatest and purest bounties, but would prefer something stronger. The officers of the House said they should be glad to gratify him, but did not know how they could with propriety pay for it out of the contingent fund. Why, said the member, under what head of appropriation do you pay for this syrup for the use of the members? Under the head of stationery, the officer said. Well, replied the member, put down a little grog under the head of fuel, and let me have it.[23]

By the latter part of the nineteenth century, Congress had come to appreciate fully the realities of the situation. It often appropriated deliberately less money than was known to be required, with the expectation of providing the remainder in deficiency bills later. In election years the legislature was tempted to take advantage of this technique to make a show of economy. It was not until the beginning of genuine budgetary practice under the Budget and Accounting Act of 1921 that the conduct of federal administration was freed from the irrationalities of such coercive deficiencies.

Administrative checks. The internal checks that were devised also proved unsatisfactory. The Treasury Department Act of 1789 established under the Secretary of the Treasury a comptroller, a treasurer, an auditor, and a bookkeeping officer. According to the underlying theory, when Congress had passed an appropriation for the use of a particular department, the Secretary of the Treasury drew a "warrant," and the comptroller

---

[22] *Ibid.*, p. 66.
[23] *Ibid.*, p. 82.

countersigned it. This established an appropriation credit with the treasurer, which the register recorded. Thereafter, until the credit was exhausted, the Secretary of the Treasury, on request of the department, would issue further warrants in favor of particular payees, which the treasurer would pay upon countersignature by the comptroller.

The request might take the form of a voucher for materials received or services performed; if so, it had first to be examined and approved—or "settled"—by the auditor and the comptroller. Commonly, however, the payment was an advance of funds to a departmental agent—or disbursing officer—who then proceeded to pay vouchers approved in the department. Because of the particularity of appropriations, disbursing officers usually held advances under several separate appropriation headings. Many of these officers, especially in the revenue and postal services, were also collectors of public funds. For both reasons they were frequently in a position, if their advances under a particular heading were exhausted, to borrow temporarily from another to meet the need for an immediate payment.

The disbursing officers were accountable to the auditor, and furnished him periodic reports listing their collections and advances, and their payments supported by paid vouchers. If the auditor disallowed a payment as unauthorized under the appropriation charged and the comptroller sustained him, the disbursing officer was personally liable. If he could not clear the disallowance by supplying further information, by charging the expenditure to another appropriation, by recovering the money from the payee, or by securing a relief act from Congress, he was bound to pay it himself. If he defaulted, the comptroller—later the Solicitor, and now the Department of Justice—was charged with the duty of collecting the debt.

Some experience with the latitude of personal responsibility of disbursing officers led to the requirement that they be bonded. In 1941, this requirement was extended to the certifying officers, who approve vouchers, in view of the mechanized and ministerial nature of the disbursing officers' duties under modern conditions. Moreover, as a part of their operating routine the departments and bureaus developed their own internal checks on the accounts of the disbursing officers before transmittal to the Treasury. The settled accounts went to the Treasury, and remained there. In theory, an analysis of them, together with the warrants issued directly, would have made it possible to determine, as of any given date, the status and uses of an appropriation. In fact, however, such information was never assembled in time to serve any comprehensive budgetary or reporting purpose.

Delay and laxity. Some frailties of this system are plain, of which the chief was its delays. As a critic remarked, the system was "the most admirable contrivance that the mind of man ever conceived to put down the sums claimed by public creditors to the smallest figures, and then to postpone to the latest possible moment the payment of what has at last been acknowledged due." [24] However, First Comptroller Elisha Whittlesey, when asked by Secretary of the Treasury Guthrie in 1854 to report improvements, responded in the sentiment that sustained the system through the nineteenth century: "The law organizing the Treasury Department . . . was framed by very wise men, who took a deep interest in the welfare and prosperity of the country. The system is based on checks to guard against dishonesty and fraud, and it has worked admirably. The Treasury Department is as pure and free from the perpetration of fraud as it was the day it went into operation. . . . The system, in my opinion, cannot be bettered, and operates as harmoniously and beautifully now, as it did sixty-five years ago." [25]

In theory, the chain of fiscal accountability began with an appropriation. But in the old days Congress was not—as it is now—in virtually continuous session; distances were great, and communications uncertain and slow. Just as the specification of appropriations annulled its purpose by its rigidity in the face of unforeseeable changes in conditions and needs, so the administrative checks and balances turned into impediments when they prevented payments that had to be made within a time limit to serve their end—food and forage for troops and animals on a western expedition, provisions for vessels about to sail, payment to France for the Louisiana Purchase, for example. The exigencies of government were at the paying, not the appropriating, end of the chain.

In an effort to meet the complaints about delays, the duties of the comptroller and the auditor were splintered at an early date. By 1836 there were six auditors and two comptrollers; yet the tempo was not quickened. As an unavoidable result, the actual sequence of events was as likely as not to start with a payment by a disbursing officer, leaving the train of authorizing warrants and appropriations to follow along by way of ratification. When this was a common occurrence, it is understandable why promptness and exacting standards in the settlement of accounts were hard to obtain.

Failure to secure dispatch and meticulous procedure, however, was disastrous to the Treasury's own accounting system. It could tell quickly enough what appropriations had been made, what advances had been issued, and what receipts had been reported. On the other hand, everything else was at large—what obligations had been incurred or were in prospect, at what rate advances would be spent, what payments and receipts were not yet reported, what reported payments would be disallowed. All of this had to wait on paperwork that would spread over the ensuing years. On this footing of sand the Secretary of the Treasury reported annually to Congress on the state of federal finances. It was an inescapable consequence that Con-

24 Renick, Edward I., "Control of National Expenditures," *Political Science Quarterly*, 1891, Vol. 6, p. 248.
25 *Annual Report of the First Comptroller*, 1854, p. 103-104.

gress could bring only a dusty vision to the business of taxing, borrowing, and appropriating.

Path of reform. Modern efforts to reform the system began with the Dockery Act of 1894, the collaborative work of Secretary of the Treasury Foster and a congressional commission, aided by outside experts. It clarified the jurisdiction of the auditors, and strengthened their supervision over disbursing officers as well as over the issuance of departmental requisitions for advances. The law consolidated the comptrollers into one, as in the institutional beginning, with appellate authority over the auditors. It made it the comptroller's duty to render advance decisions on request from department heads or disbursing officers, and gave him power to prescribe the forms of keeping and rendering all public accounts. Finally, the new legislation centralized all bookkeeping in the Treasury in a reorganized Division of Warrants, Estimates and Appropriations.

Under the dispensation of 1894, the comptroller's main function was to provide a uniform construction of the appropriation laws, conclusive and binding upon all the departments. There had been earlier conflict over the finality of determinations by department heads when challenged by the comptroller, as happened on occasion. The Dockery Act did not touch this ambiguity, which entered the picture especially whenever the comptroller asked the Attorney General to collect by suit a payment disallowed on a construction of the law by the comptroller that the Attorney General disagreed with.[26] As to the comptroller's status, although he and the auditors were subordinates of the Secretary of the Treasury, the spoils system—as a rule with relatively few exceptions—yielded far enough to keep them in office with successive changes in the political control of the government. Like other bureau chiefs, they were ordinarily patronage appointees.

At this stage of the development, the movement leading to the passage of the Budget and Accounting Act of 1921 overtook the accounting system of the government. It was by then a system that imposed on each individual disbursing officer a tiresomely detailed and long drawn-out accountability to Treasury officials for every payment made, applying the test of statutory authorization only, and seemingly unconcerned with administrative results achieved or operating standards applied. It put almost no organizational responsibility on the departments and bureaus for the effective handling of their fiscal affairs. This was the more serious because, until the recent emergence of departmental management in a fairly inclusive sense, all the bureaus were nearly autonomous operating entities.

Equally important, the accounting system left the Treasury, as the central fiscal agency of the government, and thus also Congress, without any adequate current and comprehensive conception of the over-all financial situation. Except for occasional and sporadic legislative intervention, the

---

[26] See Mansfield, Harvey C., *The Comptroller General*, ch. 4, New Haven: Yale University Press, 1939.

system reserved for the executive branch all administrative determinations as to how and whether congressional mandates attached to appropriations were observed. While this would have been a proper arrangement if bolstered by some kind of subsequent review, there was actually no provision whatever for securing to Congress the benefits of an independent inquiry and opinion on such matters. True, these are hindsight judgments. In the light of contemporary opinion, and in the absence of the financial strains under which European governments operated, the system was not viewed with any marked dissatisfaction in the country.

Formation of the General Accounting Office. The Budget and Accounting Act of 1921 made two important changes in the scheme of financial accountability, one of them fundamental. First, it rolled together into a single establishment the combined functions, personnel, and records of the former comptroller and the six auditors, without modifying substantially the definitions of basic powers and duties as these had developed over the years. This new establishment was the General Accounting Office, under a single head —the Comptroller General. Second, the act described the General Accounting Office as "independent of the executive departments." This theory was reinforced by the stipulation that the functions of the General Accounting Office be performed "without direction from any other officer." As a tangible institutional guarantee of independence, the act gave the Comptroller General a fifteen-year term of office, making him irremovable except by joint resolution of Congress for cause and after hearing.

Adoption by Congress of Title III of the Budget and Accounting Act, containing these changes, was not preceded by any real debate of its provisions, except for the question of the Comptroller General's tenure. The fifteen-year term was a compromise between the views of the House leadership intent upon an indefinite term—"during good behavior"—and the Senators who wanted one of seven years. The House also talked of vesting the appointment in Congress. However, it was deterred by the argument that as one Congress could not bind the next, a maximum term of only two years could be assured that way.

Before the bill finally passed, there was an unsuccessful move to hand the power of appointment to the Supreme Court. Although emphatically in favor of the reform measure, President Wilson in 1920 vetoed the bill as originally passed. He protested that the restriction on his removal power was unconstitutional—a question the legislative arrangement was designed to avoid. But when the law was repassed the next year with only a slight and hardly consequential change, President Harding accepted it. The constitutional point is likely to remain moot.[27]

When voting on the law, few members of Congress realized that the establishment of an independent General Accounting Office was simply

---

[27] *Ibid.*, ch. 3.

creating a separation of powers within the administrative structure as complete and thorough as that prevailing in the constitutional system. This took the place of the former division of labor that afforded internal checks in an administration ultimately responsible to the President. The proponents of the new scheme, experts and Congressmen alike, had talked of the need for an "independent" audit on behalf of Congress—and frequently invoked the English example in complete misunderstanding of its most basic features. What the act in fact did was to institute an independent administrative control over expenditures, exercised from the standpoint of their legality.

Control versus audit. The distinction is basic. The important power of the Comptroller General, as of the comptroller before him, is to "settle" accounts. Settlement has always meant, as Wilmerding puts it, "the final administrative determination of the balances due to or from the United States on accounts between itself and its debtors and creditors." [28] An audit, on the other hand, is "an examination made on behalf of a principal of the transactions of an agent as recorded in an account." [29] The Comptroller General conducts an examination of the payments made by administrative officers, not on behalf of Congress but as an incident to the exercise of his power as a principal to settle accounts. He also determines the amounts to be paid on claims submitted to his office for direct settlement. There is hence no audit report to Congress on the amounts finally allowed as charges against appropriations; and the Comptroller General would be the last person suitable to do so, since he himself makes the determinations that would be reviewed in such an audit. As one of the effects of this confusion of audit and control, the existence of the Comptroller General has given Congress a comforting and illusory sense of security, warranted only on the supposition that the Comptroller General is infallible.

The legislature has set up no machinery in the nature of a public-accounts committee to provide an orderly instrument for making use of pertinent information for control purposes. In 1920 the Senate, and in 1927 the House, adopted resolutions consolidating their several previous committees on appropriations into one each. The evidence is clear, however, that both committees have been generally inactive in the area of fiscal accountability—rather completely so in the Senate and in the House confined to occasional investigations. A lawmaking body needs staff assistance in so intricate a field as financial control. While this general proposition has been gaining some acceptance in connection with the legislative consideration of the budget, it has made little headway as applied to control based on audit.

In the conduct of public management, the strictures imposed by the separation of powers within the administrative structure have been produc-

---

[28] *Op. cit.* above in note 16, p. 259.
[29] *Ibid.*, p. 273.

tive of much controversy. This was true particularly under the regime of Comptroller General McCarl, spanning most of the period from 1921 until World War II. The General Accounting Office increasingly substituted its determinations for those of operating officials on questions of fact as well as of law involved in ruling on the availability of appropriations.[30] The adoption of rules and forms was designed to bring to the General Accounting Office a much greater proportion of the immense mass of under-lying data on which its determinations are based. Moreover, the departments were urged—and legislation was unsuccessfully sought to compel them—to submit their vouchers for preaudit in advance of payment. This invitation was accepted in only a very small proportion of the total volume of transactions.

The immediate consequences of all these policies were to draw attention to arguments over jurisdiction and to paperwork about details handled at a point too remote from their operating origin, to the detriment of good management. It soon became apparent also that the Comptroller General's independence left a good deal of room within the interstices of the law for the expression of views on public policy in social and economic fields. Such expressions did not necessarily coincide with prevailing attitudes in either the executive or the legislative branch. The Comptroller General tangled early with Congress over veterans' payments, and later with the executive branch over the Tennessee Valley Authority and other New Deal measures.

Safeguarding operational responsibility. One by-product was no doubt a stimulus to the improvement of Treasury accounting and the development of departmental management in order to meet more effectively the Comptroller General's encroachments on operating discretion. In addition, his restrictive approach furnished a marked impetus to both the establishment of agencies and the organization of activities in corporate form outside his purview. A further method of mitigating his influence was the enactment of legislation specifically making the findings of particular agency heads on particular types of questions conclusive on the Comptroller General. In this fashion the bulk of payments in World War II was made subject to his scrutiny only in very limited degrees or not at all. On a direct test of the central issue he was expressly foreclosed from reviewing war-contract termination payments, except on the narrowest grounds, by the Contract Settlement Act of 1944. Here effective use was made in legislative debate of the prospects of delay and of "unemployment by audit," if the Comptroller General were permitted to question the bases of settlements previously arrived at. This prohibition operated to throw out baby and

---

[30] A large body of case law has been built up in this field. Annual increments will be found in the published volumes of the decisions of the Comptroller General. For some informative sketches of General Accounting Office work, see Schulsinger, Gerald G., *The General Accounting Office: Two Glimpses,* Inter-University Case Program, Case No. 35, University, Ala.: University of Alabama Press, 1956.

bath together—the scope of the audit would not reach beyond the settlement which represented the terminal point of a complex series of prior transactions.

Recognizing the undesirability of the general state of affairs, and recapturing some of the ground previously yielded to executive freedom of action, Congress undertook to push in a different direction in passing the Government Corporation Control Act of 1945.[31] Statutory precedents for this venture existed in the instructions given the Comptroller General to audit, but not to settle, the accounts of the Shipping Board and the Emergency Fleet Corporation after World War I, and also of the Tennessee Valley Authority under its basic statute of 1933. But Comptroller General McCarl had made these instructions instruments of controversy rather than of constructive innovation. In addition to preventing the establishment of new government corporations without express statutory sanction in the future, the Government Corporation Control Act directed the Comptroller General to conduct a commercial type of audit of each of the existing corporations to be considered permanent, giving due recognition to their needs for operating flexibility. The results he was to report to Congress. All corporate transactions were opened to his examination, but he was given no power to settle the accounts.

Balance sheet of audit and settlement of accounts. To replace accountability to the General Accounting Office by accountability to the legislature, the President's Committee on Administrative Management in 1937 proposed a reorganization of fiscal administration, based on the divorce of the Comptroller General's audit and settlement powers [32] and the establishment of accountability to Congress through a Joint Committee on Public Accounts. The House bill to give effect to these recommendations failed of passage. The Reorganization Act of 1939 left the matter untouched. In the Reorganization Act of 1945, Congress made plain its intent to preclude any changes affecting the status of the General Accounting Office. The Legislative Reorganization Act of 1946 did little toward a true solution. One of its provisions encouraged the Comptroller General to audit the operations of federal agencies and government corporations.

Audits adjudging the administrative performance of an agency or government corporation have helped to reorient the working perspective of the General Accounting Office toward the conduct of administrative operations. In the consideration of the audit findings, a field has opened up for collaboration between the General Accounting Office and the Bureau of the Budget. In addition, the General Accounting Office has made great strides in carrying its examination of agency accounts into the very sites of agency activities, including regional and field offices. Another factor

---

[31] See also Chapter 11, "Government Corporations."

[32] See President's Committee on Administrative Management, *Report with Special Studies*, p. 15 *ff.*, 49 *ff.*, 139 *ff.*, 173 *ff.*, Washington: Government Printing Office, 1937.

in the development of the General Accounting Office's attitude toward its responsibilities has been the Joint Accounting Program, previously mentioned.

Unfortunately, the Legislative Reorganization Act does not separate the Comptroller General's audit functions from his settlement duties. These duties alone represent a business of enormous proportions. Moreover, the act does not bring significantly nearer any real working integration of the audit function with the exercise of congressional oversight and control; for this purpose a mechanism such as a legislative committee on public accounts to whom the Comptroller General could regularly report is indispensable. Despite failure to come to grips with this basic problem, the relationship between the Comptroller General and the executive branch changed significantly for the better during the twenty years that followed the publication of the report of the President's Committee on Administrative Management (1937). Perhaps the main reason was the inevitable reaction to the "McCarl regime" of the thirties, which came close to converting the General Accounting Office into a policy brake, thus promoting irresponsibility instead of accountability. A change in institutional climate took place, prompted evidently in large part by the Comptroller General's previous excesses in interfering with the conduct of administration. A supporting factor was the gradual consolidation of the whole appropriation structure, linking it more closely to agency programs, with the interrelated by-products of giving programs a broader money basis and defining fund purposes in more general appropriation language. Finally, the rise of the contract device—in such fields as the atomic energy program and research and technical development in general—may have been a contributing element. As earlier the government corporation had moved out of the reach of traditional financial controls, so a similar effect was achieved when important governmental functions came to be managed in the primary sense by private contractors, getting paid for completed performance or in lump-sum instalments.

The emphasis in the Legislative Reorganization Act upon a redirection of the audit function away from the detail and toward the general may prove a lasting contribution. Full accountability for the level of efficiency throughout the executive branch is woven into the tenets of representative government. The more closely the United States approximates a satisfactory solution of this problem, the less ground will there be for the ill-considered contention that inefficiency is the price of democracy.

Index